企业大数据处理实战派

基于阿里云大数据平台

赵渝强 ◎ 著

电子工业出版社
Publishing House of Electronics Industry
北京·BEIJING

内 容 简 介

本书基于作者多年的教学与实践经验编写，重点介绍阿里云大数据体系的核心原理与架构，内容涉及开发、运维、管理与架构。全书分为 4 篇，共 13 章：第 1 篇（第 1~2 章）介绍大数据技术基础；第 2 篇（第 3~8 章）介绍阿里云大数据的离线计算服务；第 3 篇（第 9~10 章）介绍阿里云大数据的实时计算服务，包括消息队列 Kafka 版和实时计算 Flink 版；第 4 篇（第 11~13 章）介绍阿里云大数据增值服务——数加平台，包括阿里云大数据集成开发平台 DataWorks、数据可视化分析平台 Quick BI 和机器学习平台 PAI。

本书适合对大数据技术感兴趣的平台架构师、运维管理人员和项目开发人员阅读。

无论读者是否接触过大数据技术，只要具备基础的 Linux 知识和 Java 基础，就能够通过本书快速掌握阿里云大数据技术并增加实战经验。根据本书中的操作步骤，读者可以在实际的项目生产环境中快速应用并实施阿里云大数据平台技术。

未经许可，不得以任何方式复制或抄袭本书之部分或全部内容。
版权所有，侵权必究。

图书在版编目（CIP）数据

企业大数据处理实战派：基于阿里云大数据平台 / 赵渝强著. —北京：电子工业出版社，2023.9

ISBN 978-7-121-46076-0

Ⅰ. ①企… Ⅱ. ①赵… Ⅲ. ①企业管理－数据处理 Ⅳ. ①F272.7

中国国家版本馆 CIP 数据核字（2023）第 144795 号

责任编辑：吴宏伟
印　　刷：天津千鹤文化传播有限公司
装　　订：天津千鹤文化传播有限公司
出版发行：电子工业出版社
　　　　　北京市海淀区万寿路 173 信箱　　邮编：100036
开　　本：787×980　1/16　印张：28.25　字数：678 千字
版　　次：2023 年 9 月第 1 版
印　　次：2023 年 9 月第 1 次印刷
定　　价：128.00 元

凡所购买电子工业出版社图书有缺损问题，请向购买书店调换。若书店售缺，请与本社发行部联系。联系及邮购电话：(010) 88254888，88258888。
质量投诉请发邮件至 zlts@phei.com.cn，盗版侵权举报请发邮件至 dbqq@phei.com.cn。
本书咨询联系方式：wuhongwei@phei.com.cn。

前言

随着信息技术的不断发展，数据量呈爆炸式增长。为了实现对大数据的高效存储与管理和快速分析与计算，出现了以 Hadoop、Spark 和 Flink 为代表的大数据平台生态圈体系。"得数据者得天下"，随着数据量的不断增长，大数据生态圈体系也不断地发展。在众多的大数据平台中，阿里云大数据平台解决了超大规模多场景融合下，用户多元化数据的计算需求问题，实现了存储、调度、元数据管理的一体化架构融合，支撑交通、金融、科研、政企等场景下数据的高效处理，是国内自主研发、应用非常广泛的一体化大数据平台。

作者拥有大数据平台方向多年的教学经验，并在实际的大数据运维和开发工作中积累了大量的实战经验，因此想编写一本系统介绍阿里云大数据生态圈体系的书籍，力求能够完整地介绍阿里云大数据平台。本书总结了作者在大数据平台方面的经验，希望本书对大数据平台方向的从业者和学习者有所帮助，为大数据生态圈体系在国内的发展贡献一份力量。相信通过本书的介绍，读者能够全面并系统地掌握大数据平台的知识，并且能够在实际工作中灵活地运用。

1. 本书特色

本书聚焦阿里云大数据平台技术，全面、深入地讲解了与大数据平台技术相关的知识，并辅以实战。本书有如下特色。

1）一线技术，系统全面

本书全面介绍了阿里云大数据平台体系的组成部分，包含大数据平台技术涉及的方方面面，力求覆盖阿里云大数据平台的核心内容。

2）精雕细琢，可读性强

本书采用通俗易懂的语言，并经过多次打磨，力求精确。同时注重前后章节的承上启下，让没有大数据方面经验的读者也可以很轻松地读懂本书。

3）从零开始，循序渐进

本书从最基础的内容开始讲解并逐步深入，先介绍大数据基础，然后全面、深入地介绍阿里云大数据平台体系，从而真正做到帮助读者从基础入门向开发高手迈进，让初级、中级、高级技术人员都可以从本书中学到干货。

4）深入原理，言简意赅

本书深入介绍了阿里云大数据平台的底层原理和机制，力求言简意赅，帮助读者提高学习效率，同时尽可能地帮助读者缩短阅读本书的时间。

5）由易到难，重点解析

本书编排由易到难，内容覆盖了阿里云大数据平台技术的各个方面。同时对重点和难点进行了详细讲解，对易错点和注意点进行了提示说明，帮助读者克服学习过程中的困难。

6）突出实战，注重效果

本书采用"理论讲解+动手实操"的方式，让读者在学习理论知识之后能够动手实操。购买本书的读者可以通过网络下载书中所有的相关资料，下载后即可运行，通过实践来加深理解。

7）实践方案，指导生产

本书以实践为主，所有的示例拿来即可运行。并且书中提供了大量的技术解决方案，可以为技术人员在实际的生产环境中提供相应的指导。

2. 阅读本书，读者能学到什么

- 掌握大数据的理论基础；
- 掌握阿里云大数据生态圈体系；
- 掌握阿里云大数据技术的使用方法；
- 掌握基于 MaxCompute 的大数据离线应用开发；
- 掌握使用 MaxCompute SQL 处理结构化数据的方法；
- 掌握 MaxCompute 的权限与安全机制；
- 掌握使用消息队列 Kafka 版的方法；
- 掌握使用消息队列 Kafka 版开发应用程序的方法；
- 掌握使用实时计算 Flink 版的方法；
- 掌握使用实时计算 Flink 版开发应用程序的方法；
- 掌握使用阿里云大数据集成开发平台 DataWorks 的方法；
- 掌握使用数据可视化分析平台 Quick BI 的方法；
- 掌握使用机器学习平台 PAI 的方法。

3. 读者对象

本书既适合阿里云大数据平台技术的初学者阅读，也适合想进一步提升阿里云大数据平台技术的中高级技术人员阅读。相信不同级别的技术从业者都能从本书中学到干货。

本书的读者对象如下：

- ◎ 初学大数据技术的自学者；
- ◎ 中高级技术人员；
- ◎ 开发工程师；
- ◎ 大数据技术爱好者；
- ◎ 培训机构的老师和学员；
- ◎ 相关专业的大学毕业生；
- ◎ 高等院校的老师和学生；
- ◎ 系统架构师；
- ◎ 测试工程师；
- ◎ 技术运维人员；
- ◎ 技术管理人员；
- ◎ 技术经理。

本书涉及的所有代码和配置文件均可按照封底的"读者服务"中的方式下载。

尽管作者在本书写作过程中尽可能地追求严谨，但难免有疏漏之处，欢迎读者通过扫描下面的二维码关注微信公众号"IT 阅读会"或加入读者微信群，进行批评与指正。

赵渝强

2023 年 3 月

目录

第 1 篇　大数据技术基础

第 1 章　大数据核心理论基础与架构 2
1.1　什么是大数据 2
1.1.1　大数据的基本概念和特性 2
1.1.2　大数据平台的核心问题——存储与计算 4
1.2　大数据的理论基础 6
1.2.1　大数据的分布式存储 6
1.2.2　大数据的分布式计算 9
1.3　大数据技术与数据仓库 12
1.3.1　什么是数据仓库 12
1.3.2　基于大数据技术实现的数据仓库 13
1.4　基于开源大数据组件的大数据平台架构 15
1.4.1　数据源层 16
1.4.2　数据采集层 16
1.4.3　大数据平台层 16
1.4.4　数据仓库层 17
1.4.5　应用层 17
1.5　自建大数据平台与租赁大数据平台 17
1.5.1　为什么推荐使用租赁的大数据平台 17
1.5.2　为什么选择阿里云大数据平台 18
1.6　阿里云大数据生态圈体系 18
1.6.1　阿里云大数据基础组件 19
1.6.2　基于阿里云大数据基础组件的数加平台 24

第 2 章 阿里云大数据技术基础——开源大数据技术生态圈 ... 27

2.1 开源大数据技术生态圈简介 ... 27
2.1.1 面向离线数据的存储计算引擎 Hadoop 生态圈体系及其组件 ... 27
2.1.2 面向批处理的大数据计算引擎 Spark 生态圈体系及其组件 ... 29
2.1.3 面向流处理的大数据计算引擎 Flink 生态圈体系及其组件 ... 30

2.2 面向离线数据的存储计算引擎 Hadoop 快速上手 ... 32
2.2.1 【实战】部署 Hadoop 集群 ... 33
2.2.2 【实战】使用 Hadoop 文件系统 HDFS 存储数据 ... 38
2.2.3 【实战】使用 Hadoop 离线计算引擎 MapReduce 处理数据 ... 46

2.3 面向批处理的大数据计算引擎 Spark 快速上手 ... 49
2.3.1 【实战】部署 Spark 集群 ... 49
2.3.2 【实战】执行 Spark 离线计算任务 ... 51
2.3.3 【实战】执行 Spark 实时计算任务 ... 57
2.3.4 【实战】使用 Spark SQL 处理结构化数据 ... 60

2.4 面向流处理的大数据计算引擎 Flink 快速上手 ... 61
2.4.1 【实战】部署 Flink 集群 ... 62
2.4.2 【实战】执行 Flink 离线计算任务 ... 63
2.4.3 【实战】执行 Flink 实时计算任务 ... 64
2.4.4 【实战】使用 Flink SQL 处理结构化数据 ... 66

2.5 大数据体系的单点故障问题 ... 66

第 2 篇 阿里云大数据的离线计算服务

第 3 章 面向离线数据存储与计算的 MaxCompute 基础 ... 70

3.1 MaxCompute 简介 ... 70
3.1.1 什么是 MaxCompute ... 70
3.1.2 MaxCompute 的特点 ... 71

3.2 初识 MaxCompute ... 71
3.2.1 MaxCompute 的架构 ... 71
3.2.2 MaxCompute 的核心概念 ... 74
3.2.3 MaxCompute 的数据类型 ... 76

- 3.3 使用 MaxCompute 的准备工作 78
  - 3.3.1 【实战】创建阿里云账号 79
  - 3.3.2 【实战】开通 MaxCompute 服务 82
  - 3.3.3 【实战】创建项目 83
  - 3.3.4 配置 MaxCompute 客户端 85
- 3.4 MaxCompute 快速上手 93
  - 3.4.1 【实战】使用命令行客户端 93
  - 3.4.2 【实战】执行 MapReduce 任务 99
  - 3.4.3 【实战】执行 Spark 任务 101
- 3.5 基于 Tunnel 的数据上传与下载 102
  - 3.5.1 Tunnel 简介 102
  - 3.5.2 【实战】使用 Tunnel 的命令行工具 103
  - 3.5.3 【实战】使用 Tunnel 的 SDK 107

第 4 章 处理结构化数据——基于 MaxCompute SQL 112

- 4.1 MaxCompute SQL 简介 112
  - 4.1.1 MaxCompute SQL 与其他 SQL 的差异 112
  - 4.1.2 MaxCompute SQL 的数据类型 114
  - 4.1.3 MaxCompute SQL 的数据类型转换 115
- 4.2 使用 MaxCompute SQL 119
  - 4.2.1 【实战】使用 DDL 语句 119
  - 4.2.2 【实战】使用 DML 语句 135
  - 4.2.3 【实战】使用 DQL 语句 140
  - 4.2.4 【实战】使用 MaxCompute SQL 的增强语法 CTE 143
- 4.3 使用 MaxCompute SQL 的内建函数 145
  - 4.3.1 【实战】日期函数 145
  - 4.3.2 【实战】窗口函数 148
  - 4.3.3 【实战】聚合函数 152
  - 4.3.4 【实战】条件判断函数 152
  - 4.3.5 数学函数和字符串函数 154
- 4.4 在 MaxCompute 中自定义 SQL 155

4.4.1 【实战】UDF 155
　　4.4.2 【实战】UDT 157
　　4.4.3 UDJ 158

第 5 章 处理离线数据——基于 MaxCompute MapReduce 159

5.1 MaxCompute MapReduce 简介 159
　　5.1.1 MaxCompute MapReduce 的处理流程 159
　　5.1.2 MaxCompute MapReduce 的使用限制 160
5.2 开发 WordCount 单词计数程序 161
　　5.2.1 WordCount 数据处理的流程 162
　　5.2.2 MaxCompute MapReduce 的编程接口 163
　　5.2.3 【实战】开发 WordCount 程序 166
5.3 MaxCompute MapReduce 的高级特性 169
　　5.3.1 【实战】实现数据排序 170
　　5.3.2 【实战】实现数据二次排序 173
　　5.3.3 【实战】使用过滤模式 MapOnly 177
　　5.3.4 【实战】使用 Join 实现多表连接 179
　　5.3.5 【实战】使用计数器 Counter 183
　　5.3.6 【实战】使用 Unique 实现数据去重 187
　　5.3.7 【实战】使用项目空间资源 193

第 6 章 处理离线数据——基于 MaxCompute Spark 196

6.1 MaxCompute Spark 基础 196
　　6.1.1 MaxCompute Spark 的系统结构 196
　　6.1.2 MaxCompute Spark 的使用限制 197
　　6.1.3 使用 spark-shell 198
6.2 MaxCompute Spark 的核心数据模型 RDD 199
　　6.2.1 什么是 RDD 200
　　6.2.2 熟悉 RDD 的算子 202
　　6.2.3 【实战】RDD 的缓存机制 209
　　6.2.4 【实战】RDD 的检查点机制 211
　　6.2.5 RDD 的依赖关系和任务执行的阶段 212

6.3 在 MaxCompute Spark 中使用 SQL 处理数据 214
6.3.1 Spark SQL 的特点 214
6.3.2 Spark SQL 的数据模型 215
6.3.3 【实战】创建 DataFrame 215
6.3.4 【实战】使用 DataFrame 处理数据 218
6.3.5 【实战】创建视图 220
6.4 【实战】MaxCompute Spark 开发案例 222
6.4.1 开发 Java 版本的单词计数程序 WordCount 222
6.4.2 开发 Scala 版本的单词计数程序 WordCount 224
6.5 诊断 MaxCompute Spark 作业 225
6.5.1 使用 Logview 工具诊断作业 226
6.5.2 使用 Spark Web UI 诊断作业 227

第 7 章 处理图数据——基于 MaxCompute Graph 229
7.1 MaxCompute Graph 基础 229
7.1.1 MaxCompute Graph 的基本概念 230
7.1.2 MaxCompute Graph 的数据结构 230
7.1.3 MaxCompute Graph 的程序逻辑 231
7.1.4 MaxCompute Graph 的 Aggregator 机制 233
7.1.5 MaxCompute Graph 的使用限制 236
7.2 使用 MaxCompute Graph 计算单源最短距离 236
7.2.1 单源最短距离算法简介 236
7.2.2 【实战】开发并运行单源最短距离算法程序 239

第 8 章 MaxCompute 的权限与安全 245
8.1 MaxCompute 的权限与安全简介 245
8.2 管理 MaxCompute 的用户 246
8.3 管理 MaxCompute 的权限 247
8.3.1 授权的三要素 248
8.3.2 项目空间内的权限 249
8.3.3 【实战】使用 ACL 授权 250

8.3.4 【实战】使用 Policy 授权 252
8.3.5 ACL 授权与 Policy 授权的区别 256
8.4 管理 MaxCompute 的角色 257
8.4.1 角色的作用 257
8.4.2 内置角色和自定义角色 258
8.4.3 【实战】使用 MaxCompute 的角色 259
8.5 LabelSecurity 260
8.5.1 LabelSecurity 简介 260
8.5.2 【实战】使用 LabelSecurity 260
8.5.3 【实战】LabelSecurity 的应用场景示例 264
8.6 使用 Package 实现跨项目空间的资源分享 265
8.6.1 什么是跨项目空间的资源分享 265
8.6.2 Package 的创建与使用 266
8.6.3 【实战】Package 的应用场景示例 268
8.7 项目空间的数据保护 270
8.7.1 MaxCompute 的数据保护机制 271
8.7.2 数据保护机制下数据的流动 271

第 3 篇　阿里云大数据的实时计算服务

第 9 章　消息队列 Kafka 版 274
9.1 消息队列基础 274
9.1.1 消息队列概述 274
9.1.2 消息队列的分类 275
9.2 消息队列 Kafka 版的体系架构 278
9.2.1 消息服务器 Broker 279
9.2.2 主题、分区与副本 279
9.2.3 消息的生产者 281
9.2.4 消息的消费者 283
9.3 快速上手消息队列 Kafka 版 285
9.3.1 快速入门操作流程 285

目录 | XIII

9.3.2 【实战】获取访问授权 286
9.3.3 【实战】购买和部署 287
9.3.4 【实战】创建资源 292
9.3.5 【实战】使用管理控制台收发消息 294
9.3.6 【实战】实例运行健康自检指南 296
9.4 消息队列 Kafka 版应用开发 298
9.4.1 【实战】开发基本的消息生产者与消费者 298
9.4.2 【实战】发送与接收自定义消息 304

第 10 章 实时计算 Flink 版 313

10.1 实时计算 Flink 版基础 313
10.1.1 什么是实时计算 Flink 版 313
10.1.2 实时计算 Flink 版的应用场景 314
10.1.3 【实战】快速上手实时计算 Flink 版 317
10.2 批处理开发——基于实时计算引擎 Flink Dataset 325
10.2.1 【实战】使用 map、flatMap 与 mapPartition 算子 326
10.2.2 【实战】使用 filter 与 distinct 算子 330
10.2.3 【实战】使用 join 算子 331
10.2.4 【实战】使用 cross 算子 333
10.2.5 【实战】使用 First-N 算子 334
10.2.6 【实战】使用外连接操作 335
10.3 流处理开发——基于实时计算引擎 Flink Datastream 338
10.3.1 【实战】开发单并行度的数据源 339
10.3.2 【实战】使用 union 算子 339
10.3.3 【实战】使用 connect 算子 341
10.4 SQL 与 Table 开发——基于实时计算引擎 Flink Table&SQL 342
10.4.1 【实战】开发 Flink Table 程序 343
10.4.2 【实战】开发 Flink SQL 程序 347
10.5 实时计算 Flink 版的高级特性 352
10.5.1 检查点设置 352
10.5.2 重启策略 354

10.5.3　分布式缓存 354
　　10.5.4　累加器 356

第 4 篇　阿里云大数据增值服务——数加平台

第 11 章　阿里云大数据集成开发平台 DataWorks 362
11.1　DataWorks 基础 362
　　11.1.1　DataWorks 功能架构 362
　　11.1.2　DataWorks 的基本概念 369
　　11.1.3　DataWorks 中的角色 371
11.2　DataWorks 中的数据集成 371
　　11.2.1　离线数据集成 372
　　11.2.2　实时数据集成 373
　　11.2.3　数据同步和数据同步作业 374
11.3　【实战】DataWorks 项目开发案例 375
　　11.3.1　准备项目开发环境 375
　　11.3.2　准备测试数据 378
　　11.3.3　开发业务流程 384
　　11.3.4　提交业务流程 390

第 12 章　数据可视化分析平台 Quick BI 393
12.1　Quick BI 简介 393
　　12.1.1　什么是 Quick BI 393
　　12.1.2　Quick BI 的基本对象 394
　　12.1.3　Quick BI 的体系架构 397
　　12.1.4　Quick BI 的应用场景 399
12.2　【实战】使用数据可视化分析平台 Quick BI 400
　　12.2.1　项目背景与需求 400
　　12.2.2　连接数据源 400
　　12.2.3　数据建模 402
　　12.2.4　数据可视化分析 405
　　12.2.5　发布共享仪表板 414

第 13 章　机器学习平台 PAI 416

13.1　机器学习基础知识 416
13.1.1　什么是机器学习 416
13.1.2　机器学习的常见算法 417

13.2　机器学习平台 PAI 基础知识 417
13.2.1　初识机器学习平台 PAI 417
13.2.2　PAI 的架构 418
13.2.3　PAI 的功能特性 419
13.2.4　PAI 的基本概念 419

13.3　使用机器学习平台 PAI 实现智能推荐 421
13.3.1　使用协同过滤算法实现商品推荐 421
13.3.2　使用 ALS 算法实现商品推荐 427

第 1 篇
大数据技术基础

第 1 章
大数据核心理论基础与架构

大数据平台的核心问题是解决数据的存储和计算,从而有了 Hadoop、Spark 和 Flink 这样的大数据框架,而这些框架都可以被看作数据仓库的一种实现方式。因此在学习大数据平台体系之前,需要对这些基本问题有一个比较清楚的了解。为什么大数据平台可以解决数据的存储和计算问题呢?它采用的是什么样的思想和原理呢?这些问题是本章重点讨论的内容。

1.1 什么是大数据

下面引用百度百科中的一段文字来介绍什么是大数据。

> 大数据(Big Data),指无法在一定时间范围内使用常规软件工具进行捕捉、管理和处理的数据集合,是需要新处理模式才能具有更强的决策能力、洞察发现能力和流程优化能力的海量、高增长率和多样化的信息资产。

IBM 又提出了大数据的 5V 特点,即 Volume(大量)、Velocity(高速)、Variety(多样)、Value(低价值密度)、Veracity(真实性)。

1.1.1 大数据的基本概念和特性

下面通过两个具体的例子来说明什么是大数据,以及大数据平台体系中要解决的核心问题。

大数据平台体系所要解决的核心问题是指从技术上要解决的问题。

1. 电商平台的推荐系统

相信读者对这个案例不会感到陌生，在任何一个电商平台上都会有推荐系统。例如，图 1-1 是某电商平台首页上推荐的商品信息。

图 1-1

在电商平台首页上，需要展示过去一个月内卖得好的商品信息。该功能的描述非常简单，但是如何实现呢？另外，任何一个推荐系统应该满足最基本的"千人千面"的要求，即不同的人看到的推荐商品信息应该是不一样的。如何根据用户的喜好来推荐，这也是在具体实现推荐系统时需要考虑的因素。

把过去一个月内卖得好的商品分析出来，并且根据用户的喜好将推荐的商品信息显示在首页上，需要基于过去一个月内交易的订单来进行分析和处理。而这样的订单量会有多少？对一个大型电商平台来说，这必将是一个非常庞大的数据量。因此在具体实现时，从技术上如何解决订单数据的存储和订单数据的分析计算，就成为推荐系统要解决的核心问题。如果可以找到相应的技术手段来解决这个问题，就可以利用机器学习中的推荐算法实现商品的推荐。

2. 基于大数据的天气预报系统

图 1-2 展示了一个天气预报系统的预报信息。例如，预报北京地区未来一周的天气情况。如何实现呢？这里可能会把北京地区各个气象观测点的天气数据汇总起来，通过气象专业知识进行分析和处理，从而做出天气预报。但是这样汇总起来的数据量也非常庞大。如何从技术上解决大量气象数据的存储和大量气象数据的分析计算，就成为天气预报系统的关键技术点。

图 1-2

通过上面的两个例子，不难总结出，在大数据平台体系中要解决的核心问题不外乎数据的存储和数据的计算。如果把握住了这两个核心的问题，就把握住了大数据平台体系中最重要的部分。

> Hadoop、Spark、Flink、Kafka 和 NoSQL 数据库这些大数据框架都是为了解决数据的存储和数据的计算这两个问题的。

1.1.2 大数据平台的核心问题——存储与计算

大数据平台体系要解决的核心问题是数据的存储和数据的计算。那么，如何解决这两个问题呢？本节将从技术实现上重点讨论解决问题的思想。

1. 数据的存储

由于数据量非常庞大，无法采用传统的单机模式来存储海量数据，因此解决方案是采用分布式系统来存储数据。简单来说就是，一台机器存储不了，就使用多台机器存储数据。Google 的 GFS（Google File System）就是一个典型的分布式文件系统。Google 将 GFS 的核心思想和原理以论文的形式发表了出来，为大数据平台体系中的数据存储奠定了基础，进而有了 Hadoop 中的分布式文件系统 HDFS（Hadoop Distributed File System）。图 1-3 展示了一个分布式文件系统的基本架构。

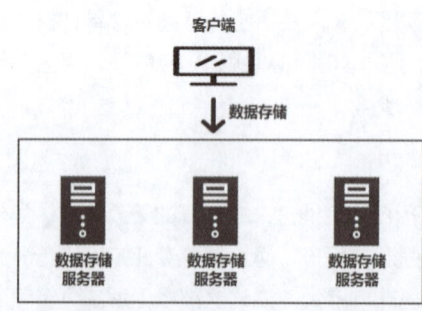

图 1-3

2. 数据的计算

与海量数据的存储所面对的问题一样,由于数据量非常庞大,无法采用单机环境完成数据的计算,因此,大数据的计算也采用了分布式计算的思想。用一句话解释分布式计算就是,一台机器无法完成计算,就使用多台机器一起计算。图 1-4 展示了一个分布式计算系统的基本架构。

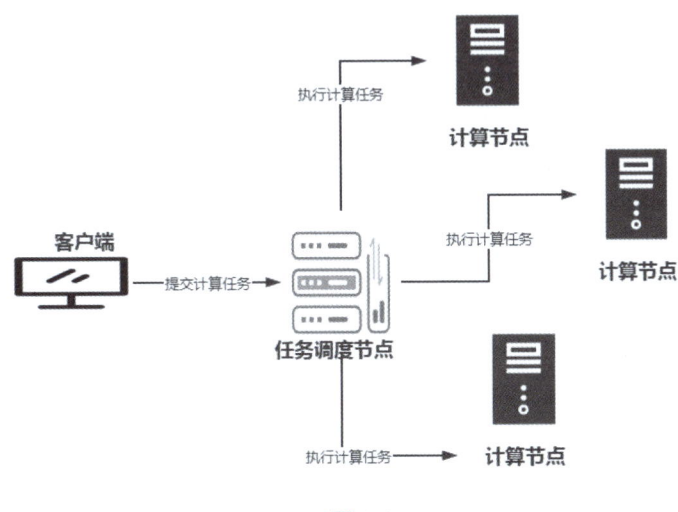

图 1-4

而大数据体系架构中的分布式计算又可以分为大数据离线计算和大数据实时计算。在学习具体的计算引擎之前,需要对一些常见的大数据计算引擎有一个初步的了解。

1)大数据离线计算

大数据离线计算也可以叫作批处理计算,它主要处理的是已经存在的历史数据。常见的大数据离线计算引擎有 Hadoop 中的 MapReduce、Spark 中的 Spark Core 和 Flink 中的 DataSet API。

 Spark 中的所有计算都是基于 Spark Core 的离线计算,也就是说,在 Spark 中没有真正的实时计算。

2)大数据实时计算

大数据实时计算也可以叫作流式计算,它主要处理的实时的流式数据,即在任务开始执行时,数据可能还不存在,一旦数据源产生了数据,就由相应的实时计算引擎完成计算。简单来说,大数据实时计算处理的是任务开始执行后产生的数据。常见的大数据实时计算引擎有 Apache Storm、Spark Streaming 和 Flink 中的 DataStream。

Spark Streaming 本质上不是真正的实时计算引擎,而是一个离线计算引擎。因为 Spark Streaming 的底层依然是 Spark Core 的离线计算引擎。因此,不能将 Spark Streaming 用于实时性很强的场景之中。

1.2 大数据的理论基础

大数据平台的核心思想是分布式集群的思想。分布式集群的思想在 Google 的技术系统中得到了很好的应用。Google 将其核心技术的思想以论文的形式公开发表出来,这就是 Google 的"三驾马车",即 Google 的 *GFS*、*MapReduce* 和 *BigTable*。这三篇论文奠定了大数据生态圈体系的技术基础,从而有了基于 Java 的大数据实现框架——Hadoop 生态圈体系。后续发展起来了 Spark 生态圈体系和 Flink 生态圈体系。

这里将重点介绍 Google 的分布式文件系统 GFS 和分布式计算模型 MapReduce。

1.2.1 大数据的分布式存储

Google 的文件系统 GFS 是一个典型的分布式文件系统,也是一个分布式存储的具体实现方式。日常的工作和生活中使用的网盘也是一个典型的分布式文件系统。图 1-5 展示了 GFS 的基本架构。

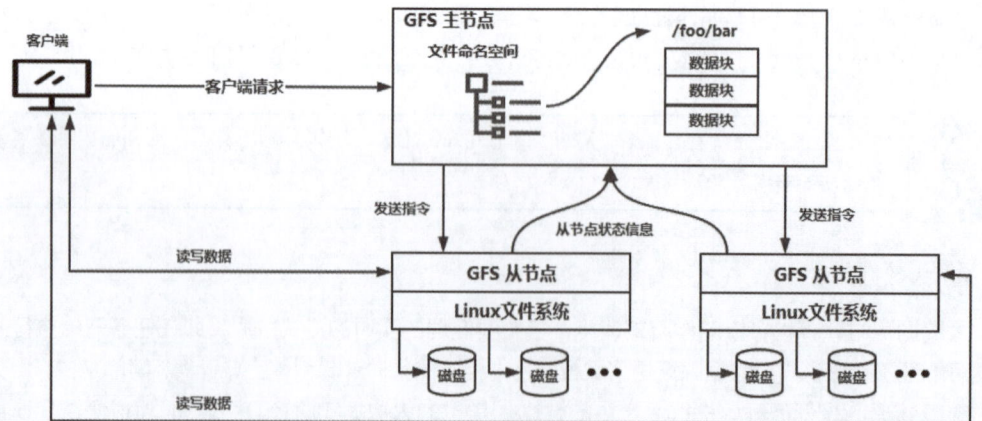

图 1-5

将数据存入一个分布式文件系统，需要解决两个问题，即如何存储海量的数据和如何保证数据的安全。如果从技术上解决了这两个问题，就能够实现一个分布式文件系统来存储大数据，并且保证数据的安全。

而解决的方案就是采用分布式集群，即采用多个节点组成一个分布式环境。下面分别讨论实现的细节，从而引出 Hadoop 的分布式文件系统 HDFS 的基本架构和实现原理。

1. **如何存储海量的数据**

因为需要存储海量的大数据，所以不能采用传统的单机模式进行存储。解决的方法也非常简单，既然一个节点或一个服务器无法存储，就采用多个节点或多个服务器一起存储，即分布式存储，进而开发一个分布式文件系统来实现数据的分布式存储。一个分布式文件系统存储数据的基本逻辑如图 1-6 所示。

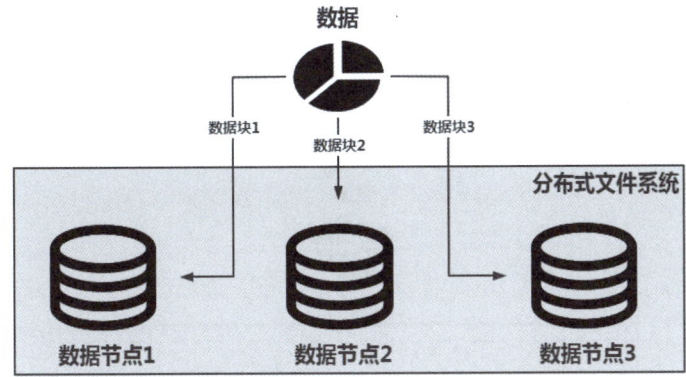

图 1-6

数据会被分隔存储到不同的数据节点上，从而实现海量数据的存储。假设数据量的大小是 20GB，而每个数据节点的存储空间只有 8GB，就无法把这些数据存储在一个节点上。

但是现在有 3 个这样的节点，假设每个节点的存储空间依然是 8GB，那么总的大小就是 24GB，就可以把这 20GB 的数据存储在由这 3 个节点组成的分布式文件系统上。

如果这 3 个数据节点都已经存储满了，就可以向该文件系统中加入新的数据节点，如数据节点 4、数据节点 5……从而实现数据节点的水平扩展。从理论上说，这样的扩展可以扩展到无穷，从而实现海量数据的存储。如果把图 1-6 架构对应到 Hadoop 的分布式文件系统 HDFS 中，数据节点就是 DataNode。

这里还有另一个问题，数据存储在分布式文件系统中的时候，是以数据块为单位进行存储的，例如：从 Hadoop 2.x 版本开始，HDFS 默认的数据块大小是 128MB。

数据块是一个逻辑单位,而不是一个物理单位,也就是说,数据块的 128MB 和数据实际的物理大小不是一一对应的。

这里举一个简单的例子。假设需要存储的数据是 300MB,使用 128MB 的数据块进行分隔存储,数据就会被分隔成 3 个单元。前两个单元的大小都是 128MB,和 HDFS 默认的数据块大小一致,而第三个单元的实际大小为 44MB,即占用的物理空间是 44MB。但是第三个单元占用的逻辑空间大小依然是一个数据块的大小,如果在 HDFS 中,就依然是 128M。换句话来说,第三个数据块没有存满。

2. 如何保证数据的安全

数据以数据块的形式存储在数据节点上,如果某个数据节点出现了问题或宕机了,就无法正常地访问存储在该节点上的数据块。如何保证数据块的安全呢?Google 的 GFS 借鉴了冗余的思想来解决这个问题。简单来说,数据块的冗余就是将同一个数据块多存储几份,并将它们存储在不同的数据节点上,这样即使某个数据节点出现了问题,也可以从其他节点上获取数据块信息,如图 1-7 所示。

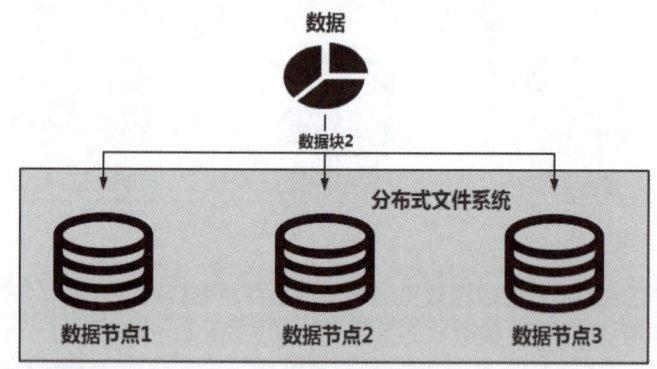

图 1-7

在图 1-7 中,数据块 2 同时存储在了 3 个数据节点上,即冗余度为 3,这样就可以从任何一个数据节点上获取该数据块的信息了。

数据冗余思想的引入解决了分布式文件系统中的数据安全问题,但是会造成存储空间的浪费。

在 Hadoop 的 HDFS 中可以通过在 hdfs-site.xml 文件中设置 dfs.replication 参数来指定数

据块的冗余度，该参数的默认值是 3。

```
<property>
    <name>dfs.replication</name>
    <value>3</value>
</property>
```

在 HDFS 体系架构中，除了前面提到的 DataNode 数据节点，还有 NameNode 和 SecondaryNameNode。HDFS 是一种主从架构，主节点是 NameNode，从节点是 DataNode。HDFS 的基本架构如图 1-8 所示。

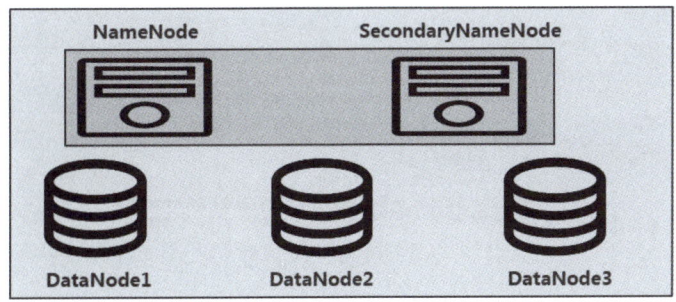

图 1-8

1.2.2　大数据的分布式计算

大数据的存储可以采用分布式文件系统，那么如何解决大数据的计算问题呢？

和大数据存储的思想一样，由于数据量庞大，无法采用单机环境来完成计算任务。既然单机环境无法完成计算任务，就使用多台服务器一起执行计算任务，从而组成一个分布式计算的集群来完成大数据的计算任务。基于这样的思想，Google 提出了 MapReduce 计算模型。

 Google 提出的 MapReduce 是一种处理大数据的计算模型，它和具体的编程语言没有关系。

Hadoop 体系中实现了 MapReduce 计算模型。Hadoop 是采用 Java 语言实现的框架，因此在 Hadoop 中开发的 MapReduce 程序也是一个 Java 程序。众所周知，MongoDB 也支持 MapReduce 计算模型，而 MongoDB 中的编程语言是 JavaScript，所以在 MongoDB 中开发 MapReduce 程序需要使用 JavaScript 语言。

Google 为什么会提出 MapReduce 计算模型呢？其主要目的是解决 PageRank 的问题，即网页排名的问题。因此在介绍 MapReduce 计算模型之前，有必要先介绍一下 PageRank。Google

作为一个搜索引擎，具有强大的搜索功能。Google 的搜索结果页面如图 1-9 所示。

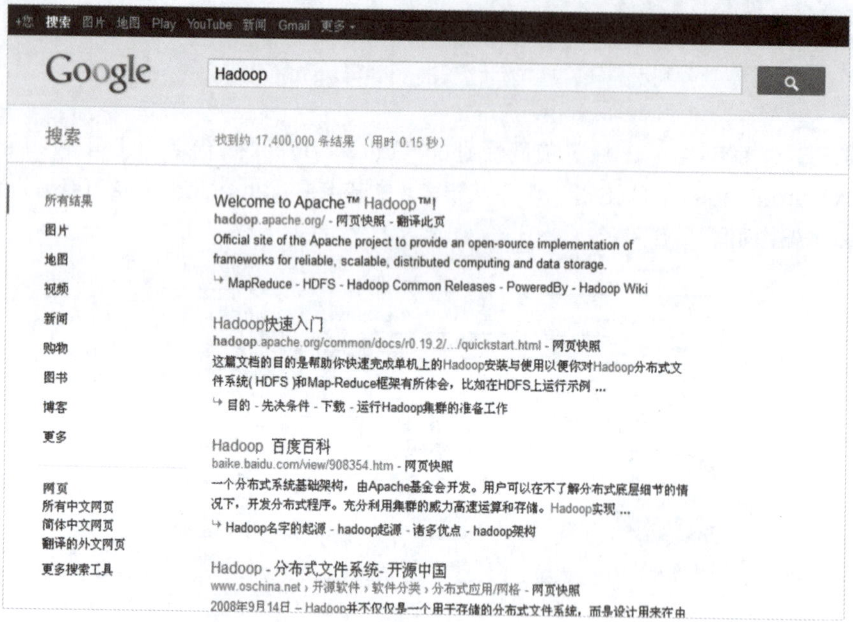

图 1-9

每一个搜索结果都是一个 HTML 网页，即 Page。那么如何决定网页的排列顺序呢？这就需要给每个网页打一个分数，即 Rank 值。Rank 值越大，对应的 Page 在搜索结果中就越靠前。PageRank 的一个简单示例如图 1-10 所示。

Google的向量矩阵

	网页1	网页2	网页3	网页4
网页1	0	1	1	1
网页2	0	0	1	1
网页3	0	0	0	0
网页4	0	0	1	0

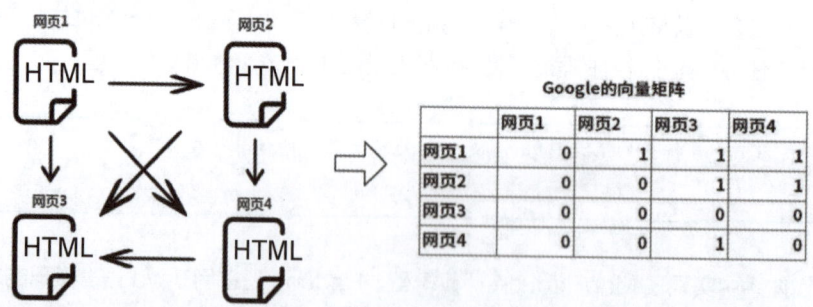

图 1-10

这个示例以 4 个 HTML 的网页来展示。网页与网页之间可以通过<a>标签的超级链接从一个网页跳转到另一个网页。

假设网页 1 链接跳转到了网页 2、网页 3 和网页 4；网页 2 链接跳转到了网页 3 和网页 4；网页 3 没有链接跳转到其他的网页；网页 4 链接跳转到了网页 3。如果用 1 表示网页之间存在链接跳转关系，用 0 表示不存在链接跳转关系，并以行为单位，就可以建立一个 Google 的向量矩阵来表示网页之间的跳转关系。这里得到的向量矩阵将是一个 4×4 的矩阵。通过计算这个矩阵就可以得到每个网页的权重值，而这个权重值就是 Rank 值，从而进行网页搜索结果的排名。

但是在实际情况下得到的这个 Google 的向量矩阵是非常庞大的。例如，网络爬虫从全世界的网站上爬取回来了 1 亿个网页，存储在分布式文件系统中，而网页之间又存在链接跳转的关系。这时候建立的 Google 的向量矩阵将会是 1 亿×1 亿的庞大矩阵。这样庞大的矩阵无法使用一台计算机来完成计算。如何解决这个庞大矩阵的计算问题将是 PageRank 的关键。在这样的问题背景下，Google 提出了 MapReduce 计算模型。

MapReduce 的核心思想其实只有 6 个字，即先拆分、再合并。通过这样的方式，不管得到的向量矩阵有多大，都可以进行计算。拆分的过程叫作 Map，而合并的过程叫作 Reduce。MapReduce 处理数据的基本过程如图 1-11 所示。

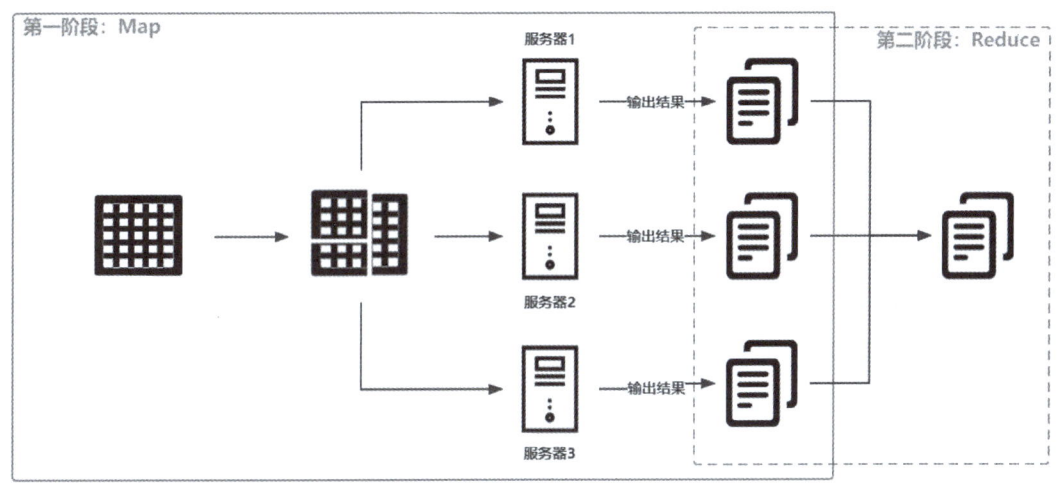

图 1-11

在图 1-11 的示例中，假设有一个庞大的矩阵要进行计算，由于无法在一台计算机上完成，因此将矩阵进行拆分，首先将其拆分为 4 个小矩阵，只要拆分到足够小，让一台计算机能够完成计算即可。每台计算机计算其中的一个小矩阵，得到部分结果，这个过程就叫作 Map，如图 1-11 中实线方框的部分。将 Map 的输出结果进行二次计算，从而得到大矩阵的结果，这个过程就叫作 Reduce，如图 1-11 中虚线方框的部分。通过 Map 和 Reduce，不管 Google 的向量矩阵有多大，都可以计算出最终的结果。在 Hadoop 中使用 Java 语言实现了这样的计算方式，这样的思想也被借鉴到了 Spark 和 Flink 中。例如，Spark 中的核心数据模型是 RDD，它由分区组成，每个分区被一个 Spark 的 Worker 从节点处理，从而实现了分布式计算。在 Hadoop 中执行

MapReduce 任务的输出日志信息如图 1-12 所示。

```
2021-01-08 20:38:28,275 INFO client.RMProxy: Connecting to ResourceManager at demo111/192.168.157.111:8032
2021-01-08 20:38:29,260 INFO mapreduce.JobResourceUploader: Disabling Erasure Coding for path: /tmp/hadoop-yarn/staging/r1
2021-01-08 20:38:30,135 INFO input.FileInputFormat: Total input files to process : 1
2021-01-08 20:38:31,099 INFO mapreduce.JobSubmitter: number of splits:1
2021-01-08 20:38:31,325 INFO mapreduce.JobSubmitter: Submitting tokens for job: job_1610109155433_0001
2021-01-08 20:38:31,327 INFO mapreduce.JobSubmitter: Executing with tokens: []
2021-01-08 20:38:31,850 INFO conf.Configuration: resource-types.xml not found
2021-01-08 20:38:31,851 INFO resource.ResourceUtils: Unable to find 'resource-types.xml'.
2021-01-08 20:38:32,691 INFO impl.YarnClientImpl: Submitted application application_1610109155433_0001
2021-01-08 20:38:32,812 INFO mapreduce.Job: The url to track the job: http://demo111:8088/proxy/application_1610109155433/
2021-01-08 20:38:32,814 INFO mapreduce.Job: Running job: job_1610109155433_0001
2021-01-08 20:38:48,485 INFO mapreduce.Job: Job job_1610109155433_0001 running in uber mode : false
2021-01-08 20:38:48,487 INFO mapreduce.Job:  map 0% reduce 0%
2021-01-08 20:38:55,717 INFO mapreduce.Job:  map 100% reduce 0%
2021-01-08 20:39:02,823 INFO mapreduce.Job:  map 100% reduce 100%
2021-01-08 20:39:04,860 INFO mapreduce.Job: Job job_1610109155433_0001 completed successfully
2021-01-08 20:39:05,034 INFO mapreduce.Job: Counters: 53
        File System Counters
                FILE: Number of bytes read=93
                FILE: Number of bytes written=432193
                FILE: Number of read operations=0
                FILE: Number of large read operations=0
                FILE: Number of write operations=0
                HDFS: Number of bytes read=159
                HDFS: Number of bytes written=55
                HDFS: Number of read operations=8
                HDFS: Number of large read operations=0
```

图 1-12

> 通过输出的日志可以看出，Hadoop 的 MapReduce 任务被拆分成了两个阶段，即 Map 阶段和 Reduce 阶段。当 Map 执行完成后，接着执行 Reduce，并且 Map 处理完的数据结果将会作为 Reduce 的输入。

1.3 大数据技术与数据仓库

大数据生态圈体系其实是数据仓库的一种实现方式。那么什么是数据仓库呢？

> 数据仓库（Data Warehouse，DW），是为企业所有级别的决策制定，提供所有类型数据支持的战略集合。它是单个数据存储，出于支持分析性报告和决策的目的而创建，为需要业务智能的企业改进业务流程提供指导，以及监视时间、成本、质量。

1.3.1 什么是数据仓库

简单来说，数据仓库就是一个数据库。在具体实现数据仓库时可以使用传统的关系型数据库，例如 Oracle 和 MySQL 等，也可以使用大数据生态圈体系来实现。在数据仓库中一般只进行数据的分析和处理，即查询操作，一般不支持修改操作，也不支持事务。利用传统的关系型数据库搭建数据仓库的过程如图 1-13 所示。

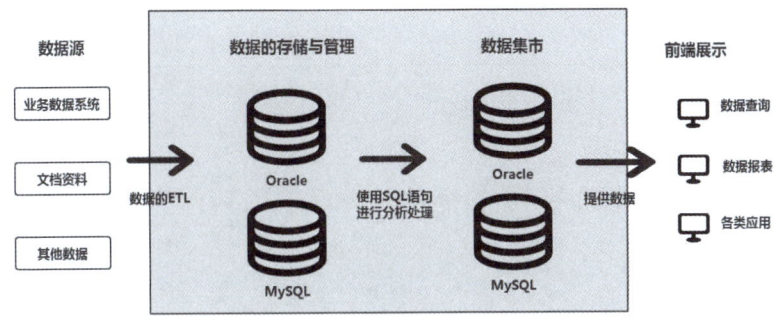

图 1-13

在搭建数据仓库时，首先需要有数据源提供各种各样的数据，例如关系型数据、文本数据等。其次需要使用 ETL 把数据源的数据采集到数据存储介质中，即抽取（Extract）、转换（Transform）和加载（Load）数据。图 1-13 中使用了传统的关系型数据库 Oracle 和 MySQL 进行数据的存储与管理。接下来，需要根据应用场景，使用 SQL 语句对原始数据进行分析和处理，把结果存入数据集市，而数据集市最大的特点就是面向主题，即面向最终业务的需要。最后把数据集市中的分析结果提供给最前端的各个业务系统。使用 Oracle 数据库创建数据仓库的界面如图 1-14 所示。

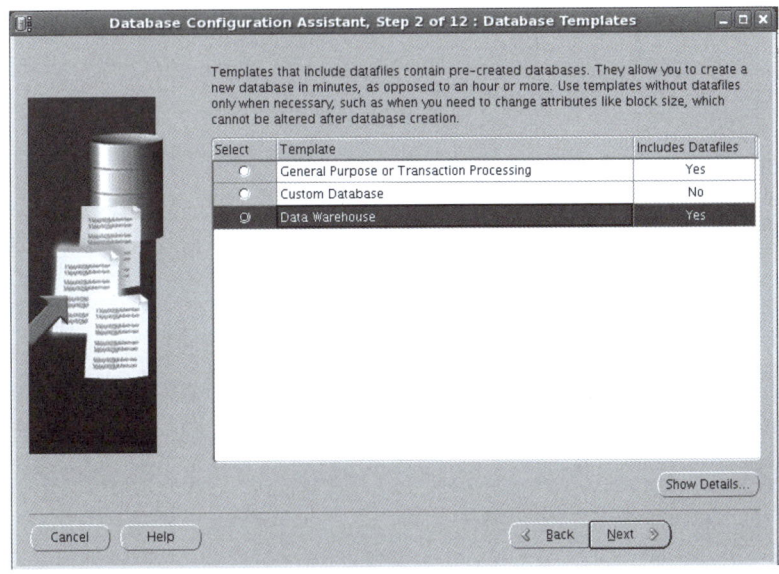

图 1-14

1.3.2 基于大数据技术实现的数据仓库

如何使用大数据生态圈体系中的组件来搭建数据仓库呢？使用大数据生态圈体系中的组件搭建

数据仓库的过程如图 1-15 所示。

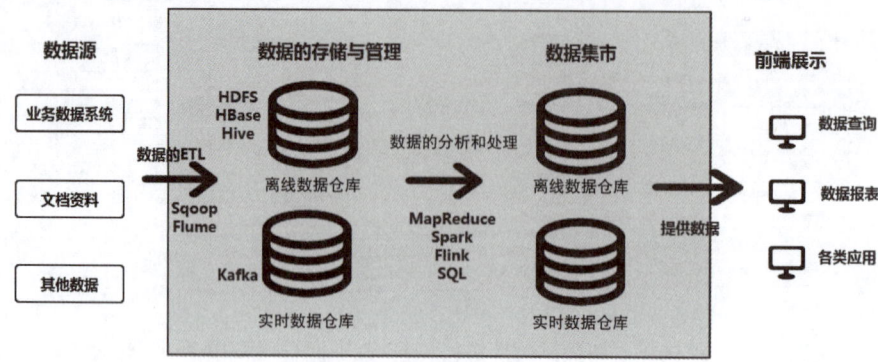

图 1-15

图 1-15 中只展示了大数据生态圈体系本身提供的组件，没有展示第三方提供的组件，在 2.1 节中将详细介绍每个组件的功能和作用。

在实现数据仓库的每个阶段，大数据生态圈体系都提供了对应的组件来实现，下面将分别进行介绍。

1. 数据的 ETL

数据的 ETL 主要完成数据的抽取、转换和加载。大数据生态圈体系提供了 Sqoop 和 Flume 完成相应的工作，但是二者的侧重点有所不同。Sqoop 的全称是 SQL to Hadoop，是一个数据交换工具，主要针对的是关系型数据库。而 Flume 主要用于采集日志数据或实时数据，数据通常是文本的形式。

2. 数据的存储和管理

这里将搭建数据仓库来实现原始数据的存储，而目前的数据仓库又可以分为离线数据仓库和实时数据仓库。离线数据仓库可以基于 HDFS、HBase 或 Hive 来实现，主要存储离线数据，从而进行数据的离线处理与计算。实时数据仓库可以基于 Kafka 消息系统来实现，主要存储实时数据或流式数据，从而进行数据的实时处理与计算。

3. 数据的分析和处理

由于数据仓库可以分为离线数据仓库和实时数据仓库，因此在进行数据分析和处理时，也可以使用不同的计算引擎。在进行离线计算时，可以使用 MapReduce、Spark Core 或 Flink DataSet API 完成。在进行实时计算时，可以使用 Storm、Spark Streaming、Flink DataStream API 完成。但大数据生态圈体系提供的计算引擎都需要开发 Java 程序或 Scala 程序，这对很多不懂编程语言的数据分析人员来说不是特别方便。因此，在大数据生态圈体系中，也可以使用 SQL 语句分析和处理数据，例如 Hive SQL、Spark SQL 和 Flink SQL。

4. 数据集市

在完成数据的分析和处理后，需要将数据存入数据集市。这里可以利用前面已经介绍过的技术、组件来搭建相应的离线数据仓库和实时数据仓库。

1.4 基于开源大数据组件的大数据平台架构

在了解了大数据技术与数据仓库的关系后，就可以利用大数据组件搭建一个大数据平台，从而实现数据的存储和数据的计算。大数据平台的整体架构如图 1-16 所示。

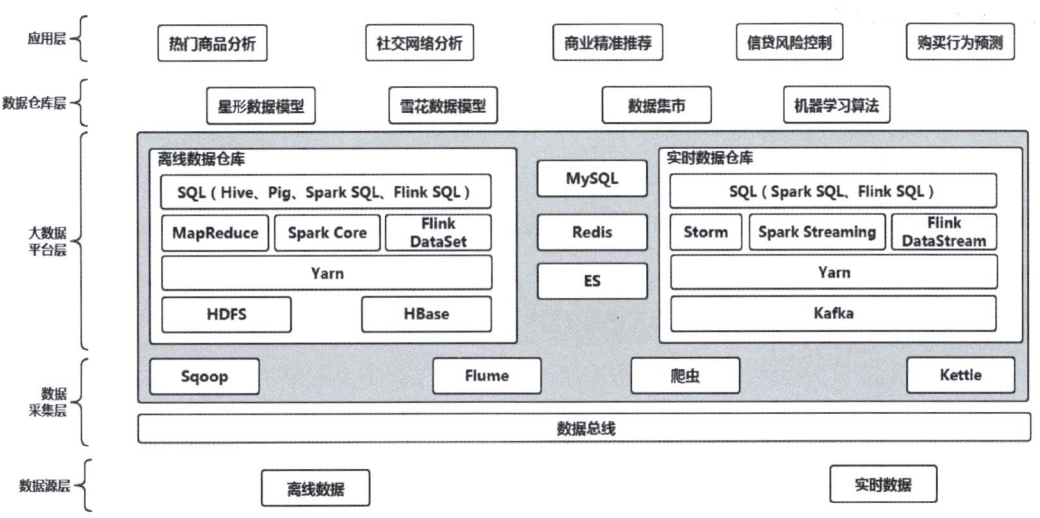

图 1-16

大数据平台的总体架构可以分为 5 层：数据源层、数据采集层、大数据平台层、数据仓库层和应用层。

图 1-16 是基于 Lambda 架构构建的大数据平台，这也是目前构建大数据平台的主流方式。Lambda 架构存在的最主要问题是需要维护离线与实时两套计算系统，从而导致批量与实时计算结果数据口径不一致。另外，维护两套计算系统增加了系统开发和维护的成本。

1.4.1 数据源层

数据源层的主要功能是提供各种需要的业务数据，例如用户订单数据、交易数据、系统的日志数据等。尽管数据源的种类多种多样，但在大数据平台体系中可以把它们划分成两大类，即离线数据源和实时数据源。顾名思义，离线数据源用于大数据离线计算，实时数据源用于大数据实时计算。

1.4.2 数据采集层

有了底层数据源提供的数据，就需要使用 ETL 工具完成数据的抽取、转换和加载，Hadoop 体系中就提供了这样的组件。例如，使用 Sqoop 完成大数据平台与关系型数据库的数据交换；使用 Flume 完成对日志数据的采集。除了大数据平台体系本身提供的这些组件，爬虫也是一种典型的数据采集方式。当然也可以使用第三方的数据采集工具，如 DataX 和 CDC 完成数据的采集工作。

> 为了降低数据源层和数据采集层之间的耦合度，可以在这两层之间加入数据总线。数据总线并不是必需的，它的引入只是为了在进行系统架构设计时，降低层与层之间的耦合度。

1.4.3 大数据平台层

大数据平台层是整个大数据体系中最核心的一层，用于完成大数据的存储和大数据的计算。由于大数据平台可以被看作数据仓库的一种实现方式，进而又可以分为离线数据仓库和实时数据仓库。下面分别进行介绍。

1. 基于大数据技术的离线数据仓库的实现方式

数据采集层得到数据后，通常先将数据存储在 HDFS 或 HBase 中，然后由离线计算引擎，如 MapReduce、Spark Core、Flink DataSet 完成离线数据的分析与处理。为了在平台上对各种计算引擎进行统一的管理和调度，可以把这些计算引擎都运行在 Yarn 上。接下来就可以使用 Java 程序或 Scala 程序来完成数据的分析与处理。为了简化应用的开发，在大数据平台体系中，也支持使用 SQL 语句来处理数据，即提供了各种数据分析引擎，例如 Hadoop 体系中的 Hive，其默认的行为是 Hive on MapReduce。这样就可以在 Hive 中书写标准的 SQL 语句，从而由 Hive 将其转换为 MapReduce，进而运行在 Yarn 上，以处理大数据。常见的大数据分析引擎除了 Hive，还有 Spark SQL 和 Flink SQL。

2. 基于大数据技术的实时数据仓库的实现方式

数据采集层得到实时数据后，为了进行数据的持久化，同时保证数据的可靠性，可以将采集的数据存入消息系统 Kafka，进而由各种实时计算引擎，如 Storm、Spark Stream 和 Flink

DataStream 进行处理。和离线数据仓库一样，这些计算引擎可以运行在 Yarn 上，同时支持使用 SQL 语句对实时数据进行处理。

> 离线数据仓库和实时数据仓库在实现的过程中，可能会用到一些公共的组件，例如使用 MySQL 存储的元信息、使用 Redis 进行缓存、使用 ElasticSearch（简称 ES）完成数据的搜索等。

1.4.4 数据仓库层

有了大数据平台层的支持就可以进一步搭建数据仓库层了。而在搭建数据仓库时，又可以基于星形模型或雪花模型搭建。前面曾经提到的数据集市和机器学习算法也可以被划归到这一层中。

1.4.5 应用层

有了数据仓库层的各种数据模型和数据后，就可以基于这些模型和数据实现各种各样的应用场景了。例如热门商品分析、社交网络分析、商业精准推荐、信贷风险控制及购买行为预测等。

1.5 自建大数据平台与租赁大数据平台

企业在构建大数据平台时，通常有两种不同的选择，即自建大数据平台和租赁大数据平台。企业在构建自己的业务应用时应该如何选择？为什么说租赁的大数据平台对企业更有意义？企业在选择租赁大数据平台时，为什么推荐使用阿里云大数据平台？本节将深入讨论这些问题。

> 租赁的大数据平台也可以叫作托管的大数据平台。

1.5.1 为什么推荐使用租赁的大数据平台

对企业的 IT 部门来说，在部署能够支持数据中心运行的大数据平台时，都希望能够快速行动，在预算紧和任务重的情况下需要快速地构建大数据平台，从而实现对数据应用的支持。而企业在构建这样一个大数据平台的过程中，不管是时间成本还是金钱成本都非常高，因此企业自建大数据平台具有一定的风险。而租赁大数据平台可以帮助企业在业务层面快速实现扩展和缩小，而不用关心底层平台架构的实现和维护。

自建大数据平台往往只适合数据量庞大的互联网企业，并且自建大数据平台的成本比租赁大数据平台的成本高出很多。因此，对绝大部分的企业来说，租赁大数据平台可能会更加适合。租赁大数据平台可以提供更高的灵活性和数据安全性，并且企业不需要对日常的 IT 运维和管理操太多的心。

 企业更适合使用哪一种方式需要从自身的业务需求及经济实力出发，进行客观的考量。

1.5.2 为什么选择阿里云大数据平台

阿里云大数据平台是阿里云自主研发的一体化大数据智能计算平台，支持百万级服务器并行计算，并提供实时离线一体、流批一体、湖仓一体、大数据+AI 一体的多场景能力。阿里云大数据平台承载了几千个客户超过 700 个项目的大数据智能计算业务。与其他大数据平台相比，阿里云大数据平台具有以下优势。

1. 成本低

企业无须组建专门的大数据平台部署和运维团队，可以按照实际需要采购存储和计算资源，因此在企业业务发展初期，极大地降低了拥有大数据平台的各项成本。

2. 效率高

通过使用阿里云大数据平台，企业可以快速构建适合业务的大数据平台架构并实现企业的业务需求。

3. 性能按需采购

阿里云大数据平台支持数据 I/O 及计算能力弹性伸缩功能，企业可以根据自身的业务需要动态进行业务的调整。

4. 安全性强

阿里云大数据平台提供数据的安全性保证，以及租户之间的安全隔离机制，并且可以实现大数据项目中不同角色的权限管理和各种数据资源的权限管理。

1.6 阿里云大数据生态圈体系

基于开源的大数据技术，阿里云开发了自己的大数据计算服务，即 MaxCompute。MaxCompute 原名 ODPS（Open Data Processing Service），它是阿里云提供的数据仓库解决方案，并提供大数据量（TB、PB、EB）的结构化数据的存储和计算服务。

由于 MaxCompute 适用于离线计算的批处理场景，因此阿里云进一步开发了实时计算 Flink 版来支持大数据的实时处理与计算。阿里云大数据的生态圈体系如图 1-17 所示。

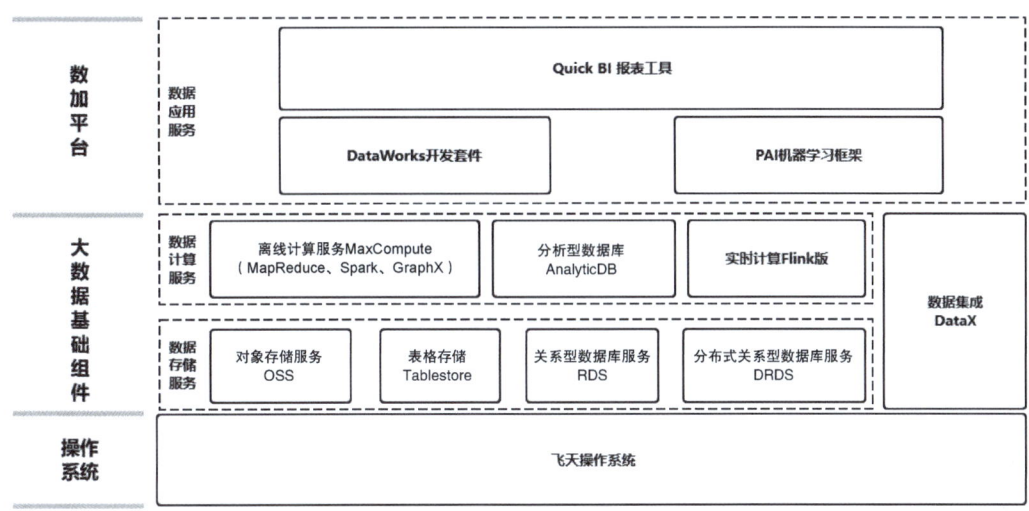

图 1-17

1.6.1 阿里云大数据基础组件

在了解了阿里云大数据生态圈体系后，下面将详细介绍阿里云提供的大数据基础组件及其功能特性。

1. 数据存储服务

阿里云大数据的数据存储服务主要包括对象存储服务 OSS、表格存储 Tablestore、关系型数据库服务 RDS 和分布式关系型数据库服务 DRDS。

1）对象存储服务 OSS

对象存储服务 OSS（Object Storage Service）是一款安全、低成本、高可靠性的云存储服务，可提供 99.9999999999%（12 个 9）的数据持久性，99.995% 的数据可用性。多种存储类型可供用户选择，全面优化存储成本。

OSS 具有与平台无关的 RESTful API 接口，用户可以在任何应用、任何时间、任何地点存储和访问任何类型的数据。用户可以使用阿里云提供的 API、SDK 接口或 OSS 迁移工具轻松地将海量数据移入或移出 OSS。将数据存储到 OSS 后，用户可以选择标准存储（Standard）作为移动应用、大型网站、图片分享或热点音视频的主要存储方式，也可以选择成本更低、存储期限更长的低频访问存储（Infrequent Access）、归档存储（Archive）、冷归档存储（Cold Archive）作为不经常访问的数据的存储方式。OSS 的管理控制台如图 1-18 所示。

图 1-18

2)表格存储 Tablestore

Tablestore 面向海量结构化数据提供 Serverless 表存储服务,同时针对物联网场景深度优化提供一站式的 IoTstore 解决方案,适用于海量账单、IM 消息、物联网、车联网、风控、推荐等场景中的结构化数据存储,提供海量数据低成本存储、毫秒级的在线数据查询和检索及灵活的数据分析功能。

Tablestore 的优势包括多模型数据存储、多元化数据索引、多计算生态接入、访问安全性等。Tablestore 的管理控制台如图 1-19 所示。

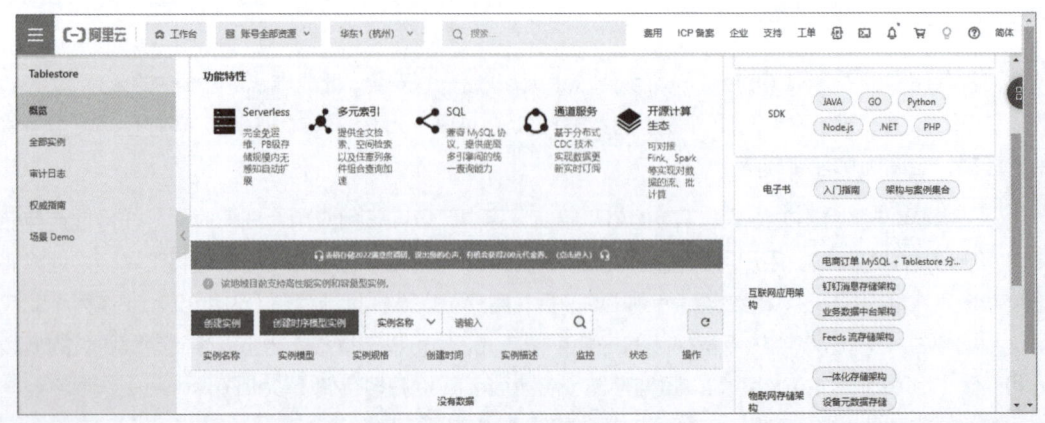

图 1-19

3)关系型数据库服务 RDS

关系型数据库服务 RDS（Relational Database Service）是一种稳定、可靠、可弹性伸缩的在线数据库服务。基于阿里云分布式文件系统和 SSD 高性能存储，RDS 支持 MySQL、SQL Server、PostgreSQL 和 MariaDB TX 引擎，并且提供了容灾、备份、恢复、监控、迁移等方面的全套解决方案，有效帮助用户解决数据库运维的相关问题。

RDS 的管理控制台如图 1-20 所示。

图 1-20

4）分布式关系型数据库服务 DRDS

分布式关系型数据库服务 DRDS（Distributed Relational Database Service）是阿里巴巴致力于解决单机数据库服务瓶颈问题而自主研发的分布式数据库产品，解决了一些传统 RDS 的痛点。

DRDS 高度兼容 MySQL 协议和语法，支持自动化水平拆分、在线平滑扩缩容、弹性扩展、透明读写分离，具备数据库全生命周期运维管控能力。

> DRDS 必须依赖 RDS。

2. 数据计算服务

阿里云大数据的数据存储服务主要包括离线计算服务 MaxCompute、分析型数据库 AnalyticDB 和实时计算 Flink 版。

1）离线计算服务 MaxCompute

离线计算服务 MaxCompute 是一种快速、完全托管的 TB/PB 级数据仓库解决方案。

MaxCompute 向用户提供了完善的数据导入方案及多种经典的分布式计算模型，能够更快速地解决用户海量数据计算的问题，有效降低企业的成本，并保障数据的安全。

MaxCompute 提供离线和流式数据的接入，具备大规模数据计算和查询加速的能力，为用户提供面向多种计算场景的数据仓库解决方案和分析建模服务。MaxCompute 还为用户提供完善的数据导入方案和多种经典的分布式计算模型，用户不必关心分布式计算和维护细节，就可以轻松完成大数据分析。

MaxCompute 适用于 100GB 以上规模的存储及计算需求，最大可达 EB 级别。MaxCompute 已经在阿里巴巴集团内部得到大规模应用。

MaxCompute 适用于大型互联网企业的数据仓库和 BI 分析、网站的日志分析、电子商务网站的交易分析、用户特征和兴趣挖掘等。MaxCompute 的管理控制台如图 1-21 所示。

图 1-21

> MaxCompute 用于离线计算的批处理场景，不能用于实时计算的流处理场景。

2）分析型数据库 AnalyticDB

分析型数据库 AnalyticDB（ADB）是阿里巴巴自主研发的海量数据实时高并发在线分析云计算服务，可以在毫秒级针对千亿级数据进行及时的多维分析透视和业务探索，具备海量数据的计算和响应计算的能力，能让用户在瞬息之间进行灵活的数据探索，快速地发现数据价值，并且可以直接嵌入业务系统为终端客户提供分析服务。

ADB 支持全面的值索引和块索引技术，并全面兼容 MySQL 协议和 SQL2003。云原生数据仓库 ADB MySQL 版的管理控制台如图 1-22 所示。

图 1-22

3）实时计算 Flink 版

实时计算 Flink 版（Alibaba Cloud Realtime Compute for Apache Flink，Powered by Ververica）是阿里云基于 Apache Flink 构建的企业级、高性能的实时大数据处理系统。它提供实时应用的作业开发、数据调试、运行与监控、自动调优、智能诊断等服务。其内核引擎 100% 兼容 Apache Flink，并有两倍性能的提升。

实时计算 Flink 版拥有 Flink CDC、动态 CEP 等企业级增值功能，内置丰富的上下游连接器，帮助企业构建高效、稳定和强大的实时数据应用。

实时计算 Flink 版的管理控制台如图 1-23 所示。

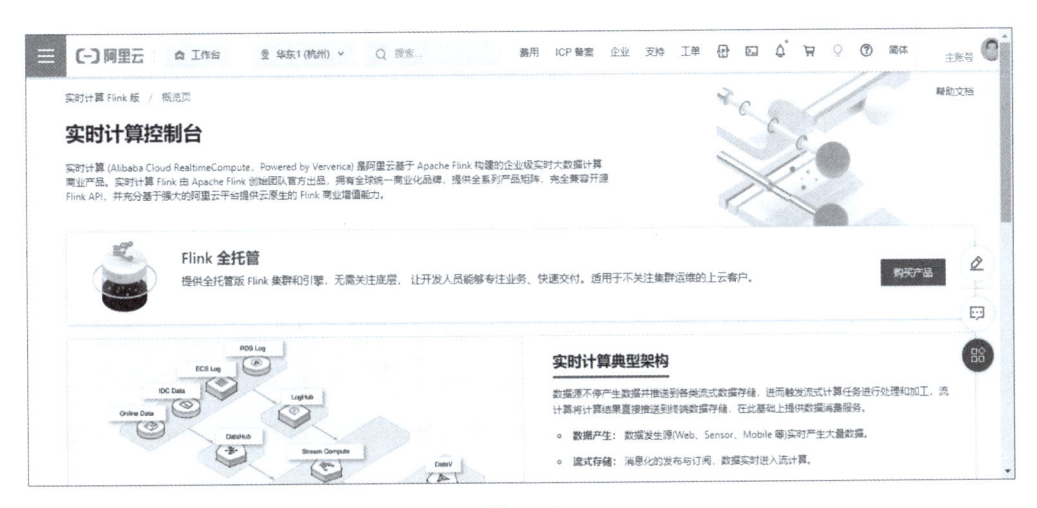

图 1-23

1.6.2 基于阿里云大数据基础组件的数加平台

数加平台基于阿里在大数据上的经验积累，在对内的平台上做了一个对外的实例，即数加。阿里云的数加平台包括多租户、账号、权限、安全、元数据、计量计费等模块，也包括算法平台 PAI。它将计算引擎、数据开发工具、数据采集和传输工具、数据分析工具、机器学习平台无缝集成，提供端到端的一站式用户体验。它让基于 Hadoop 自建数据平台成为往事，让客户专注于业务系统开发。

1. 大数据开发治理平台 DataWorks

DataWorks 基于 MaxCompute、Hologres、EMR、AnalyticDB、CDP 等大数据引擎，为数据仓库、数据湖、湖仓一体等解决方案提供统一的全链路大数据开发治理平台。

从 2009 年起，DataWorks 不断沉淀阿里巴巴大数据建设方法论，支撑数据中台建设，同时与数万名各行业的客户携手，不断提高数据应用效率，助力产业数字化升级。

DataWorks 的管理控制台页面如图 1-24 所示。

图 1-24

DataWorks 具有强大的基础能力，可以使用户大幅度提高工作效率，保障数据准时产出，助力数据治理，让用户零成本构建数据服务。它具有以下特性。

（1）学习成本低。非技术人员 1~2 小时即可掌握完整的数据开发、治理流程，告别传统命令行，节省巨大的学习成本。用户可以在同一 DAG（Directed Acyclic Graph，有向无环图）中，构建异构计算引擎形成混编任务流，无须分别维护各技术栈，帮助用户高效组合混编任务流。

（2）人效提升快。一键开通即可搭建开箱即用的数仓技术架构，告别繁重的自研、部署、维护工作，为企业免去数十人的运维开发团队开销。

（3）产品功能全。功能涵盖数据传输、开发、生产、治理、安全领域，每个领域深度覆盖大数据全生命周期，帮助企业轻松应对在搭建数仓、搭建数据中台、数字化转型项目中遇到的难题。

2. 数据可视化分析平台 Quick BI

Quick BI 是一款全场景数据消费式的 BI 平台，秉承"全场景消费数据，让业务决策触手可及"的使命，通过智能的数据分析和可视化能力帮助企业构建数据分析系统。用户可以使用 Quick BI 制作漂亮的仪表板、格式复杂的电子表格、酷炫的大屏、有分析思路的数据门户，也可以将报表集成在业务流程中，并且通过邮件、钉钉、企业微信等分享给同事和合作伙伴。使用 Quick BI 可以让企业的数据资产快速地流动起来。结合使用 BI 和 AI，挖掘数据背后的价值，可以加深并加速在企业内部各种场景的数据消费。

Quick BI 从阿里巴巴内部的 BI 工具发展而来。阿里巴巴内部在 2014 年前还在使用传统的 BI 工具来做报表和获取数据，但传统 BI 工具无法满足阿里巴巴内部丰富的场景、快速变化的业务和海量数据的查询等诉求，从 2014 年开始阿里巴巴内部开始出现各种自建的可视化工具，例如服务于有 Excel 经验人员的在线电子表格，支持"双 11"和"618 大促"活动的可视化大屏，快速构建报表和仪表板的工具等。Quick BI 的"模板市场"页面如图 1-25 所示。

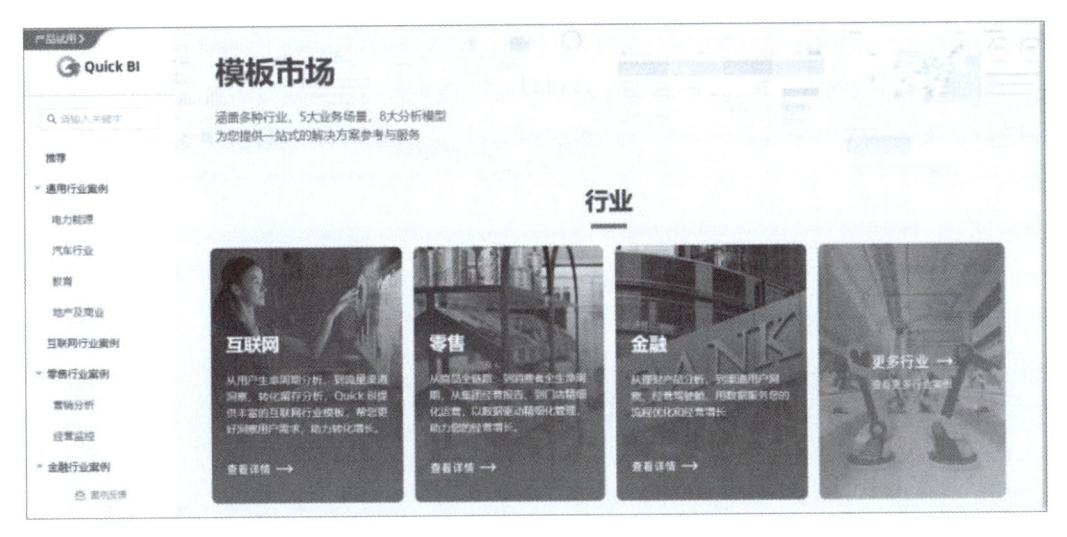

图 1-25

3. 机器学习平台 PAI

机器学习平台 PAI（Platform of Artificial Intelligence）是面向开发者和企业的机器学习/深度学习工程平台，提供包含数据标注、模型构建、模型训练、模型部署、推理优化在内的 AI 开发全链路服务，内置 140 多种优化算法，具备丰富的行业场景插件，为用户提供低门槛、高性能的云原生 AI 工程化能力。

机器学习平台 PAI 的"工作空间详情"页面如图 1-26 所示。

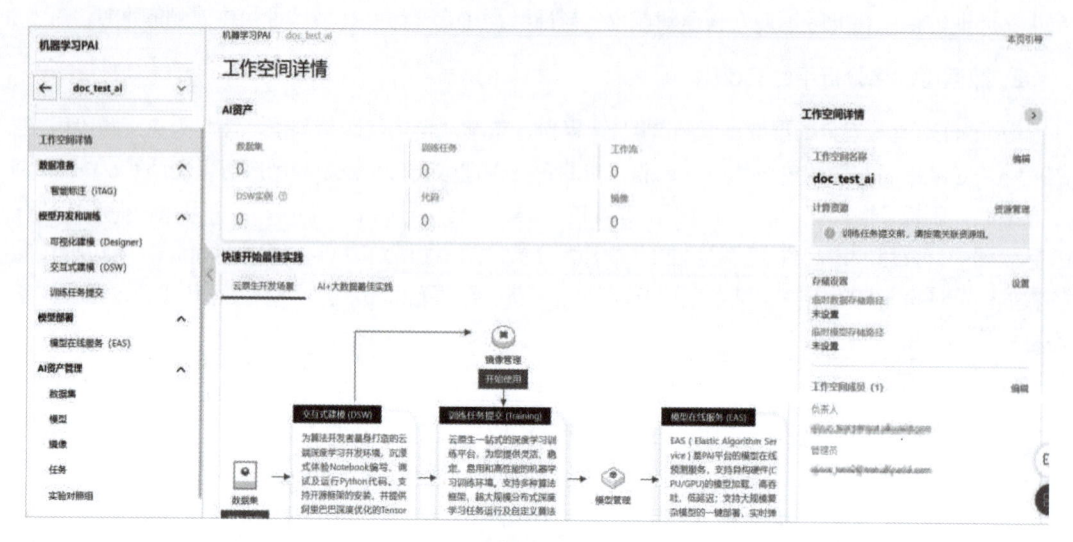

图 1-26

第 2 章
阿里云大数据技术基础——开源大数据技术生态圈

2.1 开源大数据技术生态圈简介

阿里云大数据生态圈体系是基于开源的大数据技术构建的。开源的大数据体系从最早的 Hadoop 生态圈体系开始，逐步有了 Spark 生态圈体系和 Flink 生态圈体系。因此在学习阿里云大数据之前，有必要了解一下开源大数据技术生态圈。

2.1.1 面向离线数据的存储计算引擎 Hadoop 生态圈体系及其组件

Hadoop 作为大数据体系中的第一代引擎，主要面向离线数据处理的场景。使用 Hadoop 既可以完成离线数据的存储，也可以完成离线数据的分析与计算。

Hadoop 生态圈体系中的主要组件，以及它们彼此之间的关系如图 2-1 所示。

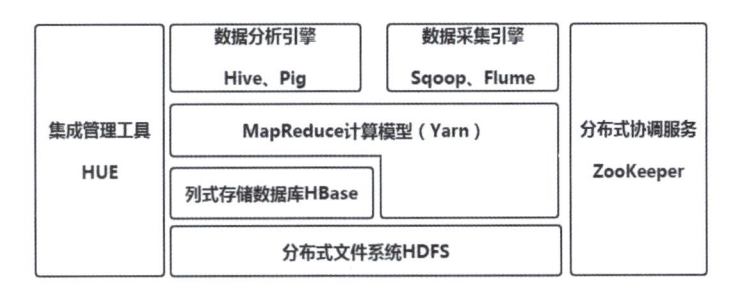

图 2-1

这里先简单说明一下 Hadoop 生态圈体系中组件的功能，在后续的章节中会进行 Hadoop 集群环境的搭建与部署。

1. 分布式文件系统 HDFS

HDFS 是 Hadoop 的分布式文件系统，用于解决大数据的存储问题。HDFS 源自 Google 的 GFS 论文，可以在低成本的通用硬件上运行，是一个具有容错性的文件系统。

2. 列式存储数据库 HBase

HBase 是基于 HDFS 的分布式列式存储 NoSQL 数据库，起源于 Google 的 BigTable 思想。由于 HBase 的底层是 HDFS，因此在 HBase 中创建的表和表中的数据最终都存储在 HDFS 上。HBase 的核心是列式存储，它适合执行查询操作。

3. MapReduce 计算模型与 Yarn

MapReduce 是一种分布式计算模型，用于进行大数据量的计算，是一种离线计算处理模型。MapReduce 分为 Map 和 Reduce 两个阶段，非常适合在大量计算机组成的分布式并行环境里进行数据处理。通过 MapReduce，既可以处理 HDFS 中的数据，也可以处理 HBase 中的数据。

Yarn（Yet Another Resource Negotiator）是 Hadoop 集群中的资源管理器。从 Hadoop 2.x 版本开始，MapReduce 默认运行在 Yarn 上。

> Hadoop 的安装包中已经集成了 HDFS 与 Yarn。因此 Hadoop 安装成功后，可以直接执行 MapReduce 任务处理 HDFS 的数据。

4. 数据分析引擎 Hive 与 Pig

Hive 是基于 HDFS 的数据仓库，支持标准的 SQL 语句。在默认情况下，Hive 的执行引擎是 MapReduce。Hive 可以把一条标准的 SQL 语句转换为 MapReduce 任务，并运行在 Yarn 上。

Pig 也是 Hadoop 中的数据分析引擎，支持 PigLatin 语句。在默认情况下，Pig 的执行引擎也是 MapReduce。Pig 允许处理结构化数据和半结构化数据。

> Hive 和 Pig 的执行引擎也可以是 Spark，即 Hive on Spark 和 Pig on Spark。

5. 数据采集引擎 Sqoop 与 Flume

Sqoop（SQL to Hadoop）是一个数据交换工具，主要针对关系型数据库，例如 Oracle、

MySQL 等。Sqoop 进行数据交换的本质是 MapReduce 程序，它充分利用了 MapReduce 的并行化和容错性，从而提高了数据交换的性能。

Flume 是一个分布式的、可靠的、可用的日志收集服务组件，可以高效地收集、聚合、移动大量的日志数据。

> Flume 进行日志采集的过程本质上并不是 MapReduce 任务。

6. 分布式协调服务 ZooKeeper

ZooKeeper 可以被当作一个数据库来使用，主要解决分布式环境下的数据管理问题，例如统一命名、状态同步、集群管理、配置同步等。在大数据架构中，利用 ZooKeeper 可以解决大数据主从架构的单点故障问题，从而实现大数据的高可用性。

7. 集成管理工具 HUE

HUE 是基于 Web 形式发布的集成管理工具，可以与大数据相关组件进行集成。使用 HUE 可以管理 Hadoop 中的相关组件，也可以管理 Spark 中的相关组件。

2.1.2 面向批处理的大数据计算引擎 Spark 生态圈体系及其组件

Spark 生态圈体系的架构与 Hadoop 略有不同。Spark 生态圈体系中只有数据的计算部分，没有数据的存储部分，因为 Spark 的核心就是它的执行引擎。

Spark 生态圈体系，以及访问每个模块的访问接口如图 2-2 所示。

数据分析引擎 Spark SQL （访问接口：SQLContext）	流式计算引擎 Spark Streaming （访问接口：StreamingContext）	机器学习框架 MLlib 图计算框架 GraphX
离线执行引擎 Spark Core （访问接口：SparkContext）		

图 2-2

这里先简单说明一下 Spark 生态圈体系中组件的功能，在后续的章节中会进行 Spark 集群环境的搭建与部署。

1. 离线执行引擎 Spark Core

Spark Core 是 Spark 的核心部分，也是 Spark 的执行引擎。在 Spark 中执行的所有计算都是由 Spark Core 完成的，它是一个离线计算引擎。Spark Core 提供了 SparkContext 访问接口，用于提交和执行 Spark 任务。通过该访问接口，既可以开发 Java 程序，也可以开发 Scala 程序，来分析和处理数据。SparkContext 也是 Spark 中最重要的一个对象。

> Spark 中的所有计算都是 Spark Core 离线计算，因此 Spark 生态圈体系中不存在真正的实时计算。

2. 数据分析引擎 Spark SQL

Spark SQL 是 Spark 处理结构化数据的一个模块，其核心数据模型是 DataFrame，其访问接口是 SQLContext。这里可以把 DataFrame 理解为一张表。当 DataFrame 创建成功后，Spark SQL 支持使用 DSL 语句和 SQL 语句来分析和处理数据。由于 Spark SQL 底层的执行引擎是 Spark Core，因此 Spark SQL 执行的本质也是执行一个 Spark 任务。

> Spark SQL 和 Hadoop 生态圈体系中的 Hive 是目前大数据生态圈体系中使用最广泛的两个大数据分析引擎。

3. 流式计算引擎 Spark Streaming

Spark Streaming 是核心 Spark API 的扩展，可以实现可扩展、高吞吐量、可容错的实时数据流处理。但是 Spark Streaming 底层的执行引擎依然是 Spark Core，这就决定了 Spark Streaming 并不是真正的流处理引擎，而是通过时间的采样间隔把流式数据转换为小批量数据进行处理，其本质仍然是批处理的离线计算。Spark Streaming 的访问接口是 StreamingContext。

4. 机器学习框架 MLlib 与图计算框架 GraphX

MLlib 是 Spark 中支持机器学习算法的框架，而 GraphX 是 Spark 中支持图计算的框架。

> MLlib 和 GraphX 主要研究的是各种算法，因此在大数据体系中不会重点介绍 MLlib 和 GraphX。

2.1.3 面向流处理的大数据计算引擎 Flink 生态圈体系及其组件

Flink 和 Spark 一样，也是大数据计算引擎，可以完成离线的批处理计算和流处理计算。Flink 的优势在它的流处理引擎 DataStream。

Flink 生态圈体系的架构如图 2-3 所示。

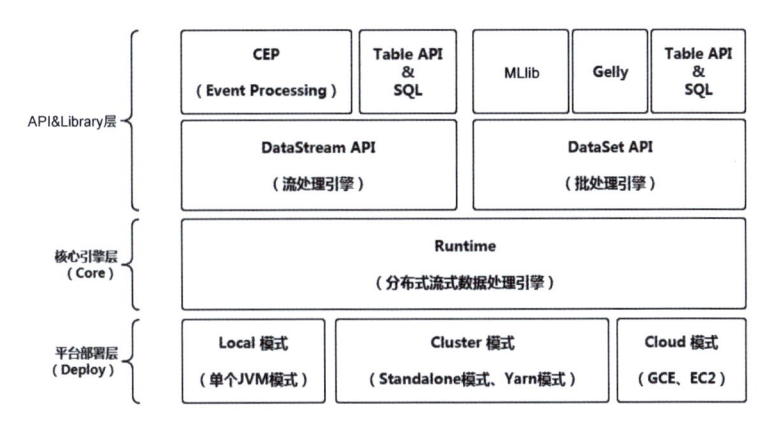

图 2-3

从下往上可以将 Flink 的生态圈体系划分为 3 层：平台部署层、核心引擎层和 API&Library 层。

1. 平台部署层

Flink 支持在不同的平台模式上部署。Flink 在各种平层模式上部署的说明如表 2-1 所示。

表 2-1

平台模式		说 明
Local 模式		Local 模式一般用于开发和测试环境中，例如我们可以在集成开发 IDE 工具中运行 Flink 程序
Cluster 模式	Standalone 模式	Standalone 模式表示 Flink 独立管理和调度 Flink 任务，不依赖其他任何组件
	Yarn 模式	Yarn 模式表示由 Yarn 管理和调度 Flink 集群的资源与任务
Cloud 模式		Cloud 模式表示可以将 Flink 部署到云环境下的虚拟容器中，除了 GCE 和 EC2，也支持 Docker 和 Kubernetes

> Flink 的 Cluster 模式和 Cloud 模式都可以用于生产环境，目前主流的 Flink 部署模式是 Yarn 模式。

2. 核心引擎层

Flink 中所有的计算任务都在核心引擎层中执行完成。部署 Flink 也是部署的这一层。

3. API&Library 层

API&Library 层主要提供给应用开发人员使用。DataStream API 是 Flink 的流处理模块，在此基础上，Flink 提供了复杂事件处理机制 CEP 与数据分析引擎工具 Table API & SQL。DataSet API 是 Flink 的批处理模块，在此基础上，Flink 提供了机器学习算法框架 MLlib、图计算框架 Gelly 和数据分析引擎工具 Table API & SQL。

2.2 面向离线数据的存储计算引擎 Hadoop 快速上手

在部署 Hadoop 集群之前，首先了解一下即将用到的实验环境。由于整套实验环境都需要在 Linux 操作系统上部署，这里将采用 RedHat Linux 作为实验所使用的操作系统。

> 这里也可以使用 CentOS 或 Ubuntu 操作系统，但不建议使用 Windows 操作系统。

实验使用的安装介质及其版本如表 2-2 所示。

表 2-2

组　　件	版　　本
操作系统	RedHat Linux 7.4 64 位
JDK	jdk-8u181-linux-x64.tar.gz
Hadoop	hadoop-3.1.2.tar.gz
Spark	spark-3.0.0-bin-hadoop3.2.tgz
Flink	flink-1.11.0-bin-scala_2.12.tgz
VMware 虚拟机	VMware Workstation 12 Pro 以上

这里将部署 3 台 Linux 操作系统的虚拟主机：bigdata111、bigdata112、bigdata113，在后续的部署过程中将陆续使用它们。每台虚拟机的安装方式完全一致，因此只需要在安装过程中为每台主机设置不同的 IP 地址和主机名即可。最终在 VMware Workstation 中安装完成的效果如图 2-4 所示。

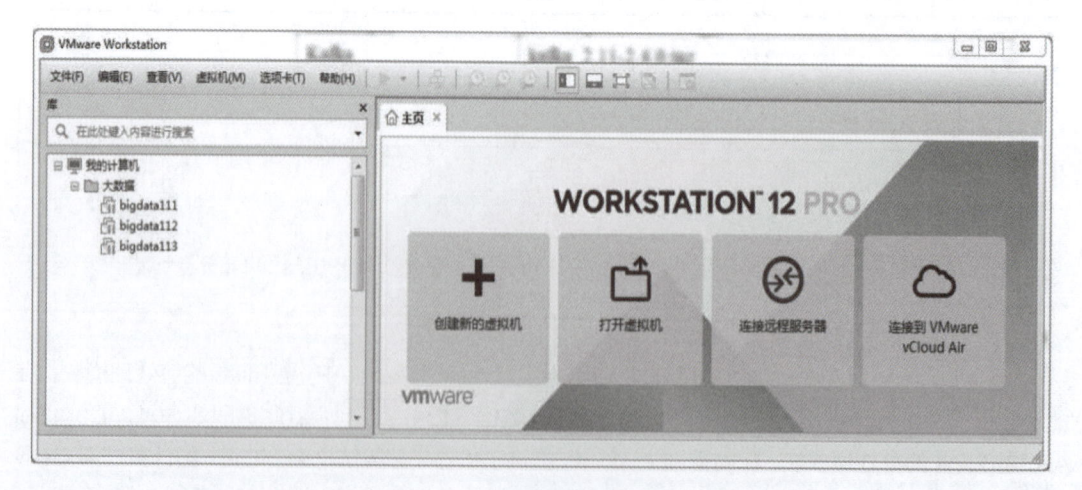

图 2-4

2.2.1 【实战】部署 Hadoop 集群

Hadoop 的安装和部署是大数据生态圈体系中最麻烦的一个。Hadoop 部署完成后，部署 Spark 和 Flink 就非常容易了。Hadoop 的部署模式分为 3 种：本地模式、伪分布模式和全分布模式。下面将演示 Hadoop 全分布模式的部署，这种模式也是在生成环境中使用的模式，本地模式和伪分布模式多用于开发和测试环境中。

1. Hadoop 的目录结构

在部署 Hadoop 之前，需要对 Hadoop 的目录结构有一定了解。先执行下面的语句将 Hadoop 的安装介质解压缩到~/training 目录中。

```
tar -zxvf hadoop-3.1.2.tar.gz -C ~/training/
```

Hadoop 的目录结构如下。

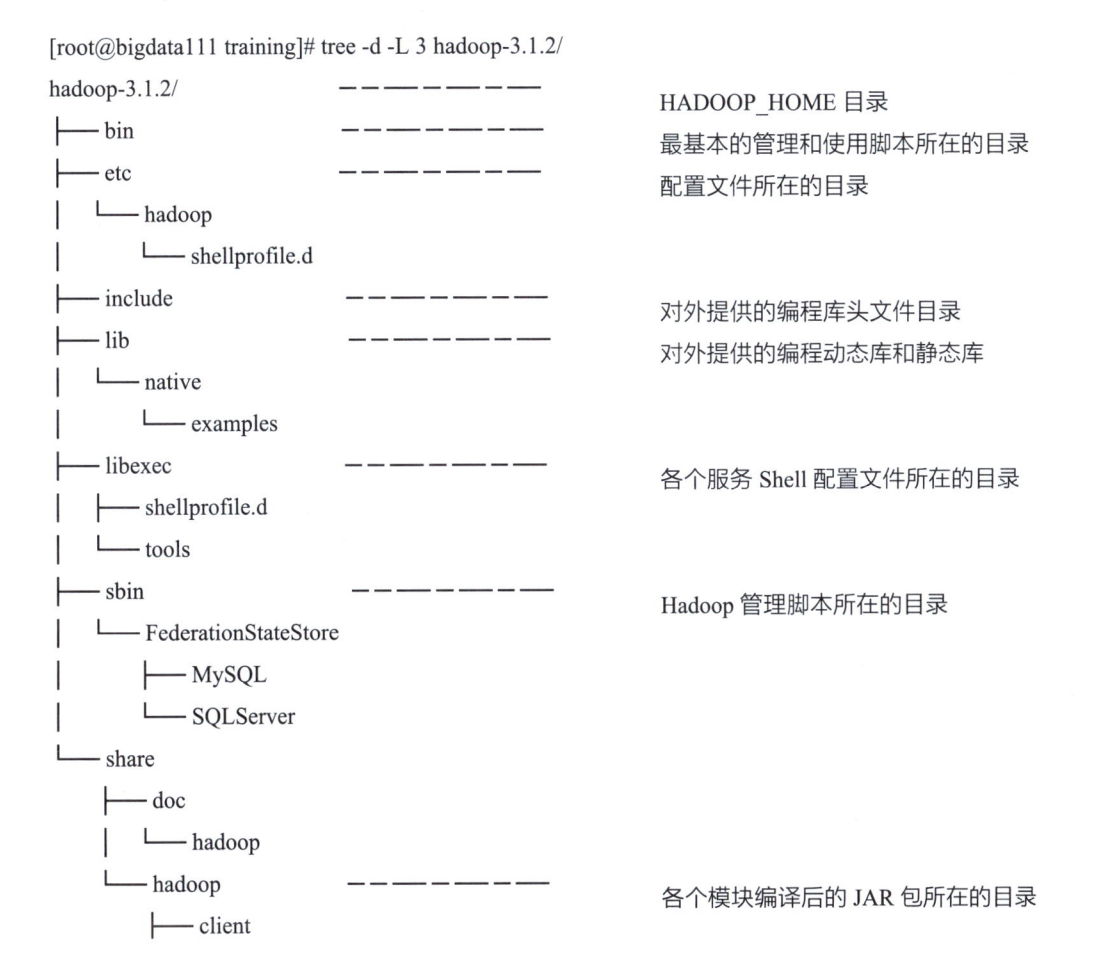

```
[root@bigdata111 training]# tree -d -L 3 hadoop-3.1.2/
hadoop-3.1.2/                      ————————    HADOOP_HOME 目录
├── bin                            ————————    最基本的管理和使用脚本所在的目录
├── etc                            ————————    配置文件所在的目录
│   └── hadoop
│       └── shellprofile.d
├── include                        ————————    对外提供的编程库头文件目录
├── lib                            ————————    对外提供的编程动态库和静态库
│   └── native
│       └── examples
├── libexec                        ————————    各个服务 Shell 配置文件所在的目录
│   ├── shellprofile.d
│   └── tools
├── sbin                           ————————    Hadoop 管理脚本所在的目录
│   └── FederationStateStore
│       ├── MySQL
│       └── SQLServer
└── share
    ├── doc
    │   └── hadoop
    └── hadoop                     ————————    各个模块编译后的 JAR 包所在的目录
        ├── client
```

```
├── common
├── hdfs
├── mapreduce
├── tools
└── yarn
```

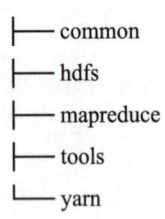

为了方便操作 Hadoop，需要设置 HADOOP_HOME 的环境变量，并把 bin 和 sbin 目录加入系统的 PATH 路径。具体的操作步骤如下。

（1）编辑/root/.bash_profile 文件。

```
vi /root/.bash_profile
```

（2）输入下面的环境变量信息，保存并退出。

```
HADOOP_HOME=/root/training/hadoop-3.1.2
export HADOOP_HOME

PATH=$HADOOP_HOME/bin:$HADOOP_HOME/sbin:$PATH
export PATH
export HDFS_DATANODE_USER=root
export HDFS_DATANODE_SECURE_USER=root
export HDFS_NAMENODE_USER=root
export HDFS_SECONDARYNAMENODE_USER=root
export YARN_RESOURCEMANAGER_USER=root
export YARN_NODEMANAGER_USER=root
```

（3）使环境变量生效。

```
source /root/.bash_profile
```

2. 部署 Hadoop 全分布模式

Hadoop 全分布模式是真正的集群模式，该模式可以用于生产环境。在这种模式下，主节点和从节点在不同主机上运行。

Hadoop 全分布模式的拓扑结构如图 2-5 所示。本节将在 bigdata111、bigdata112 和 bigdata113 上完成相应的配置与部署。

（1）关闭每台主机的防火墙，设置每台主机的主机名和 IP 地址的映射关系，安装 JDK，设置环境变量并配置每台主机之间的免密码登录。

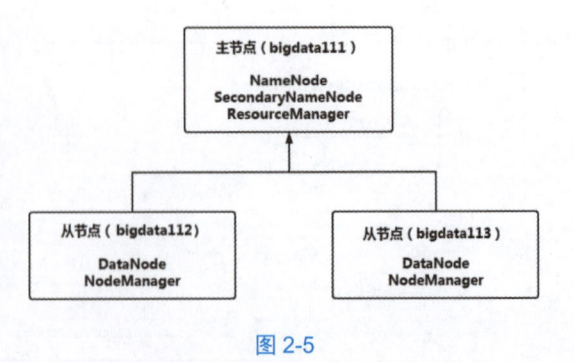

主节点（bigdata111）
NameNode
SecondaryNameNode
ResourceManager

从节点（bigdata112）
DataNode
NodeManager

从节点（bigdata113）
DataNode
NodeManager

图 2-5

(2)在 bigdata111 上创建 /root/training 目录。

```
mkdir /root/training
```

(3)将 Hadoop 安装包解压缩到 ~/training 目录下,并创建 HDFS 对应的操作系统目录。

```
tar -zxvf hadoop-3.1.2.tar.gz -C ~/training/
mkdir /root/training/hadoop-3.1.2/tmp
```

(4)进入 Hadoop 配置文件所在的目录。

```
cd /root/training/hadoop-3.1.2/etc/hadoop/
```

(5)修改 hadoop-env.sh 文件,设置 JAVA_HOME。

```
export JAVA_HOME=/root/training/jdk1.8.0_181
```

(6)修改 hdfs-site.xml 文件,增加以下内容。

```
<!--数据块的冗余度,默认为 3-->
<!--原则上,数据块冗余度跟数据节点的个数一致,但最大不超过 3-->
<property>
    <name>dfs.replication</name>
    <value>2</value>
</property>

<!--禁用了 HDFS 的权限功能-->
<!--开发环境设置为 false-->
<!--生产环境设置为 true-->
<property>
    <name>dfs.permissions</name>
    <value>false</value>
</property>
```

(7)修改 core-site.xml 文件,增加以下内容。

```
<!--设置 NameNode 的地址-->
<property>
    <name>fs.defaultFS</name>
    <value>hdfs://bigdata111:9000</value>
</property>

<!--设置 HDFS 对应的操作系统目录-->
<property>
    <name>hadoop.tmp.dir</name>
    <value>/root/training/hadoop-3.1.2/tmp</value>
</property>
```

(8)修改 mapred-site.xml 文件,增加以下内容。

```xml
<!--配置 MapReduce 运行的框架-->
<property>
    <name>mapreduce.framework.name</name>
    <value>yarn</value>
</property>

<!--配置 Hadoop 的环境变量-->
<property>
    <name>yarn.app.mapreduce.am.env</name>
    <value>HADOOP_MAPRED_HOME=${HADOOP_HOME}</value>
</property>

<property>
    <name>mapreduce.map.env</name>
    <value>HADOOP_MAPRED_HOME=${HADOOP_HOME}</value>
</property>

<property>
    <name>mapreduce.reduce.env</name>
    <value>HADOOP_MAPRED_HOME=${HADOOP_HOME}</value>
</property>
```

(9)修改 yarn-site.xml 文件,增加以下内容。

```xml
<!--配置的 ResourceManager 的地址-->
<property>
    <name>yarn.resourcemanager.hostname</name>
    <value>bigdata111</value>
</property>

<!--NodeManager 采用 shuffle 洗牌的方式来执行任务-->
<property>
    <name>yarn.nodemanager.aux-services</name>
    <value>mapreduce_shuffle</value>
</property>
```

(10)修改 workers 文件,输入从节点的信息。

```
bigdata112
bigdata113
```

(11)格式化 NameNode。

```
hdfs namenode -format
```

格式化成功后,将看到如下日志信息。

```
Storage directory /root/training/hadoop-3.1.2/tmp/dfs/name has been
successfully formatted.
```

（12）将在 bigdata111 上配置好的 Hadoop 目录复制到 bigdata112 和 bigdata113 上。

```
cd /root/training
scp -r hadoop-3.1.2/ root@bigdata112:/root/training
scp -r hadoop-3.1.2/ root@bigdata113:/root/training
```

（13）在主节点 bigdata111 上启动集群，如图 2-6 所示。

```
start-all.sh
```

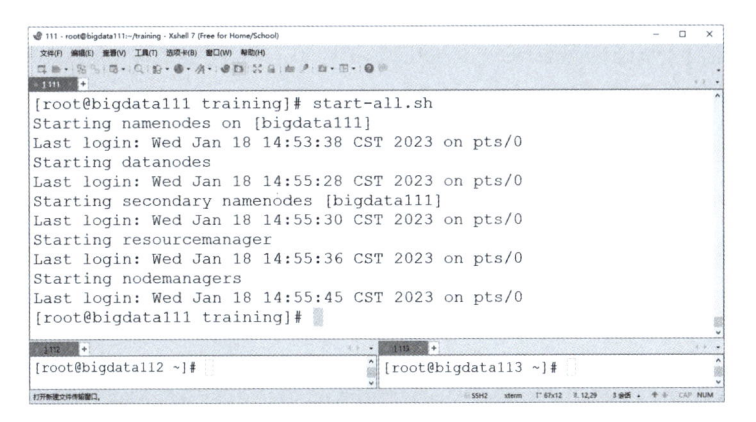

图 2-6

（14）在每台主机上执行 jps 命令，观察后台的进程，如图 2-7 所示。

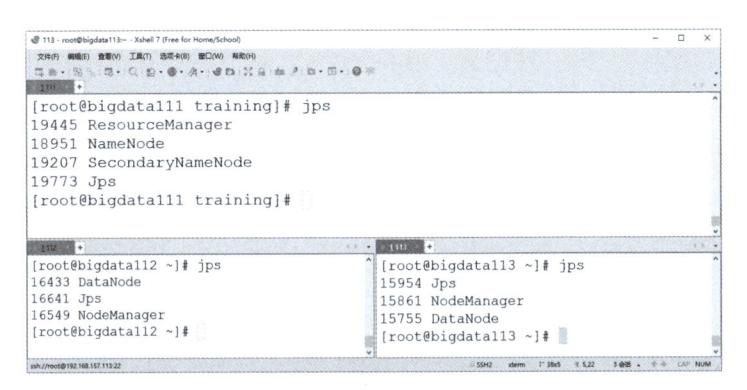

图 2-7

> 主节点 bigdata111 上有 NameNode、SecondaryNameNode 和 ResourceManager 三个进程，两个从节点 bigdata112 和 bigdata113 上有 DataNode、NodeManager 两个进程。

2.2.2 【实战】使用 Hadoop 文件系统 HDFS 存储数据

在搭建好 Hadoop 的环境后，可以通过 3 种不同的方式来操作 HDFS：HDFS 命令行、Java API 和 Web Console。这里以 HDFS 命令行和 Web Console 两种方式来演示如何使用 HDFS。

1. 以 HDFS 命令行方式使用 HDFS

HDFS 的命令可以分为普通操作命令和管理命令，它们分别以 hdfs dfs 和 hdfs dfsadmin 开头。使用 hdfs dfs 命令（也可以使用 hadoop fs 命令）列出所有的操作命令，如下所示。

```
[root@bigdata111 ~]# hdfs dfs
Usage: hadoop fs [generic options]
[-appendToFile <localsrc> ... <dst>]
[-cat [-ignoreCrc] <src> ...]
[-checksum <src> ...]
[-chgrp [-R] GROUP PATH...]
[-chmod [-R] <MODE[,MODE]... | OCTALMODE> PATH...]
[-chown [-R] [OWNER][:[GROUP]] PATH...]
[-copyFromLocal[-f][-p][-l][-d][-t <threadcount>]<localsrc> ...<dst>]
[-copyToLocal [-f] [-p] [-ignoreCrc] [-crc] <src> ... <localdst>]
[-count [-q] [-h] [-v] [-t [<storage type>]] [-u] [-x] [-e] <path> ...]
[-cp [-f] [-p | -p[topax]] [-d] <src> ... <dst>]
[-createSnapshot <snapshotDir> [<snapshotName>]]
[-deleteSnapshot <snapshotDir> <snapshotName>]
[-df [-h] [<path> ...]]
[-du [-s] [-h] [-v] [-x] <path> ...]
[-expunge]
[-find <path> ... <expression> ...]
[-get [-f] [-p] [-ignoreCrc] [-crc] <src> ... <localdst>]
[-getfacl [-R] <path>]
[-getfattr [-R] {-n name | -d} [-e en] <path>]
[-getmerge [-nl] [-skip-empty-file] <src> <localdst>]
[-head <file>]
[-help [cmd ...]]
[-ls [-C] [-d] [-h] [-q] [-R] [-t] [-S] [-r] [-u] [-e] [<path> ...]]
[-mkdir [-p] <path> ...]
[-moveFromLocal <localsrc> ... <dst>]
[-moveToLocal <src> <localdst>]
[-mv <src> ... <dst>]
[-put [-f] [-p] [-l] [-d] <localsrc> ... <dst>]
[-renameSnapshot <snapshotDir> <oldName> <newName>]
[-rm [-f] [-r|-R] [-skipTrash] [-safely] <src> ...]
[-rmdir [--ignore-fail-on-non-empty] <dir> ...]
[-setfattr {-n name [-v value] | -x name} <path>]
```

```
[-setrep [-R] [-w] <rep> <path> ...]
[-stat [format] <path> ...]
[-tail [-f] <file>]
[-test -[defsz] <path>]
[-text [-ignoreCrc] <src> ...]
[-touch [-a] [-m] [-t TIMESTAMP ] [-c] <path> ...]
[-touchz <path> ...]
[-truncate [-w] <length> <path> ...]
[-usage [cmd ...]]
```

使用 hdfs dfsadmin 命令列出所有的管理命令，如下所示。

```
[root@bigdata111 ~]# hdfs dfsadmin
Usage: hdfs dfsadmin
Note: Administrative commands can only be run as the HDFS superuser.
    [-report [-live] [-dead] [-decommissioning] [-enteringmaintenance]
[-inmaintenance]]
    [-safemode <enter | leave | get | wait>]
    [-saveNamespace [-beforeShutdown]]
    [-rollEdits]
    [-restoreFailedStorage true|false|check]
    [-refreshNodes]
    [-setQuota <quota> <dirname>...<dirname>]
    [-clrQuota <dirname>...<dirname>]
    [-setSpaceQuota <quota> [-storageType <storagetype>] <dirname>...<dirname>]
    [-clrSpaceQuota [-storageType <storagetype>] <dirname>...<dirname>]
    [-finalizeUpgrade]
    [-rollingUpgrade [<query|prepare|finalize>]]
    [-upgrade <query | finalize>]
    [-refreshServiceAcl]
    [-refreshUserToGroupsMappings]
    [-refreshSuperUserGroupsConfiguration]
    [-refreshCallQueue]
    [-refresh <host:ipc_port> <key> [arg1..argn]
    [-reconfig <namenode|datanode> <host:ipc_port> <start|status|properties>]
    [-printTopology]
    [-refreshNamenodes datanode_host:ipc_port]
    [-getVolumeReport datanode_host:ipc_port]
    [-deleteBlockPool datanode_host:ipc_port blockpoolId [force]]
    [-setBalancerBandwidth <bandwidth in bytes per second>]
    [-getBalancerBandwidth <datanode_host:ipc_port>]
    [-fetchImage <local directory>]
    [-allowSnapshot <snapshotDir>]
    [-disallowSnapshot <snapshotDir>]
```

```
[-shutdownDatanode <datanode_host:ipc_port> [upgrade]]
[-evictWriters <datanode_host:ipc_port>]
[-getDatanodeInfo <datanode_host:ipc_port>]
[-metasave filename]
[-triggerBlockReport [-incremental] <datanode_host:ipc_port>]
[-listOpenFiles [-blockingDecommission] [-path <path>]]
[-help [cmd]]
```

下面给出了一些命令的使用示例。

（1）-mkdir：创建一个目录。可选的参数-p 表示如果父目录不存在，则先创建目录。

```
#在HDFS的根目录下创建a1目录，在a1目录下创建b1目录，在b1目录下创建c1目录
hdfs dfs -mkdir -p /a1/b1/c1
```

（2）-ls：查看目录。可选的参数-R 表示查看子目录。

```
#查看HDFS的根目录，包括根目录下的子目录
hdfs dfs -ls -R /

#上面的命令可以简写成下面的形式
hdfs dfs -lsr /
```

（3）-put、-copyFromLocal、-moveFromLocal 这 3 个命令都是将文件上传到 HDFS 中的命令。

```
#在本地编辑data.txt文件，并输入以下内容
vi data.txt
I love Beijing
I love China
Beijing is the capital of China

#在HDFS中创建/input目录
hdfs dfs -mkdir /input

#将data.txt文件上传到/input目录中
hdfs dfs -put data.txt /input
```

> 使用-moveFromLocal 命令上传文件会删除本地的文件，相当于执行了剪切操作。

（4）-get、-copyToLocal：从 HDFS 中下载文件。

```
#将HDFS的/input/data.txt文件下载到当前目录中
hdfs dfs -get /input/data.txt .
```

> 该命令最后必须有一个点，它表示当前目录。

（5）-rm：删除一个空目录。-rmr：删除目录，包括子目录。

```
#删除前面创建的/a1目录及其子目录
hdfs dfs -rmr /a1
```

（6）-getmerge：将 HDFS 目录下的文件先合并，再下载。

```
#在本地编辑students01.txt和students02.txt文件
#students01.txt文件的内容如下
1,Tom,23
2,Mary,22

#students02.txt文件的内容如下
3,Mike,24

#在HDFS上创建/students目录，并上传数据文件
hdfs dfs -mkdir /students
hdfs dfs -put students0*.txt /students

#使用getmerge下载数据
hdfs dfs -getmerge /students ./allstudents.txt

#查看allstudents.txt文件，内容如下
1,Tom,23
2,Mary,22
3,Mike,24
```

（7）-cp：复制文件。

```
#将/input/data.txt文件复制到/input/a1.txt文件中
hdfs dfs -cp /input/data.txt /input/a1.txt
```

（8）-mv：移动文件。如果目的地与源目录相同，则执行重命名操作。

```
#将/input/a1.txt重命名为/input/a2.txt
hdfs dfs -mv /input/a1.txt /input/a2.txt
```

（9）-count：统计目录下的文件信息。

```
hdfs dfs -count /students
```

输出信息如下。

```
1             2                29 /students
```

> 输出信息中的2表示文件个数，29表示总的字节大小。

（10）-du：显示 HDFS 目录下文件的详细信息。

```
#查看/students 目录下文件的详细信息
hdfs dfs -du /students
```

输出信息如下。

```
19  19  /students/students01.txt
10  10  /students/students02.txt
```

（11）-text、-cat：查看文件的内容。

```
hdfs dfs -cat /input/data.txt
```

输出信息如下。

```
I love Beijing
I love China
Beijing is the capital of China
```

（12）-report：一个管理命令，可以查看 HDFS 集群的信息。

```
hdfs dfsadmin -report
```

输出信息如下。

```
Configured Capacity: 39746781184 (37.02 GB)
Present Capacity: 26564603904 (24.74 GB)
DFS Remaining: 26183876608 (24.39 GB)
DFS Used: 380727296 (363.09 MB)
DFS Used%: 1.43%
Replicated Blocks:
    Under replicated blocks: 20
    Blocks with corrupt replicas: 0
    Missing blocks: 0
    Missing blocks (with replication factor 1): 0
    Low redundancy blocks with highest priority to recover: 20
    Pending deletion blocks: 0
Erasure Coded Block Groups:
    Low redundancy block groups: 0
    Block groups with corrupt internal blocks: 0
    Missing block groups: 0
    Low redundancy blocks with highest priority to recover: 0
```

```
    Pending deletion blocks: 0

-------------------------------------------------
Live datanodes (1):

Name: 192.168.157.111:9866 (bigdata111)
Hostname: bigdata111
Decommission Status : Normal
Configured Capacity: 39746781184 (37.02 GB)
DFS Used: 380727296 (363.09 MB)
Non DFS Used: 13182177280 (12.28 GB)
DFS Remaining: 26183876608 (24.39 GB)
DFS Used%: 0.96%
DFS Remaining%: 65.88%
Configured Cache Capacity: 0 (0 B)
Cache Used: 0 (0 B)
Cache Remaining: 0 (0 B)
Cache Used%: 100.00%
Cache Remaining%: 0.00%
Xceivers: 1
Last contact: Wed May 12 14:04:29 CST 2021
Last Block Report: Wed May 12 13:36:59 CST 2021
Num of Blocks: 252
```

> 使用-report 命令可以看到 HDFS 容量的大小、已使用的空间、数据节点的相关信息等。

（13）-safemode：一个管理命令，可以查看和操作 HDFS 的安全模式。

```
#查看当前 HDFS 安全模式的状态
hdfs dfsadmin -safemode get
```

输出信息如下。

```
Safe mode is OFF
```

> 在 HDFS 正常运行期间，安全模式一定是关闭的状态。如果 HDFS 处于安全模式，则整个 HDFS 文件系统是只读的状态。

2. 以 Web Console 方式使用 HDFS

HDFS 也可以使用 Web Console 方式来访问，默认端口号是 9870。

> 在 Hadoop 3.x 以前的版本中，HDFS Web Console 的默认端口号是 50070。

下面分别介绍 HDFS Web Console 的几个主要页面。

1）Overview 页面

Overview 页面是 HDFS Web Console 的首页，如图 2-8 所示。该页面显示了 HDFS 启动的时间、版本信息、安全模式的状态、集群的容量等信息。

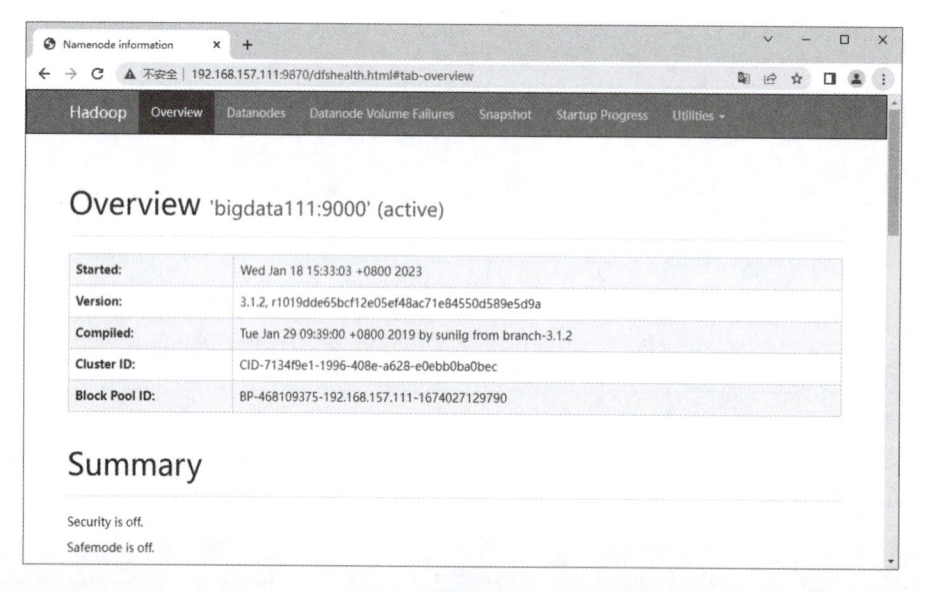

图 2-8

> Overview 页面展示的信息与使用 HDFS 管理命令 -report 输出的信息类似。

2）Datanodes 页面

Datanodes 页面显示 HDFS 数据节点的详细信息。由于这里使用的是 Hadoop 全分布模式的环境，因此可以看到有两个 Node，如图 2-9 所示。

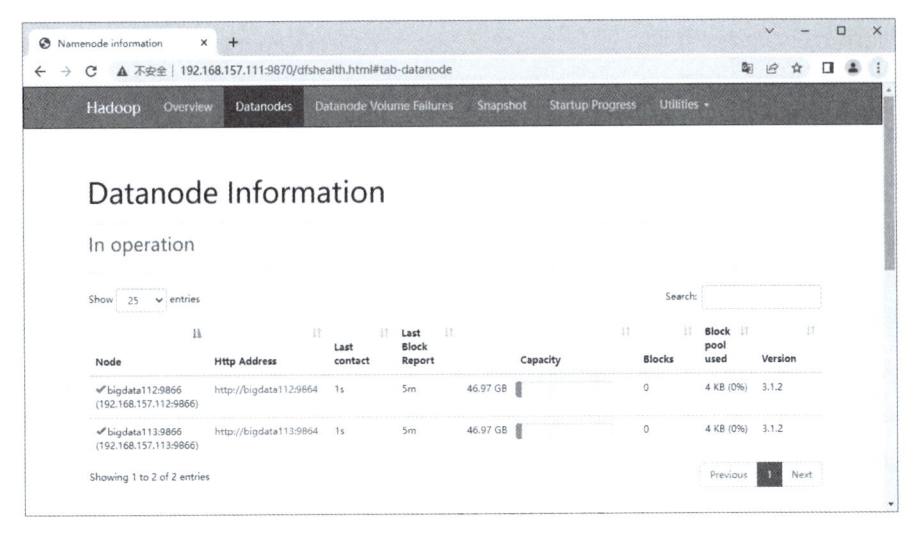

图 2-9

3）Snapshot 页面

Snapshot 页面是 HDFS 的快照页面。快照是 HDFS 提供的一种备份方式，可以防止因误操作而造成数据丢失。由于默认情况下 HDFS 的快照是关闭的，因此在这个界面上没有显示与快照相关的信息，如图 2-10 所示。

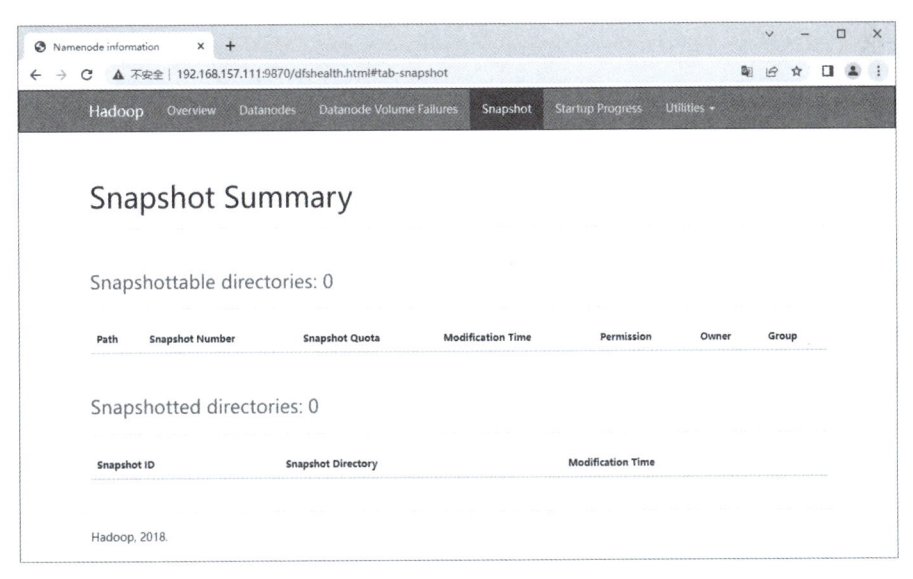

图 2-10

4）Startup Progress 页面

在 Startup Progress 页面上可以观察到整个 HDFS 的启动过程，如图 2-11 所示。

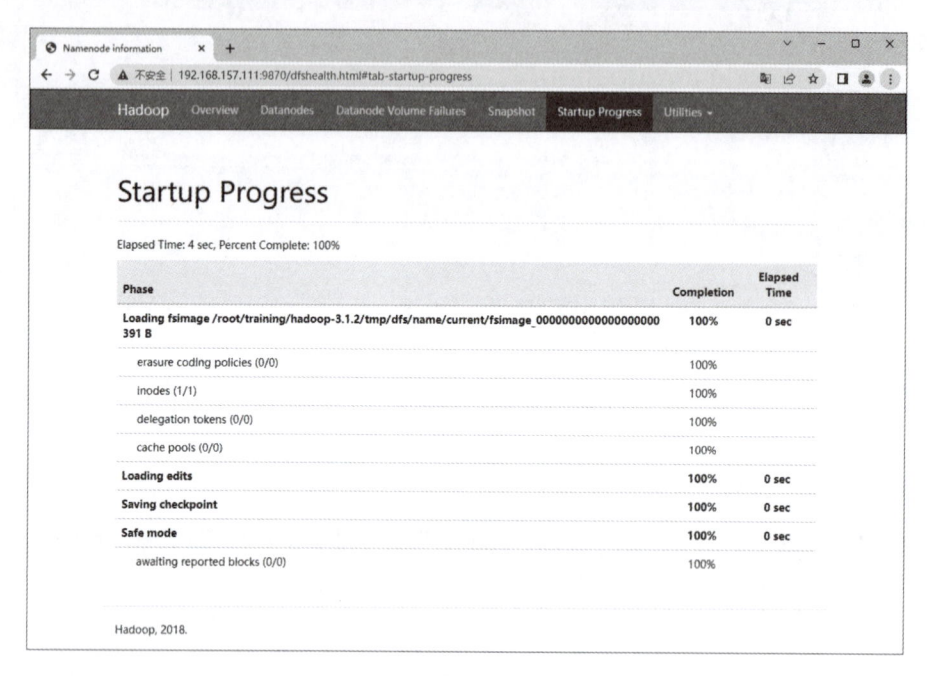

图 2-11

> 通过 Startup Progress 页面可以看出，HDFS 的启动一共分为 4 个阶段：Loading fsimage、Loading edits、Saving checkpoint 和 Safe mode。

2.2.3 【实战】使用 Hadoop 离线计算引擎 MapReduce 处理数据

在 Hadoop 安装部署完成后，就可以直接执行 MapReduce 任务来处理 HDFS 的数据了。MapReduce 非常经典的入门案例就是 WordCount——单词计数的应用程序。在搭建好的 Hadoop 环境中，可以直接运行 WordCount Example 进行单词的统计。

> 虽然 WordCount 应用程序非常简单，但它却包含了 MapReduce 处理数据的核心过程。

根据下面的步骤运行 Hadoop 自带的 WordCount Example。这里将在搭建好的 Hadoop 全分布模式下运行。

(1)启动 Hadoop 集群。

```
start-all.sh
```

(2)编辑 data.txt 文件,输入下面的内容。

```
I love Beijing
I love China
Beijing is the capital of China
```

(3)将 data.txt 文件上传到 HDFS 中。

```
hdfs dfs -mkdir /input
hdfs dfs -put data.txt /input
```

(4)执行 WordCount Example,执行过程的输出日志如图 2-12 所示。

```
cd $HADOOP_HOME/share/hadoop/mapreduce/
hadoop jar hadoop-mapreduce-examples-3.1.2.jar wordcount /input /output/wc
```

> 该命令的参数说明如下。
>
> /input:任务的输入路径。该参数可以是一个目录,也可以是一个文件。如果是一个目录,则在执行任务时读取目录下的所有文件;如果是一个文件,则在执行任务时只读取这一个文件。
>
> /output/wc:任务的输出路径。如果该目录已经存在,则在执行过程中会抛出异常。

```
[root@bigdata111 mapreduce]#
[root@bigdata111 mapreduce]# hadoop jar hadoop-mapreduce-examples-3.1.2.jar wordcount /input /output/wc
2021-05-20 20:05:45,814 INFO client.RMProxy: Connecting to ResourceManager at bigdata111/192.168.157.111:8032
2021-05-20 20:05:46,688 INFO mapreduce.JobResourceUploader: Disabling Erasure Coding for path: /tmp/hadoop-yarn/stagi
ng/root/.staging/job_1621512300466_0002
2021-05-20 20:05:47,553 INFO input.FileInputFormat: Total input files to process : 1
2021-05-20 20:05:48,477 INFO mapreduce.JobSubmitter: number of splits:1
2021-05-20 20:05:49,104 INFO mapreduce.JobSubmitter: Submitting tokens for job: job_1621512300466_0002
2021-05-20 20:05:49,108 INFO mapreduce.JobSubmitter: Executing with tokens: []
2021-05-20 20:05:49,382 INFO conf.Configuration: resource-types.xml not found
2021-05-20 20:05:49,383 INFO resource.ResourceUtils: Unable to find 'resource-types.xml'.
2021-05-20 20:05:49,970 INFO impl.YarnClientImpl: Submitted application application_1621512300466_0002
2021-05-20 20:05:50,144 INFO mapreduce.Job: The url to track the job: http://bigdata111:8088/proxy/application_162151
2300466_0002/
2021-05-20 20:05:50,145 INFO mapreduce.Job: Running job: job_1621512300466_0002
2021-05-20 20:06:01,519 INFO mapreduce.Job: Job job_1621512300466_0002 running in uber mode : false
2021-05-20 20:06:01,523 INFO mapreduce.Job:  map 0% reduce 0%
2021-05-20 20:06:06,678 INFO mapreduce.Job:  map 100% reduce 0%
2021-05-20 20:06:11,745 INFO mapreduce.Job:  map 100% reduce 100%
2021-05-20 20:06:13,828 INFO mapreduce.Job: Job job_1621512300466_0002 completed successfully
2021-05-20 20:06:13,936 INFO mapreduce.Job: Counters: 53
        File System Counters
                FILE: Number of bytes read=93
                FILE: Number of bytes written=432809
                FILE: Number of read operations=0
                FILE: Number of large read operations=0
                FILE: Number of write operations=0
                HDFS: Number of bytes read=162
                HDFS: Number of bytes written=55
                HDFS: Number of read operations=8
                HDFS: Number of large read operations=0
                HDFS: Number of write operations=2
```

图 2-12

（5）打开 Web Console，可以监控 MapReduce 任务执行的过程，如图 2-13 所示。

图 2-13

（6）任务执行成功后，查看输出的结果。

```
hdfs dfs -ls /output/wc
```

输出的信息如下。

```
Found 2 items
-rw-r--r-- 1 root supergroup  0 2021-05-20 20:06 /output/wc/_SUCCESS
-rw-r--r-- 1 root supergroup 55 2021-05-20 20:06 /output/wc/part-r-00000
```

> 结果输出了两个文件，这里重点说明一下 part-r-00000 文件。MapReduce 在执行的过程中会产生分区，在默认的情况下只有一个分区。这里的分区其实就是一个输出文件，也可以在执行 MapReduce 任务时自定义分区。如果定义了多个分区，就会有多个输出文件。

（7）执行命令，查看统计结果。

```
hdfs dfs -cat /output/wc/part-r-00000
```

输出的信息如下。

```
[root@bigdata111 mapreduce]# hdfs dfs -cat /output/wc/part-r-00000
Beijing         2
China           2
```

```
I           2
capital     1
is          1
love        2
of          1
the         1
```

> 从结果中可以看出，MapReduce 在执行过程中会进行排序。因为这里处理的是字符串，所以默认的排序规则就是字典顺序。

2.3 面向批处理的大数据计算引擎 Spark 快速上手

相对于 Hadoop 的部署，Spark 的部署就简单很多了。与 Hadoop 的部署类似，Spark 的部署也分为本地模式、伪分布模式和全分布模式。

> 这里将以 Spark 全分布模式进行部署，这种模式也是在生成环境中使用的模式。而 Spark 的本地模式和伪分布模式多用于开发和测试环境中。

2.3.1 【实战】部署 Spark 集群

和 Hadoop 的全分布模式一样，Spark 的全分布模式也需要使用 3 台主机来部署。Spark 全分布模式的拓扑结构如图 2-14 所示。

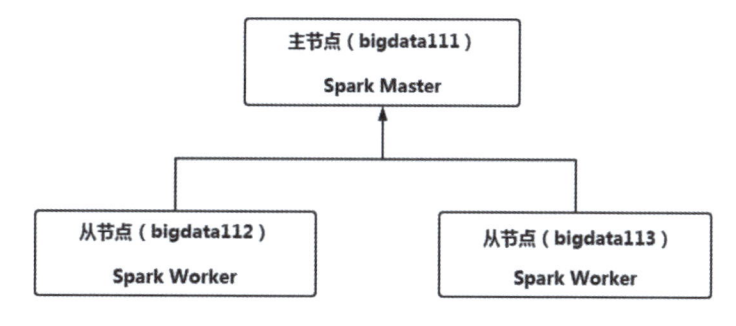

图 2-14

下面通过具体的步骤来演示如何部署 Spark 的全分布模式。

> 下面的配置步骤都是在 bigdata111 上进行的。

(1) 将 Spark 安装包解压缩到 ~/training 目录下。

```
tar -zxvf spark-3.0.0-bin-hadoop3.2.tgz -C ~/training/
```

(2) 进入 Spark 配置文件所在的目录。

```
cd /root/training/spark-3.0.0-bin-hadoop3.2/
```

(3) 修改配置文件 spark-env.sh。

```
mv spark-env.sh.template spark-env.sh
vi spark-env.sh
```

(4) 在 spark-env.sh 文件最后增加以下配置,保存并退出。

```
export JAVA_HOME=/root/training/jdk1.8.0_181
export SPARK_MASTER_HOST=bigdata111
export SPARK_MASTER_PORT=7077
```

(5) 修改配置文件 slaves。

```
mv slaves.template slaves
vi slaves
```

(6) 在 slaves 文件中增加从节点的地址。

```
bigdata112
bigdata113
```

(7) 将在 bigdata111 上配置好的 Spark 目录复制到 bigdata112 和 bigdata113 上。

```
cd /root/training
scp -r spark-3.0.0-bin-hadoop3.2/ root@bigdata112:/root/training
scp -r spark-3.0.0-bin-hadoop3.2/ root@bigdata113:/root/training
```

(8) 在 bigdata111 上启动 Spark 集群。

```
cd /root/training/spark-3.0.0-bin-hadoop3.2/
sbin/start-all.sh
```

(9) 在每台主机上执行 jps 命令,观察后台的进程,如图 2-15 所示。

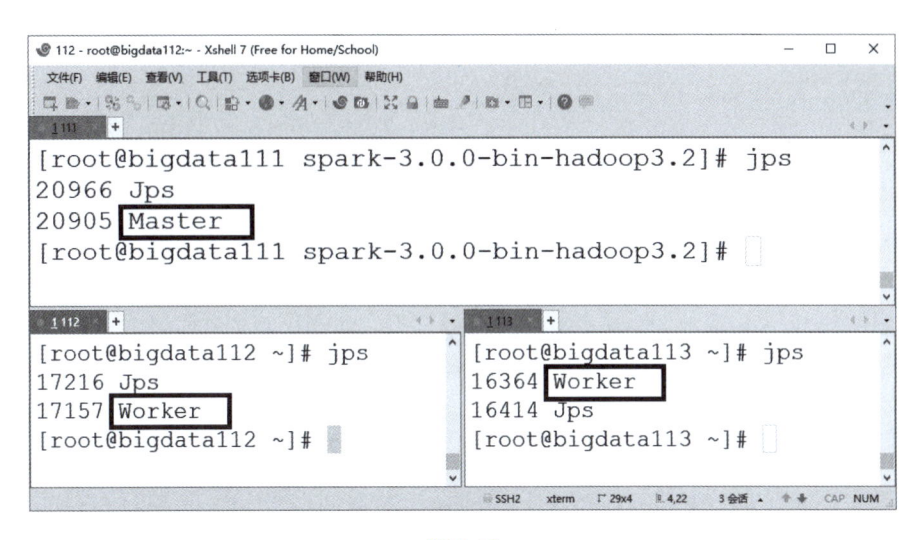

图 2-15

（10）通过 8080 端口访问 Spark Web Console，如图 2-16 所示。

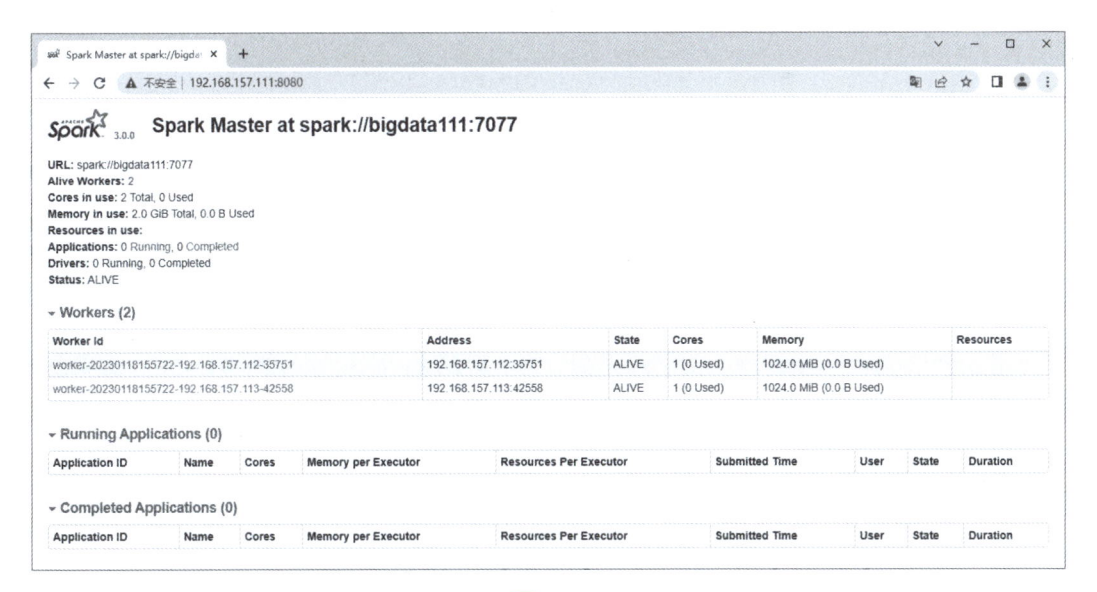

图 2-16

2.3.2 【实战】执行 Spark 离线计算任务

在部署完 Spark 集群后，就可以通过 Spark 的客户端来提交、执行 Spark 任务了。Spark

的客户端叫作 Driver Program，可以通过 Spark 的客户端工具 spark-submit 和 spark-shell 来启动。

1. 使用 spark-submit 提交 Spark 任务

当应用程序开发完成后，需要先将其打包成 JAR 文件，然后通过 Spark 的客户端工具 spark-submit 将 JAR 文件提交到集群上运行。不管是单节点的伪分布模式，还是全分布的集群模式，spark-submit 的使用方式都是一样的。

> spark-submit 位于 Spark 的 bin 目录中，使用该脚本工具可以将一个打包好的 Spark 任务，以 JAR 文件的形式提交到 Spark 集群上运行。

下面通过具体的步骤来演示如何使用 spark-submit 提交 Spark 任务。

（1）启动 Spark 集群。

```
cd /root/training/spark-3.0.0-bin-hadoop3.2/
sbin/start-all.sh
```

（2）使用 spark-submit 提交任务。

```
bin/spark-submit --master spark://bigdata111:7077 \
--class org.apache.spark.examples.SparkPi \
examples/jars/spark-examples_2.12-3.0.0.jar 100
```

> 这里使用了 Spark 自带的 SparkPi Example 演示，并使用 spark-submit 将任务提交到集群上运行。其中，参数 100 表示循环迭代的次数，这个值越大，计算出来的圆周率越准确。

Spark 已经提供了编译好的 JAR 文件，该文件位于 examples/jars 目录下。SparkPi 的源代码如下所示。

```
package org.apache.spark.examples

import scala.math.random

import org.apache.spark.sql.SparkSession

/** Computes an approximation to pi */
object SparkPi {
  def main(args: Array[String]): Unit = {
```

```scala
    val spark = SparkSession
      .builder
      .appName("Spark Pi")
      .getOrCreate()
    val slices = if (args.length > 0) args(0).toInt else 2
    //avoid overflow
    val n = math.min(100000L * slices, Int.MaxValue).toInt
    val count = spark.sparkContext.parallelize(1 until n, slices)
                  .map { i =>
      val x = random * 2 - 1
      val y = random * 2 - 1
      if (x*x + y*y <= 1) 1 else 0
    }.reduce(_ + _)
    println(s"Pi is roughly ${4.0 * count / (n - 1)}")
    spark.stop()
  }
}
```

（3）在 Spark Web Console 的页面中可以监控 Spark 任务的运行状态，如图 2-17 所示。

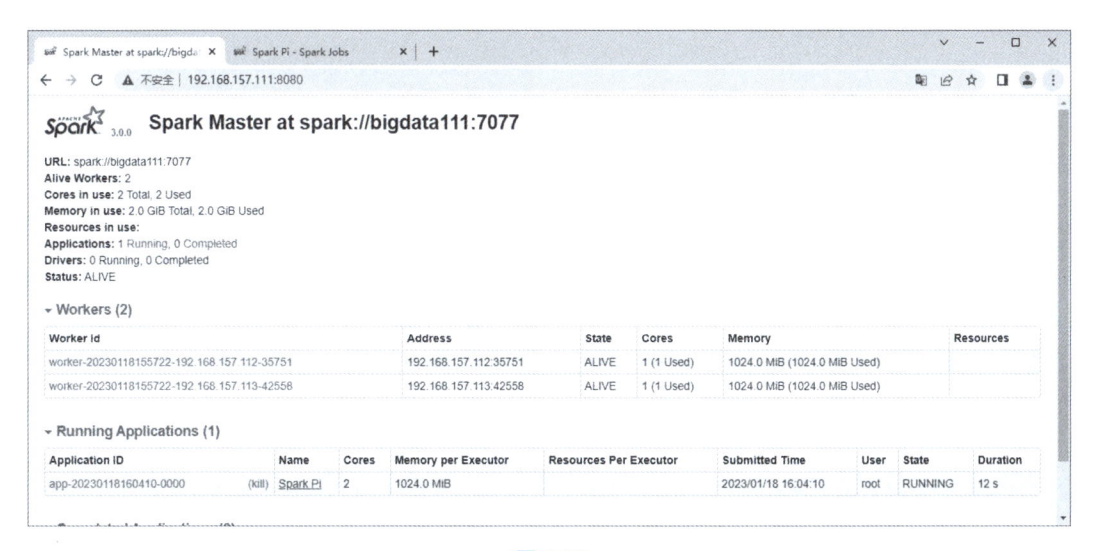

图 2-17

（4）单击 Running Applications 列表中任务的名称，如 Spark Pi，可以查看任务执行过程的详细信息，如图 2-18 所示。

（5）观察命令行的输出信息，如图 2-19 所示。

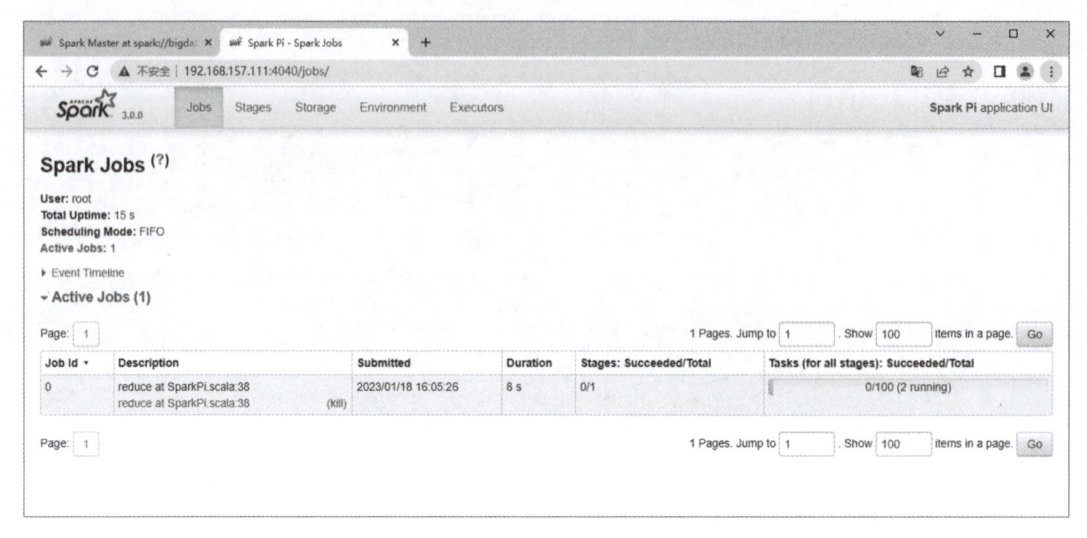

图 2-18

图 2-19

> 通过命令行的输出信息可以看到,Spark Pi 任务将计算出来的圆周率近似值直接显示在了屏幕上。

2. 使用 spark-shell 交互式命令行工具

spark-shell 是 Spark 提供的交互式分析数据的强大工具。使用 spark-shell 可以非常有效地学习 Spark RDD 的算子,它支持 Scala 语言和 Python 语言。spark-shell 有两种不同的运行模式:本地模式和集群模式。

1）使用 spark-shell 的本地模式

在本地模式下执行的 Spark 任务会在本地运行，不会被提交到集群上。这种模式与在 IDE 环境中执行程序的本质是一样的，因此本地模式多用于开发和测试环境中。

可以通过下面的方式来启动 spark-shell 的本地模式。整个启动过程输出的日志如图 2-20 所示。

```
bin/spark-shell
```

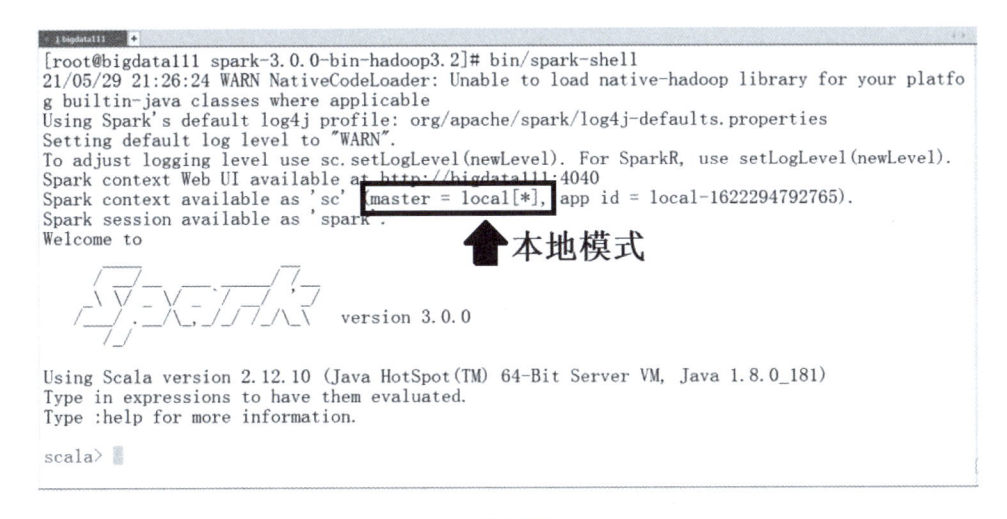

图 2-20

spark-shell 在启动时创建了两个对象：SparkContext 和 SparkSession。它们分别通过变量 sc 和 spark 来引用。SparkContext 是 Spark Core 的访问接口，它是整个 Spark 体系中最重要的一个访问接口；而 SparkSession 是从 Spark 2.x 版本开始提供的一个统一访问入口，通过 SparkSession 可以访问 Spark 的各个功能模块，包括 Spark Core、Spark SQL 和 Spark Streaming。

> 在输出日志中还可以看到 master 的地址是 local，这也说明了这时运行的模式是本地模式。

使用下面的语句可以退出 spark-shell。

```
Scala> :quit
```

2）使用 spark-shell 的集群模式

与本地模式不同，集群模式需要将 spark-shell 作为客户端连接到 Spark 集群上。这时所有在 spark-shell 中编写、执行的任务都会在集群上运行。启动 spark-shell 的集群模式需要使用

--master 选项。

```
bin/spark-shell --master spark://bigdata111:7077
```

整个启动过程输出的日志如图 2-21 所示。

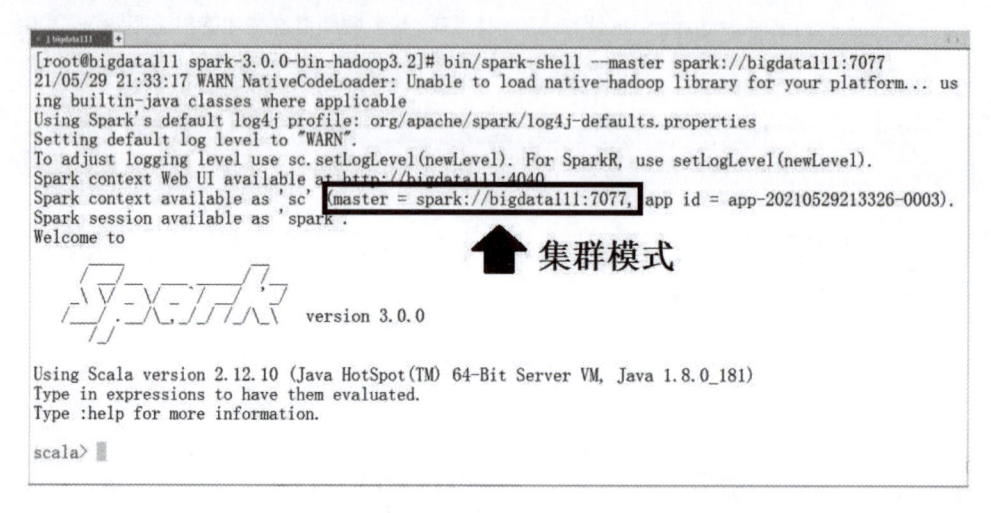

图 2-21

通过输出的日志可以看到，master 的地址变成了 spark://bigdata111:7077，说明 spark-shell 运行的模式是集群模式。这一点也可以在 Spark Web Console 的页面中观察到，如图 2-22 所示。

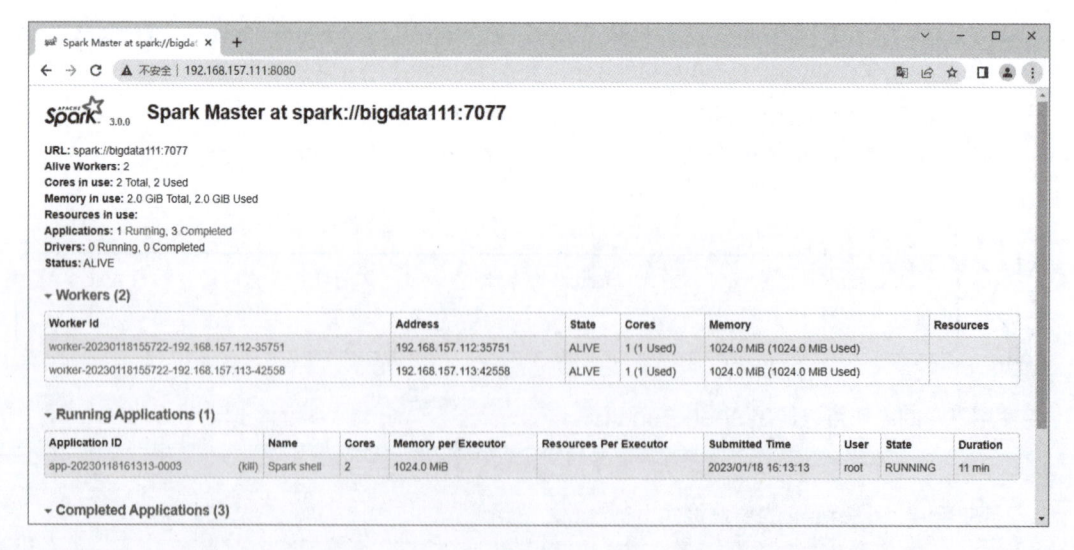

图 2-22

下面使用 Scala 编程语言，开发一个简单的 WordCount 程序来统计每个单词出现的频率。

（1）启动 Hadoop 环境。

```
start-all.sh
```

（2）在 spark-shell 中编写如下代码。通过这段代码读取 HDFS 中的数据，执行完成后，将结果保存到 HDFS 中。

```
scala> sc.textFile("hdfs://bigdata111:9000/input/data.txt")
    .flatMap(_.split(" ")).map((_,1)).reduceByKey(_+_)
    .saveAsTextFile("hdfs://bigdata111:9000/output/spark/wc")
```

> 由于 Spark 兼容 Hadoop，因此可以直接访问 HDFS 中的数据，也可以将 Spark 运行在 Yarn 上。

（3）在 HDFS 上查看统计的结果，如图 2-23 所示。

```
[root@bigdata111 ~]# hdfs dfs -ls /output/spark/wc
Found 3 items
-rw-r--r--   3 root supergroup          0 2021-05-29 21:41 /output/spark/wc/_SUCCESS
-rw-r--r--   3 root supergroup         40 2021-05-29 21:41 /output/spark/wc/part-00000
-rw-r--r--   3 root supergroup         31 2021-05-29 21:41 /output/spark/wc/part-00001
[root@bigdata111 ~]# hdfs dfs -cat /output/spark/wc/part-00000
(is,1)
(love,2)
(capital,1)
(Beijing,2)
[root@bigdata111 ~]# hdfs dfs -cat /output/spark/wc/part-00001
(China,2)
(I,2)
(of,1)
(the,1)
[root@bigdata111 ~]#
```

图 2-23

2.3.3 【实战】执行 Spark 实时计算任务

Spark 生态圈体系中提供了 Spark Streaming，使 Spark 能够支持大数据的流式计算。但是从本质上看，Spark Streaming 底层依赖的依然是 Spark Core，因此其本质上依然是一个批处理的离线计算。

Spark Example 提供了一个 Spark Streaming 的示例程序——NetworkWordCount。该示例程序会从网络上接收发送来的字符串数据，并统计每个单词出现的频率。运行该示例程序需要使用 Netcat 工具来发送数据。

> Netcat 是一款简单的 UDP 和 TCP 工具,可以将 Netcat 用作网络的测试工具,来模拟一个消息服务器,用户使用它可以轻易地建立任何连接。

这里直接在部署好的 Spark 全分布环境中运行 NetworkWordCount 示例程序。下面列出执行 NetworkWordCount 示例程序的步骤,以及需要注意的问题。

(1)启动 Spark 环境。

```
cd /root/training/spark-3.0.0-bin-hadoop3.2/sbin/start-all.sh
```

(2)新开一个命令行窗口启动 Netcat,并将其运行在本机的 1234 端口上。

```
nc -l -p 1234
```

(3)执行 Spark Streaming 的示例程序——NetworkWordCount,如图 2-24 所示。

```
bin/run-example streaming.NetworkWordCount localhost 1234
```

图 2-24

(4)在 Netcat 窗口中发送测试数据,并观察 NetworkWordCount 窗口中的输出,如图 2-25 所示。

图 2-25

这时发现在 Spark Streaming NetworkWordCount 的运行窗口中并没有得到相应的输出结果。为什么会出现这样的问题？核心的原因是：运行 Spark Streaming 程序至少应保证两个以上的线程。当只有一个线程时，如果该线程负责接收数据，则没有可用线程负责处理数据。官方文档中做出了如下说明。

When running a Spark Streaming program locally, do not use "local" or "local[1]" as the master URL. Either of these means that only one thread will be used for running tasks locally. If you are using an input DStream based on a receiver (e.g. sockets, Kafka, etc.), then the single thread will be used to run the receiver, leaving no thread for processing the received data. Hence, when running locally, always use "local[n]" as the master URL, where n > number of receivers to run (see Spark Properties for information on how to set the master).

以上官方的解释对应到搭建的虚拟机环境上，虚拟机至少要有两个 CPU 内核，才能保证 Spark Streaming 程序正常执行。

（5）关闭虚拟机并将处理器的数量修改为 2，如图 2-26 所示。

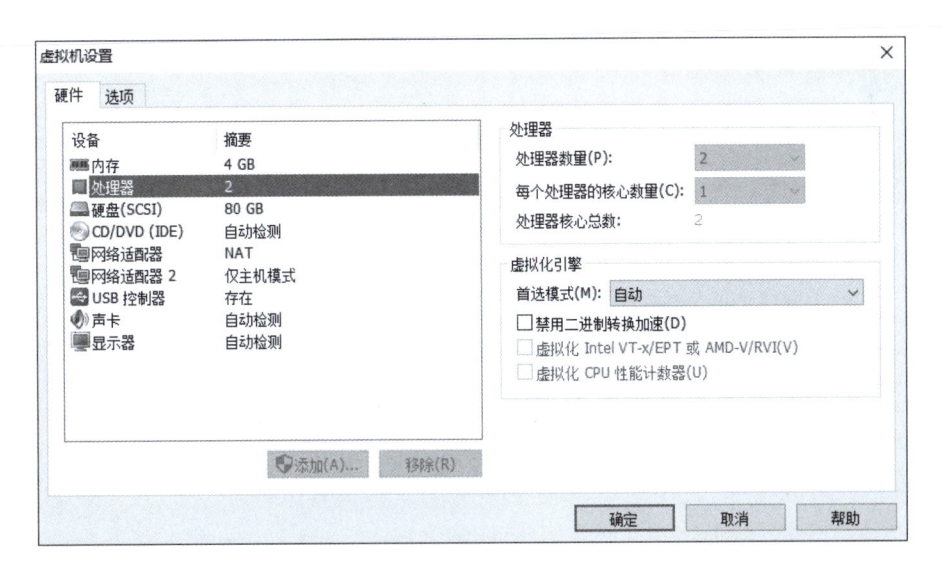

图 2-26

（6）重新执行 NetworkWordCount 示例程序。这时就可以观察到正常输出的结果，通过输出的时间戳可以看出，程序每隔一秒钟处理一次数据，如图 2-27 所示。

```
[root@bigdata111 ~]# nc -l -p 1234
I love Beijing and love China
```

```
-------------------------------------------
Time: 1623594243000 ms
-------------------------------------------
(love, 2)
(Beijing, 1)
(China, 1)
(I, 1)
(and, 1)
```

图 2-27

2.3.4 【实战】使用 Spark SQL 处理结构化数据

Spark SQL 是 Spark 用来处理结构化数据的一个模块，它提供了一个编程抽象——DataFrame。这里的 DataFrame 就是 Spark SQL 的数据模型，可以把它理解成一张表。因此可以将 Spark SQL 理解成 Spark 提供的分布式 SQL 查询引擎。

Spark 提供了结构化的示例数据文件，利用这些结构化的数据文件可以直接创建 DataFrame，这些文件位于 Spark 安装目录下的 examples/src/main/resources 目录中。下面是 people.json 文件中的数据内容。

```
{"name":"Michael"}
{"name":"Andy", "age":30}
{"name":"Justin", "age":19}
```

由于数据源文件本身具有格式，因此可以直接创建 DataFrame。下面是具体的步骤。

（1）为了便于操作，将 people.json 文件复制到/root 目录下。

```
cp people.json /root
```

（2）使用 spark-shell 直接创建 DataFrame。这里加载的文件可以在本地目录，也可以在 HDFS。

```
scala> val people = spark.read.json("file:///root/people.json")
```

（3）执行一个简单的查询。

```
scala> people.show
```

输出的结果如下。

```
+----+-------+
| age|   name|
```

```
+----+-------+
|null|Michael|
| 30|   Andy|
| 19| Justin|
+----+-------+
```

（4）查询用户的姓名。

```
scala> people.select("name").show
```

输出的结果如下。

```
+-------+
|   name|
+-------+
|Michael|
|   Andy|
| Justin|
+-------+
```

（5）创建一个视图，并使用标准的 SQL 语句查询。

```
scala> people.createOrReplaceTempView("mypeople")
scala> spark.sql("select * from mypeople").show
```

输出的结果如下。

```
+----+-------+
| age|   name|
+----+-------+
|null|Michael|
| 30|   Andy|
| 19| Justin|
+----+-------+
```

2.4 面向流处理的大数据计算引擎 Flink 快速上手

有了前面部署 Hadoop 和 Spark 的基础后，部署 Flink 环境就更加容易了。Flink 的部署模式也分为本地模式、伪分布模式和全分布模式。

> 这里将使用 Flink 全分布模式进行部署，这种模式也是在生成环境中使用的模式，在开发和测试环境中经常使用本地模式和伪分布模式。

2.4.1 【实战】部署 Flink 集群

Flink 全分布模式的部署与 Spark 完成相同，下面的步骤将把 Flink 的主节点 JobManager 部署在 bigdata111 上，在 bigdata112 和 bigdata112 上各部署一个从节点。

（1）在 bigdata111 上，将 Flink 的安装包解压缩到/root/training 目录下。

```
tar -zxvf flink-1.11.0-bin-scala_2.12.tgz -C /root/training/
```

（2）修改 Flink 的核心配置文件 flink-conf.yaml。

```
cd /root/training/flink-1.11.0/conf
vi flink-conf.yaml
```

（3）将 flink-conf.yaml 文件中 JobManager 的地址设置为当前的主机名。

```
jobmanager.rpc.address: bigdata111
```

（4）在 works 文件中指定从节点的地址。

```
bigdata112
bigdata113
```

（5）将 bigdata111 中的 Flink 目录复制到 bigdata112 和 bigdata113 上。

```
cd /root/training
scp -r flink-1.11.0/ root@bigdata112:/root/training
scp -r flink-1.11.0/ root@bigdata113:/root/training
```

（6）在 bigdata111 上启动 Flink，如图 2-28 所示。

```
cd /root/training/flink-1.11.0
bin/start-cluster.sh
```

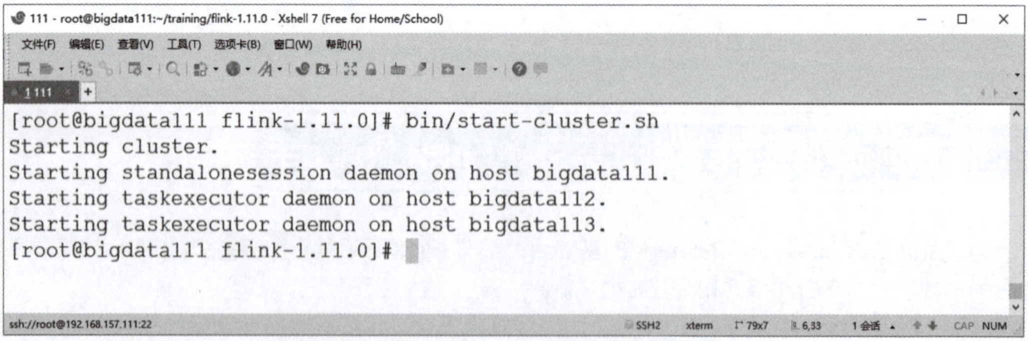

图 2-28

（7）在每台主机上执行 jps 命令，观察后台的进程，如图 2-29 所示。

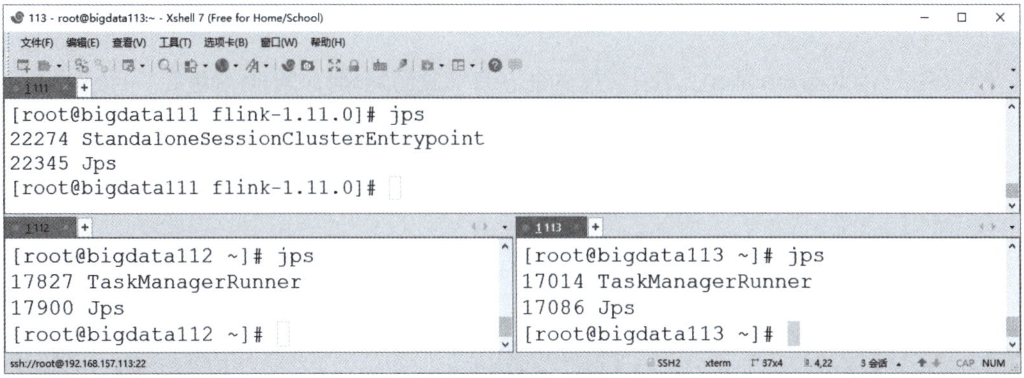

图 2-29

（8）通过端口 8081 访问 Flink Web Console，如图 2-30 所示。

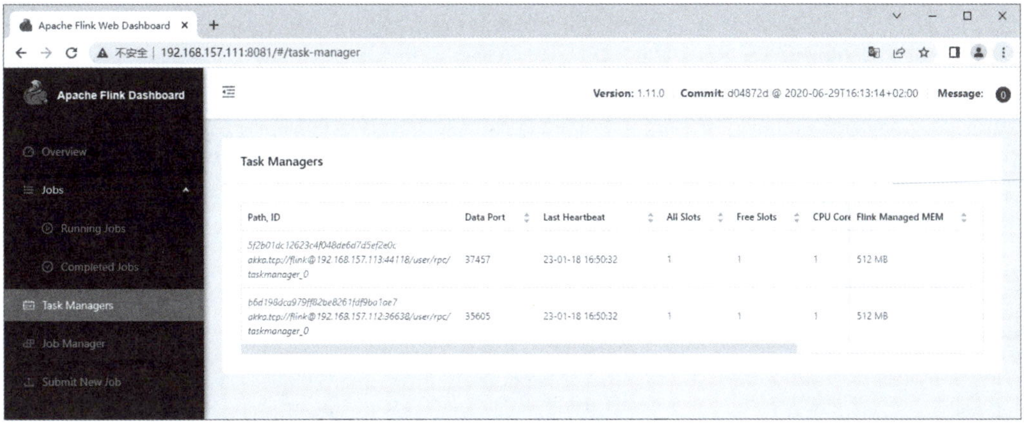

图 2-30

> 从 Flink Web Console 上可以看到有 2 个从节点，分别位于 bigdata112 和 bigdata113 主机上。

2.4.2 【实战】执行 Flink 离线计算任务

Flink 是流批一体的大数据计算引擎，提供了相应的示例程序来演示 Flink 批处理计算功能和流处理计算功能。

> 由于 Flink 没有与 Hadoop 进行集成，因此在 Flink 中访问 HDFS，或者运行 Flink on Yarn，需要手动将 Flink 与 Hadoop 进行集成。

下面是执行 Flink 批处理任务具体的操作步骤。

（1）集成 Flink 与 Hadoop，将官方提供的 JAR 包复制到 Flink 的 lib 目录下。

```
cp flink-shaded-hadoop-2-uber-2.8.3-10.0.jar \
/root/training/flink-1.11.0/lib
```

（2）启动 Flink。

```
cd /root/training/flink-1.11.0/
bin/start-cluster.sh
```

（3）启动 HDFS。这里主要是为了通过 Flink 访问 HDFS 中的数据并执行批处理计算。

```
start-dfs.sh
```

（4）执行批处理的 WordCount 示例程序，如图 2-31 所示。

```
bin/flink run examples/batch/WordCount.jar \
-input hdfs://bigdata111:9000/input/data.txt \
-output hdfs://bigdata111:9000/flink/wc
```

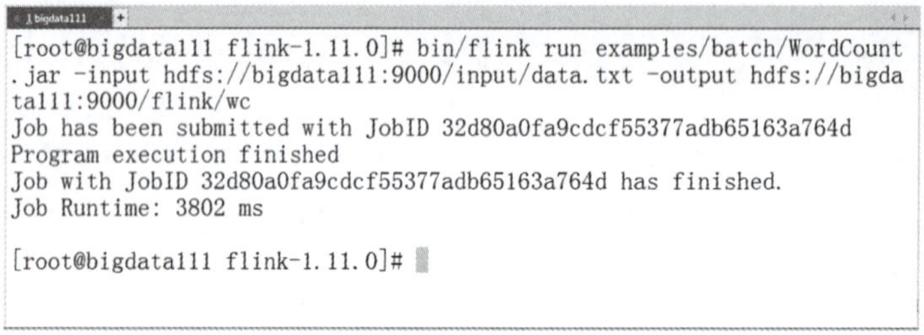

图 2-31

（5）查看批处理任务的结果，如图 2-32 所示。

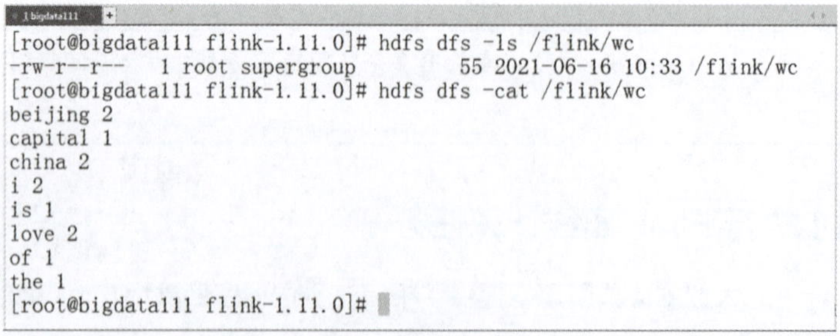

图 2-32

2.4.3 【实战】执行 Flink 实时计算任务

Flink 除了可以执行批处理的离线计算任务，还可以使用 DataStream API 执行流处理任务。

下面通过使用 Flink 提供的流处理的示例程序来演示具体的操作步骤。

（1）新打开一个命令行窗口，启动 Netcat 并监听本机的 1234 端口。

```
nc -l -p 1234
```

（2）执行流处理的 WordCount 示例程序。

```
bin/flink run examples/streaming/SocketWindowWordCount.jar --port 1234
```

（3）在 Netcat 中输入一些测试数据。

```
I love Beijing and love China
```

（4）查看流处理任务的结果，如图 2-33 所示。

```
cd /root/training/flink-1.11.0/log/
tail -f flink-root-taskexecutor-0-bigdata111.out
```

图 2-33

（5）打开 Flink Web Console 查看执行的任务，可以看到已经完成的批处理任务和正在执行的流处理任务，如图 2-34 所示。

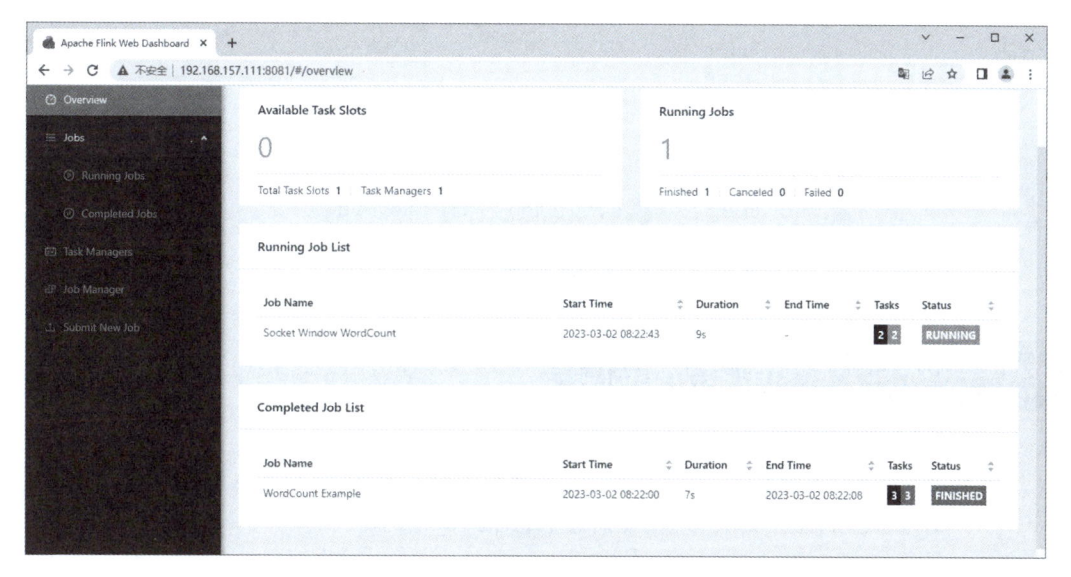

图 2-34

2.4.4 【实战】使用 Flink SQL 处理结构化数据

Flink SQL 是 Flink 为简化计算模型、降低用户使用实时计算门槛而设计的一套符合标准 SQL 语义的开发语言。使用 Flink 提供的 SQL Client 可以很方便地书写、调试一个任务，并将任务提交到 Flink 集群运行。

下面是使用 Flink SQL 处理结构化数据的示例。

（1）启动 Flink 集群。

```
cd /root/training/flink-1.11.0/
bin/start-cluster.sh
```

（2）启动 Flink SQL Client。

```
bin/sql-client.sh embedded
```

（3）执行 SQL 语句。

```
Flink SQL> select name, count(*) as cnt
> from (values ('bob'), ('alice'), ('greg'), ('bob')) as nametable(name)
> group by name;
```

输出的结果如图 2-35 所示。

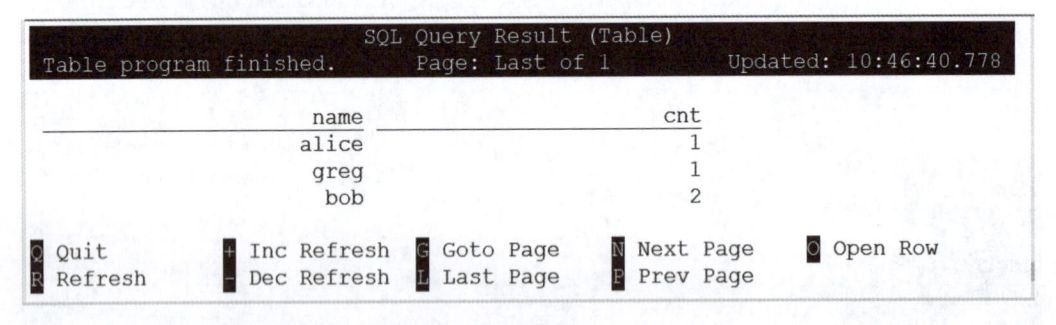

图 2-35

2.5 大数据体系的单点故障问题

大数据体系架构中的核心组件都是主从架构（即存在一个主节点和多个从节点，从而组成一个分布式环境）。大数据体系中主从架构的相关组件如图 2-36 所示。

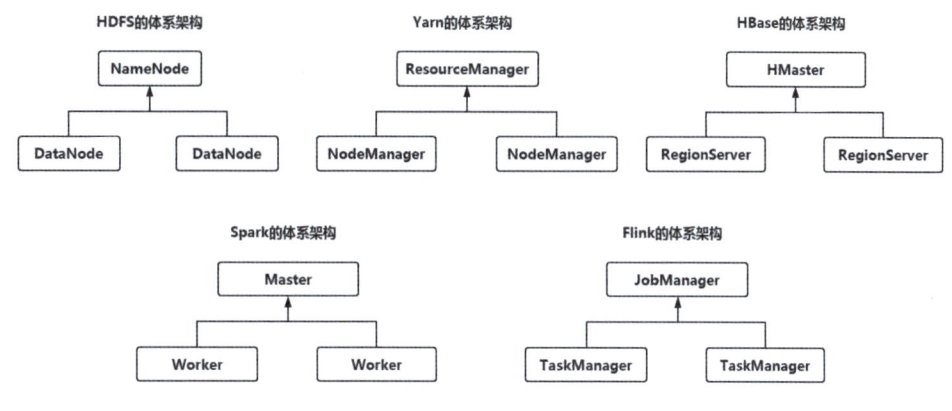

图 2-36

只要是主从架构，就存在单点故障的问题：整个集群中只存在一个主节点，如果这个主节点出现故障或发生宕机，就会造成整个集群无法正常工作。因此，在实际的生产环境中，需要实现大数据的 HA（High Availablity，高可用性）架构。

HA 的思想其实非常简单：既然整个集群中只有一个主节点存在单点故障的问题，那么只需要搭建多个主节点就可以解决这个问题了。

> 由于大数据 HA 的实现需要使用 ZooKeeper，因此 ZooKeeper 在整个大数据技术体系中有着非常重要的作用。

基于 ZooKeeper 的 HDFS HA 架构如图 2-37 所示。

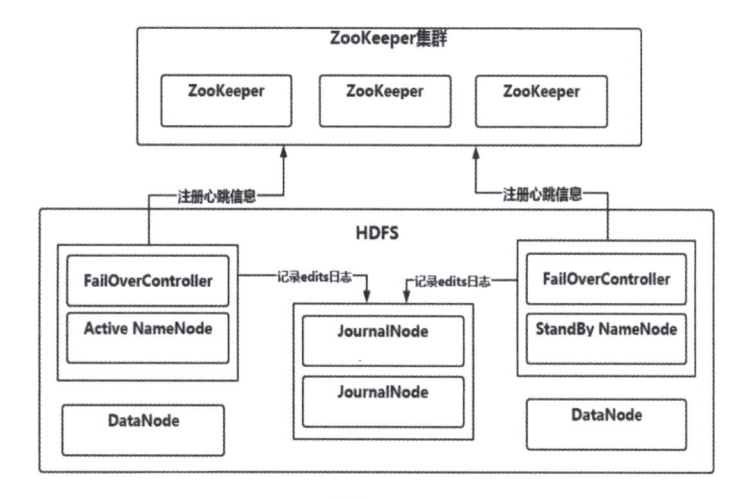

图 2-37

在 HDFS HA 架构中引入了双 NameNode 的架构：通过将两个 NameNode 分别配置为 Active 和 StandBy 状态来解决了 HDFS 的单点故障问题。StandBy NameNode 作为 Active NameNode 的热备份，能够在 NameNode 发生宕机或发生故障时，通过 ZooKeeper 的选举机制自动切换为 Active NameNode。

为了实现 HA 的主备切换，整个架构中还增加了失败迁移控制器 FailOverController。它负责与 ZooKeeper 通信并将 NameNode 的心跳信息注册到 ZooKeeper 中。如果 Active NameNode 发生故障，ZooKeeper 无法通过 FailOverController 接收 Active NameNode 的心跳信息，ZooKeeper 会找到另外一个 FailOverController，从而进行 NameNode 的切换。在 NameNode 进行主备切换时，架构中的 JournalNode 用于实现 HDFS 元数据的同步。

> HDFS HA 架构是大数据架构体系中最复杂的一种。Spark HA 和 Flink HA 架构相对比较简单。

第 2 篇
阿里云大数据的离线计算服务

第 3 章

面向离线数据存储与计算的 MaxCompute 基础

MaxCompute 是面向企业级的云数据仓库，以 Serverless 架构提供快速、全托管的在线数据仓库服务，消除了传统数据平台在资源扩展性和弹性方面的限制。通过 MaxCompute，用户只需要投入少量的运维成本，就可以经济并高效地分析、处理海量数据。数以万计的企业正基于 MaxCompute 进行数据计算与分析，将数据高效转换为业务洞察。

3.1 MaxCompute 简介

MaxCompute 是一种快速、全托管的 TB/PB 级数据仓库解决方案。MaxCompute 向用户提供了完善的数据导入方案，以及多种经典的分布式计算模型，能够更快速地解决用户海量数据的计算问题，有效降低企业成本，并保障数据安全。

3.1.1 什么是 MaxCompute

随着数据收集手段的不断丰富，行业数据的大量积累，数据规模已增长到了传统软件行业无法承载的海量数据（TB、PB、EB）级别。MaxCompute 致力于批量结构化数据的存储和计算，提供海量数据仓库的解决方案及分析建模服务。

由于单台服务器的处理能力有限，海量数据的分析需要使用分布式计算模型。分布式计算模型对数据分析人员要求较高且不易维护。数据分析人员不仅需要了解业务需求，还需要熟悉底层的分布式计算模型。MaxCompute 为用户提供完善的数据导入方案，以及多种经典的分布式计算模型，使用户不必关心分布式计算和维护细节，就可以轻松完成大数据分析。

目前，MaxCompute 服务已覆盖全球 16 个国家和地区，客户遍及金融、互联网、生物医疗、能源、交通、传媒等行业，为全球用户提供海量数据存储与计算服务。

3.1.2　MaxCompute 的特点

MaxCompute 具有以下特点。

（1）适用于大规模分布式存储与计算。MaxCompute 适用于 100GB 以上规模的存储与计算需求，最大可达 EB 级别。

（2）支持多种易用计算模型。MaxCompute 支持 SQL、MapReduce、UDF（Java/Python）、Graph 和 Spark 多种任务的执行，并简化了企业大数据平台的应用架构。

（3）数据安全性高。MaxCompute 已稳定支撑阿里全部数据仓库业务 9 年以上，提供多层沙箱防护、细粒度权限管理及监控。MaxCompute 通过了独立的第三方审计师针对阿里云对 AICPA 可信服务标准中关于安全性、可用性和机密性原则符合性描述的审计。

（4）成本低。与企业自建大数据平台相比，MaxCompute 的存储更高效，可以大幅降低采购和运维成本。

（5）用户无须关心底层分布式架构及运维。基于 MaxCompute 的 Serverless 设计思路，用户只需要关心作业和数据，而无须关心底层分布式架构及运维。

（6）拥有极致的弹性扩展。MaxCompute 提供按量付费模式下的作业级别的资源管理。用户无须受困于资源扩展难题，系统会自动扩展计算、存储、网络等资源。

3.2　初识 MaxCompute

在使用 MaxCompute 之前，需要先了解 MaxCompute 的体系架构，以及其中涉及的相关术语。

> 云原生大数据计算服务 MaxCompute 是构建在阿里云的飞天操作系统之上的大数据计算引擎。

3.2.1　MaxCompute 的架构

MaxCompute 的架构体系如图 3-1 所示，它由 4 部分组成：计算与存储层（MaxCompute Core）、逻辑层（MaxCompute Server）、接入层（MaxCompute FrontEnd）和客户端

（MaxCompute Client）。

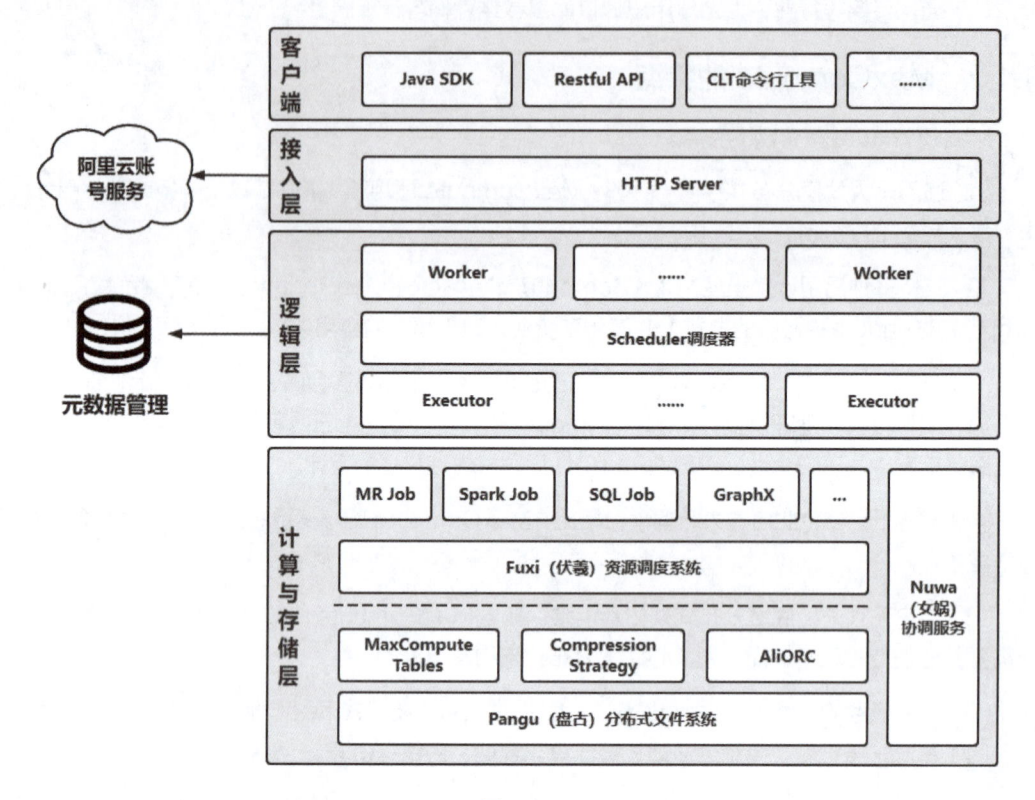

图 3-1

下面对这 4 层分别进行介绍。

1. 计算与存储层

MaxCompute 的底层存储使用阿里云自主研发的分布式文件系统 Pangu，它类似于 Hadoop 中的 HDFS。在 MaxCompute 中，数据存储具有以下特点。

（1）基于 MaxCompute Tables。MaxCompute 的数据存储单元都是以表的形式存在的。在 MaxCompute 中，不同类型作业的操作对象（输入、输出）都是表。

（2）采用 Compression Strategy。MaxCompute 采用列压缩存储格式，通常情况下具备 5 倍压缩能力。

（3）数据存储可升级为 AliORC。MaxCompute 数据存储格式全面升级为 AliORC，具备更高的存储性能。

基于 MaxCompute 底层存储的数据，MaxCompute 使用资源管理和调度系统伏羲（Fuxi）对各种计算任务进行统一管理和调度，包括 MapReduce Job、Spark Job、SQL Job、GraphX Job 等。

> 资源管理和调度系统伏羲，类似于 Hadoop 中的 Yarn。它目前以管理和调度高吞吐的离线数据处理任务为主。

为了实现集群的高可用服务，在 MaxCompute 的体系架构中还使用了分布式协调服务女娲（Nuwa）。它类似于 Hadoop 生态圈体系中的 ZooKeeper，可以使分布式集群的各个进程协调工作。

2. 逻辑层

MaxCompute 的逻辑层主要实现项目空间与对象的管理、命令的解析与执行逻辑、数据对象的访问控制与授权等功能。在逻辑层有 Worker（请求处理器）、Scheduler（调度器）和 Executor（作业执行管理器）三个角色。

（1）Worker 处理所有客户端的请求，包括用户空间（Project）管理操作、资源（Resource）管理操作、作业管理等。对于 SQL 语句、MapReduce 任务等启动任务的作业，Scheduler 会做进一步处理。

（2）Scheduler 负责伏羲的调度，包括将任务分解为执行单元、对等待提交的执行单元进行排序，以及向伏羲询问执行单元的资源占用情况，并进行流量控制。

（3）Executor 负责启动具体的任务执行单元，向伏羲提交任务执行单元，监控这些任务的运行。

在了解了逻辑层的组成部分后，这里将进一步讨论逻辑层的处理流程。当用户提交一个 MaxCompute 作业请求时，接入层先进行用户认证，然后将作业请求发送给逻辑层的 Worker。Worker 判断是否为同步请求，如果是同步请求，则本地执行并返回；如果是异步请求，则 Worker 会先做一些检查（如表是否存在、版本号是否最新等），并生成任务的 ID，然后把请求进一步发送给 Scheduler，并返回客户端一个确认信息。Scheduler 把作业分解成各个任务执行单元，Executor 主动轮询 Scheduler，获取相应的任务执行单元，提交给计算层执行，并定时将自己持有的任务执行单元的状态汇报给 Scheduler。

3. 接入层

接入层的主要作用是接收客户端的访问请求，并通过阿里云账号服务对客户端请求中的签名信息进行验证，从而实现对客户端的控制，如图 3-2 所示。接入层提供的功能包括接收 HTTP 请求、数据缓存、Load Balance 负载均衡、用户认证和服务层面的访问控制。

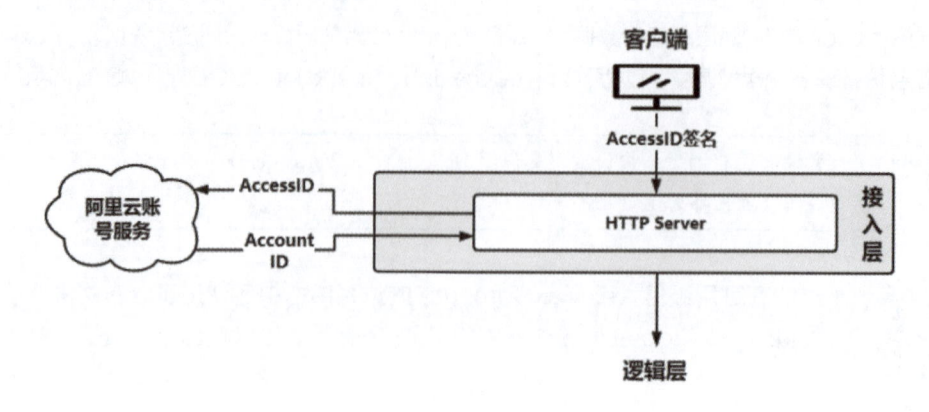

图 3-2

图 3-2 中的 AccountID 和 AccessID 有什么区别呢？

一个 AccountID 可以对应多个 AccessID 和 AccessKey，用户的权限数据都是和 AccountID 对应的。也就是说，假设某个用户被授权访问某个 MaxCompute 服务，而该用户有多对 AccessID 和 AccessKey，则可以使用任何一对 AccessID 和 AccessKey 来访问 MaxCompute 服务。

一个 AccountID 对应多个 AccessID 是从云计算的安全角度考虑的。比如：一个用户可以访问 5 个项目空间，每个项目空间可以通过不同的 AccessID 和 AccessKey 来访问。如果某个项目空间的 AccessID 和 AccessKey 泄露了，则可以删除该项目空间的 AccessID 和 AccessKey，而不用修改其他项目空间的访问方式。

4. 客户端

MaxCompute 的客户端有 4 种形式：MaxCompute Web、MaxCompute SDK、MaxCompute CLT 和 MaxCompute IDE。每种客户端的说明如表 3-1 所示。

表 3-1

客户端	说明
MaxCompute Web	MaxCompute 以 Web RESTful API 的方式提供离线数据处理服务
MaxCompute SDK	MaxCompute 对 RESTful API 的封装，目前有 Java、Python 等版本的实现
MaxCompute CLT	CLT（Command Line Tool）是 MaxCompute 运行在 Windows 或 Linux 下的命令行客户端工具。通过 CLT 可以提交命令完成项目空间的管理、DDL 和 DML 等操作
MaxCompute IDE	MaxCompute 提供了可视化的 ETL/BI 工具，即"采云间"，用户可以基于"采云间"完成数据同步、任务调度、报表生成等常见操作

3.2.2 MaxCompute 的核心概念

MaxCompute 中的概念和术语非常多，这里列举一些核心概念，这对于进一步掌握和使用

MaxCompute 非常重要。MaxCompute 的核心概念具有层次结构，通过了解其结构，可以为后期项目规划、安全管理等提供思路。

MaxCompute 核心概念的层次结构如图 3-3 所示。

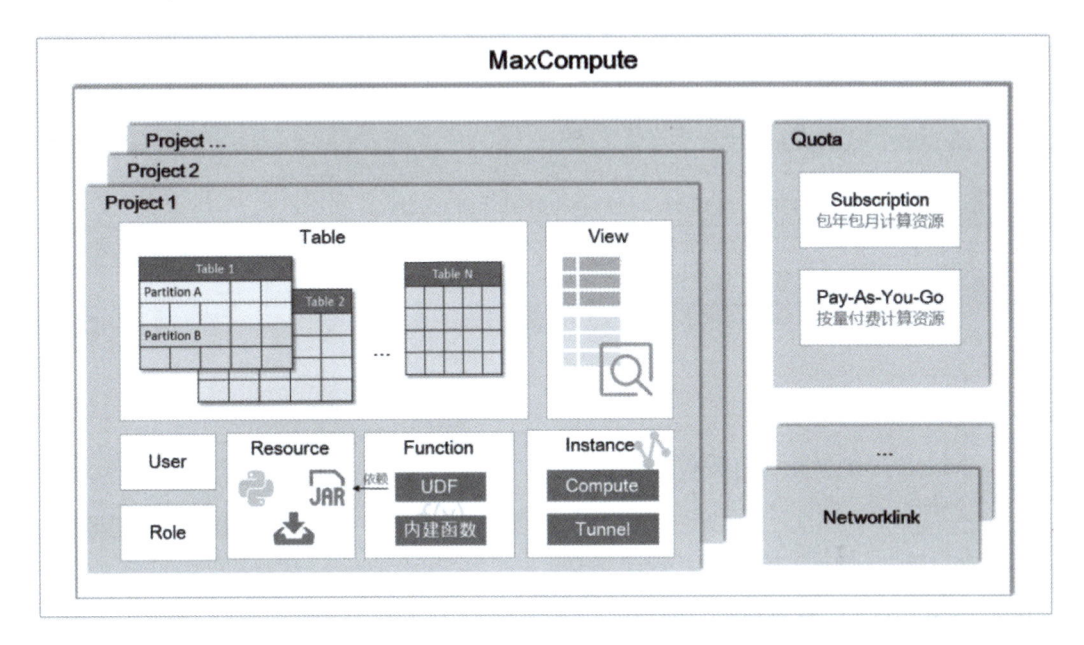

图 3-3

图 3-3 中涉及的核心概念的说明如表 3-2 所示。

表 3-2

核心概念	说明
Project（项目）	项目是 MaxCompute 的基本组织单元，类似于传统数据库的 Database 或 Schema 的概念。Project 是进行多用户的逻辑隔离和访问控制的主要边界
Table（表）	表是 MaxCompute 的数据存储单元
Partition（分区）	分区是指一张表下，根据分区字段（一个或多个字段的组合）对数据存储进行划分。如果表没有分区，则数据被存储在表所在的目录下。如果表有分区，每个分区对应表下的一个目录，则数据被分别存储在不同的分区目录下
View（视图）	视图是在表之上建立的虚拟表，它的结构和内容都来自表。一个视图可以对应一张表或多张表。如果想保留查询结果，但不想创建表占用存储，可以通过视图实现
User（用户）	用户是 MaxCompute 安全功能中的概念，MaxCompute 支持通过阿里云账号、RAM（Resource Access Management）用户或 RAM 角色访问 MaxCompute。非 MaxCompute 项目所有者（Project Owner）的用户必须被加入 MaxCompute 项目，且被授予相应的权限，才能操作 MaxCompute 项目中的数据、作业、资源及函数。 关于 MaxCompute 的用户将在第 8 章中进行介绍

续表

核心概念	说明
Role（角色）	角色是 MaxCompute 安全功能中的概念，可以理解为拥有相同权限的用户的集合。多个用户可以同时存在于一个角色下，一个用户也可以隶属于多个角色。给角色授权后，该角色下的所有用户拥有相同的权限。 关于 MaxCompute 的角色将在第 8 章中进行介绍
Resource（资源）	资源是 MaxCompute 中特有的概念。使用 MaxCompute 的服务功能需要依赖资源来完成，如 CPU 和内存都是资源
Function（函数）	MaxCompute 提供函数功能，函数包括内建函数和 UDF。 关于 MaxCompute 的函数将在第 4 章中进行介绍
Instance（实例）	实例是实际运行作业的一个具体对象，与 Hadoop MapReduce 中 Job 的概念相似
Quota（配额）	配额是 MaxCompute 的计算资源池，提供作业运行所需的计算资源
Networklink（网络连接）	MaxCompute 默认未建立与外部网络或 VPC 网络间的网络连接。当需要访问外部网络或阿里云中的其他服务时，需要单独建立网络连接
Schema	MaxCompute 支持 Schema，在项目之下对表、资源、函数进行归类

3.2.3　MaxCompute 的数据类型

MaxCompute 提供了丰富的数据类型，这些数据类型类似于关系型数据库提供的数据类型。这些数据类型主要分为两种：基本数据类型和复杂数据类型。

MaxCompute 的数据类型如图 3-4 所示。

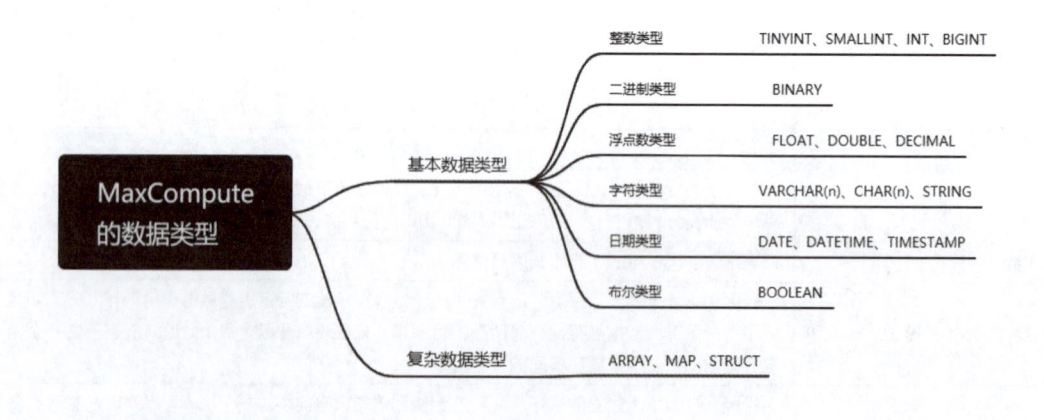

图 3-4

这里重点说明 MaxCompute 提供的 3 种复杂数据类型。

1. 数组类型 ARRAY

数组类型 ARRAY 将使用指定的值构造 ARRAY 数组，其命令格式如下。

```
array(<value>,<value>[, ...])
```

其中，value 为必填项，可以是任意类型。但所有 value 的数据类型必须一致。

例如，下面的命令构造了一个简单的整数类型数组。

```
array(1, 2, 3)
```

> 数组类型 ARRAY 可以嵌套其他的 MaxCompute 复杂数据类型，例如：
> array(struct(1, 2), struct(3, 4))
> 这条命令构造的 ARRAY 数组中就嵌套了结构类型的数据。

2. 集合类型 MAP

集合类型 MAP 将使用指定的数据构造键值对的数据集合，其命令格式如下。

```
map(K <key1>, V <value1>, K <key2>, V <value2>[, ...])
```

其中，key 为必填项，所有 key 的数据类型一致（包括隐式转换后类型一致），必须是基本数据类型。value 为必填项，所有 value 的数据类型一致（包括隐式转换后类型一致），可以是任意数据类型。

下面给出了两个构造 MAP 的具体示例。

构造 MAP 的语法格式如下。

```
map<string, string>
map<smallint, array<string>>
```

示例如下。

```
map("k1", "v1", "k2", "v2")
map(1S, array('a', 'b'), 2S, array('x', 'y'))
```

3. 结构类型 STRUCT

结构类型 STRUCT 将使用指定的数据列表构造结构，其命令格式如下。

```
struct(<value1>,<value2>[, ...])
```

其中，value 为必填项，可以是任意数据类型。

下面给出了两个构造 STRUCT 的具体示例。

构造 STRUCT 的语法格式如下。

```
struct<x:int, y:int>
struct<field1:bigint, field2:array<int>, field3:map<int, int>>
```

示例如下。

```
named_struct('x', 1, 'y', 2)
named_struct('field1', 100L, 'field2', array(1, 2), 'field3', map(1, 100, 2, 200))
```

3.3 使用 MaxCompute 的准备工作

在开始使用 MaxCompute 前，用户需要提前进行规划，然后按照操作流程执行操作。需要提前进行的规划如表 3-3 所示。

表 3-3

准备项	说明
用户	使用 MaxCompute 产品的人员名单，以便于准备阿里云账号或 RAM 用户
MaxCompute 项目	根据业务诉求，规划待创建的 MaxCompute 项目的归属地域、计费模式、采用的数据类型版本等，以便于创建 MaxCompute 项目
角色与权限	根据权限最小化原则，规划用户角色和权限
环境及工具	根据业务诉求选择合适的工具，如 MaxCompute Web 控制台、命令行客户端、DataWorks 或 MaxCompute IDE

使用阿里云 MaxCompute 的准备工作基本操作流程如图 3-5 所示。

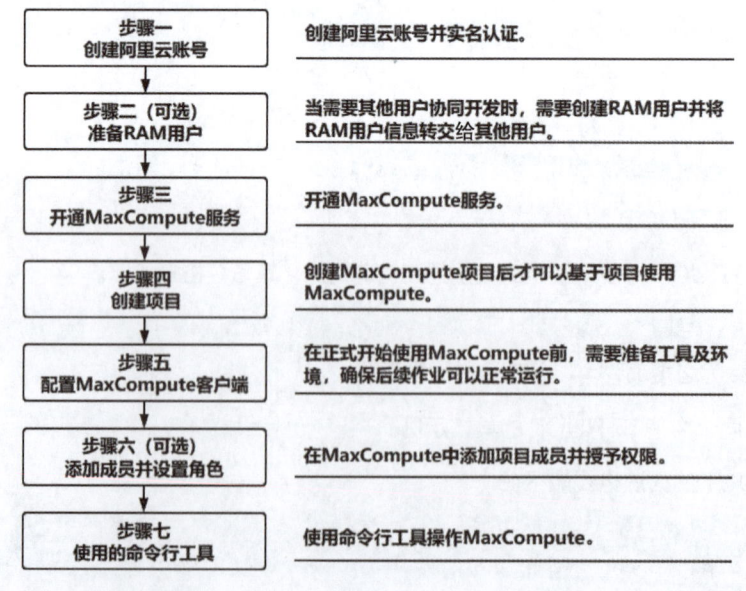

步骤一 创建阿里云账号：创建阿里云账号并实名认证。

步骤二（可选） 准备RAM用户：当需要其他用户协同开发时，需要创建RAM用户并将RAM用户信息转交给其他用户。

步骤三 开通MaxCompute服务：开通MaxCompute服务。

步骤四 创建项目：创建MaxCompute项目后才可以基于项目使用MaxCompute。

步骤五 配置MaxCompute客户端：在正式开始使用MaxCompute前，需要准备工具及环境，确保后续作业可以正常运行。

步骤六（可选） 添加成员并设置角色：在MaxCompute中添加项目成员并授予权限。

步骤七 使用的命令行工具：使用命令行工具操作MaxCompute。

图 3-5

> 下面的实战步骤省去了操作流程中的可选步骤。

3.3.1 【实战】创建阿里云账号

在使用 MaxCompute 前,需要准备好阿里云账号。下面介绍如何创建阿里云账号并完成相关准备工作。

(1)打开阿里云官网,单击阿里云官网右上角的"立即注册"按钮,如图 3-6 所示。

图 3-6

(2)在"账号注册"页面中,按照操作提示完成账号注册。

> 创建成功的阿里云账号会作为阿里云系统识别的资源消费账户,阿里云账号拥有该账户的所有权限。

(3)进入"账号中心"页面,在左侧的导航栏中选择"实名认证"选项,按照操作提示完成阿里云账号实名认证。企业用户推荐进行企业认证,以便获取更多便利。

> 为保证后续操作顺利进行,请务必完成实名认证操作。在实名制认证后,用户才可以购买和使用阿里云的产品。

（4）在阿里云管理控制台，将鼠标指针移动到页面右上角的账号信息上，在弹出的下拉列表中选择"AccessKey 管理"选项，如图 3-7 所示，进入"AccessKey"页面。

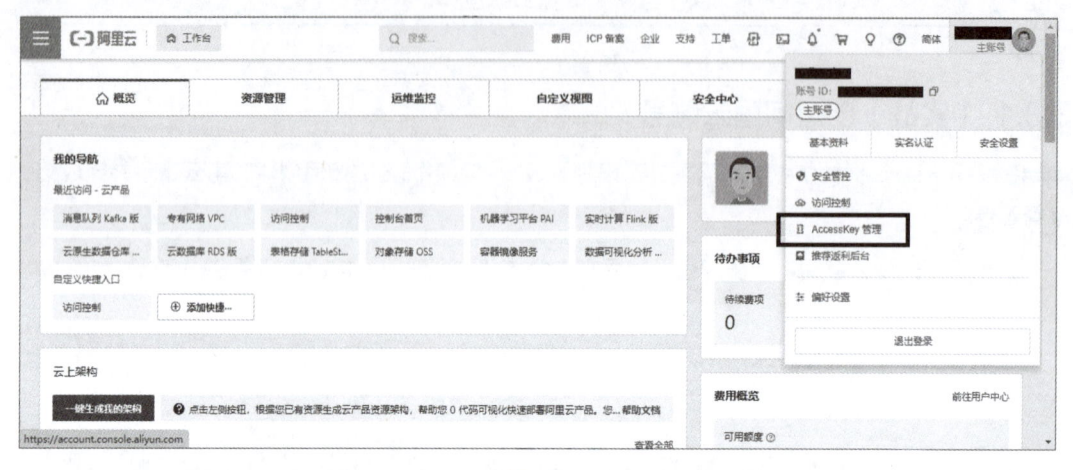

图 3-7

（5）在"AccessKey"页面中，单击"创建 AccessKey"按钮自动创建 AccessKey，如图 3-8 所示。

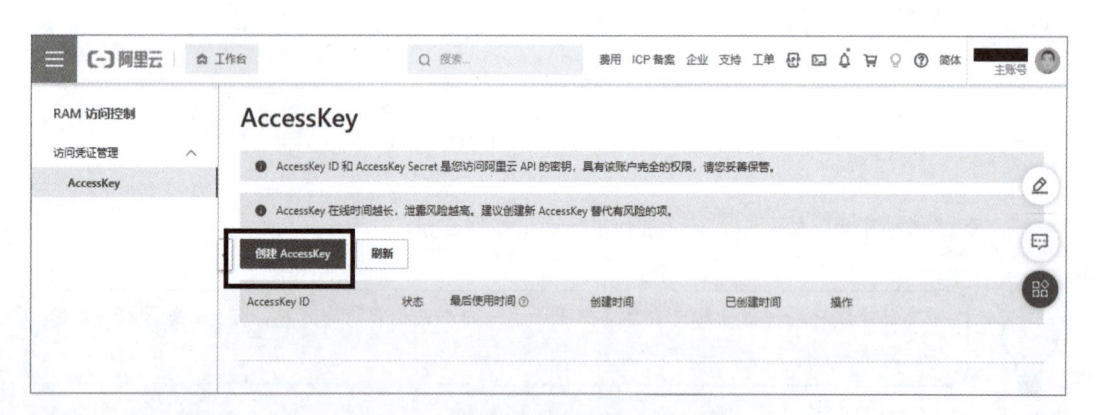

图 3-8

（6）AccessKey 创建成功后如图 3-9 所示。

（7）单击"查看 Secret"文字链接，在弹出的对话框中进行手机验证，如图 3-10 所示。

（8）在"查看 Secret"对话框中，单击"下载 CSV 文件"或"复制"文字链接保存创建的 AccessKey 信息，并单击"确定"按钮，关闭对话框，如图 3-11 所示

第 3 章 面向离线数据存储与计算的 MaxCompute 基础 | 81

图 3-9

图 3-10

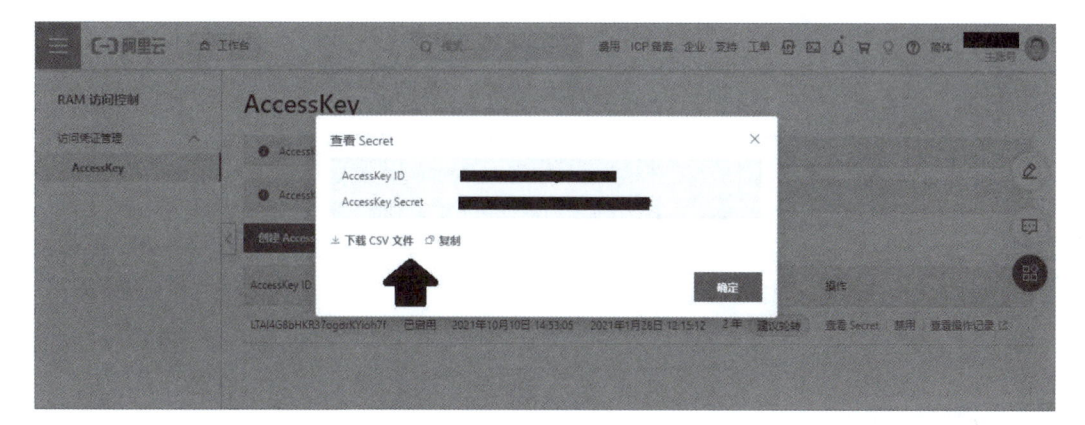

图 3-11

> 用户可以在"AccessKey"页面中查看已经创建的 AccessKey 的状态,并对其执行禁用、删除操作。
>
> 一旦 AccessKey 被禁用,则使用该 AccessKey 的服务将运行失败并报错。如果 AccessKey 状态有变更,用户需要及时关注使用该 AccessKey 的产品和服务。

3.3.2 【实战】开通 MaxCompute 服务

用户需要开通 MaxCompute 服务才可以使用 MaxCompute。如果第一次使用阿里云大数据产品,推荐使用阿里云账号开通 MaxCompute 服务。下面将详细介绍如何开通 MaxCompute。

(1)登录阿里云官网,选择"产品"→"大数据计算"→"数据计算与分析"→"云原生大数据计算服务 MaxCompute"选项,进入"云原生大数据计算服务 MaxCompute"首页,单击"立即开通"按钮。

(2)在购买页面选择"商品类型"和"区域",并勾选服务协议,单击"确认订单并支付"按钮,如图 3-12 所示。

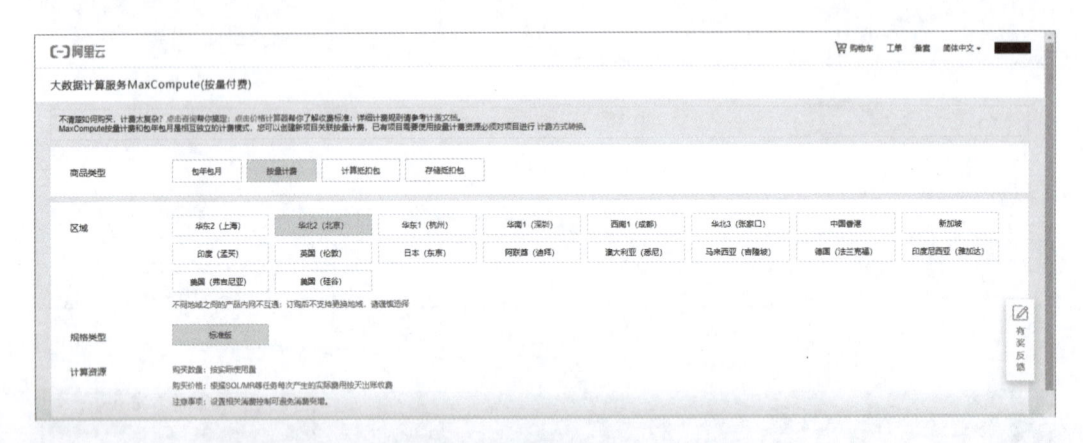

图 3-12

> 购买页面默认提供的产品规格类型为 MaxCompute 按量计费标准版+DataWorks 基础版。
>
> MaxCompute 的项目管理和查询、编辑功能集成了 DataWorks,因此在开通 MaxCompute 时会默认开通 DataWorks 基础版服务。
>
> DataWorks 基础版是 0 元开通,如果不使用数据集成、不执行调度任务,就不会产生费用。
>
> 在选择区域时需要考虑的最主要的因素是 MaxCompute 与其他阿里云产品之间的关系,例如数据所在区域。

（3）在"支付"页面中单击"支付"按钮，即可开通 MaxCompute 服务，如图 3-13 所示。

图 3-13

> 如果在选择的区域首次开通 MaxCompute 和 DataWorks 服务，且没有存量项目，则开通服务成功后，系统会自动创建一个默认项目，项目名称为"default_project_系统随机码"，该项目默认仅阿里云账号可见。

3.3.3 【实战】创建项目

项目是 MaxCompute 的基本组织单元，是进行多用户隔离和访问控制的主要边界。在开通 MaxCompute 服务后，需要通过项目使用 MaxCompute。下面将通过具体的步骤来介绍如何创建 MaxCompute 项目。

> 用户可以使用 MaxCompute 控制台或 DataWorks 创建 MaxCompute 项目空间。由于 MaxCompute 管理控制台的项目管理和查询、编辑功能是由 DataWorks 实现的，所以在创建 MaxCompute 项目时，需要先创建 DataWorks 工作空间。

（1）登录 MaxCompute 管理控制台，在左上方选择区域，在左侧的导航栏中选择"数据管理"→"项目管理"选项，在"项目管理"页面中单击"新建项目"按钮，如图 3-14 所示。

（2）在"新建项目"对话框中输入"项目名称"，其他配置项保持默认。单击"确定"按钮，如图 3-15 所示。

（3）创建成功后，即可在"项目管理"页面中查看新创建的 MaxCompute 项目，如图 3-16 所示。

图 3-14

图 3-15

图 3-16

3.3.4 配置 MaxCompute 客户端

在正式使用 MaxCompute 项目处理数据前，需要根据业务需要选择开发工具并准备相应的环境。

在 MaxCompute 中常用的工具及它们的应用场景如表 3-4 所示。

表 3-4

工具	是否需要手动安装	应用场景
命令行客户端（odpscmd）	是	MaxCompute 的命令行客户端适用于任意场景，使用者可以专注于编写命令，以完成数据处理
MaxCompute Studio	是	MaxCompute Studio 基于流行的集成开发平台 IntelliJ IDEA 的开发插件，帮助用户便捷、快速地进行数据开发。如果用户可以熟练使用 IntelliJ IDEA，推荐使用该工具
DataWorks	否	DataWorks 基于 MaxCompute 项目，以可视化方式实现全方位的数据开发、数据集成、数据服务等功能。当需要周期性调度作业时，推荐使用该工具

> 下面将重点介绍命令行客户端和 MaxCompute Studio 的使用方法。DataWorks 的使用方法将在第 11 章进行介绍。

1. 实战命令行客户端

通过 MaxCompute 的命令行客户端，可以访问 MaxCompute 项目并运行命令。这里将介绍如何安装、配置和运行客户端。

（1）从 Github 上下载 MaxCompute 命令行客户端安装包。

> MaxCompute 命令行客户端安装包可以在 GitHub 上搜索关键字 "aliyun-odps-console" 找到。

（2）解压缩下载的安装包文件，得到 bin、conf、lib 和 plugins 文件夹。

（3）进入 conf 文件夹，配置 odps_config.ini 文件，配置信息如下。

```
project_name=demo_maxcompute_001
access_id=<你的 AccessID>
access_key=<你的 AccessKey>
end_point=http://service.odps.aliyun.com/api
log_view_host=http://logview.odps.aliyun.com
https_check=true
# confirm threshold for query input size(unit: GB)
data_size_confirm=100.0
# this url is for odpscmd update
update_url=http://repo.aliyun.com/odpscmd
# download sql results by instance tunnel
use_instance_tunnel=true
# the max records when download sql results by instance tunnel
instance_tunnel_max_record=10000
# IMPORTANT:
# If leaving tunnel_endpoint untouched, console will try to
# automatically get one from odps service, which might charge networking
# fees in some cases.
# Please refer to https://help.aliyun.com/document_detail/34951.html
# tunnel_endpoint=

# use set.<key>=<value> to set flags when console launched
# e.g. set.odps.sql.select.output.format=csv
```

odps_config.ini 文件中的参数及其说明如表 3-5 所示。

表 3-5

参　数	说　明
project_name	访问的 MaxCompute 项目的名称
access_id	阿里云账号或 RAM 用户的 AccessKey ID
access_key	AccessKey ID 对应的 AccessKey Secret
end_point	MaxCompute 服务的地址，需要根据创建 MaxCompute 项目时选择的区域及网络连接方式配置 end_point

续表

参　　数	说　　明
log_view_host	Logview 地址，用户可以通过该地址查看作业的详细运行信息并为报错处理提供依据。该参数为固定取值
https_check	是否开启 HTTPS 访问机制，对访问 MaxCompute 项目的请求进行加密。默认值为 False
data_size_confirm	输入数据量的最大值，单位为 GB。取值范围无限制，推荐设置为 100GB
update_url	预留参数，暂时无须关注
use_instance_tunnel	是否使用 InstanceTunnel 下载 SQL 执行结果，默认值为 False
instance_tunnel_max_record	客户端返回的 SQL 执行结果的最大记录数。如果 use_instance_tunnel 的值为 True，则需要配置该参数。最大值为 10000
tunnel_endpoint	Tunnel 服务的外部网络访问链接。如果未配置 Tunnel Endpoint，Tunnel 会自动路由到 MaxCompute 服务所在网络对应的 Tunnel Endpoint。如果配置了 Tunnel Endpoint，则以配置为准，不进行自动路由
set.<key>=<value>	设置 MaxCompute 项目的属性

（4）为了方便操作，在本地的宿主机上设置命令行客户端的环境变量，如图 3-17 所示。

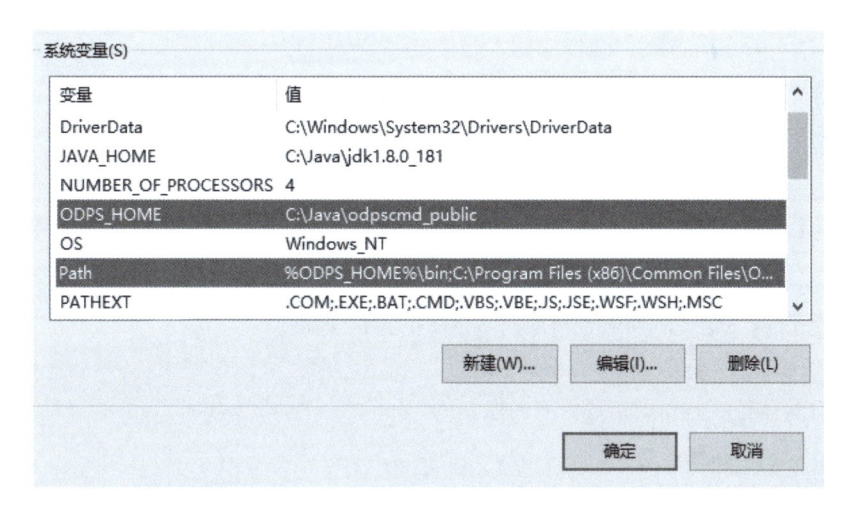

图 3-17

（5）打开一个新的 CMD 命令行窗口，输入下面的命令。

```
D:\>odpscmd
```

此时将成功连接 MaxCompute 项目空间，如图 3-18 所示。

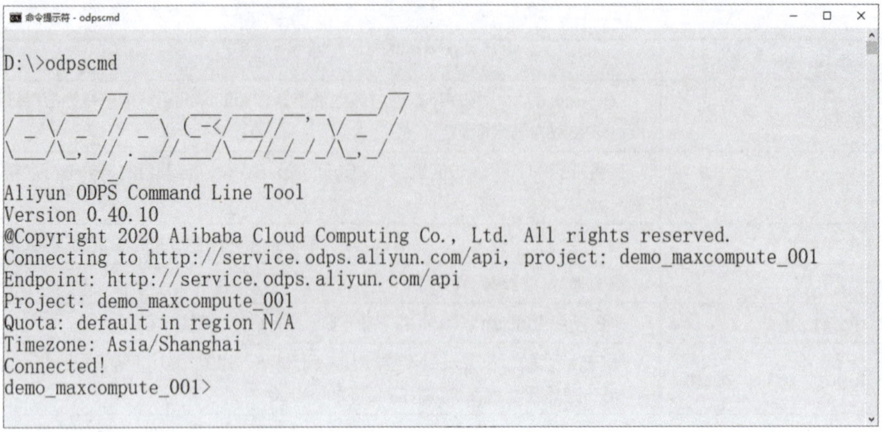

图 3-18

（6）执行下面的命令，在命令行客户端中获取当前登录用户的信息。

```
demo_maxcompute_001>whoami;
```

输出的信息如下。

```
demo_maxcompute_001>whoami;
Name: ALIYUN$*******
Source IP: 123.117.181.105
End_Point: http://service.odps.aliyun.com/api
Project: demo_maxcompute_001
demo_maxcompute_001>
```

输出信息中的每项说明如下。

- Name：当前登录的账号信息。
- Source IP：MaxCompute 客户端所在设备的 IP 地址。
- End_Point：MaxCompute 服务的地址。
- Project：MaxCompute 项目的名称。

（7）退出命令行客户端

```
demo_maxcompute_001>quit;
```

2. 实战 MaxCompute Studio

MaxCompute Studio 是阿里云 MaxCompute 平台提供的安装在开发者客户端的大数据集成开发环境工具，是一套基于流行的集成开发平台 IntelliJ IDEA 的开发插件，帮助应用开发人员便捷、快速地进行数据开发。

这里将介绍 MaxCompute Studio 的功能界面和常用的应用场景。

配置 MaxCompute Studio 的具体操作步骤如下。

（1）下载 IntelliJ IDEA。请根据操作系统（Windows、macOS、Linux）下载对应 IntelliJ IDEA 版本。这里以 Windows 操作系统为例，支持 IntelliJ IDEA 14.1.4 以上版本。

（2）下载完成后双击安装程序，安装 IntelliJ IDEA。

> 安装过程中使用默认选项即可。

（3）启动 IntelliJ IDEA 并在启动界面中选择"Plugins"选项，如图 3-19 所示。

图 3-19

> MaxCompute Studio 是 IntelliJ IDEA 的插件，可以通过在线方式或本地方式安装。

（4）在界面中间的列表上方的搜索框中输入"MaxCompute Studio"，使用在线方式安装 MaxCompute Studio，如图 3-20 所示。

图 3-20

（5）单击"Install"按钮进行安装，安装完成后重新启动 IntelliJ IDEA。

（6）在 IntelliJ IDEA 的欢迎界面上，单击"New Project"按钮，如图 3-21 所示。

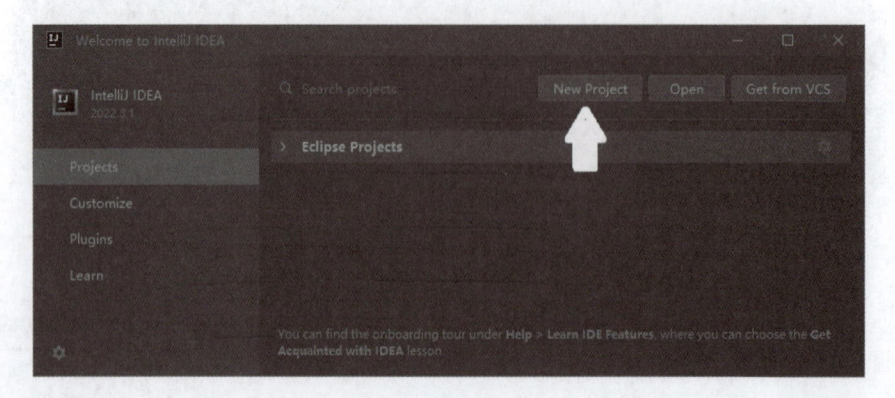

图 3-21

(7)选择左侧"Generator"区域中的"MaxCompute Studio"选项,单击"Next"按钮,如图 3-22 所示。

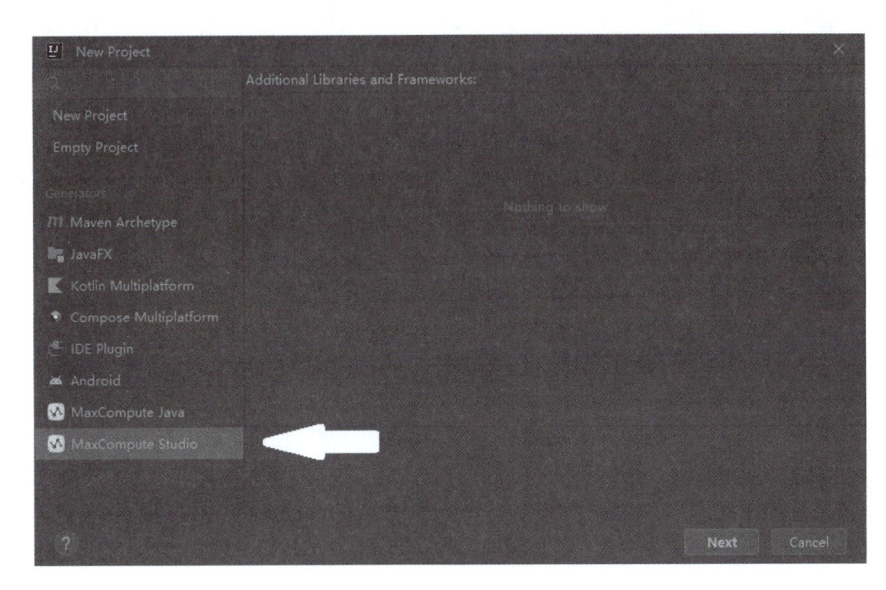

图 3-22

(8)在"New Project"对话框中输入项目名称,单击"Create"按钮,如图 3-23 所示。

图 3-23

(9)项目创建成功后,在顶部菜单栏中选择"View"→"Tool Windows"→"Project Explorer"命令,如图 3-24 所示。

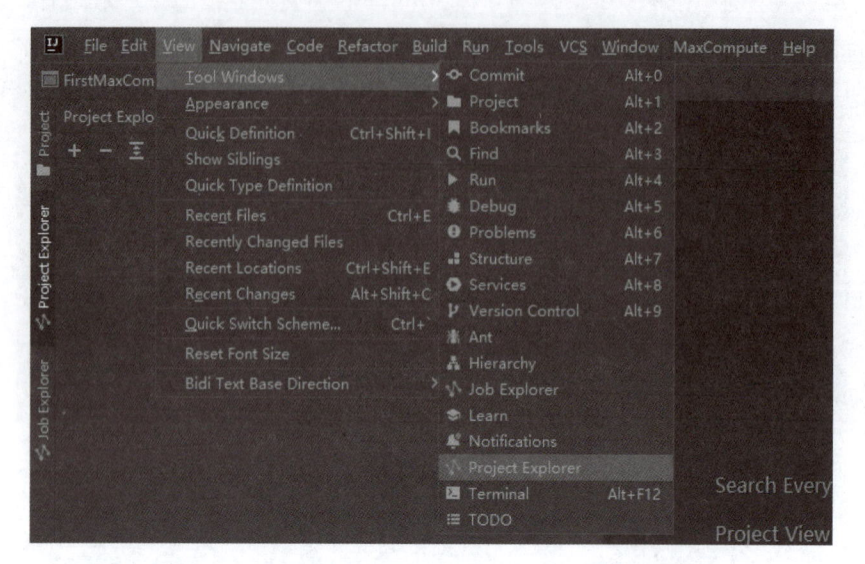

图 3-24

（10）单击左上角的"+"按钮，在弹出的下拉列表中选择"Add project from accessId/Key"选项，弹出"Add MaxCompute project"对话框，输入"Access Id"、"Access Key"和"Project Name"，单击"OK"按钮，如图 3-25 所示。

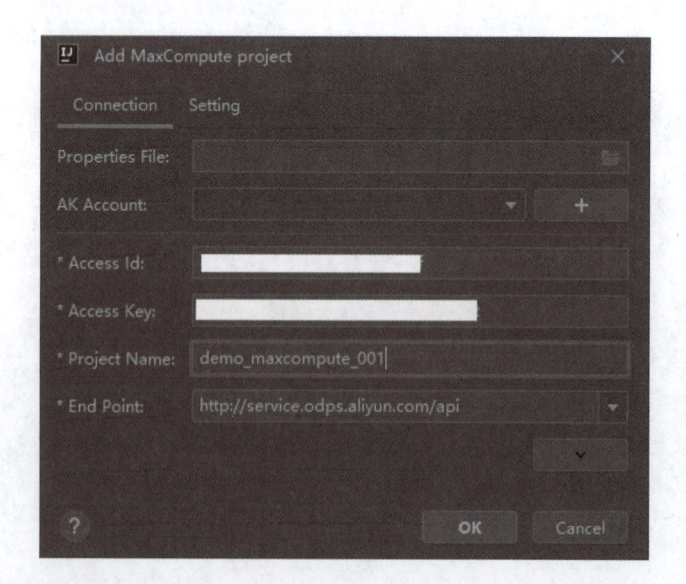

图 3-25

（11）配置完成后单击"OK"按钮，在左侧"Project Explorer"窗格中会显示 MaxCompute 项目的信息，包括该项目中的表、视图、函数及资源，如图 3-26 所示。

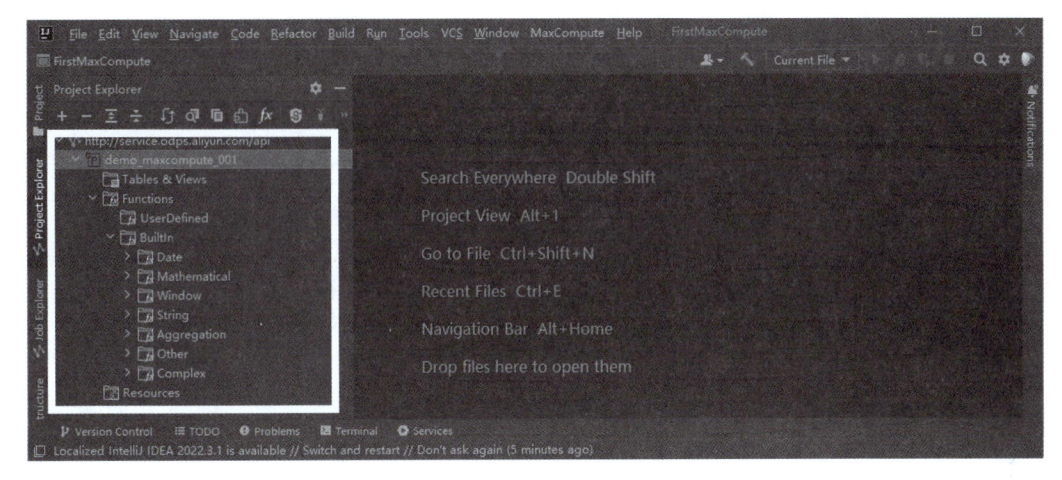

图 3-26

3.4 MaxCompute 快速上手

在配置了 MaxCompute 的客户端工具后，用户就可以非常方便地操作 MaxCompute 项目了。这里重点以命令行客户端为例进行演示和说明。

3.4.1 【实战】使用命令行客户端

MaxCompute 命令行客户端从 v0.28.0 版本开始支持 JDK 1.9 版本，v0.28.0 以下版本只支持 JDK 1.8 版本。

启动 MaxCompute 客户端后，用户可以在命令行界面查看客户端的版本号，也可以执行更多的 MaxCompute 操作。

下面通过具体的操作步骤来演示如何使用 MaxCompute 命令行客户端。

（1）启动 MaxCompute 命令行客户端。

```
D:\>odpscmd
```

（2）在 MaxCompute 客户端中查看命令帮助信息。

```
demo_maxcompute_001>help;
```

等价于如下命令。

```
demo_maxcompute_001>h;
```

输出的信息如下。

```
demo_maxcompute_001>help;
Usage: odpscmd [OPTION]...
where options include:
   --help                           (-h)for help
   --config=<config_file>               specify another config file
   --project=<prj_name>                 use project
   --endpoint=<http://host:port>        set endpoint
   -r <n>                               set retry times
   -f <"file_path;">                    execute command in file
   -e <"command;[command;]...">         execute command
...
```

（3）通过指定关键字查看相关命令的帮助信息，例如获取与表操作相关的命令的帮助信息。

```
demo_maxcompute_001>help tables;
```

输出的信息如下。

```
Usage:
  show tables [in <project name>] [like '<prefix>']
Examples:
  show tables;
  show tables like my_%;
  show tables in my_project;
  show tables in my_project.my_schema;
```

（4）创建员工表。

```
demo_maxcompute_001>create table emp
>(empno BIGINT,       -- 员工号
>ename STRING,        -- 员工姓名
>job STRING,          -- 员工职位
>mgr BIGINT,          -- 员工的老板
>hiredate STRING,     -- 入职日期
>sal BIGINT,          -- 月薪
>comm BIGINT,         -- 奖金
>deptno BIGINT);      -- 部门号
```

（5）创建部门表。

```
demo_maxcompute_001>create table dept
>(deptno BIGINT,      -- 部门号
>dname STRING,        -- 部门名称
>loc STRING);         -- 部门地址
```

（6）查看创建的表。

```
demo_maxcompute_001>list tables;
```

输出的信息如下。

```
ALIYUN$collenzhao:dept
ALIYUN$collenzhao:emp
OK
```

（7）查看员工表的表结构。

```
demo_maxcompute_001>desc emp;
```

员工表的表结构如图 3-27 所示。

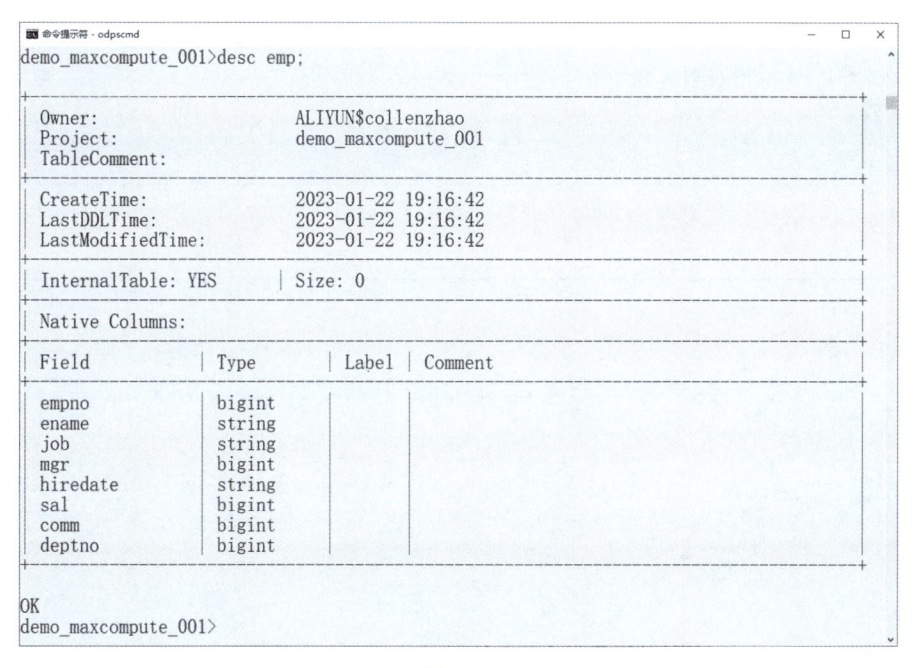

图 3-27

（8）准备员工表数据（emp.csv）和部门表数据（dept.csv），并将其存放在 D:\download 目录下。下面展示了 emp.csv 文件和 dept.csv 文件的内容。

- 员工表数据 emp.csv 文件的内容。

```
7369,SMITH,CLERK,7902,1980/12/17,800,0,20
7499,ALLEN,SALESMAN,7698,1981/2/20,1600,300,30
7521,WARD,SALESMAN,7698,1981/2/22,1250,500,30
7566,JONES,MANAGER,7839,1981/4/2,2975,0,20
7654,MARTIN,SALESMAN,7698,1981/9/28,1250,1400,30
7698,BLAKE,MANAGER,7839,1981/5/1,2850,0,30
7782,CLARK,MANAGER,7839,1981/6/9,2450,0,10
7788,SCOTT,ANALYST,7566,1987/4/19,3000,0,20
```

```
7839,KING,PRESIDENT,-1,1981/11/17,5000,0,10
7844,TURNER,SALESMAN,7698,1981/9/8,1500,0,30
7876,ADAMS,CLERK,7788,1987/5/23,1100,0,20
7900,JAMES,CLERK,7698,1981/12/3,950,0,30
7902,FORD,ANALYST,7566,1981/12/3,3000,0,20
7934,MILLER,CLERK,7782,1982/1/23,1300,0,10
```

- 部门表数据 dept.csv 文件的内容。

```
10,ACCOUNTING,NEW YORK
20,RESEARCH,DALLAS
30,SALES,CHICAGO
40,OPERATIONS,BOSTON
```

（9）将 emp.csv 文件导入员工表。

```
demo_maxcompute_001>tunnel upload D:\download\emp.csv emp;
```

> Tunnel 是 MaxCompute 提供的一个数据上传与下载的工具。Tunnel 的详细内容将在 3.5 节中介绍。

输出的信息如下。

```
Upload session: 20230122192623a7a9ca0b03347cd4
Start upload:D:\download\emp.csv
Using \r\n to split records
Upload in strict schema mode: true
Total bytes:629   Split input to 1 blocks
2023-01-22 19:26:24     scan block: '1'
2023-01-22 19:26:24     scan block complete, block id: 1
2023-01-22 19:26:24     upload block: '1'
2023-01-22 19:26:24     upload block complete, block id: 1
upload complete, average speed is 629 bytes/s
OK
```

（10）将 dept.csv 文件导入部门表。

```
demo_maxcompute_001>tunnel upload D:\download\dept.csv dept;
```

输出的信息如下。

```
Upload session: 20230122192816d2c5ca0b0334a228
Start upload:D:\download\dept.csv
Using \r\n to split records
Upload in strict schema mode: true
Total bytes:84   Split input to 1 blocks
2023-01-22 19:28:16     scan block: '1'
2023-01-22 19:28:16     scan block complete, block id: 1
```

```
2023-01-22 19:28:16     upload block: '1'
2023-01-22 19:28:16     upload block complete, block id: 1
upload complete, average speed is 84 bytes/s
OK
```

> 除了通过客户端导入数据，用户也可以使用 MaxCompute Studio、Tunnel SDK、数据集成、Sqoop、Fluentd、Flume、LogStash 等工具将数据导入 MaxCompute。

（11）执行一个简单的多表查询。

```
demo_maxcompute_001>select dept.dname "部门名称",emp.ename "姓名"
>from emp,dept
>where emp.deptno=dept.deptno;
```

输出的信息如下。

```
ID = 20230122113118249gb3lwhn2sjg
Log view:
http://logview.odps.aliyun.com/logview/?h=http://service.odps.aliyun.com
/api&p=demo_maxcompute_001&i=20230122113118249gb3lwhn2sjg&token=dzlmT0lodjR0
N3ZCTzlIbmFHUVpBZUM5a2ZRPSxPRFBTX09CTzoxMTI0ODcyNzc4NjgzMDQ2LDE2NzY5NzkwNzgs
eyJTdGF0ZW1lbnQiOiJt7IkFjdGlvbiI6WyJvZHBzOlJlYWQiXSwiRWZmZWN0IjoiQWxsb3ciLCJS
ZXNvdXJjZSI6WyJhY3M6b2RwczoqOnByb2plY3RzL2RlbW9fbWF4Y29tcHV0ZV8wMDEvaW5zdGFu
Y2VzLzIwMjMwMTIyMTEzMTE4MjQ5Z2IzbHdobjJzamciXX1dLCJWZXJzaW9uIjoiMSJ9
Job Queueing...
Summary:
resource cost: cpu 0.02 Core * Min, memory 0.02 GB * Min
inputs:
        demo_maxcompute_001.dept: 4 (714 bytes)
        demo_maxcompute_001.emp: 14 (1611 bytes)
outputs:
Job run time: 1.000
Job run mode: service job 2.0
Job run engine: execution engine
M1:
        bubble: 0
        instance count: 1
        run time: 1.000
        instance time:
                min: 1.000, max: 1.000, avg: 1.000
        ...
M2_1:
        bubble: 0
        instance count: 1
```

```
        run time: 0.000
        instance time:
                min: 0.000, max: 0.000, avg: 0.000
        ...
+--------------+----------+
| 部门名称     | 姓名     |
+--------------+----------+
| RESEARCH     | SMITH    |
| SALES        | ALLEN    |
| SALES        | WARD     |
| RESEARCH     | JONES    |
| SALES        | MARTIN   |
| SALES        | BLAKE    |
| ACCOUNTING   | CLARK    |
| RESEARCH     | SCOTT    |
| ACCOUNTING   | KING     |
| SALES        | TURNER   |
| RESEARCH     | ADAMS    |
| SALES        | JAMES    |
| RESEARCH     | FORD     |
| ACCOUNTING   | MILLER   |
+--------------+----------+
A total of 14 records fetched by instance tunnel. Max record number: 10000
```

（12）使用浏览器打开任务的日志查看器，如图 3-28 所示。

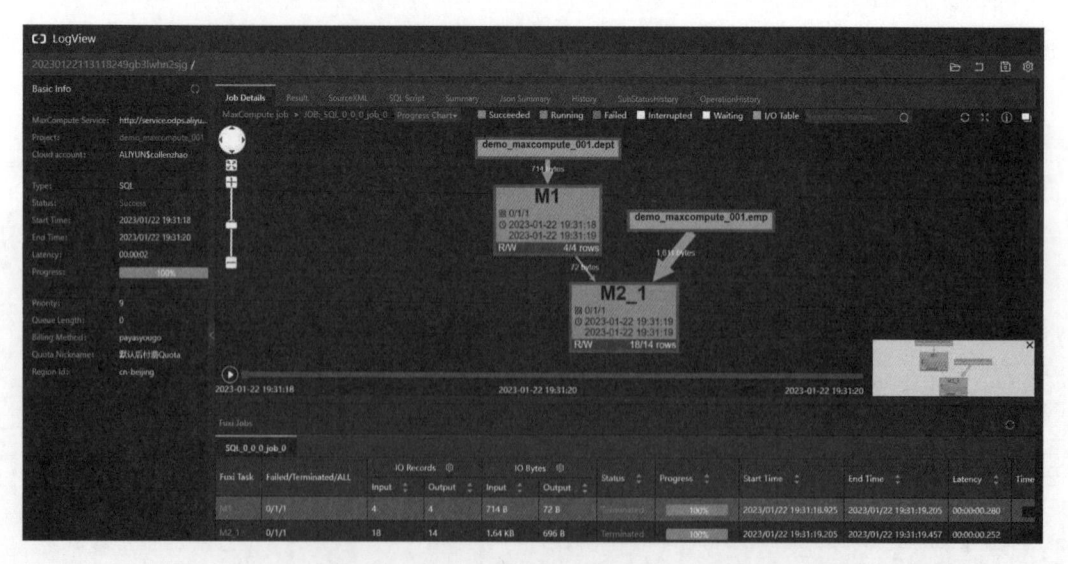

图 3-28

> 日志查看的 URL 地址可以在第（10）步中输出的"Log view"中找到。

3.4.2 【实战】执行 MapReduce 任务

在创建好的 MaxCompute 项目空间中，可以执行 MapReduce 任务来处理数据。这里将以 WordCount 单词计数程序为例来进行演示。

（1）在本地的 D:\download 目录下准备测试数据文件 data.txt，并输入下面的测试数据。

```
I love Beijing
I love China
Beijing is the capital of China
```

（2）在 MaxCompute 的项目空间中创建一张输入表，用于保存要处理的数据。

```
demo_maxcompute_001>create table testdata(data string);
```

（3）将 data.txt 文件导入输入表 testdata。

```
demo_maxcompute_001>tunnel upload d:\download\data.txt testdata;
```

（4）查询输入表 testdata 中的数据。

```
demo_maxcompute_001>select * from testdata;
```

输出的信息如下。

```
...
outputs:
+---------------------------------+
| data                            |
+---------------------------------+
| I love Beijing                  |
| I love China                    |
| Beijing is the capital of China |
+---------------------------------+
A total of 3 records fetched by instance tunnel. Max record number: 10000
```

（5）将开发好的 MapReduce 任务的 JAR 文件上传到 MaxCompute 项目空间中。

```
demo_maxcompute_001>add jar d:\download\mydemo_odps_wc.jar -f;
OK: Resource 'mydemo_odps_wc.jar' have been updated.
demo_maxcompute_001>
```

> mydemo_odps_wc.jar 是开发完成的 MapReduce 任务程序，读者可以在本章的资料中找到。关于 MapReduce 任务的开发将在第 5 章中介绍。

（6）创建结果输出表。

```
demo_maxcompute_001>create table wordcount(word string,total bigint);
```

（7）MapReduce 执行任务。

```
demo_maxcompute_001>jar    -resources    mydemo_odps_wc.jar    -classpath
d:\download\mydemo_odps_wc.jar demo.wc.WordCountMain testdata wordcount;
```

输出的信息如图 3-29 所示。

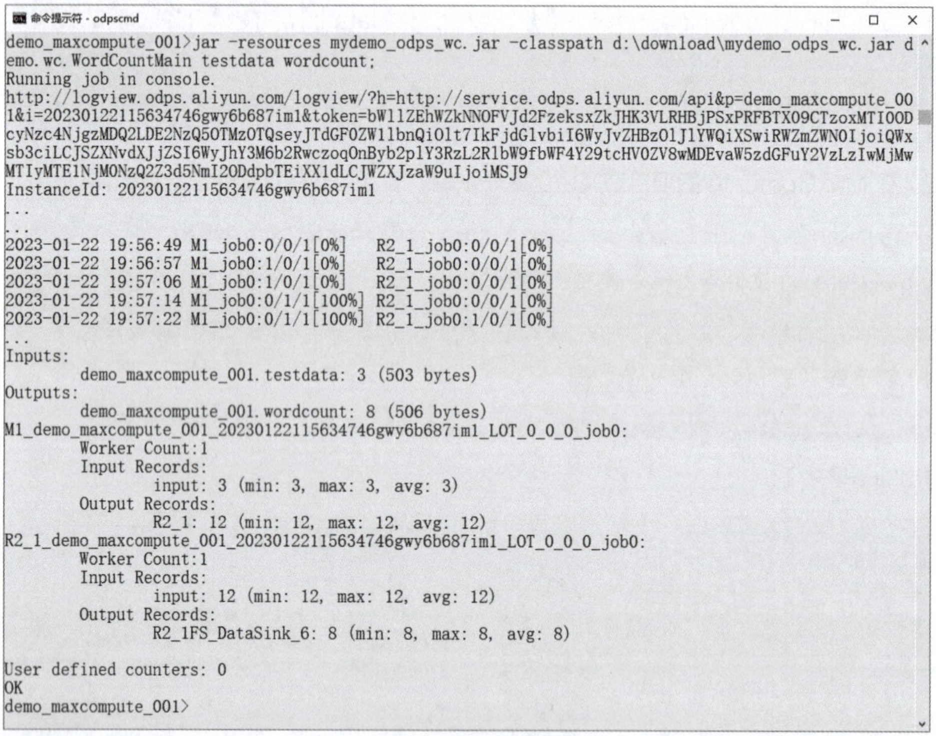

```
命令提示符 - odpscmd
demo_maxcompute_001>jar -resources mydemo_odps_wc.jar -classpath d:\download\mydemo_odps_wc.jar d
emo.wc.WordCountMain testdata wordcount;
Running job in console.
http://logview.odps.aliyun.com/logview/?h=http://service.odps.aliyun.com/api&p=demo_maxcompute_00
1&i=20230122115634746gwy6b687im1&token=bW1lZEhWZkNNOFVJd2FzeksxZkJHK3VLRHBjPSxPRFBTX09CTzoxMTI0OD
cyNzc4NjgzMDQ2LDE2NzQ5OTMzOTQseyJTdGF0ZW1lbnQiOlt7IkFjdGlvbiI6WyJvZHBzOlJlYWQiXSwiRWZmZWN0IjoiQWx
sb3ciLCJSZXNvdXJjZSI6WyJhY3M6b2RwczoqOnByb2plY3RzL2RlbW9fbWF4Y29tcHV0ZV8wMDEvaW5zdGFuY2VzLzIwMjMw
MTIyMTE1NjM0NzQ2Z3d5NmI2ODdpbTEiXX1dLCJWZXJzaW9uIjoiMSJ9
InstanceId: 20230122115634746gwy6b687im1
...
...
2023-01-22 19:56:49 M1_job0:0/0/1[0%]    R2_1_job0:0/0/1[0%]
2023-01-22 19:56:57 M1_job0:1/0/1[0%]    R2_1_job0:0/0/1[0%]
2023-01-22 19:57:06 M1_job0:1/0/1[0%]    R2_1_job0:0/0/1[0%]
2023-01-22 19:57:14 M1_job0:0/1/1[100%]  R2_1_job0:0/0/1[0%]
2023-01-22 19:57:22 M1_job0:0/1/1[100%]  R2_1_job0:1/0/1[0%]
...
Inputs:
        demo_maxcompute_001.testdata: 3 (503 bytes)
Outputs:
        demo_maxcompute_001.wordcount: 8 (506 bytes)
M1_demo_maxcompute_001_20230122115634746gwy6b687im1_LOT_0_0_0_job0:
        Worker Count:1
        Input Records:
                input: 3 (min: 3, max: 3, avg: 3)
        Output Records:
                R2_1: 12 (min: 12, max: 12, avg: 12)
R2_1_demo_maxcompute_001_20230122115634746gwy6b687im1_LOT_0_0_0_job0:
        Worker Count:1
        Input Records:
                input: 12 (min: 12, max: 12, avg: 12)
        Output Records:
                R2_1FS_DataSink_6: 8 (min: 8, max: 8, avg: 8)

User defined counters: 0
OK
demo_maxcompute_001>
```

图 3-29

（8）验证数据处理的结果。

```
demo_maxcompute_001>select * from wordcount;
```

输出的信息如下。

```
...
outputs:
+------------+----------+
| word       | total    |
+------------+----------+
```

```
| Beijing     | 2        |
| China       | 2        |
| I           | 2        |
| capital     | 1        |
| is          | 1        |
| love        | 2        |
| of          | 1        |
| the         | 1        |
+-------------+----------+
A total of 8 records fetched by instance tunnel. Max record number: 10000
```

> 从输出的结果可以看出，在 wordcount 表中得到了每个单词出现的频率，并且输出的结果按照字母顺序进行了排序。

3.4.3 【实战】执行 Spark 任务

MaxCompute Spark 是 MaxCompute 提供的兼容开源 Spark 的计算服务。它在统一的计算资源和数据集权限体系之上提供 Spark 计算框架，支持用户以熟悉的开发、使用方式提交和执行 Spark 作业，满足更丰富的数据处理分析需求。

> 关于 MaxCompute Spark 的详细内容将在第 6 章介绍。

下面通过具体的步骤演示来说明如何执行 MaxCompute Spark 任务。

（1）确保本地已安装 JDK 1.8 或以上版本。

（2）下载 MaxCompute Spark 客户端安装包，这里以 Spark-2.3.0 版本为例进行说明。

> MaxCompute Spark 客户端安装包可以在阿里云官网上，搜索 "spark-2.3.0-odps0.33.0.tar.gz" 找到。

（3）将 MaxCompute Spark 客户端包解压缩至 D:\download 目录下。

（4）第一次使用 MaxCompute Spark 客户端时，需要配置 spark-defaults.conf 文件。

```
# OdpsAccount Info Setting
spark.hadoop.odps.project.name = demo_maxcompute_001
spark.hadoop.odps.access.id = <你的 AccessID>
spark.hadoop.odps.access.key = <你的 AccessKey>
```

> SPARK_HOME/conf 路径下存在 spark-defaults.conf.template 文件，可以将其作为 spark-defaults.conf 的模板进行相关配置。

（5）完成以上工作后，执行任务测试，验证 MaxCompute Spark 是否可以端到端连通。以 Spark-2.x 版本为例，验证功能是否正常，提交命令如下。

```
D:\download>cd spark-2.3.0-odps0.33.0
D:\download\spark-2.3.0-odps0.33.0>bin\spark-submit ^
--master yarn-cluster ^
--class com.aliyun.odps.spark.examples.SparkPi ^
 examples\spark-examples_2.11-3.3.12-shaded.jar
```

如果看到以下日志，则表明任务执行成功。

```
23/01/24 21:17:21 INFO Client:
 client token: N/A
 diagnostics: N/A
 ApplicationMaster host: master34b597d0-7523-44-51
 ApplicationMaster RPC port: 8088
 queue: queue
 start time: 1674566153170
 final status: SUCCEEDED
```

3.5 基于 Tunnel 的数据上传与下载

MaxCompute 提供了 3 种数据上传与下载的通道。

（1）DataHub：实时数据通道，包含的工具有 OGG 插件、Flume 插件、LogStash 插件和 Fluentd 插件。

（2）Tunnel：批量数据通道，包含的工具有 MaxCompute 客户端、DataWorks、DTS、Sqoop、Kettle 插件和 MMA 迁移工具。

（3）Streaming Tunnel：流式数据写入通道，支持实时计算 Flink、数据通道 DataHub、数据传输服务 DTS、实时数据同步、Kafka 消息系统。

下面重点介绍如何使用 Tunnel 完成 MaxCompute 项目空间中数据的上传与下载。

3.5.1 Tunnel 简介

Tunnel 是 MaxCompute 的数据通道，用户可以通过 Tunnel 上传或下载数据。

3.5.2 【实战】使用 Tunnel 的命令行工具

下面通过具体的步骤来演示如何使用 Tunnel 的命令行工具完成数据的上传与下载。

（1）查看 Tunnel 的帮助信息。

```
demo_maxcompute_001>tunnel help;
```

输出的信息如下。

```
Usage: tunnel <subcommand> [options] [args]
Type 'tunnel help <subcommand>' for help on a specific subcommand.

Available subcommands:
    upload (u)
    download (d)
    resume (r)
    show (s)
    purge (p)
    help (h)
tunnel is a command for uploading data to / downloading data from ODPS.
```

（2）创建分区表 emp_part。

```
demo_maxcompute_001>create table emp_part
>(empno BIGINT,
>ename STRING,
>job STRING,
>mgr BIGINT,
>hiredate STRING,
>sal BIGINT,
>comm BIGINT)
>partitioned by(deptno BIGINT);
```

（3）为分区表 emp_part 添加分区。

```
demo_maxcompute_001>alter table emp_part add partition(deptno=10);
demo_maxcompute_001>alter table emp_part add partition(deptno=20);
demo_maxcompute_001>alter table emp_part add partition(deptno=30);
```

（4）准备需要上传的数据文件 emp10.csv、emp20.csv 和 emp30.csv，内容如下所示，并将其保存到 D:\download 目录下。

```
#emp10.csv
7782,CLARK,MANAGER,7839,1981/6/9,2450,0
7839,KING,PRESIDENT,-1,1981/11/17,5000,0
7934,MILLER,CLERK,7782,1982/1/23,1300,0
```

```
#emp20.csv
7369,SMITH,CLERK,7902,1980/12/17,800,0
7566,JONES,MANAGER,7839,1981/4/2,2975,0
7788,SCOTT,ANALYST,7566,1987/4/19,3000,0
7876,ADAMS,CLERK,7788,1987/5/23,1100,0
7902,FORD,ANALYST,7566,1981/12/3,3000,0

#emp30.csv
7499,ALLEN,SALESMAN,7698,1981/2/20,1600,300
7521,WARD,SALESMAN,7698,1981/2/22,1250,500
7654,MARTIN,SALESMAN,7698,1981/9/28,1250,1400
7698,BLAKE,MANAGER,7839,1981/5/1,2850,0
7844,TURNER,SALESMAN,7698,1981/9/8,1500,0
7900,JAMES,CLERK,7698,1981/12/3,950,0
```

（5）为了模拟执行出错，这里可以任意删除一个员工的某个属性。例如，删除 emp10.csv 文件中的某一列。

（6）使用 upload 命令将数据文件 emp10.csv 上传至分区表 emp_part。

```
demo_maxcompute_001>tunnel upload d:\download\emp10.csv emp_part/deptno=10;
```

（7）由于 emp10.csv 文件中有脏数据，因此数据导入失败。此时 Tunnel 会给出 Session ID 及错误提示信息，如下所示。

```
...
Caused by: org.apache.commons.cli.ParseException: ERROR: column mismatch,
expected 7 columns, 6 columns found, please check data or delimiter
 content: 7782,CLARK,MANAGER,1981/6/9,2450,0
...
```

（8）使用 show 命令查询上传失败的 Session ID。

```
demo_maxcompute_001>tunnel show history;
```

输出的信息如下。

```
202301222111521ebdca0b03383a34  failed  'upload d:\download\emp10.csv emp_part/deptno=10'
2023012219462811bdca0b03355d4e  success 'upload d:\download\data.txt testdata'
20230122192816d2c5ca0b0334a228  success 'upload D:\download\dept.csv dept'
20230122192623a7a9ca0b03347cd4  success 'upload D:\download\emp.csv emp'
```

> 这里的执行失败的 Session ID 是 202301222111521ebdca0b03383a34

（9）修改示例数据文件 emp10.csv，使其符合 emp_part 的表结构。

（10）使用 resume 命令修复执行上传数据。

```
demo_maxcompute_001>tunnel resume 202301222111521ebdca0b03383a34;
```

其中，202301222111521ebdca0b03383a34 为上传失败的 Session ID。

输出的信息如下。

```
start resume 202301222111521ebdca0b03383a34
Upload session: 202301222111521ebdca0b03383a34
Start upload:d:\download\emp10.csv
Using \r\n to split records
Upload in strict schema mode: true
Resume 1 blocks
2023-01-22 21:16:31    scan block: '1'
2023-01-22 21:16:31    scan block complete, block id: 1
2023-01-22 21:16:31    upload block: '1'
2023-01-22 21:16:31    upload block complete, block id: 1
upload complete, average speed is 0 bytes/s
OK
```

（11）验证数据上传是否成功。

```
demo_maxcompute_001>select * from emp_part where deptno=10;
```

执行结果如图 3-30 所示。

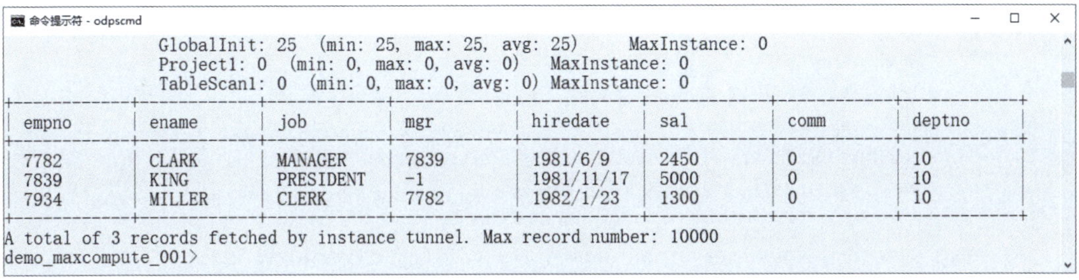

图 3-30

（12）使用同样的方式上传 emp20.csv 和 emp30.csv 文件的数据。

```
demo_maxcompute_001>tunnel upload d:\download\emp20.csv
                    emp_part/deptno=20;
demo_maxcompute_001>tunnel upload d:\download\emp30.csv
                    emp_part/deptno=30;
```

（13）执行一个简单的 SQL 查询，通过集合运算得到 emp20.csv 和 emp30.csv 文件中的员工数据。

```
demo_maxcompute_001>select * from emp_part where deptno=10
>union
>select * from emp_part where deptno=20;
```

执行结果如图 3-31 所示。

图 3-31

（14）使用 explain 命令查看 SQL 的执行计划。

```
demo_maxcompute_001>explain select * from emp_part where deptno=10
>union select * from emp_part where deptno=20;
```

输出的执行计划如下。

```
...
In Task M1_U0:
    TS: demo_maxcompute_001.emp_part/deptno=10
        Statistics: Num rows: 3.0, Data size: 996.0
        SEL: empno, ename, job, mgr, hiredate, sal, comm, 10L deptno
            Statistics: Num rows: 3.0, Data size: 1020.0
        LocalSortBy: order: ++++++++
                nullDirection: ********
                keys:empno, ename, job, mgr, hiredate, sal, comm, deptno
            Statistics: Num rows: 3.0, Data size: 1020.0
            UNION
                Sort
                keys:
                        empno
                        ename
                        job
                        mgr
```

```
                             hiredate
                             sal
                             comm
                             deptno

            Statistics: Num rows: 8.0, Data size: 2720.0
            AGGREGATE:    group   by:empno,ename,job,mgr,hiredate,sal,
comm,deptno
            Statistics: Num rows: 2.0, Data size: 680.0
        FS: output: Screen
            schema:
              empno (bigint)
              ename (string)
              job (string)
              mgr (bigint)
              hiredate (string)
              sal (bigint)
              comm (bigint)
              deptno (bigint)

            Statistics: Num rows: 2.0, Data size: 680.0
...
```

（15）使用 download 命令下载查询结果数据。

```
demo_maxcompute_001>tunnel download
>instance://20230122132743420gcirt84nqcg d:\download\result.txt;
```

其中，20230122132743420gcirt84nqcg 为执行的 SQL 语句对应的实例 ID。

（16）查看下载的查询结果数据，其中的内容如下。

```
7369,SMITH,CLERK,7902,1980/12/17,800,0,20
7566,JONES,MANAGER,7839,1981/4/2,2975,0,20
7782,CLARK,MANAGER,7839,1981/6/9,2450,0,10
7788,SCOTT,ANALYST,7566,1987/4/19,3000,0,20
7839,KING,PRESIDENT,-1,1981/11/17,5000,0,10
7876,ADAMS,CLERK,7788,1987/5/23,1100,0,20
7902,FORD,ANALYST,7566,1981/12/3,3000,0,20
7934,MILLER,CLERK,7782,1982/1/23,1300,0,10
```

3.5.3 【实战】使用 Tunnel 的 SDK

MaxCompute 提供的数据上传与下载工具是基于 Tunnel SDK 编写的。Tunnel SDK 的主要接口如表 3-6 所示。

表 3-6

接口名称	说明
TableTunnel	访问 MaxCompute Tunnel 表服务的入口类。可以通过公网或阿里云内网环境对 MaxCompute 及其 Tunnel 进行访问。当在阿里云内网环境中使用 Tunnel 内网连接下载数据时，MaxCompute 不会将该操作产生的流量计费
TableTunnel.UploadSession	表示一个向 MaxCompute 表中上传数据的会话
TableTunnel.DownloadSession	表示一个从 MaxCompute 表中下载数据的会话
InstanceTunnel	访问 MaxCompute Tunnel 实例服务的入口类。可以通过公网或阿里云内网环境对 MaxCompute 及其 Tunnel 进行访问。当在阿里云内网环境中使用 Tunnel 内网连接下载数据时，MaxCompute 不会将该操作产生的流量计费
InstanceTunnel.DownloadSession	表示一个从 MaxCompute Instance 中下载数据的会话，但只能下载以 SELECT 关键字开头的用于获取数据的 SQL Instance

为了简化 Tunnel SDK 应用程序的开发，可以使用 Maven 搭建 Tunnel 的开发环境。在 pom.xml 文件中需要加入以下依赖。

```xml
<dependency>
    <groupId>com.aliyun.odps</groupId>
    <artifactId>odps-sdk-core</artifactId>
    <version>0.24.0-public</version>
</dependency>
```

下面通过具体的步骤来演示如何开发使用 Tunnel 完成 MaxCompute 项目空间数据的上传与下载的 Java 程序。

> 这里将以 3.4.1 节中创建的部门表 dept 为例来完成数据的上传与下载。

（1）使用 Tunnel SDK 开发 Java 应用程序以完成数据的上传。

```java
import com.aliyun.odps.Odps;
import com.aliyun.odps.account.Account;
import com.aliyun.odps.account.AliyunAccount;
import com.aliyun.odps.data.Record;
import com.aliyun.odps.data.RecordWriter;
import com.aliyun.odps.tunnel.TableTunnel;
import com.aliyun.odps.tunnel.TableTunnel.UploadSession;

public class UploadSample {
    //指定访问的地址信息和相应的 Key
    private static String accessId = "你的 AccessID";
    private static String accessKey = "你的 AccessKey";
```

```java
private static String odpsUrl =
                "http://service.odps.aliyun.com/api";
private static String tunnelUrl =
                "http://dt.cn-beijing.maxcompute.aliyun.com";

//指定项目和表
private static String project = "demo_maxcompute_001";
private static String table = "dept";

public static void main(String args[]) {
    Account account = new AliyunAccount(accessId, accessKey);
    Odps odps = new Odps(account);
    odps.setEndpoint(odpsUrl);
    odps.setDefaultProject(project);
    try {
        TableTunnel tunnel = new TableTunnel(odps);
        //设置tunnelUrl
        tunnel.setEndpoint(tunnelUrl);

        UploadSession uploadSession =
                    tunnel.createUploadSession(project, table);
        //获取Session的状态
        System.out.println("Session Status is : " +
                    uploadSession.getStatus().toString());

        //创建输出流
        RecordWriter recordWriter =
                    uploadSession.openBufferedWriter();

        //创建上传的数据记录
        Record record = uploadSession.newRecord();
        record.setBigint(0, 10L);
        record.setString(1, "My Dept");
        record.setString(2, "Beijing China");

        //上传数据并提交
        recordWriter.write(record);
        recordWriter.close();
        uploadSession.commit();

        System.out.println("upload success!");
    } catch (Exception e) {
        e.printStackTrace();
    }
}
```

        }
}

输出的信息如下。

```
Session Status is : NORMAL
upload success!
```

（2）使用命令行客户端验证插入的数据。

```
demo_maxcompute_001>select * from dept;
```

输出的信息如下。

```
...
outputs:
+------------+----------+---------------+
| deptno     | dname    | loc           |
+------------+----------+---------------+
| 10         | My Dept  | Beijing China |
| 10         | ACCOUNTING| NEW YORK     |
| 20         | RESEARCH | DALLAS        |
| 30         | SALES    | CHICAGO       |
| 40         | OPERATIONS| BOSTON       |
+------------+----------+---------------+
A total of 5 records fetched by instance tunnel. Max record number: 10000
```

（3）使用 Tunnel SDK 开发 Java 应用程序以完成数据的下载。

```
import com.aliyun.odps.Odps;
import com.aliyun.odps.account.Account;
import com.aliyun.odps.account.AliyunAccount;
import com.aliyun.odps.data.Record;
import com.aliyun.odps.data.RecordReader;
import com.aliyun.odps.tunnel.TableTunnel;
import com.aliyun.odps.tunnel.TableTunnel.DownloadSession;

public class DownloadSample {
    //指定访问的地址信息和相应的 Key
    private static String accessId = "你的 AccessID";
    private static String accessKey = "你的 AccessKey";
    private static String odpsUrl =
                "http://service.odps.aliyun.com/api";
    private static String tunnelUrl =
                "http://dt.cn-beijing.maxcompute.aliyun.com";

    //指定项目和表
    private static String project = "demo_maxcompute_001";
```

```java
    private static String table = "dept";

public static void main(String args[]) throws Exception {
    Account account = new AliyunAccount(accessId, accessKey);
    Odps odps = new Odps(account);
    odps.setEndpoint(odpsUrl);
    odps.setDefaultProject(project);
    TableTunnel tunnel = new TableTunnel(odps);
    //设置 tunnelUrl
    tunnel.setEndpoint(tunnelUrl);

    //创建 DownloadSession
    DownloadSession downloadSession =
            tunnel.createDownloadSession(project, table);
    System.out.println("Session Status is : " +
            downloadSession.getStatus().toString());

    //获取表中的记录数
    long count = downloadSession.getRecordCount();
    System.out.println("RecordCount is: " + count);

    //创建下载的输出流
    RecordReader recordReader = downloadSession.
                        openRecordReader(0, count);

    //下载的数据
    Record record;
    while ((record = recordReader.read()) != null) {
        long deptno = record.getBigint(0);
        String dname = record.getString(1);
        String loc = record.getString(2);
        System.out.println(deptno+"\t"+dname+"\t"+loc);
    }
    recordReader.close();
}
}
```

输出的信息如下。

```
Session Status is : NORMAL
RecordCount is: 5
10      My Dept         Beijing China
10      ACCOUNTING      NEW YORK
20      RESEARCH        DALLAS
30      SALES           CHICAGO
40      OPERATIONS      BOSTON
```

第 4 章
处理结构化数据——基于 MaxCompute SQL

MaxCompute SQL 采用的是类似 SQL 的语法。它的语法是标准语法 ANSI SQL92 的一个子集，并有自己的扩展。

本章将介绍 MaxCompute SQL 的使用场景、使用向导、支持的工具，帮助读者快速了解 MaxCompute SQL，为后续使用 MaxCompute SQL 提供帮助。

4.1 MaxCompute SQL 简介

MaxCompute SQL 适用于海量数据（GB、TB、EB 级别）离线批量计算的场景。在提交 MaxCompute 作业后，会存在几十秒到数分钟不等的排队调度，所以适合处理批作业（提交一次作业批量处理海量数据），不适合直接对接需要每秒处理几千至数万笔事务的前台业务系统。

4.1.1 MaxCompute SQL 与其他 SQL 的差异

由于不同的数据分析引擎的标准语法 ANSI SQL92 实现的方式略有差异，并且 MaxCompute SQL 是 ANSI SQL92 的一个子集。因此，这里将 MaxCompute SQL 的语法与其他数据分析引擎所支持的 SQL 语法做一个对比，主要包括 DDL、DML 和 SCRIPTING 的语法差异。

MaxCompute DDL 语法与其他数据分析引擎所支持的 DDL 语法的对比如表 4-1 所示。

表 4-1

语　法	数据分析引擎				
	MaxCompute	Hive	MySQL	Oracle	SQL Server
CREATE TABLE—PRIMARY KEY	N	N	Y	Y	Y
CREATE TABLE—NOT NULL	Y	N	Y	Y	Y
CREATE TABLE—CLUSTER BY	Y	Y	N	Y	Y
CREATE TABLE—EXTERNAL TABLE	Y	Y	N	Y	N
CREATE TABLE—TEMPORARY TABLE	N	Y	Y	Y	Y
INDEX—CREATE INDEX	N	Y	Y	Y	Y
VIRTUAL COLUMN	N	N	N	Y	Y

MaxCompute DML 语法与其他数据分析引擎所支持的 DML 语法的对比如表 4-2 所示。

表 4-2

语　法	数据分析引擎				
	MaxCompute	Hive	MySQL	Oracle	SQL Server
CTE	Y	Y	Y	Y	Y
SELECT—recursive CTE	N	N	N	Y	Y
SELECT—GROUP BY ROLL UP	Y	Y	Y	Y	Y
SELECT—GROUP BY CUBE	Y	Y	N	Y	Y
SELECT—GROUPING SET	Y	Y	N	Y	Y
SELECT—IMPLICT JOIN	Y	Y	N	Y	Y
SELECT—PIVOT	N	N	N	Y	Y
SEMI JOIN	Y	Y	Y	N	N
SELECT TRANSFORM	Y	Y	N	N	N
SELECT—corelated subquery	Y	Y	Y	Y	Y
ORDER BY NULLS FIRST/LAST	N	Y	Y	Y	Y
LATERAL VIEW	Y	Y	N	Y	Y
SET OPERATOR—UNION (disintct)	Y	Y	Y	Y	Y
SET OPERATOR—INTERSECT	Y	N	N	Y	Y
SET OPERATOR—MINUS/EXCEPT	Y	N	N	Y	Y
INSERT INTO ... VALUES	Y	Y	Y	Y	Y
INSERT INTO (ColumnList)	Y	Y	Y	Y	Y
UPDATE … WHERE	Y	Y	Y	Y	Y
DELETE … WHERE	Y	Y	Y	Y	Y

续表

语　　法	数据分析引擎				
	MaxCompute	Hive	MySQL	Oracle	SQL Server
MERGE INTO	Y	Y	N	Y	Y
ANALYTIC—reusable WINDOWING CLAUSE	Y	Y	N	N	N
ANALYTIC—CURRENT ROW	Y	Y	N	Y	Y
ANALYTIC—UNBOUNDED	Y	N	Y	Y	Y
ANALYTIC—RANGE …	N	Y	N	Y	Y
WHILE DO	N	N	Y	Y	Y
VIEW WITH PARAMETERS	Y	N	N	N	N

MaxCompute SCRIPTING 语法与其他数据分析引擎所支持的 SCRIPTING 语法的对比如表 4-3 所示。

表 4-3

语　　法	数据分析引擎				
	MaxCompute	Hive	MySQL	Oracle	SQL Server
TABLE VARIABLE	Y	Y	Y	Y	Y
SCALER VARIABLE	Y	Y	Y	Y	Y
ERROR HANDLING—RAISE ERROR	N	N	Y	Y	Y
ERROR HANDLING—TRY CATCH	N	N	N	Y	Y
FLOW CONTROL—LOOP	N	N	Y	Y	Y
CURSOR	N	N	Y	Y	Y

4.1.2　MaxCompute SQL 的数据类型

MaxCompute 2.0 版本推出了兼容开源主流产品的 2.0 数据类型和 Hive 兼容数据类型两个数据类型版本，再加上原有的 1.0 数据类型版本，目前 MaxCompute 一共支持 3 个数据类型版本。MaxCompute 设置数据类型版本的属性共有 3 个，如表 4-4 所示。

表 4-4

属　　性	说　　明
odps.sql.type.system.odps2	2.0 数据类型版本的开关，属性值为 True 或 False
odps.sql.decimal.odps2	2.0 数据类型版本的 Decimal 数据类型的开关，属性值为 True 或 False
odps.sql.hive.compatible	Hive 兼容（即部分数据类型和 SQL 行为兼容 Hive）数据类型版本的开关，属性值为 True 或 False

如果需要设置项目空间所支持的数据类型，则可以在 MaxCompute 的命令行工具中使用 setproject 命令。下面是该命令的帮助信息。

```
demo_maxcompute_001>help setproject;
Usage: setproject <key>=<value> [<key>=<value>]
```

例如，如果需要使用 1.0 数据类型版本，可以执行下面的命令。

```
--关闭 MaxCompute 2.0 数据类型
demo_maxcompute_001>setproject odps.sql.type.system.odps2=false;
--关闭 Decimal 2.0 数据类型
demo_maxcompute_001>setproject odps.sql.decimal.odps2=false;
--关闭 Hive 兼容模式
demo_maxcompute_001>setproject odps.sql.hive.compatible=false;
```

如果需要使用 2.0 数据类型版本，可以执行下面的命令。

```
--打开 MaxCompute 2.0 数据类型
demo_maxcompute_001>setproject odps.sql.type.system.odps2=true;
--打开 Decimal 2.0 数据类型
demo_maxcompute_001>setproject odps.sql.decimal.odps2=true;
--关闭 Hive 兼容模式
demo_maxcompute_001>setproject odps.sql.hive.compatible=false;
```

下面的命令将使用 Hive 兼容数据类型版本。

```
--打开 MaxCompute 2.0 数据类型版本
demo_maxcompute_001>setproject odps.sql.type.system.odps2=true;
--打开 Decimal 2.0 数据类型版本
demo_maxcompute_001>setproject odps.sql.decimal.odps2=true;
--打开 Hive 兼容数据类型版本
demo_maxcompute_001>setproject odps.sql.hive.compatible=true;
```

> MaxCompute 支持的具体数据类型请参考 3.2.3 节的介绍。

4.1.3 MaxCompute SQL 的数据类型转换

MaxCompute SQL 允许数据类型之间的转换，转换方式包括显式类型转换和隐式类型转换。

1. 显式类型转换

显式类型转换是指通过 CAST 函数将一种数据类型的值转换为另一种数据类型的值，在 MaxCompute SQL 中支持的显式类型转换如表 4-5 所示。

表 4-5

From	To					
	BIGINT	DOUBLE	STRING	DATETIME	BOOLEAN	DECIMAL	FLOAT
BIGINT	/	Y	Y	N	Y	Y	Y
DOUBLE	Y	/	Y	N	Y	Y	Y
STRING	Y	Y	/	Y	Y	Y	Y
DATETIME	N	N	Y	/	N	N	N
BOOLEAN	Y	Y	Y	N	/	Y	Y
DECIMAL	Y	Y	Y	N	Y	/	Y
FLOAT	Y	Y	Y	N	Y	Y	/

其中，Y 表示可以转换，N 表示不可以转换，/表示不需要转换。不支持的显式类型转换会失败并报错退出。

下面是几个使用显示类型转换的示例及其运行的结果。

示例 1。

```
demo_maxcompute_001>
>select cast('2015-10-01 00:00:00' as datetime) as new_date;
```

该示例将一个字符串类型的数据显示转换为一个日期类型的数据，输出的结果如下。

```
+---------------------+
| new_date            |
+---------------------+
| 2015-10-01 00:00:00 |
+---------------------+
```

示例 2。

```
demo_maxcompute_001>select cast(array(1,2,3) as array<string>);
```

该示例将一个整数类型的数组转换为一个字符串类型的数组，输出的结果如下。

```
+---------------+
| _c0           |
+---------------+
| ["1","2","3"] |
+---------------+
```

示例 3。

```
demo_maxcompute_001>
>select concat_ws(',', cast(array(1, 2) as array<string>));
```

该示例将一个整数类型数组中的元素拼接成字符串并生成了一个字符串类型的数组，输出的结果如下。

```
+-----------+
| _c0       |
+-----------+
| 1,2       |
+-----------+
```

2. 隐式类型转换

隐式类型转换是指在运行时，由 MaxCompute 依据上下文使用环境及类型转换规则自动进行的类型转换。布尔类型和数值类型的隐式转换规则如表 4-6 所示。

表 4-6

From	To					
	BOOLEAN	TINYINT	SMALLINT	INT	BIGINT	FLOAT
BOOLEAN	Y	N	N	N	N	N
TINYINT	N	Y	Y	Y	Y	Y
SMALLINT	N	N	Y	Y	Y	Y
INT	N	N	Y	Y	Y	Y
BIGINT	N	N	N	N	Y	Y
FLOAT	N	N	N	N	Y	Y

双精度类型、字符串类型和日期类型的隐式转换规则如表 4-7 所示。

表 4-7

From	To					
	DOUBLE	DECIMAL	STRING	VARCHAR	TIMESTAMP	BINARY
DOUBLE	Y	Y	Y	Y	N	N
DECIMAL	N	Y	Y	Y	N	N
STRING	Y	Y	Y	Y	N	N
VARCHAR	Y	Y	N	N	/	/
TIMESTAMP	N	N	Y	Y	Y	N
BINARY	N	N	N	N	N	Y

其中，Y 表示可以转换，N 表示不可以转换，/表示不需要转换。不支持的隐式类型转换会导致异常。如果在执行时转换失败，也会导致异常。

下面是几个使用隐式类型转换的示例及其运行的结果。

下面使用的 emp 表为 3.4.1 节中创建的员工表。

示例 1。

```
demo_maxcompute_001>
>select empno+sal+'12345', concat(ename,empno,sal) from emp;
```

此处，empno+sal+'12345'完成数字的加法运算，自动将字符串'12345'转换为数字；concat(ename,empno,sal)将完成字符串拼接，自动将 empno 和 sal 转换为字符串。输出的结果如下。

```
+------------+---------------+
| _c0        | _c1           |
+------------+---------------+
| 20514.0    | SMITH7369800  |
| 21444.0    | ALLEN74991600 |
| 21116.0    | WARD75211250  |
| 22886.0    | JONES75662975 |
| 21249.0    | MARTIN76541250|
| 22893.0    | BLAKE76982850 |
| 22577.0    | CLARK77822450 |
| 23133.0    | SCOTT77883000 |
| 25184.0    | KING78395000  |
| 21689.0    | TURNER78441500|
| 21321.0    | ADAMS78761100 |
| 21195.0    | JAMES7900950  |
| 23247.0    | FORD79023000  |
| 21579.0    | MILLER79341300|
+------------+---------------+
```

示例 2。

```
demo_maxcompute_001>
>select empno,ename,job,sal from emp where deptno='10';
```

这里将查询 10 号部门的员工信息，where 条件中自动将'10'转换为数字 10。该语句等价于下面的语句。

```
demo_maxcompute_001>
>select empno,ename,job,sal from emp where deptno=10;
```

输出的结果如下。

```
+-----------+-----------+-----------+-----------+
| empno     | ename     | job       | sal       |
```

```
+----------+----------+-----------+----------+
| 7782     | CLARK    | MANAGER   | 2450     |
| 7839     | KING     | PRESIDENT | 5000     |
| 7934     | MILLER   | CLERK     | 1300     |
+----------+----------+-----------+----------+
```

MaxCompute SQL 也支持 STRING 类型和 DATETIME 类型之间的转换。转换时使用的格式为 yyyy-mm-dd hh:mi:ss。转换格式的含义如表 4-8 所示。

表 4-8

单位	年	月	日	时	分	秒
字符串（忽略大小写）	yyyy	mm	dd	hh	mi	ss
有效值域	0001~9999	01~12	01~28/29/30/31	00~23	00~59	00~59

> 如果要将不满足日期格式的 STRING 类型数据转换为 DATETIME 类型，MaxCompute 提供了 TO_DATE 函数，通过显示类型转换的方式进行转换。

4.2 使用 MaxCompute SQL

SQL（Structure Query Language，结构化查询语言）分为 3 种类型，即 DDL（Data Definition Language，数据定义语言）、DML（Data Manipulation Language，数据操作语言）和 DQL（Data Query Language，数据查询语言）。MaxCompute SQL 实现了标准的 SQL 语法，并有一定的扩展。这里将通过具体的步骤来介绍 MaxCompute SQL 的使用方法。

4.2.1 【实战】使用 DDL 语句

MaxCompute SQL 中的 DDL 可以分为不同的操作类型，如表操作、表克隆、分区和列操作、生命周期操作、视图操作、物化视图操作等。

1. 表操作

表是 MaxCompute 的数据存储单元。数据仓库的开发、分析及运维都需要对表数据进行处理。表操作包括创建表、修改表的所有人、修改表的注释、修改表的修改时间、修改表的聚簇属性、重命名表、清空非分区表里的数据、删除表、查看表或视图信息、查看分区信息、查看建表语句、列出项目下的表和视图、列出所有分区。

下面通过具体的示例来演示表操作。

（1）创建表的语法格式如下。

```
--创建新表
create [external] table [if not exists] <table_name>
[(<col_name> <data_type> [not null] [default <default_value>] [comment <col_comment>], ...)]
[comment <table_comment>]
[partitioned by (<col_name> <data_type> [comment <col_comment>], ...)]
--用于创建聚簇表时设置表的Shuffle和Sort属性
[clustered by | range clustered by (<col_name> [, <col_name>, ...]) [sorted by (<col_name> [asc | desc] [, <col_name> [asc | desc] ...])] into <number_of_buckets> buckets]
--仅限外部表
[stored by StorageHandler]
--仅限外部表
[with serdeproperties (options)]
--仅限外部表
[location <osslocation>]
--指定表为Transactional表，后续可以对该表执行更新或删除表数据操作，但是Transactional表有部分使用限制，请根据需求创建
[tblproperties("transactional"="true")]
[lifecycle <days>];

--基于已存在的表创建新表并复制数据，但不复制分区属性。支持外部表和湖仓一体外部项目中的表
create table [if not exists] <table_name> [lifecycle <days>] as <select_statement>;

--基于已存在的表创建具备相同结构的新表，但不复制数据，支持外部表和湖仓一体外部项目中的表
create table [if not exists] <table_name> like <existing_table_name> [lifecycle <days>];
```

（2）创建非分区表test1。

```
demo_maxcompute_001>create table test1 (key STRING);
```

（3）创建分区表sale_detail。

```
demo_maxcompute_001>create table if not exists sale_detail(
>shop_name      STRING,
>customer_id    STRING,
>total_price    DOUBLE)
>partitioned by (sale_date STRING, region STRING);
```

（4）创建一张新表sale_detail_ctas1，将分区表sale_detail的数据复制到sale_detail_ctas1中，并设置生命周期。

```
demo_maxcompute_001>
>create table sale_detail_ctas1 lifecycle 10 as select * from sale_detail;
```

（5）创建一张新表 sale_detail_ctas2，在 select 子句中使用常量作为列的值。

```
--指定列的名字
demo_maxcompute_001>create table sale_detail_ctas2
>as
>select shop_name, customer_id, total_price,
>         '2013' as sale_date, 'China' as region
>from sale_detail;

--不指定列的名字
demo_maxcompute_001>create table sale_detail_ctas3
>as
>select shop_name, customer_id, total_price, '2013', 'China'
>from sale_detail;
```

（6）创建一张新表 sale_detail_like，使其与分区表 sale_detail 具有相同的表结构，并设置生命周期。

```
demo_maxcompute_001>
>create table sale_detail_like like sale_detail lifecycle 10;
```

（7）查看分区表 sale_detail 的建表语句。

```
demo_maxcompute_001>show create table sale_detail;
```

输出的信息如下。

```
ID = 20230123054407589gh6wrdgioqt5
CREATE TABLE IF NOT EXISTS demo_maxcompute_001.sale_detail(shop_name
STRING,customer_id STRING,total_price DOUBLE) PARTITIONED BY (sale_date
STRING,region STRING) STORED AS ALIORC;

OK
```

（8）查看表 sale_detail_like 的结构和所有人信息。

```
demo_maxcompute_001>desc sale_detail_like;
```

输出的信息如下。

```
+------------------------------------------------+
| Owner:            ALIYUN$collenzhao           |
| Project:          demo_maxcompute_001         |
| TableComment:                                  |
+------------------------------------------------+
| CreateTime:       2023-01-23 13:43:55         |
```

```
| LastDDLTime:              2023-01-23 13:43:55    |
| LastModifiedTime:         2023-01-23 13:43:55    |
| Lifecycle:                10                     |
+--------------------------------------------------+
| InternalTable: YES       | Size: 0               |
+--------------------------------------------------+
| Native Columns:                                  |
+--------------------------------------------------+
| Field          | Type    | Label  | Comment      |
+--------------------------------------------------+
| shop_name      | string  |        |              |
| customer_id    | string  |        |              |
| total_price    | double  |        |              |
+--------------------------------------------------+
| Partition Columns:                               |
+--------------------------------------------------+
| sale_date      | string  |                       |
| region         | string  |                       |
+--------------------------------------------------+

OK
```

（9）列出项目下所有的表和视图。

```
demo_maxcompute_001>show tables;
```

输出的信息如下。

```
ALIYUN$collenzhao:dept
ALIYUN$collenzhao:emp
ALIYUN$collenzhao:emp_part
ALIYUN$collenzhao:sale_detail
ALIYUN$collenzhao:sale_detail_like
ALIYUN$collenzhao:sales
ALIYUN$collenzhao:test1
ALIYUN$collenzhao:testdata
ALIYUN$collenzhao:wordcount

OK
```

> 在使用 show tables 语句时，也可以使用通配符进行查询。例如，列出项目下表名与 sale* 匹配的表，* 表示任意字段。
>
> ```
> demo_maxcompute_001>show tables like 'sale*';
> ```

（10）列出分区表 emp_part 中的所有分区。

```
demo_maxcompute_001>show partitions emp_part;
```

输出的信息如下。

```
deptno=10
deptno=20
deptno=30

OK
```

（11）查看分区表 emp_part 中的分区信息。

```
demo_maxcompute_001>desc emp_part partition(deptno=10);
```

输出的信息如下。

```
+------------------------------------------+
| PartitionSize: 1188                      |
+------------------------------------------+
| CreateTime:          2023-01-22 21:11:22 |
| LastDDLTime:         2023-01-22 21:11:22 |
| LastModifiedTime:    2023-01-22 21:16:32 |
+------------------------------------------+

OK
```

（12）使用 alter table 语句修改表的所有人。

```
--将表 test1 的所有人修改为 ALIYUN$xxx@aliyun.com
demo_maxcompute_001>
>alter table test1 changeowner to 'ALIYUN$xxx@aliyun.com';
```

（13）为表 sale_detail 添加注释。

```
demo_maxcompute_001>
>alter table sale_detail set comment '为表 sale_detail 添加的注释';
```

在使用 desc 语句查看表结构时，可以看到以下注释信息。

```
+------------------------------------------+
| Owner:              ALIYUN$collenzhao    |
| Project:            demo_maxcompute_001  |
| TableComment: 为表 sale_detail 添加的注释 |
+------------------------------------------+
```

（14）重命名分区表 sale_detail。

```
demo_maxcompute_001>
>alter table sale_detail rename to sale_detail_rename;
```

（15）使用 drop table 语句删除分区表 sale_detail。

```
--删除表 sale_detail。无论 sale_detail 表是否存在，均返回成功
demo_maxcompute_001>drop table if exists sale_detail;
Confirm to "drop table if exists sale_detail" (yes/no)? yes
...
OK
```

> 请谨慎使用删除表操作，在确认表可以删除后，再执行删除操作。
>
> 如果误删除了表，但项目空间开启了备份恢复功能，且删除操作未超过项目设置的备份数据保留天数，则可以恢复表。

2. 表克隆

当需要将一张表中的数据复制到另一张表中时，可以使用 MaxCompute 的 clone table 功能，这样可以提高数据迁移效率。这里将介绍 clone table 的功能、使用限制、命令格式及使用示例。

clone table 的语法格式如下。

```
clone table
<[<src_project_name>.]<src_table_name>> [partition(<pt_spec>), ...]
 to
<[<dest_project_name>.]<dest_table_name>>
[if exists [overwrite | ignore]] ;
```

clone table 语法中各个参数及其说明如表 4-9 所示。

表 4-9

参数	说明
src_project_name	可选。源表所属 MaxCompute 项目的名称。不指定时，默认为当前项目。当源表与目标表不属于同一个 MaxCompute 项目时，需要使用此参数
src_table_name	必填。源表的名称
pt_spec	可选。源表的分区信息。 格式为(partition_col1 = partition_col_value1, partition_col2 = partition_col_value2, ...)。partition_col 是分区字段，partition_col_value 是分区值
dest_project_name	可选。目标表所属 MaxCompute 项目的名称。不指定时，默认为当前项目。当源表与目标表不属于同一个 MaxCompute 项目时，需要使用此参数
dest_table_name	必填。目标表的名称

下面通过具体的示例来演示表克隆。

（1）创建一张分区表 sale_detail。

```
demo_maxcompute_001>create table if not exists sale_detail
```

```
>(
>shop_name       string,
>customer_id     string,
>total_price     double
>)partitioned by (sale_date string, region string);
```

（2）给分区表 sale_detail 添加分区。

```
demo_maxcompute_001>alter table sale_detail
>add partition (sale_date='2013', region='china')
>    partition (sale_date='2014', region='shanghai');
```

（3）向分区表 sale_detail 追加数据。

```
demo_maxcompute_001>insert into sale_detail
>partition (sale_date='2013', region='china')
>values ('s1','c1',100.1),('s2','c2',100.2),('s3','c3',100.3);

demo_maxcompute_001>insert into sale_detail
>partition (sale_date='2014', region='shanghai')
>values ('null','c5',null),('s6','c6',100.4),('s7','c7',100.5);
```

（4）查询分区表 sale_detail 中的数据。

```
demo_maxcompute_001>select * from sale_detail;
```

此时将得到下面的错误信息。

```
FAILED: ODPS-0130071:[0,0] Semantic analysis exception - physical plan generation failed:
java.lang.RuntimeException: Table(demo_maxcompute_001,sale_detail) is full scan with all partitions, please specify partition predicates.
```

允许执行全表扫描，并重新执行查询。

```
demo_maxcompute_001>set odps.sql.allow.fullscan=true;
```

输出的结果如下。

```
+-----------+-----------+-----------+----------+-----------+
| shop_name |customer_id| total_price| sale_date | region    |
+-----------+-----------+-----------+----------+-----------+
| s1        | c1        | 100.1     | 2013     | china     |
| s2        | c2        | 100.2     | 2013     | china     |
| s3        | c3        | 100.3     | 2013     | china     |
| null      | c5        | NULL      | 2014     | shanghai  |
| s6        | c6        | 100.4     | 2014     | shanghai  |
| s7        | c7        | 100.5     | 2014     | shanghai  |
+-----------+-----------+-----------+----------+-----------+
```

(5)创建一张非分区表 sale_detail_np,并向表中追加数据。

```
demo_maxcompute_001>create table if not exists sale_detail_np
>(
shop_name      string,
>customer_id    string,
total_price    double
>);

demo_maxcompute_001>insert into sale_detail_np
>values ('s4','c4',100.4);
```

(6)查询非分区表 sale_detail_np 中的数据。

```
demo_maxcompute_001>select * from sale_detail_np;
```

输出的结果如下。

```
+-----------+-------------+-------------+
| shop_name | customer_id | total_price |
+-----------+-------------+-------------+
| s4        | c4          | 100.4       |
+-----------+-------------+-------------+
```

(7)将非分区表 sale_detail_np 的数据全量复制到目标表 sale_detail_np_clone 中。

```
--复制表数据
demo_maxcompute_001>clone table sale_detail_np to sale_detail_np_clone;
--查看复制后目标表 sale_detail_np_clone 的信息,验证数据的准确性
demo_maxcompute_001>select * from sale_detail_np_clone;
```

输出的结果如下。

```
+-----------+-------------+-------------+
| shop_name | customer_id | total_price |
+-----------+-------------+-------------+
| s4        | c4          | 100.4       |
+-----------+-------------+-------------+
```

(8)将分区表 sale_detail 指定分区的数据复制到目标表 sale_detail_clone 中。

```
--复制表数据
demo_maxcompute_001>clone table sale_detail
>partition (sale_date='2013', region='china')
>to sale_detail_clone if exists overwrite;

--查看复制后目标表 sale_detail_clone 的信息,验证数据的准确性
demo_maxcompute_001>select * from sale_detail_clone;
```

输出的结果如下。

```
+-------------+-------------+-------------+-----------+----------+
| shop_name   | customer_id | total_price | sale_date | region   |
+-------------+-------------+-------------+-----------+----------+
| s1          | c1          | 100.1       | 2013      | china    |
| s2          | c2          | 100.2       | 2013      | china    |
| s3          | c3          | 100.3       | 2013      | china    |
+-------------+-------------+-------------+-----------+----------+
```

（9）将分区表 sale_detail 的数据全量复制到目标表 sale_detail_clone 中，并跳过目标表中已存在的分区。

```
--复制表数据
demo_maxcompute_001>clone table sale_detail
>to sale_detail_clone if exists ignore;

--查看复制后目标表 sale_detail_clone 的信息，验证数据的准确性
demo_maxcompute_001>select * from sale_detail_clone;
```

输出的结果如下。

```
+-------------+-------------+-------------+-----------+----------+
| shop_name   | customer_id | total_price | sale_date | region   |
+-------------+-------------+-------------+-----------+----------+
| s1          | c1          | 100.1       | 2013      | china    |
| s2          | c2          | 100.2       | 2013      | china    |
| s3          | c3          | 100.3       | 2013      | china    |
| null        | c5          | NULL        | 2014      | shanghai |
| s6          | c6          | 100.4       | 2014      | shanghai |
| s7          | c7          | 100.5       | 2014      | shanghai |
+-------------+-------------+-------------+-----------+----------+
```

（10）将分区表 sale_detail 的数据全量复制到目标表 sale_detail_clone1 中。

```
--复制表数据
demo_maxcompute_001>clone table sale_detail to sale_detail_clone1;

--查看复制后目标表 sale_detail_clone1 的信息，验证数据的准确性
demo_maxcompute_001>select * from sale_detail_clone1;
```

输出的结果如下。

```
+-----------+------------+------------+-----------+----------+
| shop_name |customer_id |total_price | sale_date | region   |
+-----------+------------+------------+-----------+----------+
| s1        | c1         | 100.1      | 2013      | china    |
| s2        | c2         | 100.2      | 2013      | china    |
```

```
| s3      | c3      | 100.3    | 2013     | china    |
| null    | c5      | NULL     | 2014     | shanghai |
| s6      | c6      | 100.4    | 2014     | shanghai |
| s7      | c7      | 100.5    | 2014     | shanghai |
+---------+---------+----------+----------+----------+
```

3. 分区和列操作

分区和列操作为用户提供了变更 MaxCompute 中表的分区或列的操作方法，用户可以根据实际业务场景执行相应操作。

下面通过具体的示例来演示分区和列操作。

（1）给表 sale_detail 添加一个分区，用来存储 2013 年 12 月杭州地区的销售记录。

```
demo_maxcompute_001>alter table sale_detail add if not exists
>partition (sale_date='201312', region='hangzhou');
```

（2）给表 sale_detail 同时添加两个分区，用来存储 2013 年 12 月北京和上海地区的销售记录。

```
demo_maxcompute_001>alter table sale_detail add if not exists
>partition (sale_date='201312', region='beijing')
>partition (sale_date='201312', region='shanghai');
```

（3）给表 sale_detail 添加分区，仅指定一个分区字段 sale_date。

```
demo_maxcompute_001>alter table sale_detail add if not exists
>partition (sale_date='20111011');
```

此时将返回下面的错误信息。需要同时指定两个分区字段 sale_date 和 region。

```
Semantic analysis exception - provided partition spec does not match table partition spec
```

（4）查看表 sale_detail 的分区。

```
demo_maxcompute_001>show partitions sale_detail;
```

输出的信息如下。

```
sale_date=2013/region=china
sale_date=201312/region=beijing
sale_date=201312/region=hangzhou
sale_date=201312/region=shanghai
sale_date=2014/region=shanghai

OK
```

（5）未指定筛选条件清空分区数据。

```
--从表sale_detail中清空一个分区,清空2013年12月杭州地区的销售记录
demo_maxcompute_001>truncate table sale_detail
>partition(sale_date='201312',region='hangzhou');

--从表sale_detail中同时清空两个分区,清空2013年12月杭州和上海地区的销售记录
demo_maxcompute_001>truncate table sale_detail
>partition(sale_date='201312',region='hangzhou'),
>partition(sale_date='201312',region='shanghai');
```

（6）指定筛选条件清空分区数据。

```
--从表sale_detail中清空多个分区,清空杭州地区下sale_date以2013开头的销售记录
demo_maxcompute_001>truncate table sale_detail
>partition(sale_date like '2013%',region='hangzhou');
```

（7）未指定筛选条件删除分区。

```
--从表sale_detail中删除一个分区,删除2013年12月杭州地区的销售记录
demo_maxcompute_001>alter table sale_detail drop if exists
>partition(sale_date='201312',region='hangzhou');

--从表sale_detail中同时删除两个分区,删除2013年12月杭州和上海地区的销售记录
demo_maxcompute_001>alter table sale_detail drop if exists
>partition(sale_date='201312',region='hangzhou'),
>partition(sale_date='201312',region='shanghai');
```

（8）指定筛选条件删除分区。

```
--创建分区表
demo_maxcompute_001>create table if not exists sale_detail1(
>shop_name      STRING,
>customer_id    STRING,
>total_price    DOUBLE)
>partitioned by (sale_date STRING);

--添加分区
demo_maxcompute_001>alter table sale_detail1 add if not exists
>partition (sale_date= '201910')
>partition (sale_date= '201911')
>partition (sale_date= '201912')
>partition (sale_date= '202001')
>partition (sale_date= '202002')
>partition (sale_date= '202003')
>partition (sale_date= '202004')
>partition (sale_date= '202005')
>partition (sale_date= '202006')
>partition (sale_date= '202007');
```

```
--批量删除分区
demo_maxcompute_001>alter table sale_detail1 drop if exists
>partition(sale_date < '201911');
demo_maxcompute_001>alter table sale_detail1 drop if exists
>partition(sale_date >= '202007');
demo_maxcompute_001>alter table sale_detail1 drop if exists
>partition(sale_date LIKE '20191%');
demo_maxcompute_001>alter table sale_detail1 drop if exists
>partition(sale_date IN ('202002','202004','202006'));
demo_maxcompute_001>alter table sale_detail1 drop if exists
>partition(sale_date BETWEEN '202001' AND '202007');
demo_maxcompute_001>alter table sale_detail1 drop if exists
>partition(substr(sale_date, 1, 4) = '2020');
demo_maxcompute_001>alter table sale_detail1 drop if exists
>partition(sale_date < '201912' OR sale_date >= '202006');
demo_maxcompute_001>alter table sale_detail1 drop if exists
>partition(sale_date > '201912' AND sale_date <= '202004');
demo_maxcompute_001>alter table sale_detail1 drop if exists
>partition(NOT sale_date > '202004');

--支持多个分区过滤表达式，表达式之间是 OR 的关系
demo_maxcompute_001>alter table sale_detail1 drop if exists
>partition(sale_date < '201911'), partition(sale_date >= '202007');

--添加其他格式分区
demo_maxcompute_001>alter table sale_detail1 add IF NOT EXISTS
>partition (sale_date= '2019-10-05')
>partition (sale_date= '2019-10-06')
>partition (sale_date= '2019-10-07');

--批量删除分区，使用正则表达式匹配分区
demo_maxcompute_001>alter table sale_detail1 drop if exists
>partition(sale_date RLIKE '2019-\\d+-\\d+');
```

（9）给表 sale_detail 添加两个列。

```
demo_maxcompute_001>alter table sale_detail
>add columns (customer_name STRING, education BIGINT);
```

（10）给表 sale_detail 添加两个列并添加列注释。

```
demo_maxcompute_001>alter table sale_detail add columns
>(customer_name1 STRING comment '客户',education1 BIGINT comment '教育');
```

（11）给表 sale_detail 添加一个复杂数据类型列。

```
demo_maxcompute_001>alter table sale_detail add columns
>(region1 struct<province:string, area:string>);
```

4. 生命周期操作

MaxCompute 提供了表数据生命周期管理功能，方便用户释放存储空间，简化回收数据的流程。用户可以在创建表时，通过 lifecycle 关键字指定生命周期。

> 在 MaxCompute 中，当表的数据被修改后，表的 LastModifiedTime 将会被更新。MaxCompute 会根据每张表的 LastModifiedTime 及生命周期的设置来判断是否回收此表。

下面通过具体的示例来演示生命周期操作。

（1）项目级别设置自动删除表。

```
demo_maxcompute_001>setproject
>odps.table.lifecycle.deletemeta.on.expiration=true;
```

（2）项目级别关闭自动删除表。

```
demo_maxcompute_001>setproject
>odps.table.lifecycle.deletemeta.on.expiration=false;
```

（3）表级别设置自动删除表。

```
demo_maxcompute_001>create table mf_delete_meta2
>(id int, name string) partitioned by (ds string)
>tblproperties ('lifecycle.deletemeta'='true') lifecycle 1;
```

（4）表级别设置关闭自动删除表。

```
demo_maxcompute_001>alter table mf_delete_meta2
>set tblproperties('lifecycle.deletemeta'='false');
```

（5）新建表 test_lifecycle，生命周期为 100 天。

```
demo_maxcompute_001>create table test_lifecycle (key string)
>lifecycle 100;
```

（6）修改表 test_lifecycle，将生命周期设置为 50 天。

```
demo_maxcompute_001>alter table test_lifecycle set lifecycle 50;
```

（7）禁止表 test_lifecycle 的生命周期功能。

```
demo_maxcompute_001>alter table test_lifecycle disable lifecycle;
```

5. 视图操作

视图是在表之上建立的虚拟表，其结构和内容都来自表。一个视图可以对应一张表或多张表。

如果用户想保留查询结果，但不想创建表占用存储，就可以通过视图实现。

下面通过具体的示例来演示视图操作。

（1）基于员工表 emp 和部门表 dept 创建视图。

```
demo_maxcompute_001>create view if not exists emp_detail_view
>(empno,ename,job,sal,dname)
>comment '基于员工表emp和部门表dept的视图'
>as
>select empno,ename,job,sal,dname
>from emp,dept
>where emp.deptno=dept.deptno;
```

（2）通过视图获取数据，输出的结果如图 4-1 所示。

```
demo_maxcompute_001>select * from emp_detail_view;
```

```
0
          TableScan1: 0   (min: 0, max: 0, avg: 0) MaxInstance: 0
+-------+----------+-----------+--------+-------------+
| empno | ename    | job       | sal    | dname       |
+-------+----------+-----------+--------+-------------+
| 7369  | SMITH    | CLERK     | 800    | RESEARCH    |
| 7499  | ALLEN    | SALESMAN  | 1600   | SALES       |
| 7521  | WARD     | SALESMAN  | 1250   | SALES       |
| 7566  | JONES    | MANAGER   | 2975   | RESEARCH    |
| 7654  | MARTIN   | SALESMAN  | 1250   | SALES       |
| 7698  | BLAKE    | MANAGER   | 2850   | SALES       |
| 7782  | CLARK    | MANAGER   | 2450   | My Dept     |
| 7782  | CLARK    | MANAGER   | 2450   | ACCOUNTING  |
| 7788  | SCOTT    | ANALYST   | 3000   | RESEARCH    |
| 7839  | KING     | PRESIDENT | 5000   | My Dept     |
| 7839  | KING     | PRESIDENT | 5000   | ACCOUNTING  |
| 7844  | TURNER   | SALESMAN  | 1500   | SALES       |
| 7876  | ADAMS    | CLERK     | 1100   | RESEARCH    |
| 7900  | JAMES    | CLERK     | 950    | SALES       |
| 7902  | FORD     | ANALYST   | 3000   | RESEARCH    |
| 7934  | MILLER   | CLERK     | 1300   | My Dept     |
| 7934  | MILLER   | CLERK     | 1300   | ACCOUNTING  |
+-------+----------+-----------+--------+-------------+
A total of 17 records fetched by instance tunnel. Max record number: 10000
demo_maxcompute_001>
```

图 4-1

（3）将视图 emp_detail_view 重命名为 emp_detail_view2。

```
demo_maxcompute_001>alter view emp_detail_view
>rename to emp_detail_view2;
```

（4）查看视图的结构。

```
demo_maxcompute_001>desc emp_detail_view2;
```

输出的结果如图 4-2 所示。

```
命令提示符 - bin\odpscmd
demo_maxcompute_001>desc emp_detail_view2;

Owner:                ALIYUN$collenzhao
Project:              demo_maxcompute_001
TableComment: 基于员工表emp和部门表dept的视图

CreateTime:           2023-01-23 14:57:14
LastDDLTime:          2023-01-23 15:01:54
LastModifiedTime:     2023-01-23 14:57:14

VirtualView  : YES
ViewText: select empno,ename,job,sal,dname from emp,dept where emp.deptno=dept.deptno

Native Columns:

Field         | Type    | Label | Comment
empno         | bigint  |       |
ename         | string  |       |
job           | string  |       |
sal           | bigint  |       |
dname         | string  |       |

OK
demo_maxcompute_001>
```

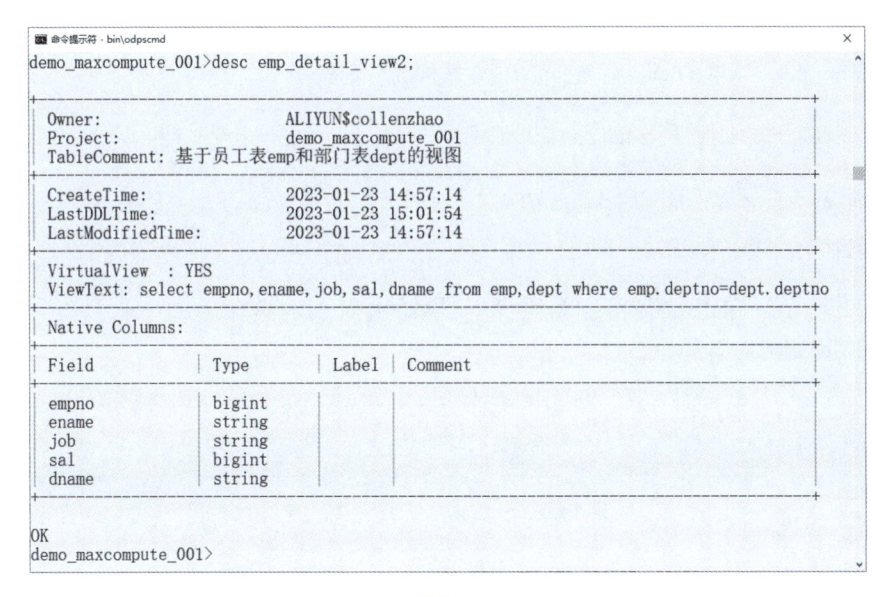

图 4-2

（5）删除视图 emp_detail_view2。

```
demo_maxcompute_001>drop view if exists emp_detail_view2;
```

> 由于视图的本质是一张虚拟表，因此视图不能缓存数据，通过视图查询数据不能提高查询的性能，但物化视图除外。

6. 物化视图操作

物化视图（Materialized View）的本质是一种预计算，即把某些耗时的操作（如 JOIN、AGGREGATE）的结果保存下来，以便在查询时直接复用，从而避免这些耗时的操作，达到加速的目的。

> 由于物化视图会将查询的结果保存下来，因此通过物化视图查询数据可以提高查询的性能。

下面通过具体的示例来演示物化视图操作。

（1）基于员工表 emp 和部门表 dept 创建物化视图。

```
demo_maxcompute_001>create materialized view
>if not exists emp_detail_view2
```

```
>(empno,ename,job,sal,dname)
>comment '基于员工表 emp 和部门表 dept 的视图'
>as
>select empno,ename,job,sal,dname
>from emp,dept
>where emp.deptno=dept.deptno;
```

（2）查询物化视图的信息。

```
demo_maxcompute_001>desc extended emp_detail_view2;
```

输出的结果如图 4-3 所示。

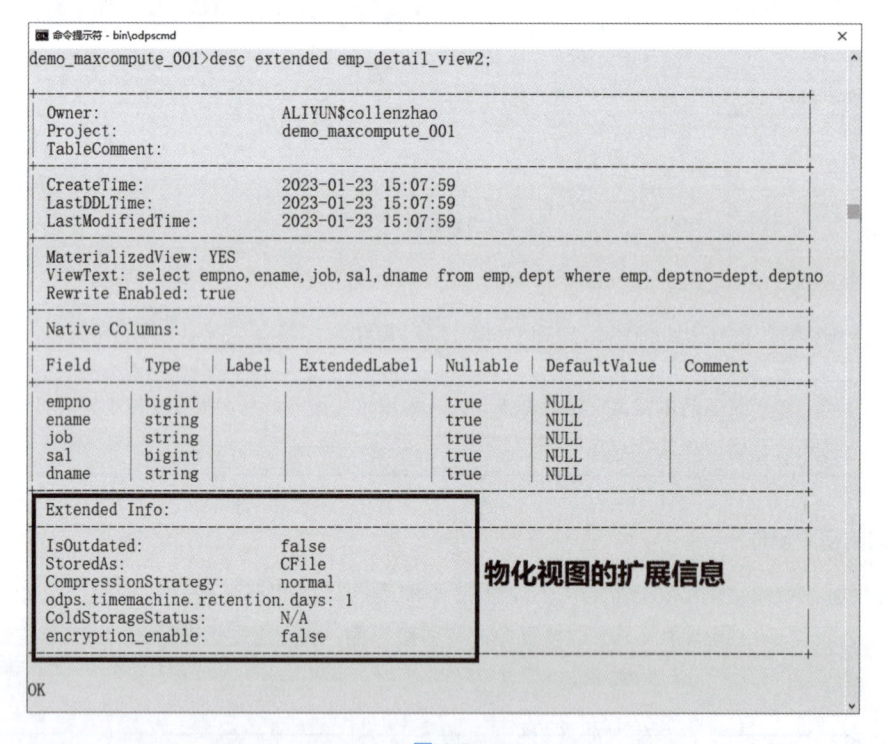

```
demo_maxcompute_001>desc extended emp_detail_view2;

Owner:                  ALIYUN$collenzhao
Project:                demo_maxcompute_001
TableComment:

CreateTime:             2023-01-23 15:07:59
LastDDLTime:            2023-01-23 15:07:59
LastModifiedTime:       2023-01-23 15:07:59

MaterializedView: YES
ViewText: select empno,ename,job,sal,dname from emp,dept where emp.deptno=dept.deptno
Rewrite Enabled: true

Native Columns:

Field    | Type    | Label | ExtendedLabel | Nullable | DefaultValue | Comment

empno      bigint                            true       NULL
ename      string                            true       NULL
job        string                            true       NULL
sal        bigint                            true       NULL
dname      string                            true       NULL

Extended Info:

IsOutdated:                    false
StoredAs:                      CFile              物化视图的扩展信息
CompressionStrategy:           normal
odps.timemachine.retention.days: 1
ColdStorageStatus:             N/A
encryption_enable:             false

OK
```

图 4-3

（3）检查 emp_detail_view2 的数据是否与原表最新的数据一致。如果一致，则返回 true，否则返回 false。

```
demo_maxcompute_001>
>select materialized_view_is_valid("emp_detail_view2");
```

输出的结果如下。

```
+------+
| _c0  |
```

```
+------+
| true |
+------+
A total of 1 records fetched by instance tunnel. Max record number: 10000
```

4.2.2 【实战】使用 DML 语句

DML 语句指的是 insert（插入）、update（更新）和 delete（删除）3 个语句。MaxCompute SQL 中的 DML 语句，除了支持标准 SQL 中的 DML 语法，还有一定扩展。

> 对于 delete（删除）和 update（更新）操作，MaxCompute SQL 仅支持在行级别删除或更新 Transactional 表。
>
> 如果更新或删除非 Transactional 表中的数据，则得到错误信息：FAILED: ODPS-0130071:[1,1] Semantic analysis exception - trying to update a non-transactional table is not allowed. Set tblproperties ("transactional" = "true") in order to use this feature。

下面通过具体的示例来演示 MaxCompute SQL 中 DML 语句的使用。

（1）创建一张非分区表 websites。

```
demo_maxcompute_001>create table if not exists websites
>(id int,
> name string,
> url string
>);
```

（2）创建一张非分区表 apps。

```
demo_maxcompute_001>create table if not exists apps
>(id int,
> app_name string,
> url string
>);
```

（3）向表 apps 中插入数据。

```
demo_maxcompute_001>insert into apps (id,app_name,url)
>values (1,'Aliyun','https://www.aliyun.com');
```

> 注意：insert into table table_name 可以简写为 insert into table_name。

（4）复制表 apps 的数据并追加至 websites 表中。

```
demo_maxcompute_001>insert into websites (id,name,url)
>select id,app_name,url from apps;
```

（5）执行 select 语句查看表 websites 中的数据。

```
demo_maxcompute_001>select * from websites;
```

输出的结果如下。

```
+-----------+-----------+------------------------+
| id        | name      | url                    |
+-----------+-----------+------------------------+
| 1         | Aliyun    | https://www.aliyun.com |
+-----------+-----------+------------------------+
```

（6）创建非分区表 acid_update 并导入数据，执行 update 操作，更新满足指定条件的行对应的列数据。

```
--创建 Transactional 表 acid_update
demo_maxcompute_001>create table if not exists
>acid_update(id bigint) tblproperties ("transactional"="true");

--插入数据
demo_maxcompute_001>insert overwrite table acid_update
>values(1),(2),(3),(2);

--查看插入结果
demo_maxcompute_001>select * from acid_update;
--输出结果如下
+-----------+
| id        |
+-----------+
| 1         |
| 2         |
| 3         |
| 2         |
+-----------+

--将所有 id 为 2 的行，id 值更新为 4
demo_maxcompute_001>update acid_update set id = 4 where id = 2;

--查看更新结果
demo_maxcompute_001>select * from acid_update;
--输出结果如下
```

```
+----------+
| id       |
+----------+
| 1        |
| 3        |
| 4        |
| 4        |
+----------+
```

update 语句有多种形式，下面展示了 update 语句更新数据时 3 种不同的形式。

```
--方式 1
update <table_name>
set <col1_name> = <value1> [, <col2_name> = <value2> ...]
[WHERE <where_condition>];

--方式 2
update <table_name>
set (<col1_name> [, <col2_name> ...]) = (<value1> [, <value2> ...])
[WHERE <where_condition>];

--方式 3
update <table_name>
set <col1_name> = <value1> [ , <col2_name> = <value2> , ... ]
[ from <additional_tables> ]
[ where <where_condition> ]
```

（7）创建非分区表 acid_delete 并导入数据，执行 delete 操作，删除满足指定条件的行数据。

```
--创建 Transactional 表 acid_delete
demo_maxcompute_001>create table if not exists
>acid_delete(id bigint) tblproperties ("transactional"="true");

--插入数据
demo_maxcompute_001>insert overwrite table
>acid_delete values(1),(2),(3),(2);

--查看插入结果
demo_maxcompute_001>select * from acid_delete;
--输出结果如下
+----------+
| id       |
+----------+
| 1        |
| 2        |
```

```
| 3          |
| 2          |
+-----------+

--删除 id 为 2 的行,如果在 MaxCompute 客户端执行,则需要输入 yes/no 确认
demo_maxcompute_001>delete from acid_delete where id = 2;

--查看删除结果
demo_maxcompute_001>select * from acid_delete;
--输出结果如下
+-----------+
| id        |
+-----------+
| 1         |
| 3         |
+-----------+
```

(8)当需要对 Transactional 表执行 insert、update 或 delete 操作时,可以通过 merge into 功能将这些操作合并为一条 SQL 语句,根据与源表关联的结果,对目标 Transactional 表执行 insert、update 或 delete 操作,提升执行效率。

```
--创建目标表 acid_address_book_base1
demo_maxcompute_001>create table if not exists acid_address_book_base1
>(id bigint,first_name string,last_name string,phone string)
>partitioned by(year string, month string, day string, hour string)
>tblproperties ("transactional"="true");

--创建源表 exists tmp_table1
demo_maxcompute_001>create table if not exists tmp_table1
>(id bigint, first_name string, last_name string,
>phone string, _event_type_ string);

--向目标表 acid_address_book_base1 插入测试数据
demo_maxcompute_001>insert overwrite table acid_address_book_base1
>partition(year='2020', month='08', day='20', hour='16')
>values (4, 'nihaho', 'li', '222'),
>       (5, 'tahao', 'ha', '333'),
>       (7, 'djh', 'hahh', '555');

--向源表 exists tmp_table1 插入测试数据
demo_maxcompute_001>insert overwrite table tmp_table1 values
>(1, 'hh', 'liu', '999', 'I'), (2, 'cc', 'zhang', '888', 'I'),
>(3, 'cy', 'zhang', '666', 'I'),(4, 'hh', 'liu', '999', 'U'),
>(5, 'cc', 'zhang', '888', 'U'),(6, 'cy', 'zhang', '666', 'U');
```

```
--执行merge into操作
demo_maxcompute_001>merge into acid_address_book_base1 as t
>using tmp_table1 as s
>on s.id = t.id and t.year='2020' and t.month='08' and t.day='20'
>and t.hour='16'
>when matched then update set t.first_name = s.first_name,
>t.last_name = s.last_name, t.phone = s.phone
>when not matched and (s._event_type_='I') then
>insert values
>(s.id, s.first_name, s.last_name,s.phone,'2020','08','20','16');

--查询目标表的数据，确认merge into操作的结果
demo_maxcompute_001>select * from acid_address_book_base1;
```

输出的结果如图 4-4 所示。

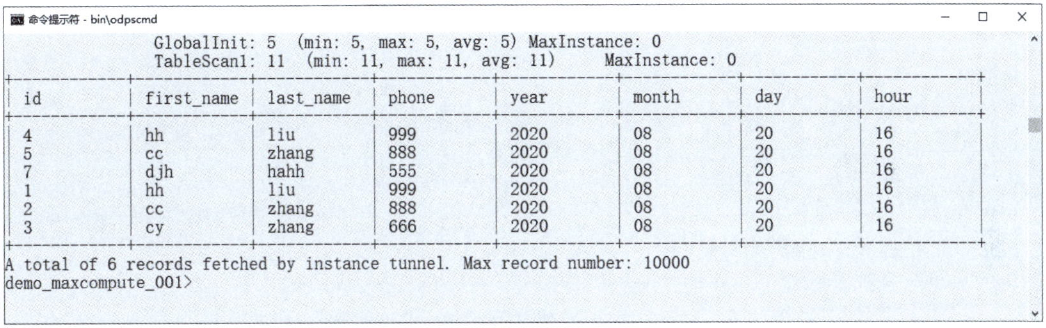

```
GlobalInit: 5   (min: 5, max: 5, avg: 5) MaxInstance: 0
TableScan1: 11  (min: 11, max: 11, avg: 11)   MaxInstance: 0
+----+------------+-----------+-------+------+-------+-----+------+
| id | first_name | last_name | phone | year | month | day | hour |
+----+------------+-----------+-------+------+-------+-----+------+
| 4  | hh         | liu       | 999   | 2020 | 08    | 20  | 16   |
| 5  | cc         | zhang     | 888   | 2020 | 08    | 20  | 16   |
| 7  | djh        | hahh      | 555   | 2020 | 08    | 20  | 16   |
| 1  | hh         | liu       | 999   | 2020 | 08    | 20  | 16   |
| 2  | cc         | zhang     | 888   | 2020 | 08    | 20  | 16   |
| 3  | cy         | zhang     | 666   | 2020 | 08    | 20  | 16   |
+----+------------+-----------+-------+------+-------+-----+------+
A total of 6 records fetched by instance tunnel. Max record number: 10000
demo_maxcompute_001>
```

图 4-4

（9）MaxCompute SQL 支持在一条 SQL 语句中通过 insert into 或 insert overwrite 操作将数据插入不同的目标表或分区，从而实现多路输出。

```
--创建表emp_multi
demo_maxcompute_001>create table emp_multi like emp_part;

--开启全表扫描，仅在此Session有效。将表emp_part中的数据插入表emp_multi
demo_maxcompute_001>set odps.sql.allow.fullscan=true;
demo_maxcompute_001>from emp_part
>insert overwrite table emp_multi partition (deptno=10)
>select empno,ename,job,mgr,hiredate,sal,comm
>insert overwrite table emp_multi partition (deptno=20)
>select empno,ename,job,mgr,hiredate,sal,comm;

--开启全表扫描，仅在此Session有效。执行select语句，查看表emp_multi中的数据
```

```
demo_maxcompute_001>set odps.sql.allow.fullscan=true;
demo_maxcompute_001>select * from emp_multi;
```

输出的结果如图 4-5 所示。

图 4-5

4.2.3 【实战】使用 DQL 语句

MaxCompute SQL 支持使用 select 语句查询数据。

> 这里将使用 3.4.1 节中创建的员工表 emp 和部门表 dept 进行演示说明。

下面介绍 select 语句的语法格式及如何实现基本查询、分组查询、排序等操作。关于 MaxCompute SQL 中 select 语句的详细用法请参考阿里云官方文档。

（1）查询所有的员工数据。

```
demo_maxcompute_001>select * from emp;
```

输出的结果如图 4-6 所示。

```
inputs:
outputs:
+-------+--------+----------+------+-----------+------+------+--------+
| empno | ename  | job      | mgr  | hiredate  | sal  | comm | deptno |
+-------+--------+----------+------+-----------+------+------+--------+
| 7369  | SMITH  | CLERK    | 7902 | 1980/12/17| 800  | 0    | 20     |
| 7499  | ALLEN  | SALESMAN | 7698 | 1981/2/20 | 1600 | 300  | 30     |
| 7521  | WARD   | SALESMAN | 7698 | 1981/2/22 | 1250 | 500  | 30     |
| 7566  | JONES  | MANAGER  | 7839 | 1981/4/2  | 2975 | 0    | 20     |
| 7654  | MARTIN | SALESMAN | 7698 | 1981/9/28 | 1250 | 1400 | 30     |
| 7698  | BLAKE  | MANAGER  | 7839 | 1981/5/1  | 2850 | 0    | 30     |
| 7782  | CLARK  | MANAGER  | 7839 | 1981/6/9  | 2450 | 0    | 10     |
| 7788  | SCOTT  | ANALYST  | 7566 | 1987/4/19 | 3000 | 0    | 20     |
| 7839  | KING   | PRESIDENT| -1   | 1981/11/17| 5000 | 0    | 10     |
| 7844  | TURNER | SALESMAN | 7698 | 1981/9/8  | 1500 | 0    | 30     |
| 7876  | ADAMS  | CLERK    | 7788 | 1987/5/23 | 1100 | 0    | 20     |
| 7900  | JAMES  | CLERK    | 7698 | 1981/12/3 | 950  | 0    | 30     |
| 7902  | FORD   | ANALYST  | 7566 | 1981/12/3 | 3000 | 0    | 20     |
| 7934  | MILLER | CLERK    | 7782 | 1982/1/23 | 1300 | 0    | 10     |
+-------+--------+----------+------+-----------+------+------+--------+
A total of 14 records fetched by instance tunnel. Max record number: 10000
demo_maxcompute_001>
```

图 4-6

（2）查询员工数据，要求显示姓名、工资、奖金、年薪和年收入。

```
demo_maxcompute_001>select ename,sal,comm,sal*12,sal*12+comm from emp;
```

（3）查询员工数据，要求显示姓名、工资、奖金、年薪和年收入，并按年收入排序。

```
demo_maxcompute_001>set odps.sql.validate.orderby.limit=false
demo_maxcompute_001>select ename,sal,comm,sal*12,sal*12+comm
>from emp order by 5;
```

输出的结果如图 4-7 所示。

```
                Project1: 0  (min: 0, max: 0, avg: 0)  MaxInstance: 0
                StreamLineRead1: 1  (min: 1, max: 1, avg: 1)  MaxInstance: 0
+--------+------+------+-------+-------+
| ename  | sal  | comm | _c3   | _c4   |
+--------+------+------+-------+-------+
| SMITH  | 800  | 0    | 9600  | 9600  |
| ALLEN  | 1600 | 300  | 19200 | 19500 |
| WARD   | 1250 | 500  | 15000 | 15500 |
| JONES  | 2975 | 0    | 35700 | 35700 |
| MARTIN | 1250 | 1400 | 15000 | 16400 |
| BLAKE  | 2850 | 0    | 34200 | 34200 |
| CLARK  | 2450 | 0    | 29400 | 29400 |
| SCOTT  | 3000 | 0    | 36000 | 36000 |
| KING   | 5000 | 0    | 60000 | 60000 |
| TURNER | 1500 | 0    | 18000 | 18000 |
| ADAMS  | 1100 | 0    | 13200 | 13200 |
| JAMES  | 950  | 0    | 11400 | 11400 |
| FORD   | 3000 | 0    | 36000 | 36000 |
| MILLER | 1300 | 0    | 15600 | 15600 |
+--------+------+------+-------+-------+
A total of 14 records fetched by instance tunnel. Max record number: 10000
demo_maxcompute_001>
```

图 4-7

> order by 子句后面的数字 5 代表 select 语句中的第 5 列，即 sal*12+comm。由于在默认情况下，order by 子句需要指定 limit 关键字，因此这里将参数 odps.sql.validate.orderby.limit 设置为了 false。

（4）查询每个部门的平均工资。

```
demo_maxcompute_001>select deptno,avg(sal) from emp group by deptno;
```

（5）按部门统计员工人数，要求显示部门号、部门名称和人数。

```
demo_maxcompute_001>
>select d.deptno "部门号",d.dname "部门名称",count(e.empno) "人数"
>from emp e,dept d
>where e.deptno=d.deptno
>group by d.deptno,d.dname;
```

输出的结果如下。

```
+-----------+----------------+--------+
| 部门号    | 部门名称       | 人数   |
+-----------+----------------+--------+
| 10        | ACCOUNTING     | 3      |
| 20        | RESEARCH       | 5      |
| 30        | SALES          | 6      |
+-----------+----------------+--------+
```

这里的输出结果是不正确的。由于部门表中存在 40 号部门，而员工表中没有 40 部门的员工，因此这里丢失了 40 号部门的数据。正确的方式是使用外连接进行查询。

```
demo_maxcompute_001>
>select d.deptno "部门号",d.dname "部门名称",count(e.empno) "人数"
>from emp e right join dept d
>on e.deptno=d.deptno
>group by d.deptno,d.dname;
```

输出的结果如下。

```
+-----------+----------------+--------+
| 部门号    | 部门名称       | 人数   |
+-----------+----------------+--------+
| 10        | ACCOUNTING     | 3      |
| 20        | RESEARCH       | 5      |
| 30        | SALES          | 6      |
| 40        | OPERATIONS     | 0      |
+-----------+----------------+--------+
```

（6）查询工资比 SCOTT 高的员工信息。

```
demo_maxcompute_001>
>select * from emp where sal>(select sal from emp where ename='SCOTT');
```

（7）查询工资高于本部门平均工资的员工信息，要求显示员工姓名、员工工资和部门平均工资。

```
demo_maxcompute_001>
>select e.ename "员工姓名",e.sal "员工工资",d.avgsal "部门平均工资"
>from emp e,(select deptno,avg(sal) avgsal from emp group by deptno) d
>where e.deptno=d.deptno and e.sal>d.avgsal;
```

输出的结果如下。

```
+----------+----------+-------------------+
| 员工姓名  | 员工工资  | 部门平均工资       |
+----------+----------+-------------------+
| ALLEN    | 1600     | 1566.6666666666667|
| JONES    | 2975     | 2175.0            |
| BLAKE    | 2850     | 1566.6666666666667|
| SCOTT    | 3000     | 2175.0            |
| KING     | 5000     | 2916.6666666666665|
| FORD     | 3000     | 2175.0            |
+----------+----------+-------------------+
```

4.2.4 【实战】使用 MaxCompute SQL 的增强语法 CTE

CTE（Common Table Expression，公用表表达式）可以被认为是在单个 DML 语句的执行范围内定义的临时结果集。CTE 类似于派生表，它不作为对象存储，并且仅在查询期间持续。在开发过程中结合 CTE，可以提高 SQL 语句的可读性，便于轻松维护复杂查询。

> CTE 是一个临时命名结果集，用于简化 SQL。MaxCompute 支持标准 SQL 的 CTE，结合 CTE 可以更好地提高 SQL 语句的可读性与执行效率。

CTE 的语法格式如下。

```
with
    <cte_name> as
    (
        <cte_query>
    )
    [,<cte_name2> as
    (
    <cte_query2>
    )
    ,……]
```

（1）cte_name：必填项。CTE 的名称，不能与当前 with 子句中的其他 CTE 的名称相同。查询中任何使用 cte_name 标识符的地方，均指 CTE。

（2）cte_query：必填项。一个 select 语句。select 的结果集用于填充 CTE。

下面通过一个示例来说明 CTE 的使用方法。

（1）使用相关子查询查询员工表中工资大于本部门平均工资的员工。

```
demo_maxcompute_001>
>select empno,ename,sal,
>       (select avg(sal) from emp where deptno=e.deptno) avgsal
>from emp e
>where sal > (select avg(sal) from emp where deptno=e.deptno);
```

输出的结果如下。

```
+-----------+------------+----------+--------------------+
| empno     | ename      | sal      | avgsal             |
+-----------+------------+----------+--------------------+
| 7499      | ALLEN      | 1600     | 1566.6666666666667 |
| 7566      | JONES      | 2975     | 2175.0             |
| 7698      | BLAKE      | 2850     | 1566.6666666666667 |
| 7788      | SCOTT      | 3000     | 2175.0             |
| 7839      | KING       | 5000     | 2916.6666666666665 |
| 7902      | FORD       | 3000     | 2175.0             |
+-----------+------------+----------+--------------------+
```

> 这里重复使用了一条语句 (select avg(sal) from emp where deptno=e.deptno)。因此可以使用 CTE 进行简化。

（2）使用 CTE 改写上面的语句。

```
demo_maxcompute_001>with
>a as (select deptno,avg(sal) avgsal from emp group by deptno),
>b as (select empno,ename,sal,a.avgsal
>      from emp join a on emp.deptno=a.deptno and emp.sal>a.avgsal)
>select * from b;
```

输出的结果如下。

```
+-----------+------------+----------+--------------------+
| empno     | ename      | sal      | avgsal             |
+-----------+------------+----------+--------------------+
| 7499      | ALLEN      | 1600     | 1566.6666666666667 |
| 7566      | JONES      | 2975     | 2175.0             |
```

```
| 7698      | BLAKE       | 2850     | 1566.6666666666667  |
| 7788      | SCOTT       | 3000     | 2175.0              |
| 7839      | KING        | 5000     | 2916.6666666666665  |
| 7902      | FORD        | 3000     | 2175.0              |
+-----------+-------------+----------+---------------------+
```

> 重写后，a 对应的子查询只需写一次，就可以在后面进行重用。可以在 CTE 的 with 子句中指定多个子查询，像使用变量一样在整个语句中反复重用。除重用外，不必反复重写该语句。

4.3 使用 MaxCompute SQL 的内建函数

MaxCompute 自身预置了许多函数，可以满足大部分业务场景的数据处理需求。MaxCompute 预置的函数类型如表 4-10 所示。

表 4-10

函 数 类 型	说　　　明
日期函数	支持处理 DATE、DATETIME、TIMESTAMP 等日期类型的数据，实现加减日期、计算日期差值、提取日期字段、获取当前时间、转换日期格式等功能
数学函数	支持处理 BIGINT、DOUBLE、DECIMAL、FLOAT 等数值类型的数据，实现转换进制、数学运算、四舍五入、获取随机数等功能
窗口函数	支持在指定的开窗列中，实现求和、求最大值、求最小值、求平均值、求中间值、数值排序、数值偏移、抽样等功能
聚合函数	支持将多条输入记录聚合成一条输出值，实现求和、求平均值、求最大值、求最小值、求平均值、参数聚合、字符串连接等功能
字符串函数	支持处理 STRING 类型的字符串，实现截取字符串、替换字符串、查找字符串、转换大小写、转换字符串格式等功能
复杂类型函数	支持处理 MAP、ARRAY、STRUCT 及 JSON 类型的数据，实现去重元素、聚合元素、元素排序、合并元素等功能
其他函数	除上述函数之外，提供支持其他业务场景的函数

4.3.1 【实战】日期函数

MaxCompute SQL 提供了常见的日期函数，用户可以根据实际需要选择合适的日期函数，完成日期计算、日期转换。MaxCompute SQL 提供的日期函数如表 4-11 所示。

表 4-11

函　数	功　能
DATEADD	按照指定的单位和幅度修改日期值
DATE_ADD	按照指定的幅度增减天数，与 DATE_SUB 函数的增减逻辑相反
DATE_FORMAT	将日期值转换为指定格式的字符串
DATE_SUB	按照指定的幅度增减天数，与 DATE_ADD 函数的增减逻辑相反
DATEDIFF	计算两个日期的差值并使用指定的单位表示
DATEPART	提取日期中符合指定时间单位的字段值
DATETRUNC	提取日期按照指定时间单位截取后的值
FROM_UNIXTIME	将数字型 UNIX 值转换为日期值
GETDATE	获取当前系统时间
ISDATE	判断一个日期字符串能否根据指定的格式串转换为一个日期值
LASTDAY	获取日期所在月的最后一天
TO_DATE	将指定格式的字符串转换为日期值
TO_CHAR	将日期按照指定格式转换为字符串
UNIX_TIMESTAMP	将日期转换为整型 UNIX 格式的日期值
WEEKDAY	返回日期值是当前周的第几天
WEEKOFYEAR	返回日期值是当年的第几周
ADD_MONTHS	计算日期值增加指定月数后的日期
CURRENT_TIMESTAMP	返回当前 TIMESTAMP 类型的时间戳
DAY	返回日期值的天
DAYOFMONTH	返回日期值的日
EXTRACT	获取日期 TIMESTAMP 中指定单位的部分
FROM_UTC_TIMESTAMP	将一个 UTC 时区的时间戳转换为一个指定时区的时间戳
HOUR	返回日期小时部分的值
LAST_DAY	返回日期值所在月份的最后一天日期
MINUTE	返回日期分钟部分的值
MONTH	返回日期值所属月份
MONTHS_BETWEEN	返回指定日期值间的月数
NEXT_DAY	返回大于日期值且与指定周相匹配的第一个日期
QUARTER	返回日期值所属季度
SECOND	返回日期秒数部分的值
TO_MILLIS	将指定日期转换为以毫秒为单位的 UNIX 时间戳
YEAR	返回日期值的年

下面通过具体的操作来演示如何使用 MaxCompute SQL 日期函数。

（1）在当前日期上加 1 天。

```
demo_maxcompute_001>select dateadd(current_timestamp(), 1, 'dd');
```

输出结果：2023-01-24 19:47:29.851。

（2）将当前时间按照指定格式转换为字符串。

```
demo_maxcompute_001>
>select date_format(current_timestamp(),'yyyy-mm-dd hh:mm:ss.SSS');
```

输出结果：2023-01-23 19:01:47.47S。

（3）在当前日期上减 1 天

```
demo_maxcompute_001>select date_sub(current_timestamp(), 1);
```

输出结果：2023-01-22。

（4）获取两个日期相差的天数。

```
demo_maxcompute_001>
>select datediff(datetime'2013-05-31 13:00:00',
>                datetime'2013-04-30 12:30:00', 'dd');
```

输出结果：31。

（5）提取日期中指定时间单位部分的值。

```
demo_maxcompute_001>
>select datepart(datetime'2013-06-08 01:10:00', 'yyyy');
```

输出结果：2013。

```
demo_maxcompute_001>
>select datepart(datetime'2013-06-08 01:10:00', 'mm');
```

输出结果：6。

```
demo_maxcompute_001>select datepart(date '2013-06-08', 'yyyy');
```

输出结果：2013。

（6）将日期按照指定的时间单位进行截取后的日期值。

```
demo_maxcompute_001>
>select datetrunc(datetime'2011-12-07 16:28:46', 'yyyy');
```

输出结果：2011-01-01 00:00:00。

```
demo_maxcompute_001>
>select datetrunc(datetime'2011-12-07 16:28:46', 'month');
```

输出结果：2011-12-01 00:00:00。

```
demo_maxcompute_001>
>select datetrunc(datetime'2011-12-07 16:28:46', 'DD');
```

输出结果：2011-12-07 00:00:00。

```
demo_maxcompute_001>select datetrunc(date '2011-12-07', 'yyyy');
```

输出结果：2011-01-01。

（7）将日期按照指定的格式转换为字符串。

```
demo_maxcompute_001>
>select to_char(current_timestamp(), 'Today is yyyy-mm*dd');
```

输出结果：Today is 2023-01*23。

（8）获取指定日期是当前周的第几天。

```
demo_maxcompute_001>select weekday (datetime '2009-03-20 11:11:00');
```

输出结果：4。

（9）获取当前日期是当年的第几周。

```
demo_maxcompute_001>select weekofyear(current_timestamp());
```

输出结果：4。

（10）在当前的日期上增加 3 个月后的日期。

```
demo_maxcompute_001>select add_months(current_timestamp(),3);
```

输出结果：2023-04-23。

4.3.2 【实战】窗口函数

用户可以在 MaxCompute SQL 中使用窗口函数对指定开窗列的数据灵活地进行分析、处理工作。MaxCompute SQL 支持的窗口函数如表 4-12 所示。

表 4-12

函　　数	功　　能
ROW_NUMBER	计算行号，从 1 开始递增
RANK	计算排名，排名可能不连续
DENSE_RANK	计算排名，排名是连续的
PERCENT_RANK	计算排名，输出百分比格式
CUME_DIST	计算累计分布
NTILE	将数据顺序切分成 N 等份，返回数据所在等份的编号（从 1 到 N）
LAG	取当前行往前（朝分区头部方向）第 N 行数据的值

续表

函　　数	功　　能
LEAD	取当前行往后（朝分区尾部方向）第 N 行数据的值
FIRST_VALUE	取当前行所对应窗口的第一条数据的值
LAST_VALUE	取当前行所对应窗口的最后一条数据的值
NTH_VALUE	取当前行所对应窗口的第 N 条数据的值
CLUSTER_SAMPLE	用户随机抽样，返回 True 表示该行数据被抽中
COUNT	计算窗口中的记录数
MIN	计算窗口中的最小值
MAX	计算窗口中的最大值
AVG	对窗口中的数据求平均值
SUM	对窗口中的数据求和
MEDIAN	计算窗口中的中位数
STDDEV	计算总体标准差，是 STDDEV_POP 的别名
STDDEV_SAMP	计算样本标准差

下面通过具体的操作来演示如何使用 MaxCompute SQL 窗口函数。

（1）查询员工数据。对各部门进行分组并显示第一行至当前行的工资汇总。

```
demo_maxcompute_001>select empno,ename, deptno,sal,
>    sum(sal) over(partition by deptno order by sal
>           rows between unbounded preceding and current row) max_sal
>from emp;
```

输出的结果如图 4-8 所示。

```
命令提示符 - bin\odpscmd                                    —   □   ×

+-------+--------+--------+------+---------+
| empno | ename  | deptno | sal  | max_sal |
+-------+--------+--------+------+---------+
| 7934  | MILLER | 10     | 1300 | 1300    |
| 7782  | CLARK  | 10     | 2450 | 3750    |
| 7839  | KING   | 10     | 5000 | 8750    |
| 7369  | SMITH  | 20     | 800  | 800     |
| 7876  | ADAMS  | 20     | 1100 | 1900    |
| 7566  | JONES  | 20     | 2975 | 4875    |
| 7788  | SCOTT  | 20     | 3000 | 7875    |
| 7902  | FORD   | 20     | 3000 | 10875   |
| 7900  | JAMES  | 30     | 950  | 950     |
| 7654  | MARTIN | 30     | 1250 | 2200    |
| 7521  | WARD   | 30     | 1250 | 3450    |
| 7844  | TURNER | 30     | 1500 | 4950    |
| 7499  | ALLEN  | 30     | 1600 | 6550    |
| 7698  | BLAKE  | 30     | 2850 | 9400    |
+-------+--------+--------+------+---------+
A total of 14 records fetched by instance tunnel. Max record number: 10000
demo_maxcompute_001>
```

图 4-8

> rows between unbounded preceding and current row 表示经过 over 分组后，每一组的第一行到当前行的数据记录。unbounded preceding 表示分组后的第一行；unbounded following 表示分组后的最后一行。current row 表示分组后的当前行。

（2）查询员工信息，并在部门内部按照工资升序排序。

```
demo_maxcompute_001>select empno,ename, deptno,sal,
>      row_number() over(partition by deptno order by sal) rownum
>from emp;
```

输出的结果如图 4-9 所示。

```
+-------+--------+--------+------+--------+
| empno | ename  | deptno | sal  | rownum |
+-------+--------+--------+------+--------+
| 7934  | MILLER | 10     | 1300 | 1      |
| 7782  | CLARK  | 10     | 2450 | 2      |
| 7839  | KING   | 10     | 5000 | 3      |
| 7369  | SMITH  | 20     | 800  | 1      |
| 7876  | ADAMS  | 20     | 1100 | 2      |
| 7566  | JONES  | 20     | 2975 | 3      |
| 7788  | SCOTT  | 20     | 3000 | 4      |
| 7902  | FORD   | 20     | 3000 | 5      |
| 7900  | JAMES  | 30     | 950  | 1      |
| 7654  | MARTIN | 30     | 1250 | 2      |
| 7521  | WARD   | 30     | 1250 | 3      |
| 7844  | TURNER | 30     | 1500 | 4      |
| 7499  | ALLEN  | 30     | 1600 | 5      |
| 7698  | BLAKE  | 30     | 2850 | 6      |
+-------+--------+--------+------+--------+
A total of 14 records fetched by instance tunnel. Max record number: 10000
demo_maxcompute_001>
```

图 4-9

> ROW_NUMBER 函数的用途非常广泛，在排序时最好使用它，它会为查询出来的每一行记录生成一个序号，依次排序且不会重复。

（3）将第 2 步中的 ROW_NUMBER 函数替换为 RANK 函数。

```
demo_maxcompute_001>select empno,ename, deptno,sal,
>      rank() over(partition by deptno order by sal) rownum
>from emp;
```

输出的结果如图 4-10 所示。

第 4 章　处理结构化数据——基于 MaxCompute SQL | 151

```
命令提示符 - bin\odpscmd                                    —  □  ×
+------+--------+-------+------+-------+
|empno |ename   |deptno |sal   |rownum |
+------+--------+-------+------+-------+
|7934  |MILLER  |10     |1300  |1      |
|7782  |CLARK   |10     |2450  |2      |
|7839  |KING    |10     |5000  |3      |
|7369  |SMITH   |20     |800   |1      |
|7876  |ADAMS   |20     |1100  |2      |
|7566  |JONES   |20     |2975  |3      |
|7788  |SCOTT   |20     |3000  |4      |
|7902  |FORD    |20     |3000  |4      |
|7900  |JAMES   |30     |950   |1      |
|7654  |MARTIN  |30     |1250  |2      |
|7521  |WARD    |30     |1250  |2      |
|7844  |TURNER  |30     |1500  |4      |
|7499  |ALLEN   |30     |1600  |5      |
|7698  |BLAKE   |30     |2850  |6      |
+------+--------+-------+------+-------+
A total of 14 records fetched by instance tunnel. Max record number: 10000
demo_maxcompute_001>
```

图 4-10

> 与 ROW_NUMBER 函数不同的是，RANK 函数考虑到了 over 子句中排序字段值相同的情况。如果使用 RANK 函数生成序号，则 over 子句中排序字段值相同的序号是一样的，后面字段值不相同的序号将跳过相同的排名号排下一个。

（4）将第 3 步中的 RANK 函数替换为 DENSE_RANK 函数。

```
demo_maxcompute_001>select empno,ename, deptno,sal,
>      dense_rank() over(partition by deptno order by sal) rownum
>from emp;
```

输出的结果如图 4-11 所示。

```
命令提示符 - bin\odpscmd                                    —  □  ×
+------+--------+-------+------+-------+
|empno |ename   |deptno |sal   |rownum |
+------+--------+-------+------+-------+
|7934  |MILLER  |10     |1300  |1      |
|7782  |CLARK   |10     |2450  |2      |
|7839  |KING    |10     |5000  |3      |
|7369  |SMITH   |20     |800   |1      |
|7876  |ADAMS   |20     |1100  |2      |
|7566  |JONES   |20     |2975  |3      |
|7788  |SCOTT   |20     |3000  |4      |
|7902  |FORD    |20     |3000  |4      |
|7900  |JAMES   |30     |950   |1      |
|7654  |MARTIN  |30     |1250  |2      |
|7521  |WARD    |30     |1250  |2      |
|7844  |TURNER  |30     |1500  |3      |
|7499  |ALLEN   |30     |1600  |4      |
|7698  |BLAKE   |30     |2850  |5      |
+------+--------+-------+------+-------+
A total of 14 records fetched by instance tunnel. Max record number: 10000
demo_maxcompute_001>
```

图 4-11

> DENSE_RANK 函数的功能与 RANK 函数类似，DENSE_RANK 函数在生成序号时是连续的，而 RANK 函数生成的序号有可能不连续。DENSE_RANK 函数在出现相同排名时，将不跳过相同排名号。

4.3.3 【实战】聚合函数

聚合函数的输入与输出是多对一的关系，即将多条输入记录聚合成一条输出值，可以与 MaxCompute SQL 中的 group by 语句配合使用。MaxCompute SQL 支持的部分聚合函数如表 4-13 所示。

表 4-13

函数	功能	函数	功能
AVG	计算平均值	MEDIAN	计算中位数
COUNT	计算记录数	STDDEV	计算总体标准差
COUNT_IF	计算指定表达式为 True 的记录数	STDDEV_SAMP	计算样本标准差
MAX	计算最大值	SUM	计算汇总值
MIN	计算最小值		

下面的查询语句将查询每个部门的最高工资、最低工资、平均工资和工资总和。

```
demo_maxcompute_001>
>select deptno 部门号,max(sal) 最高工资,
>       min(sal) 最低工资,avg(sal) 平均工资,sum(sal) 工资总和
>from emp group by deptno;
```

输出的结果如下。

```
+--------+----------+----------+--------------------+------------+
| 部门号 | 最高工资 | 最低工资 | 平均工资           | 工资总和   |
+--------+----------+----------+--------------------+------------+
| 10     | 5000     | 1300     | 2916.6666666666665 | 8750       |
| 20     | 3000     | 800      | 2175.0             | 10875      |
| 30     | 2850     | 950      | 1566.6666666666667 | 9400       |
+--------+----------+----------+--------------------+------------+
A total of 3 records fetched by instance tunnel. Max record number: 10000
```

4.3.4 【实战】条件判断函数

MaxCompute SQL 提供了 DECODE 函数实现 if-then-else 分支选择的功能。该函数的语法格式如下。

```
decode(<expression>, <search>, <result>[, <search>, <result>]...[, <default>])
```

(1) expression：必填项。要比较的表达式。

(2) search：必填项。与 expression 进行比较的搜索项。

(3) result：必填项。当 search 和 expression 的值匹配时的返回值。

(4) default：可选项。如果所有的搜索项都不匹配，则返回 default 值，如果未指定，则返回 NULL。

下面通过具体的操作来演示如何使用 DECODE 函数。

(1) 制作工资报表，按照员工职位给员工涨工资。如果员工职位是总裁，则涨 1000 元；如果员工职位是经理，则涨 800 元；否则涨 400 元。

```
demo_maxcompute_001>
>select ename 姓名,job 职位,sal 涨前工资,
>decode(job,'PRESIDENT',1000,
>        'MANAGER',800,
>        400) 涨后工资
>from emp;
```

输出的结果如下。

```
+----------+-----------+----------+----------+
| 姓名     | 职位      | 涨前工资 | 涨后工资 |
+----------+-----------+----------+----------+
| SMITH    | CLERK     | 800      | 400      |
| ALLEN    | SALESMAN  | 1600     | 400      |
| WARD     | SALESMAN  | 1250     | 400      |
| JONES    | MANAGER   | 2975     | 800      |
| MARTIN   | SALESMAN  | 1250     | 400      |
| BLAKE    | MANAGER   | 2850     | 800      |
| CLARK    | MANAGER   | 2450     | 800      |
| SCOTT    | ANALYST   | 3000     | 400      |
| KING     | PRESIDENT | 5000     | 1000     |
| TURNER   | SALESMAN  | 1500     | 400      |
| ADAMS    | CLERK     | 1100     | 400      |
| JAMES    | CLERK     | 950      | 400      |
| FORD     | ANALYST   | 3000     | 400      |
| MILLER   | CLERK     | 1300     | 400      |
+----------+-----------+----------+----------+
A total of 14 records fetched by instance tunnel. Max record number: 10000
```

(2) 上面的语句也可以写成下面的形式。

```
demo_maxcompute_001>select ename 姓名,job 职位,sal 涨前工资,
    >case job when 'PRESIDENT' then sal+1000
```

```
>             when 'MANAGER' then sal+800
>             else sal+400
>end 涨后工资
>from emp;
```

> 第 1 步和第 2 步的主要区别在于，DECODE 是一个函数，而 case 是一个表达式。

4.3.5 数学函数和字符串函数

MaxCompute SQL 提供了常见的数学函数，在开发过程中，用户可以根据实际需要选择合适的数学函数进行数据计算、数据转换等操作。MaxCompute SQL 支持的部分数学函数如表 4-14 所示。

表 4-14

函　数	功　能	函　数	功　能
ABS	计算绝对值	CONV	计算进制转换值
ACOS	计算反余弦值	COS	计算余弦值
ASIN	计算反正弦值	COSH	计算双曲余弦值
ATAN	计算反正切值	COT	计算余切值
CEIL	计算向上取整值	EXP	计算指数值

MaxCompute SQL 也提供了字符串函数对指定字符串进行灵活处理。MaxCompute SQL 支持的部分字符串函数如表 4-15 所示。

表 4-15

函　数	功　能
ASCII	返回字符串第一个字符的 ASCII 码
CHAR_MATCHCOUNT	计算 A 字符串出现在 B 字符串中的字符个数
CHR	将指定 ASCII 码转换为字符
CONCAT	将字符串连接在一起
CONCAT_WS	将参数中的所有字符串按照指定的分隔符连接在一起
ENCODE	将字符串按照指定的编码格式编码
FIND_IN_SET	在以逗号分隔的字符串中查找指定字符串的位置
FORMAT_NUMBER	将数字转换为指定格式的字符串
FROM_JSON	根据给定的 JSON 字符串和输出格式信息，返回 ARRAY、MAP 或 STRUCT 类型
GET_JSON_OBJECT	在一个标准 JSON 字符串中，按照指定方式抽取指定的字符串

4.4 在 MaxCompute 中自定义 SQL

MaxCompute 允许用户使用自定义 SQL 来满足一些特殊场景的需要。MaxCompute 中自定义 SQL 有 3 种不同的类型：UDF（User Defined Function，用户自定义函数）、UDT（User Defined Type，用户自定义类型）和 UDJ（User Defined Join，用户自定义连接）。下面重点介绍 UDF 的使用。

4.4.1 【实战】UDF

MaxCompute 产品提供多种类型的内建函数来满足用户的业务需求，当内建函数无法支撑业务实现时，用户可以自行编写代码逻辑来创建自定义函数，以满足多样化需求。

用户在开发 UDF 时，需要将下面的依赖加入 Java 开发工程。

```
<dependency>
    <groupId>com.aliyun.odps</groupId>
    <artifactId>odps-sdk-udf</artifactId>
    <version>0.29.10-public</version>
</dependency>
```

下面通过开发两个具体的 UDF 来演示开发部署的流程。

（1）开发 UDF，完成两个字符串的拼接。

```
package demo.udf;
import com.aliyun.odps.udf.UDF;
public class MyConcatString extends UDF {
    public String evaluate(String a,String b){
        return a+"****"+b;
    }
}
```

（2）开发 UDF，根据员工的工资判断级别。

```
package demo.udf;
import com.aliyun.odps.udf.UDF;
public class CheckSalaryGrade extends UDF {
    public String evaluate(String salary){
        double sal = Double.parseDouble(salary);
        if(sal <= 1000) {
            return "Grade A";
        }else if(sal > 1000 && sal <= 3000) {
            return "Grade B";
        }else {
```

```
            return "Grade C";
        }
    }
}
```

(3）将 Java 代码打包成 udf.jar。

(4）将 udf.jar 上传到 MaxCompute 的项目空间中。

```
demo_maxcompute_001>create resource jar d:\download\udf.jar -f;
```

(5）查看项目空间中的资源。

```
demo_maxcompute_001>list resources;
```

输出的信息如下。

```
Resource Name           Owner                  ... Type ...
mydemo_odps_wc.jar      ALIYUN$collenzhao      ... jar  ...
udf.jar                 ALIYUN$collenzhao      ... jar  ...
2 resources
```

(6）创建自定义函数。

```
demo_maxcompute_001>
>create function myconcat as demo.udf.MyConcatString using udf.jar;
demo_maxcompute_001>
>create function checkgrade as demo.udf.CheckSalaryGrade using udf.jar;
```

(7）在查询中使用自定义函数 myconcat()。

```
demo_maxcompute_001>select myconcat(ename,job) from emp;
```

输出的信息如下。

```
+--------------------+
| _c0                |
+--------------------+
| SMITH****CLERK     |
| ALLEN****SALESMAN  |
| WARD****SALESMAN   |
| JONES****MANAGER   |
| MARTIN****SALESMAN |
| BLAKE****MANAGER   |
| CLARK****MANAGER   |
| SCOTT****ANALYST   |
| KING****PRESIDENT  |
| TURNER****SALESMAN |
| ADAMS****CLERK     |
| JAMES****CLERK     |
```

```
| FORD****ANALYST    |
| MILLER****CLERK    |
+--------------------+
A total of 14 records fetched by instance tunnel. Max record number: 10000
```

（8）在查询中使用自定义函数 checkgrade()。

`demo_maxcompute_001>select empno,ename,sal,checkgrade(sal) from emp;`

输出的信息如下。

```
+--------+-------+------+---------+
| empno  | ename | sal  | _c3     |
+--------+-------+------+---------+
| 7369   | SMITH | 800  | Grade A |
| 7499   | ALLEN | 1600 | Grade B |
| 7521   | WARD  | 1250 | Grade B |
| 7566   | JONES | 2975 | Grade B |
| 7654   | MARTIN| 1250 | Grade B |
| 7698   | BLAKE | 2850 | Grade B |
| 7782   | CLARK | 2450 | Grade B |
| 7788   | SCOTT | 3000 | Grade B |
| 7839   | KING  | 5000 | Grade C |
| 7844   | TURNER| 1500 | Grade B |
| 7876   | ADAMS | 1100 | Grade B |
| 7900   | JAMES | 950  | Grade A |
| 7902   | FORD  | 3000 | Grade B |
| 7934   | MILLER| 1300 | Grade B |
+--------+-------+------+---------+
A total of 14 records fetched by instance tunnel. Max record number: 10000
```

4.4.2 【实战】UDT

MaxCompute 基于新一代的 SQL 引擎推出新功能 UDT。MaxCompute 的 UDT 功能允许用户在 SQL 中直接调用第三方语言的类，使用其方法或直接使用第三方对象，以获取其数据内容。

下面通过一个简单的示例来演示如何在 MaxCompute SQL 中调用 Java 语言。

（1）打开数据类型支持开关。

`demo_maxcompute_001>set odps.sql.type.system.odps2=true;`

（2）在 MaxCompute SQL 调用 Java 的数据类型。

`demo_maxcompute_001>select java.lang.Integer.MAX_VALUE;`

输出的结果如下。

```
+-------------+
| max_value   |
+-------------+
| 2147483647  |
+-------------+
```

（3）和 Java 语言一样，java.lang 包可以省略，所以上述示例可以简写为如下语句。

```
demo_maxcompute_001>select Integer.MAX_VALUE;
```

> 💡 UDT 除了支持直接调用第三方语言，还支持一些复杂的操作，如操作 Java 数组和 JSON 数据、聚合操作、使用表值函数、函数重载等。

4.4.3　UDJ

MaxCompute 内置了多种 Join 操作，包括 Inner/Right Join、Outer/Left Join、Outer/Full Join、Outer/semi/Anti-semi Join 等。这些内置的 Join 操作功能强大，但由于其标准的 Join 实现，无法满足很多跨表操作的需求场景。

而 UDF 框架主要针对在单个数据表上的操作而设计，在多表操作的场景中，MaxCompute SQL 通过支持开发 MapReduce 任务来实现跨表操作，但这无疑提高了 MaxCompute SQL 的使用门槛。

> 💡 关于 MaxCompute MapReduce 任务开发的内容，将在第 5 章中介绍。

基于 MaxCompute 2.0 计算引擎，MaxCompute 在 UDF 框架中引入了新的扩展机制 UDJ，以实现灵活的跨表、多表自定义操作，同时减少通过 MapReduce 等方式对分布式系统底层细节的操作。

第 5 章

处理离线数据——基于 MaxCompute MapReduce

Google 为了解决 PageRank 的计算问题，提出了 MapReduce 计算模型，这是一种分布式计算的模型。简单来说就是，使用一台服务器不能完成计算，就搭建一个集群，使用多台服务器一起执行计算，其核心思想就是先拆分再合并。MaxCompute MapReduce 兼容原生的 MapReduce 接口，并提供更加强大的功能与特性。

> MapReduce 是一种离线数据处理模型，或者说是一种批处理引擎，它不适合进行实时的流式计算。

5.1 MaxCompute MapReduce 简介

MaxCompute 提供两个版本的 MapReduce 编程接口。

（1）MaxCompute MapReduce：MaxCompute 的原生接口，执行速度快、开发快捷、不暴露文件系统。

（2）MaxCompute 扩展 MapReduce（MR2）：对 MaxCompute MapReduce 的扩展，支持更复杂的作业调度逻辑。MapReduce 的实现方式与 MaxCompute 原生接口一致。

5.1.1 MaxCompute MapReduce 的处理流程

MapReduce 处理数据过程主要分成 Map 和 Reduce 两个阶段。先执行 Map 阶段，再执行 Reduce 阶段。Map 阶段和 Reduce 阶段的处理逻辑由用户自定义实现，但要符合 MapReduce

框架的约定。

MapReduce 处理数据的完整流程分为以下几个步骤。

（1）输入数据。对文本进行分片，所谓分片，就是将输入数据切分为大小相等的数据块，每一块作为单个 Mapper 的输入被处理，分片完成后，多个 Mapper 就可以同时工作。

（2）Map 阶段。每个 Mapper 在读入各自的数据后，进行计算处理，最终输出给 Reduce 阶段。Mapper 在输出数据时，需要为每一条输出数据指定一个 Key，这个 Key 值决定了这条数据将会被发送给哪一个 Reducer。Key 值和 Reducer 是多对一的关系，Key 值相同的数据会被发送给同一个 Reducer，单个 Reducer 有可能会接收多个 Key 值的数据。

（3）Reduce 预处理阶段。在进入 Reduce 阶段之前，MapReduce 框架会对数据按照 Key 值排序，使具有相同 Key 值的数据相邻。如果指定了合并操作（Combiner），框架会调用 Combiner，将具有相同 Key 值的数据进行聚合。Combiner 的逻辑可以由用户自定义实现。与经典的 MapReduce 框架协议不同，在 MaxCompute 中，Combiner 的输入、输出的参数必须与 Reduce 保持一致，这部分的处理通常也叫作洗牌（Shuffle）。

（4）Reduce 阶段。进入 Reduce 阶段，Key 值相同的数据会被发送到同一个 Reducer。同一个 Reducer 会接收来自多个 Mapper 的数据。每个 Reducer 会对 Key 值相同的多个数据进行 Reduce 操作。最后，具有相同 Key 值的多条数据在 Reduce 操作后，将变成一个值。

（5）输出结果数据。

> 在 5.2 节中将结合 WordCount 单词计数来详细分析数据处理的这 5 个步骤。

5.1.2　MaxCompute MapReduce 的使用限制

MaxCompute MapReduce 在使用时有一些限制。这些限制主要体现 MaxCompute MapReduce 的使用限制项和输入与输出两个不同的方面。

1. MaxCompute MapReduce 的使用限制项

MapReduce 使用限制项的说明如表 5-1 所示，不遵循使用限制可能导致业务受到影响。

表 5-1

边 界 名	边 界 值	默 认 值	是否可配置
Instance 内存占用	[256MB,12GB]	2048MB + 1024MB	是
Resource 数量	256 个	无	否

续表

边 界 名	边 界 值	默 认 值	是否可配置
输入路数和输出路数	1024 个和 256 个	无	否
Counter 数量	64 个	无	否
Map Instance	[1,100000]	无	是
Reduce Instance	[0,2000]	无	是
重试次数	3	无	否
Local Debug 模式	Instance 个数不超过 100	无	否
重复读取 Resource 次数	64 次	无	否
Resource 字节数	2GB	无	否
Split Size	大于等于 1	256MB	是
STRING 列内容长度	8MB	无	否
Worker 运行超时时间	[1,3600]	600	否
MapReduce 引用 Table 资源支持的字段类型	BIGINT、DOUBLE、STRING、DATETIME、BOOLEAN	无	否

MapReduce 不支持 MaxCompute 2.0 新类型，也不支持读取 OSS 数据。

2. MaxCompute MapReduce 的输入与输出

下面列举了在开发 MapReduce 任务程序时，MaxCompute 对输入与输出的限制规定。

（1）MaxCompute MapReduce 的输入与输出支持 MaxCompute 内置类型的 Bigint、Double、String、Datetime 和 Boolean 类型，不支持用户自定义数据类型。

（2）接受多表输入，且输入表的 Schema 可以不同。在 Map 函数中，用户可以获取当前 Record 对应的 Table 信息。

（3）输入可以为空，不支持将视图作为输入。

（4）Reduce 接受多路输出，可以输出到不同表或同一张表的不同分区中。不同输出的 Schema 可以不同。不同输出间通过 label 进行区分，默认输出不必加 label，但目前不接受没有输出的情况。

5.2 开发 WordCount 单词计数程序

本节将从 WordCount 程序出发，详细介绍 MaxCompute MapReduce 的编程知识。

5.2.1　WordCount 数据处理的流程

在 3.4.2 小节中已经演示了 WordCount 单词计数的示例程序。在开发自己的 WordCount 程序之前，有必要先对 MapReduce 数据处理的流程进行分析。了解了数据的处理流程，开发 MapReduce 程序就会非常简单。WordCount 程序进行数据处理的流程如图 5-1 所示。

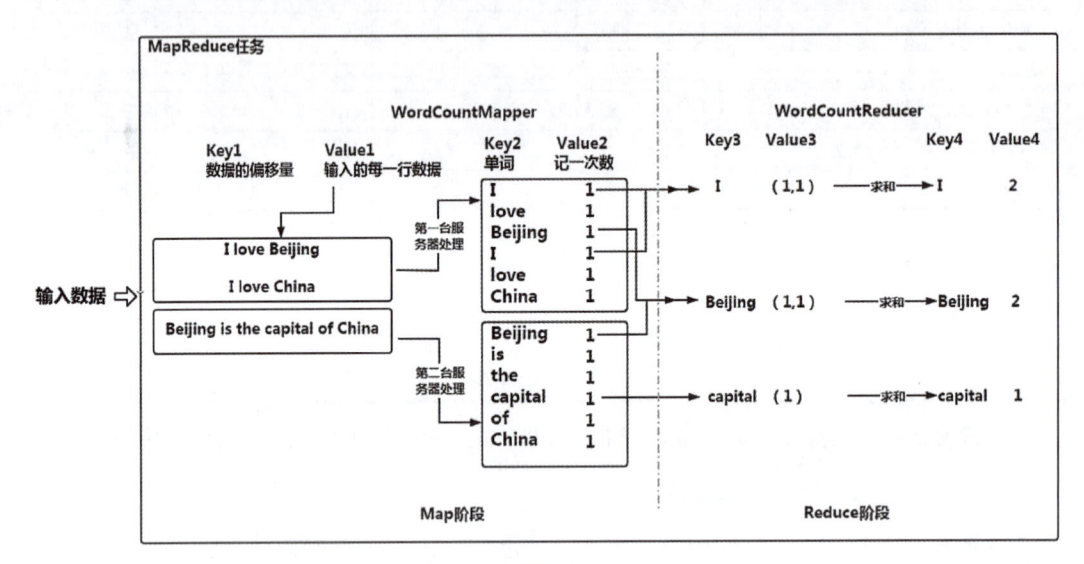

图 5-1

整个 MapReduce 任务被分为了 Map 阶段和 Reduce 阶段。Map 阶段相当于一个循环，通过 Mapper 对每一行数据进行处理；Reducer 阶段是一个聚合操作，用于统计相同单词出现的频率。详细的处理流程如下。

（1）首先通过 Mapper 读取 MaxCompute 项目空间表中的每一行数据。

（2）Mapper 的输入是一个<Key,Value>键值对，这里是<Key1,Value1>。Key1 表示的数据在该文件中的偏移量，Value1 表示读入的每一行文本数据。

> 一般在处理数据时并不关心 Key1 的偏移量，更关心如何处理 Value1 的数据。

（3）由于需要处理的数据量通常比较庞大，Mapper 需要将数据拆分到不同的节点进行处理，如图 5-1 所示。假设通过 Mapper 的拆分，把前两句话拆分给第一台服务器处理，而第三句话拆分给第二台服务器处理。

（4）在每台服务器上需要完成对数据的处理。这里的处理方式就是"分词操作"。通过分词得到了这句话中的每个单词，并且每个单词计一次数。从而得到 Mapper 的输出。

（5）Mapper 的输出也是<Key,Value>键值对，这里是<Key2,Value2>。

（6）接着，将<Key2,Value2>输出到 Reduce 阶段。

> 这里已经由 MapReduce 框架实现了处理的逻辑，即相同的 Key2，它的 Value2 会被同一个 Reducer 处理。其本质就是按照 Key2 进行了分组，从而得到了 Reducer 的输入。

（7）Reducer 的输入也是<Key,Value>键值对，这里是<Key3,Value3>。Key3 其实就是 Key2；而 Value3 是一个集合，该集合中的每一个元素就是 Value2。

（8）Reducer 的处理逻辑就是对 Value3 求和，从而得到每个单词出现的频率，并且把单词和单词出现的频率作为 Reducer 的输出。

（9）Reducer 的输出也是<Key,Value>键值对，这里是<Key4,Value4>。

（10）最终，将 Reducer 的输出保存到目的地，例如输出到 MaxCompute 的目的地表中。

5.2.2 MaxCompute MapReduce 的编程接口

在开发具体的代码程序之前，需要对 MaxCompute 提供的 MapReduce 编程接口有一定了解，这有助于开发应用程序。这些编程接口主要包括 MapperBase、ReducerBase、TaskContext、JobClient、JobConf、RunningJob、InputUtis 和 OutputUtils，如表 5-2 所示。

表 5-2

主要接口	描述
MapperBase	用户自定义的 Map 函数需要继承此类。将输入表的记录对象加工处理成键值对集合并输出到 Reduce 阶段，或者不经过 Reduce 阶段直接将结果记录输出到结果表中。不经过 Reduce 阶段而直接输出计算结果的作业，也可以称为 MapOnly 作业
ReducerBase	用户自定义的 Reduce 函数需要继承此类。对与一个键（Key）关联的一组数值集（Values）进行归约计算
TaskContext	MapperBase 及 ReducerBase 多个成员函数的输入参数之一，含有任务运行的上下文信息
JobClient	用于提交和管理作业，提交方式包括阻塞（同步）方式及非阻塞（异步）方式
JobConf	描述一个 MapReduce 任务的配置，通常在主程序（Main 函数）中定义 JobConf 对象，然后通过 JobClient 将作业提交给 MaxCompute 服务
RunningJob	作业运行时对象，用于跟踪运行中的 MapReduce 作业实例
InputUtils	数据输入工具类
OutputUtils	数据输出工具类

MapperBase 接口的主要函数接口如表 5-3 所示。

表 5-3

主要函数接口	描述
void cleanup(TaskContext context)	在 Map 阶段结束时调用
void map(long key, Record record, TaskContext context)	Map 阶段处理数据的方法
void setup(TaskContext context)	在 Map 阶段开始时调用

ReducerBase 接口的主要函数接口如表 5-4 所示。

表 5-4

主要函数接口	描述
void cleanup(TaskContext context)	在 Reduce 阶段结束时调用
void reduce (Record key,Iterator<Record > values, TaskContext context)	Reduce 阶段处理数据的方法
void setup(TaskContext context)	在 Reduce 阶段开始时调用

TaskContext 接口的主要函数接口如表 5-5 所示。

表 5-5

主要函数接口	描述
TableInfo[] getOutputTableInfo()	获取输出的表信息
Record createOutputRecord()	创建默认输出表的记录对象
Record createOutputRecord(String label)	创建给定 label 输出表的记录对象
Record createMapOutputKeyRecord()	创建 Map 输出 Key 的记录对象
Record createMapOutputValueRecord()	创建 Map 输出 Value 的记录对象
void write(Record record)	写记录到默认输出，用于 Reduce 端写出数据，可在 Reduce 端多次调用
void write(Record record, String label)	写记录到给定标签输出，用于 Reduce 端写出数据，可在 Reduce 端多次调用
void write(Record key, Record value)	写记录到中间结果，用于 Map 端写出数据，可在 Map 端多次调用
BufferedInputStream readResourceFileAsStream (String resourceName)	读取文件类型资源
Iterator<Record > readResourceTable (String resourceName)	读取表类型资源
Counter getCounter(Enum<? > name)	获取给定名称的 Counter 对象
Counter getCounter(String group, String name)	获取给定组名和名称的 Counter 对象
void progress()	向 MapReduce 框架报告心跳信息。如果用户方法处理时间很长，可调用这个方法避免 Task 超时，框架默认 600s 超时

JobClient 接口的主要函数接口如表 5-6 所示。

表 5-6

主要函数接口	描 述
static RunningJob runJob(JobConf job)	阻塞（同步）方式提交 MapReduce 作业后立即返回
static RunningJob submitJob(JobConf job)	非阻塞（异步）方式提交 MapReduce 作业后立即返回

JobConf 接口的主要函数接口如表 5-7 所示。

表 5-7

主要函数接口	描 述
void setResources(String resourceNames)	声明作业使用的资源。只有声明的资源才能在运行 Mapper/Reducer 时通过 TaskContext 对象读取
void setMapOutputKeySchema(Column[] schema)	设置 Mapper 输出到 Reducer 的 Key 属性
void setMapOutputValueSchema(Column[] schema)	设置 Mapper 输出到 Reducer 的 Value 属性
void setOutputKeySortColumns(String[] cols)	设置 Mapper 输出到 Reducer 的 Key 排序列
void setOutputGroupingColumns(String[] cols)	设置 Key 分组列
void setMapperClass(Class<? extends Mapper > > > theClass)	设置作业的 Mapper 函数
void setPartitionColumns(String[] cols)	设置作业指定的分区列，默认是 Mapper 输出 Key 的所有列
void setReducerClass(Class<? extends Reducer > theClass)	设置作业的 Reducer
void setCombinerClass(Class<? extends Reducer > theClass)	设置作业的 Combiner
void setSplitSize(long size)	设置输入分片大小，单位为 MB，默认值为 256MB
void setNumReduceTasks(int n)	设置 Reducer 任务数，默认为 Mapper 任务数的 1/4
void setMemoryForMapTask(int mem)	设置 Mapper 任务中单个 Worker 的内存大小，单位为 MB，默认值为 2048MB
void setMemoryForReduceTask(int mem)	设置 Reducer 任务中单个 Worker 的内存大小，单位为 MB，默认值为 2048MB
void setOutputSchema(Column[] schema, String label)	设置指定 label 的输出属性。多路输出时，每一路输出对应一个 label

RunningJob 接口的主要函数接口如表 5-8 所示。

表 5-8

主要函数接口	描 述
String getInstanceID()	获取作业运行实例的 ID，用于查看运行日志和作业管理
boolean isComplete()	查询作业是否结束
boolean isSuccessful()	查询作业实例是否运行成功
void waitForCompletion()	等待直至作业实例结束。通常用于以异步方式提交的作业
JobStatus getJobStatus()	查询作业实例的运行状态
void killJob()	结束此作业
Counters getCounters()	获取 Counters 计数器的信息

InputUtils 接口的主要函数接口如表 5-9 所示。

表 5-9

主要函数接口	描 述
static void addTable (TableInfo table, JobConf conf)	将表 Table 添加到任务输入，可以被调用多次，新加入的表以 Append 方式添加到输入队列中
static void setTables (TableInfo [] tables, JobConf conf)	将多张表添加到任务输入中

OutputUtils 接口的主要函数接口如表 5-10 所示。

表 5-10

主要函数接口	描 述
static void addTable (TableInfo table, JobConf conf)	将表 table 添加到任务输出，可以被调用多次，新加入的表以 Append 方式添加到输出队列中
static void setTables (TableInfo [] tables, JobConf conf)	将多张表添加到任务输出中

5.2.3 【实战】开发 WordCount 程序

在了解了 MaxCompute MapReduce 的编程接口后，下面将基于 MaxCompute MapReduce 提供的编程接口开发 WordCount 程序。

（1）创建 Java Maven 工程，并在 pom.xml 文件中添加下面的依赖。

```xml
<dependency>
    <groupId>com.aliyun.odps</groupId>
    <artifactId>odps-sdk-mapred</artifactId>
    <version>0.36.4-public</version>
</dependency>
```

第 5 章　处理离线数据——基于 MaxCompute MapReduce | 167

```xml
<dependency>
    <groupId>com.aliyun.odps</groupId>
    <artifactId>odps-sdk-commons</artifactId>
    <version>0.36.4-public</version>
</dependency>
<dependency>
    <groupId>com.aliyun.odps</groupId>
    <artifactId>odps-sdk-core</artifactId>
    <version>0.36.4-public</version>
</dependency>
```

> JDK 需要保证为 JDK 1.8 或以上版本。

（2）开发 WordCountMappe.java 程序。

```java
package demo.wc;

import java.io.IOException;
import com.aliyun.odps.data.Record;
import com.aliyun.odps.mapred.MapperBase;

public class WordCountMapper extends MapperBase {
    private Record word;
    private Record one;
    @Override
        public void setup(TaskContext context) throws IOException {
        word = context.createMapOutputKeyRecord();
        one = context.createMapOutputValueRecord();
        one.set(new Object[] {1L});
    }

    @Override
    public void map(long key, Record record, TaskContext context)
        throws IOException {
        for(int i=0;i<record.getColumnCount();i++) {
            //得到每一列的数据
            String data = record.get(i).toString();
            //执行分词，得到这一句话中的每个单词
            String[] words = data.split(" ");
            //输出<key2, value2>，即每一个单词计一次数
            for(String w:words) {
```

```
            word.set(new Object[] { w});
            context.write(word,one);
        }
      }
   }
}
```

（3）开发 WordCountReducer.java 程序。

```
package demo.wc;

import java.io.IOException;
import java.util.Iterator;
import com.aliyun.odps.data.Record;
import com.aliyun.odps.mapred.ReducerBase;

public class WordCountReducer extends ReducerBase {

    private Record result = null;

    @Override
    public void setup(TaskContext context) throws IOException {
        result = context.createOutputRecord();
    }

    @Override
    public void reduce(Record key3, Iterator<Record> values3,
                       TaskContext context) throws IOException {
        long count = 0;
     //将 values3 中的元素求和
        while (values3.hasNext()) {
            Record val = values3.next();
            count += (Long) val.get(0);
        }
     //输出 key4 和 value4
        result.set(0, key3.get(0));
        result.set(1, count);
        context.write(result);
    }
}
```

（4）开发 WordCountMain.java 程序。

```
package demo.wc;
```

```java
import com.aliyun.odps.OdpsException;
import com.aliyun.odps.data.TableInfo;
import com.aliyun.odps.mapred.JobClient;
import com.aliyun.odps.mapred.conf.JobConf;
import com.aliyun.odps.mapred.utils.InputUtils;
import com.aliyun.odps.mapred.utils.OutputUtils;
import com.aliyun.odps.mapred.utils.SchemaUtils;

public class WordCountMain {
    public static void main(String[] args) throws OdpsException {
        JobConf job = new JobConf();
        //设置任务的 Mapper 和 Reducer
        job.setMapperClass(WordCountMapper.class);
        job.setReducerClass(WordCountReducer.class);

        //设置 Mapper 中间结果的 key 和 value 的 Schema
        //Mapper 中间结果的输出也是 Record 的形式
        job.setMapOutputKeySchema
                (SchemaUtils.fromString("word:string"));
        job.setMapOutputValueSchema
                (SchemaUtils.fromString("count:bigint"));

        //设置输入和输出的表信息
        InputUtils.addTable(TableInfo.builder()
                            .tableName(args[0]).build(), job);
        OutputUtils.addTable(TableInfo.builder()
                            .tableName(args[1]).build(), job);
        //执行任务
        JobClient.runJob(job);
    }
}
```

（5）将 Java 程序打包生成 JAR 文件，并按照 3.4.2 节的步骤将其提交到 MaxCompute 项目空间中运行。

5.3　MaxCompute MapReduce 的高级特性

MaxCompute MapReduce 除了提供最基本的 Map 和 Reduce 处理能力，还提供了很多高级功能和特性，以帮助用户处理一些复杂情况下的数据。本节将通过具体的编程案例来介绍并演示这些高级功能和特性。

5.3.1 【实战】实现数据排序

MaxCompute MapReduce 会根据 Key2 对处理的数据进行排序。这里的 Key2 就是 Map 输出的 Key。

下面的示例将对员工表 emp 中的数据按照员工的工资进行排序，并输出员工的工资和员工的姓名。这里的员工表 emp 在 3.4.1 节中已经创建。

（1）创建输出结果表，用于保存员工的工资和员工的姓名。

```
demo_maxcompute_001>create table sort_emp(sal bigint,ename string);
```

（2）开发 SortMapper.java 程序。

```java
package demo.sort;

import java.io.IOException;
import com.aliyun.odps.data.Record;
import com.aliyun.odps.mapred.MapperBase;

public class SortMapper extends MapperBase {
    private Record key;
    private Record value;

    @Override
    public void setup(TaskContext context) throws IOException {
        key = context.createMapOutputKeyRecord();
        value = context.createMapOutputValueRecord();
    }

    @Override
    public void map(long recordNum, Record record, TaskContext context)
        throws IOException {
        //将员工的工资设置为 Mapper 输出的 Key
        key.set(new Object[] { (Long) record.get(5) });
        //将员工的姓名设置为 Mapper 输出的 Value
        value.set(new Object[] { (String) record.get(1) });
        context.write(key, value);
    }
}
```

> 按照 MaxCompute MapReduce 对数据排序的要求，SortMapper.java 程序中将员工的工资设置为 Mapper 输出的 Key，即 Key2。

(3)开发 SortReducer.java 程序。

```java
package demo.sort;

import java.io.IOException;
import java.util.Iterator;
import com.aliyun.odps.data.Record;
import com.aliyun.odps.mapred.ReducerBase;

public class SortReducer extends ReducerBase {
    private Record result = null;

    @Override
    public void setup(TaskContext context) throws IOException {
        result = context.createOutputRecord();
    }

    //将所有的 Key 和 Value 直接输出
    @Override
    public void reduce(Record key, Iterator<Record> values,
                       TaskContext context) throws IOException {
        result.set(0, key.get(0));
        while (values.hasNext()) {
            Record val = values.next();
            result.set(1, val.get(0));
            context.write(result);
        }
    }
}
```

> SortReducer.java 程序中没有任何处理逻辑，直接将 SortMapper.java 输入的数据输出。

(4)开发 SortMain.java 主程序。

```java
package demo.sort;

import com.aliyun.odps.data.TableInfo;
import com.aliyun.odps.mapred.JobClient;
import com.aliyun.odps.mapred.conf.JobConf;
import com.aliyun.odps.mapred.utils.InputUtils;
import com.aliyun.odps.mapred.utils.OutputUtils;
import com.aliyun.odps.mapred.utils.SchemaUtils;
```

```java
import java.util.Date;

public class SortMain {
    public static void main(String[] args) throws Exception {
        JobConf jobConf = new JobConf();
        jobConf.setMapperClass(SortMapper.class);
        jobConf.setReducerClass(SortReducer.class);

        //为了全局有序,这里将Reducer的个数设置为1
        //此时所有的数据都会集中到一个Reducer中处理
        jobConf.setNumReduceTasks(1);

        jobConf.setMapOutputKeySchema(
                    SchemaUtils.fromString("key:bigint"));
        jobConf.setMapOutputValueSchema(
                    SchemaUtils.fromString("value:string"));
        InputUtils.addTable(TableInfo.builder()
                        .tableName(args[0]).build(), jobConf);
        OutputUtils.addTable(TableInfo.builder()
                        .tableName(args[1]).build(), jobConf);

        Date startTime = new Date();
        System.out.println("Job started: " + startTime);
        JobClient.runJob(jobConf);
        Date end_time = new Date();
        System.out.println("Job ended: " + end_time);
        System.out.println("The job took " +
                (end_time.getTime() - startTime.getTime()) / 1000
                + " seconds.");
    }
}
```

(5)将 MapReduce 程序打包成 sort.jar 文件。

(6)使用 MaxCompute 命令行工具将 sort.jar 文件上传到项目空间中。

```
demo_maxcompute_001>add jar d:\download\sort.jar -f;
```

(7)执行 MapReduce 任务,对数据进行排序。

```
demo_maxcompute_001>jar -resources sort.jar -classpath
>d:\download\sort.jar demo.sort.SortMain emp sort_emp;
```

输出的信息如下。

```
Running job in console.
Job started: Tue Jan 24 13:30:59 CST 2023
```

```
......
Job ended: Tue Jan 24 13:32:13 CST 2023
The job took 73 seconds.
```

（8）执行查询，验证数据排序的结果。

```
demo_maxcompute_001>select * from sort_emp;
```

输出的结果如下。

```
+----------+----------+
| sal      | ename    |
+----------+----------+
| 800      | SMITH    |
| 950      | JAMES    |
| 1100     | ADAMS    |
| 1250     | WARD     |
| 1250     | MARTIN   |
| 1300     | MILLER   |
| 1500     | TURNER   |
| 1600     | ALLEN    |
| 2450     | CLARK    |
| 2850     | BLAKE    |
| 2975     | JONES    |
| 3000     | SCOTT    |
| 3000     | FORD     |
| 5000     | KING     |
+----------+----------+
```

5.3.2 【实战】实现数据二次排序

在对数据进行排序操作时，有时需要按照多个列进行排序，即数据的二次排序。例如，下面的查询语句在查询员工信息时，先按照了部门号进行排序。如果部门号相同，再按照工资排序。

```
demo_maxcompute_001>select deptno,sal,ename from emp
>order by deptno,sal;
```

输出的结果如下。

```
+----------+----------+----------+
| deptno   | sal      | ename    |
+----------+----------+----------+
| 10       | 1300     | MILLER   |
| 10       | 2450     | CLARK    |
| 10       | 5000     | KING     |
| 20       | 800      | SMITH    |
| 20       | 1100     | ADAMS    |
```

```
| 20        | 2975       | JONES      |
| 20        | 3000       | SCOTT      |
| 20        | 3000       | FORD       |
| 30        | 950        | JAMES      |
| 30        | 1250       | MARTIN     |
| 30        | 1250       | WARD       |
| 30        | 1500       | TURNER     |
| 30        | 1600       | ALLEN      |
| 30        | 2850       | BLAKE      |
+-----------+------------+------------+
```

使用 MaxCompute MapReduce 也可以实现相同的功能。由于 MaxCompute MapReduce 会按照 Map 输出的 Key2 进行排序，因此此时需要将员工的部门号和工资组合起来作为 Key2。具体的代码程序如下。

（1）创建输出结果表，用于保存二次排序后的数据结果。

```
demo_maxcompute_001>create table secondary_sort_emp
>(deptno bigint,sal bigint,ename string);
```

（2）开发 SecondarySortMapper.java 程序。

```java
package demo.secondarysort;

import java.io.IOException;

import com.aliyun.odps.data.Record;
import com.aliyun.odps.mapred.MapperBase;

public class SecondarySortMapper extends MapperBase {
    private Record key;
    private Record value;

    @Override
    public void setup(TaskContext context) throws IOException {
        key = context.createMapOutputKeyRecord();
        value = context.createMapOutputValueRecord();
    }

    @Override
    public void map(long recordNum, Record record, TaskContext context)
        throws IOException {
        //将员工的部门号和工资设置为 Mapper 输出的 Key
        key.set(new Object[] {(Long) record.get(7),
                              (Long) record.get(5) });
```

```java
        //将员工的姓名设置为 Mapper 输出的 Value
        value.set(new Object[] { (String) record.get(1) });
        context.write(key, value);
    }
}
```

（3）开发 SecondarySortReducer.java 程序。

```java
package demo.secondarysort;

import java.io.IOException;
import java.util.Iterator;

import com.aliyun.odps.data.Record;
import com.aliyun.odps.mapred.ReducerBase;

public class SecondarySortReducer extends ReducerBase {
    private Record result = null;

    @Override
    public void setup(TaskContext context) throws IOException {
        result = context.createOutputRecord();
    }

    //将所有的 Key 和 Value 直接输出
    @Override
    public void reduce(Record key, Iterator<Record> values,
                       TaskContext context) throws IOException {
        result.set(0,key.get(0));
        while (values.hasNext()) {
            result.set(1,key.get(1));
            Record val = values.next();
            result.set(2, val.get(0));
            context.write(result);
        }
    }
}
```

（4）开发 SecondarySortMain.java 主程序。

```java
package demo.secondarysort;

import com.aliyun.odps.data.TableInfo;
import com.aliyun.odps.mapred.JobClient;
import com.aliyun.odps.mapred.conf.JobConf;
import com.aliyun.odps.mapred.utils.InputUtils;
```

```java
import com.aliyun.odps.mapred.utils.OutputUtils;
import com.aliyun.odps.mapred.utils.SchemaUtils;

public class SecondarySortMain {
    public static void main(String[] args) throws Exception {
        JobConf job = new JobConf();
        job.setMapperClass(SecondarySortMapper.class);
        job.setReducerClass(SecondarySortReducer.class);

        //将多列设置为Key并给列起名
        job.setOutputKeySortColumns(new String[] { "deptno", "sal" });

        //设置第一个排序的列
        job.setPartitionColumns(new String[] { "deptno" });
        job.setOutputGroupingColumns(new String[] { "deptno" });

        //设置Mapper输出的Key2
        //此时的Key2组合了员工的部门号和员工的工资两列
        job.setMapOutputKeySchema(
            SchemaUtils.fromString("deptno:bigint,sal:bigint"));
        //设置Mapper输出的Value2
        job.setMapOutputValueSchema(
            SchemaUtils.fromString("ename:string"));

        InputUtils.addTable(TableInfo.builder()
            .tableName(args[0]).build(), job);
        OutputUtils.addTable(TableInfo.builder()
            .tableName(args[1]).build(), job);
        JobClient.runJob(job);
    }
}
```

（5）将程序打包为 secondarysort.jar。

（6）将 secondarysort.jar 上传到 MaxCompute 的项目空间中。

```
demo_maxcompute_001>add jar d:\download\secondarysort.jar -f;
```

（7）执行 MapReduce 任务，对数据进行二次排序。

```
demo_maxcompute_001>jar    -resources    secondarysort.jar    -classpath d:\download\secondarysort.jar    demo.secondarysort.SecondarySortMain    emp secondary_sort_emp;
```

（8）查询表 secondary_sort_emp 的数据，验证二次排序的结果。

5.3.3 【实战】使用过滤模式 MapOnly

MapOnly 作业中只有 Map，没有 Reduce。任务通过 Map 直接将<Key,Value>信息输出到 MaxCompute 的表中。因此在使用 MapOnly 时只需要指定输出表，无须指定 Map 输出的 Key 和 Value 元信息。

> 使用 MapOnly 可以实现 SQL 语句中 where 子句的过滤功能。

下面的示例将查询员工表中工资大于或等于 2000 元的员工的信息。

（1）创建输出结果表，用于保存过滤的数据结果。

```
demo_maxcompute_001>create table maponly_emp like emp;
```

（2）开发 MapOnlyMapper.java 程序。

```java
package demo.maponly;

import java.io.IOException;

import com.aliyun.odps.data.Record;
import com.aliyun.odps.mapred.MapperBase;

public class MapOnlyMapper extends MapperBase {

    @Override
    public void map(long recordNum, Record record, TaskContext context)
        throws IOException {
        //获取员工的工资
        Long sal = (Long) record.get(5);
        //设置过滤条件
        if (sal >= 2000) {
            Record result = context.createOutputRecord();
            result.set(0, record.get(0));
            result.set(1, record.get(1));
            result.set(2, record.get(2));
            result.set(3, record.get(3));
            result.set(4, record.get(4));
            result.set(5, record.get(5));
            result.set(6, record.get(6));
            result.set(7, record.get(7));
            context.write(result);
```

        }
    }
}

（3）开发 MapOnlyMain.java 主程序。

```java
package demo.maponly;

import com.aliyun.odps.OdpsException;
import com.aliyun.odps.data.TableInfo;
import com.aliyun.odps.mapred.JobClient;
import com.aliyun.odps.mapred.conf.JobConf;
import com.aliyun.odps.mapred.utils.InputUtils;
import com.aliyun.odps.mapred.utils.OutputUtils;

public class MapOnlyMain {

    public static void main(String[] args) throws OdpsException {
        JobConf job = new JobConf();
        job.setMapperClass(MapOnlyMapper.class);
        //对于MapOnly的作业，必须显式设置Reducer的个数为0
        job.setNumReduceTasks(0);

        //设置输入表和输出表的信息
        InputUtils.addTable(TableInfo.builder()
                            .tableName(args[0]).build(), job);
        OutputUtils.addTable(TableInfo.builder()
                            .tableName(args[1]).build(), job);
        JobClient.runJob(job);
    }
}
```

（4）将程序打包为 maponly.jar。

（5）将 maponly.jar 上传到 MaxCompute 的项目空间中。

```
demo_maxcompute_001>add jar d:\download\maponly.jar -f;
```

（6）执行 MapReduce 任务，对数据进行过滤。

```
demo_maxcompute_001>jar -resources maponly.jar -classpath
>d:\download\maponly.jar demo.maponly.MapOnlyMain emp maponly_emp;
```

（7）查询表 maponly_emp 的数据，验证过滤后的结果。

```
demo_maxcompute_001>select * from maponly_emp;
```

输出的结果如图 5-2 所示。

第 5 章　处理离线数据——基于 MaxCompute MapReduce | 179

```
Summary:
resource cost: cpu 0.00 Core * Min, memory 0.00 GB * Min
inputs:
outputs:
+-------+-------+-----------+------+-----------+------+------+--------+
| empno | ename | job       | mgr  | hiredate  | sal  | comm | deptno |
+-------+-------+-----------+------+-----------+------+------+--------+
| 7566  | JONES | MANAGER   | 7839 | 1981/4/2  | 2975 | 0    | 20     |
| 7698  | BLAKE | MANAGER   | 7839 | 1981/5/1  | 2850 | 0    | 30     |
| 7782  | CLARK | MANAGER   | 7839 | 1981/6/9  | 2450 | 0    | 10     |
| 7788  | SCOTT | ANALYST   | 7566 | 1987/4/19 | 3000 | 0    | 20     |
| 7839  | KING  | PRESIDENT | -1   | 1981/11/17| 5000 | 0    | 10     |
| 7902  | FORD  | ANALYST   | 7566 | 1981/12/3 | 3000 | 0    | 20     |
+-------+-------+-----------+------+-----------+------+------+--------+
A total of 6 records fetched by instance tunnel. Max record number: 10000
demo_maxcompute_001>
```

图 5-2

5.3.4 【实战】使用 Join 实现多表连接

MaxCompute MapReduce 框架自身并不支持 Join 逻辑，但用户可以在自己的 Map 或 Reduce 函数中实现数据的 Join。

> 在自己的 Map 或 Reduce 函数中实现数据的 Join，可以实现类似于 SQL 中的多表查询功能。

下面通过具体的示例来演示如何在 MaxCompute MapReduce 中实现数据的 Join。

（1）在本地准备测试需要的数据文件 data1.txt 和 data2.txt。将其存放在 D:\download 目录下，文件内容如下。

```
#data1.txt
1,hello
2,odps

#data2.txt
1,odps
3,hello
4,odps
```

（2）在 MaxCompute 项目空间中创建两张输入表，用于保存输入数据。

```
demo_maxcompute_001>
>create table mr_Join_src1(key bigint, value string);
demo_maxcompute_001>
>create table mr_Join_src2(key bigint, value string);
```

(3)将本地的数据文件上传到输入表中。

```
demo_maxcompute_001>tunnel upload d:\download\data1.txt mr_Join_src1;
demo_maxcompute_001>tunnel upload d:\download\data2.txt mr_Join_src2;
```

(4)创建输出表,用于保存 Join 连接后的执行结果。

```
demo_maxcompute_001>create table mr_Join_out
>(key bigint, value1 string, value2 string);
```

(5)开发 JoinMapper.java 程序。

```java
package demo.join;

import java.io.IOException;
import com.aliyun.odps.data.Record;
import com.aliyun.odps.mapred.MapperBase;

public class JoinMapper extends MapperBase {
    private Record mapkey;
    private Record mapvalue;
    private long tag;
    @Override
    public void setup(TaskContext context) throws IOException {
        mapkey = context.createMapOutputKeyRecord();
        mapvalue = context.createMapOutputValueRecord();
        //获取设置tag标签
        tag = context.getInputTableInfo()
                    .getLabel().equals("left") ? 0 : 1;
    }
    @Override
    public void map(long key, Record record, TaskContext context)
    throws IOException {
        mapkey.set(0, record.get(0));
        mapkey.set(1, tag);
        for (int i = 1; i < record.getColumnCount(); i++) {
            mapvalue.set(i - 1, record.get(i));
        }
        context.write(mapkey, mapvalue);
    }
}
```

(6)开发 JoinReducer.java 程序。

```java
package demo.join;

import java.io.IOException;
```

```java
import java.util.ArrayList;
import java.util.Iterator;
import java.util.List;

import com.aliyun.odps.data.Record;
import com.aliyun.odps.mapred.ReducerBase;

public class JoinReducer extends ReducerBase {
    private Record result = null;
    @Override
        public void setup(TaskContext context) throws IOException {
        result = context.createOutputRecord();
    }
    //reduce()函数每次的输入是key值相同的所有Record
    @Override
        public void reduce(Record key, Iterator<Record> values,
            TaskContext context)
        throws IOException {
        long k = key.getBigint(0);
        List<Object[]> leftValues = new ArrayList<Object[]>();
        //设置outputKeySortColumn是key+tag组合
        //这样可以保证reduce()函数的输入Record中
        //left表的Record数据在前面
        while (values.hasNext()) {
            Record value = values.next();
            long tag = (Long) key.get(1);
            //左表的数据会先缓存到内存中
            if (tag == 0) {
                leftValues.add(value.toArray().clone());
            } else {
                //右表的数据会与所有左表的数据进行Join输出
                //此时左表的数据已经全部在内存里了
                for (Object[] leftValue : leftValues) {
                    int index = 0;
                    result.set(index++, k);
                    for (int i = 0; i < leftValue.length; i++) {
                        result.set(index++, leftValue[i]);
                    }
                    for (int i = 0; i < value.getColumnCount(); i++) {
                        result.set(index++, value.get(i));
                    }
                    context.write(result);
                }
            }
        }
```

            }
        }
}
```

（7）开发 JoinMain.java 程序。

```java
package demo.join;

import com.aliyun.odps.data.TableInfo;
import com.aliyun.odps.mapred.JobClient;
import com.aliyun.odps.mapred.conf.JobConf;
import com.aliyun.odps.mapred.utils.InputUtils;
import com.aliyun.odps.mapred.utils.OutputUtils;
import com.aliyun.odps.mapred.utils.SchemaUtils;

public class JoinMain {
    public static void main(String[] args) throws Exception {
        if (args.length != 3) {
            System.err.println(
                "Usage: Join <input table1> <input table2> <out>");
            System.exit(2);
        }
        JobConf job = new JobConf();
        job.setMapperClass(JoinMapper.class);
        job.setReducerClass(JoinReducer.class);
        job.setMapOutputKeySchema(
                SchemaUtils.fromString("key:bigint,tag:bigint"));
        job.setMapOutputValueSchema(
                SchemaUtils.fromString("value:string"));
        job.setPartitionColumns(new String[] { "key" });
        job.setOutputKeySortColumns(new String[] { "key", "tag" });
        job.setOutputGroupingColumns(new String[] { "key" });
        job.setNumReduceTasks(1);
        InputUtils.addTable(TableInfo.builder().tableName(args[0])
                            .label("left").build(), job);
        InputUtils.addTable(TableInfo.builder().tableName(args[1])
                            .label("right").build(), job);
        OutputUtils.addTable(TableInfo.builder()
                            .tableName(args[2]).build(), job);
        JobClient.runJob(job);
    }
}
```

（8）将 MapReduce 程序打包为 join.jar 文件。

（9）将 join.jar 文件上传到 MaxCompute 的项目空间中。
```

(10)输入下面的命令,实现数据的 Join。

```
demo_maxcompute_001>jar -resources join.jar -classpath
>d:\download\join.jar demo.join.JoinMain
>mr_Join_src1 mr_Join_src2 mr_Join_out;
```

(11)执行下面的查询语句,验证 Join 的输出结果。

```
demo_maxcompute_001>select * from mr_Join_out;
```

输出结果如下。

```
......
inputs:
outputs:
+-----------+-----------+------------+
| key       | value1    | value2     |
+-----------+-----------+------------+
| 1         | hello     | odps       |
+-----------+-----------+------------+
A total of 1 records fetched by instance tunnel. Max record number: 10000
```

5.3.5 【实战】使用计数器 Counter

计数器 Counter 是用来记录任务的执行进度和状态的。开发人员可以在程序的某个位置插入计数器,记录数据或进度的变化情况。

> 计数器 Counter 提供了一个用于观察 Job 运行期间各种细节数据的窗口,对性能调优很有帮助。

下面的示例程序改造了 5.3.2 节中数据二次排序的代码,使用了计数器 Counter 统计任务在执行过程中 Map 任务的数量、Reduce 任务的数量和任务的总数量。

(1)为了方便统计不同任务的数量,定义一个枚举类型 MyCounter,用于代表不同的任务类型。

```
package demo.counter;

public enum MyCounter {
    TOTAL_TASKS, MAP_TASKS, REDUCE_TASKS
}
```

(2)开发 MyCountertMapper.java 程序。

```
package demo.counter;

import java.io.IOException;
```

```java
import com.aliyun.odps.counter.Counter;
import com.aliyun.odps.data.Record;
import com.aliyun.odps.mapred.MapperBase;

public class MyCountertMapper extends MapperBase {
    private Record key;
    private Record value;

    @Override
    public void setup(TaskContext context) throws IOException {
        key = context.createMapOutputKeyRecord();
        value = context.createMapOutputValueRecord();
        //获取并设置计数器的值
        Counter map_tasks = context.getCounter(MyCounter.MAP_TASKS);
        Counter total_tasks = context.getCounter(MyCounter.TOTAL_TASKS);
        map_tasks.increment(1);
        total_tasks.increment(1);
    }

    @Override
    public void map(long recordNum, Record record, TaskContext context)
        throws IOException {
        //将员工的部门号和工资设置为 Mapper 输出的 Key
        key.set(new Object[] {(Long) record.get(7),
                              (Long) record.get(5) });

        //将员工的姓名设置为 Mapper 输出的 Value
        value.set(new Object[] { (String) record.get(1) });
        context.write(key, value);
    }
}
```

（3）开发 MyCountertReducer.java 程序。

```java
package demo.counter;

import java.io.IOException;
import java.util.Iterator;

import com.aliyun.odps.counter.Counter;
import com.aliyun.odps.data.Record;
import com.aliyun.odps.mapred.ReducerBase;

public class MyCounterReducer extends ReducerBase {
```

```java
    private Record result = null;

    @Override
    public void setup(TaskContext context) throws IOException {
        result = context.createOutputRecord();
        //获取并设置计数器的值
        Counter reduce_tasks =
                        context.getCounter(MyCounter.REDUCE_TASKS);
        Counter total_tasks =
                        context.getCounter(MyCounter.TOTAL_TASKS);
        reduce_tasks.increment(1);
        total_tasks.increment(1);
    }

    //将所有的Key和Value直接输出
    @Override
    public void reduce(Record key, Iterator<Record> values,
                    TaskContext context) throws IOException {
        result.set(0,key.get(0));
        while (values.hasNext()) {
            result.set(1,key.get(1));
            Record val = values.next();
            result.set(2, val.get(0));
            context.write(result);
        }
    }
}
```

（4）开发 MyCountertMain.java 程序。

```java
package demo.counter;

import com.aliyun.odps.counter.Counters;
import com.aliyun.odps.data.TableInfo;
import com.aliyun.odps.mapred.JobClient;
import com.aliyun.odps.mapred.RunningJob;
import com.aliyun.odps.mapred.conf.JobConf;
import com.aliyun.odps.mapred.utils.InputUtils;
import com.aliyun.odps.mapred.utils.OutputUtils;
import com.aliyun.odps.mapred.utils.SchemaUtils;

public class MyCounterMain {
    public static void main(String[] args) throws Exception {
        JobConf job = new JobConf();
        job.setMapperClass(MyCountertMapper.class);
```

```java
        job.setReducerClass(MyCounterReducer.class);

        //将多列设置为Key并给列起名
        job.setOutputKeySortColumns(new String[] { "deptno", "sal" });

        //设置第一个排序的列
        job.setPartitionColumns(new String[] { "deptno" });
        job.setOutputGroupingColumns(new String[] { "deptno" });

        //设置Mapper输出的Key2
        //此时的Key2组合了员工的部门号和员工的工资两列
        job.setMapOutputKeySchema(
            SchemaUtils.fromString("deptno:bigint,sal:bigint"));
        //设置Mapper输出的Value2
        job.setMapOutputValueSchema(
            SchemaUtils.fromString("ename:string"));

        InputUtils.addTable(
            TableInfo.builder().tableName(args[0]).build(), job);
        OutputUtils.addTable(
            TableInfo.builder().tableName(args[1]).build(), job);
        RunningJob rJob = JobClient.runJob(job);

        //在作业成功结束后,可以获取Job里自定义Counter的值
        Counters counters = rJob.getCounters();
        long mapTask =
            counters.findCounter(MyCounter.MAP_TASKS).getValue();
        long reduceTask =
            counters.findCounter(MyCounter.REDUCE_TASKS).getValue();
        long totalTask =
            counters.findCounter(MyCounter.TOTAL_TASKS).getValue();
        System.out.println("Map Tasks:" + mapTask);
        System.out.println("Reduce Tasks:" + reduceTask);
        System.out.println("Total Tasks:" + totalTask);
    }
}
```

> 计数器Counter的值在任务执行完成后才能获取。

（5）将MaxCompute MapReduce任务打包成count.jar文件。

（6）将count.jar文件上传到MaxCompute的项目空间中。

```
demo_maxcompute_001>add jar d:\download\counter.jar -f;
```

（7）执行 MaxCompute MapReduce 任务。

```
demo_maxcompute_001>jar -resources counter.jar -classpath
>d:\download\counter.jar demo.counter.MyCounterMain
>emp secondary_sort_emp;
```

输出的结果如下。

```
......
Map Tasks:1
Reduce Tasks:1
Total Tasks:2
```

5.3.6 【实战】使用 Unique 实现数据去重

MaxCompute MapReduce 在处理数据时，Map 阶段的输出是 Reduce 阶段的输入。同时，相同的 Key2 所对应的 Value2 会被同一个 Reducer 处理。利用这个特点可以在数据处理的过程中实现数据去重的功能。下面通过一个简单的示例来说明这个问题。

（1）根据员工表 emp 创建一张新表作为输入表的数据。

```
demo_maxcompute_001>
create table emp_unique as select deptno,sal from emp;
```

表 emp_unique 中的数据如下，其中包含了重复的数据。

```
+----------+----------+
| deptno   | sal      |
+----------+----------+
| 20       | 800      |
| 30       | 1600     |
| 30       | 1250     |
| 20       | 2975     |
| 30       | 1250     |
| 30       | 2850     |
| 10       | 2450     |
| 20       | 3000     |
| 10       | 5000     |
| 30       | 1500     |
| 20       | 1100     |
| 30       | 950      |
| 20       | 3000     |
| 10       | 1300     |
+----------+----------+
```

（2）创建一张输出表，用于保存去重后的数据结果。

```
demo_maxcompute_001>create table unique_out(key bigint, value bigint);
```

（3）开发 UniqueMapper.java 程序。

```java
package demo.unique;

import java.io.IOException;
import com.aliyun.odps.data.Record;
import com.aliyun.odps.mapred.MapperBase;

public class UniqueMapper extends MapperBase {
    private Record key;
    private Record value;

    @Override
    public void setup(TaskContext context) throws IOException {
        key = context.createMapOutputKeyRecord();
        value = context.createMapOutputValueRecord();
    }

    @Override
    public void map(long recordNum, Record record, TaskContext context)
        throws IOException {
        long left = 0;
        long right = 0;
        if (record.getColumnCount() > 0) {
            left = (Long) record.get(0);
            if (record.getColumnCount() > 1) {
                right = (Long) record.get(1);
            }
            key.set(new Object[] { (Long) left, (Long) right });
            value.set(new Object[] { (Long) left, (Long) right });
            context.write(key, value);
        }
    }
}
```

（4）开发 UniqueReducer.java 程序。

```java
package demo.unique;

import java.io.IOException;
import java.util.Iterator;
import com.aliyun.odps.data.Record;
```

```java
import com.aliyun.odps.mapred.ReducerBase;

public class UniqueReducer extends ReducerBase {
    private Record result = null;

    @Override
    public void setup(TaskContext context) throws IOException {
        result = context.createOutputRecord();
    }

    @Override
    public void reduce(Record key, Iterator<Record> values, TaskContext
                       context) throws IOException {
        result.set(0, key.get(0));
        while (values.hasNext()) {
            Record value = values.next();
            result.set(1, value.get(1));
        }
        context.write(result);
    }
}
```

(5)开发 UniqueMain.java 程序。

```java
package demo.unique;

import com.aliyun.odps.OdpsException;
import com.aliyun.odps.data.TableInfo;
import com.aliyun.odps.mapred.JobClient;
import com.aliyun.odps.mapred.conf.JobConf;
import com.aliyun.odps.mapred.utils.InputUtils;
import com.aliyun.odps.mapred.utils.OutputUtils;
import com.aliyun.odps.mapred.utils.SchemaUtils;

public class UniqueMain {

    public static void main(String[] args) throws Exception {
        if (args.length > 3 || args.length < 2) {
            System.err.println(
                    "Usage: unique <in> <out> [key|value|all]");
            System.exit(2);
        }
        String ops = "all";
        if (args.length == 3) {
            ops = args[2];
```

```java
}

//按照key进行数据的去重
if (ops.equals("key")) {
    JobConf job = new JobConf();
    job.setMapperClass(UniqueMapper.class);
    job.setReducerClass(UniqueReducer.class);
    job.setMapOutputKeySchema(
            SchemaUtils.fromString("key:bigint,value:bigint"));
    job.setMapOutputValueSchema(
            SchemaUtils.fromString("key:bigint,value:bigint"));
    job.setPartitionColumns(new String[] { "key" });
    job.setOutputKeySortColumns(new String[] { "key", "value" });
    job.setOutputGroupingColumns(new String[] { "key" });
    job.set("tablename2", args[1]);
    job.setNumReduceTasks(1);
    job.setInt("table.counter", 0);
    InputUtils.addTable(
      TableInfo.builder().tableName(args[0]).build(), job);
    OutputUtils.addTable(
      TableInfo.builder().tableName(args[1]).build(), job);
    JobClient.runJob(job);
}
//按照(key,value)进行数据的去重
if (ops.equals("all")) {
    JobConf job = new JobConf();
    job.setMapperClass(UniqueMapper.class);
    job.setReducerClass(UniqueReducer.class);
    job.setMapOutputKeySchema(
      SchemaUtils.fromString("key:bigint,value:bigint"));
    job.setMapOutputValueSchema(
      SchemaUtils.fromString("key:bigint,value:bigint"));
    job.setPartitionColumns(new String[] { "key" });
    job.setOutputKeySortColumns(new String[] { "key", "value" });
    job.setOutputGroupingColumns(
                    new String[] { "key", "value" });
    job.set("tablename2", args[1]);
    job.setNumReduceTasks(1);
    job.setInt("table.counter", 0);
    InputUtils.addTable(
      TableInfo.builder().tableName(args[0]).build(), job);
    OutputUtils.addTable(
      TableInfo.builder().tableName(args[1]).build(), job);
    JobClient.runJob(job);
```

```
        }
        //按照value进行数据的去重
        if (ops.equals("value")) {
            JobConf job = new JobConf();
            job.setMapperClass(UniqueMapper.class);
            job.setReducerClass(UniqueReducer.class);
            job.setMapOutputKeySchema(
                SchemaUtils.fromString("key:bigint,value:bigint"));
            job.setMapOutputValueSchema(
                SchemaUtils.fromString("key:bigint,value:bigint"));
            job.setPartitionColumns(new String[] { "value" });
            job.setOutputKeySortColumns(new String[] { "value" });
            job.setOutputGroupingColumns(new String[] { "value" });
            job.set("tablename2", args[1]);
            job.setNumReduceTasks(1);
            job.setInt("table.counter", 0);
            InputUtils.addTable(
                TableInfo.builder().tableName(args[0]).build(), job);
            OutputUtils.addTable(
                TableInfo.builder().tableName(args[1]).build(), job);
            JobClient.runJob(job);
        }
    }
}
```

(6)将 MapReduce 程序打包为 unique.jar 文件。

(7)将 unique.jar 文件上传到 MaxCompute 的项目空间中。

```
demo_maxcompute_001>add jar d:\download\unique.jar -f;
```

(8)执行 MaxCompute MapReduce 任务,按照 key 进行数据的去重。

```
demo_maxcompute_001>jar -resources unique.jar -classpath
>d:\download\unique.jar demo.unique.UniqueMain
>emp_unique unique_out key;
```

(9)查看 unique_out 表中数据去重后的结果。

```
demo_maxcompute_001>select * from unique_out;
```

输出的信息如下。

```
+----------+----------+
| key      | value    |
+----------+----------+
| 10       | 5000     |
```

```
| 20        | 3000      |
| 30        | 2850      |
+-----------+-----------+
```

（10）执行 MaxCompute MapReduce 任务，按照 value 进行数据的去重。

```
demo_maxcompute_001>jar -resources unique.jar -classpath
>d:\download\unique.jar demo.unique.UniqueMain
>emp_unique unique_out value;
```

（11）查看 unique_out 表中数据去重后的结果。

```
demo_maxcompute_001>select * from unique_out;
```

输出的信息如下。

```
+-----------+-----------+
| key       | value     |
+-----------+-----------+
| 20        | 800       |
| 30        | 950       |
| 20        | 1100      |
| 30        | 1250      |
| 10        | 1300      |
| 30        | 1500      |
| 30        | 1600      |
| 10        | 2450      |
| 30        | 2850      |
| 20        | 2975      |
| 20        | 3000      |
| 10        | 5000      |
+-----------+-----------+
```

（12）再次执行 MaxCompute MapReduce 任务，按照(key,value)进行数据的去重。

```
demo_maxcompute_001>jar -resources unique.jar -classpath
>d:\download\unique.jar demo.unique.UniqueMain
>emp_unique unique_out all;
```

（13）查看 unique_out 表中数据去重后的结果。

```
demo_maxcompute_001>select * from unique_out;
```

输出的信息如下。

```
+-----------+-----------+
| key       | value     |
+-----------+-----------+
| 10        | 1300      |
| 10        | 2450      |
```

```
| 10       | 5000      |
| 20       | 800       |
| 20       | 1100      |
| 20       | 2975      |
| 20       | 3000      |
| 30       | 950       |
| 30       | 1250      |
| 30       | 1500      |
| 30       | 1600      |
| 30       | 2850      |
+----------+-----------+
```

5.3.7 【实战】使用项目空间资源

MaxCompute MapReduce 在执行程序的过程中会获取项目空间资源，例如，读取项目空间中已经存在的文件。

下面通过具体的示例来演示如何在 MaxCompute MapReduce 程序中读取项目空间中的文件，并将读取到的文件写入表。

（1）根据员工表 emp 的结构创建一张新表。

```
demo_maxcompute_001>create table emp_upload like emp;
```

（2）将员工数据文件 emp.csv 上传到项目空间中。

```
demo_maxcompute_001>add file d:\download\emp.csv -f;
```

（3）开发 ResourceMapper.java 程序。

```java
package demo.resource;

import java.io.BufferedInputStream;
import java.io.FileNotFoundException;
import java.io.IOException;
import com.aliyun.odps.data.Record;
import com.aliyun.odps.mapred.MapperBase;

public class ResourceMapper extends MapperBase {
    @Override
    public void setup(TaskContext context) throws IOException {
        //在setup()方法中完成项目空间资源的读取
        Record record = context.createOutputRecord();
        StringBuilder importdata = new StringBuilder();
        BufferedInputStream bufferedInput = null;
        try {
            byte[] buffer = new byte[1024];
```

```java
            int bytesRead = 0;
            String filename = context.getJobConf()
                                    .get("import.filename");
            bufferedInput = context.readResourceFileAsStream(filename);
            while ((bytesRead = bufferedInput.read(buffer)) != -1) {
                String chunk = new String(buffer, 0, bytesRead);
                importdata.append(chunk);
            }
            String lines[] = importdata.toString().split("\n");
            for (int i = 0; i < lines.length; i++) {
                String[] ss = lines[i].split(",");
                //构造员工数据
                record.set(0, Long.parseLong(ss[0].trim()));//员工号
                record.set(1, ss[1].trim());//姓名
                record.set(2, ss[2].trim());//职位
                record.set(3, Long.parseLong(ss[3].trim()));//老板号
                record.set(4, ss[4].trim());//入职日期
                record.set(5, Long.parseLong(ss[5].trim()));//工资
                record.set(6, Long.parseLong(ss[6].trim()));//奖金
                record.set(7, Long.parseLong(ss[7].trim()));//部门号
                context.write(record);
            }
        } catch (FileNotFoundException ex) {
            throw new IOException(ex);
        } catch (IOException ex) {
            throw new IOException(ex);
        } finally {
        }
    }

    @Override
    public void map(long recordNum, Record record, TaskContext context)
        throws IOException {
        //由于不需要对数据进行处理，因此不需要实现map()方法
    }
}
```

（4）开发 ResourceMain.java 程序。

```java
package demo.resource;

import com.aliyun.odps.data.TableInfo;
import com.aliyun.odps.mapred.JobClient;
import com.aliyun.odps.mapred.conf.JobConf;
import com.aliyun.odps.mapred.utils.InputUtils;
```

```java
import com.aliyun.odps.mapred.utils.OutputUtils;
import com.aliyun.odps.mapred.utils.SchemaUtils;

public class ResourceMain {
    public static void main(String[] args) throws Exception {
        if (args.length != 2) {
            System.err.println(
                    "Usage: Upload <import_txt> <out_table>");
            System.exit(2);
        }
        JobConf job = new JobConf();
        job.setMapperClass(ResourceMapper.class);
        //设置资源名字
        job.set("import.filename", args[0]);
        //由于任务中没有Reducer，因此maponly作业需要显式设置Reducer的数目为0
        job.setNumReduceTasks(0);

        job.setMapOutputKeySchema(
            SchemaUtils.fromString("key:bigint"));
        job.setMapOutputValueSchema(
            SchemaUtils.fromString("value:string"));
        InputUtils.addTable(
            TableInfo.builder().tableName(args[1]).build(), job);
        OutputUtils.addTable(
            TableInfo.builder().tableName(args[1]).build(), job);
        JobClient.runJob(job);
    }
}
```

（5）将 MapReduce 程序打包成 resource.jar 文件。

（6）将 resource.jar 文件上传到 MaxCompute 的项目空间中。

```
demo_maxcompute_001>add jar d:\download\resource.jar -f;
```

（7）执行 MapReduce 任务，读取项目空间中的文件。

```
demo_maxcompute_001>jar -resources resource.jar,emp.csv -classpath
>d:\download\resource.jar demo.resource.ResourceMain
>emp.csv emp_upload;
```

（8）查询表 emp_upload，验证读取的结果。

```
demo_maxcompute_001>select * from emp_upload;
```

第 6 章
处理离线数据——基于 MaxCompute Spark

MaxCompute Spark 是 MaxCompute 提供的兼容开源 Spark 的计算服务。它在统一的计算资源和数据集权限体系之上，提供 Spark 计算框架，支持用户以熟悉的开发使用方式提交、运行 Spark 作业，满足更丰富的数据处理、分析需求。

6.1 MaxCompute Spark 基础

MaxCompute Spark 是阿里云提供的 Spark on MaxCompute 的解决方案，让原生 Spark 能够在 MaxCompute 中运行。MaxCompute Spark 支持以下场景。

（1）离线计算场景，例如 GraphX、MLlib、RDD、Spark-SQL、PySpark 等。

（2）读写 MaxCompute Table。

（3）引用 MaxCompute 中的文件资源。

（4）读写 VPC 环境下的服务，例如 RDS、Redis、HBase、ECS 上部署的服务等。

（5）读写 OSS 非结构化存储。

（6）读 OSS、Hologres 及 HBase 外部表。

6.1.1 MaxCompute Spark 的系统结构

MaxCompute Spark 的系统结构如图 6-1 所示。其中，左侧是原生 Spark 的架构图，右侧是 Spark on MaxCompute 运行在阿里云自主研发的 Cupid 平台上的架构图，Cupid 平台可以原生支持开源社区 Yarn 所支持的计算框架。

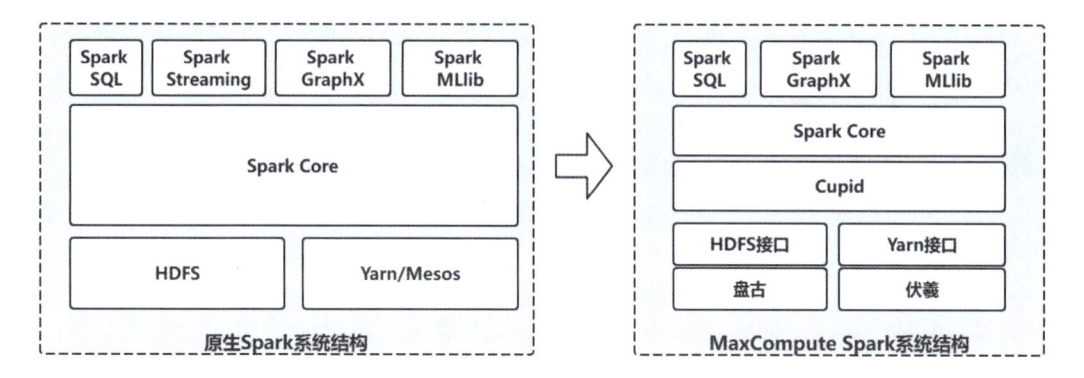

图 6-1

MaxCompute 支持社区原生 Spark 并完全兼容 Spark 的 API，还支持多个 Spark 版本同时运行。MaxCompute Spark 提供原生的 Spark Web UI 供用户查看。同时，与 MaxCompute SQL、MapReduce 等作业类型类似，MaxCompute Spark 运行在 MaxCompute 项目统一开通的计算资源中，并遵循 MaxCompute 项目的权限体系，用户在访问权限范围内可以安全地查询数据。MaxCompute Spark 与社区开源 Spark 保持相同的体验，完全符合 Spark 用户的使用习惯。开源应用的调试过程中需要使用开源 UI，MaxCompute Spark 提供原生的开源实时 UI 和查询历史日志的功能，对于部分开源应用还支持交互式体验，在后台引擎运行后即可进行实时交互。

> Spark 推荐使用 Scala 编程语言开发应用程序。Scala 是一门基于 Java 语言的多范式的编程语言，支持面向对象编程和函数式编程两种不同的编程方式。

6.1.2　MaxCompute Spark 的使用限制

MaxCompute Spark 暂不支持以下场景。

（1）交互式和流式计算类需求，例如 Spark-Shell、Spark-SQL-Shell、PySpark-Shell、Spark Streaming 等。

（2）不支持访问 MaxCompute 除 OSS、Hologres 及 HBase 外部表之外的外部表、内建函数和自定义函数。

（3）不支持在使用按量计费开发者版本资源的项目中执行 Spark 作业。按量计费开发者版本仅支持 MaxCompute SQL（支持使用 UDF）、PyODPS 作业。

MaxCompute Spark 不支持 Checkpoint（检查点）功能。

> 检查点是 Spark 提供的一种容错机制。由于 Spark 的计算是在内存中完成的，因此任务执行的生命周期越长，执行出错的概率就越大。Spark 通过检查点机制，将内存中的数据写入磁盘进行持久化的保存，从而支持容错。如果在检查点之后有节点出现了问题，Spark 只需要从检查点的位置开始重新执行。

6.1.3 使用 spark-shell

在使用本地模式运行 MaxCompute Spark 时，可以使用 spark-shell 交互式命令行工具，从而方便开发和调试应用程序代码。

启动 spark-shell，可以执行下面的命令。

```
D:\>cd download\spark-2.3.0-odps0.33.0
D:\download\spark-2.3.0-odps0.33.0>bin\spark-shell
```

启动成功后，输出的信息如下。

```
Spark context Web UI available at http://localhost:4040
Spark context available as 'sc' (master = local[*], app id = local-167450).
Spark session available as 'spark'.
Welcome to
      ____              __
     / __/__  ___ _____/ /__
    _\ \/ _ \/ _ `/ __/  '_/
   /___/ .__/\_,_/_/ /_/\_\   version 2.3.0-odps0.33.0
      /_/

Using Scala version 2.11.8
(Java HotSpot(TM) 64-Bit Server VM, Java 1.8.0_181)
Type in expressions to have them evaluated.
Type :help for more information.

scala>
```

spark-shell 在启动成功后，会创建两个非常重要的对象：SparkContext 和 SparkSession，分别通过变量 sc 和 spark 来引用。

> 通过下面这一行输出的信息，也可以看出当前的 spark-shell 是使用本地模式运行的。
> Spark context available as 'sc' (master = local[*],……)

在 spark-shell 中执行下面的 Scala 程序。

```
scala> sc.textFile("d:\\download\\data.txt").flatMap(_.split(" ")).map((_,1)).reduceByKey(_+_).collect
```

输出结果如下。

```
res3: Array[(String, Int)] = Array((is,1), (love,2), (capital,1), (Beijing,2), (China,2), (I,2), (of,1), (the,1))
```

> 💡 这里使用 Scala 编程语言开发了单词计数的 WordCount 程序，并将结果直接显示在了屏幕上。与 MaxCompute MapReduce 的 WordCount 程序相比，这里的 Scala 程序简洁了很多。这是因为 Scala 编程语言最大的特点就是可以利用函数式编程来简化应用程序代码。

打开浏览器，访问 http://localhost:4040，可以监控在本地模式下运行的 Spark 任务，如图 6-2 所示。

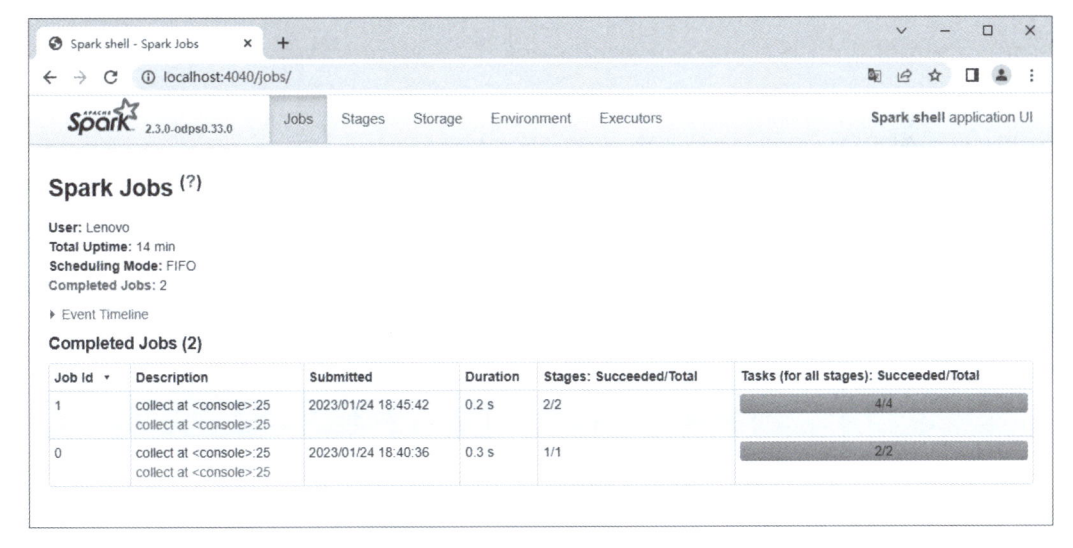

图 6-2

6.2　MaxCompute Spark 的核心数据模型 RDD

RDD（Resilient Distributed Datasets，弹性分布式数据集）是 MaxCompute Spark 核心的数据模型，是整个 MaxCompute Spark 生态圈体系中最重要的部分。MaxCompute Spark 最终会将数据模型转换成 RDD 的方式来处理，包括 Spark SQL 中的 DataFrame 和 Spark Streaming

中的 DStream。

本节将重点介绍 RDD 的核心概念及其特性，以及如何使用相应的算子来处理 RDD 中的数据。

6.2.1 什么是 RDD

RDD 是 MaxCompute Spark 中最基本，也是最重要的数据模型。它由分区组成，每个分区被一个 Spark 的 Worker 从节点处理，从而支持分布式的并行计算。

RDD 通过检查点机制提供自动容错的功能，并且具有位置感知性调度和可伸缩的特性。RDD 也提供缓存的机制，可以极大地提高数据处理的速度。

1. RDD 的组成

在 WordCount 示例中，每一步都会生成一个新的 RDD，用于保存这一步的结果。

创建 RDD 可以使用下面的方式。

```scala
scala> val myrdd = sc.parallelize(Array(1,2,3,4,5,6,7,8),2)
```

这行代码创建了一个名为 myrdd 的 RDD，该 RDD 中包含一个数组，并且这个 RDD 由两个分区组成。

通过查看 RDD 的 partitions 算子可以查看分区的长度。

```scala
scala> myrdd.partitions.length
res0: Int = 2
```

那么 RDD、分区和 Worker 节点之间是什么关系呢？这里以创建的 myrdd 为例来说明它们之间的关系，如图 6-3 所示。

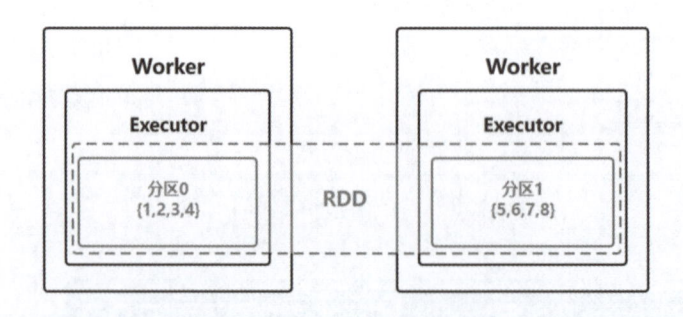

图 6-3

假设有两个 Worker 节点。myrdd 又包含了两个分区，每个分区会有一个分区号，分区号从零开始。从图 6-3 可以看出，在第一个 Worker 节点上处理的是分区 0 中的数据，即{1,2,3,4}，而在第二个 Worker 节点上处理的是分区 1 中的数据，即{5,6,7,8}。

> 这里可以把分区理解成一个物理概念,它里面的数据由 Worker 节点上 Executor 执行的任务处理。虚线方框表示的是 RDD,可以看出它其实是一个逻辑概念。

2. RDD 的特性

RDD 具有什么特性呢?Spark RDD 的源码中对 RDD 的特性做了如下解释。

```
* Internally, each RDD is characterized by five main properties:
*
*  - A list of partitions
*  - A function for computing each split
*  - A list of dependencies on other RDDs
*  - Optionally, a Partitioner for key-value RDDs
(e.g. to say that the RDD is hash-partitioned)
*  - Optionally, a list of preferred locations to compute each
split on (e.g. block locations for an HDFS file)
```

通过这段注释可以了解到 RDD 具有以下 5 个基本的特性。

1)由一组分区组成

对 RDD 来说,每个分区都会被一个计算任务处理并决定并行计算的粒度。用户可以在创建 RDD 时指定 RDD 的分区个数,如果没有指定,则采用默认值。默认值就是程序分配到的 CPU 内核的数目。

2)一个计算每个分区的函数

MaxCompute Spark 中 RDD 的计算是以分区为单位的。每个 RDD 都需要实现 Compute 函数,从而达到处理数据的目的。

3)RDD 之间的依赖关系

可以把 WordCount 程序代码拆开,从而单步执行。在每次转换时,可以定义一个新的 RDD 来保存这一步的结果,如下所示。

```
scala> val rdd1 = sc.textFile("d:\\download\\data.txt")
scala> val rdd2 = rdd1.flatMap(_.split(" "))
scala> val rdd3 = rdd2.map((_,1))
scala> val rdd4 = rdd3.reduceByKey(_+_)
scala> rdd4.collect
```

这里一共定义了 4 个 RDD,分别是 rdd1、rdd2、rdd3 和 rdd4,其中,rdd4 依赖 rdd3,rdd3 依赖 rdd2,而 rdd2 依赖 rdd1。根据依赖关系的不同,可以划分任务执行的阶段,从而支持检查点机制。

> 如果在计算过程中丢失了某个分区的数据，MaxCompute Spark 可以通过这个依赖关系重新进行计算，而不是对 RDD 的所有分区重新进行计算。

4）一个 Partitioner

Partitioner 是 RDD 的分区函数，其内部实现了两种类型的分区函数：①基于哈希算法的 HashPartitioner；②基于范围的 RangePartitioner。继承 Partitioner 也可以实现自定义的分区函数。分区函数不但决定了 RDD 本身的分区数量，也决定了 RDD Shuffle 输出时的分区数量。

5）一个存储了读取每个分区优先位置（Preferred Location）的列表

根据这个列表的信息，MaxCompute Spark 在进行任务调度时会尽可能地将计算任务分配到要处理的数据块的存储位置，这样可以提高处理数据的效率。

6.2.2 熟悉 RDD 的算子

RDD 由分区组成，要处理分区中的数据就需要开发相应的函数或方法。这些函数或方法叫作算子。MaxCompute Spark 的算子分为两种类型：Transformation 和 Action。

> 所有的 Transformation 算子并不会直接触发计算，即 Transformation 算子都是延迟计算的，它们只是记录在 RDD 数据集上的操作动作，只有在发生了一个 Action 操作时，这些 Transformation 操作才会真正运行，才会真正触发 Spark 执行计算。延时计算让 Spark 更有效率地运行。

1. Transformation 算子和 Action 算子

RDD 的 Transformation 算子及其作用如表 6-1 所示。

表 6-1

Transformation 算子	作 用
map(func)	返回一个新的 RDD，该 RDD 由每一个输入元素经过 func 函数转换后组成
filter(func)	返回一个新的 RDD，该 RDD 由经过 func 函数计算后返回值为 true 的输入元素组成
flatMap(func)	类似于 map(func)算子，但是每一个输入元素可以被映射为 0 或多个输出元素（所以 func 函数应该返回一个序列，而不是单一元素）
mapPartitions(func)	类似于 map(func)算子，但独立地在 RDD 的每一个分区上运行，因此在类型为 T 的 RDD 上运行时，func 函数的类型必须是 Iterator[T] => Iterator[U]

续表

Transformation 算子	作用
mapPartitionsWithIndex(func)	类似于 mapPartitions(func)算子，但 func 函数带有一个整数参数表示分区的索引值，因此在类型为 T 的 RDD 上运行时，func 函数的类型必须是(Int, Interator[T]) => Iterator[U]
sample(withReplacement, fraction, seed)	根据 fraction 指定的比例对数据进行采样，可以选择是否使用随机数进行替换，seed 用于指定随机数生成器种子
union(otherDataset)	对原 RDD 和参数 RDD 求并集后返回一个新的 RDD
intersection(otherDataset)	对原 RDD 和参数 RDD 求交集后返回一个新的 RDD
distinct([numTasks])	对原 RDD 进行去重后返回一个新的 RDD
groupByKey([numTasks])	在一个(K,V)的 RDD 上调用，返回一个(K, Iterator[V])的 RDD
reduceByKey(func, [numTasks])	在一个(K,V)的 RDD 上调用，返回一个(K,V)的 RDD，使用指定的 Reduce 函数，将相同 key 的值聚合到一起，与 groupByKey 算子类似，Reduce 任务的个数可以通过第二个可选的参数来设置
aggregateByKey(zeroValue)(seqOp, combOp, [numTasks])	针对 RDD 中(K,V)类型的数据，先进行局部聚合操作，再进行全局聚合操作
sortByKey([ascending], [numTasks])	在一个(K,V)的 RDD 上调用，K 必须实现 Ordered 接口，返回一个按照 key 进行排序的(K,V)的 RDD
sortBy(func,[ascending], [numTasks])	与 sortByKey 算子类似，但是更灵活
join(otherDataset, [numTasks])	在类型为(K,V)和(K,W)的 RDD 上调用，返回一个相同 key 对应的所有元素对在一起的(K,(V,W))的 RDD
cogroup(otherDataset, [numTasks])	在类型为(K,V)和(K,W)的 RDD 上调用，返回一个(K,(Iterable<V>,Iterable<W>))类型的 RDD
cartesian(otherDataset)	生成笛卡儿积
coalesce(numPartitions)	将 RDD 中的分区进行重分区，默认不会进行 Shuffle
repartition(numPartitions)	将 RDD 中的分区进行重分区，会进行 Shuffle
aggregate()	针对 RDD 中的每个分区，先进行局部聚合操作，再进行全局聚合操作

RDD 的 Action 算子及其作用如表 6-2 所示。

表 6-2

Action 算子	作用
reduce(func)	通过 func 函数聚集 RDD 中的所有元素，该功能必须是可交换且可并联的
collect()	在驱动程序中，以数组的形式返回数据集的所有元素
count()	返回 RDD 的元素个数
first()	返回 RDD 的第一个元素（类似于 take(1)）

续表

Action 算子	作　　用
take(n)	返回一个由数据集的前 n 个元素组成的数组
takeSample(withReplacement,num, [seed])	返回一个数组，该数组由从数据集中随机采样的 num 个元素组成，可以选择是否用随机数替换不足的部分。其中，seed 用于指定随机数生成器种子
saveAsTextFile(path)	将数据集的元素以 textfile 的形式保存到 HDFS 文件系统或其他支持的文件系统中。对于每个元素，Spark 都会调用 toString()方法，将其转换为文件中的文本
saveAsSequenceFile(path)	将数据集中的元素以 Hadoop sequencefile 的格式保存到指定目录下。该目录可以是 HDFS 中的目录，也可以是其他 Hadoop 支持的目录
countByKey()	针对(K,V)类型的 RDD，返回一个(K,Int)的 map，表示每一个 Key 对应的元素个数
foreach(func)	在数据集的每一个元素上运行 func 函数，以进行更新
top()	返回集合中元素降序排序后的最前面的元素

2. 使用 RDD 的算子处理数据

本节将通过具体步骤来演示 RDD 算子的使用方法，这里的示例代码可以直接在 spark-shell 中运行。

1）使用 Transformation 的基础算子

（1）map(func)算子会将输入的每个元素重写，组合成一个元组。

```
scala> val rdd1 = sc.parallelize(Array(1,2,3,4,5,6,7,8))
scala> val rdd2 = rdd1.map((_ * 10))
scala> rdd2.collect
res0: Array[Int] = Array(10, 20, 30, 40, 50, 60, 70, 80)
```

> 这里的代码会将数组中的每个元素乘 10。

（2）filter(func)算子将返回一个新的 RDD，该 RDD 由经过 func 函数计算后返回值为 true 的元素组成。

```
scala> val rdd1 = sc.parallelize(Array(1,2,3,4,5,6,7,8))
scala> val rdd3 = rdd1.filter(_ > 5)
scala> rdd3.collect
res1: Array[Int] = Array(6, 7, 8)
```

> 这里的代码会返回大于 5 的元素。

（3）flatMap(func)算子将数据元素进行压平操作。

```
scala> val books = sc.parallelize(List("Hadoop","Hive","HDFS"))
scala> books.flatMap(_.toList).collect
res2: Array[Char] = Array(H, a, d, o, o, p, H, i, v, e, H, D, F, S)
```

（4）union(otherDataset)算子类似于 SQL 语句中的并集运算。

```
scala> val rdd4 = sc.parallelize(List(5,6,4,7))
scala> val rdd5 = sc.parallelize(List(1,2,3,4))
scala> val rdd6 = rdd4.union(rdd5)
scala> rdd6.collect
res3: Array[Int] = Array(5, 6, 4, 7, 1, 2, 3, 4)
```

（5）intersection(otherDataset)算子类似于 SQL 语句中的交集运算。

```
scala> val rdd7 = rdd5.intersection(rdd4)
scala> rdd7.collect
res4: Array[Int] = Array(4)
```

（6）distinct([numTasks])算子将去掉集合中的重复数据。

```
scala> val rdd8 = sc.parallelize(List(5,6,4,7,5,5,5))
scala> rdd8.distinct.collect
res5: Array[Int] = Array(4, 6, 7, 5)
```

（7）groupByKey([numTasks])算子将对一个<Key,Value>类型的 RDD，按照 Key 进行分组。

```
scala> val rdd9 = sc.parallelize(Array(("I",1),("love",2),("I",3)))
scala> rdd9.groupByKey.collect
res6: Array[(String, Iterable[Int])] = Array((love,CompactBuffer(2)), (I,CompactBuffer(1, 3)))
```

（8）cartesian(otherDataset)算子将生成笛卡儿积。

```
scala> val rdd10 = sc.parallelize(List("tom", "jerry"))
scala> val rdd11 = sc.parallelize(List("tom", "kitty", "shuke"))
scala> val rdd12 = rdd10.cartesian(rdd11)
scala> rdd12.collect
res9: Array[(String, String)] = Array((tom,tom), (tom,kitty), (tom,shuke), (jerry,tom), (jerry,kitty), (jerry,shuke))
```

2）使用 Transformation 的高级算子

（1）使用 mapPartitionsWithIndex(func)算子。

针对 RDD 中每个带有下标号的分区以某种方式进行计算。mapPartitionsWithIndex(func)算子的 API 说明如下。

```
def mapPartitionsWithIndex[U](f: (Int, Iterator[T]) => Iterator[U],
                preservesPartitioning: Boolean = false)
               (implicit arg0: ClassTag[U]): RDD[U]
```

其中最主要的参数是第一个参数 f: (Int, Iterator[T]) => Iterator[U]，这是一个函数参数。该函数的第一个参数是 Int 类型，表示分区号，第二个参数 Iterator[T]表示该分区中的元素，该分区的元素处理完成后返回的结果使用 Iterator[U]表示。

下面的代码会将每个分区中的元素和分区号显示出来。

```
#创建一个 RDD
scala> val rdd1 = sc.parallelize(List(1,2,3,4,5,6,7,8,9), 2)

#定义一个函数 func1()，将分区号和分区中的元素拼接成一个字符串
scala> def func1(index:Int, iter:Iterator[Int]):Iterator[String] ={
   iter.toList.map( x => "[PartID:" + index +
", value=" + x + "]" ).iterator
}

#调用 mapPartitionsWithIndex(func1)，并将结果输出到屏幕
scala> rdd1.mapPartitionsWithIndex(func1).collect
```

代码执行的结果如图 6-4 所示。

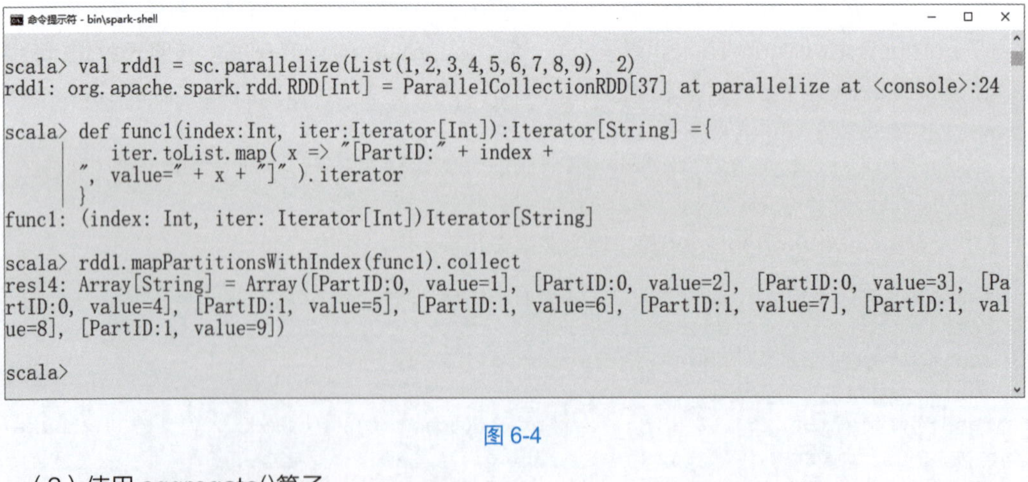

图 6-4

（2）使用 aggregate()算子。

针对 RDD 中的每个分区先进行局部聚合操作，再进行全局聚合操作。aggregate()算子的 API 说明如下。

```
def aggregate[U](zeroValue: U)(seqOp: (U, T)=>U,
                               combOp: (U, U)=>U)
                              (implicit arg0: ClassTag[U]): U
```

其中，参数 zeroValue: U 表示聚合操作时的初始值；参数 seqOp: (U, T)=>U 表示局部执行的操作；参数 combOp: (U, U)=>U 表示全局执行的操作。

下面通过一个示例来说明 aggregate() 算子的执行过程，如图 6-5 所示。

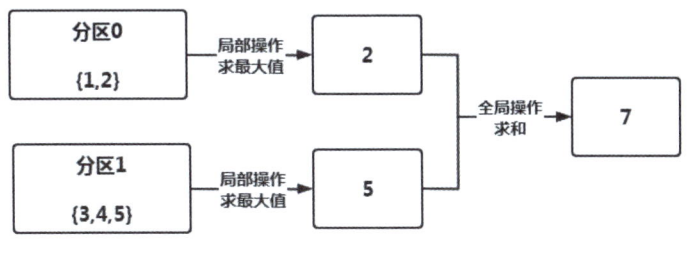

图 6-5

图 6-5 表示求 RDD 中每个分区最大值的和。假设 RDD 包含两个分区，在分区 0 中含有元素 {1,2}，在分区 1 中含有元素 {3,4,5}。通过局部操作先求出每个分区的最大值，即 2 和 5。再执行全局的求和操作，最后得到结果 7。

上面的示例可以通过下面的代码来实现。

```
scala> val rdd2 = sc.parallelize(List(1,2,3,4,5),2)
scala> rdd2.aggregate(0)(math.max(_,_),_+_)
res10: Int = 7
```

下面是一个复杂一点的示例，该示例将在 aggregate() 算子中使用字符串类型的数据。

```
scala> val rdd3 = sc.parallelize(List("12","23","345","4567"),2)
scala> rdd3.aggregate("")((x,y) =>
     math.max(x.length, y.length).toString, (x,y) => x + y)
res11: String = 24

scala> val rdd4 = sc.parallelize(List("12","23","345",""),2)
scala> rdd4.aggregate("")((x,y) =>
     math.min(x.length, y.length).toString, (x,y) => x + y)
res12: String = 10
```

或者

```
res17: String = 01
```

（3）使用 aggregateByKey(zeroValue)(seqOp,combOp,[numTasks]) 算子。

aggregateByKey(zeroValue)(seqOp,combOp,[numTasks]) 算子的作用与 aggregate() 算

子完全相同，只不过它处理的是<Key,Value>类型的数据。下面通过具体的代码来说明。

```
#创建一个 RDD
scala> val pairRDD = sc.parallelize(List( ("cat",2), ("cat", 5),
                                    ("mouse", 4),("cat", 12),
                                    ("dog", 12), ("mouse", 2)),
                                    2)

#将每个分区中的元素和分区号拼接为一个字符串
scala> def func2(index: Int, iter: Iterator[(String, Int)])
       :Iterator[String] = {
  iter.toList.map(x => "[partID:" + index + ", val: " + x + "]").iterator
}

#调用 mapPartitionsWithIndex（func2）查看分区中的元素
scala> pairRDD.mapPartitionsWithIndex(func2).collect
res13: Array[String] = Array([partID:0, val: (cat,2)], [partID:0, val:
(cat,5)], [partID:0, val: (mouse,4)], [partID:1, val: (cat,12)], [partID:1,
val: (dog,12)], [partID:1, val: (mouse,2)])

#将每个分区中数量最多的动物数进行求和
scala> pairRDD.aggregateByKey(0)(math.max(_,_),_+_).collect
res14: Array[(String, Int)] = Array((dog,12), (cat,17), (mouse,6))

#求每种动物的和
scala> pairRDD.aggregateByKey(0)(_+_,_+_).collect
res15: Array[(String, Int)] = Array((dog,12), (cat,19), (mouse,6))
```

（4）使用 coalesce(numPartitions)算子与 repartition(numPartitions)算子。

coalesce(numPartitions)算子与 repartition(numPartitions)算子会将 RDD 中的分区进行重分区。二者区别是：coalesce(numPartitions)算子默认不会进行 shuffle，即不会真正执行重分区；repartition(numPartitions)算子会进行 shuffle，即会将数据真正地进行重分区。

```
scala> val rdd5 = sc.parallelize(List(1,2,3,4,5,6,7,8,9), 2)
scala> val rdd6 = rdd5.repartition(3)
scala> rdd6.partitions.length
res16: Int = 3
```

> 注意，下面两句话是等价的。
> scala> val rdd6 = rdd5.repartition(3)
> scala> val rdd7 = rdd5.coalesce(3,true);

3）使用 Action 算子

（1）collect()算子将触发计算并以数组的形式返回数据集的所有元素。

```
scala> val rdd1 = sc.parallelize(List(1,2,3,4,5), 2)
rdd1.collect
res17: Array[Int] = Array(1, 2, 3, 4, 5)
```

（2）reduce(func)算子将集合中的所有元素进行某种操作。例如，下面的代码会对集合中的所有元素进行求和。

```
scala> val rdd2 = rdd1.reduce(_+_)
rdd2: Int = 15
```

（3）count()算子返回 RDD 的元素个数。

```
scala> rdd1.count
res18: Long = 5
```

（4）top()算子返回集合中元素降序排序后的最前面的元素。下面的代码将返回集合中最大的两个元素。

```
scala> rdd1.top(2)
res19: Array[Int] = Array(5, 4)
```

（5）take(n)算子将按照插入顺序取出前面的 n 个元素。下面的代码将返回集合中的前两个元素。

```
scala> rdd1.take(2)
res20: Array[Int] = Array(1, 2)
```

（6）first()算子将按照插入顺序取出第一个元素。

```
scala> rdd1.first
res21: Int = 1
```

6.2.3 【实战】RDD 的缓存机制

RDD 通过 persist()方法或 cache()方法可以将计算结果缓存，但是并不是这两个方法被调用时立即缓存，而是触发后面的 Action 时，RDD 才会被缓存在计算节点的内存中并供后面重用。下面是 persist()方法或 cache()方法的函数定义。

```
def persist(): this.type = persist(StorageLevel.MEMORY_ONLY)
def cache(): this.type = persist()
```

可以发现，cache()方法最终也是调用了 persist()方法，默认的存储级别都是仅在内存存储一份，Spark 在 object StorageLevel 中定义了缓存的存储级别。下面是在 StorageLevel 中定义的缓存级别。

```
val NONE = new StorageLevel(false, false, false, false)
val DISK_ONLY = new StorageLevel(true, false, false, false)
val DISK_ONLY_2 = new StorageLevel(true, false, false, false, 2)
val MEMORY_ONLY = new StorageLevel(false, true, false, true)
val MEMORY_ONLY_2 = new StorageLevel(false, true, false, true, 2)
val MEMORY_ONLY_SER = new StorageLevel(false, true, false, false)
val MEMORY_ONLY_SER_2 = new StorageLevel(false, true, false, false, 2)
val MEMORY_AND_DISK = new StorageLevel(true, true, false, true)
val MEMORY_AND_DISK_2 = new StorageLevel(true, true, false, true, 2)
val MEMORY_AND_DISK_SER = new StorageLevel(true, true, false, false)
val MEMORY_AND_DISK_SER_2=new StorageLevel(true, true, false, false, 2)
valOFF_HEAP = new StorageLevel(true, true, true, false, 1)
```

> 需要说明的是，使用 RDD 的缓存机制，数据可能丢失，或者会由于内存的不足而造成数据被删除。使用 RDD 的检查点机制可以保证缓存的容错，即使缓存丢失了也能保证计算的正确执行。

下面是使用 RDD 缓存机制的一个示例。这里使用 RDD 读取一个大的文件，该文件中包含 918843 条记录。通过 Spark Web Console 可以对比在不使用缓存和使用缓存时，执行效率的差别。

（1）读取一个大文件。

```
scala> val rdd1 = sc.textFile("d:\\download\\sales")
```

（2）触发一个计算，这里没有使用缓存。

```
scala> rdd1.count
```

（3）调用 cache()方法标识该 RDD 可以被缓存。

```
scala> rdd1.cache
```

（4）第二次触发计算，计算完成后会将结果缓存。

```
scala> rdd1.count
```

（5）第三次触发计算，这里会直接从之前的缓存中获取结果。

```
scala> rdd1.count
```

（6）访问 Spark Web Console，观察这 3 次 count 计算的执行时间，可以看到，最后一次 count 计算只耗费了 31ms，如图 6-6 所示。

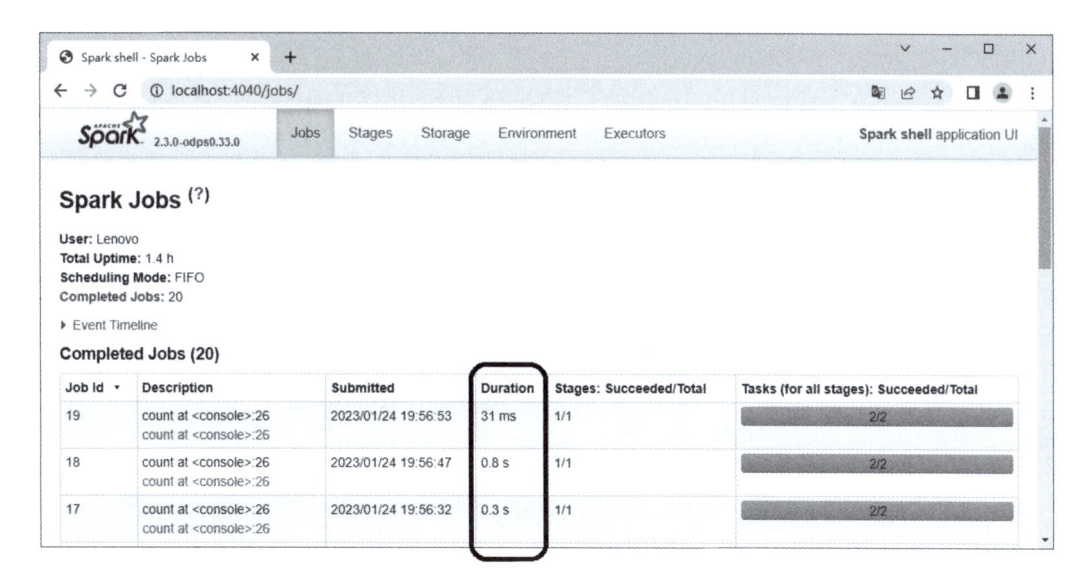

图 6-6

6.2.4 【实战】RDD 的检查点机制

由于 MaxCompute Spark 的计算是在内存中完成的，因此任务执行的生命周期 lineage（血统）越长，执行出错的概率就会越大。MaxCompute Spark 通过检查点机制，将 RDD 的状态写入磁盘进行持久化的保存从而支持容错。如果在检查点之后有节点出现了问题，MaxCompute Spark 只需要从检查点的位置开始重新执行 lineage。

> 建议在生产系统中采用具有容错能力、高可靠的文件系统作为检查点保存的目的地。

下面的代码使用了本地目录作为 RDD 检查点的目录

（1）设置检查点目录。

```
scala> sc.setCheckpointDir("d:\\download\\checkpoint")
```

（2）创建 RDD。

```
scala> val rdd1 = sc.textFile("d:\\download\\sales")
```

（3）标识 RDD 的检查点。

```
scala> rdd1.checkpoint
```

（4）执行计算。

```
scala> rdd1.count
```

（5）计算完成后，本地的 D:\download\checkpoint 目录下生成了相应的检查点信息，如图 6-7 所示。

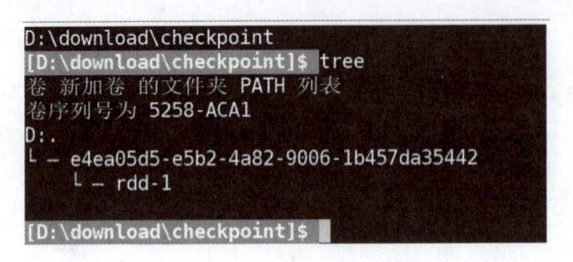

图 6-7

6.2.5　RDD 的依赖关系和任务执行的阶段

RDD 彼此之间会存在一定的依赖关系。依赖关系有两种不同的类型：窄依赖和宽依赖。如果父 RDD 的每一个分区最多只被一个子 RDD 的分区使用，这样的依赖关系就是窄依赖；如果父 RDD 的每一个分区被多个子 RDD 的分区使用，这样的依赖关系就是宽依赖。

map、filter、union 等操作都是典型的窄依赖操作。每一个父 RDD 的分区都只被一个子 RDD 的分区使用，如图 6-8 所示。

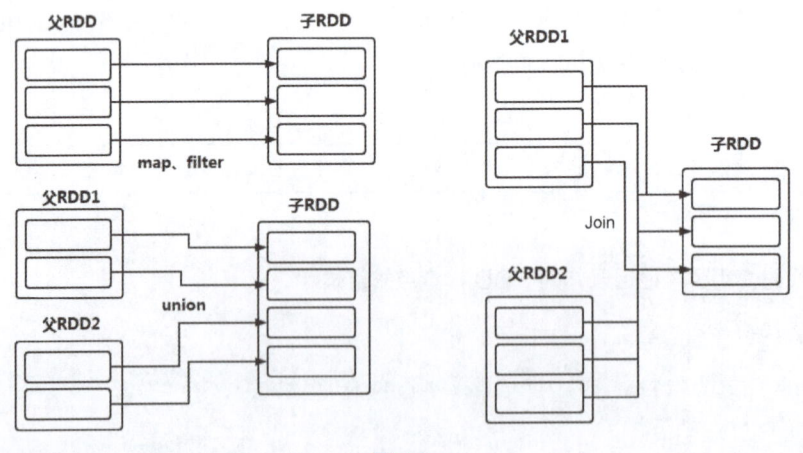

图 6-8

> Join 操作可能会比较特殊，有些情况的 Join 操作是窄依赖操作，有些情况的 Join 操作是宽依赖操作，需要具体问题具体分析。

宽依赖最典型的操作就是分组，如图 6-9 所示，父 RDD 的每一个分区都被多个子 RDD 的分区使用。

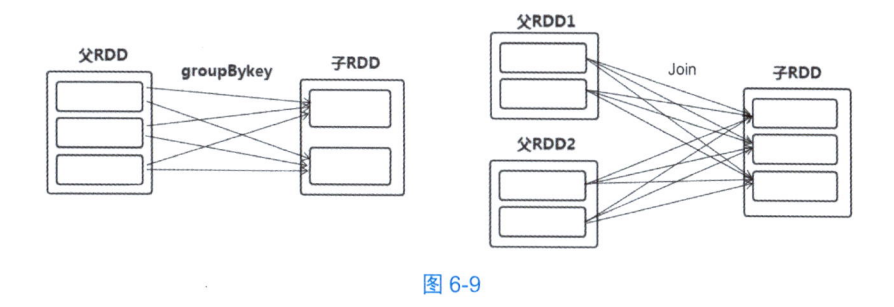

图 6-9

> 这里的 Join 操作就是一个宽依赖操作。

有了 RDD 之间不同的依赖关系，就可以划分任务执行的阶段，从而构建任务执行的 DAG。对于窄依赖，分区的转换处理在同一个阶段中完成计算；对于宽依赖，由于 Shuffle 的存在，在父 RDD 处理完成后，子 RDD 才能开始计算，因此宽依赖是划分任务阶段的标准。图 6-10 中的任务一共被划分成了 3 个不同阶段来执行。

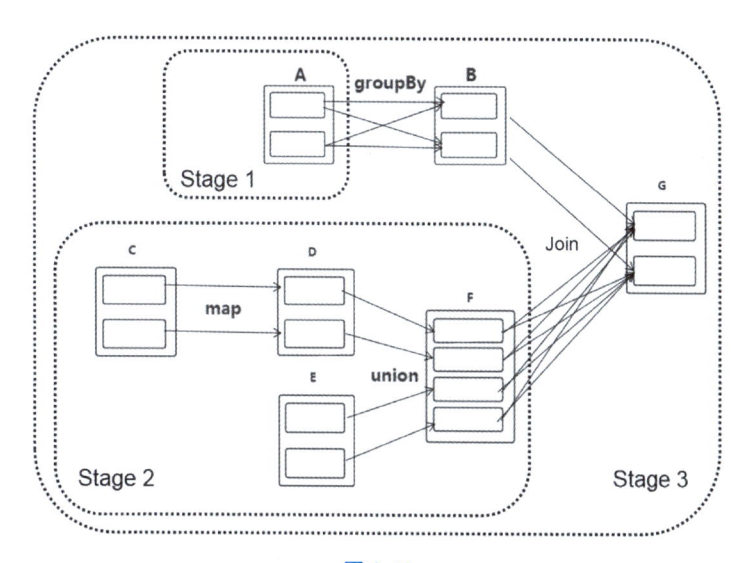

图 6-10

通过 Spark Web Console 可以很方便地查看到任务被划分的阶段及 DAG。在 Spark Web Console 查看之前 WordCount 任务的 DAG，如图 6-11 所示。

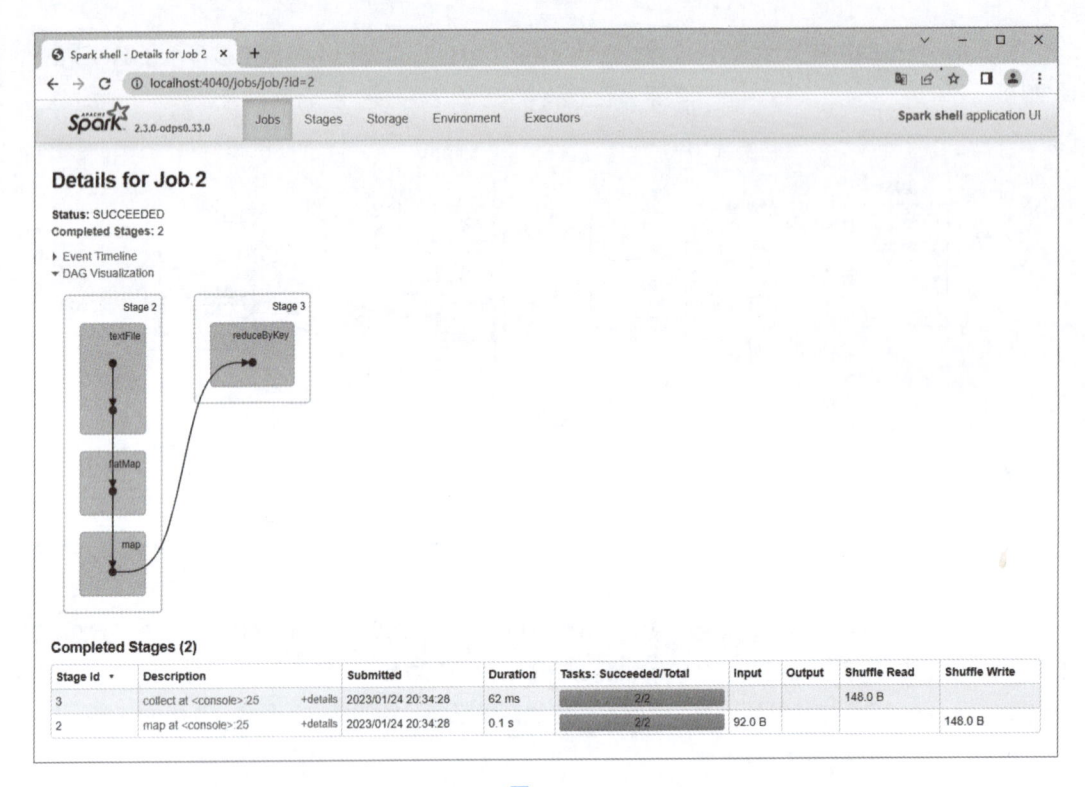

图 6-11

6.3 在 MaxCompute Spark 中使用 SQL 处理数据

Spark SQL 是 MaxCompute Spark 处理结构化数据的一个模块，它提供了一个编程抽象叫作 DataFrame。这里的 DataFrame 就是 Spark SQL 的数据模型，可以把它理解成是一张表。并且 Spark SQL 将提供分布式 SQL 查询引擎的作用。

6.3.1 Spark SQL 的特点

Spark SQL 具有以下的特性。

1. 容易整合

Spark SQL 无论是在原生的 Spark 生态圈体系中，还是在 MaxCompute 中，都已经被集成到 MaxCompute Spark 的环境中，不需要单独安装。在开通了 MaxCompute 服务以后就可以直接使用 Spark SQL。

2. 提供统一的数据访问方式

Spark SQL 主要用于处理结构化数据，结构化数据也包含很多类型，如 JSON 文件、CSV 文件、Parquet 文件或关系型数据库中的数据。Spark SQL 提供了 DataFrame 的数据抽象，用于代表不同的结构化数据。创建和使用 DataFrame 就能够处理不同类型的结构化数据。

3. 兼容 Hive

Hive 是基于 HDFS 的数据仓库，可以被当作一个数据库来使用。将数据存储在 Hive 的表中，通过 Spark SQL 来处理 Hive 中的数据。

4. 支持标准的数据连接

Spark SQL 支持标准的数据连接方式，如 JDBC 和 ODBC。

6.3.2 Spark SQL 的数据模型

通过 SQL 语句处理数据的前提是创建一张表，在 Spark SQL 中，表被定义为 DataFrame，它由两部分组成：表结构的 Schema 和数据集合 RDD，如图 6-12 所示。

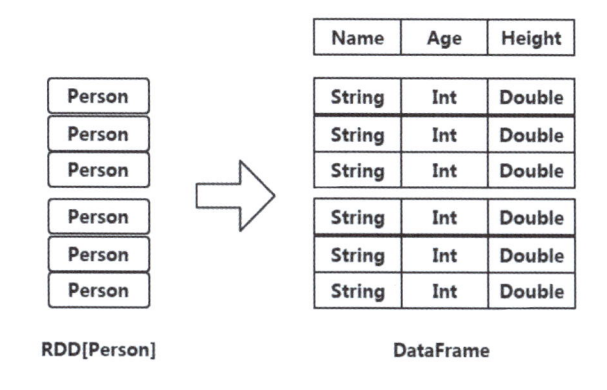

图 6-12

从图 6-12 中可以看出，RDD 是一个 Java 对象的数据集合，而 DataFrame 增加了 Schema 的结构信息，因此可以把 DataFrame 看成一张表，而 DataFrame 的表现形式也可以看成 RDD。DataFrame 除了具有 RDD 的特性，还提供了更加丰富的算子，可以提升执行效率、减少数据读取及进行执行计划的优化。

6.3.3 【实战】创建 DataFrame

DataFrame 可以通过 3 种不同的方式来创建，这里以之前的员工数据 CSV 文件为例，举例进行说明如何使用 spark-shell 在 Spark SQL 中创建 DataFrame。

1. 使用 case class 定义表结构

（1）定义员工表的结构 Schema。

```
scala> case class Emp(empno:Int,ename:String,job:String,mgr:Int,
hiredate:String,sal:Int,comm:Int,deptno:Int)
```

（2）将员工数据读入 RDD。

```
scala> val rdd1 =
sc.textFile("d:\\download\\emp.csv").map(_.split(","))
```

（3）关联 RDD 和 Schema。

```
scala> val emp = rdd1.map(x=>Emp(x(0).toInt,x(1),x(2),x(3).toInt,x(4),
x(5).toInt,x(6).toInt,x(7).toInt))
```

（4）生成 DataFrame。

```
scala> val df = emp.toDF
```

（5）查询员工表中的数据。

```
scala> df.show
```

输出的结果如图 6-13 所示。

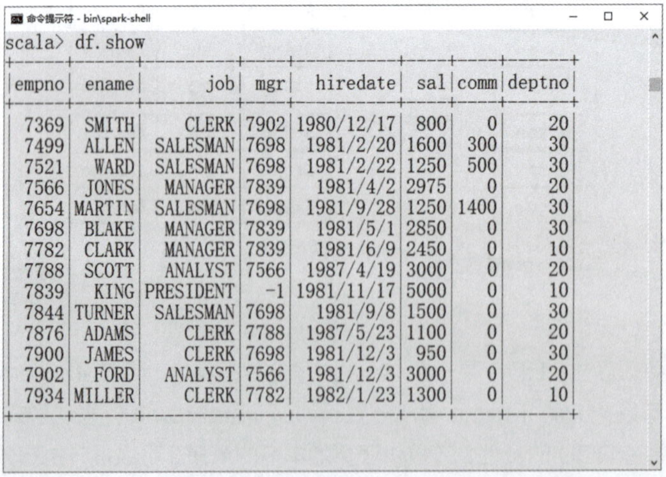

命令提示符 - bin\spark-shell

scala> df.show

empno	ename	job	mgr	hiredate	sal	comm	deptno
7369	SMITH	CLERK	7902	1980/12/17	800	0	20
7499	ALLEN	SALESMAN	7698	1981/2/20	1600	300	30
7521	WARD	SALESMAN	7698	1981/2/22	1250	500	30
7566	JONES	MANAGER	7839	1981/4/2	2975	0	20
7654	MARTIN	SALESMAN	7698	1981/9/28	1250	1400	30
7698	BLAKE	MANAGER	7839	1981/5/1	2850	0	30
7782	CLARK	MANAGER	7839	1981/6/9	2450	0	10
7788	SCOTT	ANALYST	7566	1987/4/19	3000	0	20
7839	KING	PRESIDENT	-1	1981/11/17	5000	0	10
7844	TURNER	SALESMAN	7698	1981/9/8	1500	0	30
7876	ADAMS	CLERK	7788	1987/5/23	1100	0	20
7900	JAMES	CLERK	7698	1981/12/3	950	0	30
7902	FORD	ANALYST	7566	1981/12/3	3000	0	20
7934	MILLER	CLERK	7782	1982/1/23	1300	0	10

图 6-13

2. 使用 StructType 定义表结构

（1）导入需要的类型。

```
scala> import org.apache.spark.sql.types._
scala> import org.apache.spark.sql.Row
```

（2）定义表结构。

```
scala> val myschema = StructType(
    List(StructField("empno",DataTypes.IntegerType),
    StructField("ename",DataTypes.StringType),
    StructField("job",DataTypes.StringType),
    StructField("mgr", DataTypes.IntegerType),
    StructField("hiredate", DataTypes.StringType),
    StructField("sal", DataTypes.IntegerType),
    StructField("comm",DataTypes.IntegerType),
    StructField("deptno", DataTypes.IntegerType)))
```

（3）将数据读入 RDD。

```
scala> val rdd2 =
    sc.textFile("d:\\download\\emp.csv").map(_.split(","))
```

（4）将 RDD 中的数据映射成 Row 对象。

```
scala> val rowRDD = rdd2.map(x=>Row(x(0).toInt,x(1),x(2),
    x(3).toInt,x(4),x(5).toInt,x(6).toInt,x(7).toInt))
```

（5）创建 DataFrame。

```
scala> val df = spark.createDataFrame(rowRDD,myschema)
```

（6）查看 DataFrame 的表结构。

```
scala> df.printSchema
```

输出的信息如下。

```
root
 |-- empno: integer (nullable = true)
 |-- ename: string (nullable = true)
 |-- job: string (nullable = true)
 |-- mgr: integer (nullable = true)
 |-- hiredate: string (nullable = true)
 |-- sal: integer (nullable = true)
 |-- comm: integer (nullable = true)
 |-- deptno: integer (nullable = true)
```

3. 直接加载带格式的数据文件

MaxCompute Spark 提供了结构化的示例数据文件，利用这些结构化的示例数据文件可以直接创建 DataFrame，这些文件位于 Spark 安装目录下的 examples/src/main/resources 目录中。下面是该目录下 people.json 文件中的数据。

```
{"name":"Michael"}
{"name":"Andy", "age":30}
```

```
{"name":"Justin", "age":19}
```

由于数据源文件本身就具有格式，因此可以直接创建 DataFrame。下面是具体的操作步骤。

（1）为了便于操作，将 people.json 文件复制到 D:\download 目录下

```
D:\>cd D:\download\spark-2.3.0-odps0.33.0\examples\src\main\resources
D:\download\spark-2.3.0-odps0.33.0\examples\src\main\resources>copy people.json D:\download\
已复制         1 个文件。
```

（2）直接创建 DataFrame。这里加载的文件在本地目录，也可以是 HDFS 中的文件。

```
scala> val people = spark.read.json("D:\\download\\people.json")
```

（3）执行一个简单的查询。

```
scala> people.show
```

输出的结果如图 6-14 所示。

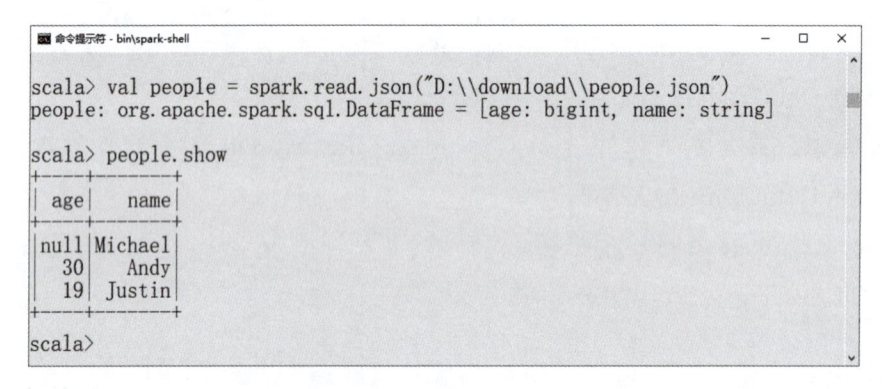

图 6-14

6.3.4 【实战】使用 DataFrame 处理数据

在默认情况下，Spark SQL 可以使用 DSL（Domain Specified Language，领域专用语言）处理 DataFrame 中的数据。

下面通过具体的示例来演示如何使用 DSL 语句，这里以前面创建好的员工表为例。

（1）查询所有的员工姓名。

```
scala> df.select("ename").show
```

或者

```
scala> df.select($"ename").show
```

（2）使用 filter() 过滤数据，查询工资大于 2000 的员工。

`scala> df.filter($"sal" > 2000).show`

执行结果如图 6-15 所示。

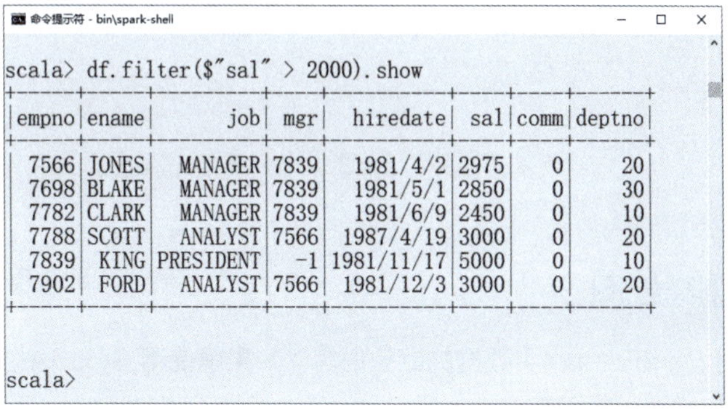

图 6-15

（3）查询所有的员工姓名和工资，并给工资加 100 元。

`scala> df.select($"ename",$"sal",$"sal"+100).show`

执行结果如图 6-16 所示。

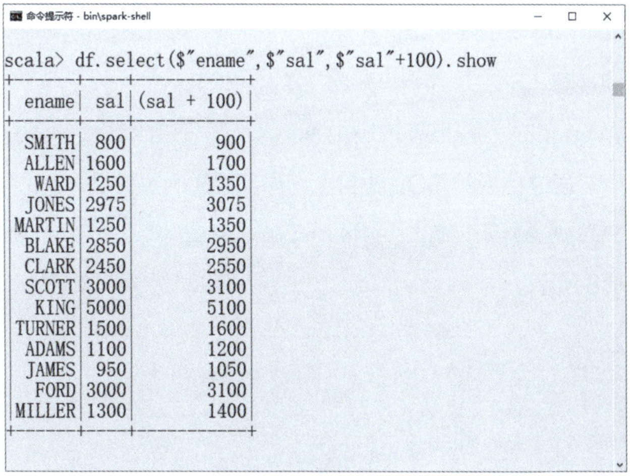

图 6-16

（4）求每个部门的员工人数。

`scala> df.groupBy($"deptno").count.show`

执行结果如图 6-17 所示。

```
scala> df.groupBy($"deptno").count.show
+------+-----+
|deptno|count|
+------+-----+
|    20|    5|
|    10|    3|
|    30|    6|
+------+-----+

scala>
```

图 6-17

6.3.5 【实战】创建视图

DSL 语句是处理 DataFrame 中数据的默认语言。如果想使用 SQL 语句来处理数据，可以基于 DataFrame 先创建视图。视图在 Spark SQL 中分为两种不同的类型，即局部视图和全局视图。局部视图只能在当前会话中使用，而全局视图可以在不同的会话中使用。

> 全局视图是创建在命名空间 global_temp 上的，因此在使用全局视图时，需要加上 global_temp 的前缀。

下面使用之前的员工数据来创建视图。

（1）创建一个局部视图

```
scala> df.createOrReplaceTempView("emp1")
```

（2）在当前会话中，通过标准的 SQL 语句查询局部视图的数据。

```
scala> spark.sql("select * from emp1 where deptno=10").show
```

执行结果如图 6-18 所示。

```
scala> spark.sql("select * from emp1 where deptno=10").show
+-----+------+---------+----+---------+----+----+------+
|empno| ename|      job| mgr| hiredate| sal|comm|deptno|
+-----+------+---------+----+---------+----+----+------+
| 7782| CLARK|  MANAGER|7839|1981/6/9 |2450|   0|    10|
| 7839|  KING|PRESIDENT|  -1|1981/11/17|5000|   0|   10|
| 7934|MILLER|    CLERK|7782|1982/1/23|1300|   0|    10|
+-----+------+---------+----+---------+----+----+------+

scala>
```

图 6-18

（3）在一个新的会话中，通过标准的 SQL 语句查询局部视图。

```
scala> spark.newSession.sql("select * from emp1 where deptno=10").show
```

输出的错误信息如图 6-19 所示。

图 6-19

（4）创建一个全局视图。

```
scala> df.createOrReplaceGlobalTempView("emp2")
```

（5）在当前会话中，通过标准的 SQL 语句查询全局视图的数据。

```
scala> spark.sql("select * from global_temp.emp2 where deptno=10").show
```

执行结果如图 6-20 所示。

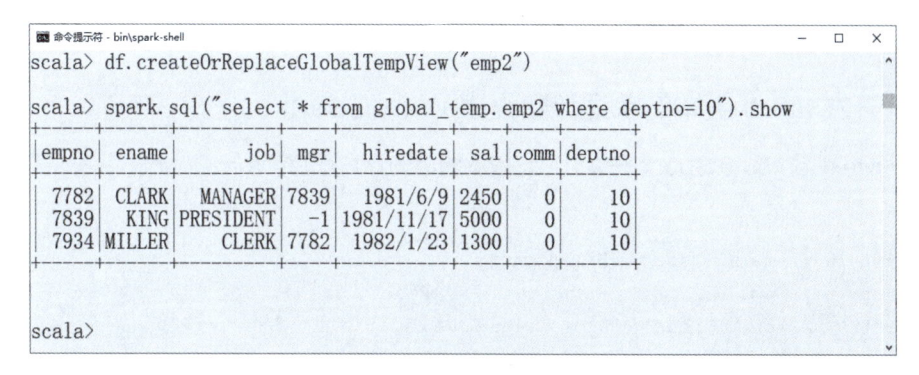

图 6-20

（6）在一个新的会话中，通过标准的 SQL 语句查询全局视图。

```
scala> spark.newSession
      .sql("select * from global_temp.emp2 where deptno=10").show
```

执行结果如图 6-21 所示。

图 6-21

6.4 【实战】MaxCompute Spark 开发案例

MaxCompute Spark 程序开发与原生 Spark 程序开发类似。下面以开发 Java 版本和 Scala 版本的单词计数程序为例，演示 MaxCompute Spark 程序开发的流程。不管是 Java 版本还是 Scala 版本的 MaxCompute Spark 程序，都可以使用 Maven 构建工程。

> Maven 的 Pom 依赖请参考本章的配套资源。

6.4.1 开发 Java 版本的单词计数程序 WordCount

基于 MaxCompute Spark 开发 Java 版本的单词计数程序 WordCount，完整的程序代码如下。

```
import org.apache.spark.SparkConf;
import org.apache.spark.api.java.JavaPairRDD;
import org.apache.spark.api.java.JavaRDD;
import org.apache.spark.api.java.JavaSparkContext;
import org.apache.spark.api.java.function.FlatMapFunction;
import org.apache.spark.api.java.function.Function2;
import org.apache.spark.api.java.function.PairFunction;
```

```java
import scala.Tuple2;

import java.util.Arrays;
import java.util.Iterator;
import java.util.List;
import java.util.regex.Pattern;

public final class JavaWordCount {
    private static final Pattern SPACE = Pattern.compile(" ");

    public static void main(String[] args) throws Exception {
        SparkConf sparkConf = new
                            SparkConf().setAppName("JavaWordCount")
                                    .setMaster("local");
        JavaSparkContext ctx = new JavaSparkContext(sparkConf);
        //读入数据
        JavaRDD<String> lines = ctx.textFile("d:\\download\\data.txt");
        //执行分词操作
        JavaRDD<String> words = lines.flatMap(
            new FlatMapFunction<String, String>() {
            @Override
            public Iterator<String> call(String s) throws Exception {
                return Arrays.asList(SPACE.split(s)).iterator();
            }


        });
        //每个单词计一次数
        JavaPairRDD<String, Integer> ones = words.mapToPair(
            new PairFunction<String, String, Integer>() {
            @Override
            public Tuple2<String, Integer> call(String s) {
                return new Tuple2<String, Integer>(s, 1);
            }
        });
        //将相同的单词进行求和
        JavaPairRDD<String, Integer> counts = ones.reduceByKey(
            new Function2<Integer, Integer, Integer>() {
            @Override
            public Integer call(Integer i1, Integer i2) {
                return i1 + i2;
            }
```

```java
        });
        //执行任务并输出结果
        List<Tuple2<String, Integer>> output = counts.collect();
        for (Tuple2<?, ?> tuple : output) {
            System.out.println(tuple._1() + ": " + tuple._2());
        }
        ctx.stop();
    }
}
```

程序运行在本地模式上的输出结果如图 6-22 所示。

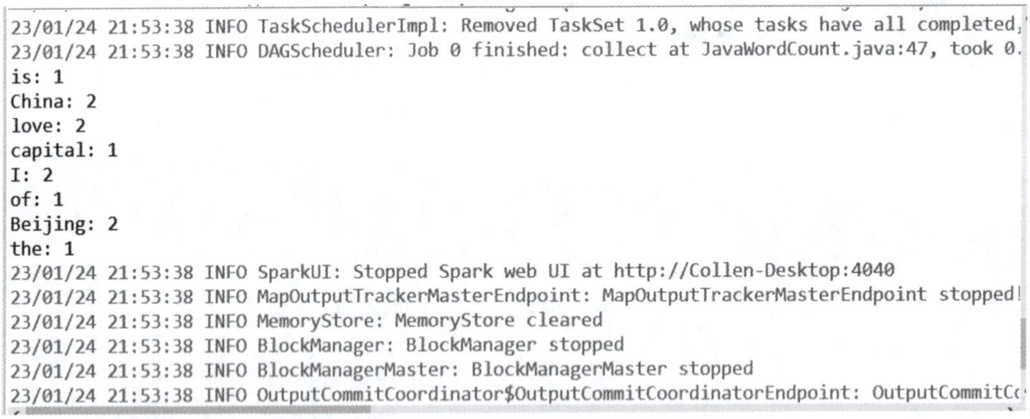

```
23/01/24 21:53:38 INFO TaskSchedulerImpl: Removed TaskSet 1.0, whose tasks have all completed,
23/01/24 21:53:38 INFO DAGScheduler: Job 0 finished: collect at JavaWordCount.java:47, took 0.
is: 1
China: 2
love: 2
capital: 1
I: 2
of: 1
Beijing: 2
the: 1
23/01/24 21:53:38 INFO SparkUI: Stopped Spark web UI at http://Collen-Desktop:4040
23/01/24 21:53:38 INFO MapOutputTrackerMasterEndpoint: MapOutputTrackerMasterEndpoint stopped!
23/01/24 21:53:38 INFO MemoryStore: MemoryStore cleared
23/01/24 21:53:38 INFO BlockManager: BlockManager stopped
23/01/24 21:53:38 INFO BlockManagerMaster: BlockManagerMaster stopped
23/01/24 21:53:38 INFO OutputCommitCoordinator$OutputCommitCoordinatorEndpoint: OutputCommitCo
```

图 6-22

如果需要将 MaxCompute Spark 程序运行在 MaxCompute 项目空间的集群环境上，则需要将加粗部分的代码修改为如下形式。

```
SparkConf sparkConf = new SparkConf().setAppName("JavaWordCount")
```

即去掉 setMaster("local") 部分。

将程序打包成 JAR 文件，再按照 3.4.3 节中的方式使用 spark-submit 提交。

6.4.2　开发 Scala 版本的单词计数程序 WordCount

基于 MaxCompute Spark 开发 Scala 版本的单词计数程序 WordCount，完整的程序代码如下。

```scala
import org.apache.spark.SparkContext
import org.apache.spark.SparkConf
import org.apache.log4j.Logger
```

```
import org.apache.log4j.Level

object WordCountDemo {
  def main(args: Array[String]): Unit = {
    Logger.getLogger("org.apache.spark").setLevel(Level.ERROR)
    Logger.getLogger("org.eclipse.jetty.server").setLevel(Level.OFF)
    //本地模式
    val conf = new SparkConf().setAppName("WordCountDemo")
                              .setMaster("local")
    //集群模式
    //val conf = new SparkConf().setAppName("WordCountDemo")

    //创建SparkContext
    val sc = new SparkContext(conf)
    val result = sc.textFile("d:\\download\\data.txt")
              .flatMap(_.split(" "))
              .map((_,1))
              .reduceByKey(_+_)
    //输出到屏幕
    result.collect.foreach(println)
    sc.stop
  }
}
```

程序运行在本地模式上的输出结果如图 6-23 所示。

```
23/01/24 22:11:48 INFO FileInputFormat: Total input
(is,1)
(China,2)
(love,2)
(capital,1)
(I,2)
(of,1)
(Beijing,2)
(the,1)
```

图 6-23

6.5 诊断 MaxCompute Spark 作业

MaxCompute 为 Spark 作业提供 Logview 工具及 Spark Web UI，帮助用户通过作业日志检

查作业是否已正常提交并执行。当通过 spark-submit 成功提交任务后，MaxCompute 会创建一个 Instance，并在日志中打印 Instance 的 Logview 和 Tracking 的 URL 地址信息。以 3.4.3 节中执行的 Spark 任务为例，任务执行时的输出日志信息如图 6-24 所示。

图 6-24

图 6-24 中方框部分即为 Logview 和 Tracking 的 URL 地址信息。

6.5.1 使用 Logview 工具诊断作业

Logview 是 MaxCompute 自主研发的分布式作业追踪工具。该工具的功能如下。

（1）获取作业的状态。

（2）获取作业各节点的起停调度信息。

（3）Logview 的时效性为 3~5 天。当本地磁盘已满时，StdOut 和 StdErr 会被清理。

（4）获取作业各节点的标准输入和标准输出日志。

> 建议将 Spark 结果输出输出到 StdOut，Spark 的 log4j 日志则默认输出到 StdErr。

在浏览器中打开日志输出的 Logview，查看 MaxCompute Spark 作业的运行情况，如图 6-25 所示。

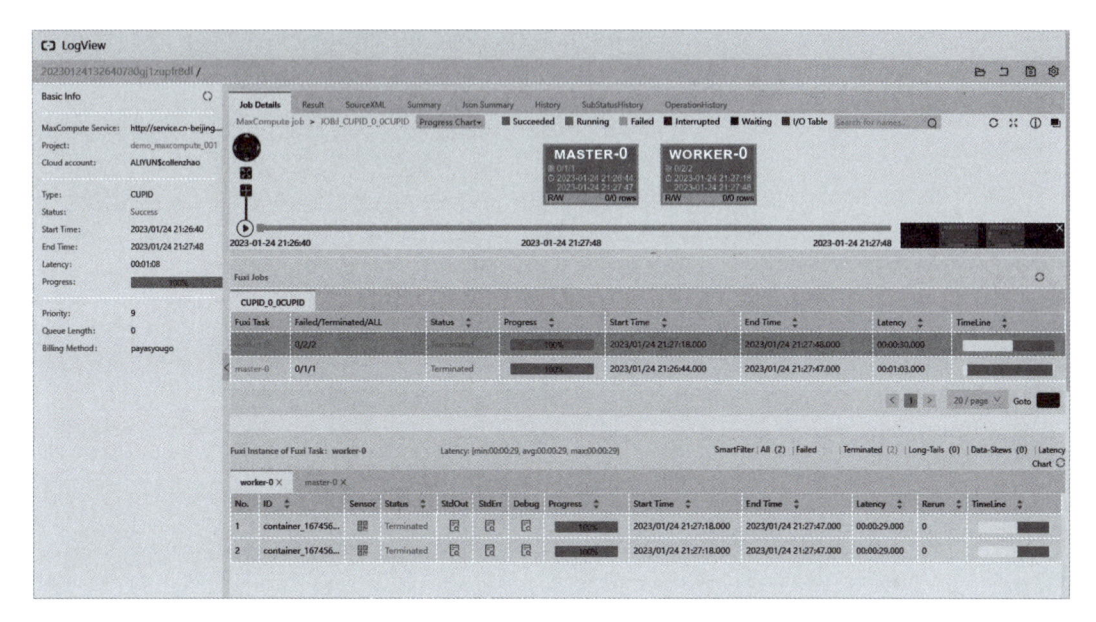

图 6-25

6.5.2 使用 Spark Web UI 诊断作业

日志输出的 Tracking URL，表示 MaxCompute Spark 任务已经提交到 MaxCompute 集群。Tracking URL 是 Spark Web UI 和 HistoryServer 的 URL。该工具的功能如下。

（1）获取原生 Spark Web UI 的所有信息。

（2）作业运行时，显示作业运行的实时信息。

（3）作业运行结束后，把事件从驱动传递到 HistoryServer 有 1~3 分钟的延迟。

> 任务运行结束后立刻打开 Tracking URL，可能会出现一个页面，显示 Application application_1560240626712_2078769635 not found. 错误，稍后重试就会正常。

在浏览器中打开日志输出的 Tracking URL，查看 MaxCompute Spark 作业的运行情况，如图 6-26 所示。

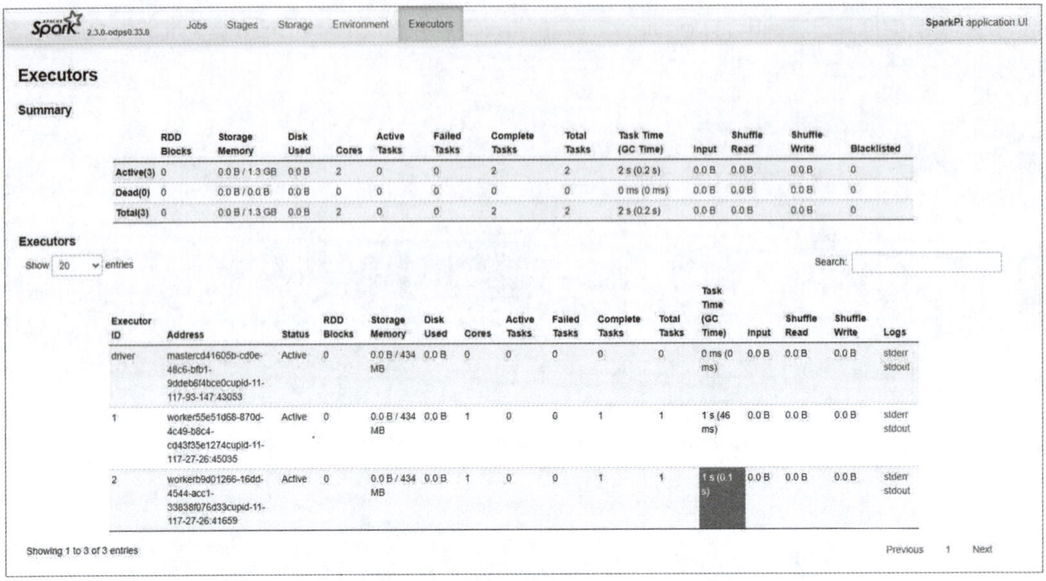

图 6-26

第 7 章
处理图数据——基于 MaxCompute Graph

MaxCompute Graph 是一套面向迭代的图计算处理框架。图计算（Graph Processing）作业使用图（Graph）进行建模，图由点（Vertex）和边（Edge）组成，点和边包含权值（Value）。

7.1 MaxCompute Graph 基础

百度百科对图计算做了如下解释。

> 图计算将数据按照图的方式建模，可以获得以往用扁平化的视角很难得到的结果。图是表示对象之间关联关系的一种抽象数据结构，使用顶点和边进行描述。顶点表示对象，边表示对象之间的关系。可抽象成用图描述的数据即为图数据。图计算就是以图作为数据模型来表达问题并予以解决的过程。以高效解决图计算问题为目标的系统软件称为图计算系统。

MaxCompute Graph 是阿里云大数据技术框架对图计算的一种实现方式，通过迭代对图进行编辑、演化，得出结果。典型应用有 PageRank、单源最短距离算法、k 均值聚类算法等。用户可以使用 MaxCompute Graph 提供的接口 Java SDK 编写图计算程序。MaxCompute Graph 支持以下图编辑操作。

（1）修改点或边的权值。

（2）增加、删除点。

（3）增加、删除边。

7.1.1 MaxCompute Graph 的基本概念

在用图表示的数据结构中,涉及很多基本的概念,因此在进一步学习 MaxCompute Graph 之前需要对这些基本概念有所了解。MaxCompute Graph 中涉及的基本概念及其含义如表 7-1 所示。

表 7-1

基 本 概 念	含 义
图	表示对象之间关联关系的一种抽象数据结构
点	在图模型中表示对象
边	在图模型中表示对象之间的关系,由源 ID、目标 ID 和与该边缘关联的数据组成的单个定向边缘
有向图	边有方向性的图模型,一条边的两个点一般为不同的角色,例如页面 A 连接向页面 B。有向图中的边分为出边和入边
无向图	边无方向性的图模型,例如用户组中的普通用户
出边	指从当前点指向其他点的边
入边	指其他点指向当前点的边
度	度表示一个点的所有边的数量
出度	一个点出边的数量
入度	一个点入边的数量
超步(SuperStep)	图进行迭代计算时,一次迭代称为一个超步

7.1.2 MaxCompute Graph 的数据结构

MaxCompute Graph 能够处理的图必须是一个由点和边组成的有向图。由于 MaxCompute 仅提供二维表的存储结构,因此需要将图数据分解为二维表并存储在 MaxCompute 中。用户需要根据自身的业务场景进行分解。

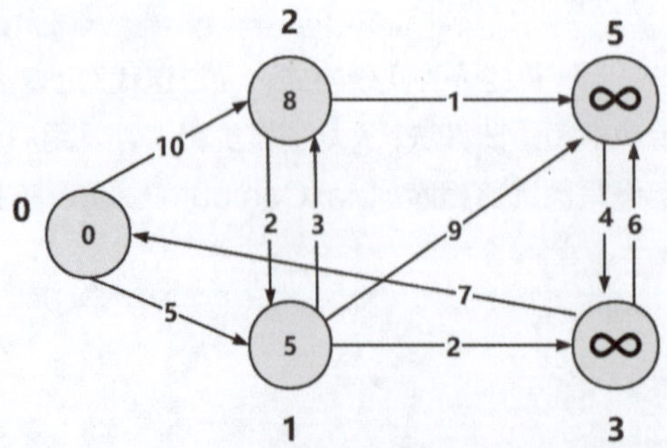

在进行图计算分析时,使用自定义的 GraphLoader 将二维表数据转换为 MaxCompute Graph 引擎中的点和边。图 7-1 展示了一个典型的图。

从图 7-1 中可以看出,图中的点和边可以采用下面的数据结构表示。

图 7-1

（1）点的结构为<ID, Value, Halted, Edges>，参数如下。

- ID：点标识符。
- Value：权值。
- Halted：状态，表示是否要停止迭代。
- Edges：出边集合，以该点为起始点的所有边列表。

（2）边的结构为<DestVertexID, Value>，参数如下。

- DestVertexID：目标点。
- Value：权值。

有了这样的数据结构表示方式，图 7-1 可以以表 7-2 的二维表格式描述。

表 7-2

Vertex	<ID, Value, Halted, Edges>
v0	<0, 0, false, [<1, 5 >, <2, 10 >]>
v1	<1, 5, false, [<2, 3>, <3, 2>, <5, 9>]>
v2	<2, 8, false, [<1, 2>, <5, 1 >]>
v3	<3, Long.MAX_VALUE, false, [<0, 7>, <5, 6>]>
v5	<5, Long.MAX_VALUE, false, [<3, 4 >]>

7.1.3　MaxCompute Graph 的程序逻辑

MaxCompute Graph 程序主要包含图加载、迭代计算、迭代终止等处理步骤。

Graph 程序的伪代码描述如下所示。

```
//1. load
for each record in input_table {
  GraphLoader.load();
}
//2. setup
WorkerComputer.setup();
for each aggr in aggregators {
  aggr.createStartupValue();
}
for each v in vertices {
  v.setup();
}
//3. superstep
for (step = 0; step < max; step ++) {
  for each aggr in aggregators {
    aggr.createInitialValue();
```

```
    }
    for each v in vertices {
        v.compute();
    }
}
//4. cleanup
for each v in vertices {
  v.cleanup();
}
WorkerComputer.cleanup();
```

1. 初始化图

初始化图包含两个步骤。

（1）图加载。框架调用自定义的 GraphLoader，将输入表的记录解析为点或边。

（2）分布式化。框架调用自定义的 Partitioner，对点进行分片（默认的分片逻辑是，根据点 ID 的哈希值对 Worker 个数取模分片），并将其分配到相应的 Worker。

假设 Worker 个数是 2，则 v0、v2 会被分配到 Worker0，因为 ID 对 2 取模结果为 0，而 v1、v3、v5 将被分配到 Worker1，因为 ID 对 2 取模结果为 1，如图 7-2 所示。

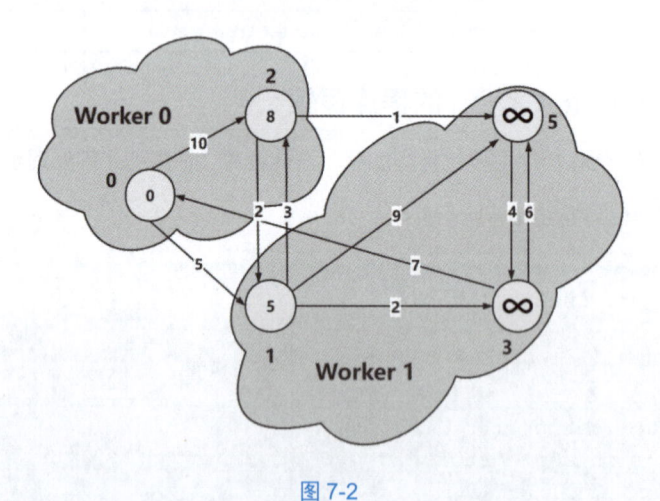

图 7-2

2. 迭代计算

一次迭代为一个超步，遍历所有非结束状态（Halted 值为 False）的点或收到消息的点（处于结束状态的点收到信息会被自动唤醒），并调用其 compute()方法。

在实现的 compute()方法中，需要完成以下步骤。

(1)处理上一个超步发送给当前点的消息。

(2)根据需要对图进行编辑,例如修改点、边的取值,发送消息给某些点,增加、删除点或边。

(3)通过 Aggregator 将信息汇总到全局信息。

> Aggregator 机制将在 7.1.4 节中介绍。

(4)设置当前点的状态,结束或非结束状态。

(5)迭代过程中,框架会将消息以异步的方式发送到对应 Worker,并在下一个超步进行处理,无须人工干预。

3. 迭代终止

满足以下任意条件,迭代就会终止。

(1)所有点处于结束状态(Halted 值为 True)且没有新消息产生。

(2)达到最大迭代次数。

(3)某个 Aggregator 的 terminate() 方法返回 True。

7.1.4 MaxCompute Graph 的 Aggregator 机制

Aggregator 是 MaxCompute Graph 作业中常用的特征,特别适用于解决机器学习问题。在 MaxCompute Graph 中,Aggregator 用于汇总并处理全局信息。

1. Aggregator 机制的处理方式

Aggregator 的处理逻辑分为两部分:一部分在所有 Worker 上执行,即分布式执行;另一部分只在 Aggregator Owner 所在的 Worker 上执行,即单点执行。

> 在所有 Worker 上执行的操作包括创建初始值及局部聚合,然后将局部聚合结果发送给 Aggregator Owner 所在的 Worker。Aggregator Owner 所在的 Worker 先聚合普通 Worker 发送过来的局部聚合对象,得到全局聚合结果,然后判断迭代是否结束。全局聚合的结果会在下一轮迭代分发给所有 Worker,供下一轮迭代使用。

Aggregator 的处理逻辑如图 7-3 所示。

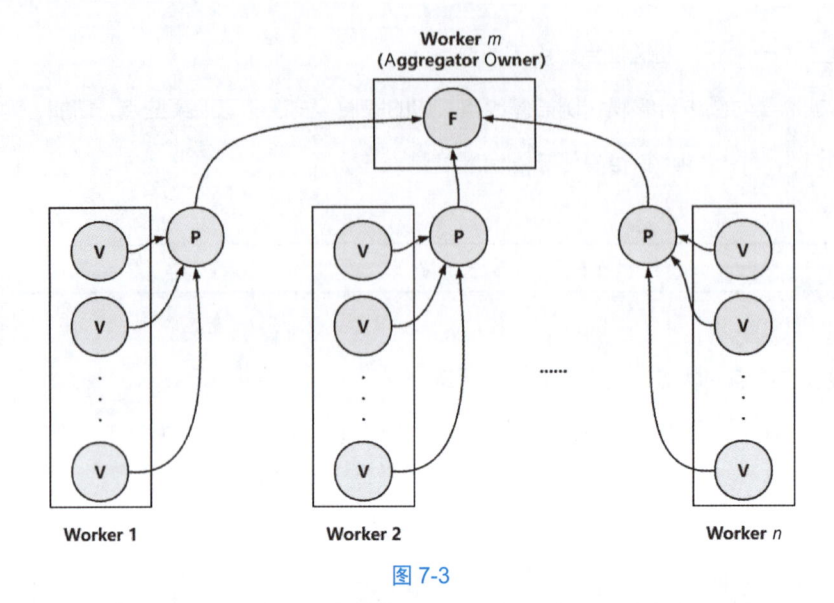

图 7-3

在了解了 Aggregator 的处理逻辑后，其完整的处理流程分为以下 6 个步骤。

（1）每个 Worker 启动时，执行 createStartupValue()用于创建 AggregatorValue。

（2）每轮迭代开始前，每个 Worker 执行 createInitialValue()来初始化本轮的 AggregatorValue。

（3）一轮迭代中，每个点通过 context.aggregate()来执行 aggregate()实现 Worker 内的局部迭代。

（4）每个 Worker 将局部迭代结果发送给 AggregatorOwner 所在的 Worker。

（5）Aggregator Owner 所在 Worker 执行多次 merge()，实现全局聚合。

（6）Aggregator Owner 所在 Worker 执行 terminate()，处理全局聚合结果，并决定是否结束迭代。

2. Aggregator 的 API

Aggregator 提供了 5 个 API 供用户使用。下面详细说明了这 5 个 API 的调用时机及常规用途。

1）createStartupValue(context)

该 API 在所有 Worker 上执行一次，在所有迭代开始前调用，通常用于初始化 AggregatorValue。在第 0 轮迭代中，调用 WorkerContext.getLastAggregatedValue()或 ComputeContext.getLastAggregatedValue()可以获取该 API 初始化的 AggregatorValue 对象。

2）createInitialValue(context)

该 API 在所有 Worker 上每轮迭代开始时调用一次，用于初始化本轮迭代所用的 AggregatorValue。通常操作是先通过 WorkerContext.getLastAggregatedValue() 得到上一轮迭代的结果，然后执行部分初始化操作。

3）aggregate(value, item)

该 API 同样在所有 Worker 上执行。与上述两个 API 不同的是，该 API 由用户显示调用 ComputeContext#aggregate(item) 来触发，而上述两个 API 由框架自动调用。该 API 用于执行局部聚合操作，其中，第 1 个参数 value 是本 Worker 在该轮迭代已经聚合的结果（初始值是 createInitialValue() 返回的对象），第 2 个参数是用户的代码调用 ComputeContext#aggregate(item) 传入的参数。该 API 中通常用 item 更新 value 以实现聚合。在所有 aggregate(value, item) 执行完后，得到的 value 就是该 Worker 的局部聚合结果，之后由框架发送给 Aggregator Owner 所在的 Worker。

4）merge(value, partial)

该 API 在 Aggregator Owner 所在 Worker 上执行，用于合并各 Worker 局部聚合的结果，得到全局聚合对象。与 aggregate(value, item) 类似，value 是已经聚合的结果，而 partial 是待聚合的对象，同样用 partial 更新 value。

假设有 3 个 Worker，分别是 w0、w1、w2，其局部聚合结果是 p0、p1、p2。例如，发送到 Aggregator Owner 所在 Worker 的顺序为 p1、p0、p2，则 merge(value, partial) 执行分为以下两个步骤。

（1）执行 merge(p1, p0)，这样 p1 和 p0 就聚合为 p1。

（2）执行 merge(p1, p2)，p1 和 p2 聚合为 p1，而 p1 即为本轮迭代全局聚合的结果。

由上述示例可见，当只有一个 Worker 时，不需要执行 merge(value, partial)，即 merge(value, partial) 不会被调用。

5）terminate(context, value)

当 Aggregator Owner 所在 Worker 执行完 merge(value, partial) 后，框架会调用 terminate(context, value) 执行最后的处理。其中，第 2 个参数 value 即为 merge(value, partial) 最后得到的全局聚合对象，在 terminate(context, value) 中可以继续修改全局聚合对象。在执行完 terminate(context, value) 后，框架会将全局聚合对象分发给所有 Worker，供下一轮迭代使用。terminate(context, value) 的一个特殊之处在于，如果返回 True，则整个作业结束迭代，否则继续执行。在机器学习场景中，通常判断收敛后返回 True 以结束作业。

7.1.5　MaxCompute Graph 的使用限制

在使用 MaxCompute Graph 时有以下限制。

（1）如果单个 Job 引用的 Resource 数量不超过 256 个，则 Table、Archive 按照一个单位计算。

（2）单个 Job 引用的 Resource 总字节数大小不超过 512MB。

（3）单个 Job 的输入路数不能超过 1024（输入表的个数不能超过 64）。单个 Job 的输出路数不能超过 256。

（4）多路输出中指定的 Label 不能为 NULL 或空字符串，长度不能超过 256 个字符，只能包括 A~Z、a~z、0~9、下画线（_）、井号（#）、英文句点（.）和短横线（-）。

（5）单个 Job 中自定义 Counter 的数量不能超过 64 个。Counter 的 group name 和 counter name 中不能带有井号，两者长度之和不能超过 100 个字符。

（6）单个 Job 的 Worker 数由框架计算得出，最大为 1000 个，超过会抛出异常。

（7）单个 Worker 占用 CPU 个数的范围为 50~800。

（8）单个 Worker 占用的 Memory 默认为 4096MB，范围为 256MB~12GB。

（9）单个 Worker 重复读一个 Resource 的次数不大于 64 次。

（10）split_size 默认为 64MB，用户可以自行设置，范围为 0<split_size ≤（9223372036854775807>>20）。

（11）MaxCompute Graph 程序中的 GraphLoader、Vertex、Aggregator 等在集群运行时，受到 Java 沙箱的限制（Graph 作业的主程序不受此限制）。

7.2　使用 MaxCompute Graph 计算单源最短距离

单源最短距离（Single Source Shortest Path，SSSP）是指给定图中一个源点，计算源点到其他所有节点的最短距离。单源就是从一个点到所有其他点的最短路径，得到的结果是一个数组，表示这个点到其他点的最短距离。常用的算法有 Dijkstra 算法和 Bellman-Ford 算法。

7.2.1　单源最短距离算法简介

Dijkstra 算法是求有向图中单源最短距离的经典算法。算法基本计算过程分为以下两个步骤。

（1）初始化：源点 s 到 s 自身的距离（d[s]=0），其他点 u 到 s 的距离为无穷（d[u]=∞）。

（2）迭代计算：如果存在一条从 u 到 v 的边，则从 s 到 v 的最短距离更新为 d[v]=min(d[v], d[u]+weight(u, v))，当所有的点到 s 的距离不再发生变化时，迭代结束。

下面以图 7-1 为例，详细说明单源最短距离进行迭代计算的过程。

图 7-1 可以由表 7-3 表示。点 0 有两条边，分别指向了点 1 和点 2，其权重分别是 5 和 10。因此，点 1 的出边集合表示为[(1:5), (2:10)]，点 1、点 2、点 3 和点 5 的出边集合以此类推。

表 7-3

点 ID	出 边 集 合
0	(1:5)(2:10)
1	(2:3)(3:2)(5:9)
2	(1:2)(5:1)
3	(0:7)(5:6)
5	(3:4)

下面以点 0 为例，计算点 0 到其他点的最短距离。具体的数据处理过程如下。

（1）初始状态。在初始状态下点 0 到其他点的距离如表 7-4 所示。选择距离值最短的点，即点 1，进行下一次迭代计算。

表 7-4

迭代次数	路　　径	点 1	点 2	点 3	点 5
初始状态	{0}	5	10	Long.MaxValue	Long.MaxValue

> Long.MaxValue 表示该点不能够直接到达。

（2）第 1 次迭代。计算点 1 到其他点的最短距离，并加上初始状态下的最短距离值 5。计算的结果如表 7-5 所示。在没有计算过的点中选择距离值最短的点，即点 3，进行下一次迭代计算。

表 7-5

迭代次数	路　　径	点 1	点 2	点 3	点 5
初始状态	{0}	5	10	Long.MaxValue	Long.MaxValue
1	{0,1}	5	8	7	14

（3）第 2 次迭代。计算点 3 到其他点的最短距离，并加上第 1 次迭代的最短距离值 7。计算的结果如表 7-6 所示。在没有计算过的点中选择距离值最短的点，即点 2，进行下一次迭代计算。

表 7-6

迭代次数	路径	点 1	点 2	点 3	点 5
初始状态	{0}	5	10	Long.MaxValue	Long.MaxValue
1	{0,1}	5	8	7	14
2	{0,1,3}	5	8	7	13

（4）第 3 次迭代。计算点 2 到其他点的最短距离，并加上第 2 次迭代的最短距离值 8。计算的结果如表 7-7 所示。在没有计算过的点中选择距离值最短的点，即点 5，进行下一次迭代计算。

表 7-7

迭代次数	路径	点 1	点 2	点 3	点 5
初始状态	{0}	5	10	Long.MaxValue	Long.MaxValue
1	{0,1}	5	8	7	14
2	{0,1,3}	5	8	7	13
3	{0,1,3,2}	5	8	9	9

> 此时没有没有计算过的点只剩下点 5。

（5）第 4 次迭代。计算点 5 到其他点的最短距离，并加上第 3 次迭代的最短距离值 9。计算的结果如表 7-8 所示。

表 7-8

迭代次数	路径	点 1	点 2	点 3	点 5
初始状态	{0}	5	10	Long.MaxValue	Long.MaxValue
1	{0,1}	5	8	7	14
2	{0,1,3}	5	8	7	13
3	{0,1,3,2}	5	8	7	9
4	{0,1,3,2,5}	5	8	7	9

最终，点 0 到其他点的最短距离如表 7-9 所示。

表 7-9

起点 ID	终点 ID	距离
0	0	0
0	1	5
0	2	8

续表

起点 ID	终点 ID	距　　离
0	3	7
0	4	9

由算法基本原理可以看出，此算法非常适合于用 MaxCompute Graph 程序进行求解。每个点维护到源点的当前最短距离值，当这个值变化时，将新值加上边的权值，发送消息通知其邻接点。在下一轮迭代时，邻接点根据收到的消息，更新其当前最短距离，当所有点的当前最短距离不再变化时，迭代结束。

7.2.2 【实战】开发并运行单源最短距离算法程序

如果用户使用 Java 的 Maven 来创建 MaxCompute Graph 工程，就可以从 Maven 库中搜索相应的 odps-sdk-graph，以获取不同版本的 Java SDK。下面是 pom.xml 文件中需要的依赖。

```xml
<dependency>
    <groupId>com.aliyun.odps</groupId>
    <artifactId>odps-sdk-graph</artifactId>
    <version>0.20.7-public</version>
</dependency>
```

MaxCompute Graph SDK 中的主要接口如表 7-10 所示。

表 7-10

主要接口	说　　明
GraphJob	GraphJob 继承自 JobConf，用于定义、提交和管理一个 MaxCompute Graph 作业
Vertex	Vertex 是图的点的抽象，包含 id、value、halted、edges 属性。通过 GraphJob 的 setVertexClass 接口提供 Vertex 实现
Edge	Edge 是图的边的抽象，包含 destVertexId、value 属性。图数据结构采用邻接表，点的出边保存在点的 edges 中
GraphLoader	GraphLoader 用于载入图。通过 GraphJob 的 setGraphLoaderClass 接口提供 GraphLoader 实现
VertexResolver	VertexResolver 用于修改自定义图拓扑。通过 GraphJob 的 setLoadingVertexResolverClass 和 setComputingVertexResolverClass 接口，提供图加载和迭代计算过程中的图拓扑修改的冲突处理逻辑
Partitioner	Partitioner 用于对图进行划分，使计算可以分片进行。通过 GraphJob 的接口提供 Partitioner 实现，默认采用 HashPartitioner，即先对点 ID 求哈希值，然后对 Worker 数目取模
WorkerComputer	WorkerComputer 允许在 Worker 开始和退出时执行用户自定义的逻辑。通过 GraphJob 的 setWorkerComputerClass 接口提供 WorkerComputer 实现
Aggregator	Aggregator 的 setAggregatorClass 定义一个或多个 Aggregator
Combiner	Combiner 的 setCombinerClass 设置 Combiner

主 要 接 口	说　明
Counters	计数器。在作业运行逻辑中，可以通过 WorkerContext 接口取得计数器并进行计数，框架会自动进行汇总
WorkerContext	上下文对象，封装了框架提供的功能。例如，修改图拓扑结构、发送消息、写结果、读取资源等

在了解了 MaxCompute Graph SDK 提供的主要接口后，按照下面的步骤来开发并运行自己的应用程序。

（1）创建输入表和输出表。

```
demo_maxcompute_001>create table sssp_in (v bigint, es string);
demo_maxcompute_001>create table sssp_out (v bigint, l bigint);
```

（2）将测试数据插入输入表 sssp_in。

```
demo_maxcompute_001>insert into sssp_in values
>(1,'2:2,3:1,4:4'),
>(2,'1:2,3:2,4:1'),
>(3,'1:1,2:2,5:1'),
>(4,'1:4,2:1,5:1'),
>(5,'3:1,4:1');
```

（3）确认输入的测试数据。

```
demo_maxcompute_001>select * from sssp_in;
```

输出的信息如下。

```
+----------+--------------+
| v        | es           |
+----------+--------------+
| 1        | 2:2,3:1,4:4  |
| 2        | 1:2,3:2,4:1  |
| 3        | 1:1,2:2,5:1  |
| 4        | 1:4,2:1,5:1  |
| 5        | 3:1,4:1      |
+----------+--------------+
```

（4）开发代码程序。

```
package demo;

import java.io.IOException;
import com.aliyun.odps.io.WritableRecord;
import com.aliyun.odps.graph.Combiner;
import com.aliyun.odps.graph.ComputeContext;
import com.aliyun.odps.graph.Edge;
```

```java
import com.aliyun.odps.graph.GraphJob;
import com.aliyun.odps.graph.GraphLoader;
import com.aliyun.odps.graph.MutationContext;
import com.aliyun.odps.graph.Vertex;
import com.aliyun.odps.graph.WorkerContext;
import com.aliyun.odps.io.LongWritable;
import com.aliyun.odps.data.TableInfo;

public class SSSP {
  public static final String START_VERTEX = "sssp.start.vertex.id";
  public static class SSSPVertex extends
      Vertex<LongWritable, LongWritable, LongWritable, LongWritable> {
    private static long startVertexId = -1;
    public SSSPVertex() {
      this.setValue(new LongWritable(Long.MAX_VALUE));
    }

    public boolean isStartVertex(ComputeContext
    <LongWritable, LongWritable, LongWritable, LongWritable> context) {
      if (startVertexId == -1) {
        String s = context.getConfiguration().get(START_VERTEX);
        startVertexId = Long.parseLong(s);
      }
      return getId().get() == startVertexId;
    }

    @Override
    public void compute(ComputeContext
    <LongWritable, LongWritable, LongWritable, LongWritable> context,
        Iterable<LongWritable> messages) throws IOException {
      long minDist = isStartVertex(context) ? 0 : Integer.MAX_VALUE;
      for (LongWritable msg : messages) {
        if (msg.get() < minDist) {
          minDist = msg.get();
        }
      }

      if (minDist < this.getValue().get()) {
        this.setValue(new LongWritable(minDist));
        if (hasEdges()) {
          for (Edge<LongWritable, LongWritable> e : this.getEdges()) {
            context.sendMessage(e.getDestVertexId(),
                          new LongWritable(minDist
              + e.getValue().get()));
```

```java
      }
    }
  } else {
    voteToHalt();
  }
}

@Override
public void cleanup(WorkerContext
<LongWritable, LongWritable, LongWritable, LongWritable> context)
    throws IOException {
  context.write(getId(), getValue());
}
}

public static class MinLongCombiner extends
    Combiner<LongWritable, LongWritable> {

  @Override
  public void combine(LongWritable vertexId,
                      LongWritable combinedMessage,
    LongWritable messageToCombine) throws IOException {
    if (combinedMessage.get() > messageToCombine.get()) {
      combinedMessage.set(messageToCombine.get());
    }
  }

}

public static class SSSPVertexReader extends
GraphLoader<LongWritable, LongWritable, LongWritable, LongWritable> {

  @Override
  public void load(
    LongWritable recordNum,
    WritableRecord record,
    MutationContext
  <LongWritable, LongWritable, LongWritable, LongWritable> context)
      throws IOException {
    SSSPVertex vertex = new SSSPVertex();
    vertex.setId((LongWritable) record.get(0));
    String[] edges = record.get(1).toString().split(",");
    for (int i = 0; i < edges.length; i++) {
      String[] ss = edges[i].split(":");
```

```java
      vertex.addEdge(new LongWritable(Long.parseLong(ss[0])),
          new LongWritable(Long.parseLong(ss[1])));
    }
    context.addVertexRequest(vertex);
  }
}

public static void main(String[] args) throws IOException {
  if (args.length < 2) {
    System.out.println("Usage: <startnode> <input> <output>");
    System.exit(-1);
  }

  GraphJob job = new GraphJob();
  job.setGraphLoaderClass(SSSPVertexReader.class);
  job.setVertexClass(SSSPVertex.class);
  job.setCombinerClass(MinLongCombiner.class);

  job.set(START_VERTEX, args[0]);
  job.addInput(TableInfo.builder().tableName(args[1]).build());
  job.addOutput(TableInfo.builder().tableName(args[2]).build());

  long startTime = System.currentTimeMillis();
  job.run();
  System.out.println("Job Finished in "
      + (System.currentTimeMillis() - startTime) / 1000.0 + " seconds");
  }
}
```

（5）将程序打包为 sssp.jar，并将任务 JAR 文件上传到 MaxCompute 的项目空间中。

```
demo_maxcompute_001>add jar D:\download\sssp.jar;
```

（6）执行计算任务。

```
demo_maxcompute_001>jar -libjars sssp.jar -classpath
>D:\download\sssp.jar demo.SSSP 1 sssp_in sssp_out;
```

> 执行任务的命令格式为 Usage: <startnode> <input> <output>
> 这里执行的命令的含义是计算点 1 到其他点的最短距离。

（7）任务计算完成后，查看计算的结果。

```
demo_maxcompute_001>select * from sssp_out;
```

输出的结果如下。

```
+----------+----------+
| v        | 1        |
+----------+----------+
| 1        | 0        |
| 2        | 2        |
| 3        | 1        |
| 4        | 3        |
| 5        | 2        |
+----------+----------+
```

从输出的结果可以看出：点 1 到点 1、点 2、点 3、点 4 和点 5 的最短距离分别是 0、2、1、3 和 2。

第 8 章 MaxCompute 的权限与安全

由于 MaxCompute 构建在阿里云的公有云环境之上，因此对 MaxCompute 项目空间中资源的保护显得格外重要。为此，MaxCompute 提供了一套非常强大的安全机制来确保项目空间的安全。

8.1 MaxCompute 的权限与安全简介

MaxCompute 提供的安全机制主要包含以下几个方面。

1. 用户管理

支持云账号和 RAM 账号两种账号体系，其中云账号也可以被叫作主账号。对于 RAM 账号，仅识别账号体系而不识别 RAM 权限体系，即可以将云账号拥有的任意 RAM 子账号加入 MaxCompute 的项目，但 MaxCompute 在对该 RAM 子账号进行权限验证时，并不会考虑 RAM 中的权限定义。

用户管理中非常重要的一个方面就是管理用户的权限。管理员可以在 MaxCompute 项目空间中对用户进行添加（Add）、移除（Remove）和授权（Grant）管理，还可以通过角色（Role）管理权限。MaxCompute 项目空间中默认有 Admin 角色。授权方式包含 ACL（Access Control List）和 Policy 两种。

ACL 使用的语法类似于 SQL92 定义的 GRANT 和 REVOKE 语法，通过简单的授权语句来完成对已存在的项目空间对象的授权或撤销授权。授权语法举例如下。

```
grant actions on object to subject;
revoke actions on object from subject;
```

> Policy 授权方式将在 8.3.4 节中介绍。

2. 标签安全策略

基于标签的安全（LabelSecurity）是项目空间级别的一种强制访问控制（Mandatory Access Control，MAC）策略，它可以让项目空间管理员更加灵活地控制用户对列级别敏感数据的访问。

3. 跨项目空间的资源分享

Package 是一种跨项目空间共享数据及资源的机制，主要用于解决跨项目空间的用户授权问题，可以将表、资源、函数等分享给其他项目，而无须对其他项目的用户进行管理。

4. 项目空间的数据保护

主要解决类似于不允许用户将数据转移到项目空间之外的需求。

8.2 管理 MaxCompute 的用户

MaxCompute 的用户管理涉及 3 个不同的方面，即用户、角色和权限。角色是权限的集合，三者紧密相连。

管理员在管理 MaxCompute 用户时，可以执行以下操作。

（1）将用户添加至 MaxCompute 项目中，并通过授权操作，授予用户指定对象的指定权限。

（2）根据用户的操作范围，快速将 MaxCompute 已定义的角色授予用户。

（3）根据业务需要自定义角色，并对角色授权后，将角色赋予用户。

（4）根据需要查看用户或角色的权限信息。

当 MaxCompute 项目需要多人维护时，非项目所有者的用户必须被加入 MaxCompute 项目，且被授予相应的权限，才能操作 MaxCompute 中的表、资源、函数或作业（实例）。

MaxCompute 支持云账号和 RAM 账号两种账号体系。二者的区别如下。

（1）创建的阿里云账号为主账号，作为阿里云系统识别的资源消费账号，主账号拥有该账户的所有权限。

（2）当需要邀请其他用户协助使用 MaxCompute 服务时，需要创建 RAM 用户，并通过主账号为 RAM 用户授权。

> RAM 是阿里云为客户提供的用户身份管理与资源访问控制服务。
>
> 通过 RAM 服务，主账号可以创建、管理用户账号（RAM 账号），控制这些用户账号对主账号下资源具有的操作权限。
>
> 从归属关系上看，云账号与 RAM 用户是一种主子关系。
>
> 从权限角度上看，云账号与 RAM 用户是一种 Root 与 User 的关系（类似于 Linux 系统中的 Root 和 User）。

当项目的所有者需要为用户授权时，需要先将该用户添加到自己的项目中，只有添加到项目中的用户才能被授权。命令格式如下。

```
add user ALIYUN$<account_name>;
```

其中，account_name 是阿里云账号的账号名称。例如 odps_test_user@aliyun.com。

下面将用户 ALIYUN$collenzhao2 添加到项目空间中。

（1）执行命令添加用户。

```
demo_maxcompute_001>add user ALIYUN$collenzhao2;
```

（2）验证用户是否添加成功。

```
demo_maxcompute_001>list users;
```

输出的信息如下。

```
ALIYUN$collenzhao2
```

（3）通过下面的语句添加 RAM 账号。

```
demo_maxcompute_001>add accountprovider ram;
```

（4）添加成功后，项目空间所有者可以执行如下命令，查看该项目支持的账号系统，确认 RAM 账号是否添加成功。

```
demo_maxcompute_001>list accountproviders;
```

输出的信息如下。

```
ALIYUN, RAM
```

8.3 管理 MaxCompute 的权限

为确保 MaxCompute 项目数据的安全性，项目所有者或具备授权权限的用户需要对项目内成员的权限进行合理管控，确保权限不会过大，也不会过小。

在将用户添加到项目中后，项目所有者或项目管理员需要为用户授权，之后用户才能执行操作。

MaxCompute 提供了 ACL 授权、Policy 授权、跨项目数据分享和项目数据保护等多种授权方式。

> 这里将重点讨论 ACL 授权和 Policy 授权。

在 ACL 授权中，MaxCompute 的主体是用户或角色，客体是项目中各种类型的对象，包括项目、表、函数、资源和实例。操作与对象类型有关，不同对象类型支持的操作不同。当对象已经存在时，才能进行授权操作。当对象被删除时，权限数据会被自动删除。

Policy 授权是一种基于策略的授权。通过 Policy 授权的权限数据（即访问策略）被看作是授权主体的一种子资源。只有当主体（用户或角色）存在时，才能进行 Policy 授权操作。当主体被删除后，权限数据会被自动删除。Policy 授权使用 MaxCompute 自定义的一种访问策略语言来进行授权，允许或禁止主体对项目空间对象的访问权限。

8.3.1 授权的三要素

授权一般涉及 3 个要素，即主体（Subject，可以是用户，也可以是角色）、客体（Object）和操作（Action）。主体、客体和操作的说明如表 8-1 所示。

表 8-1

授权要素	说　　明
主体	被授予权限的用户或角色，即被授权人。 需要注意的是： ● 被授权人必须已添加至 MaxCompute 项目中。 ● 使用阿里云账号执行授权操作时，支持为当前账号下的 RAM 用户和其他阿里云账号授权。 ● 使用 RAM 账号执行授权操作时，仅支持为隶属同一个阿里云账号的其他 RAM 用户授权，不支持为其他账号授权
客体	主要指 MaxCompute 项目中的对象或行为。 下面是 MaxCompute 中的对象。 ● 项目：MaxCompute 项目。 ● 表：MaxCompute 项目中的表或视图。在 MaxCompute 项目中，视图是虚拟表，权限操作与表相同（如果视图 Owner 缺失视图引用表的 Select 权限，则视图不可用）。 ● 函数：MaxCompute 项目中用户自定义的函数。 ● 资源：MaxCompute 项目中上传的资源，例如 JAR 包、ZIP 包。 ● 实例：MaxCompute 作业运行时生成的实例。 下面是 MaxCompute 中常见的行为。 ● Tunnel 下载：下载表、资源或实例。 ● 访问敏感数据：如访问表或表的列级敏感数据。 ● 分享 Package：实现跨项目访问资源。 ● 管理权限：对权限执行某种操作
操作	操作与客体类型有关，不同客体类型所支持的操作不相同。例如表的读、写、查操作

8.3.2 项目空间内的权限

MaxCompute 项目及项目内的权限如表 8-2 所示。

表 8-2

客体	操作	说明
项目	Read	查看项目自身（不包括项目中的任何对象）的信息
	Write	更新项目自身（不包括项目中的任何对象）的信息
	List	查看项目所有类型的对象列表。例如 show tables;、show functions;
	CreateTable	在项目中创建表。例如 create table <table_name>...;
	CreateInstance	在项目中创建实例，即运行作业
	CreateFunction	在项目中创建自定义函数。例如 create function <function_name> ...;
	CreateResource	在项目中添加资源。例如 add file|archive|py|jar <local_file>... ;、add table <table_name> ...;
	All	具备上述 Project 的所有权限
表	Describe	读取表的元数据信息，包括表结构、创建时间、修改时间、表数据大小等。例如 desc <table_name>;
	Select	查看表的数据。例如 select * from <table_name>;
	Alter	修改表的元数据信息，包括修改表所有人、修改表名称、修改列名、添加或删除分区等。例如 alter table <table_name> add if not exists partition ...;
	Update	更新表数据。例如 insert into|overwrite table <table_name> ...;、update <table_name> set ...;、delete from <table_name> where ...;
	Drop	删除表。例如 drop table <table_name>;
	ShowHistory	查看表的备份数据信息。例如 show history for table <table_name>;
	All	具备上述 Table 的所有权限
函数	Read	读取自定义函数的程序文件
	Write	更新自定义函数
	Delete	删除自定义函数。例如 drop function <function_name>;
	Execute	调用自定义函数。例如 select <function_name> from ...;
	All	具备上述 Function 的所有权限
资源	Read	读取资源
	Write	更新资源
	Delete	删除资源。例如 drop resource <resource_name>;
	All	具备上述 Resource 的所有权限
实例	Read	读取实例
	Write	更新实例
	All	具备上述 Instance 的所有权限

8.3.3 【实战】使用 ACL 授权

MaxCompute 支持通过 ACL 方式授予用户或角色对指定对象执行指定操作的权限。ACL 权限控制为白名单授权机制。ACL 权限控制方式简单明了，可以实现精准授权。

1. ACL 授权的使用场景

在创建 MaxCompute 项目后，ACL 权限控制功能默认为打开状态。项目所有者可以在 MaxCompute 项目中执行以下命令开启或关闭 ACL 权限控制功能。

```
set CheckPermissionUsingACL=true|false;
```

ACL 权限控制适用于以下两种不同的场景。

（1）为用户授权：直接为单个用户授予对指定对象执行单个或多个操作的权限。

（2）基于角色为用户授权：先为单个角色授予对指定对象执行单个或多个操作的权限，再将角色绑定至多个用户，用户即可具备角色的权限。

> 关于角色的知识将在 8.4 节中进行介绍。

2. 示例

在进行具体的 ACL 授权之前，需要对 ACL 权限控制命令的格式有一定的了解。

ACL 授权与撤销 ACL 授权的命令格式如下。

```
#ACL 授权
grant <actions> on <object_type> <object_name>
[(<column_list>)] to <subject_type> <subject_name>
[privilegeproperties(
"conditions" = "<conditions>", "expires"="<days>")];

#撤销 ACL 授权
revoke <actions> on <object_type> <object_name>
[(<column_list>)] from <subject_type> <subject_name>;

#列级别权限控制
grant <actions> on table <table_name> (<column_list>)
to <subject_type> <subject_name>;
revoke <actions> on table <table_name> (<column_list>)
from <subject_type> <subject_name>;
```

下面将通过具体的实例来演示如何完成 ACL 授权与撤销 ACL 授权。

1）场景 1

为用户 Alice 授予表的读取元数据和表数据的权限。具体的操作步骤如下。

（1）创建一张分区表 sale_detail。

```
demo_maxcompute_001>create table if not exists sale_detail
>(
>shop_name      string,
>customer_id    string,
>total_price    double
>)
>partitioned by (sale_date string, region string);
```

（2）将用户 Alice 添加为项目成员。

```
demo_maxcompute_001>add user aliyun$alice@aliyun.com;
```

（3）为 Alice 授予权限。

```
demo_maxcompute_001>grant Describe, Select on table sale_detail
>to user aliyun$alice@aliyun.com;
```

（4）查看用户 Alice 的授权结果。

```
demo_maxcompute_001>show grants for aliyun$alice@aliyun.com;
```

输出的结果如下。

```
Authorization Type: ACL
[user/ALIYUN$alice@aliyun.com]
A  projects/demo_maxcompute_001/tables/sale_detail: Describe | Select
```

2）场景 2

在表 sale_detail 的基础上，为用户 Tom 授予表 sale_detail 中 shop_name 和 customer_id 两列的所有操作权限。具体的操作步骤如下。

（1）将用户 Tom 添加为项目成员。

```
demo_maxcompute_001>add user aliyun$tom@aliyun.com;
```

（2）为 Tom 授予权限。

```
demo_maxcompute_001>grant All on table
>sale_detail (shop_name, customer_id) to user aliyun$tom@aliyun.com;
```

（3）查看用户 Tom 的授权结果。

```
demo_maxcompute_001>show grants for aliyun$tom@aliyun.com;
```

输出的结果如下。

```
Authorization Type: ACL
[user/ALIYUN$tom@aliyun.com]
A       projects/demo_maxcompute_001/tables/sale_detail/customer_id: All
A       projects/demo_maxcompute_001/tables/sale_detail/shop_name: All
```

3）场景 3

撤销对用户 Alice 和 Tom 的授权。具体的操作步骤如下。

（1）撤销对 Alice 的授权。

```
demo_maxcompute_001>revoke Describe, Select on table sale_detail
>(shop_name, customer_id) from user aliyun$alice@aliyun.com;
```

（2）撤销对 Tom 的授权。

```
demo_maxcompute_001>revoke All on table sale_detail
>(shop_name, customer_id) from user aliyun$tom@aliyun.com;
```

（3）查看撤销用户 Alice 授权的结果。权限列表无 Describe、Select 权限信息。

```
demo_maxcompute_001>show grants for aliyun$alice@aliyun.com;
```

（4）查看撤销用户 Tom 授权的结果。权限列表无 All 权限信息。

```
demo_maxcompute_001>show grants for aliyun$tom@aliyun.com;
```

8.3.4 【实战】使用 Policy 授权

MaxCompute 支持通过 Policy 权限控制方案，允许或禁止角色对指定对象执行指定操作，在将角色绑定至用户后，用户权限即可生效。Policy 权限控制支持白名单授权机制，即通过使用白名单来控制用户对指定对象执行的操作。

在创建 MaxCompute 项目后，Policy 权限控制功能默认为打开状态。项目所有者可以在 MaxCompute 项目中执行以下命令开启或关闭 Policy 权限控制功能。

```
set CheckPermissionUsingPolicy=true|false;
```

下面通过几个具体的示例来演示如何使用 Policy 授权机制。

1. 基于角色为用户授权，创建黑名单用户

禁止 Tom 删除以 tb_开头的表，具体的操作步骤如下。

（1）创建角色 Worker。

```
demo_maxcompute_001>create role Worker;
```

> 关于角色的内容将在 8.4 节中介绍。

（2）将角色 Worker 绑定至用户 Tom。

```
demo_maxcompute_001>grant Worker TO aliyun$tom@aliyun.com;
```

> 在对用户进行授权操作前，需要保证已经将该用户加入了项目空间。例如，这里的用户 Tom 必须是该项目空间中的用户。

（3）禁止角色 Worker 删除项目空间中以 tb_ 开头的表。

```
demo_maxcompute_001>grant Drop on table tb_* to
>ROLE Worker privilegeproperties("policy" = "true", "allow"="false");
```

（4）查看用户 Tom 的授权结果。

```
demo_maxcompute_001>show grants for aliyun$tom@aliyun.com;
```

输出的结果如下。

```
[roles]
worker

Authorization Type: ACL
[user/ALIYUN$tom@aliyun.com]
A       projects/demo_maxcompute_001/tables/sale_detail/customer_id: All
A       projects/demo_maxcompute_001/tables/sale_detail/shop_name: All

Authorization Type: Policy
[role/worker]
D       projects/demo_maxcompute_001/tables/tb_*: Drop
```

通过这里输出的信息，可以看到用户 Tom 有一项 Policy 授权。其中，D 表示禁止，即禁止删除项目空间 demo_maxcompute_001 中以 tb_ 开头的表。

2. 撤销 Policy 授权，删除黑名单用户

撤销对用户 Tom 的 Policy 授权，具体的操作步骤如下。

（1）收回用户 Tom 绑定的角色 Worker。

```
demo_maxcompute_001>revoke Worker from aliyun$tom@aliyun.com;
```

（2）查看用户 Tom 的授权结果。权限列表无 Drop 权限信息。

```
demo_maxcompute_001>show grants for aliyun$tom@aliyun.com;
```

3. 基于角色为用户授权，创建白名单用户

允许 Tom 修改以 tb_ 开头的表的数据，具体的操作步骤如下。

（1）将角色 Worker 绑定至用户 Tom。

```
demo_maxcompute_001>grant Worker TO aliyun$tom@aliyun.com;
```

（2）允许角色 Worker 修改项目空间中以 tb_ 开头的表的数据。

```
demo_maxcompute_001>grant Update on table tb_* to ROLE
>Worker privilegeproperties("policy" = "true", "allow"="true");
```

（3）查看用户 Tom 的授权结果。

```
demo_maxcompute_001>show grants for aliyun$tom@aliyun.com;
```

输出的结果如下。

```
......
Authorization Type: Policy
[role/worker]
A        projects/demo_maxcompute_001/tables/tb_*: Update
```

其中，A 表示允许，即允许更新项目空间 demo_maxcompute_001 中以 tb_ 开头的表的数据。

4. 撤销 Policy 授权，删除白名单用户

撤销对用户 Tom 的 Policy 授权，具体的操作步骤如下。

（1）收回用户 Tom 绑定的角色 Worker。

```
demo_maxcompute_001>revoke Worker from aliyun$tom@aliyun.com;
```

（2）查看用户 Tom 的授权结果。权限列表无 Update 权限信息。

```
demo_maxcompute_001>show grants for aliyun$tom@aliyun.com;
```

5. 使用 JSON 文件为用户进行精细化授权

Policy 授权可以使用访问策略语言描述权限，这里的访问策略语言其实就是一个 JSON 文件。基本语法如下。

```
#读取项目空间的 Policy
get policy;

#设置（覆盖）项目空间的 Policy
put policy <policy file>;

#读取项目空间中某个角色的 Policy
get policy on role <role name>;

#设置（覆盖）项目空间中某个角色的 Policy
put policy <policy file> on role <role name>;
```

授予项目空间中的所有成员，只能够读取项目空间中的表和资源的权限，具体的操作步骤如下。

（1）在 D:\download 目录下创建 myaccess.json 文件用于描述权限的访问信息，文件的内容如下。

```
{"Version": "1",
"Statement":
[{
   "Effect":"Allow",
   "Principal":"*",
   "Action":["odps:Read"],
   "Resource":"acs:odps:*:projects/demo_maxcompute_001/tables/*"
},
{
   "Effect":"Allow",
   "Principal":"*",
   "Action":["odps:Read"],
   "Resource":"acs:odps:*:projects/demo_maxcompute_001/resources/*"
}]
}
```

（2）执行命令，使用 Policy 机制完成授权。

```
demo_maxcompute_001>put policy d:\download\myaccess.json;
```

> 这里也可以设置（覆盖）项目空间中某个角色的 Policy。例如：
> put policy <policy file> on role <role name>;

（3）查看项目空间中的 Policy。

```
demo_maxcompute_001>get policy;
```

输出信息如下。

```
demo_maxcompute_001>get policy;
{
   "Statement": [{
         "Action": ["odps:Read"],
         "Effect": "Allow",
         "Principal": ["*"],
         "Resource":
["acs:odps:*:projects/demo_maxcompute_001/tables/*"]},
      {
```

```
            "Action": ["odps:Read"],
            "Effect": "Allow",
            "Principal": ["*"],
            "Resource":
["acs:odps:*:projects/demo_maxcompute_001/resources/*"]}],
        "Version": "1"}
```

8.3.5　ACL 授权与 Policy 授权的区别

ACL 授权与 Policy 授权是 MaxCompute 中主要的两种授权方式。这两种授权方式的特点如下。

1. ACL 授权的特点

（1）在授权或撤销授权时，Grantee（如 User 或 Role）和 Object（如 Table）必须已经存在。这点与 Oracle 授权特性相似，可以避免删除并重建同名对象所带来的安全风险。

（2）在删除一个对象时，自动撤销与该对象关联的所有授权。

（3）仅支持 Allow（白名单）授权，不支持 Deny（黑名单）授权。

（4）使用经典的 Grant、Revoke 授权命令进行授权，命令简单，使用时不易出错。不支持带限制条件的授权。

（5）适合简单的授权需求：授权不带限制条件，不需要 Deny，并只需要对已存在对象进行授权。

2. Policy 授权的特点

（1）授权或撤销授权时，不关心 Grantee 或 Object 存在与否。授权对象可以支持以通配符（*）来表达。例如，projects/tbproj/tables/taobao*，表示项目空间 tbproj 中所有以 taobao 开头的表。这点与 MySQL 授权特性相似，允许对不存在的对象授权，授权者应考虑到删除并重建同名对象所带来的安全风险。

（2）在删除一个对象时，与该对象关联的 Policy 授权不会被删除。

（3）同时支持 Allow（白名单）和 Deny（黑名单）授权。当 Allow 和 Deny 授权同时存在时，遵循 Deny 优先原则。

（4）支持带限制条件的授权。授权者可以对 Allow 或 Deny 授权施加条件限制（目前支持 20 种条件操作）。例如，允许请求者的 IP 地址在指定的 IP 地址范围内，同时，访问时间必须在 2017-11-11 23:59:59 之前。

（5）适合相对复杂的授权需求，例如带授权限制条件、有 Deny 授权需求、希望支持对未来的对象授权。

（6）使用 Policy 授权命令进行授权，命令较复杂。

8.4 管理 MaxCompute 的角色

角色是权限的集合，当需要对一组用户授予相同的权限时，可以使用角色来授权。基于角色的授权可以简化授权流程，降低授权管理成本。对多个用户执行相同授权操作时，应优先考虑使用角色授权。

> MaxCompute 的角色管理分为项目级别和租户级别。
> （1）MaxCompute 角色的项目级别管理方式，可以先在 MaxCompute 项目中创建角色并为角色授权，然后将角色绑定至用户，用户会同时具备角色相应的权限。
> （2）MaxCompute 角色的租户级别管理方式，可以实现一个账号管理多个 Project 对象权限，提升权限管理的便捷性。

8.4.1 角色的作用

MaxCompute 角色包括管理类（Admin）角色和资源类（Resource）角色。

1. 管理类角色

管理类角色可以通过 Policy 方式授予管理类权限，不支持对管理类角色授予资源权限，不支持通过 ACL 方式进行管理类权限授权。

2. 资源类角色

资源类角色可以通过 Policy 或 ACL 方式进行资源类权限授权，不支持对其进行管理类权限授权。

MaxCompute 使用角色的主要目的是简化对用户权限的管理。

考虑图 8-1 中的场景。用户 David 和用户 Rachel 是 HR 部门的普通员工，拥有选择雇员和更新雇员的权限；用户 Jenny 是 HR 部门的经理，拥有删除雇员和插入雇员的权限。用户 Jenny 作为经理也应当拥有选择雇员和更新雇员的权限。为了实现这样的权限管理策略，引入了两个角色 HR_MGR 和 HR_CLERK。将选择雇员和更新雇员的权限授予 HR_CLERK 角色，而将删除雇员和插入雇员的权限授予 HR_MGR 角色，同时 HR_MGR 角色继承了 HR_CLERK 角色。这样再把 HR_MGR 角色授予 Jenny，把 HR_CLERK 角色授予 David 和 Rachel，就实现了要求的权限策略。

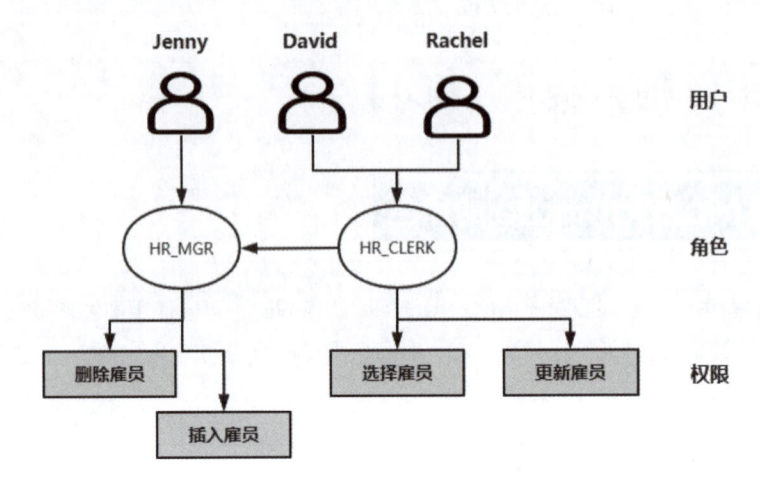

图 8-1

8.4.2 内置角色和自定义角色

MaxCompute 内置了很多角色方便用户使用，也允许用户根据实际的需要创建自己的角色。

1. 内置角色

MaxCompute 在项目级别和租户级别内置了两个管理角色 Super_Administrator 和 Admin。这两个角色的区别如表 8-3 所示。

表 8-3

角色类别	角色名称	角色类型	角色说明
项目级别	Super_Administrator	Admin	MaxCompute 内置的管理角色。拥有操作项目内所有资源类权限和管理类权限
	Admin	Admin	MaxCompute 内置的管理角色。拥有操作项目内所有资源类权限和部分基础管理类权限
租户级别	Super_Administrator	Admin	拥有租户级用户管理、角色管理权限，可以将租户级内置角色赋予其他用户
	Admin	Admin	拥有租户级用户管理、角色管理权限，仅支持将租户级自定义角色赋予其他用户

2. 自定义角色

MaxCompute 支持用户根据实际业务情况自定义管理类角色和资源类角色，对用户进行分类管理。

项目级别与租户级别的自定义角色的区别如表 8-4 所示。

表 8-4

角色类别	角色名称	角色类型	角色说明
项目级别	自定义角色	Admin、Resource	非 MaxCompute 内置的角色，支持对 Project 管理操作的权限定义（管理类角色），也支持对 Project 内对象资源的权限定义（资源类角色）
租户级别	自定义角色	Resource	非 MaxCompute 内置角色，支持对 Quota、Networklink、Project 等对象资源的权限定义（资源类角色）

8.4.3 【实战】使用 MaxCompute 的角色

下面将通过具体的步骤来演示如何使用 MaxCompute 的角色。

假设项目空间的管理员需要为 3 个新加入的项目组的成员 Alice、Bob 和 Charlie 分配对应的角色，这 3 名成员的角色是数据审查员，都需要申请查看 Table 列表、提交作业和读取表 emp 的权限。具体的操作步骤如下。

（1）查看项目空间中的角色。

```
demo_maxcompute_001>list roles;
```

输出的信息如下。

```
admin
super_administrator
```

> 这两个角色都是项目级别的内置角色。

（2）将用户加入项目空间。

```
demo_maxcompute_001>add user aliyun$alice@aliyun.com;
demo_maxcompute_001>add user aliyun$bob@aliyun.com;
demo_maxcompute_001>add user aliyun$charlie@aliyun.com;
```

（3）创建自定义角色。

```
demo_maxcompute_001>create role tableviewer;
```

（4）授予角色权限。

```
demo_maxcompute_001>grant List, CreateInstance
>on project demo_maxcompute_001 to role tableviewer;

demo_maxcompute_001>grant Describe, Select on table emp
>to role tableviewer;
```

（5）将用户赋予角色 tableviewer。

```
demo_maxcompute_001>grant tableviewer to aliyun$alice@aliyun.com;
demo_maxcompute_001>grant tableviewer to aliyun$bob@aliyun.com;
demo_maxcompute_001>grant tableviewer to aliyun$charlie@aliyun.com;
```

8.5 LabelSecurity

MaxCompute 通过 LabelSecurity 实现用户对列级别敏感数据的访问。LabelSecurity 是项目级别的一种强制访问控制策略，它为表或表的列设置敏感等级标签（Label），用户仅可以访问 MaxCompute 项目中敏感等级小于或等于自身访问许可等级的表或列数据。

8.5.1 LabelSecurity 简介

Label 权限控制即 LabelSecurity。在创建 MaxCompute 项目后，LabelSecurity 默认为关闭状态。项目所有者可以在 MaxCompute 项目的项目级别，执行 Set LabelSecurity=true|false;命令，以开启或关闭 LabelSecurity。

如果开启了 LabelSecurity，则项目所有者需要定义明确的表或表的列敏感等级、用户访问许可等级划分标准，并分别为表或表的列、用户或角色，设置敏感等级标签、访问许可等级标签。当用户访问设置了敏感等级标签的数据时，除必须拥有目标表的 SELECT 权限外，仅能访问敏感等级小于或等于自身访问许可等级的表或列数据。

LabelSecurity 对敏感数据的支持能力如下。

（1）最小支持粒度为列级别，即对表的列设置敏感等级标签。

（2）支持对表的任何列设置敏感等级标签。一张表可以由不同敏感等级的列构成。

（3）支持对视图设置敏感等级标签。视图的敏感等级标签和视图对应的源表的敏感等级标签是独立的。

8.5.2 【实战】使用 LabelSecurity

下面通过具体的示例来演示如何在 MaxCompute 项目空间中使用 LabelSecurity。

首先需要开启 LabelSecurity 安全机制。

```
demo_maxcompute_001>set labelsecurity=true;
```

> 默认情况下 labelsecurity 为 false。该操作必须由项目所有者完成。

1. 为用户设置访问许可等级标签

为用户设置访问许可等级标签的语法格式如下。

```
set label <number> to [user|role] <name>;
```

其中，number 的取值范围为 0~9。以下操作只能由项目所有者或 Admin 角色完成。

（1）添加云账号用户 yunma，默认的访问许可等级为 0 级。

```
demo_maxcompute_001>add user aliyun$yunma@aliyun.com;
```

（2）添加 yunma@aliyun.com 的 RAM 子账号用户 allen。

```
demo_maxcompute_001>add user ram$yunma@aliyun.com:allen;
```

（3）将 yunma 的访问许可等级设置为 3 级，该用户能访问访问许可等级不超过 3 级的数据。

```
demo_maxcompute_001>set label 3 to user aliyun$yunma@aliyun.com;
```

（4）将 yunma 子账号用户 allen 的访问许可等级设置为 1 级，该用户能访问访问许可等级不超过 1 级的数据。

```
demo_maxcompute_001>set label 1 to user ram$yunma@aliyun.com:allen;
```

2. 为数据设置敏感等级标签

下面展示了为数据设置敏感等级标签的语法格式。

```
set label <number> to table tablename(column_list);
```

其中，number 取值范围为 0~9。

以下操作只能够由项目所有者或 Admin 角色完成。

（1）将表 t1 的敏感等级设置为 1 级。

```
demo_maxcompute_001>set label 1 to table emp;
```

（2）将表 t1 的 ename 和 job 两列的敏感等级设置为 2 级。

```
demo_maxcompute_001>set label 2 to table emp(ename, job);
```

（3）将表 emp 的敏感等级设置为 3 级。

```
demo_maxcompute_001>set label 3 to table emp;
```

> 注意，此时 ename 和 job 两列的敏感等级仍为 2 级

(4)查看表 emp 中所有列的敏感等级。

```
demo_maxcompute_001>desc emp;
```

输出的信息如下。

```
......
+-------------------------------------------------+
| Native Columns:                                 |
+-------------------------------------------------+
| Field        | Type      | Label | Comment      |
+-------------------------------------------------+
| empno        | bigint    | 3     |              |
| ename        | string    | 2     |              |
| job          | string    | 2     |              |
| mgr          | bigint    | 3     |              |
| hiredate     | string    | 3     |              |
| sal          | bigint    | 3     |              |
| comm         | bigint    | 3     |              |
| deptno       | bigint    | 3     |              |
+-------------------------------------------------+
```

3. 显式授权低级别用户访问高敏感等级数据表

下面展示了相关语句的语法格式。

```
#授予权限
grant label <number> on table <tablename>[(column_list)]
to [user|role] <name> [with exp <days>];
```

其中,默认过期时间是 180 天。

```
#撤销授权
revoke label on table <tablename>[(column_list)]
from [user|role] <name>;
```

```
#清理过期的授权
clear expired grants;
```

具体的操作步骤如下。

(1)显式授权 Alice 访问表 emp 中敏感等级不超过 2 级的数据,授权有效期为 1 天。

```
demo_maxcompute_001>grant label 2 on table emp
>to user aliyun$alice@aliyun.com with exp 1;
```

(2)显式授权 Alice 访问表 emp 中敏感等级不超过 3 级的数据,授权有效期为 1 天。

```
demo_maxcompute_001>grant label 3 on table emp
>to user aliyun$alice@aliyun.com with exp 1;
```

（3）查看 Alice 可以访问的敏感数据集。

```
demo_maxcompute_001>show label grants for aliyun$alice@aliyun.com;
```

输出的信息如下。

```
User Label: 0

+-----------+--------------+---------------------------+
| TableName | GrantedLabel | Expires                   |
+-----------+--------------+---------------------------+
| emp       | 3            | 2023-01-27T15:28:37+0800  |
+-----------+--------------+---------------------------+
```

（4）查看 Alice 可以访问的表 emp 的所有列。

```
demo_maxcompute_001>show label grants on table emp
>for user aliyun$alice@aliyun.com;
```

输出的信息如下。

```
User Label: 0
+-----------+--------------+---------------------------+
| Column    | GrantedLabel | Expires                   |
+-----------+--------------+---------------------------+
| comm      | 3            | 2023-01-27T15:28:37+0800  |
+-----------+--------------+---------------------------+
| deptno    | 3            | 2023-01-27T15:28:37+0800  |
+-----------+--------------+---------------------------+
| empno     | 3            | 2023-01-27T15:28:37+0800  |
+-----------+--------------+---------------------------+
| ename     | 3            | 2023-01-27T15:28:37+0800  |
+-----------+--------------+---------------------------+
| hiredate  | 3            | 2023-01-27T15:28:37+0800  |
+-----------+--------------+---------------------------+
| job       | 3            | 2023-01-27T15:28:37+0800  |
+-----------+--------------+---------------------------+
| mgr       | 3            | 2023-01-27T15:28:37+0800  |
+-----------+--------------+---------------------------+
| sal       | 3            | 2023-01-27T15:28:37+0800  |
+-----------+--------------+---------------------------+
```

（5）撤销 Alice 对表 emp 的敏感数据访问。

```
demo_maxcompute_001>revoke label on table emp
>from user aliyun$alice@aliyun.com;
```

8.5.3 【实战】LabelSecurity 的应用场景示例

在 8.5.2 节中详细介绍了如何使用 LabelSecurity，这里将通过一个具体的示例来说明 LabelSecurity 的应用场景。

假设 user_profile 是某项目中的一张含有敏感数据的表，它包含 100 列，其中，id_card、credit_card、mobile、user_addr、birthday 五列包含敏感数据。当前已经授权了所有用户对该表的 Select 操作。项目所有者希望除拥有 Admin 角色之外的用户不被允许访问敏感数据。

项目所有者执行如下命令进行设置。执行下述命令后，所有非 Admin 角色的用户将无法访问敏感数据。如果由于业务需要，需要访问这些敏感数据，则需要获得项目所有者或 Admin 角色用户的授权。

（1）开启 LabelSecurity 安全机制。

```
demo_maxcompute_001>set LabelSecurity=true;
```

（2）将指定列的敏感等级设置为 2。

```
demo_maxcompute_001>set label 2 to table
>user_profile(mobile, user_addr, birthday);
```

（3）将指定列的敏感等级设置为 3。

```
demo_maxcompute_001>set label 3 to table
>user_profile(id_card, credit_card);
```

（4）Alice 是项目中的一员，由于业务需要，她要申请访问 mobile 列的数据，访问时间为 1 周。项目管理员需执行如下命令授权。

```
demo_maxcompute_001>grant label 2 on table user_profile
>to user aliyun$alice@aliyun.com with exp 7;
```

此时，Alice 由于业务需要而获得了访问敏感等级为 2 的数据的权限。但项目管理员仍然担心 Alice 可能会将 user_profile 表中的敏感等级为 2 的数据复制到她自己新建的另一张表 user_profile_copy 中，进一步将 user_profile_copy 表自主授权给 Bob 访问，因此需要限制 Alice 对敏感数据的复制与传播。

考虑到安全易用性和管理成本，LabelSecurity 的默认安全策略允许 WriteDown，即允许用户向敏感等级不高于用户等级的数据列写入数据，因此 MaxCompute 还无法从根本上解决此问题。但这里可以限制用户的自主授权行为，即只允许对象创建者访问自己创建的数据，而不允许将该对象授权给其他用户。具体的操作如下。

（1）允许对象创建者操作对象。

```
demo_maxcompute_001>set ObjectCreatorHasAccessPermission=true;
```

（2）不允许对象创建者将对象授权给其他用户。

```
demo_maxcompute_001>set ObjectCreatorHasGrantPermission=false;
```

8.6 使用 Package 实现跨项目空间的资源分享

当用户需要跨项目访问资源时，如果未被加入目标资源所属项目，则用户无法直接访问资源。MaxCompute 提供了 Package 授权机制，可以将资源及相应权限打包为 Package，其他项目安装此 Package 后，即可解决跨项目空间访问资源的问题。

8.6.1 什么是跨项目空间的资源分享

假设你是项目空间所有者或管理员（Admin 角色），某个主账号下有多个项目空间，其中一个项目空间里有一些资源（包括 Tables、Resources），现在需要将这些资源分享给其他项目空间，如图 8-2 所示。

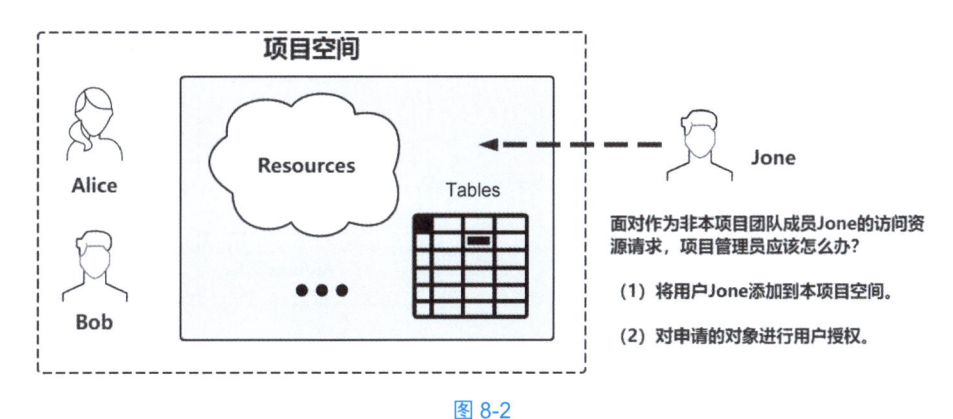

图 8-2

项目管理员可以使用下面两种不同的方法。

（1）将其他项目空间的用户都添加到这个项目空间并逐个进行授权操作。此方法比较烦琐，不推荐在跨项目空间资源分享场景下使用。如果资源需要精细控制单人使用，且申请人是本业务项目团队成员，那么建议使用此方法。

（2）对申请访问的资源对象逐一进行用户授权。

> 很明显这两种方式都没有很好地解决这个问题。为了解决这个问题，MaxCompute 提供了基于 Package 的跨项目空间的资源分享。

8.6.2 Package 的创建与使用

Package 是一种跨项目空间共享数据及资源的机制，主要用于解决跨项目空间的用户授权问题。Package 的使用涉及两个主体：Package 创建者和 Package 使用者。

（1）Package 创建者所在的项目空间是资源提供方。它先将需要分享的资源及其访问权限进行打包，然后许可 Package 使用者安装使用。

（2）Package 使用者所在的项目空间是资源使用方。它在安装了资源提供方发布的 Package 之后，就可以直接跨项目空间访问资源。

在使用 Package 之后，其他项目空间的管理员可以先对项目空间中需要使用的对象进行打包授权（即创建一个 Package），然后许可其他项目空间安装此 Package。其他项目空间的管理员安装了 Package 后，就可以自行管理 Package，进一步授权给自己项目空间中的用户。

使用 Package 实现跨项目空间资源分享的完整流程如图 8-3 所示。

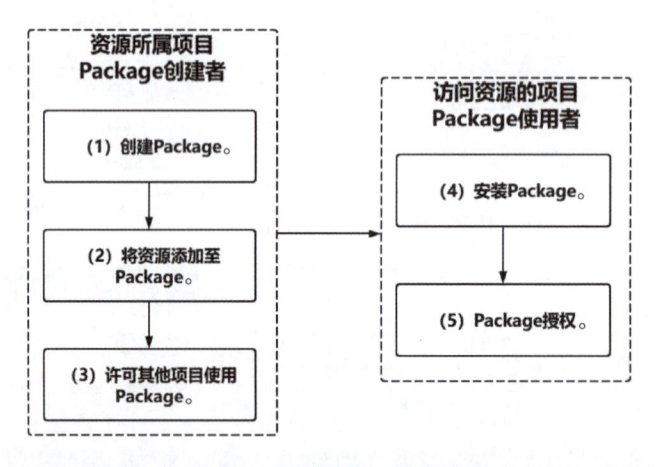

图 8-3

下面将介绍 Package 创建者和 Package 使用者使用的命令。

1. Package 创建者使用的命令

下面介绍了 Package 创建者使用的命令。

（1）创建 Package。

```
create package <pkgname>;
```

其中，pkgname 是 Package 的名称。

> 目前创建的 Package 的名称不能超过 128 个字符。只有项目空间的所有者才有权限执行此命令。

（2）将分享的资源添加到 Package 中。

```
--将对象添加到 Package 中
add project_object to package package_name [with privileges privileges];

--将对象从 Package 中移除
remove project_object from package package_name;
project_object ::= table table_name |
            instance inst_name |
            function func_name |
            resource res_name
privileges ::= action_item1, action_item2, ...
```

（3）许可其他项目空间使用 Package。

```
allow project <prjname> to install package <pkgname> [using label <number>];
```

（4）撤销其他项目空间使用 Package 的许可。

```
disallow project <prjname> to install package <pkgname>;
```

（5）删除 Package。

```
delete package <pkgname>;
```

（6）查看已创建和已安装的 Package。

```
show packages;
```

（7）查看 Package 的详细信息。

```
describe package <pkgname>;
```

2. Package 使用者使用的命令

下面介绍了 Package 使用者使用的命令。

（1）安装 Package。

```
install package <pkgname>;
```

其中，安装 Package 时要求 pkgname 的格式为<projectname>.<packagename>。

> 只有项目空间所有者才有权限执行该操作。

（2）卸载 Package。

```
uninstall package <pkgname>;
```

（3）查看已创建和已安装的 Package。

```
show packages;
```

（4）查看 Package 的详细信息。

```
describe package <pkgname>;
```

8.6.3 【实战】Package 的应用场景示例

下面通过一个示例来演示如何在 MaxCompute 项目中基于 Package 实现跨项目空间的资源分享。

Jack 是项目空间 demo_maxcompute_001 的管理员。John 是项目空间 demo_maxcompute_002 的管理员。由于业务需要，Jack 希望将其项目空间 demo_maxcompute_001 中的某些资源（如员工表 emp、部门表 dept 和资源 mydemo_odps_wc.jar）分享给 John 的项目空间 demo_maxcompute_002。如果项目空间 demo_maxcompute_002 的用户 Bob 需要访问这些资源，则管理员 John 可以通过 ACL 为 Bob 自主授权，无须 Jack 参与。

具体的操作步骤如下。

（1）Jack 在项目空间 demo_maxcompute_001 中创建 Package。

```
--创建一个 Package
demo_maxcompute_001>create package datamining;

--将资源添加到 Package
demo_maxcompute_001>add resource mydemo_odps_wc.jar
>to package datamining;

--将表添加到 Package
demo_maxcompute_001>add table emp to package datamining;
demo_maxcompute_001>add table dept to package datamining;
```

（2）Jack 查看自己创建的 Package。

```
demo_maxcompute_001>describe package demo_maxcompute_001.datamining;
```

输出的结果如图 8-4 所示。

```
demo_maxcompute_001>describe package demo_maxcompute_001.datamining;
CreateTime:        2023-01-26T16:08:30+0800
PackageName:       datamining
SourceProject:     demo_maxcompute_001
Object List
+--------------+---------------------------------------------------------+------------------+
| ObjectType   | ObjectName                                              | ObjectPrivileges |
+--------------+---------------------------------------------------------+------------------+
| RESOURCE     | mydemo_odps_wc.jar                                      | Read             |
| TABLE        | dept                                                    | Describe,Select  |
| TABLE        | emp                                                     | Describe,Select  |
| TABLE_COLUMN | projects/demo_maxcompute_001/resources/mydemo_odps_wc.jar |                |
+--------------+---------------------------------------------------------+------------------+

Allowed Project List
+-------------+-----------+
| ProjectName | UserLabel |
+-------------+-----------+
|             |           |
+-------------+-----------+
```

图 8-4

（3）Jack 将 Package 分享给项目空间 demo_maxcompute_002。

```
demo_maxcompute_001>allow project demo_maxcompute_002
>to install package datamining;
```

（4）John 在项目空间 demo_maxcompute_002 中安装 Package。

```
--安装 Package
demo_maxcompute_002>install package demo_maxcompute_001.datamining;
```

（5）John 查看自己项目空间中的 Package。

```
demo_maxcompute_002>show packages;
```

输出的信息如图 8-5 所示。

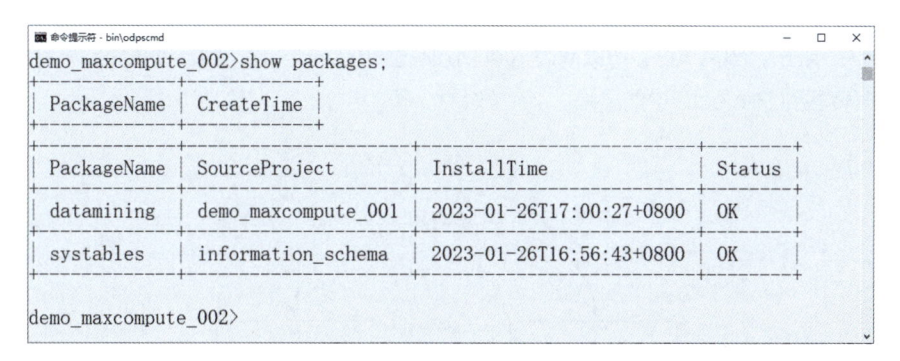

```
demo_maxcompute_002>show packages;
+-------------+-------------+
| PackageName | CreateTime  |
+-------------+-------------+
+-------------+---------------------+-------------------------+--------+
| PackageName | SourceProject       | InstallTime             | Status |
+-------------+---------------------+-------------------------+--------+
| datamining  | demo_maxcompute_001 | 2023-01-26T17:00:27+0800 | OK     |
| systables   | information_schema  | 2023-01-26T16:56:43+0800 | OK     |
+-------------+---------------------+-------------------------+--------+
demo_maxcompute_002>
```

图 8-5

（6）John 查看 demo_maxcompute_001.datamining 的详细信息。

```
demo_maxcompute_002>describe package demo_maxcompute_001.datamining;
```

输出的信息如图 8-6 所示。

```
demo_maxcompute_002>describe package demo_maxcompute_001.datamining;
CreateTime:         2023-01-26T16:08:30+0800
PackageName:        datamining
SourceProject:      demo_maxcompute_001
Object List
+--------------+-------------------------------------------------------------+-------------------+
| ObjectType   | ObjectName                                                  | ObjectPrivileges  |
+--------------+-------------------------------------------------------------+-------------------+
| RESOURCE     | mydemo_odps_wc.jar                                          | Read              |
| TABLE        | dept                                                        | Describe,Select   |
| TABLE        | emp                                                         | Describe,Select   |
| TABLE_COLUMN | projects/demo_maxcompute_001/resources/mydemo_odps_wc.jar   |                   |
+--------------+-------------------------------------------------------------+-------------------+
```

图 8-6

（7）John 通过 ACL 授权 Bob 使用 Package。

```
--通过 ACL 授权 Bob 使用 Package
demo_maxcompute_002>grant Read on package
>demo_maxcompute_001.datamining to user aliyun$bob@aliyun.com;
```

8.7 项目空间的数据保护

部分公司对数据安全非常敏感。例如，不允许员工将工作带回家而只允许在公司内部进行操作；禁用公司所有计算机上的 USB 存储接口。这样做的目的是防止员工泄露敏感数据。作为 MaxCompute 项目空间管理员，也会遇到与不允许用户将数据转移到项目空间之外类似的安全问题。

如图 8-7 所示，用户 Alice 可以同时访问 Project1 和 Project2，则存在 Alice 将 Project1 中的敏感数据转移到 Project2 中的风险。

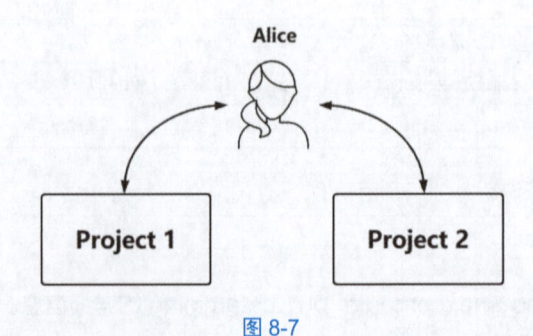

图 8-7

如果 Alice 拥有 Project1.table1 的 Select 权限，也拥有在 Project2 的 CreateTable 权限，则 Alice 可以使用如下语句将 Project1 的数据转移到 Project2。

```
create table project2.table2 as select * from project1.table1;
```

如果项目空间中的数据非常敏感，不允许流出到其他项目空间，MaxCompute 提供了数据保护机制，以确保敏感数据的安全。

8.7.1　MaxCompute 的数据保护机制

同时在多个项目空间中拥有访问权限的用户，可以自由地使用任意支持跨项目空间的数据访问操作来转移项目空间中的数据。如果项目空间中的数据高度敏感，则需要管理员自行设置 ProjectProtection。

在项目空间中执行如下命令，开启 ProjectProtection。

```
set projectProtection=true;
```

在使用 ProjectProtection 时，需要注意以下几点。

（1）ProjectProtection 的默认值为 false。

（2）设置 ProjectProtection 后，项目空间中的数据流向就会得到控制，数据只能流入，不能流出。

（3）跨项目空间的数据访问操作将失效，因为它们违背了 ProjectProtection 规则。

（4）ProjectProtection 是对数据流向的控制，而不是访问控制。只有在用户能访问数据的前提下，控制数据流向才是有意义的。

8.7.2　数据保护机制下数据的流动

项目空间被设置了 ProjectProtection 后，MaxCompute 提供了两种数据流出途径：设置 Exception Policy（例外策略）和设置 TrustedProject（项目互信）。

1. 设置 Exception Policy

在设置 ProjectProtection 时可以附带一个 Exception Policy，命令如下。

```
set ProjectProtection=true with exception <policyFile>;
```

下面通过一个示例来说明 policyFile 文件的格式。

例如，项目管理员允许云账号 Alice@aliyun.com 通过 SQL 任务对表 alipay.table_test 执行查询数据操作时将数据流出 alipay 项目空间。

```
{"Version": "1",
```

```
"Statement":
[{
    "Effect":"Allow",
    "Principal":"ALIYUN$Alice@aliyun.com",
    "Action":["odps:Select"],
    "Resource":"acs:odps:*:projects/alipay/tables/table_test",
    "Condition":{
        "StringEquals": {
            "odps:TaskType":["DT", "SQL"]
        }
    }
}]}
```

2. 设置 TrustedProject

如果当前项目空间处于受保护状态，且将数据流出的目标项目空间设置为当前项目空间的 TrustedProject，那么数据流向目标项目空间将不会被视为触犯 ProjectProtection 规则。如果多个项目空间之间两两互相设置为 TrustedProject，那么这些项目空间就形成了一个 TrustedProject Group，数据可以在这个 TrustedProject Group 内流动，但禁止流出 TrustedProject Group。

下面通过具体的操作来演示如何使用 TrustedProject。

（1）查看当前项目空间中的所有 TrustedProject。

```
demo_maxcompute_001>list trustedprojects;
```

输出的信息如下。

```
Trusted project list:
<empty>
```

（2）在当前项目空间中添加一个 TrustedProject。

```
demo_maxcompute_001>add trustedproject demo_maxcompute_002;
```

（3）重新查看当前项目空间中的所有 TrustedProject。

```
demo_maxcompute_001>list trustedprojects;
```

输出的信息如下。

```
Trusted project list:
demo_maxcompute_002
```

（4）从当前项目空间中移除一个 TrustedProject。

```
remove trustedproject demo_maxcompute_002;
```

第3篇
阿里云大数据的实时计算服务

第 9 章
消息队列 Kafka 版

消息队列 Kafka 版是阿里云基于 Apache Kafka 构建的高吞吐量、高可扩展性的分布式消息队列服务，广泛用于日志收集、监控数据聚合、流式数据处理、在线和离线分析等场景，是大数据生态圈中不可或缺的产品之一。

9.1 消息队列基础

在介绍消息队列 Kafka 版之前，需要对消息队列的一些基本知识有所了解，这有助于学习消息队列 Kafka 版。

9.1.1 消息队列概述

维基百科中对消息队列的解释如下。

> 消息队列提供了一种异步通信协议，这意味着消息的发送者和接收者不需要同时与消息保持联系，发送者发送的消息会存储在消息系统中，直到接收者接收它。

消息的发送者被称为生产者（Producer），消息的接收者被称为消费者（Consumer）。通常生产者的生产速度和消费者的消费速度是不相等的。如果两个程序始终保持同步沟通，则势必会有一方存在空等时间。如果两个程序持续运行，则消费者的消费速度一定要大于生产者的生产速度，否则消息会越来越多。当然，如果消费者没有时效性需求，则可以把消息囤积在消息队列中，从而集中进行消费。

根据生产者和消费者作用范围的不同，一般可以把消息队列分为以下 3 类。

（1）第 1 类是在一个应用程序内部（进程之间或线程之间），生产者负责生产消息，并将生产的消息放到缓冲区（如共享数组）；消费者从缓冲区取出消息。这个缓冲区被称为消息队列。

（2）第 2 类是第 1 类的特例，就像用户经常把操作系统和应用程序区别对待一样，操作系统要处理无数繁杂的事务，各进程、线程之间的数据交换少不了消息队列的支持。

（3）第 3 类是通用意义上的消息队列，这类系统主要作用于不同应用程序，特别是跨机器、跨平台的应用程序，这令数据的交换更加广泛。一般一款独立的消息队列除了实现消息的传递，还提供相应的可靠性、事务、分布式等特性，将生产者和消费者在相互作用的过程中进行解耦。在这类消息队列中，根据系统是否开源又可分为两类：商业的专有软件，如 Oracle WebLogic、IBM WebSphere MQ 等；开源的软件，如 ActiveMQ、RabbitMQ、Apache Kafka 等。

在了解了消息队列的基本概念后，下面通过一个例子来说明一个消息队列的典型应用架构，如图 9-1 所示。

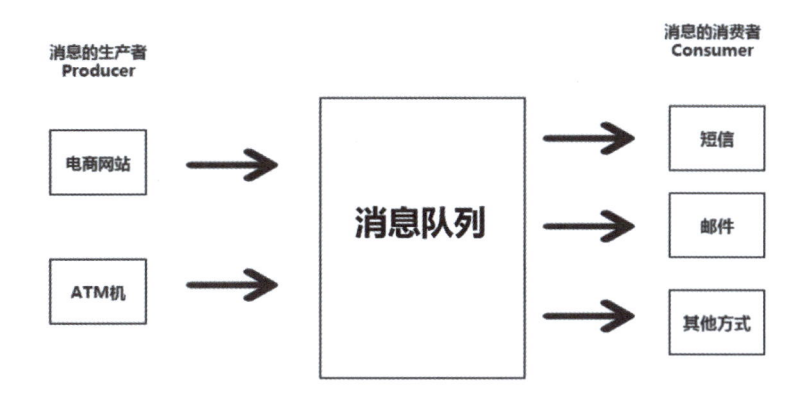

图 9-1

这个例子以一个银行系统为例。当用户在电商网站上进行消费或从银行的 ATM 机上取钱时，银行都会通知到用户，这时就可以把电商网站和 ATM 机看作银行消息队列的消息生产者。当用户使用了银行账户的存款后，生产者就会产生一个消息并发送到银行的消息队列中，并由该消息队列进行处理，从而通过不同的方式通知用户，如短信、邮件等。用户就可以把这些通知看作银行消息队列的消息消费者，它们负责接收由消息队列转发处理的消息。

> 通过这样的一个例子也说明了作为一个消息队列，其最基本的组成就包括消息生产者、消息消费者和消息队列，这里的消息队列其实就是消息服务器。

9.1.2 消息队列的分类

消息队列负责将消息数据从一个应用程序传输到另一个应用程序，因此应用程序可以专注于数据，而不必担心如何共享数据。消息队列可以按照不同的方式进行划分，如同步消息和异步消息、队列消息和主题消息。下面分别进行介绍。

1. 同步消息与异步消息

同步消息是指两个应用程序之间必须进行同步，且两个应用程序必须一直处于正常运行的状态。发送程序在向接收程序发送消息后，先阻塞自身与其他应用程序的通信进程，等待接收程序的返回消息，然后继续执行下一个业务。图 9-2 展示了一个同步消息队列的典型架构。

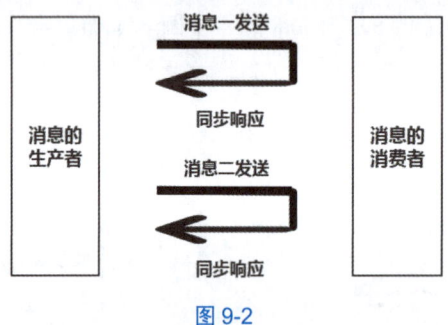

图 9-2

异步消息是指两个应用程序之间可以不用同时在线等待，任何一方只处理自己的业务而不用等待对方的响应。发送程序在向接收程序发送消息后，不用等待接收程序的返回消息，就可以继续执行下一个业务。图 9-3 展示了一个异步消息队列的典型架构。

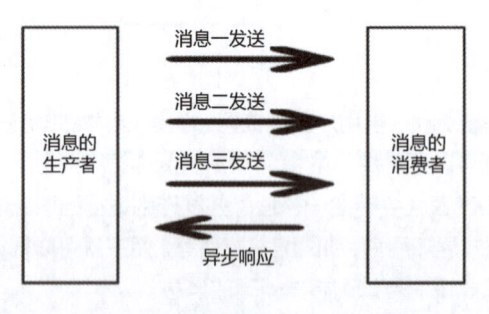

图 9-3

在了解到了同步消息与异步消息的基本知识后，下面通过具体的例子来说明同步消息和异步消息的区别。

1）同步消息

在付款的时候，用户 A 已经付款了，这时如果没有收到支付成功的状态提示，用户 A 就会在想自己是否支付成功了呢？就会一直处于等待状态。系统反馈一个消息，要么是支付成功，要么是支付失败，之后才会进行后续的操作，这就是同步消息机制。

2）异步消息

用户 A 给用户 B 发送一封电子邮件，用户 A 不需要知道用户 B 是否收到了电子邮件，用户 A 只是把自己的信息传递出去，这样的场景就是异步消息。因为在这个过程中，用户 A 在乎的是把信息传递出去，而不在乎其他人的状态。贴张告示也是这样，不需要了解每个人是否已知晓这则告示的内容，只将告示贴出去就可以了。

那么异步消息有什么样的优点和缺点呢？异步消息有一些优点：更灵活，并且提供更高的可用性，系统对信息采取行动的压力较小；在使用异步消息时，关闭一个系统也不会影响另一个系统；异步消息传递允许更多的并行性，由于进程不阻塞，所以它可以在消息传输时进行一些计算。异步消息的缺点是缺乏直接性，应用程序之间没有直接的相互作用。考虑一下你与你的朋友使用即时通信软件或电话聊天，除非你的朋友及时回复你，否则这不是聊天或谈话，这正是同步消息的优点。

> 消息队列 Kafka 版既支持同步消息的发送与接收，也支持异步消息的发送与接收。

2. 队列消息与主题消息

队列（Queue）类型的消息，也可以叫作点对点的消息。通过该消息传递模型，一个应用程序（生产者）可以向另外一个应用程序（消费者）发送消息。消息首先被传送至消息服务器特定的队列中，然后将消息传送至监听此队列的某个消费者。同一个队列可以关联多个生产者和消费者，但一条消息仅能传递给一个消费者。如果多个消费者正在监听队列，则消息服务器将根据"先来者优先"的原则确定由哪个消费者接收下一条消息。如果没有消费者监听队列，则消息将保留在队列中，直至消费者连接队列为止。这种消息传递模型就是传统意义上的懒模型或轮询模型。在此模型中，消息不是自动推送给消费者的，而是消费者从队列中请求获得的。

主题（Topic）类型的消息，也可以叫作发布与订阅的消息。通过该消息传递模型，应用程序能够将一条消息发送给多个消费者。生产者先将消息发布至消息服务器特定的主题中，然后由消息服务器将消息传递给所有订阅此主题的消费者。在该模型中，消息会自动广播，消费者无须通过主动请求或轮询主题的方法来获得新的消息。

> 消息队列 Kafka 版只支持主题类型的消息。

图 9-4 展示了一个典型的主题类型的消息队列。

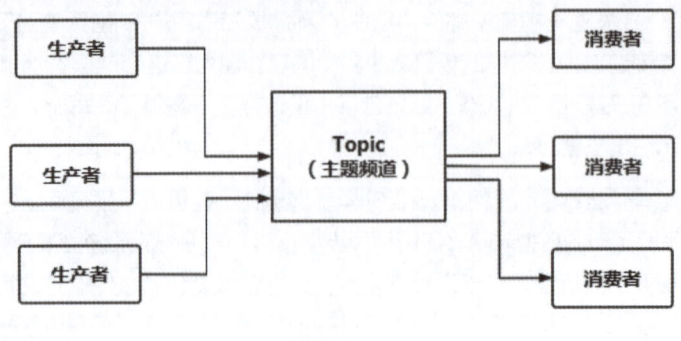

图 9-4

9.2 消息队列 Kafka 版的体系架构

消息队列 Kafka 版是一个典型的分布式系统，其组成部分包括生产者、消费者、消息服务器及分布式协调服务 ZooKeeper。

消息队列 Kafka 版集群的架构如图 9-5 所示。

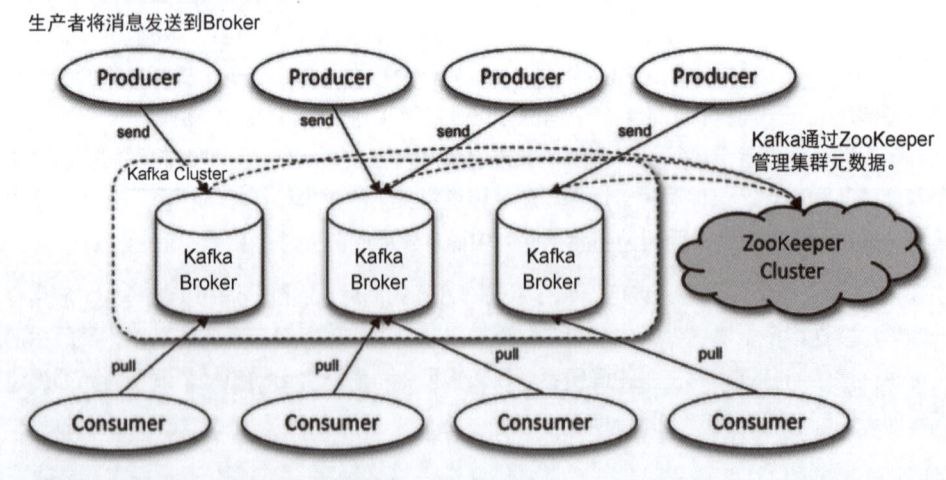

图 9-5

消息队列 Kafka 版中的一些术语如表 9-1 所示，这些术语对于掌握消息队列 Kafka 版的内容非常重要。

表 9-1

术　语	说　明
Broker（消息服务器）	Kafka 集群包含一个或多个消息服务器，这种消息服务器被称为 Broker
Topic（主题）	每条发送到 Kafka 集群的消息都有一个类别，这个类别被称为主题。不同主题的消息在物理上是分开存储的，逻辑上一个主题的消息虽然存储于一个或多个 Broker 上，但用户只需指定消息的主题，就可以生产或消费数据而不必关心数据存储于何处
Partition（分区）	分区是物理上的概念，每个主题包含一个或多个分区，并且同一个分区可能存在多个副本
Producer（生产者）	生产者负责将消息发送到 Broker
Consumer（消费者）	消费者负责从 Broker 读取消息
Consumer Group（消费者组）	每个消费者属于一个特定的消费者组。可以为每个消费者指定 Group Name，如果不指定 Group Name，则属于默认的 Group

9.2.1　消息服务器 Broker

Broker 是消息服务器。生产者向 Broker 中的指定主题写入消息，消费者先从 Broker 中拉取指定主题的消息，然后进行业务处理。Broker 在中间起到代理存储消息的作用。

Broker 没有副本机制，因此，一旦 Broker 宕机，则该 Broker 的消息都将不可用。消费者可以回溯到任意位置重新从 Broker 中进行消息的消费。当消费者发生故障时，可以选择最小的消息偏移地址重新消费消息。

9.2.2　主题、分区与副本

消息队列 Kafka 版中的消息以主题为单位进行归类，生产者负责将消息发送到特定的主题，而消费者负责订阅主题并进行消费。主题可以分为多个分区，一个分区只属于某个主题。

主题和分区的关系如下。

（1）同一个主题下的不同分区包含的消息不同。生产者发送给主题的消息都是具体发送到某个分区中的。

（2）消息被追加到主题的某个分区时，Broker 会为消息分配一个特定的偏移地址，该地址是消息在分区中的唯一标识，通过它来保证消息在分区中的顺序性。

（3）偏移地址不能跨越分区，即偏移地址保证的是分区有序而不是主题有序。

主题与分区之间的关系如图 9-6 所示。

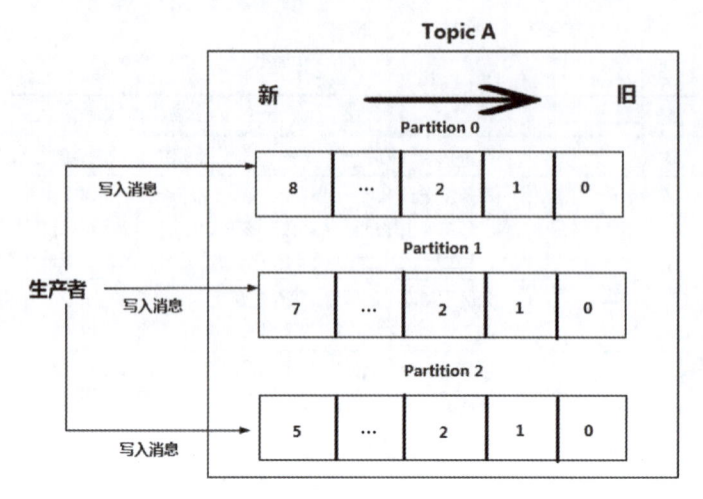

图 9-6

在这个例子中，Topic A 有 3 个分区。消息由生产者按顺序追加到每个分区日志文件的尾部。不同的分区可以分布在不同的 Broker 上，从而支持负载均衡和容错的功能。也就是说，主题是一个逻辑概念，它可以横跨多个 Broker。

说完了主题和分区，再来说说副本。每个主题可以有多个分区，每个分区又可以有多个副本。在这多个副本中，只有一个副本的角色是 Leader，而其他副本的角色都是 Follower。仅 Leader 副本所在的 Broker 可以对外提供服务。Follower 副本通常不会存放在 Leader 副本所在的 Broker 上。通过这样的机制实现了高可用。当 Leader 副本所在的 Broker 宕机后，Follower 副本所在的 Broker 就能够被选举成为新的 Leader。Kafka 分区的副本机制如图 9-7 所示。

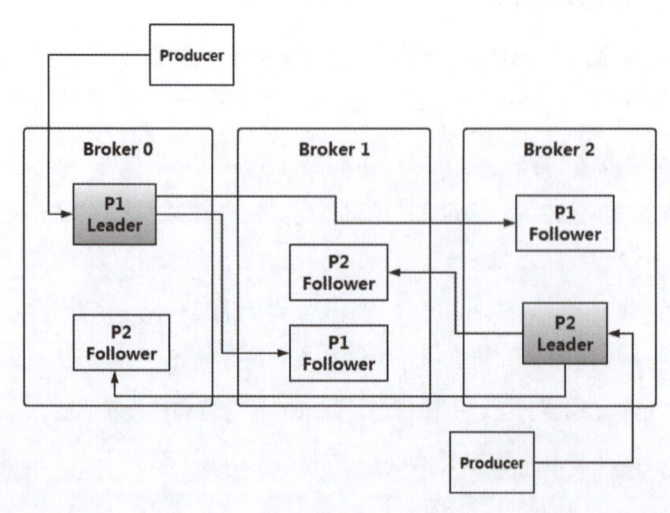

图 9-7

图 9-7 中的主题由 P1 和 P2 两个分区组成。每个分区有 3 个副本。每个分区中都将由 Leader 副本所在的 Broker 负责对外提供服务。

9.2.3 消息的生产者

消息的生产者负责将消息发送到消息队列 Kafka 版的 Broker 上。生产者生产的消息可以是字符串类型的消息，也可以是一个对象。

1. 生产者的执行过程

生产者将消息序列化之后，发送到对应主题的指定分区上。整个生产者客户端由两个线程协调运行，这两个线程分别为主线程和 Sender 线程。生产者的执行过程如图 9-8 所示。

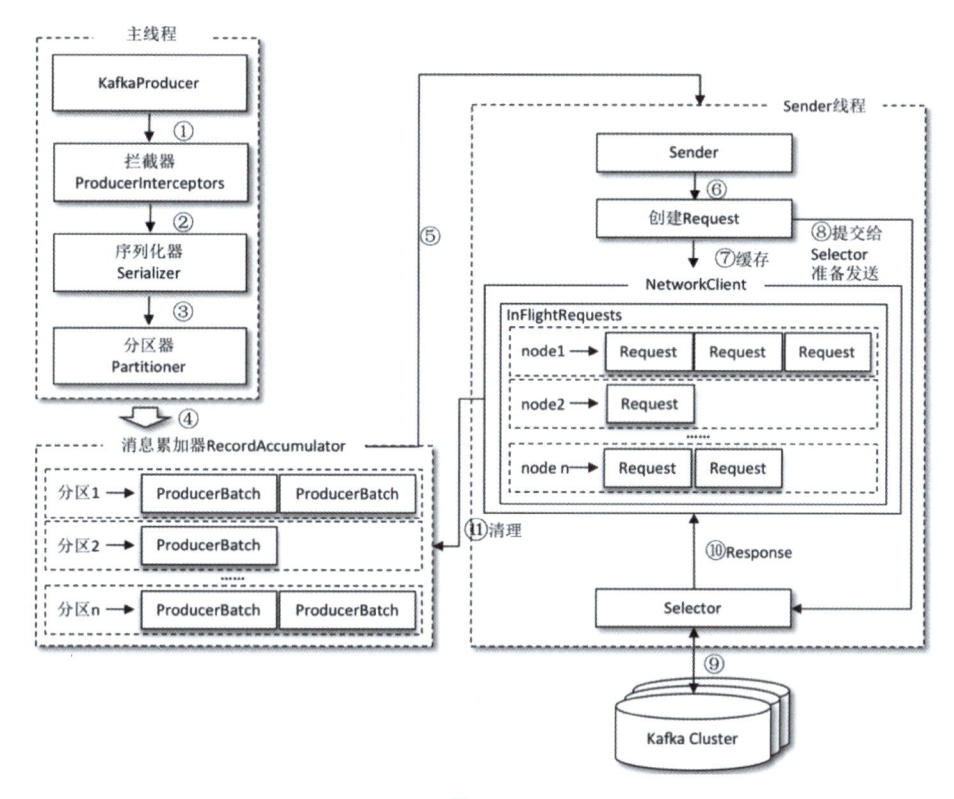

图 9-8

整个生产者客户端由两个线程协调运行，下面分别讨论一下这两个线程。

1）主线程

在主线程中将创建一个 KafkaProducer 对象，并由 KafkaProducer 创建一个

ProducerRecord 对象。该对象代表了生产者发送到消息服务器 Broker 的一个消息对象。ProducerRecord 对象是一个 Key-Value 键值对的对象，其中包含了主题名称、主题中的分区号、时间戳及其他 Key-Value 键值对，其中最重要的就是消息服务器的主题名称。

ProducerRecord 对象在创建成功后，需要拦截器、序列化器将其转换为字节数组，之后才能在网络上传输。分区器的作用是根据发送过程中指定的有效的分区号，将 ProducerRecord 对象发送到相应的分区中。如果没有指定主题中的分区号，则会根据 Key 进行哈希运算，将 ProducerRecord 对象映射到一个对应的分区。ProducerRecord 对象最终使用的时间戳取决于主题的配置。主题时间戳的两种配置如表 9-2 所示。

表 9-2

主题时间戳	说　　明
CreateTime	在生产者中创建 ProducerRecord 对象的时间戳
LogAppendTime	在将 ProducerRecord 对象添加到日志文件中时，生产者记录的时间戳

2）Sender 线程

KafkaProducer 创建的消息最终会缓存到生产者的消息累加器中，由发送线程负责从消息累加器中获取消息并将其发送到 Broker 中。Broker 在收到消息时会返回一个响应给 KafkaProducer。如果消息写入成功，则 Broker 会返回一个 RecordMetaData 对象，它包含了主题和分区信息，以及消息在分区里的偏移量，同时时间戳也会返回给用户；如果消息写入失败，则 Broker 会返回一个错误，生产者在收到错误之后会尝试重新发送消息，几次之后如果消息还是写入失败，则生产者就返回错误消息。

2. 生产者的消息发送方式

生产者有 3 种消息发送方式，这 3 种方式的区别在于对消息是否正常到达的处理，如表 9-3 所示。

表 9-3

消息发送方式	说　　明
fire-and-forget	该方式把消息发送给 Broker 之后不关心其是否正常到达。在大多数情况下消息会正常到达，即使出错了，生产者也会自动重试。但这种方式可能造成 Broker 没有接收到生产者的消息，因此这种方式适用于允许消息丢失并对吞吐量要求大的场景，比如上传大量用户的访问日志数据
同步发送	生产者使用 send 方法发送一条消息，该方法会返回一个 Future 对象。调用该对象的 get 方法可以阻塞当前线程并等待返回。这种方式适用于对消息可靠性要求高的场景，比如支付的场景，这种场景要求消息不可丢失，如果丢失了，则回滚相关的业务操作
异步发送	生产者在使用 send 方法发送一条消息时指定回调函数，该函数在 Broker 返回结果时被调用。这个回调函数可以进行错误日志的记录或重试。这种方式牺牲了一部分可靠性，但吞吐量会比同步发送高很多

9.2.4 消息的消费者

消息的消费者负责接收消费和处理消息。消息队列 Kafka 版采用消费者组的方式来管理消费者。

1. 消费者与消费者组

消费者就是从消息队列 Kafka 版集群消费数据的客户端。消费者从主题中消费数据的模型如图 9-9 所示。

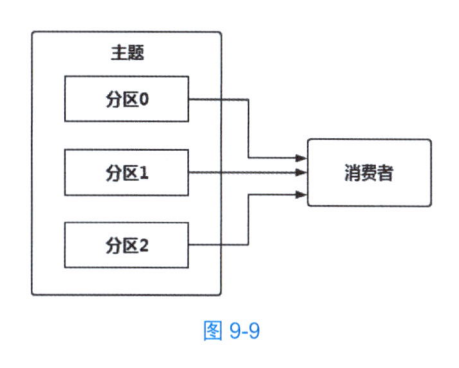

图 9-9

> 图 9-9 展示的是单消费者模型。单消费者模型存在一个问题：如果上游生产数据的速度很快，超过了单个消费者的消费速度，则会导致数据堆积。

为了解决单消费者模型存在的问题，消息队列 Kafka 版提出了消费者组的概念。消费者组就是一组消费者的集合。消费者以消费者组的方式工作，即一个消费者组由一个或多个消费者组成，它们共同消费一个主题中的消息。在同一个时间点，主题中分区的消息只能由一个消费者组中的一个消费者进行消费，而同一个分区的消息可以被不同消费者组中的消费者消费，如图 9-10 所示。

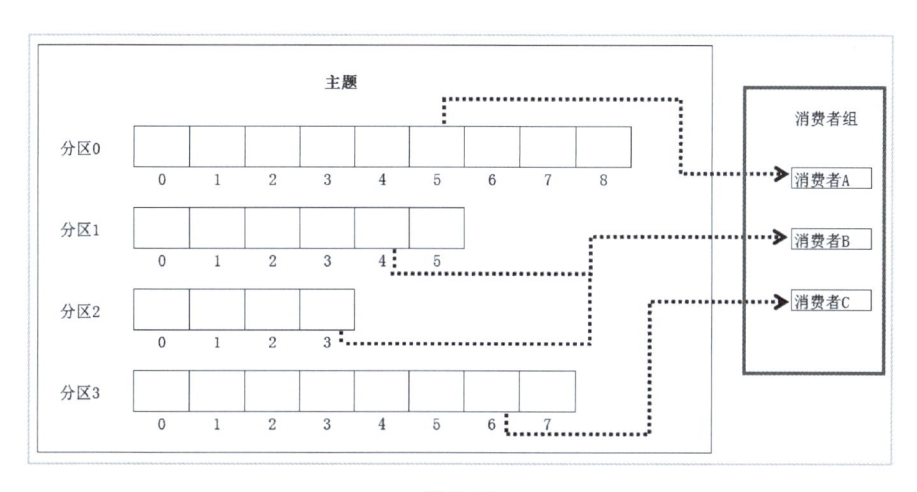

图 9-10

图 9-10 中的消费者组由 3 个消费者组成，主题由 4 个分区组成。其中，消费者 A 读取一个分区的数据，消费者 B 读取两个分区的数据，消费者 C 读取一个分区的数据。在这种情况下，消费者可以通过水平扩展的方式同时读取大量的消息。另外，如果一个消费者读取失败了，那么消费者组的其他成员会自动读取这个消费者读取失败的分区数据。

> 消息队列 Kafka 版使用消费者组来允许多个消费者共同消费和处理同一个主题中的消息。消费者组的成员是动态维护的，如果一个消费者处理失败了，则之前分配给它的分区将被重新分配给组中的其他消费者。同样，如果消费者组中加入了新的消费者，则将触发整个分区的重新分配，每个消费者将尽可能地分配到相同数目的分区，以达到新的均衡状态。

2. 消息的消费模式

消费者组中消息的消费模式有两种，即推送模式（Push）和拉取模式（Pull）。

1）推送模式

推送模式需要记录消费者消费的消息状态。当把一条消息推送给消费者后，需要维护消息的状态。如果这条消息已经被消费，则消息将被标记。这种方式无法很好地保证消息被处理。如果要保证消息被处理，则在发送完消息后需要将其状态设置为已发送，在收到消费者的确认后才将其状态更新为已消费。这就需要 Broker 记录所有消息的消费状态，显然这种方式不可取。这种方式还存在一个明显的缺点：消息被标记为已消费后，其他消费者就不能再消费它了。

2）拉取模式

由于推送模式存在一定的缺点，因此消息队列 Kafka 版采用了拉取模式来消费消息。该模式由每个消费者维护自己的消费状态，并且每个消费者互相独立地按顺序拉取每个分区中的消息。消费者通过偏移量来控制从 Broker 中消费的消息，如图 9-11 所示。

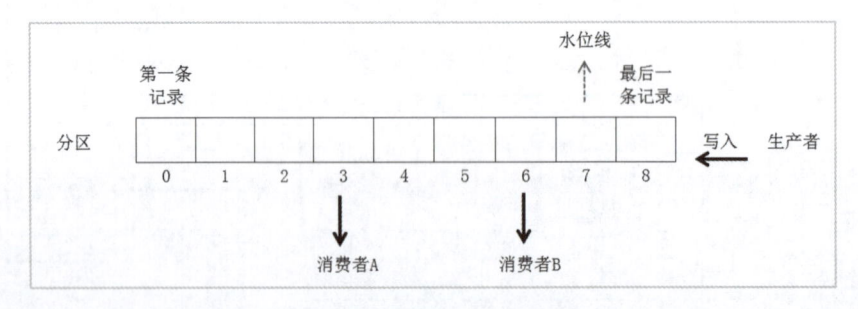

图 9-11

由消费者通过偏移量进行消息消费的优点在于，消费者可以按照任意的顺序消费消息。例如，消费者可以通过重置偏移量重新处理已被消费的消息，或者直接跳转到某个偏移量位置并开始消费。

> 如果生产者最新写入的消息没有达到备份数量，则其对消费者是不可见的。

另外，如果消费者已经对消息进行了消费，消息队列 Kafka 版并不会立即将消息删除，而是将所有的消息保存。消息将持久化保存到消息日志中。不管消息有没有被消费，用户都可以通过设置保留时间来清理过期的消息。

9.3 快速上手消息队列 Kafka 版

在了解了消息系统的基本知识和消息队列 Kafka 版的体系架构后，本节将通过具体的操作来演示如何使用消息队列 Kafka 版。

9.3.1 快速入门操作流程

网络类型不同，消息队列 Kafka 版快速入门的操作流程也有所不同。消息队列 Kafka 版快速入门操作流程如图 9-12 所示。

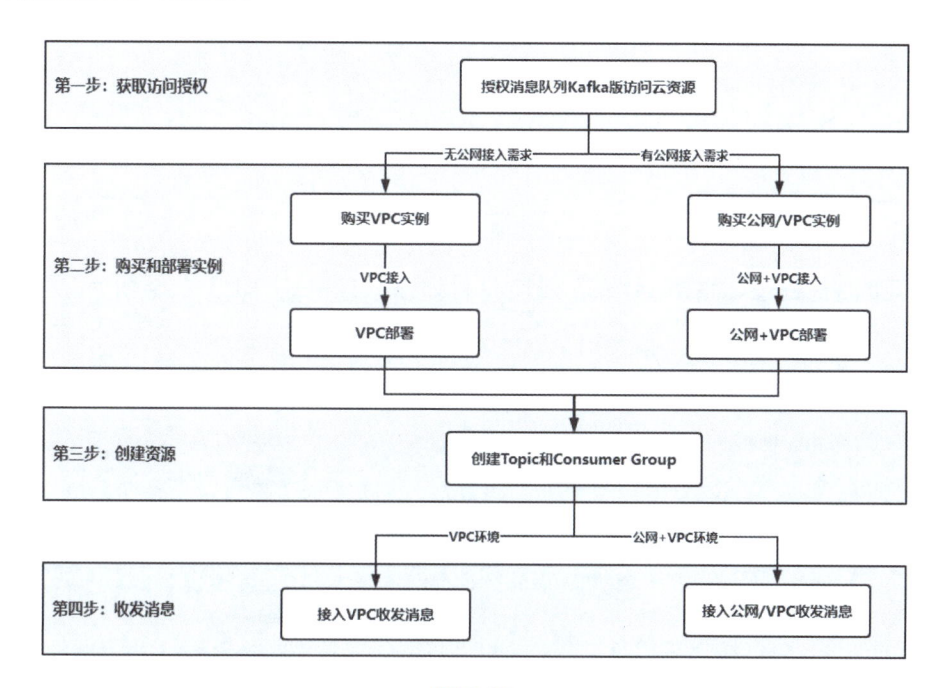

图 9-12

> VPC 是 Virtual Private Cloud 的缩写，代表虚拟专有网络。

9.3.2 【实战】获取访问授权

开通消息队列 Kafka 版服务需要使用阿里云其他云产品中的资源，因此需要先授权消息队列 Kafka 版访问用户所拥有的其他阿里云资源。具体的操作步骤如下。

（1）登录阿里云官网并开通消息队列 Kafka 版。当第一次访问消息队列 Kafka 版的管理控制台时，会自动打开"云资源访问授权"页面，如图 9-13 所示，单击"同意授权"按钮。

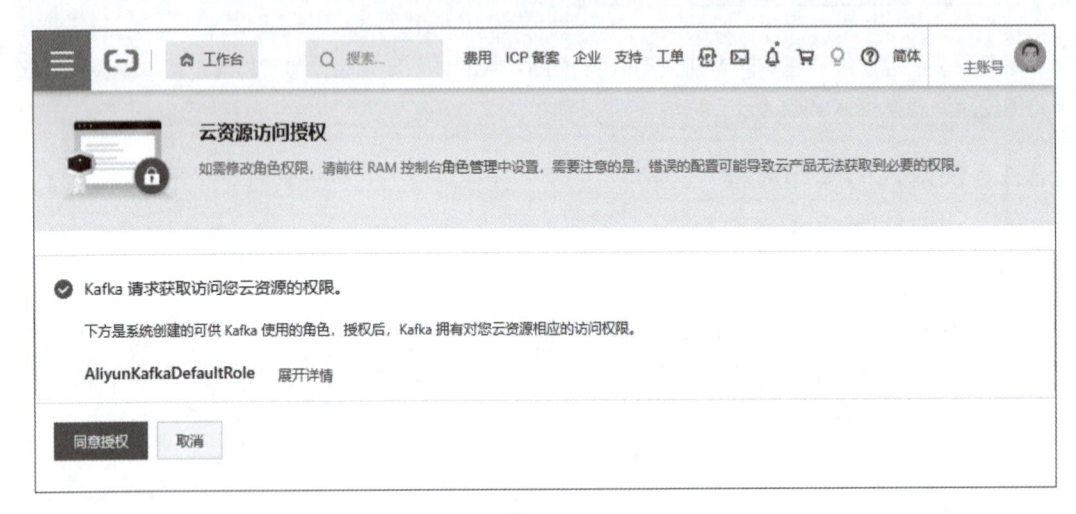

图 9-13

（2）完成授权后，页面跳转到消息队列 Kafka 版的管理控制台，如图 9-14 所示。

图 9-14

9.3.3 【实战】购买和部署

在授权消息队列 Kafka 版访问其他阿里云资源后，用户需要根据网络环境购买并部署消息队列 Kafka 版的实例。如果仅需要在 VPC 网络接入消息队列 Kafka 版，则可以购买并部署 VPC 实例；如果需要同时在 VPC 网络和公网接入消息队列 Kafka 版，则需要购买并部署公网/VPC 实例。具体的操作步骤如下。

> 这里将以同时在 VPC 网络和公网接入消息队列 Kafka 版为例进行演示说明。

（1）登录消息队列 Kafka 版的管理控制台，在左侧的导航栏中选择"实例列表"选项。在"实例列表"页面的顶部菜单栏中选择地域，如"华北 2（北京）"，如图 9-15 所示。

图 9-15

（2）单击"购买实例"按钮。在弹出的"请选择您要创建的实例的付费方式"对话框中选择要创建的实例的付费方式，如"按量付费"，如图 9-16 所示，单击"确定"按钮。

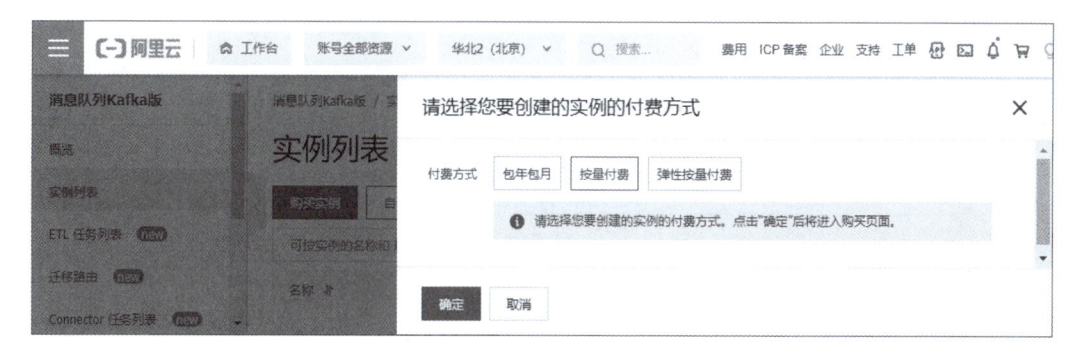

图 9-16

（3）在购买对话框中选择"公网/VPC 实例"选项，其他配置根据自身业务需求进行选择，如图 9-17 所示。

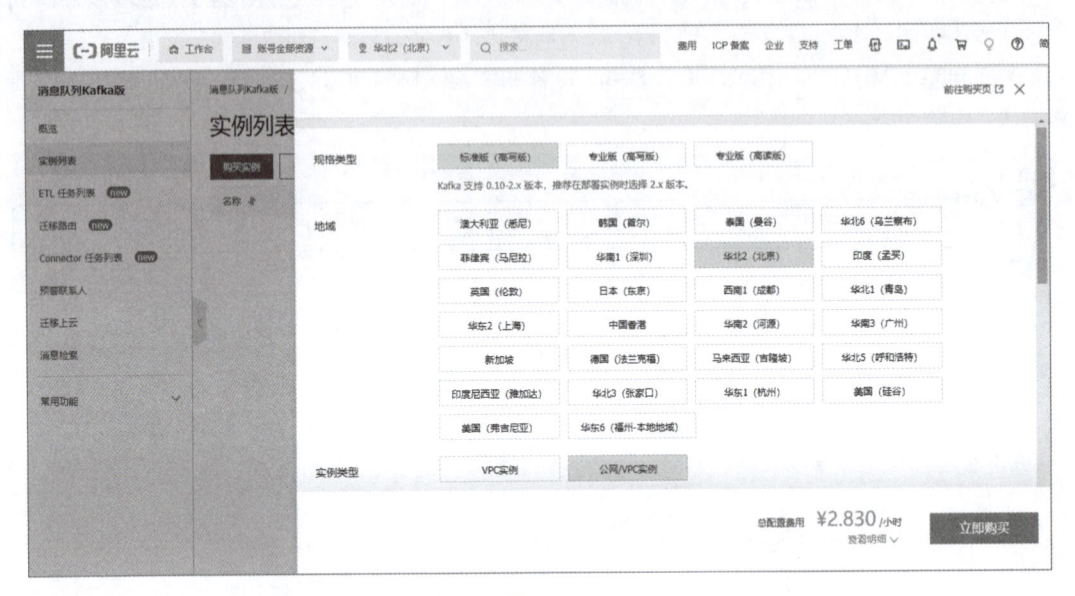

图 9-17

（4）单击"立即购买"按钮并完成支付。此时，"实例列表"页面如图 9-18 所示。

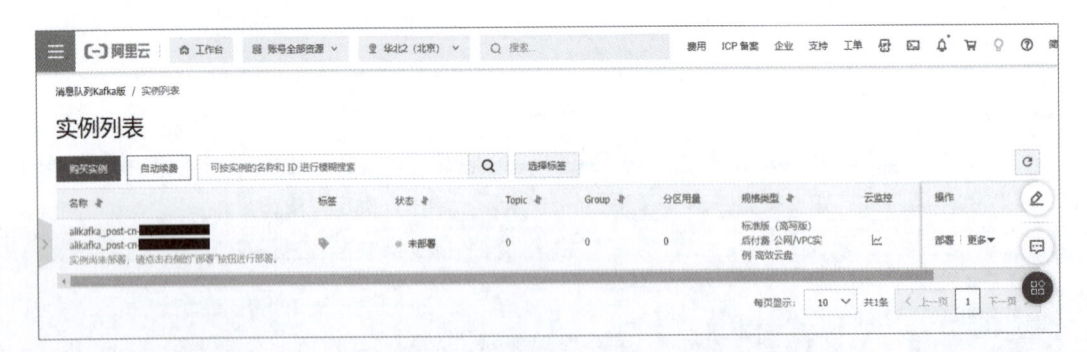

图 9-18

> 此时实例的状态为"未部署"，需要将其部署在相应的网络环境中。

（5）通过阿里云首页登录 VPC 网关控制台，并在顶部菜单栏中选择搭建的 VPC 网络所在的地域，如图 9-19 所示。

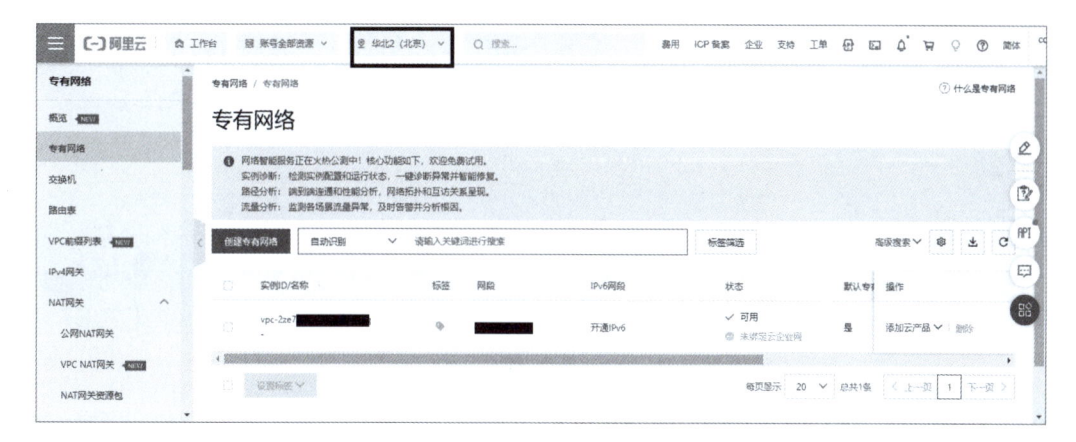

图 9-19

（6）在左侧的导航栏中选择"交换机"选项，如图 9-20 所示。

图 9-20

> 在"交换机"页面查看目标交换机的 ID 和 VPC ID，其中，"实例 ID/名称"列出了交换机 ID（即 vSwitch ID），"专有网络"列出了交换机所在的 VPC ID。

（7）回到消息队列 Kafka 版的管理控制台，找到状态为"未部署"的实例并单击"部署"文字链接，如图 9-21 所示。

（8）弹出"Kafka 服务关联角色"对话框，单击"确认"按钮，如图 9-22 所示。

（9）在部署实例对话框中确定部署的相关配置信息，单击"确定"按钮，如图 9-23 所示。

> 如果用户已经完成了 VPC 网关的配置，则在确定部署的相关配置信息时，VPC ID 和 vSwitch ID 将被自动填入。

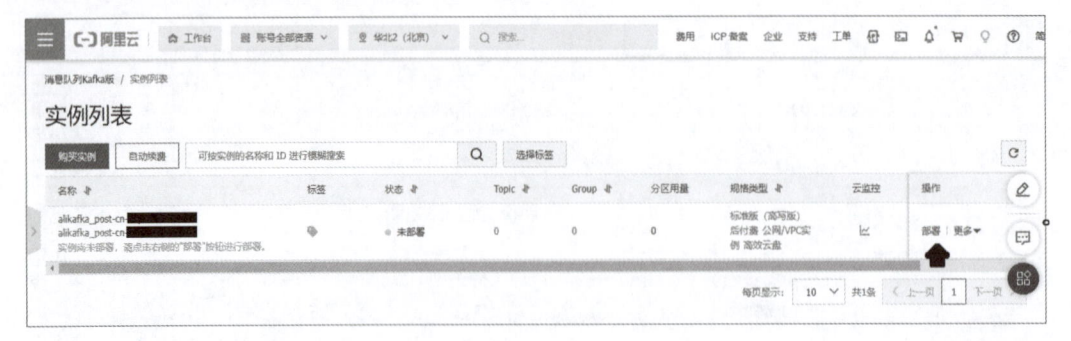

图 9-21

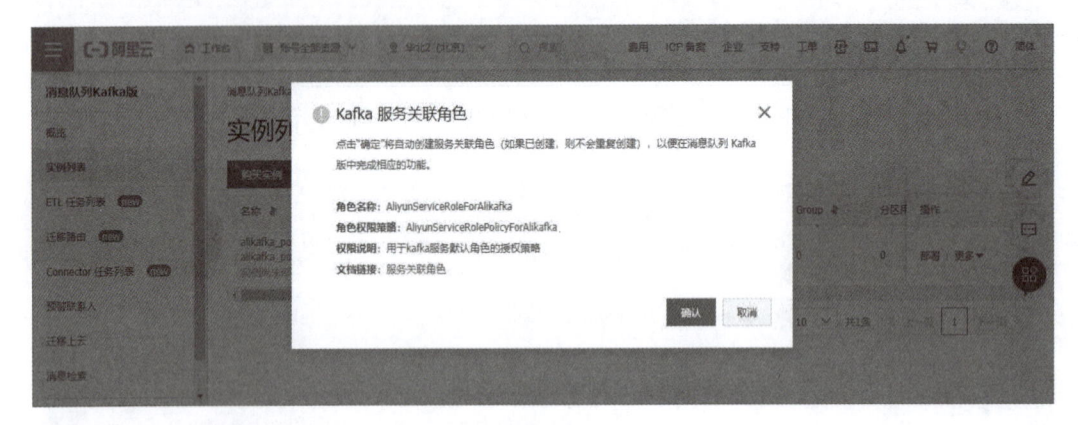

图 9-22

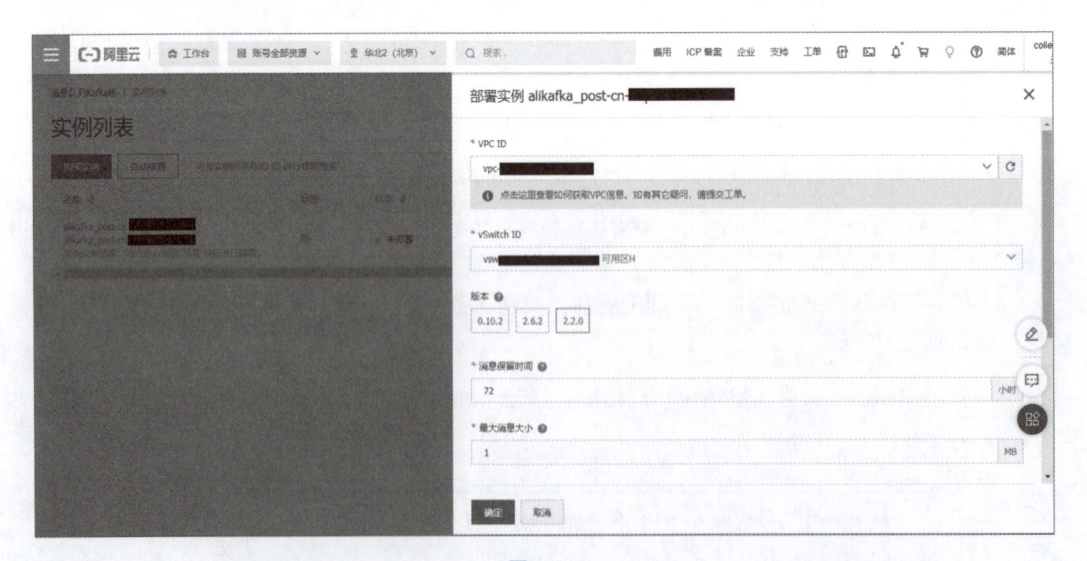

图 9-23

（10）部署完成后的页面如图 9-24 所示。

图 9-24

> 此时实例的状态为"服务中"，表示该实例已经正常运行，并且可以对外提供服务。

（11）单击实例名称进入"实例详情"页面，查看"接入点信息"，如图 9-25 所示。

图 9-25

> 为了在公网环境中访问消息队列 Kafka 版，后续的步骤都将使用公网环境下的接入点配置，即 SSL 接入点。

（12）在本地开启 Telnet，使用 SSL 接入点测试是否可以连接消息队列 Kafka 版。

```
C:\> telnet alikafka-post-cn-******-1.alikafka.aliyuncs.com:9093
```

以下输出信息表示已经成功连接消息队列 Kafka 版的消息服务器 Broker。

```
Host 'alikafka-post-cn-******-1.alikafka.aliyuncs.com' resolved
Connecting to ******:9093...
Connection established.
To escape to local shell, press 'Ctrl+Alt+]'.
```

9.3.4 【实战】创建资源

在使用消息队列 Kafka 版发送与接收消息之前，需要先在消息队列 Kafka 版的管理控制台上创建相应的资源，否则将无法通过鉴权认证及使用相关的管控运维功能。

> 这里的资源指的是需要创建相应的主题和消费者组信息。

主题和消费者组的创建均使用管理控制台完成，具体的操作步骤如下。

（1）在"实例详情"页面，在左侧的导航栏中选择"Topic 管理"选项，进入"Topic 管理"页面，单击"创建 Topic"按钮，如图 9-26 所示。

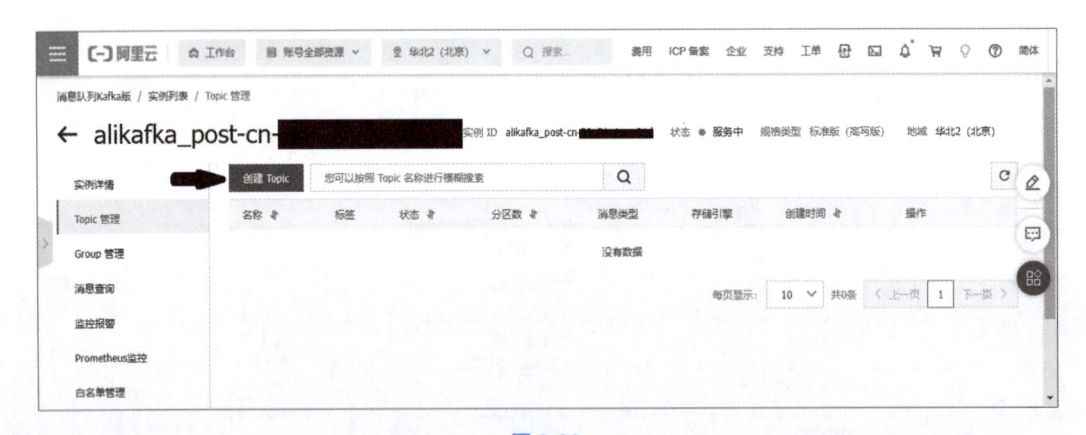

图 9-26

（2）在"创建 Topic"对话框中输入 Topic 的相关信息，并单击"确定"按钮，如图 9-27 所示。

（3）创建的 Topic 的信息如图 9-28 所示。

（4）在左侧的导航栏中选择"Group 管理"选项，打开"Group 管理"页面，单击"创建 Group"按钮，如图 9-29 所示。

图 9-27

图 9-28

图 9-29

（5）在"创建 Group"对话框中输入 Group 的相关信息，单击"确定"按钮，如图 9-30 所示。

图 9-30

（6）创建完成的 Group 的信息如图 9-31 所示。

图 9-31

9.3.5 【实战】使用管理控制台收发消息

在成功创建了消息队列 Kafka 版的资源后，就可以直接使用管理控制台进行消息的发送与订阅。具体的步骤如下。

（1）进入"Topic 管理"页面，单击右侧的"更多"文字链接，在弹出的下拉列表中选择"体验发送消息"选项，如图 9-32 所示。

（2）在"快速体验消息收发"对话框中输入"消息 Key"和"消息内容"，单击"确定"按钮，如图 9-33 所示。

（3）在左侧的导航栏中选择"消息查询"选项，打开"消息查询"页面，查看第（2）步中发送的消息，如图 9-34 所示。

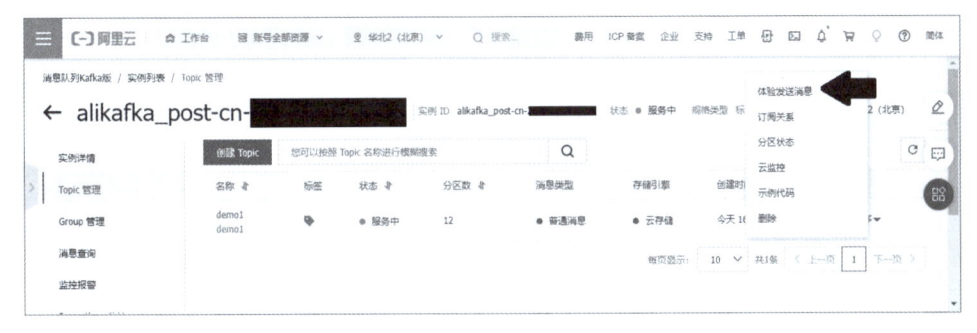

图 9-32

图 9-33

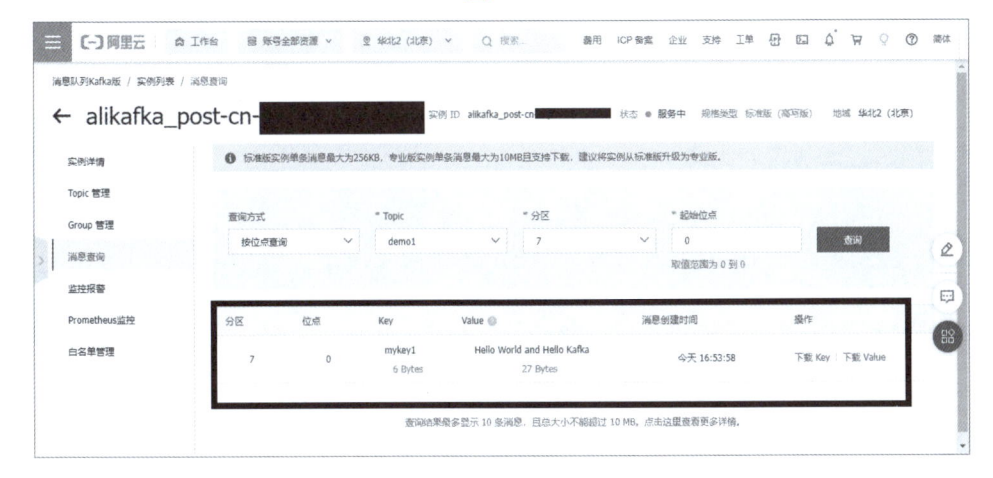

图 9-34

9.3.6 【实战】实例运行健康自检指南

当实例运行出现异常时,用户可以使用消息队列 Kafka 版提供的自检工具对实例的健康状态进行自检。下面通过具体的步骤来演示如何使用该自检工具。

(1)安装 1.8 或以上版本的 JDK。

(2)下载自检工具 kafka-checker.zip 并解压缩。

> kafka-checker.zip 可以从消息队列 Kafka 版的产品文档中下载。

(3)在消息队列 Kafka 版的"实例详情"页面确定域名接入点,如图 9-35 所示。

类型	网络	协议	域名接入点	操作
默认接入点	VPC	PLAINTEXT	alikafka-post-cn-██████-1-vpc.alikafka.aliyuncs.com:9092,alikafka-post-cn-██████-2-vpc.alikafka.aliyuncs.com:9092,alikafka-post-cn-██████-3-vpc.alikafka.aliyuncs.com:9092	管理白名单
SSL接入点	公网	SASL_SSL	alikafka-post-cn-██████-1.alikafka.aliyuncs.com:9093,alikafka-post-cn-██████-2.alikafka.aliyuncs.com:9093,alikafka-post-cn-██████-3.alikafka.aliyuncs.com:9093	管理白名单

图 9-35

(4)执行自检命令,测试是否可以连接消息队列 Kafka 版。

```
D:\download\kafka-checker>java -jar KafkaChecker.jar telnet -s ^
alikafka-post-cn-******-1.alikafka.aliyuncs.com:9093,^
alikafka-post-cn-******-2.alikafka.aliyuncs.com:9093,^
alikafka-post-cn-******-3.alikafka.aliyuncs.com:9093
```

输出的信息如下。

```
[2023-01-19 17:24:40,052] INFO Parameter level = INFO (client.BossCommand)
[2023-01-19 17:24:40,052] INFO Parameter servers =
alikafka-post-cn-******-1.alikafka.aliyuncs.com:9093,
alikafka-post-cn-******-2.alikafka.aliyuncs.com:9093,
alikafka-post-cn-******-3.alikafka.aliyuncs.com:9093 (client.BossCommand)
[0;32mtelnet alikafka-post-cn-******-1.****** 9093 success[0m
[0;32mtelnet alikafka-post-cn-******-2.****** 9093 success[0m
[0;32mtelnet alikafka-post-cn-******-3.****** 9093 success[0m
```

（5）执行自检命令，测试是否可以发送消息到消息队列 Kafka 版。

```
D:\download\kafka-checker> java -jar KafkaChecker.jar send ^
-sm PLAIN -ss true ^
-u 用户名 -psw 密码 ^
-s alikafka-post-cn-******-1.alikafka.aliyuncs.com:9093,^
alikafka-post-cn-******-2.alikafka.aliyuncs.com:9093,^
alikafka-post-cn-******-3.alikafka.aliyuncs.com:9093 ^
--topic demo1
```

如果提示与下方信息类似的信息，则说明消息发送成功。

```
Produce ok number:3 p:0 offset:9 response:demo1-0@9 cost:9810 ms
Produce ok number:3 p:4 offset:5 response:demo1-4@5 cost:9810 ms
Produce ok number:4 p:3 offset:12 response:demo1-3@12 cost:20 ms
Produce ok number:4 p:4 offset:6 response:demo1-4@6 cost:20 ms
Produce ok number:5 p:6 offset:6 response:demo1-6@6 cost:10 ms
Produce ok number:5 p:10 offset:10 response:demo1-10@10 cost:10 ms
Produce ok number:6 p:10 offset:11 response:demo1-10@11 cost:20 ms
Produce ok number:6 p:1 offset:17 response:demo1-1@17 cost:20 ms
Produce ok number:7 p:9 offset:11 response:demo1-9@11 cost:30 ms
Produce ok number:7 p:6 offset:7 response:demo1-6@7 cost:30 ms
Produce ok number:8 p:5 offset:12 response:demo1-5@12 cost:10 ms
Produce ok number:8 p:6 offset:8 response:demo1-6@8 cost:10 ms
Produce ok number:9 p:6 offset:9 response:demo1-6@9 cost:30 ms
Produce ok number:9 p:4 offset:7 response:demo1-4@7 cost:30 ms
```

（6）执行自检命令，测试是否可以从消息队列 Kafka 版消费消息。

```
D:\download\kafka-checker> java -jar KafkaChecker.jar pull ^
-sm PLAIN -ss true ^
-u 用户名 -psw 密码 ^
-s alikafka-post-cn-******-1.alikafka.aliyuncs.com:9093,^
alikafka-post-cn-******-2.alikafka.aliyuncs.com:9093,^
alikafka-post-cn-******-3.alikafka.aliyuncs.com:9093 ^
--topic demo1 --group group_demo1 --partition 0 --offset 0 --count 12
```

如果提示与下方信息类似的信息，则说明消费成功。

```
INFO Check Metadata Start ====== (client.KafkaPuller)
Pull Succ topic:demo1 partition:0 offset:0 ******
Pull Succ topic:demo1 partition:0 offset:1 ******
Pull Succ topic:demo1 partition:0 offset:2 ******
Pull Succ topic:demo1 partition:0 offset:3 ******
Pull Succ topic:demo1 partition:0 offset:4 ******
Pull Succ topic:demo1 partition:0 offset:5 ******
```

```
Pull Succ topic:demo1 partition:0 offset:6 ******
Pull Succ topic:demo1 partition:0 offset:7 ******
Pull Succ topic:demo1 partition:0 offset:8 ******
Pull Succ topic:demo1 partition:0 offset:9 ******
Pull Succ topic:demo1 partition:0 offset:10 ******
Pull Succ topic:demo1 partition:0 offset:11 ******
Pull Succ topic:demo1 partition:0 offset:12 ******
INFO Check pollData End ====== (client.KafkaPuller)
```

9.4 消息队列 Kafka 版应用开发

消息队列 Kafka 版支持多语言的 SDK 开发，包括 Java SDK、Python SDK、C++ SDK 和 Go SDK 等。这里以 Java SDK 为例来介绍如何使用 Java 编程语言开发消息队列 Kafka 版的应用程序。首先需要在 Maven 的 pom.xml 文件中添加下面的依赖信息。

```
<dependency>
    <groupId>org.apache.kafka</groupId>
    <artifactId>kafka-clients</artifactId>
    <version>0.10.2.2</version>
</dependency>
<dependency>
    <groupId>org.slf4j</groupId>
    <artifactId>slf4j-log4j12</artifactId>
    <version>1.7.6</version>
</dependency>
```

9.4.1 【实战】开发基本的消息生产者与消费者

利用 Java 语言可以开发消息队列 Kafka 版的生产者和消费者程序。下面示例中的生产者程序将每隔 1 秒钟发送 1 条消息数据，而消费者将从对应的主题中接收消息数据。

（1）从 GitHub 上下载 SSL 根证书文件 only.4096.client.truststore.jks，将其保存到 D:\download\kafkademo 目录下。

> 在 GitHub 的 aliware-kafka-demos/kafka-java-demo/vpc-ssl/src/main/resources/ 目录下可以找到 only.4096.client.truststore.jks 文件。

（2）将 SSL 根证书文件重命名为 kafka.client.truststore.jks。

(3) 创建 JAAS 配置文件 kafka_client_jaas.conf，将其保存到 D:\kafkademo 目录下。

```
KafkaClient {
  org.apache.kafka.common.security.plain.PlainLoginModule required
  username="在 Kafka 版实例详情中的配置信息中可以找到"
  password="在 Kafka 版实例详情中的配置信息中可以找到";
};
```

(4) 在 Java 的 Maven 工程中创建 Log4j 配置文件 log4j.properties，输入以下配置信息。

```
log4j.rootLogger=INFO, STDOUT

log4j.appender.STDOUT=org.apache.log4j.ConsoleAppender
log4j.appender.STDOUT.layout=org.apache.log4j.PatternLayout
log4j.appender.STDOUT.layout.ConversionPattern=[%d] %p %m (%c)%n
```

(5) 在 Java 的 Maven 工程中创建配置文件 kafka.properties，输入以下配置信息。

```
## 通过管理控制台获取 SSL 接入点信息
bootstrap.servers=*********
## 主题的名称
topic=demo1
## 消费者组的名称
group.id=group_demo1
## SSL 根证书
ssl.truststore.location=D:/kafkademo/kafka.client.truststore.jks
## JAAS 配置文件
java.security.auth.login.config=D:/kafkademo/kafka_client_jaas.conf
```

(6) 创建配置文件加载程序 JavaKafkaConfigurer.java。

```java
package demo;
import java.util.Properties;

public class JavaKafkaConfigurer {

    private static Properties properties;

    public static void configureSasl() {
        if (null == System.getProperty
                        ("java.security.auth.login.config")) {
            //这个路径必须是一个文件系统可读的路径，不能被打包到 JAR 文件中
            System.setProperty("java.security.auth.login.config",
                    getKafkaProperties()
                    .getProperty("java.security.auth.login.config"));
        }
```

```java
    }
    public synchronized static Properties getKafkaProperties() {
        if (null != properties) {
            return properties;
        }
        //获取配置文件kafka.properties的内容
        Properties kafkaProperties = new Properties();
        try {
            kafkaProperties.load(JavaKafkaConfigurer.class
                        .getClassLoader()
                        .getResourceAsStream("kafka.properties"));
        } catch (Exception e) {
            //没加载到文件,程序要考虑退出
            e.printStackTrace();
        }
        properties = kafkaProperties;
        return kafkaProperties;
    }
}
```

(7)开发消息的生产者程序 ProducerDemo.java。

```java
package demo;
import java.util.Properties;
import org.apache.kafka.clients.CommonClientConfigs;
import org.apache.kafka.clients.producer.KafkaProducer;
import org.apache.kafka.clients.producer.ProducerConfig;
import org.apache.kafka.clients.producer.ProducerRecord;
import org.apache.kafka.common.config.SaslConfigs;
import org.apache.kafka.common.config.SslConfigs;

public class ProducerDemo {
    public static void main(String args[]) {
        //设置JAAS配置文件的路径
        JavaKafkaConfigurer.configureSasl();

        //加载配置文件kafka.properties
        Properties kafkaProperties = JavaKafkaConfigurer
                        .getKafkaProperties();

        Properties props = new Properties();
        //设置接入点,请通过管理控制台获取对应Topic的接入点
```

```java
props.put(ProducerConfig.BOOTSTRAP_SERVERS_CONFIG,
        kafkaProperties.getProperty("bootstrap.servers"));
//设置 SSL 根证书的路径,请记得修改为自己的路径
//与 SASL 路径类似,该文件也不能被打包到 JAR 文件中
props.put(SslConfigs.SSL_TRUSTSTORE_LOCATION_CONFIG,
    kafkaProperties.getProperty("ssl.truststore.location"));
//根证书 store 的密码,保持不变
props.put(SslConfigs.SSL_TRUSTSTORE_PASSWORD_CONFIG,
        "KafkaOnsClient");
//接入协议,目前支持使用 SASL_SSL 协议接入
props.put(CommonClientConfigs.SECURITY_PROTOCOL_CONFIG,
        "SASL_SSL");
//SASL 鉴权方式,保持不变
props.put(SaslConfigs.SASL_MECHANISM, "PLAIN");

//消息队列 Kafka 版消息的序列化方式
props.put(ProducerConfig.KEY_SERIALIZER_CLASS_CONFIG,
    "org.apache.kafka.common.serialization.StringSerializer");
props.put(ProducerConfig.VALUE_SERIALIZER_CLASS_CONFIG,
    "org.apache.kafka.common.serialization.StringSerializer");

//构造 Producer 对象。该对象是线程安全的
//一般来说,在一个进程内构造一个 Producer 对象即可
//如果想提高性能,可以多构造几个对象,但不要太多,最好不要超过 5 个
KafkaProducer<String, String> producer =
                new KafkaProducer<String, String>(props);

//构造一个消息队列 Kafka 版消息
String topic = kafkaProperties.getProperty("topic");
//消息的内容
String value = "Hello Aliyun Kafka";
try {
    for (int i = 0; i < 10; i++) {
        //发送消息
        ProducerRecord<String, String> kafkaMessage =
            new ProducerRecord<String, String>(topic,value + ": " + i);
        producer.send(kafkaMessage);
        //睡眠一秒钟
        Thread.sleep(1000);
            }
    producer.flush();
} catch (Exception e) {
```

```
            System.out.println("error occurred");
            e.printStackTrace();
        }
    }
}
```

(8) 开发消息的消费者程序 ConsumerDemo.java。

```java
package demo;
import java.util.ArrayList;
import java.util.List;
import java.util.Properties;
import org.apache.kafka.clients.CommonClientConfigs;
import org.apache.kafka.clients.consumer.ConsumerConfig;
import org.apache.kafka.clients.consumer.ConsumerRecord;
import org.apache.kafka.clients.consumer.ConsumerRecords;
import org.apache.kafka.clients.consumer.KafkaConsumer;
import org.apache.kafka.clients.producer.ProducerConfig;
import org.apache.kafka.common.config.SaslConfigs;
import org.apache.kafka.common.config.SslConfigs;

public class ConsumerDemo {
    public static void main(String[] args) {
        //设置 JAAS 配置文件的路径
        JavaKafkaConfigurer.configureSasl();

        //加载配置文件 kafka.properties
        Properties kafkaProperties =
                        JavaKafkaConfigurer.getKafkaProperties();

        Properties props = new Properties();
        //设置接入点，请通过管理控制台获取对应 Topic 的接入点
        props.put(ProducerConfig.BOOTSTRAP_SERVERS_CONFIG,
            kafkaProperties.getProperty("bootstrap.servers"));
        //设置 SSL 根证书的路径，请记得修改为自己的路径
        //与 SASL 路径类似，该文件也不能被打包到 JAR 文件中
        props.put(SslConfigs.SSL_TRUSTSTORE_LOCATION_CONFIG,
            kafkaProperties.getProperty("ssl.truststore.location"));
        //根证书存储的密码，保持不变
        props.put(SslConfigs.SSL_TRUSTSTORE_PASSWORD_CONFIG,
            "KafkaOnsClient");
        //接入协议，目前支持使用 SASL_SSL 协议接入
        props.put(CommonClientConfigs.SECURITY_PROTOCOL_CONFIG,
```

```java
            "SASL_SSL");
//SASL 鉴权方式，保持不变
props.put(SaslConfigs.SASL_MECHANISM, "PLAIN");
//消息的反序列化方式
props.put(ConsumerConfig.KEY_DESERIALIZER_CLASS_CONFIG,
    "org.apache.kafka.common.serialization.StringDeserializer");
props.put(ConsumerConfig.VALUE_DESERIALIZER_CLASS_CONFIG,
    "org.apache.kafka.common.serialization.StringDeserializer");
//当前消费实例所属的消费者组。属于同一个消费者组的消费实例会负载消费消息
props.put(ConsumerConfig.GROUP_ID_CONFIG,
            kafkaProperties.getProperty("group.id"));
//构造消费对象，即生成一个消费实例
KafkaConsumer<String, String> consumer =
                    new KafkaConsumer<String, String>(props);
//设置消费者组订阅的 Topic，可以订阅多个
//如果 GROUP_ID_CONFIG 相同，则建议将订阅的 Topic 也设置成相同的
List<String> subscribedTopics = new ArrayList<String>();
//如果需要订阅多个 Topic，在这里加进去即可
subscribedTopics.add(kafkaProperties.getProperty("topic"));
consumer.subscribe(subscribedTopics);

//循环消费消息
while (true) {
    try {
        ConsumerRecords<String, String> records =
                                    consumer.poll(1000);
        //输出收到的消息信息
        for (ConsumerRecord<String, String> record : records) {
            System.out.println(record.key() +
                            " " +
                            record.value());
        }
    } catch (Exception e) {
        //处理异常
        e.printStackTrace();
    }
}
```

（9）启动消息的消费者与生产者程序，观察消费者端输出的结果，如图 9-36 所示。

图 9-36

9.4.2 【实战】发送与接收自定义消息

消息队列 Kafka 版生产者发送的消息必须经过序列化。实现序列化可以简单总结为以下两步。

（1）实现序列化接口 Serializer，将指定数据类型序列化为字节数组，以实现消息数据的序列化。

（2）实现反序列化接口 Deserializer，将指定的字节数组反序列化为指定数据类型，以实现消息数据的反序列化。

使用 Java 语言实现数据的序列化和反序列化有很多种不同的方式，这里将介绍基于 FastJson 的序列化方式。

> FastJson 是阿里巴巴开发的一个 Java 库，它可以将 Java 对象序列化为 JSON 格式的字符串，也可以将 JSON 格式的字符串反序列化为 Java 对象。

使用 FastJson，需要在 Maven 工程的 pom.xml 文件中加入以下依赖。

```xml
<dependency>
    <groupId>com.alibaba</groupId>
    <artifactId>fastjson</artifactId>
    <version>1.2.68</version>
</dependency>
```

下面通过一个示例来演示如何使用 FastJson 对一个员工对象进行序列化，并将其作为生产者的消息发送到 Kafka 版的消息集群上。

测试使用的员工数据，每个字段的说明如表 9-4 所示。

表 9-4

字　　段	类　　型	说　　明
empno	int	员工号
ename	String	员工姓名
job	String	员工职位
mgr	int	员工经理的员工号
hiredate	String	入职日期
sal	int	月薪
comm	int	奖金
deptno	int	部门号

具体的开发步骤如下。

（1）开发 Employee 类，用于封装员工对象。

```
package emp;

public class Employee {
    private int empno;
    private String ename;
    private String job;
    private int mgr;
    private String hiredate;
    private int sal;
    private int comm;
    private int deptno;

    public Employee() {    }

    @Override
    public String toString() {
        return "Employee [empno=" + empno + ", ename=" + ename
                + ", job=" + job + ", mgr=" + mgr + ", hiredate="
                + hiredate + ", sal=" + sal + ", comm="
                + comm + ", deptno=" + deptno + "]";
    }

    public int getEmpno() {
        return empno;
    }

    public void setEmpno(int empno) {
```

```java
        this.empno = empno;
    }

    public String getEname() {
        return ename;
    }

    public void setEname(String ename) {
        this.ename = ename;
    }

    public String getJob() {
        return job;
    }

    public void setJob(String job) {
        this.job = job;
    }

    public int getMgr() {
        return mgr;
    }

    public void setMgr(int mgr) {
        this.mgr = mgr;
    }

    public String getHiredate() {
        return hiredate;
    }

    public void setHiredate(String hiredate) {
        this.hiredate = hiredate;
    }

    public int getSal() {
        return sal;
    }

    public void setSal(int sal) {
        this.sal = sal;
    }

    public int getComm() {
```

```
        return comm;
    }

    public void setComm(int comm) {
        this.comm = comm;
    }

    public int getDeptno() {
        return deptno;
    }

    public void setDeptno(int deptno) {
        this.deptno = deptno;
    }
}
```

> Employee 类为了方便输出结果，重写了 toString()方法。

（2）开发 EmployeeJSONSerializer 类，用于将 Employee 对象序列化。

```
package emp;

import java.util.Map;
import org.apache.kafka.common.serialization.Serializer;
import com.alibaba.fastjson.JSON;

public class EmployeeJSONSerializer implements Serializer<Employee> {

    @Override
    public byte[] serialize(String topic, Employee data) {
    //将数据进行序列化操作
        return JSON.toJSONBytes(data);
    }

    @Override
    public void configure(Map<String, ?> configs, boolean isKey) {

    }

    @Override
    public void close() {
```

    }
}
```

> EmployeeJSONSerializer 类使用了 serialize()方法，将员工对象序列化为一个 JSON 格式的字节数组。

（3）开发 EmployeeProducer 类，用于将 Employee 对象发送到 Kafka 集群上。

```java
package emp;

import java.util.Properties;
import org.apache.kafka.clients.CommonClientConfigs;
import org.apache.kafka.clients.producer.KafkaProducer;
import org.apache.kafka.clients.producer.Producer;
import org.apache.kafka.clients.producer.ProducerConfig;
import org.apache.kafka.clients.producer.ProducerRecord;
import org.apache.kafka.common.config.SaslConfigs;
import org.apache.kafka.common.config.SslConfigs;
import demo.JavaKafkaConfigurer;

public class EmployeeProducer {

    public static void main(String[] args) throws Exception {
        //设置 JAAS 配置文件的路径
        JavaKafkaConfigurer.configureSasl();
        //加载配置文件 kafka.properties
        Properties kafkaProperties =
                        JavaKafkaConfigurer.getKafkaProperties();
        Properties props = new Properties();
        //设置接入点，请通过管理控制台获取对应 Topic 的接入点
        props.put(ProducerConfig.BOOTSTRAP_SERVERS_CONFIG,
                kafkaProperties.getProperty("bootstrap.servers"));
        //设置 SSL 根证书的路径，请记得修改为自己的路径
        //与 SASL 路径类似，该文件也不能被打包到 JAR 文件中
        props.put(SslConfigs.SSL_TRUSTSTORE_LOCATION_CONFIG,
                kafkaProperties.getProperty("ssl.truststore.location"));
        //根证书 store 的密码，保持不变
        props.put(SslConfigs.SSL_TRUSTSTORE_PASSWORD_CONFIG,
                "KafkaOnsClient");
        //接入协议，目前支持使用 SASL_SSL 协议接入
        props.put(CommonClientConfigs.SECURITY_PROTOCOL_CONFIG,
                "SASL_SSL");
        //SASL 鉴权方式，保持不变
```
```

```java
        props.put(SaslConfigs.SASL_MECHANISM, "PLAIN");

        props.setProperty(ProducerConfig.KEY_SERIALIZER_CLASS_CONFIG,
            "org.apache.kafka.common.serialization.StringSerializer");
        //使用 EmployeeJSONSerializer
        props.setProperty(ProducerConfig.VALUE_SERIALIZER_CLASS_CONFIG,
            "emp.EmployeeJSONSerializer");

        //创建生产者
        Producer<String, Employee> producer =
                        new KafkaProducer<String, Employee>(props);
        //构造一个消息队列 Kafka 版消息
        String topic = kafkaProperties.getProperty("topic");
        //发送 10 个员工对象
        for (int i = 0; i < 10; i++) {
            Employee emp = new Employee();
            emp.setEmpno(i);//设置员工号
            emp.setEname("Ename" + i);//设置员工姓名
            emp.setJob("Job" + i);//设置员工职位
            emp.setMgr(1000 + i);//设置员工经理的员工号
            emp.setHiredate("2023-01-01");//设置入职日期
            emp.setSal(6000);//设置月薪
            emp.setComm(2000);//设置奖金
            emp.setDeptno(10);//设置部门号
            //发送消息
            ProducerRecord<String, Employee> kafkaMessage =
                    new ProducerRecord<String, Employee>(topic,emp);
            producer.send(kafkaMessage);
            //每两秒发送一个 Employee 对象
            Thread.sleep(2000);
        }
        producer.close();
    }
}
```

（4）开发 EmployeeJSONDeserializer 类，用于反序列化。

```java
package emp;

import java.util.Map;
import org.apache.kafka.common.serialization.Deserializer;
import com.alibaba.fastjson.JSON;

public class EmployeeJSONDeserializer implements Deserializer<Employee> {
```

```java
    @Override
    public void configure(Map<String, ?> configs, boolean isKey) {

    }

    @Override
    public Employee deserialize(String topic, byte[] data) {
        //将数据进行反序列化操作,生成一个 Employee 类的实例对象。
        return JSON.parseObject(data,Employee.class);
    }

    @Override
    public void close() {

    }
}
```

> EmployeeJSONDeserializer 类使用 deserialize()方法将一个 JSON 格式的字节数组反序列化为一个员工对象。

(5)开发 EmployeeConsumer 类,用于消费消息。

```java
package emp;

import java.util.ArrayList;
import java.util.List;
import java.util.Properties;
import org.apache.kafka.clients.CommonClientConfigs;
import org.apache.kafka.clients.consumer.ConsumerConfig;
import org.apache.kafka.clients.consumer.ConsumerRecord;
import org.apache.kafka.clients.consumer.ConsumerRecords;
import org.apache.kafka.clients.consumer.KafkaConsumer;
import org.apache.kafka.clients.producer.ProducerConfig;
import org.apache.kafka.common.config.SaslConfigs;
import org.apache.kafka.common.config.SslConfigs;
import demo.JavaKafkaConfigurer;

public class EmployeeConsumer {

    public static void main(String[] args) {
        //设置 JAAS 配置文件的路径
        JavaKafkaConfigurer.configureSasl();
```

```java
//加载配置文件 kafka.properties
Properties kafkaProperties =
                    JavaKafkaConfigurer.getKafkaProperties();

Properties props = new Properties();
//设置接入点，请通过管理控制台获取对应 Topic 的接入点
props.put(ProducerConfig.BOOTSTRAP_SERVERS_CONFIG,
        kafkaProperties.getProperty("bootstrap.servers"));
//设置 SSL 根证书的路径，请记得修改为自己的路径
//与 SASL 路径类似，该文件也不能被打包到 JAR 文件中
props.put(SslConfigs.SSL_TRUSTSTORE_LOCATION_CONFIG,
        kafkaProperties.getProperty("ssl.truststore.location"));
//根证书存储的密码，保持不变
props.put(SslConfigs.SSL_TRUSTSTORE_PASSWORD_CONFIG,
        "KafkaOnsClient");
//接入协议，目前支持使用 SASL_SSL 协议接入
props.put(CommonClientConfigs.SECURITY_PROTOCOL_CONFIG,
        "SASL_SSL");
//SASL 鉴权方式，保持不变
props.put(SaslConfigs.SASL_MECHANISM, "PLAIN");
//指定 Key 的反序列化方式
props.setProperty(ConsumerConfig.KEY_DESERIALIZER_CLASS_CONFIG,
    "org.apache.kafka.common.serialization.StringDeserializer");
//使用 EmployeeJSONDeserializer
props.setProperty(ConsumerConfig.VALUE_DESERIALIZER_CLASS_CONFIG,
    "emp.EmployeeJSONDeserializer");

//当前消费实例所属的消费者组。属于同一个消费者组的消费实例会负载消费消息
props.put(ConsumerConfig.GROUP_ID_CONFIG,
        kafkaProperties.getProperty("group.id"));
//构造消费对象，即生成一个消费实例
KafkaConsumer<String, Employee> consumer =
                    new KafkaConsumer<String, Employee>(props);
//设置消费者组订阅的 Topic，可以订阅多个
//如果 GROUP_ID_CONFIG 相同，则建议将订阅的 Topic 也设置成相同的
List<String> subscribedTopics = new ArrayList<String>();
//如果需要订阅多个 Topic，在这里加进去即可
subscribedTopics.add(kafkaProperties.getProperty("topic"));
consumer.subscribe(subscribedTopics);

while (true) {
    ConsumerRecords<String, Employee> records = consumer.poll(1000);
    for (ConsumerRecord<String, Employee> r : records) {
        System.out.println("收到员工对象: "
```

```
                            + r.key() + "\t" + r.value());
                }
            }
        }
    }
```

（6）启动 EmployeeProducer 和 EmployeeConsumer，程序运行的输出如图 9-37 所示。

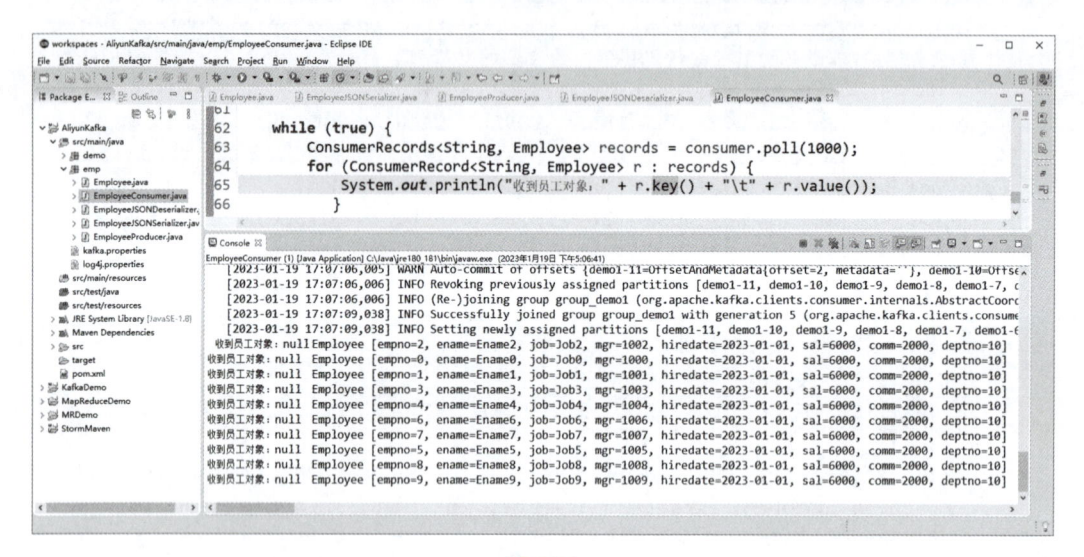

图 9-37

> 从图 9-37 中可以看出，消费者从 Broker 上正常接收到了生产者发送的员工对象数据，并将其直接显示了出来。

第 10 章
实时计算 Flink 版

实时计算 Flink 版是阿里云提供的、全托管 Serverless 的 Flink 云服务，具备实时应用的作业开发、数据调试、运行与监控、自动调优、智能诊断等全生命周期能力。其内核引擎 100% 兼容 Apache Flink。与 Apache Flink 相比，实时计算 Flink 版有约两倍性能的提升，拥有 Flink CDC、动态 CEP 等企业级增值功能，内置了丰富的上下游连接器，能助力企业构建高效、稳定和强大的实时数据应用。

10.1 实时计算 Flink 版基础

实时计算 Flink 版是阿里云基于 Apache Flink 构建的企业级、高性能的实时大数据处理系统。

10.1.1 什么是实时计算 Flink 版

实时计算 Flink 版提供端到端亚秒级实时数据分析能力，并通过标准 SQL 降低业务开发门槛，助力企业向实时化、智能化大数据计算升级转型。

实时计算 Flink 版的产品架构如图 10-1 所示。

实时计算 Flink 版进行流式计算，可以处理多种实时数据，包括 ECS 在线服务日志、IoT 场景下的传感器数据等，同时，可以订阅云上数据库 RDS、PolarDB 等关系型数据库中 binlog 的更新。Flink 通过 DataHub 数据总线产品、SLS 日志服务、开源的 Kafka 消息队列产品等订阅实时数据，并收录进实时计算产品中，进行实时的数据分析和处理，最终将分析结果写入不同的数据服务中（例如 MaxCompute、MaxCompute-Hologres 交互式分析、PAI 机器学习、Elasticsearch 等）。

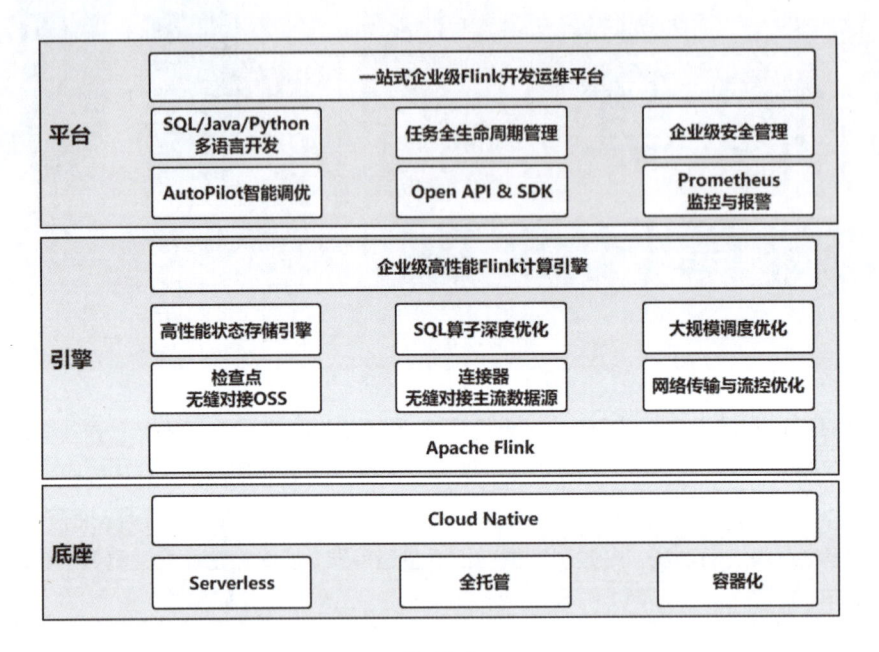

图 10-1

实时计算 Flink 版主要的应用场景是将各种不同的实时数据源中的数据进行实时的订阅、处理和分析，并把得到的结果写入其他的在线存储中让用户直接使用。整个系统具有速度快、数据准、云原生架构及智能化等特点，是一款非常具有竞争力的企业级产品。产品运行在阿里云的容器服务和 ECS 等 IaaS 系统上，和阿里云的各项系统天然打通，方便用户在更多场景下使用。

10.1.2　实时计算 Flink 版的应用场景

实时计算 Flink 版广泛被应用于大数据的实时处理，从而进一步实现流批一体的应用场景。这里将从 3 个场景详细介绍实时计算 Flink 版的应用。

1. 数据集成的流批一体

在大数据场景下经常需要数据同步或数据集成，即将数据库中的数据同步到大数据的数仓或其他存储中。

图 10-2 的上方是传统的经典数据集成架构，全量同步和实时同步实际上是两套技术，需要定期将全量同步的数据和实时同步的数据合并，不断地迭代来把数据库的数据同步到数据仓库中。

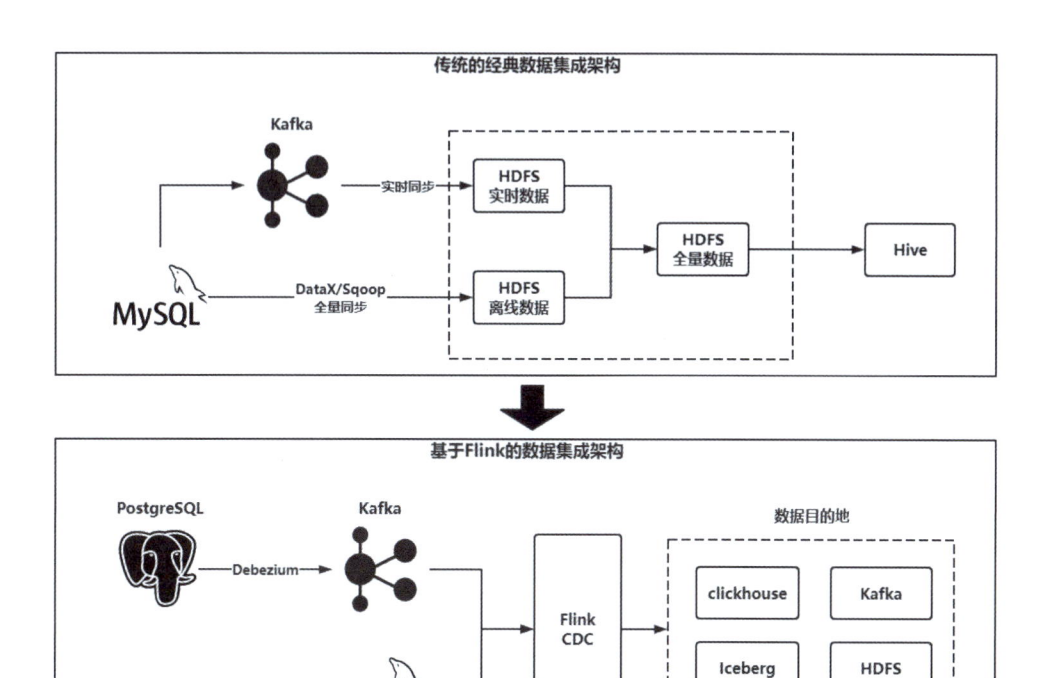

图 10-2

基于实时计算 Flink 版的数据集成架构则不同。因为 Flink SQL 也支持数据库（如 MySQL 和 PG）的 CDC 语义，所以，可以使用 Flink SQL 将数据库的数据一键同步到 Hive、ClickHouse、TiDB 等开源的数据库或开源的 KV 存储中。在实时计算 Flink 版流批一体架构的基础上，实时计算 Flink 版的 connector 也是流批混合的，它会先读取数据库全量数据并同步到数仓中，然后自动切换到增量模式，通过 CDC 读取 Binlog 并进行全量和增量的同步，内部可以自动协调，这就是流批一体的价值。

2. 数仓架构的流批一体

目前主流数仓架构都是一套典型的离线数仓和一套新的实时数仓，但这两套技术栈是分开的。在离线数仓中，习惯使用 Hive 或 Spark；在实时数仓中，习惯使用实时计算 Flink 版和消息队列 Kafka 版。

主流数仓架构有 3 个问题需要解决：两套开发流程，成本高；数据链路冗余，两套链路将数据相关的操作做了两遍；数据口径的一致性难以保证，因为它是由两套引擎计算出来的。传统的数仓架构与流批一体数仓架构的区别如图 10-3 所示。

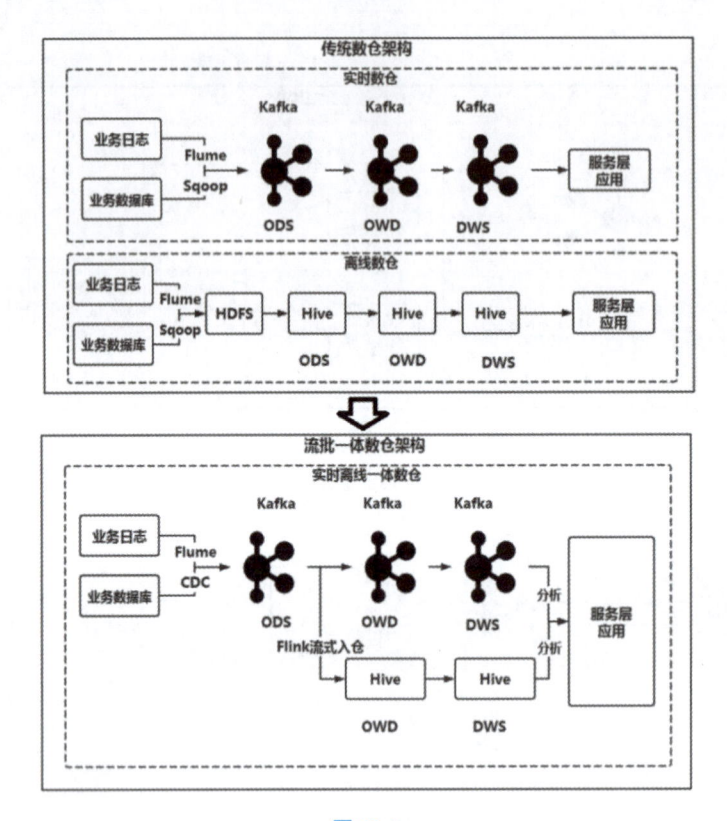

图 10-3

以上问题可以使用流批一体架构来解决，原因如下。

（1）实时计算 Flink 版是使用一套 Flink SQL 开发的，不存在两套开发成本。一个开发团队，一套技术栈，就可以做所有的离线和实时业务统计。

（2）数据链路不存在冗余，明细层的计算进行一次即可，不需要离线再算一遍。

（3）数据口径天然一致。无论是离线的流程，还是实时的流程，都是一套引擎，一套 SQL，一套 UDF，一套开发人员，所以它天然是一致的，不存在实时和离线数据口径不一致的问题。

3. 数据湖的流批一体

Hive 元数据的管理是瓶颈，因为 Hive 作为离线数据分析引擎，不支持数据的实时更新，因此，Hive 也就不具备创建实时数仓的能力。

数据湖架构可以解决更具扩展性的元数据的问题，而且，数据湖中存储的数据支持实时更新，是一个流批一体的存储。数据湖存储与实时计算 Flink 版结合，可以将实时离线一体化的数仓架构演变成实时离线一体化的数据湖架构。

基于实时计算 Flink 版的流批一体数据湖架构如图 10-4 所示。

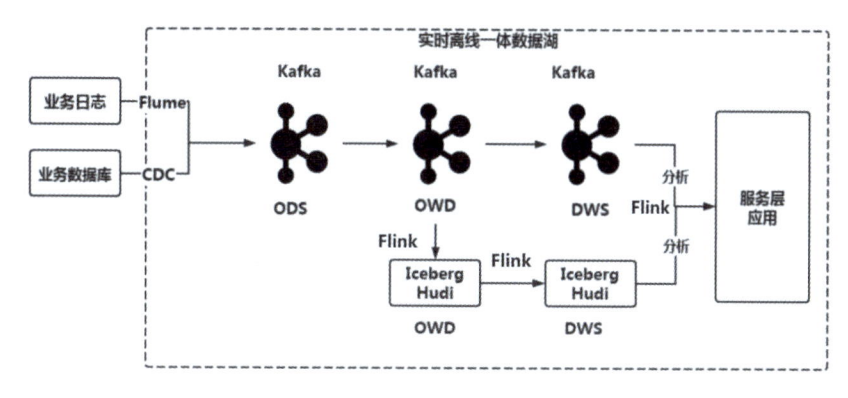

图 10-4

10.1.3 【实战】快速上手实时计算 Flink 版

在使用实时计算 Flink 版之前，需要先开通相应的服务，之后就可以在实时计算 Flink 版的管理控制台上很方便地使用实时计算 Flink 版提供的各项功能。

1. 开通实时计算 Flink 版

开通实时计算 Flink 版服务的步骤如下。

（1）在实时计算 Flink 版的主页上单击"立即开通"按钮，如图 10-5 所示。

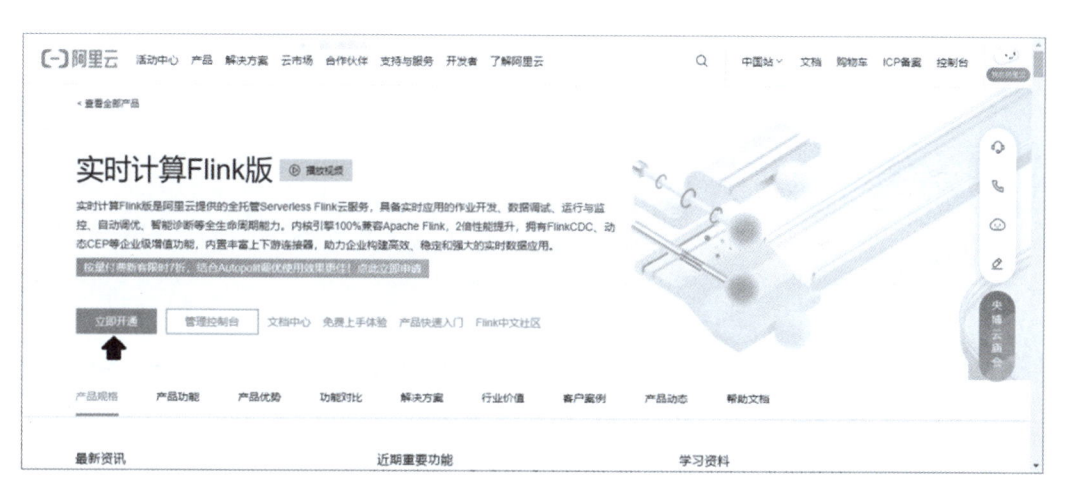

图 10-5

（2）进入"授权请求"页面，单击"前往 RAM 进行授权"按钮，如图 10-6 所示。

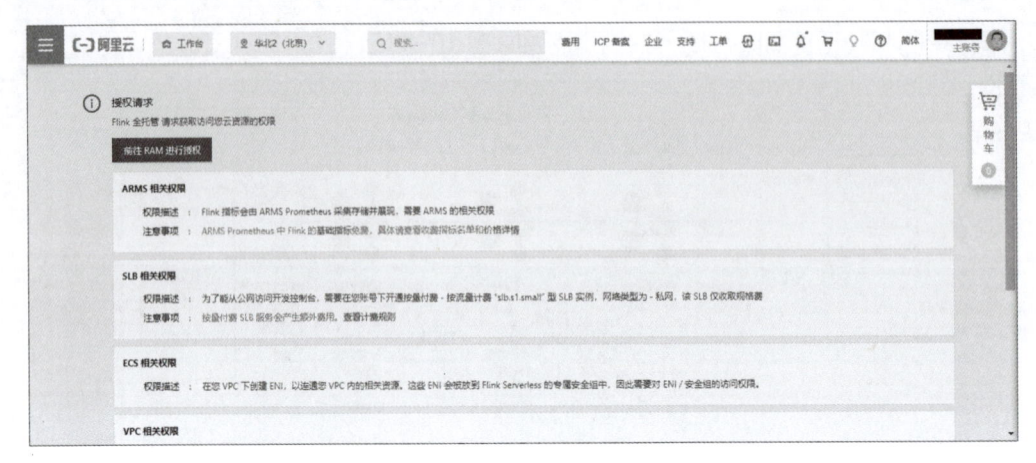

图 10-6

> RAM 授权是为了使实时计算 Flink 版可以访问阿里云上的其他服务。

（3）进入"云资源访问授权"页面，单击"同意授权"按钮，如图 10-7 所示。

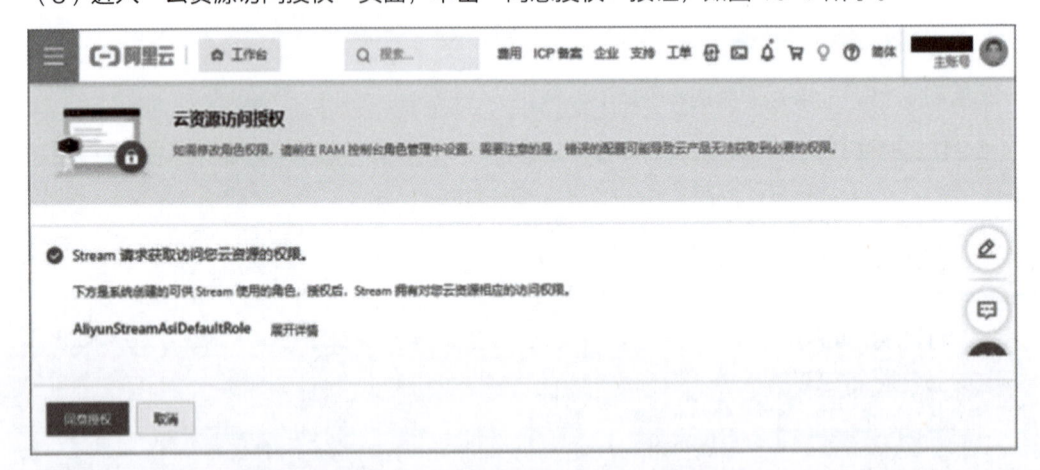

图 10-7

（4）进入"实时计算控制台"页面，单击"Flink 全托管"右侧的"立即购买"按钮。进入"Flink 全托管"页面，购买实时计算 Flink 版服务，如图 10-8 所示。

（5）在完成了相应的支付操作后，在"Flink 全托管"页面中就可以看到正在创建的 Flink 实例，如图 10-9 所示。

（6）在 Flink 实例创建成功后，单击右侧的"控制台"文字链接，进入实时计算 Flink 版的管理控制台，如图 10-10 所示。

图 10-8

图 10-9

图 10-10

2. 运行 Flink JAR 作业

Flink 全托管支持通过 JAR 代码编辑和运行作业。下面来演示如何执行 JAR 流作业与批作业的创建和上线运行等操作。

（1）在实时计算 Flink 版管理控制台左侧的导航栏中选择"资源上传"选项，进入"资源上传"页面，上传 JAR 文件和需要用到的测试数据文件，如图 10-11 所示。

图 10-11

（2）在左侧的导航栏中选择"作业开发"选项，进入"作业开发"页面创建 JAR 流作业。

（3）单击"新建"按钮，在"新建文件"对话框中填写 JAR 流作业的信息，如图 10-12 所示。

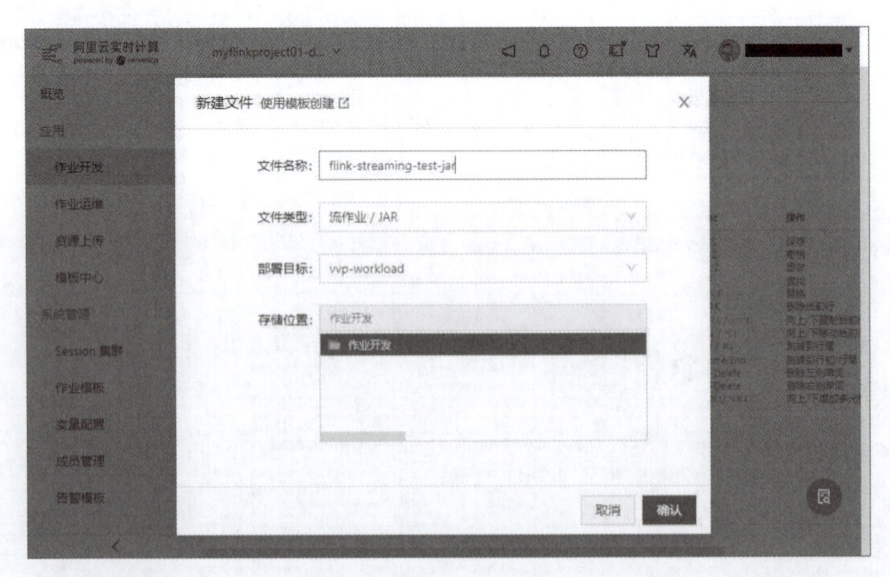

图 10-12

(4)在"作业开发"页面中填写 JAR 流作业的配置信息，如图 10-13 所示。

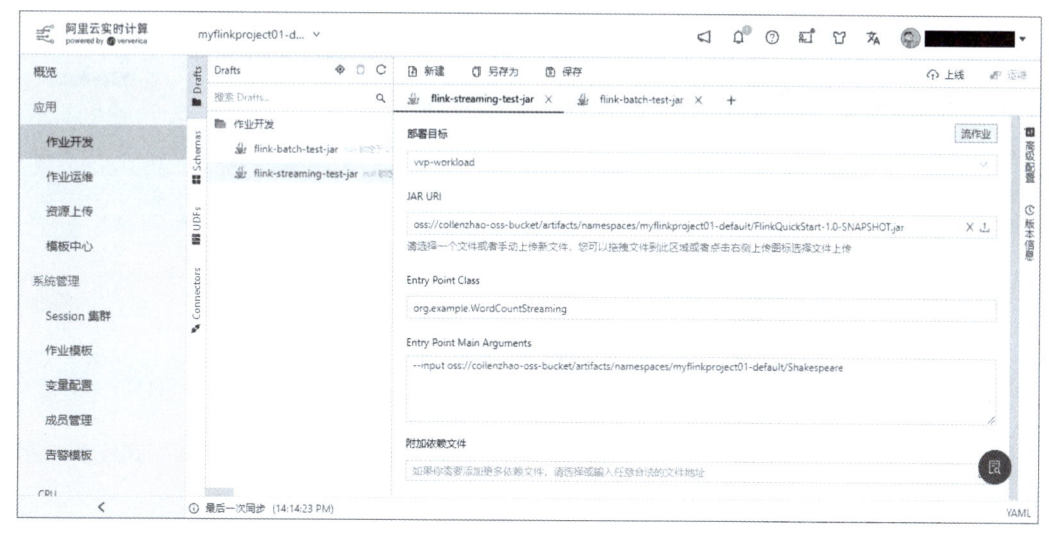

图 10-13

(5)单击"上线"按钮完成 JAR 流作业的部署。

(6)按照类似的方式部署 JAR 批作业，JAR 批作业的配置信息如图 10-14 所示。

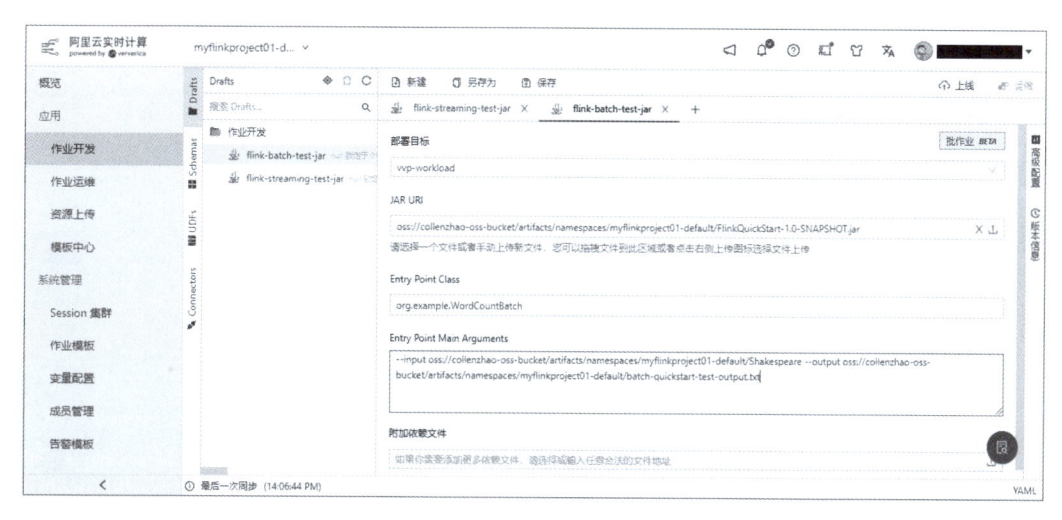

图 10-14

(7)单击"上线"按钮完成 JAR 批作业的部署。

（8）在左侧的导航栏中选择"作业运维"选项，进入"作业运维"页面，可以看到创建的流作业和批作业，如图 10-15 所示。

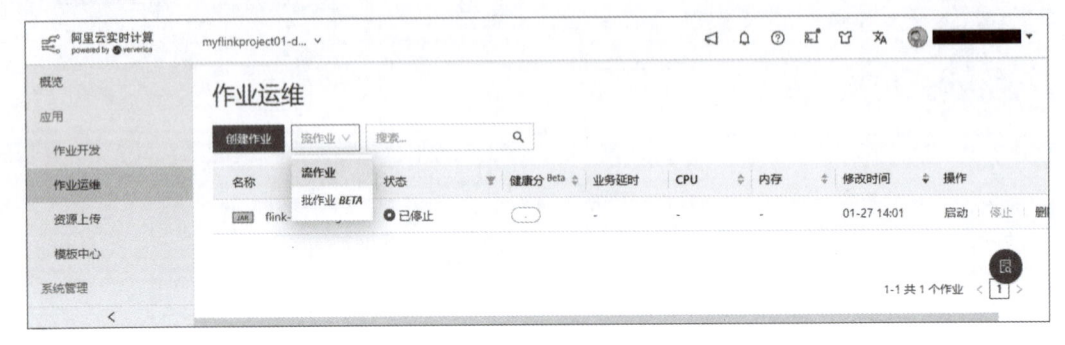

图 10-15

（9）单击流作业的"启动"文字链接运行流作业。如果作业状态变为"运行中"，则代表作业运行正常。

（10）在流作业运行过程中，通过 Task Manager 查看以 .out 结尾的日志文件，搜索 shakespeare，查看流作业的输出结果，如图 10-16 所示。

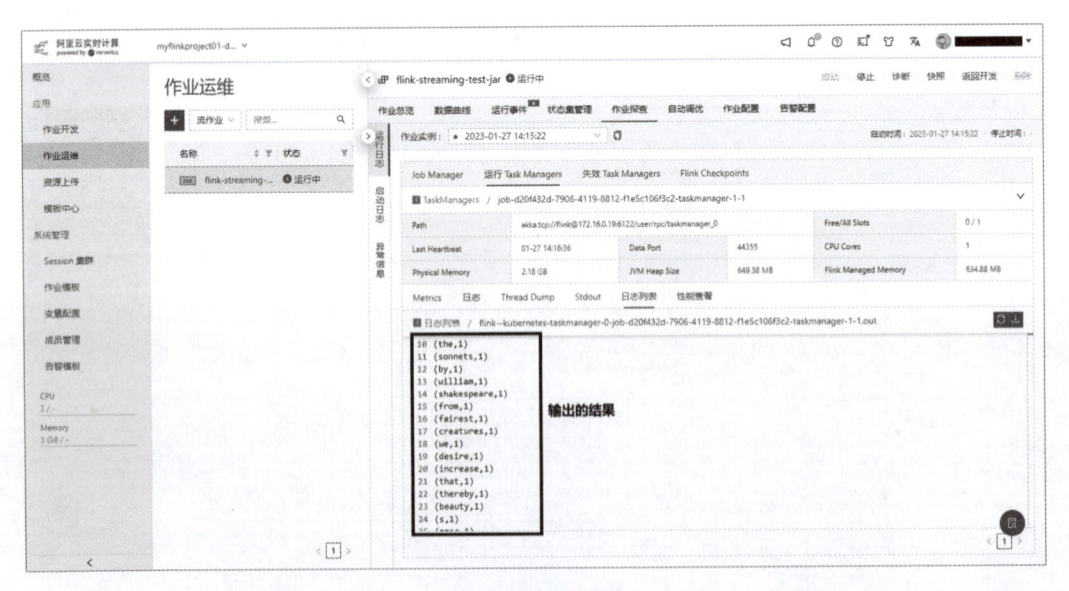

图 10-16

（11）启动批作业，并通过 OSS 查看批作业的输出结果，如图 10-17 所示。

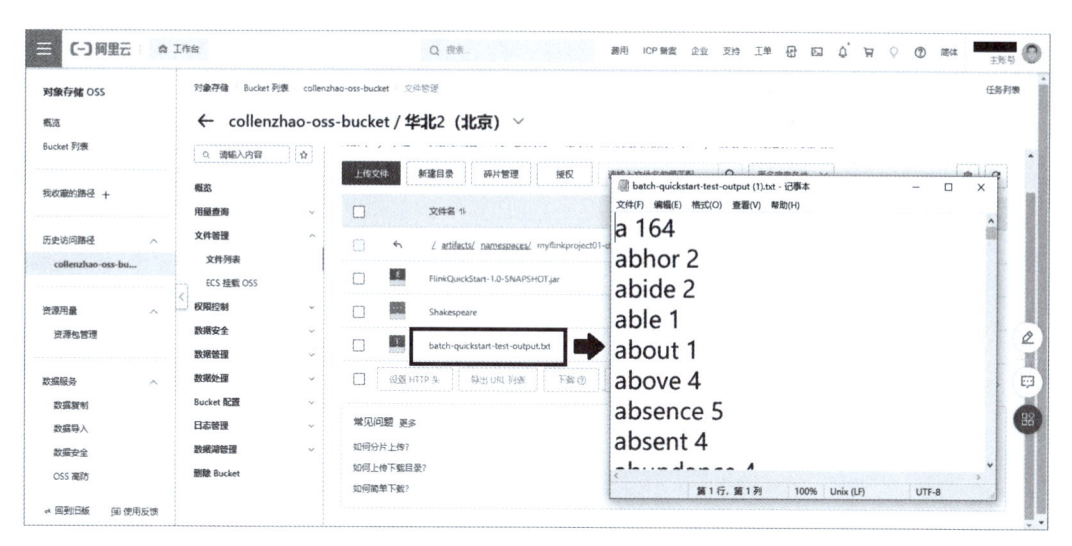

图 10-17

3. 运行 Flink SQL 作业

Flink 全托管支持通过 SQL 代码编辑和运行作业。下面来演示如何执行 SQL 作业的创建和上线运行等操作。

（1）在实时计算 Flink 版管理控制台左侧的导航栏中选择"作业开发"选项，进入"作业开发"页面，创建 SQL 流作业。

（2）单击"新建"按钮，在"新建文件"对话框中填写 SQL 流作业的信息，如图 10-18 所示。

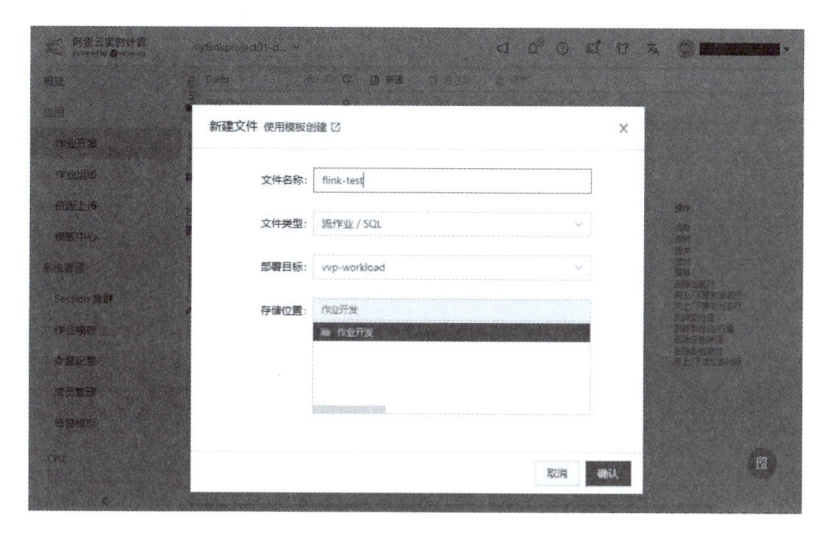

图 10-18

（3）创建一个产生随机数据的 datagen 源表，将 datagen 源表中 randstr 字段的数据打印出来。将以下作业代码复制到作业文本编辑区。

```sql
create temporary table datagen_source(
  randstr varchar
) with (
  'connector' = 'datagen'
);

create temporary table print_table(
  randstr  varchar
) with (
  'connector' = 'print',
  'logger' = 'true'
);

insert into print_table
select substring(randstr,0,8) from datagen_source;
```

（4）单击"验证"按钮，进行语法检查。验证通过后，单击"上线"按钮，在"上线新版本"对话框中单击"确认"按钮。

（5）在左侧的导航栏中选择"作业运维"选项，进入"作业运维"页面，查看 Flink SQL 作业计算结果，如图 10-19 所示。

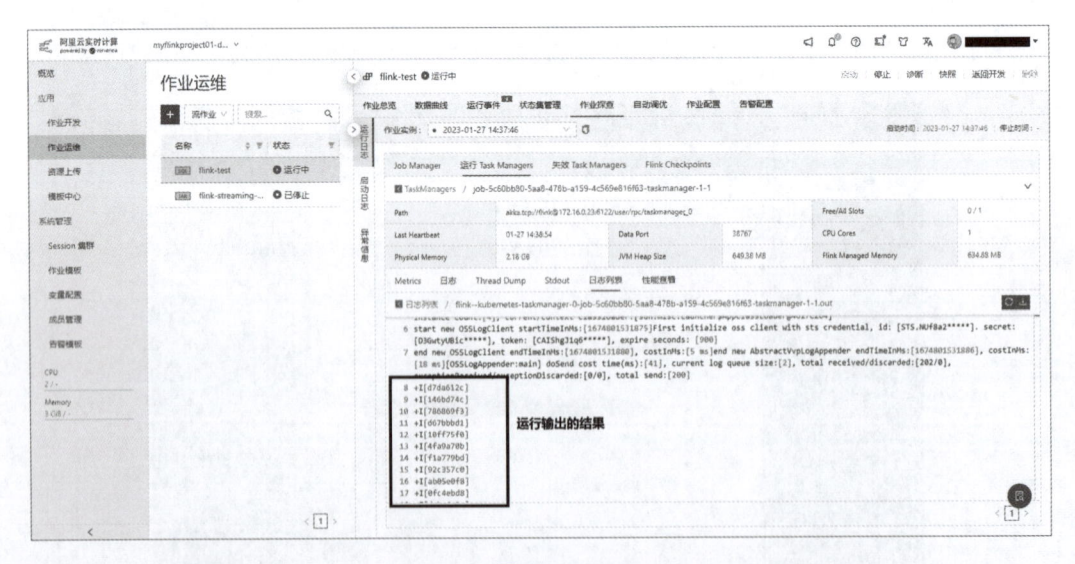

图 10-19

10.2 批处理开发——基于实时计算引擎 Flink Dataset

实时计算 Flink 版完全兼容开源的 Flink 版本，因此在开发 Flink 应用程序前，需要确定实时计算 Flink 版中使用的版本与开发工程 pom.xml 文件中使用的版本是否相同。

在"作业开发"页面右侧的导航栏中，选择"高级配置"选项，并在"常规配置"选区的"引擎版本"列表中选择版本，如图 10-20 所示。

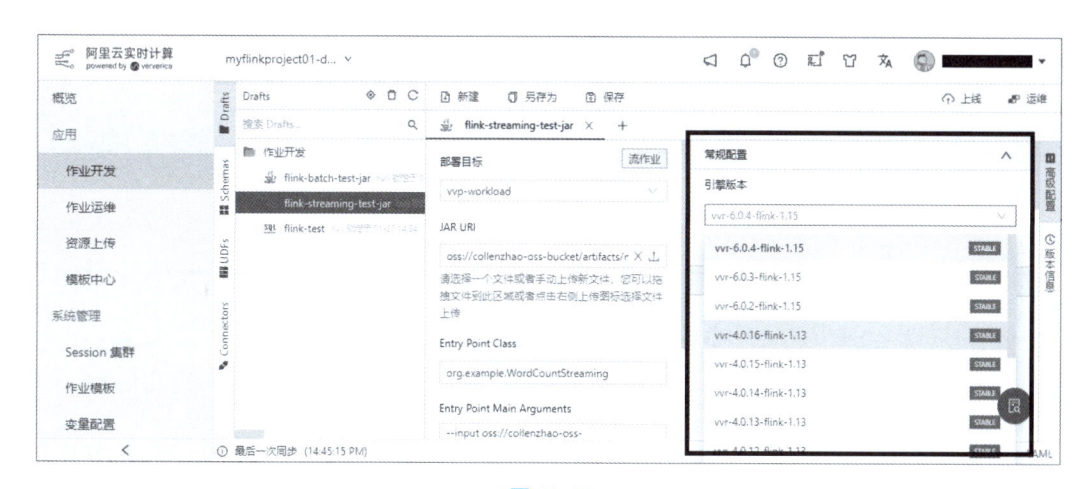

图 10-20

确定了 Flink 版本信息后，就可以使用下面的 pom.xml 文件来构建 Java 工程了。

```
<dependency>
    <groupId>org.apache.flink</groupId>
    <artifactId>flink-streaming-java_2.11</artifactId>
    <version>1.13.6</version>
    <scope>provided</scope>
</dependency>
<dependency>
    <groupId>org.apache.flink</groupId>
    <artifactId>flink-clients_2.11</artifactId>
    <version>1.13.6</version>
    <scope>provided</scope>
</dependency>
```

Flink DataSet API 是处理有边界数据流的功能模块，其本质是执行批处理的离线计算，这一点与 Hadoop 中的 MapReduce 和 Spark 中的 Spark Core 其实是一样的。

Flink DataSet API 中一些常见的算子如表 10-1 所示。

表 10-1

算子	说明
map	输入一个元素，然后返回一个元素，中间可以进行清洗、转换等操作
flatMap	输入一个元素，可以返回零个、一个或多个元素
mapPartition	类似于 map，一次处理一个分区的数据
filter	过滤操作，对传入的数据进行判断，不符合条件的数据会被过滤
reduce	结合当前元素和上一次 reduce 返回的值进行聚合操作，然后返回一个新的值
aggregate	聚合操作，如 sum、max、min 等
distinct	返回一个数据集去重之后的元素
join	多表链接
OuterJoin	外连接
cross	获取两个数据集的笛卡儿积
union	返回两个数据集的总和，数据类型需要一致
First-N	获取集合中的前 N 个元素

10.2.1 【实战】使用 map、flatMap 与 mapPartition 算子

map、flatMap 与 mapPartition 的作用类似，可以把这 3 个算子处理数据的方式看成一个循环。下面通过具体的示例进行说明。

1. map 算子

map 算子相当于一个循环。使用 map 算子能够对数据流集合中的每一个元素进行处理，处理完成后返回一个新的数据流集合。

下面是一段 map 算子的示例程序。

```java
import java.util.ArrayList;
import java.util.List;

import org.apache.flink.api.common.functions.RichMapFunction;
import org.apache.flink.api.java.DataSet;
import org.apache.flink.api.java.ExecutionEnvironment;

public class FlinkMapDemo {

    public static void main(String[] args) throws Exception {
        ExecutionEnvironment env = ExecutionEnvironment
                                    .getExecutionEnvironment();
        DataSet<String> source = env.fromElements
                                    ("I love Beijing",
```

```
                            "I love China",
                            "Beijing is the capital of China");

        //map 算子
        source.map(new RichMapFunction<String, List<String>>() {

            @Override
            public List<String> map(String value) throws Exception {
                //分词
                String[] words = value.split(" ");

                List<String> result = new ArrayList<String>();
                for(String w:words) {
                    result.add("单词是: " + w);
                }
                return result;
            }
        }).print();
    }
}
```

输出的结果如下。

```
[单词是: I, 单词是: love, 单词是: Beijing]
[单词是: I, 单词是: love, 单词是: China]
[单词是: Beijing, 单词是: is, 单词是: the, 单词是: capital, 单词是: of, 单词是: China]
```

2. flatMap 算子

flatMap 算子在 map 算子的基础上加上了一个压平操作。这里可以把压平操作理解为将多个集合合并为一个集合。下面是 flatMap 算子的示例程序。

```
import org.apache.flink.api.common.functions.FlatMapFunction;
import org.apache.flink.api.java.DataSet;
import org.apache.flink.api.java.ExecutionEnvironment;
import org.apache.flink.util.Collector;

public class FlinkFlatMapDemo {
    public static void main(String[] args) throws Exception {
        ExecutionEnvironment env = ExecutionEnvironment
                                    .getExecutionEnvironment();
        //数据源
        DataSet<String> source = env.fromElements
                                    ("I love Beijing",
```

```
                                    "I love China",
                                    "Beijing is the capital of China");
        source.flatMap(new FlatMapFunction<String, String>() {
            @Override
            public void flatMap(String value, Collector<String> out)
            throws Exception {
                String[] words = value.split(" ");
                for(String w:words) {
                    out.collect(w);
                }
            }
        }).print();
    }
}
```

输出的结果如下。

```
I
love
Beijing
I
love
China
Beijing
is
the
capital
of
China
```

3. mapPartition 算子

mapPartition 算子针对 DataSet 集合中的每一个分区处理数据。

> 这里可以把 DataSet 理解为由分区组成，这一点与 Spark RDD 的概念类似。下面是一段 mapPartition 的测试代码。其中，MapPartitionFunction 的第一个泛型参数表示分区中元素的类型，而第二个泛型参数表示处理后的数据类型。

下面是使用 mapPartition 算子的一个示例。

```
import java.util.Iterator;

import org.apache.flink.api.common.functions.MapPartitionFunction;
import org.apache.flink.api.java.DataSet;
import org.apache.flink.api.java.ExecutionEnvironment;
```

```java
import org.apache.flink.util.Collector;

public class FlinkMapPartitionDemo {

    public static void main(String[] args) throws Exception {
        ExecutionEnvironment env = ExecutionEnvironment
                                    .getExecutionEnvironment();

        //数据源
        DataSet<String> source = env.fromElements
                                ("I love Beijing",
                                 "I love China",
                                 "Beijing is the capital of China");

        source.mapPartition(new MapPartitionFunction<String, String>() {
            //分区号
            private int index = 0;

            @Override
            public void mapPartition(Iterable<String> values,
                    Collector<String> out) throws Exception {
                //针对分区中的元素进行操作
                Iterator<String> its = values.iterator();
                while(its.hasNext()) {
                    String line = its.next();
                    String[] words = line.split(" ");
                    for(String w:words) {
                        out.collect("分区 "+index+" 中的元素: " + w);
                    }
                    index ++;
                    out.collect("=================");
                }
            }
        }).print();

    }
}
```

输出的结果如下。

分区 0 中的元素: I
分区 0 中的元素: love
分区 0 中的元素: Beijing
=================
分区 1 中的元素: I

```
分区 1 中的元素: love
分区 1 中的元素: China
==================
分区 2 中的元素: Beijing
分区 2 中的元素: is
分区 2 中的元素: the
分区 2 中的元素: capital
分区 2 中的元素: of
分区 2 中的元素: China
==================
```

10.2.2 【实战】使用 filter 与 distinct 算子

filter 算子类似于 SQL 语句中的 where 条件，可以过滤数据集中的元素。distinct 算子则完成数据去重的工作。下面的代码程序演示了 filter 算子和 distinct 算子的用法。

```java
import org.apache.flink.api.common.functions.FilterFunction;
import org.apache.flink.api.common.functions.FlatMapFunction;
import org.apache.flink.api.java.DataSet;
import org.apache.flink.api.java.ExecutionEnvironment;
import org.apache.flink.util.Collector;

public class FlinkFilterDistinctDemo {
    public static void main(String[] args) throws Exception {
        ExecutionEnvironment env = ExecutionEnvironment
                                    .getExecutionEnvironment();
        DataSet<String> source = env.fromElements
                            ("I love Beijing",
                             "I love China",
                             "Beijing is the capital of China");

        //得到数据集中的每一个单词
        DataSet<String> flatResult =source.flatMap(
            new FlatMapFunction<String, String>() {
            @Override
            public void flatMap(String value, Collector<String> out)
            throws Exception {
                String[] words = value.split(" ");
                for (String w : words) {
                    out.collect(w);
                }
            }
        });
        //选择长度大于 5 的单词
        flatResult.filter(new FilterFunction<String>() {
```

```
            @Override
            public boolean filter(String value) throws Exception {
                return value.length() >= 5 ? true : false;
            }
        }).print();

        System.out.println("--------------------------");
        //去掉重复的单词
        flatResult.distinct().print();
    }
}
```

输出的结果如下。

```
Beijing
China
Beijing
capital
China
--------------------------
China
is
of
Beijing
I
love
the
capital
```

10.2.3 【实战】使用 join 算子

与 SQL 语句中的多表查询一样，使用 Flink DataSet API 中的 join 算子能够完成多表链接操作。在下面的示例代码中，首先构造了两张表，然后使用 join 算子完成了多表的链接。

```
import java.util.ArrayList;

import org.apache.flink.api.common.functions.JoinFunction;
import org.apache.flink.api.java.DataSet;
import org.apache.flink.api.java.ExecutionEnvironment;
import org.apache.flink.api.java.tuple.Tuple2;
import org.apache.flink.api.java.tuple.Tuple3;

public class FlinkJoinDemo {

    public static void main(String[] args) throws Exception {
        ExecutionEnvironment env = ExecutionEnvironment
```

```java
                                .getExecutionEnvironment();

//创建用户表(用户ID,姓名)
ArrayList<Tuple2<Integer, String>> list1 =
                    new ArrayList<Tuple2<Integer,String>>();
list1.add(new Tuple2<Integer, String>(1,"Tom"));
list1.add(new Tuple2<Integer, String>(2,"Mike"));
list1.add(new Tuple2<Integer, String>(3,"Mary"));
list1.add(new Tuple2<Integer, String>(4,"Jone"));

//创建地区表（用户ID,地区）
ArrayList<Tuple2<Integer, String>> list2 =
                    new ArrayList<Tuple2<Integer,String>>();
list2.add(new Tuple2<Integer, String>(1,"北京"));
list2.add(new Tuple2<Integer, String>(2,"北京"));
list2.add(new Tuple2<Integer, String>(3,"上海"));
list2.add(new Tuple2<Integer, String>(4,"广州"));

DataSet<Tuple2<Integer, String>> table1 =
                    env.fromCollection(list1);
DataSet<Tuple2<Integer, String>> table2 =
                    env.fromCollection(list2);
//执行Join等值连接
//where(0).equalTo(0)表示使用第1张表的第1列,连接第2张表的第1列
table1.join(table2).where(0).equalTo(0)
/*
 * JoinFunction 的3个泛型参数的含义如下
 * 第1个泛型参数表示第1张表
 * 第2个泛型参数表示第2张表
 * 第3个泛型参数表示Join操作后输出结果
 */
.with(new JoinFunction<Tuple2<Integer, String>,
                Tuple2<Integer, String>,
                Tuple3<Integer, String, String>>() {
    @Override
    public Tuple3<Integer, String, String> join(
            Tuple2<Integer, String> first,
            Tuple2<Integer, String> second)
        throws Exception {
        //返回用户ID、姓名、地区
        return new Tuple3<Integer, String, String>
                (first.f0,first.f1,second.f1);
    }
}).print();
```

        }
    }

输出的结果如下。

(3,Mary,上海)
(1,Tom,北京)
(2,Mike,北京)
(4,Jone,广州)

10.2.4 【实战】使用 cross 算子

在 SQL 语句中，在执行多表链接操作时，如果没有链接条件，则会得到多表链接的笛卡儿积。Flink DataSet API 也提供了 cross 算子来得到多表链接的笛卡儿积。

```java
import java.util.ArrayList;
import org.apache.flink.api.java.DataSet;
import org.apache.flink.api.java.ExecutionEnvironment;
import org.apache.flink.api.java.tuple.Tuple2;
public class FlinkCrossDemo {
    public static void main(String[] args) throws Exception {
        ExecutionEnvironment env = ExecutionEnvironment.getExecutionEnvironment();
        //创建用户表(用户ID,姓名)
        ArrayList<Tuple2<Integer, String>> list1 =
                            new ArrayList<Tuple2<Integer,String>>();
        list1.add(new Tuple2<Integer, String>(1,"Tom"));
        list1.add(new Tuple2<Integer, String>(2,"Mike"));
        list1.add(new Tuple2<Integer, String>(3,"Mary"));
        list1.add(new Tuple2<Integer, String>(4,"Jone"));
        //创建地区表（用户ID,地区）
        ArrayList<Tuple2<Integer, String>> list2 =
                            new ArrayList<Tuple2<Integer,String>>();
        list2.add(new Tuple2<Integer, String>(1,"北京"));
        list2.add(new Tuple2<Integer, String>(2,"北京"));
        list2.add(new Tuple2<Integer, String>(3,"上海"));
        list2.add(new Tuple2<Integer, String>(4,"广州"));

        DataSet<Tuple2<Integer, String>> table1 =
                                    env.fromCollection(list1);
        DataSet<Tuple2<Integer, String>> table2 =
                                    env.fromCollection(list2);
        //生成笛卡儿积
        table1.cross(table2).print();
    }
}
```

输出的结果如下。

```
((1,Tom),(1,北京))
((1,Tom),(2,北京))
((1,Tom),(3,上海))
((1,Tom),(4,广州))
((2,Mike),(1,北京))
((2,Mike),(2,北京))
((2,Mike),(3,上海))
((2,Mike),(4,广州))
((3,Mary),(1,北京))
((3,Mary),(2,北京))
((3,Mary),(3,上海))
((3,Mary),(4,广州))
((4,Jone),(1,北京))
((4,Jone),(2,北京))
((4,Jone),(3,上海))
((4,Jone),(4,广州))
```

10.2.5 【实战】使用 First-N 算子

First-N 操作也叫作 Top-N 操作。它先按照某种规律对数据集中的元素进行排序，然后取出排在最前面的几个元素。

```java
import org.apache.flink.api.common.operators.Order;
import org.apache.flink.api.java.DataSet;
import org.apache.flink.api.java.ExecutionEnvironment;
import org.apache.flink.api.java.tuple.Tuple3;

public class FlinkFirstNDemo {
    public static void main(String[] args) throws Exception {
        ExecutionEnvironment env = ExecutionEnvironment
                                    .getExecutionEnvironment();

        //构造一张表，包含姓名、工资、部门号这3个字段
        DataSet<Tuple3<String, Integer, Integer>> source =
            env.fromElements(
                new Tuple3<String, Integer, Integer>("SMITH",1000,10),
                new Tuple3<String, Integer, Integer>("KING",5000,10),
                new Tuple3<String, Integer, Integer>("Ford",3000,20),
                new Tuple3<String, Integer, Integer>("JONE",2500,30),
                new Tuple3<String, Integer, Integer>("CLARK",1000,10));
        //按照插入顺序，取出前3条记录
        source.first(3).print();
```

```
        System.out.println("**********************");
        //先按照部门号排序,再按照工资排序
        source.sortPartition(2, Order.ASCENDING)
                .sortPartition(1, Order.DESCENDING).print();
        System.out.println("**********************");
        //按照部门号分组,取每组中的第 1 条记录
        source.groupBy(2).first(1).print();
    }
}
```

输出的结果如下。

```
(SMITH,1000,10)
(KING,5000,10)
(Ford,3000,20)
**********************
(KING,5000,10)
(SMITH,1000,10)
(CLARK,1000,10)
(Ford,3000,20)
(JONE,2500,30)
**********************
(JONE,2500,30)
(SMITH,1000,10)
(Ford,3000,20)
```

10.2.6 【实战】使用外连接操作

外连接操作是一种特殊的连接操作。通过外连接操作可以把连接条件不成立的记录包含在连接的结果中。外链接分为左外连接、右外连接和全外连接。

(1) 左外连接的示例代码如下。

```java
import java.util.ArrayList;
import org.apache.flink.api.common.functions.JoinFunction;
import org.apache.flink.api.java.DataSet;
import org.apache.flink.api.java.ExecutionEnvironment;
import org.apache.flink.api.java.tuple.Tuple2;
import org.apache.flink.api.java.tuple.Tuple3;

public class FlinkOuterJoinDemo {

    public static void main(String[] args) throws Exception {
        ExecutionEnvironment env = ExecutionEnvironment
                                    .getExecutionEnvironment();
```

```java
//创建两张表
//1.用户表(用户ID,姓名),注意这里没有2号用户
ArrayList<Tuple2<Integer, String>> list1 =
                    new ArrayList<Tuple2<Integer,String>>();
list1.add(new Tuple2<Integer, String>(1,"Tom"));
list1.add(new Tuple2<Integer, String>(3,"Mary"));
list1.add(new Tuple2<Integer, String>(4,"Jone"));

//2.地区表(用户ID,地区),注意这里没有3号用户
ArrayList<Tuple2<Integer, String>> list2 =
                    new ArrayList<Tuple2<Integer,String>>();
list2.add(new Tuple2<Integer, String>(1,"北京"));
list2.add(new Tuple2<Integer, String>(2,"北京"));
list2.add(new Tuple2<Integer, String>(4,"广州"));

DataSet<Tuple2<Integer, String>> table1 =
                                    env.fromCollection(list1);
DataSet<Tuple2<Integer, String>> table2 =
                                    env.fromCollection(list2);

//左外连接
table1.leftOuterJoin(table2).where(0).equalTo(0)
    .with(new JoinFunction<Tuple2<Integer, String>,
                Tuple2<Integer, String>,
                Tuple3<Integer, String, String>>() {

    @Override
    public Tuple3<Integer, String, String> join(
            Tuple2<Integer, String> first,
            Tuple2<Integer, String> second)throws Exception {
        if(second == null) {
        return new Tuple3<Integer, String, String>
                (first.f0,first.f1,null);
        }else {
        return new Tuple3<Integer, String, String>
                (first.f0,first.f1,second.f1);
        }
    }
}).print();
}
}
```

输出的结果如下。

```
(3,Mary,null)
(1,Tom,北京)
(4,Jone,广州)
```

（2）右外连接的示例代码如下。

```
//右外连接
table1.rightOuterJoin(table2).where(0).equalTo(0)
    .with(new JoinFunction<Tuple2<Integer, String>,
                    Tuple2<Integer, String>,
                    Tuple3<Integer, String, String>>() {

    @Override
    public Tuple3<Integer, String, String> join(
            Tuple2<Integer, String> first,
            Tuple2<Integer, String> second)    throws Exception {
        if(first == null) {
            return new Tuple3<Integer, String, String>
                        (second.f0,null,second.f1);
        }else {
            return new Tuple3<Integer, String, String>
                        (first.f0,first.f1,second.f1);
        }
    }
}).print();
```

输出的结果如下。

```
(1,Tom,北京)
(2,null,北京)
(4,Jone,广州)
```

（3）全外连接的示例代码如下。

```
//全外连接
table1.fullOuterJoin(table2).where(0).equalTo(0)
    .with(new JoinFunction<Tuple2<Integer, String>,
                    Tuple2<Integer, String>,
                    Tuple3<Integer, String, String>>() {

    @Override
    public Tuple3<Integer, String, String> join(
                    Tuple2<Integer, String> first,
                    Tuple2<Integer, String> second)
            throws Exception {
        if(first == null) {
            return new Tuple3<Integer, String, String>
```

```
                              (second.f0,null,second.f1);
        }else if(second == null) {
            return new Tuple3<Integer, String, String>
                              (first.f0,first.f1,null);
        }else {
            return new Tuple3<Integer, String, String>
                              (first.f0,first.f1,second.f1);
        }
    }
})).print();
```

输出的结果如下。

```
(3,Mary,null)
(1,Tom,北京)
(2,null,北京)
(4,Jone,广州)
```

10.3 流处理开发——基于实时计算引擎 Flink Datastream

Flink DataStream API 可以从多种数据源（如消息队列 Kafka 版、文件流和 Socket 连接等）创建 DataStreamSource。然后，通过 Transformation 的转换操作进行流式数据的处理。最后由 Sink 组件将处理的结果输出。

与 Flink DataSet API 类似，在 Flink DataStream API 中也提供了相应的 Transformation 操作。Flink DataStream API 中一些常见的算子如表 10-2 所示。

表 10-2

算子	说明
map	输入一个元素，经过转换后返回一个新元素
flatmap	输入一个元素，经过转换后返回零个、一个或多个元素
filter	过滤操作，对传入的数据进行判断，不符合条件的数据会被过滤
keyBy	根据指定的 key 进行分组
reduce	对数据进行聚合操作
aggregations	聚合操作，如 sum、min、max 等
union	合并多个流，新的流会包含所有流中的数据
connect	和 union 类似，但是只能连接两个流，两个流的数据类型可以不同
split	根据规则把一个数据流切分为多个流
select	和 split 配合使用，选择切分后的流

> 与 Flink DataSet API 类似的算子在这里就不再介绍了。

10.3.1 【实战】开发单并行度的数据源

为了方便测试，首先开发一个单并行度的数据源。通过实现 SourceFunction 接口能够实现并行度为 1 的数据源。在使用 Flink DataStream API 算子时，可以使用该数据源的数据。

> 单并行度的数据源不能指定其并行度，否则程序会抛出异常。

```java
import org.apache.flink.streaming.api.functions.source.*;

//自定义实现并行度为 1 的数据源，每秒产生一条 Long 类型的数据
//注意：SourceFunction 和 SourceContext 都需要指定数据类型
//如果不指定，则代码运行时会报错
public class MyNoParalleSource implements SourceFunction<Long>{
  private long count = 1;
  private boolean isRunning = true;

  //主要的方法，启动一个数据源
  public void run(SourceContext<Long> ctx) throws Exception {
      while(isRunning){
          ctx.collect(count);
          count++;
          //每秒产生一条数据
          Thread.sleep(1000);
      }
  }
  //在取消一个 cancel 时会调用的方法
  public void cancel() {
      isRunning = false;
  }
}
```

10.3.2 【实战】使用 union 算子

union 算子可以合并多个流，生成一个新的流，新的流会包含多个流中的数据，但合并的每个流中数据的类型必须一致。

下面的示例代码演示了如何使用 union 算子，其中使用了 10.3.1 节中创建的单并行度数据源

MyNoParalleSource。

```java
import org.apache.flink.api.common.functions.RichMapFunction;
import org.apache.flink.streaming.api.datastream.DataStream;
import org.apache.flink.streaming.api.datastream.DataStreamSource;
import org.apache.flink.streaming.api.environment.StreamExecutionEnvironment;

public class FlinkDataStreamUnionDemo {
    public static void main(String[] args) throws Exception {
        StreamExecutionEnvironment sEnv = StreamExecutionEnvironment
                                            .getExecutionEnvironment();
        //创建数据源
        DataStreamSource<Long> source1 = sEnv
                            .addSource(new MyNoParalleSource());
        DataStreamSource<Long> source2 = sEnv
                            .addSource(new MyNoParalleSource());
        //union 算子可以合并多个流，但合并的每个流中数据的类型必须一致
        DataStream<Long> data = source1.union(source2);

        //输出 union 操作后的结果
        data.map(new RichMapFunction<Long, Long>() {
            @Override
            public Long map(Long value) throws Exception {
                System.out.println("收到的数据是:" + value);
                return value;
            }
        });
        sEnv.execute("FlinkDataStreamUnionDemo");
    }
}
```

输出的结果如下。

```
收到的数据是:1
收到的数据是:1
收到的数据是:2
收到的数据是:2
收到的数据是:3
收到的数据是:3
收到的数据是:4
收到的数据是:4
收到的数据是:5
收到的数据是:5
......
```

10.3.3 【实战】使用 connect 算子

connect 算子只能连接两个流，两个流中数据的类型可以不同，并且可以针对两个流中的数据分别进行处理。

在下面的代码中，数据源 source1 中数据的类型是 Long，而数据源 source2 中数据的类型是 String。在使用 connect 算子后，可以分别对不同的数据类型进行处理。

```java
import org.apache.flink.api.common.functions.RichMapFunction;
import org.apache.flink.streaming.api.datastream.DataStream;
import org.apache.flink.streaming.api.datastream.DataStreamSource;
import org.apache.flink.streaming.api.environment.StreamExecutionEnvironment;
import org.apache.flink.streaming.api.functions.co.CoMapFunction;

public class FlinkDataStreamConnectDemo {
    public static void main(String[] args) throws Exception {
        //connect算子只能连接两个流，两个流中数据的类型可以不同
        //可以针对两个流中的数据分别进行处理
        StreamExecutionEnvironment sEnv = StreamExecutionEnvironment
                                        .getExecutionEnvironment();

        //创建数据源
        DataStreamSource<Long> source1 = sEnv
                    .addSource(new MyNoParalleSource());
        DataStream<String> source2 = sEnv
                    .addSource(new MyNoParalleSource())
                    .map(new RichMapFunction<Long, String>() {
            @Override
            public String map(Long value) throws Exception {
                return "String" + value;
            }
        });
        //连接两个流，可以针对这两个流进行不同的处理
        source1.connect(source2).map(
                new CoMapFunction<Long, String, Object>() {
                    @Override
                    public Object map1(Long value) throws Exception {
                        return "对Integer进行处理：" + value;
                    }
                    @Override
                    public Object map2(String value) throws Exception {
                        return "对String进行处理：" + value;
                    }
```

```
        }).print();
        sEnv.execute("FlinkDataStreamConnectDemo");
    }
}
```

输出的结果如下。

```
1> 对 String 进行处理：String1
4> 对 Integer 进行处理：1
1> 对 Integer 进行处理：2
2> 对 String 进行处理：String2
2> 对 Integer 进行处理：3
3> 对 String 进行处理：String3
3> 对 Integer 进行处理：4
4> 对 String 进行处理：String4
4> 对 Integer 进行处理：5
1> 对 String 进行处理：String5
...
```

10.4 SQL 与 Table 开发——基于实时计算引擎 Flink Table&SQL

与 Hadoop 的 Hive 和 Spark SQL 类似，在 Flink 的生态圈体系中也提供了两个关系型操作的 API——Flink Table API 和 Flink SQL API。Flink Table API 是用于 Scala 和 Java 语言的查询 API，允许以非常直观的方式组合关系运算符的查询，如 select、filter 和 join；Flink SQL API 实现了标准 SQL 接口，通过 Flink SQL API 能够使用 SQL 语句处理 DataSet 数据流和 DataStream 数据流。

使用 Flink Table API 和 Flink SQL API 需要将以下依赖引入项目。

```xml
<dependency>
    <groupId>org.apache.flink</groupId>
    <artifactId>flink-table-api-java-bridge_2.11</artifactId>
    <version>1.13.6</version>
    <scope>provided</scope>
</dependency>

<dependency>
    <groupId>org.apache.flink</groupId>
    <artifactId>flink-table-planner_2.11</artifactId>
    <version>1.13.6</version>
    <scope>provided</scope>
</dependency>
```

```xml
<dependency>
    <groupId>org.apache.flink</groupId>
    <artifactId>flink-table-planner-blink_2.11</artifactId>
    <version>1.13.6</version>
    <scope>provided</scope>
</dependency>
```

10.4.1 【实战】开发 Flink Table 程序

本节通过具体的示例来展示如何使用 Flink Table API 进行批处理的离线计算和流处理的实时计算。

1. 使用 Flink Table API 开发 Java 版本的批处理 WordCount

```java
import org.apache.flink.api.common.functions.FlatMapFunction;
import org.apache.flink.api.java.DataSet;
import org.apache.flink.api.java.ExecutionEnvironment;
import org.apache.flink.table.api.Table;
import org.apache.flink.table.api.bridge.java.BatchTableEnvironment;
import org.apache.flink.util.Collector;

public class WordCountBatchTableAPI {
    public static void main(String[] args) throws Exception {
        ExecutionEnvironment env = ExecutionEnvironment
                                    .getExecutionEnvironment();
        BatchTableEnvironment tEnv = BatchTableEnvironment.create(env);
        DataSet<String> text = env.fromElements
                                ("I love Beijing",
                                 "I love China",
                                 "Beijing is the capital of China");
        DataSet<WordCount> input = text.flatMap(new MySplitter());
        Table table = tEnv.fromDataSet(input);
        Table data = table.groupBy("word")
                        .select("word, frequency.sum as frequency");
        DataSet<WordCount> result =
                        tEnv.toDataSet(data, WordCount.class);
        result.print();
    }
    public static class MySplitter implements
                            FlatMapFunction<String, WordCount> {
        public void flatMap(String value, Collector<WordCount> out)
        throws Exception {
            for (String word : value.split(" ")) {
                out.collect(new WordCount(word,1));
```

```
            }
        }
    }

    public static class WordCount {
        public String word;
        public long frequency;
        public WordCount() {}
        public WordCount(String word, long frequency) {
            this.word = word;
            this.frequency = frequency;
        }
        @Override
        public String toString() {
            return "WordCount Result: " + word + " " + frequency;
        }
    }
}
```

输出的结果如下。

```
WordCount Result: China 2
WordCount Result: is 1
WordCount Result: of 1
WordCount Result: Beijing 2
WordCount Result: I 2
WordCount Result: love 2
WordCount Result: the 1
WordCount Result: capital 1
```

2. 使用 Flink Table API 开发 Java 版本的流处理 WordCount

```
import org.apache.flink.api.common.functions.FlatMapFunction;
import org.apache.flink.streaming.api.datastream.DataStream;
import org.apache.flink.streaming.api.datastream.DataStreamSource;
import org.apache.flink.streaming.api.environment.*;
import org.apache.flink.table.api.EnvironmentSettings;
import org.apache.flink.table.api.Table;
import org.apache.flink.table.api.bridge.java.StreamTableEnvironment;
import org.apache.flink.util.Collector;

public class WordCountStreamTableAPI {
    public static void main(String[] args) throws Exception {
        StreamExecutionEnvironment env = StreamExecutionEnvironment
                                    .getExecutionEnvironment();
        //得到 Table 的运行环境
        StreamTableEnvironment stEnv = StreamTableEnvironment
```

```java
                                .create(env);//得到输入流
        DataStreamSource<String> source = Env
                    .socketTextStream(netcat 服务器地址, 1234);
        DataStream<WordWithCount> input = source.flatMap(
                    new FlatMapFunction<String, WordWithCount>() {
            public void flatMap(String data,
                        Collector<WordWithCount> output)
            throws Exception {
                String[] words = data.split(" ");
                for(String word:words){
                    output.collect(new WordWithCount(word,1));
                }
            }
        });
        Table table = stEnv.fromDataStream(input,"word,frequncy");
        Table result = table.groupBy("word")
                        .select("word,frequncy.sum")
                        .as("word","frequncy");

        stEnv.toRetractStream(result, WordWithCount.class).print();
        env.execute();
    }

    public static class WordWithCount{
        public String word;
        public int frequncy;
        public WordWithCount(){}
        public WordWithCount(String word,int frequncy){
            this.word = word;
            this.frequncy = frequncy;
        }
        @Override
        public String toString() {
            return "WordCount [word=" + word + ", frequncy="
                        + frequncy + "]";
        }
    }
}
```

程序中使用网络工具 Netcat 作为消息数据源的服务器。

在 Netcat 中输入以下数据。

I love Beijing and love China

程序运行的结果如下。

```
2> (true,WordCount [word=love, frequncy=1])
1> (true,WordCount [word=I, frequncy=1])
1> (true,WordCount [word=Beijing, frequncy=1])
2> (false,WordCount [word=love, frequncy=1])
2> (true,WordCount [word=love, frequncy=2])
1> (true,WordCount [word=and, frequncy=1])
2> (true,WordCount [word=China, frequncy=1])
```

3. 使用 Flink Table API 开发 Scala 版本的批处理 WordCount

```scala
import org.apache.flink.api.scala._
import org.apache.flink.table.api._
import org.apache.flink.table.api.bridge.scala.BatchTableEnvironment

object WordCountBatchTable {
  def main(args: Array[String]): Unit = {
    val env = ExecutionEnvironment.getExecutionEnvironment
    val tEnv = BatchTableEnvironment.create(env)
    val text = env.fromElements("I love Beijing",
                                "I love China",
                                "Beijing is the capital of China")
    val input = text.flatMap(_.split(" ")).map(word => WordCount(word,1))
    //使用隐式转换将 DataSet 转换为 Table
    val table = tEnv.fromDataSet(input)
    val data = table.groupBy("word")
                    .select("word, frequency.sum as frequency");
    tEnv.toDataSet[WordCount](data).print()
  }
}
case class WordCount(word:String,frequency:Integer)
```

4. 使用 Flink Table API 开发 Scala 版本的流处理 WordCount

```scala
import org.apache.flink.streaming.api.scala._
import org.apache.flink.table.api.TableEnvironment
import org.apache.flink.api.scala._
import org.apache.flink.table.api.bridge.scala.StreamTableEnvironment

object WordCountStreamTable {
  def main(args: Array[String]): Unit = {
    //获取运行环境
    val env: StreamExecutionEnvironment =
              StreamExecutionEnvironment.getExecutionEnvironment
    val tEnv = StreamTableEnvironment.create(env)
    //链接 socket 获取输入数据
    val source = env.socketTextStream("bigdata111",1234)
```

```scala
//注意：必须添加这一行隐式转行，否则在执行下面的flatmap()方法时会报错
import org.apache.flink.api.scala._
//生成DataStream，并通过隐式转换生成表
val dataStream = source.flatMap(line => line.split(" "))
                      .map(w => WordCount(w,1))
val table = tEnv.fromDataStream(dataStream)
val data = table.groupBy("word")
                .select("word,frequency.sum")
                .as("word", "frequency")
//执行查询，并输出
val result = tEnv.toRetractStream[WordCount](data)
result.print
env.execute()
}
case class WordCount(word: String, frequency: Integer)
}
```

10.4.2 【实战】开发 Flink SQL 程序

在进行数据分析和处理时，更常用的方式是使用 SQL 语句来分析和处理数据。

下面的代码展示了如何使用 Flink SQL API 进行批处理的离线计算和流处理的实时计算。

1. 使用 Flink SQL API 开发 Java 版本的批处理 WordCount

```java
import org.apache.flink.api.common.functions.FlatMapFunction;
import org.apache.flink.api.common.functions.MapFunction;
import org.apache.flink.api.java.DataSet;
import org.apache.flink.api.java.ExecutionEnvironment;
import org.apache.flink.api.java.tuple.Tuple2;
import org.apache.flink.table.api.Table;
import org.apache.flink.table.api.bridge.java.BatchTableEnvironment;
import org.apache.flink.util.Collector;

public class WordCountBatchSQL {
    public static void main(String[] args) throws Exception {
        //设置运行环境
        ExecutionEnvironment env = ExecutionEnvironment
                                    .getExecutionEnvironment();
        BatchTableEnvironment tEnv = BatchTableEnvironment.create(env);
        //准备数据
        DataSet<String> text = env.fromElements
                            ("I love Beijing",
                             "I love China",
                             "Beijing is the capital of China");
    DataSet<WordCount> input = text.flatMap(new MySplitter());
```

```java
        //注册表
        tEnv.registerDataSet("WordCount", input, "word,frequency");
        //执行 SQL,并输出
        Table table = tEnv.sqlQuery(
            "select word,sum(frequency) as frequency from WordCount "
            +
            "group by word");
        DataSet<WordCount> result = tEnv.toDataSet(table,
                                                    WordCount.class);
        result.print();
    }
    public static class MySplitter
                    implements FlatMapFunction<String, WordCount> {
        public void flatMap(String value, Collector<WordCount> out)
        throws Exception {
            for (String word : value.split(" ")) {
                out.collect(new WordCount(word,1));
            }
        }
    }
    public static class WordCount {
        public String word;
        public long frequency;
        public WordCount() {}
        public WordCount(String word, long frequency) {
            this.word = word;
            this.frequency = frequency;
        }
        @Override
        public String toString() {
            return word + " " + frequency;
        }
    }
}
```

输出的结果如下。

```
China 2
is 1
of 1
Beijing 2
I 2
love 2
the 1
capital 1
```

2. 使用 Flink SQL API 开发 Java 版本的流处理 WordCount

```java
import org.apache.flink.api.common.functions.FlatMapFunction;
import org.apache.flink.streaming.api.datastream.DataStream;
import org.apache.flink.streaming.api.datastream.DataStreamSource;
import org.apache.flink.streaming.api.environment.*;
import org.apache.flink.table.api.Table;
import org.apache.flink.table.api.TableEnvironment;
import org.apache.flink.table.api.bridge.java.StreamTableEnvironment;
import org.apache.flink.util.Collector;

public class WordCountStreamSQL {
    public static void main(String[] args) throws Exception {
        StreamExecutionEnvironment env =
                    StreamExecutionEnvironment.getExecutionEnvironment();
        //得到 Table 的运行环境
        StreamTableEnvironment stEnv = StreamTableEnvironment
                                        .create(env);
        //得到输入流
        DataStreamSource<String> source =
                        env.socketTextStream("bigdata111", 1234);
        DataStream<WordWithCount> input = source.flatMap(
         new FlatMapFunction<String, WordWithCount>() {
            public void flatMap(String data,
                            Collector<WordWithCount> output)
            throws Exception {
                String[] words = data.split(" ");
                for(String word:words){
                    output.collect(new WordWithCount(word,1));
                }
            }
        });
        Table table = stEnv.fromDataStream(input,"word,frequncy");
        Table result = stEnv.sqlQuery
                        ("select word,sum(frequncy) as frequncy from "
                        + table + " group by word");
        stEnv.toRetractStream(result, WordWithCount.class).print();
        env.execute();
    }

    public static class WordWithCount{
        public String word;
        public int frequncy;
        public WordWithCount(){}
        public WordWithCount(String word,int frequncy){
```

```java
            this.word = word;
            this.frequncy = frequncy;
        }
        @Override
        public String toString() {
            return "WordCount [word=" + word + ", frequncy="
                + frequncy + "]";
        }
    }
}
```

在 Netcat 中输入下面的测试数据。

```
I love Beijing and love China
I love Beijing
I love China
```

处理的结果如下。

```
2> (true,WordCount [word=love, frequncy=1])
1> (true,WordCount [word=I, frequncy=1])
1> (true,WordCount [word=Beijing, frequncy=1])
1> (true,WordCount [word=and, frequncy=1])
2> (false,WordCount [word=love, frequncy=1])
2> (true,WordCount [word=love, frequncy=2])
2> (true,WordCount [word=China, frequncy=1])
1> (false,WordCount [word=I, frequncy=1])
2> (false,WordCount [word=love, frequncy=2])
1> (true,WordCount [word=I, frequncy=2])
2> (true,WordCount [word=love, frequncy=3])
1> (false,WordCount [word=Beijing, frequncy=1])
1> (true,WordCount [word=Beijing, frequncy=2])
1> (false,WordCount [word=I, frequncy=2])
1> (true,WordCount [word=I, frequncy=3])
2> (false,WordCount [word=love, frequncy=3])
2> (true,WordCount [word=love, frequncy=4])
2> (false,WordCount [word=China, frequncy=1])
2> (true,WordCount [word=China, frequncy=2])
```

3. 使用 Flink SQL API 开发 Scala 版本的批处理 WordCount

```scala
import org.apache.flink.api.scala._
import org.apache.flink.table.api.TableEnvironment
import org.apache.flink.table.api.bridge.scala.BatchTableEnvironment

object WordCountBatchSQLAPI {
  def main(args: Array[String]): Unit = {
```

```
    val env = ExecutionEnvironment.getExecutionEnvironment
    val tEnv = BatchTableEnvironment.create(env)
    val text = env.fromElements
                        ("I love Beijing",
                        "I love China",
                        "Beijing is the capital of China")
    val input = text.flatMap(_.split(" "))
            .map(word => WordCount(word, 1))
    val table = tEnv.fromDataSet(input)
    //注册表
    tEnv.registerTable("mytable", table)
    val result = tEnv.sqlQuery(
        "select word, sum(frequency) from mytable group by word")
    tEnv.toDataSet[WordCount](result).print()
  }
  case class WordCount(word: String, frequency: Integer)
}
```

4. 使用 Flink SQL API 开发 Scala 版本的批处理 WordCount

```
import org.apache.flink.streaming.api.scala._
import org.apache.flink.table.api.TableEnvironment
import org.apache.flink.api.scala._
import org.apache.flink.table.api.bridge.scala.StreamTableEnvironment

object WordCountStreamSQL {
  def main(args: Array[String]): Unit = {
    //获取运行环境
    val env: StreamExecutionEnvironment =
            StreamExecutionEnvironment.getExecutionEnvironment
    val tEnv = StreamTableEnvironment.create(env)
    //链接 socket 获取输入数据
    val source = env.socketTextStream("bigdata111",1234)
    //注意：必须添加这一行隐式转行，否则在执行下面的 flatmap()方法时会报错
    import org.apache.flink.api.scala._
    //生成 DataStream，并注册 DataStream
    val dataStream = source.flatMap(line => line.split(" "))
                    .map(w => WordCount(w,1))
    tEnv.registerDataStream("mytable", dataStream)
    //执行查询，并输出
    val data = tEnv.sqlQuery(
     "select word,sum(frequency) as frequency from mytable group by word")
    //执行查询，并输出
    val result = tEnv.toRetractStream[WordCount](data)
    result.print
    env.execute()
```

```
  }
  case class WordCount(word: String, frequency: Integer)
}
```

10.5 实时计算 Flink 版的高级特性

实时计算 Flink 版提供大量的特性来帮助用户开发应用程序。这些特性包括检查点设置、重启策略、分布式缓存和累加器等。下面分别进行介绍。

10.5.1 检查点设置

由于 Flink 是在内存中完成计算的，为了保证容错性，Flink 可以通过检查点对内存中的数据进行持久化的保存。检查点是 Flink 实现容错机制最核心的功能，通过检查点可以周期性地将内存中的数据保存起来，从而生成内存中数据的快照。当 Flink 程序意外崩溃时，重新运行程序后可以有选择地从这些快照进行恢复，从而修正故障导致的程序数据异常。

在应用程序代码级别可以启用检查点。在下面的代码中，每 1000ms 执行一个检查点。启用检查点后，状态在执行持久化保存时，默认会保存在 TaskManager 的内存中。

```
StreamExecutionEnvironment sEnv = 
StreamExecutionEnvironment.getExecutionEnvironment();
sEnv.enableCheckpointing(1000);
```

在实时计算 Flink 版的管理控制台上也可以很方便地设置检查点，如图 10-21 所示。

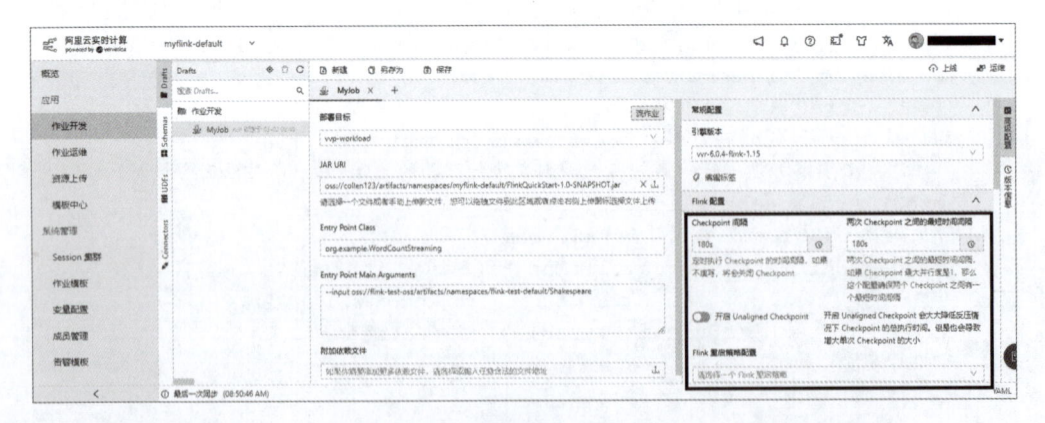

图 10-21

开源版本的 Flink 支持 3 种不同的后端存储方式，用于将内存中的数据进行持久化操作，如表 10-3 所示。

表 10-3

后端存储方式	描 述 信 息
MemoryStateBackend	状态数据保存在 Java 的堆内存中，在执行检查点时，会将状态数据保存到 TaskManager 的内存中。这种方式不建议在生产环境中使用
FsStateBackend	状态数据保存在 TaskManager 的内存中，在执行检查点时，会将状态数据保存到相应的文件系统中，如 HDFS，比较适合在生产中使用
RocksDBStateBackend	RocksDB 是一个为更快速存储而生的、可嵌入的、持久型的 Key-Value 存储数据库。这种方式克服了状态受内存限制的缺点，又能持久化到远端系统中。因此与 FsStateBackend 一样，比较适合在生产中使用

可以通过以下两个不同的级别来配置检查点的后端存储方式。

1. 应用程序代码级别

```
sEnv.setStateBackend(new FsStateBackend("HDFS 的路径"));
```

或者：

```
sEnv.setStateBackend(new MemoryStateBackend());
```

或者：

```
sEnv.setStateBackend(new RocksDBStateBackend(filebackend, true));
```

2. Flink 系统级别

通过修改 Flink 的配置文件 flink-conf.yaml，也能实现检查点后端存储的配置。

```
#==============================================================
# Fault tolerance and checkpointing
#==============================================================
# The backend that will be used to store operator state checkpoints if
# checkpointing is enabled.
# Supported backends are 'jobmanager', 'filesystem', 'rocksdb',
# or the <class-name-of-factory>.
#
# state.backend: filesystem

# Directory for checkpoints filesystem, when using any of the
# default bundled state backends.
#
# state.checkpoints.dir: hdfs://namenode-host:port/flink-checkpoints
```

这里的核心配置参数是 state.backend 和 state.checkpoints.dir。例如下面的代码使用了 HDFS 作为检查点的后端存储。

```
state.backend: filesystem
state.checkpoints.dir: hdfs://bigdata111:9000/flink/checkpoints
```

> state.backend 的值可以是下面几种。
> （1）jobmanager：使用 MemoryStateBackend。
> （2）filesystem：使用 FsStateBackend。
> （3）rocksdb：使用 RocksDBStateBackend。

10.5.2 重启策略

有了检查点的支持，当任务执行失败时，Flink 就可以使用不同的重启策略重启失败的任务。Flink 常用的重启策略有固定间隔（Fixed delay）、失败率（Failure rate）和无重启（No restart）。用户可以在应用程序代码级别，或者在实时计算 Flink 版的管理控制台上，来指定使用哪一种重启策略。

> 如果没有启用检查点，则需要使用无重启的策略；如果启用了检查点，则默认使用固定间隔的策略。

（1）在应用程序的代码级别配置重启策略。

```
sEnv.setRestartStrategy(RestartStrategies.fixedDelayRestart(
    3, //尝试重启的次数
    Time.of(10, TimeUnit.SECONDS)  //每次重启的间隔
));
```

（2）在实时计算 Flink 版的管理控制台上配置重启策略，如图 10-22 所示。

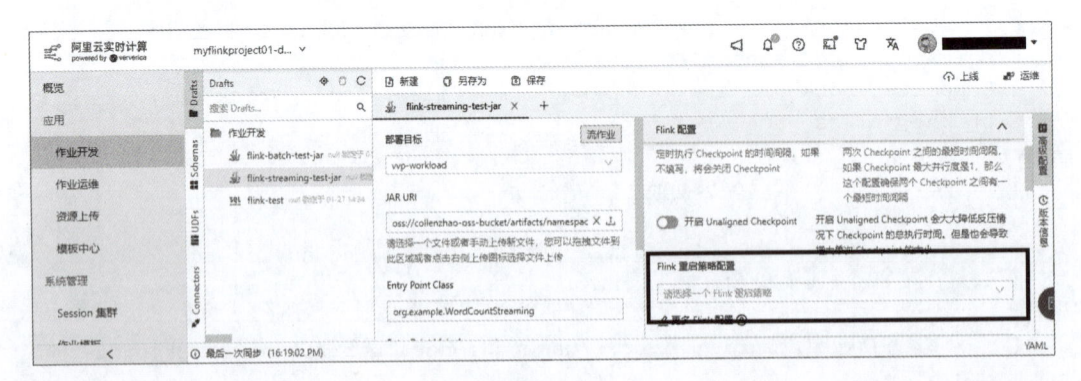

图 10-22

10.5.3 分布式缓存

Flink 版提供了一个分布式缓存，可以使用户在并行函数中很方便地读取本地文件。这种功能类

似于 Hadoop 中的 MapJoin，因此适用于链接一张大表和一张小表的情况。Flink 分布式缓存的过程机制如图 10-23 所示。

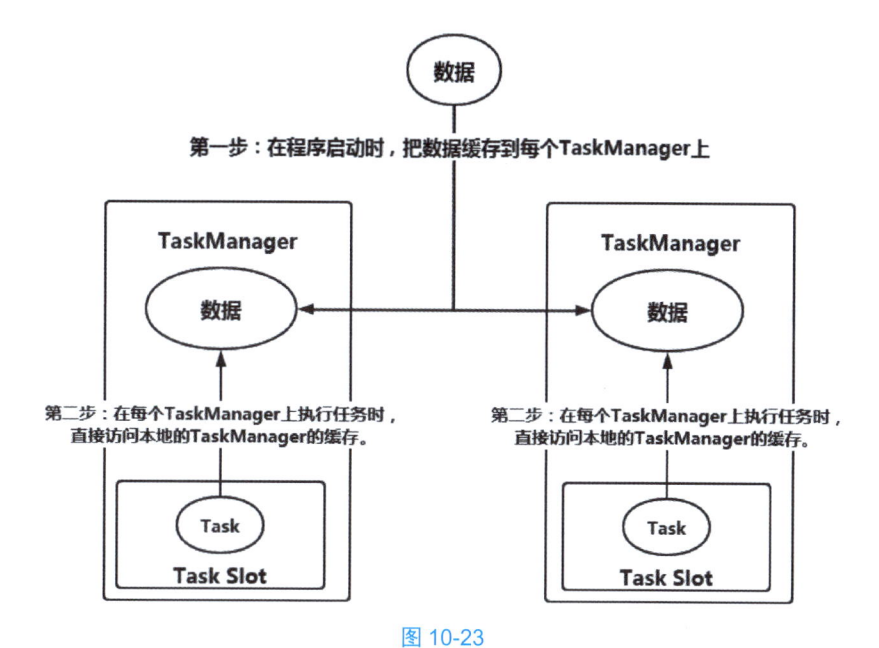

图 10-23

下面的代码在启动阶段将本地文件（D:\\data.txt）中的数据缓存到了每个 TaskManager 上，这样在执行任务时，直接读取本地缓存的数据即可。通过这样的方式可以提高程序执行的效率。

```java
import java.io.File;
import java.util.List;
import org.apache.commons.io.FileUtils;
import org.apache.flink.api.common.functions.RichMapFunction;
import org.apache.flink.api.java.DataSet;
import org.apache.flink.api.java.ExecutionEnvironment;
import org.apache.flink.configuration.Configuration;

public class DistributedCacheDemo {
    public static void main(String[] args) throws Exception {
        //创建一个方位接口的对象:DataSet API
        ExecutionEnvironment env = ExecutionEnvironment
                                        .getExecutionEnvironment();
        //注册需要缓存的数据
        env.registerCachedFile("d:\\data.txt", "localfile");
        //执行一个简单的计算
        DataSet<Integer> source = env
                                    .fromElements(1,2,3,4,5,6,7,8,9,10);
```

```
            //需要使用 RichMapFunction 的 open()方法在初始化时读取缓存的数据文件
            source.map(new RichMapFunction<Integer, String>() {
                private String shareData = "";
                @Override
                public void open(Configuration parameters)
                throws Exception {
                    //读取分布式缓存的数据
                    File file = getRuntimeContext().getDistributedCache()
                                        .getFile("localfile");
                    //读取文件的内容
                    List<String> lines = FileUtils.readLines(file);
                    //得到数据
                    shareData = lines.get(0);
                }
                @Override
                public String map(Integer value) throws Exception {
                    return shareData + "\t" + value;
                }}).print();
        }
    }
```

输出的结果如下。

```
I love Beijing    1
I love Beijing    2
I love Beijing    3
I love Beijing    4
I love Beijing    5
I love Beijing    6
I love Beijing    7
I love Beijing    8
I love Beijing    9
I love Beijing    10
```

10.5.4 累加器

累加器（Accumulator）类似于 MapReduce Counter，程序代码可以在 Flink 任务的算子中操作累加器的值，但是在任务执行结束之后才能获得累加器的最终结果。由于 Flink 是一个分布式计算引擎，所以使用累加器可以保证在全局范围内数据的一致性。而计数器（Counter）是累加器的一个实现方式，具体分为 IntCounter、LongCounter 和 DoubleCounter。

下面通过一个具体的示例来对比在 Flink 计算中不使用累加器和使用累加器的区别。

（1）不使用累加器，开发程序完成计数操作。代码如下所示。

```
01  import org.apache.flink.api.common.functions.RichMapFunction;
02  import org.apache.flink.api.java.DataSet;
03  import org.apache.flink.api.java.ExecutionEnvironment;
04
05  public class NoAccumulatorDemo {
06      public static void main(String[] args) throws Exception {
07          //访问接口 ExecutionEnvironment
08          ExecutionEnvironment env = ExecutionEnvironment
                                            .getExecutionEnvironment();
09
10          //数据源
11          DataSet<String> source = Env
                            .fromElements("Tom","Mary","Mike","Jone");
12
13          //统计集合中的个数
14          DataSet<Integer> result = source.map(
             new RichMapFunction<String, Integer>() {
15              private int total = 0;
16
17              @Override
18              public Integer map(String value) throws Exception {
19                  //计数
20                  total ++;
21                  return total;
22              }
23          }).setParallelism(1);
24          result.print();
25      }
26  }
```

（2）运行代码会统计 DataSet 集合中元素的个数，输出的结果如下。

```
1
2
3
4
```

> 这里的第 23 行代码设置了任务的并行度为 1，这时执行程序可以得到正确的结果。

（3）将任务的并行度设置为一个大于 1 的数字，例如设置为 3，这时统计的结果就不正确了。输出的结果如下。

```
1
2
1
1
```

> 结果不正确的根本原因是，设置了任务的并行度为 3，这等同于有 3 个任务的实例在同时计数，造成了数据的不一致。

（4）使用累加器解决数据不一致的问题，代码如下。

```
01  import org.apache.flink.api.common.JobExecutionResult;
02  import org.apache.flink.api.common.accumulators.IntCounter;
03  import org.apache.flink.api.common.functions.RichMapFunction;
04  import org.apache.flink.api.java.DataSet;
05  import org.apache.flink.api.java.ExecutionEnvironment;
06  import org.apache.flink.configuration.Configuration;
07
08  public class AccumulatorDemo {
09      public static void main(String[] args) throws Exception {
10          //访问接口 ExecutionEnvironment
11          ExecutionEnvironment env = ExecutionEnvironment
                                            .getExecutionEnvironment();
12
13          //数据源
14          DataSet<String> source = Env
                            .fromElements("Tom","Mary","Mike","Jone");
15
16          //统计集合中的个数
17          DataSet<Integer> result = source.map(
                            new RichMapFunction<String, Integer>() {
18              //定义一个累加器
19              private IntCounter intCount = new IntCounter();
20
21              @Override
22              public void open(Configuration parameters)
                    throws Exception {
23                  //将累加器注册到任务
24                  this.getRuntimeContext()
                        .addAccumulator("myaccumulator", intCount);
25              }
26
27              @Override
28              public Integer map(String value) throws Exception {
```

```
29                    //在具体任务中操作累加器
30                    this.intCount.add(1);
31                    return 0;
32                }
33          }).setParallelism(3);
34
35          result.writeAsText("d:\\result.txt");
36
37          //获取累加器的值
38          JobExecutionResult finalResult =  Env
                                        .execute("AccumulatorDemo");
39          int total = finalResult
                        .getAccumulatorResult("myaccumulator");
40          System.out.println("结果是:" + total );
41
42      }
43  }
```

> 这里的第 33 行代码设置了任务的并行度为 3，这时执行程序将得到正确的结果"结果是：4"。即使修改任务的并行度，程序的结果也不会发生变化。

第 4 篇
阿里云大数据增值服务
——数加平台

第 11 章
阿里云大数据集成开发平台 DataWorks

DataWorks 基于 MaxCompute、Hologres、EMR、AnalyticDB、CDP 等大数据引擎，为数据仓库、数据湖、湖仓一体等解决方案提供统一的全链路大数据集成开发平台。

11.1 DataWorks 基础

DataWorks 是阿里云重要的 PaaS（Platform as a Service）平台产品，为用户提供数据集成、数据开发、数据地图、数据质量和数据服务等全方位的产品服务，它具有一站式开发管理的界面，可以帮助企业专注于数据价值的挖掘和探索。

DataWorks 支持多种计算和存储引擎服务，包括离线计算 MaxCompute、开源大数据引擎 E-MapReduce、基于 Flink 的实时计算、机器学习 PAI、图计算服务 Graph Compute 和交互式分析服务等，并且支持用户自定义接入计算和存储服务。DataWorks 可以为用户提供全链路智能大数据及 AI 开发和治理服务。

用户可以使用 DataWorks 对数据进行传输、转换和集成等操作，从不同的数据存储引入数据，并进行转化和开发，最后将处理好的数据同步至其他数据系统。

11.1.1 DataWorks 功能架构

DataWorks 提供 9 个核心功能模块，整体功能架构如图 11-1 所示。

图 11-1

1. 数据集成

DataWorks 的数据集成功能模块是稳定高效、弹性伸缩的数据同步平台,致力于提供复杂网络环境下丰富的异构数据源之间高速稳定的数据移动及同步能力。DataWorks 数据集成支持离线同步、实时同步,以及离线和实时一体化的全增量同步。DataWorks 数据集成的主页面如图 11-2 所示。

图 11-2

2. 数据加工

DataWorks 的数据开发功能模块是数据加工的开发平台,运维中心功能模块是数据加工的管理平台。基于这两个功能模块，用户可以在 DataWorks 上规范、高效地构建和运维数据开发工作流。

> DataWorks 的数据开发平台可以使用工具 DataStudio。

DataStudio 数据开发工具提供的功能如下。

（1）DataStudio 支持 MaxCompute、EMR、CDH、Hologres、AnalyticDB、ClickHouse 等多种计算引擎，支持在统一的平台上进行各类引擎任务的开发、测试、发布和运维等操作。

（2）DataStudio 支持智能编辑器、可视化依赖编排，调度能力经过阿里集团内调度任务、复杂业务依赖的反复验证。

（3）DataStudio 提供隔离的开发和生产环境，结合版本管理、代码评审、冒烟测试、发布管控、操作审计等配套功能，帮助企业规范地完成数据开发。

DataStudio 数据开发工具的主页面如图 11-3 所示。

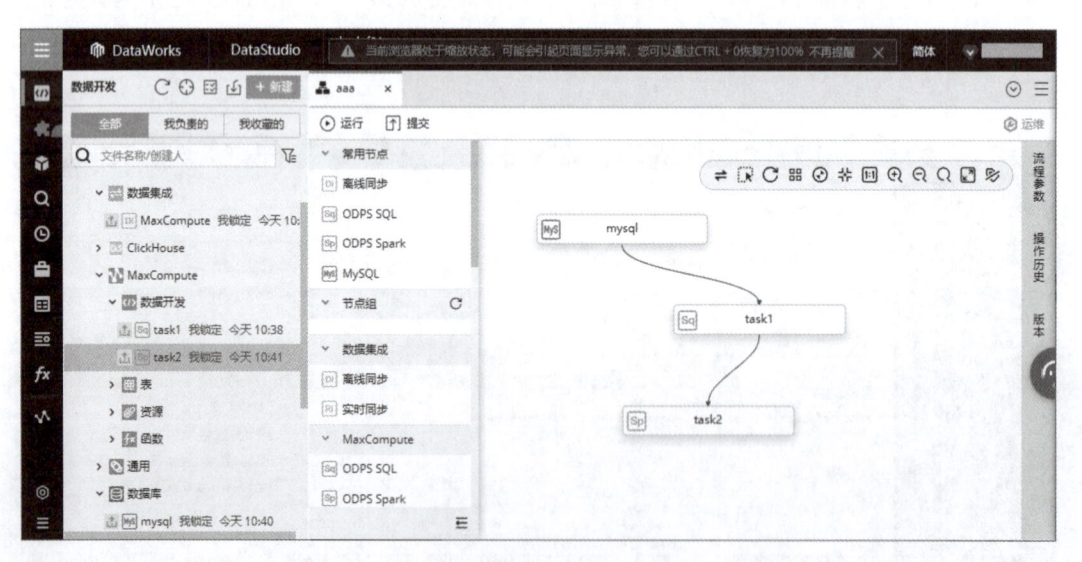

图 11-3

DataWorks 运维中心提供数据时效性保障、任务诊断、影响分析、自动运维、移动运维等功能。DataWorks 运维中心的主页面如图 11-4 所示。

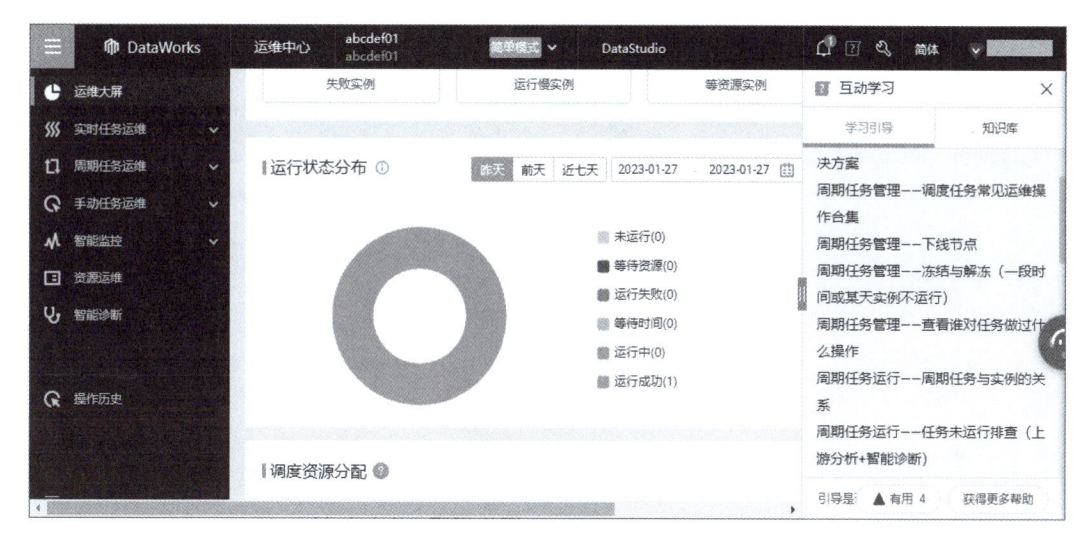

图 11-4

3. 数据建模

数据建模是阿里云 DataWorks 自主研发的智能数据建模产品，沉淀了阿里巴巴十多年来数仓建模方法论的最佳实践，包含数仓规划、数据标准、维度建模及数据指标四大模块，帮助企业在搭建数据中台和建设数据集市过程中提升建模及逆向建模的能力，并通过数据建模快速构建企业数据资产。

DataWorks 数据建模可以助力企业提高自身建模能力，挖掘企业的数据资产价值。它支持以下的场景。

1）海量数据的标准化管理

企业业务越庞大，数据结构就越复杂，企业数据量会随着企业业务的快速发展而迅速增长，如何有序地管理和存储数据是每个企业都将面临的一个挑战。

2）业务数据互联互通，打破信息壁垒

公司内部各业务、各部门之间数据独立自主，形成了数据孤岛，导致决策层无法清晰、快速地了解公司各类数据的情况。如何打破部门或业务领域之间的信息孤岛是企业数据管理的一大难题。

3）数据标准整合，统一灵活对接

同一数据具有不同的描述，企业数据管理难、内容重复、结果不准确。如何制定统一的数据标准又不打破原有的系统架构，实现灵活对接上下游业务，是标准化管理的核心之一。

4）数据价值最大化，企业利润最大化

在最大程度上用好企业各类数据，使企业数据价值最大化，为企业提供更高效的数据服务。

DataWorks 数据建模的主页面如图 11-5 所示。

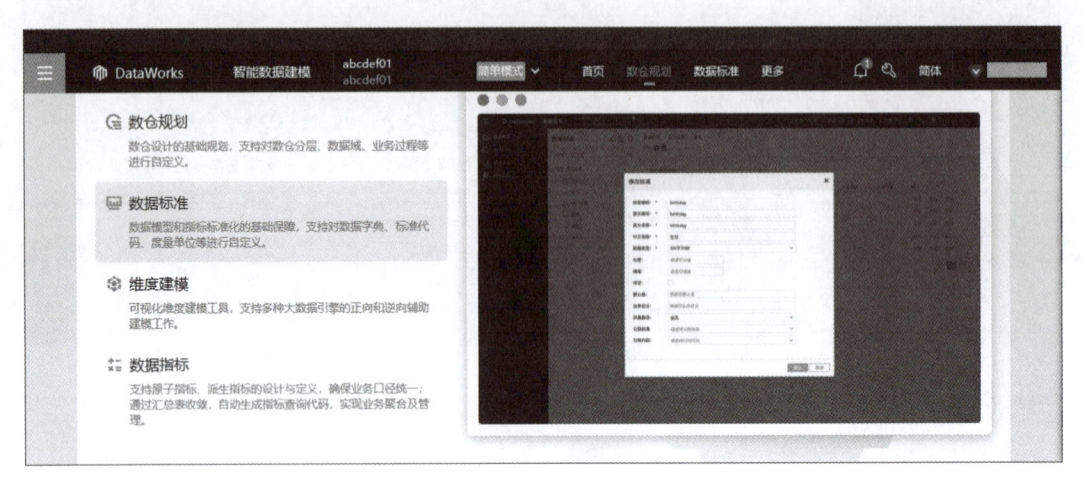

图 11-5

4. 数据分析

数据分析基于"人人都是数据分析师"的产品目标，旨在为更多非专业数据开发人员，如数据分析、产品、运营等工作人员，提供更加简洁高效的取数、用数工具，提高大家日常取数分析效率。数据分析支持基于个人视角的数据上传、公共数据集、表搜索与收藏、在线 SQL 取数、SQL 文件共享、SQL 查询结果下载及使用电子表格进行大屏幕数据查看等功能。

DataWorks 数据分析的主页面如图 11-6 所示。

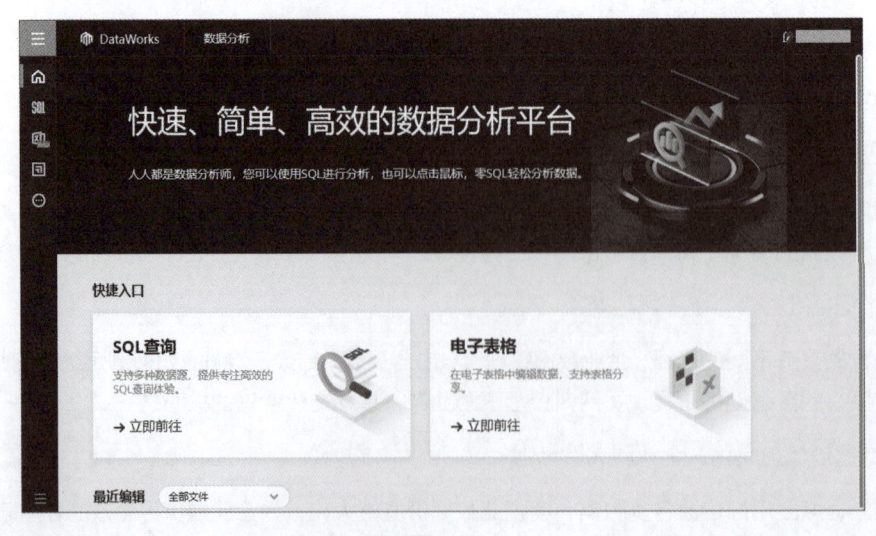

图 11-6

5. 数据质量

DataWorks 的全流程数据质量监控功能模块为用户提供多种预设表级别、字段级别和自定义的监控模板。数据质量可以帮助用户第一时间感知到源端数据的变更与 ETL（Extract Transformation Load）中产生的脏数据，自动拦截问题任务，有效阻止脏数据向下游蔓延。

数据质量以数据集（DataSet）为监控对象，支持监控 MaxCompute 数据表和 DataHub 实时数据流。当离线 MaxCompute 数据发生变化时，数据质量会对数据进行校验，并阻塞生产链路，以避免问题数据污染扩散。同时，数据质量提供历史校验结果的管理，以便用户对数据质量进行分析和定级。

DataWorks 数据质量的"任务查询"页面如图 11-7 所示。

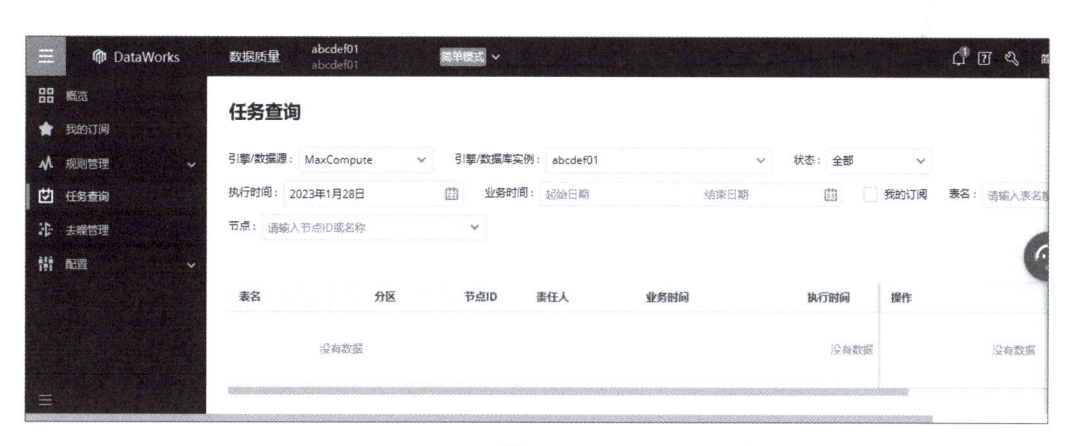

图 11-7

6. 数据地图

DataWorks 的数据地图功能模块可以实现对数据的统一管理和血缘的跟踪。数据地图以数据搜索为基础，提供表使用说明、数据类目、数据血缘、字段血缘等工具，帮助数据表的使用者和拥有者更好地管理数据、协作开发。DataWorks 数据地图的主页面如图 11-8 所示。

7. 数据服务

DataWorks 的数据服务功能模块是灵活轻量、安全稳定的数据 API 构建平台，旨在为企业提供全面的数据共享服务，帮助用户从发布审批、授权管控、调用计量、资源隔离等方面实现数据价值输出及共享开放。DataWorks 数据服务的主页面如图 11-9 所示。

8. 数据迁移

DataWorks 的数据迁移功能模块通过使用迁移助手，支持将开源调度引擎的作业迁移至 DataWorks，支持作业跨云、跨 Region、跨账号迁移，实现 DataWorks 作业快速克隆部署。同时 DataWorks 团队联合大数据专家服务团队，上线迁云服务，帮助用户快速实现数据与任务的上云。DataWorks 数据迁移的主页面如图 11-10 所示。

图 11-8

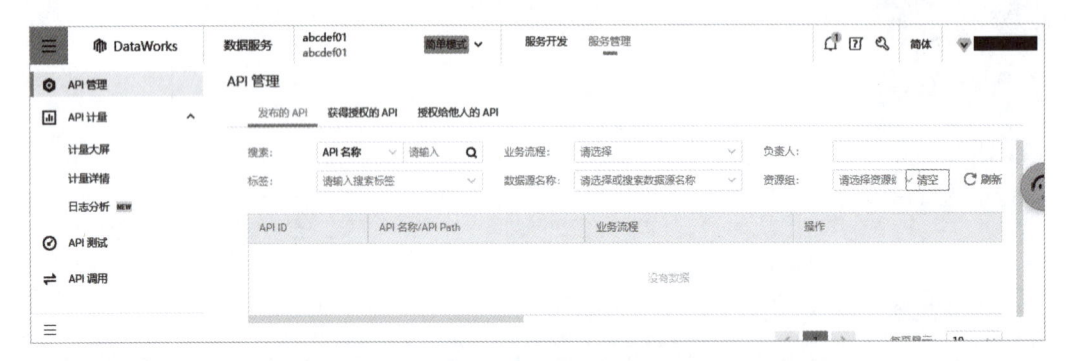

图 11-9

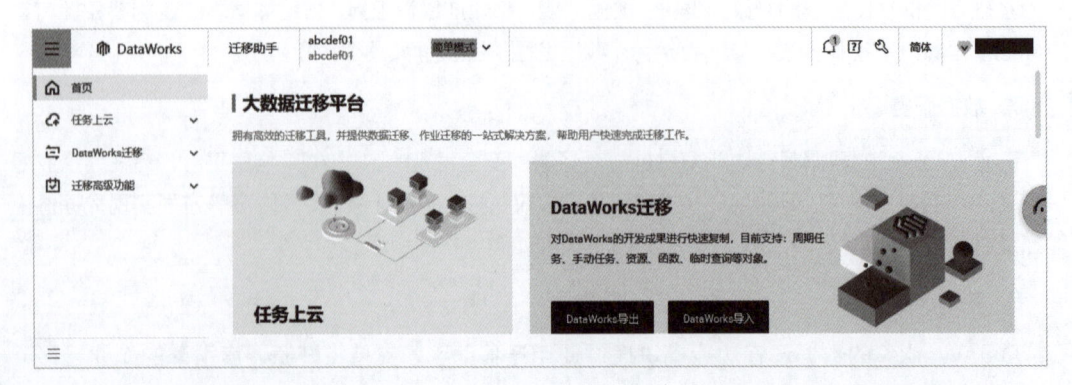

图 11-10

9. 开放平台

DataWorks 开放平台是 DataWorks 对外提供数据和服务的开放通道。DataWorks 开放平台提供开放 API（OpenAPI）、开放事件（OpenEvent）、扩展程序（Extensions）服务，可以帮助用户快速实现各类应用系统与 DataWorks 的对接，方便快捷地进行数据流程管控、数据治理和运维，及时响应应用系统对接 DataWorks 的业务状态变化。DataWorks 开放平台的"开发者后台"页面如图 11-11 所示。

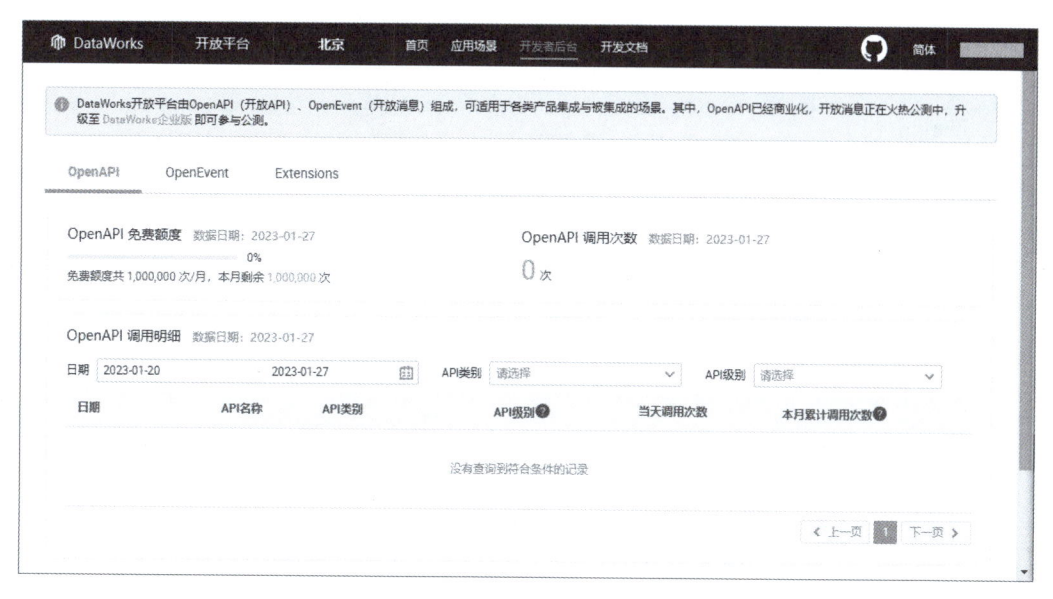

图 11-11

11.1.2　DataWorks 的基本概念

DataWorks 中的基本概念主要包括工作空间、业务流程、解决方案、组件、任务、实例、提交、脚本开发、资源和函数、输出名称、元数据、补数据等，如表 11-1 所示。

表 11-1

基本概念	说　　明
工作空间	工作空间是 DataWorks 管理任务、成员，分配角色和权限的基本单元。工作空间管理员可以将成员加入工作空间，并赋予成员工作空间管理员、开发、运维、部署、安全管理员或访客角色，以实现多角色协同工作。一个工作空间支持绑定 MaxCompute 和实时计算等多种类型的计算引擎实例。绑定引擎实例后，即可在工作空间开发和调度引擎任务
业务流程	针对业务实体，抽象出业务流程的概念，帮助用户从业务视角组织代码的开发，提高任务管理效率
解决方案	用户可以将部分业务流程自定义组合为一个解决方案。一个解决方案可以包括多个业务流程，且解决方案之间可以复用相同的业务流程

续表

基本概念	说明
组件	用户可以将 SQL 中的通用逻辑抽象为组件，以提高代码的复用性。SQL 代码的处理过程通常是引入一个或多个源数据表，通过过滤、连接和聚合等操作，加工出新业务需要的目标表。组件是带有多个输入参数和输出参数的 SQL 代码过程模板
任务（Task）	任务是对数据执行的操作的定义。每个任务使用 0 或 0 个以上的数据表（数据集）作为输入，生成一个或多个数据表（数据集）作为输出。任务主要分为节点任务（Node Task）、工作流任务（Flow Task）和内部节点（Inner Node）
实例（Instance）	实例是某个任务在某时某刻执行的一个快照。调度系统中的任务，经过调度系统、手动触发运行后，会生成一个实例。实例中会有任务的运行时间、运行状态和运行日志等信息。 例如，设置每天 2:00 运行 Task1 实例，调度系统会在每天 23:30 根据周期节点定义好的时间，自动生成一个快照，即 Task1 第二天 2:00 运行的实例。在第二天 2:00 时，如果判断上游实例已经完成，Task1 实例就会如期启动运行
提交（Submit）	提交是指开发的节点任务、业务流程，从 DataWorks 开发环境发布至调度系统的过程。完成提交后，相应的代码、调度配置全部合并至调度系统中，调度系统根据相关配置进行调度操作
脚本开发（Script）	脚本开发是为数据分析提供的一个代码存储空间。脚本开发的代码无法发布到调度系统，无法进行调度参数配置，仅可以进行部分数据的查询、分析工作
资源和函数	资源、函数都是 MaxCompute 的概念。用户可以在 DataWorks 中，通过界面管理资源和函数。如果通过 MaxCompute 的其他方式管理资源和函数，则无法在 DataWorks 中进行相关的查询
输出名称	输出名称是每个任务输出点的名称，它是用户在设置任务依赖关系时，用于连接上下游两个任务的虚拟实体。当用户在设置某任务与其他任务形成上下游依赖关系时，必须根据输出名称（而不是节点名称或节点 ID）来完成设置。设置完成后，该任务的输出名称也作为其下游节点的输入名称
元数据	元数据是数据的描述数据，可以说明数据的属性（名称、大小、数据类型等），或结构（字段、类型、长度等），或其相关数据（位于何处、拥有者、产出任务、访问权限等）。在 DataWorks 中，元数据主要指与库、表相关的信息，元数据管理对应的主要功能模块是数据地图
补数据	完成周期任务的开发，将任务提交发布之后，任务会按照调度配置定时运行。如果用户希望对历史时间段内的数据进行计算，可以使用补数据功能。补数据操作生成的补数据实例将按照指定的业务日期运行

节点任务、工作流任务、内部节点的区别如表 11-2 所示。

表 11-2

任务类型	任务描述
节点任务	一个数据执行的操作，可以与其他节点任务、工作流任务配置依赖关系，组成 DAG
工作流任务	满足一个业务场景需求的一组内部节点，组成一个工作流任务，建议工作流任务小于 10 个。工作流任务的内部节点无法被其他工作流任务、节点任务依赖。工作流任务可以与其他工作流任务、节点任务配置依赖关系，组成 DAG
内部节点	工作流任务内部的节点，与节点任务的功能基本一致。用户可以通过拖曳形成依赖关系，其调度周期会继承工作流任务的调度周期，无法进行单独配置

11.1.3 DataWorks 中的角色

DataWorks 中包含 7 种不同的角色,而每种角色具有不同的职责,如表 11-3 所示。

表 11-3

角色	职责
项目所有者	项目所有者拥有工作空间的所有权限,可以新建计算引擎、新建项目空间、新建调度资源、添加组织成员、为组织成员赋予项目管理员角色、配置数据类目等,即阿里云主账号的角色,此角色不能赋予其他账号
项目管理员	除拥有开发角色和运维角色的全部权限外,还可以进行添加/移出工作空间成员并授予角色、创建自定义资源组等操作。可以对该项目空间的基本属性、数据源、当前项目空间计算引擎配置和项目成员等进行管理,并为项目成员赋予项目管理员、开发、运维、部署、访客角色
开发	负责数据开发页面的设计和维护工作。能够创建工作流、脚本文件、资源和 UDF,新建、删除表,同时可以创建发布包,但不能执行发布操作
运维	负责在运维中心页面管理全部任务的运行情况并进行相应处理。由项目管理员分配运维权限,拥有发布及线上运维的操作权限,没有数据开发的操作权限
部署	仅在多工作空间模式时审核任务代码并决定是否提交运维。与运维角色相似,但是没有线上运维的操作权限
访客	仅有只读权限,可以查看数据开发页面的业务流程设计和代码。没有权限编辑工作流和代码
安全管理员	仅有数据保护伞模块的操作权限,无其他模块权限。用于敏感规则配置、数据风险审计等

11.2 DataWorks 中的数据集成

数据集成是稳定高效、弹性伸缩的数据同步平台,致力于提供复杂网络环境下丰富的异构数据源之间高速稳定的数据移动及同步能力。

使用 DataWorks 的数据集成时需要注意下面的问题。

(1)支持且仅支持结构化(如 RDS、DRDS 等)、半结构化、无结构化(如 OSS、TXT 等,要求具体同步数据必须抽象为结构化数据)的数据的同步。即数据集成仅支持将能够抽象为逻辑二维表的数据同步至 MaxCompute,不支持将 OSS 中存放的完全非结构化数据(如一段 MP3)同步至 MaxCompute。

(2)支持单地域内及部分跨地域的数据存储相互同步、交换的需求。部分地域之间可以通过经典网络传输,但不能保证其连通性。如果经典网络不通,建议使用公网方式进行连接。

(3)数据集成仅完成数据同步(传输),本身不提供数据流的消费方式。

DataWorks 数据集成的入口如图 11-12 所示。

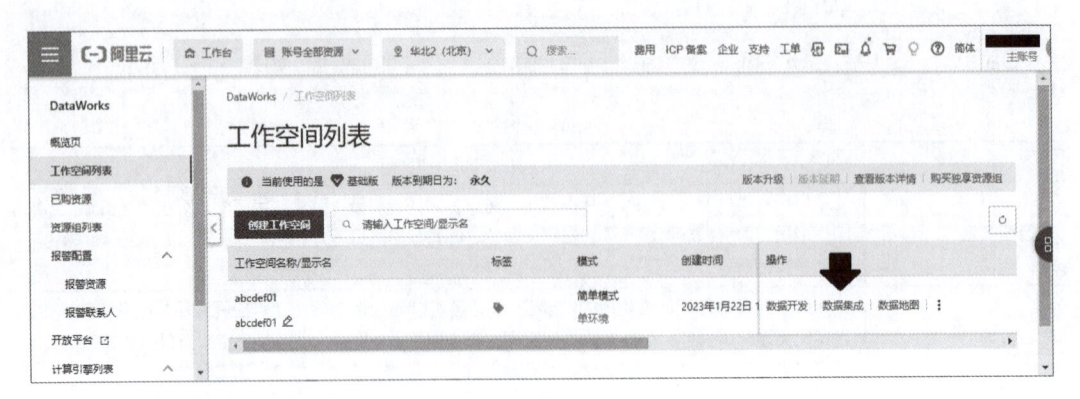

图 11-12

11.2.1 离线数据集成

离线数据集成，也叫作离线数据同步或批量数据同步。它通过定义数据来源和去向的数据源与数据集，提供一套抽象化的数据抽取插件（Reader）、数据写入插件（Writer），并基于此框架设计一套简化版的中间数据传输格式，从而实现任意结构化、半结构化数据源之间的数据传输。

离线数据集成的架构如图 11-13 所示。

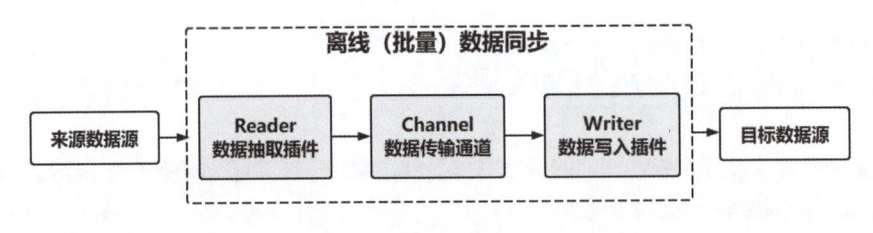

图 11-13

> 在 DataWorks 中已经集成了 DataX，用于完成离线数据集成。

DataX 是一个异构数据源离线同步工具，致力于实现包括关系型数据库（MySQL、Oracle 等）、HDFS、Hive、ODPS、HBase、FTP 等各种异构数据源之间稳定高效的数据同步功能。

为了解决异构数据源同步问题，DataX 将复杂的网状的同步链路变成了星形数据链路，DataX 作为中间传输载体，负责连接各种数据源。当需要接入一个新的数据源时，只需要将此数据源对接到 DataX，就能跟已有的数据源做到无缝数据同步。DataX 的星形数据链路如图 11-14 所示。

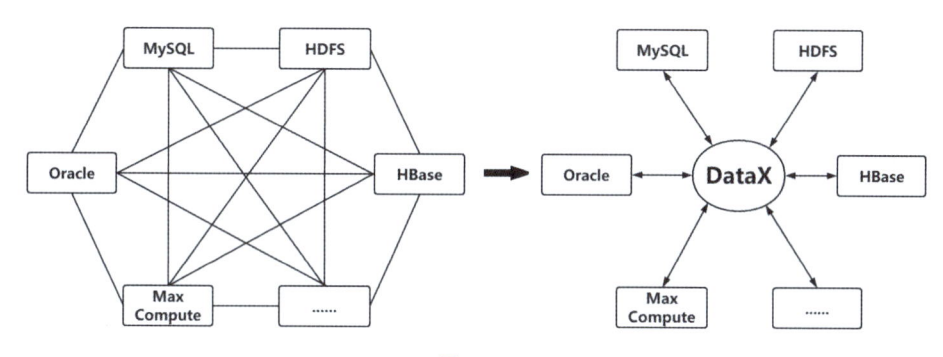

图 11-14

DataX 本身作为离线数据同步框架，采用 Framework + Plugin 架构构建。将数据源读取和写入抽象为 Reader 和 Writer 插件，纳入整个同步框架中。DataX 的体系架构如图 11-15 所示。

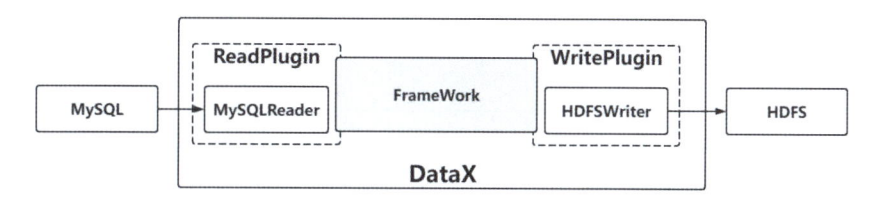

图 11-15

在 DataX 的体系架构中，各模块的说明如下。

（1）Reader：数据读取模块，负责采集数据源的数据，将数据发送给 Framework。

（2）Writer：数据写入模块，负责不断从 Framework 中获取数据，并将数据写入目的端。

（3）Framework：用于连接 Reader 和 Writer，作为两者的数据传输通道，并处理缓冲、流控、并发、数据转换等核心技术问题。

11.2.2 实时数据集成

实时数据集成支持用户将多种输入及输出数据源搭配组成同步链路，进行单表或整库数据的实时增量同步。用户可以根据数据源的支持情况，配置实时同步任务。数据集成的实时同步包括实时读取、转换和写入 3 种基础插件，插件之间通过内部定义的中间数据格式进行交互。一个实时数据集成任务支持多个转换插件进行数据清洗，并支持多个写入插件实现多路输出功能。同时，针对某些场景，支持整库实时同步解决方案，用户可以一次性实时同步多个表。

实时数据集成根据集成的数据类型，可以通过很多种方式实现。例如，可以通过使用 Flink CDC 的方式完成对数据库的实时数据集成。基于 Flink CDC 的实时数据集成如图 11-16 所示。

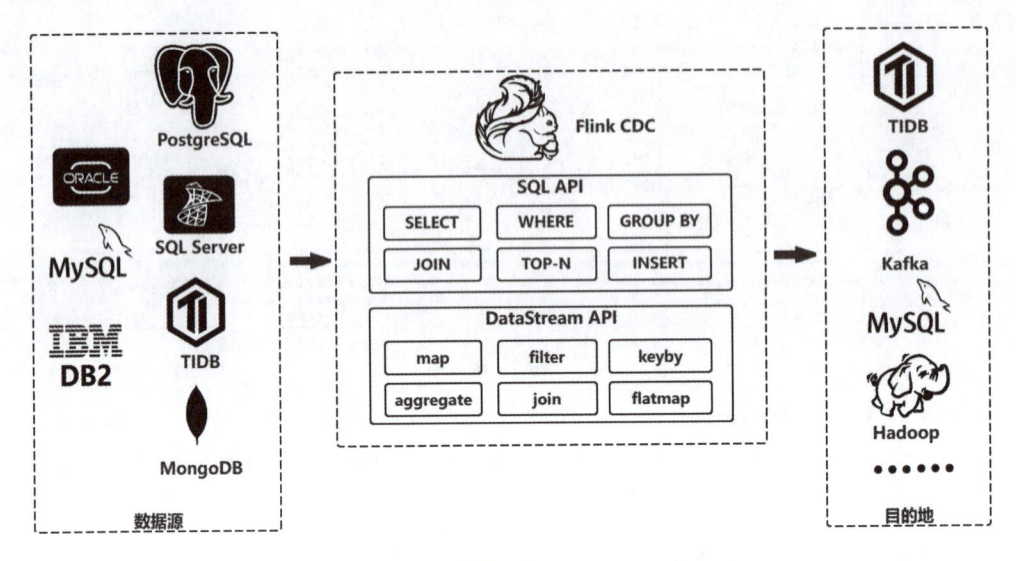

图 11-16

> CDC（Change Data Capture，变更数据捕获）的核心思想是监测并捕获数据库的变动（包括数据或数据表的插入、更新及删除等），并将这些变动按发生的顺序完整记录下来，写入消息中间件中，以供其他服务订阅及消费。因此，CDC 主要用于数据库的实时数据集成的场景。

11.2.3 数据同步和数据同步作业

在使用数据集成完成数据同步前，还需要区分数据同步和数据同步作业这两个基本的概念。

1. 数据同步

数据同步是指为保证两端数据一致性而进行的数据传输过程。一般来讲，数据集成的数据同步是为了保证源端、目的端数据逻辑的一致性，将数据从源端移动到目的端，并伴随一定的数据转换或清洗的过程。在数据集成的功能边界中，数据同步被定义为云上各种存储产品之间的数据转移过程。

数据同步类型可以分为离线数据同步和流式数据同步。数据同步的三要素是：数据源、数据转换过程、数据目的端。

2. 数据同步作业

数据同步作业是数据集成进行数据批量同步的基本业务单位，数据集成的数据同步作业面向表级数据同步，它描述了一个数据同步作业完成一次数据同步所需要的信息，包括 E（Extract）、

T（Transform）、L（Loading）这 3 个阶段的信息，也包含作业的运行信息。下面详细介绍这 3 个阶段。

1）数据抽取（Extract）

数据抽取是指从数据源获取所需数据的过程。在数据抽取过程中会过滤目标数据集中不需要的源数据字段或数据记录。数据抽取可以采用 Pull 和 Push 两种方式：Push 就是由源系统按照双方定义的数据格式，主动将符合要求的数据抽取出来，形成接口数据表或数据视图供 ETL 系统使用；而 Pull 则是由 ETL 系统直接访问数据源来获取数据。

2）数据转换（Transform）

数据转换按照目标表的数据结构，对一个或多个源数据的字段进行翻译、匹配、聚合等操作，得到目标数据的字段。数据转换主要包括格式转换、字段合并与拆分、数据翻译、数据匹配、数据聚合和其他的一些复杂计算。

3）数据装载（Loading）

把源数据转换为目标数据后，就可以直接通过数据加载工具加载到目标数据库中。数据加载工作一般分为以下 3 步。

（1）Re-Load：删除源数据索引。

（2）Load ：将源数据加载到目标数据库的表中。

（3）Post-Load：在目标数据库中重新生成索引。

11.3 【实战】DataWorks 项目开发案例

在掌握了 DataWorks 的相关知识后，下面通过一个数据开发案例来演示 DataWorks 提供的强大功能。

11.3.1 准备项目开发环境

在使用 DataWorks 之前需要开通 DataWorks 服务，并创建工作空间。DataWorks 提供了组合购买 DataWorks 和计算引擎、单独购买 DataWorks 两种方式，用户可根据需要选择任意方式开通 DataWorks 服务。下面是具体的操作步骤。

> 由于开通 DataWorks 服务比较简单，所以这里将直接从创建 DataWorks 的工作空间开始进行演示。

（1）在 DataWorks 的"工作空间列表"页面中，单击"创建工作空间"按钮，如图 11-17 所示。

图 11-17

（2）在"创建工作空间"对话框中输入工作空间名称，其他选项保持为默认值，单击"提交"按钮，如图 11-18 所示。

图 11-18

（3）工作空间创建成功后，需要绑定到特定队列大数据执行引擎上，才能执行相应的任务。这里选择 MaxCompute，单击"立即绑定"按钮，如图 11-19 所示。

（4）在"绑定 MaxCompute"页面中输入相关信息后，单击"完成绑定"按钮，如图 11-20 所示。

图 11-19

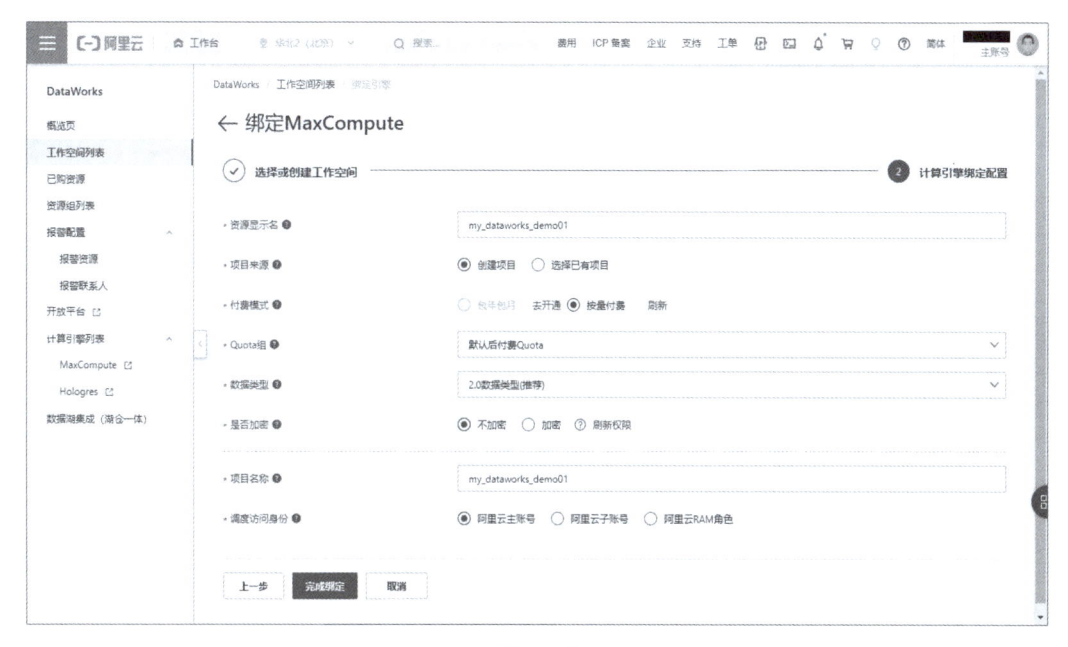

图 11-20

（5）绑定成功后，返回"工作空间列表"页面，就可以看到新创建的工作空间，如图 11-21 所示。

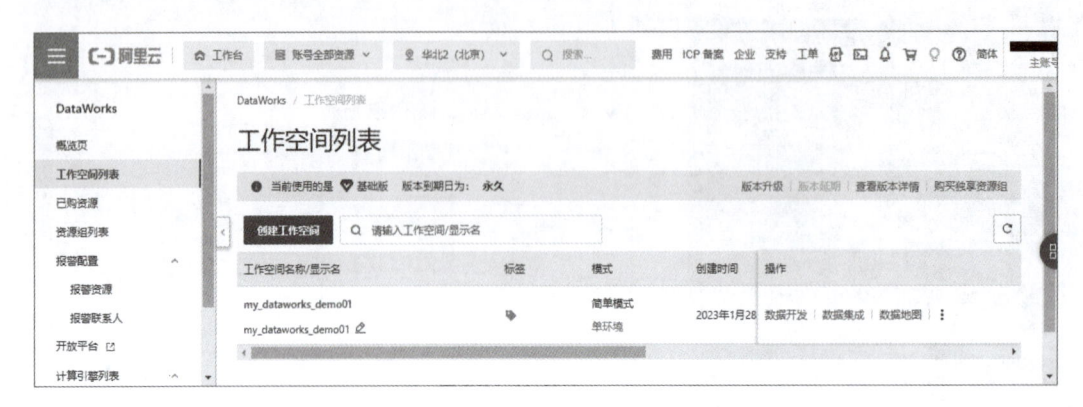

图 11-21

（6）打开 MaxCompute 管理控制台，就可以看到与 DataWorks 工作空间绑定的项目，如图 11-22 所示。

图 11-22

11.3.2 准备测试数据

在 DataWorks 工作空间创建成功后，就可以准备项目中需要使用的数据了。这里将创建两张 MaxCompute 表，分别作为任务的输入表和输出表。

（1）进入 DataWorks 的"工作空间列表"页面，单击"数据开发"文字链接，如图 11-23 所示。

第 11 章　阿里云大数据集成开发平台 DataWorks | 379

图 11-23

（2）进入"数据开发"页面后，单击"新建"按钮，在弹出的下拉列表中选择"新建业务流程"选项，如图 11-24 所示。

图 11-24

（3）在"新建业务流程"对话框中输入业务名称，单击"新建"按钮，如图 11-25 所示。

图 11-25

（4）右击"表"，在弹出的快捷菜单中选择"新建表"命令，新建一张表作为任务的输入数据，如图 11-26 所示。

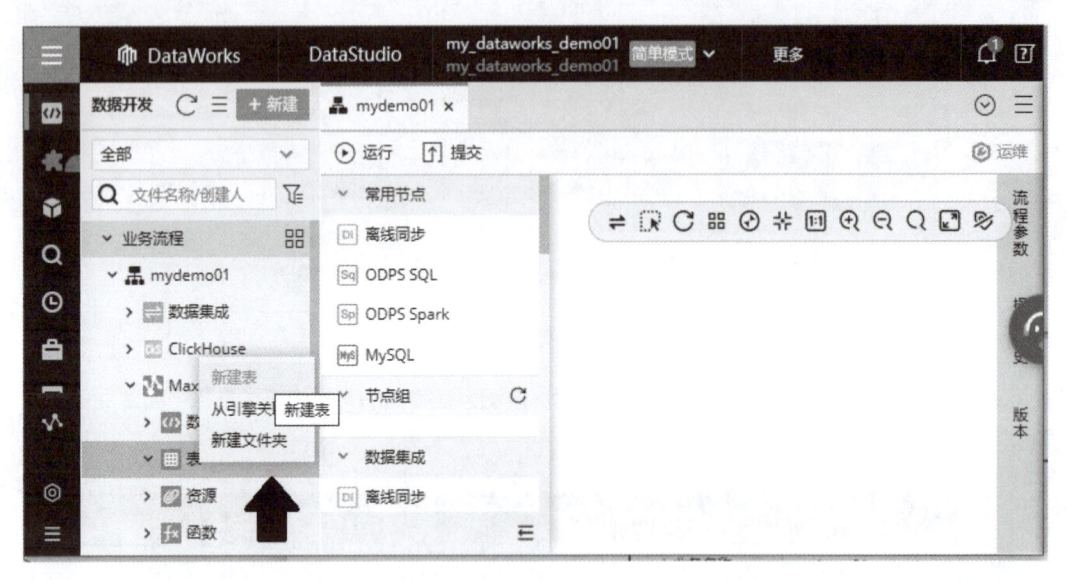

图 11-26

（5）在"新建表"对话框中输入名称，如 bank_data，单击"新建"按钮，如图 11-27 所示。

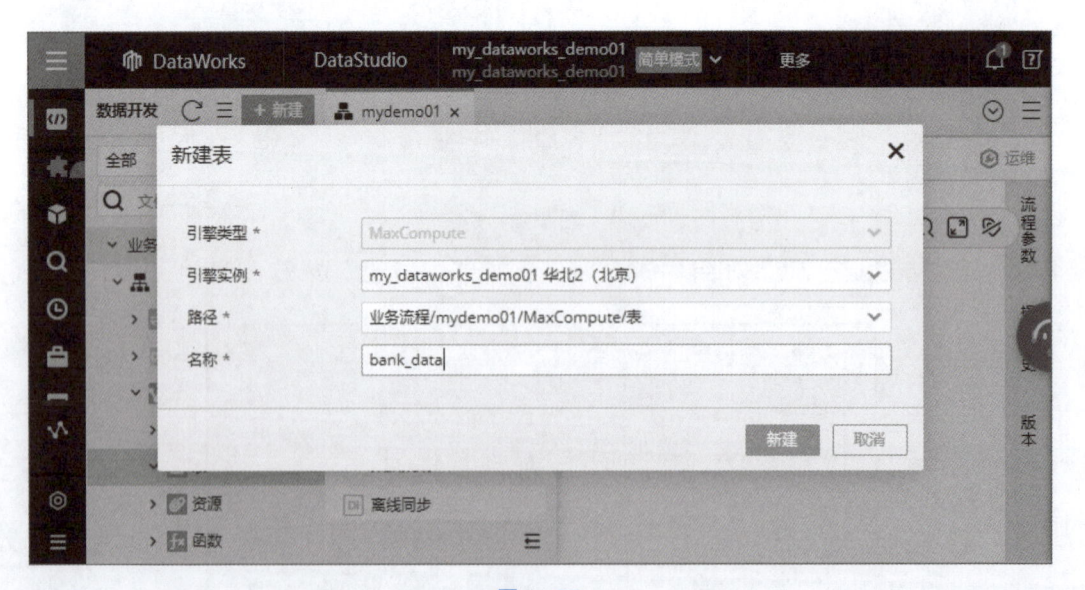

图 11-27

（6）在表 bank_data 的配置页面中，单击"DDL"按钮，如图 11-28 所示。

图 11-28

（7）在"DDL"对话框中输入下面的语句创建 bank_data 表结构，并单击"生成表结构"按钮。

```
CREATE TABLE IF NOT EXISTS bank_data
(
    age              BIGINT COMMENT '年龄',
    job              STRING COMMENT '工作类型',
    marital          STRING COMMENT '婚否',
    education        STRING COMMENT '教育程度',
    default          STRING COMMENT '是否有信用卡',
    housing          STRING COMMENT '房贷',
    loan             STRING COMMENT '贷款',
    contact          STRING COMMENT '联系途径',
    month            STRING COMMENT '月份',
    day_of_week      STRING COMMENT '星期几',
    duration         STRING COMMENT '持续时间',
    campaign         BIGINT COMMENT '本次活动联系的次数',
    pdays            DOUBLE COMMENT '与上一次联系的时间间隔',
    previous         DOUBLE COMMENT '之前与客户联系的次数',
    poutcome         STRING COMMENT '之前市场活动的结果',
    emp_var_rate     DOUBLE COMMENT '就业变化速率',
    cons_price_idx   DOUBLE COMMENT '消费者物价指数',
    cons_conf_idx    DOUBLE COMMENT '消费者信心指数',
    euribor3m        DOUBLE COMMENT '欧元存款利率',
    nr_employed      DOUBLE COMMENT '职工人数',
    y                BIGINT COMMENT '是否有定期存款'
);
```

(8)单击"提交到生成环境"按钮确认表的创建,如图 11-29 所示。

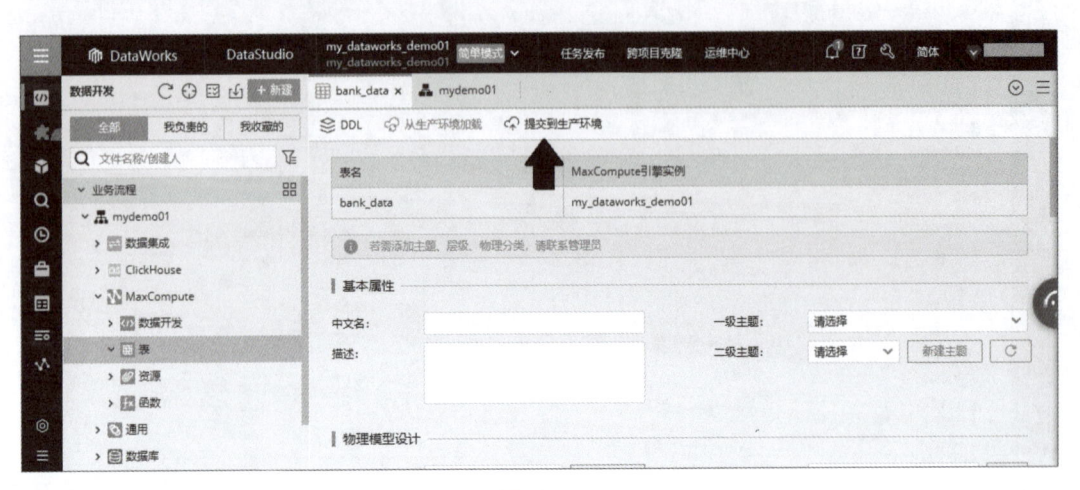

图 11-29

(9)按照同样的方式创建任务输出表 result_table,其 DDL 语句如下。

```
CREATE TABLE IF NOT EXISTS result_table
(
    education   STRING COMMENT '教育程度',
    num         BIGINT COMMENT '人数'
);
```

(10)单击左上角的"导入数据"按钮,将测试数据导入 bank_data 表中,如图 11-30 所示。

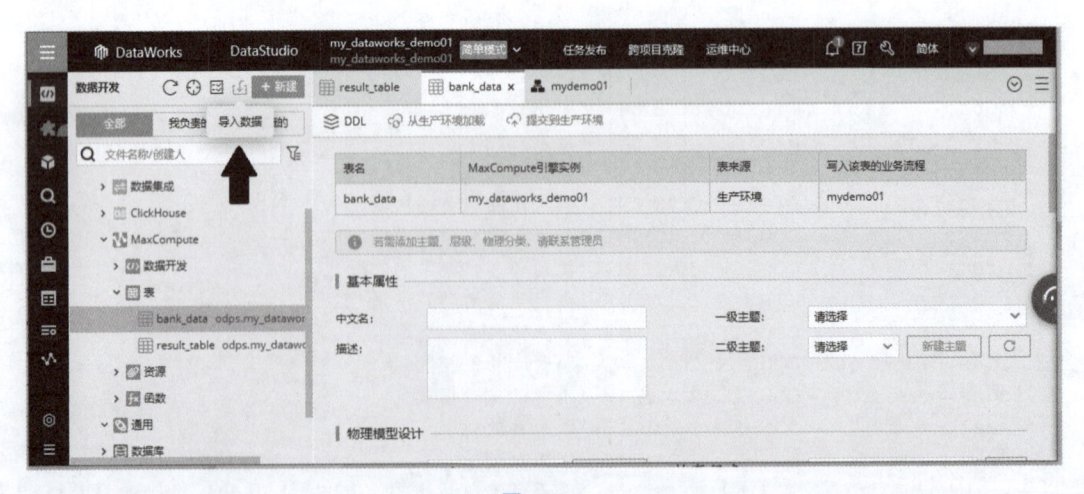

图 11-30

（11）弹出"将本地数据导入开发表"对话框，选择"bank_data"选项，并单击"下一步"按钮，如图 11-31 所示。

图 11-31

（12）导入数据文件 banking.txt，单击"下一步"按钮，如图 11-32 所示。

图 11-32

（13）在"选择目标表字段与源字段的匹配方式"选区中选中"按名称匹配"单选按钮，单击"导入数据"按钮，如图 11-33 所示。

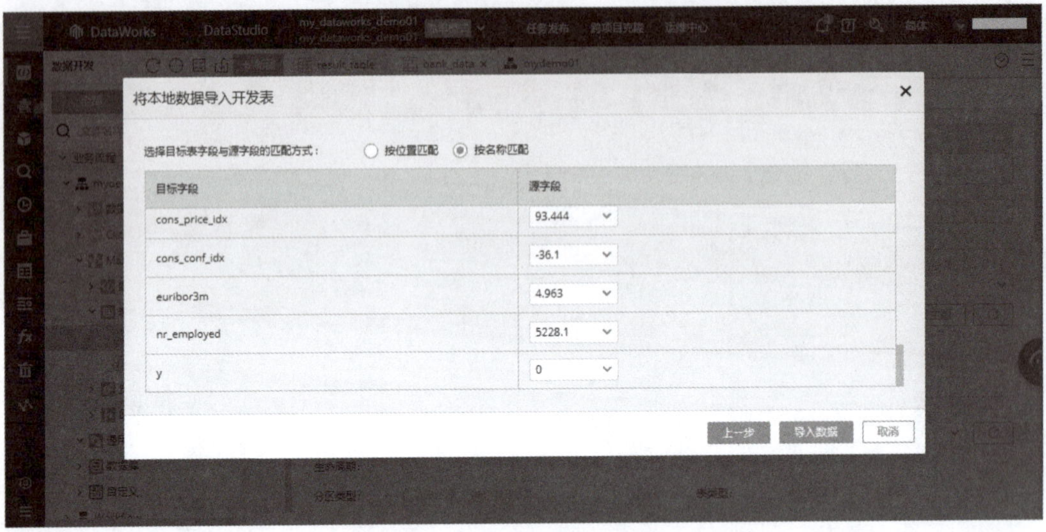

图 11-33

（14）在数据导入成功后，可以通过 MaxCompute 命令行工具进行确认。

```
my_dataworks_demo01>show tables;
ALIYUN$collenzhao:bank_data
ALIYUN$collenzhao:result_table
OK
my_dataworks_demo01>select count(*) from bank_data;
+------------+
| _c0        |
+------------+
| 41187      |
+------------+
```

11.3.3 开发业务流程

用户可以利用 DataWorks 完成数据开发的工作：通过在业务流程中创建任务节点并配置依赖关系来完成业务流程，并可以对工作空间的数据进行深入分析和计算。DataStudio 通过可视化拖曳来完成节点间的依赖设置，从而实现数据的处理。

下面通过执行一个简单的 SQL 任务来说明业务流程的开发过程。

（1）在业务流程开发面板上，将"虚拟节点"拖曳到开发面板上，如图 11-34 所示。

第 11 章　阿里云大数据集成开发平台 DataWorks | 385

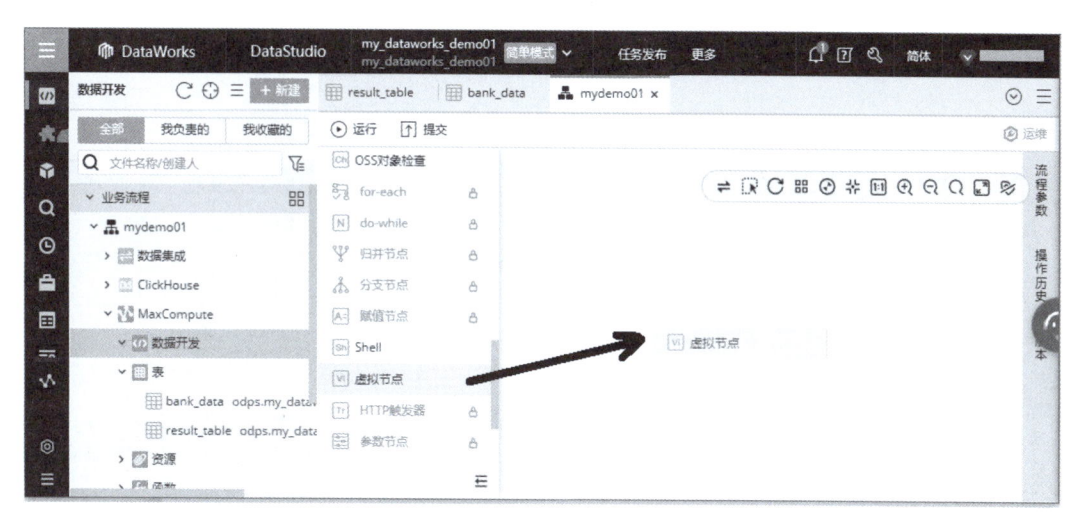

图 11-34

> 虚拟节点属于控制类型的节点。在业务流程运行过程中，它不会对数据产生任何影响，仅用于实现对下游节点的运维控制。业务流程中，虚拟节点的上游节点通常会被设置为工作空间根节点。

（2）在"新建节点"对话框中输入虚拟节点的名称，如 start，单击"确认"按钮，如图 11-35 所示。

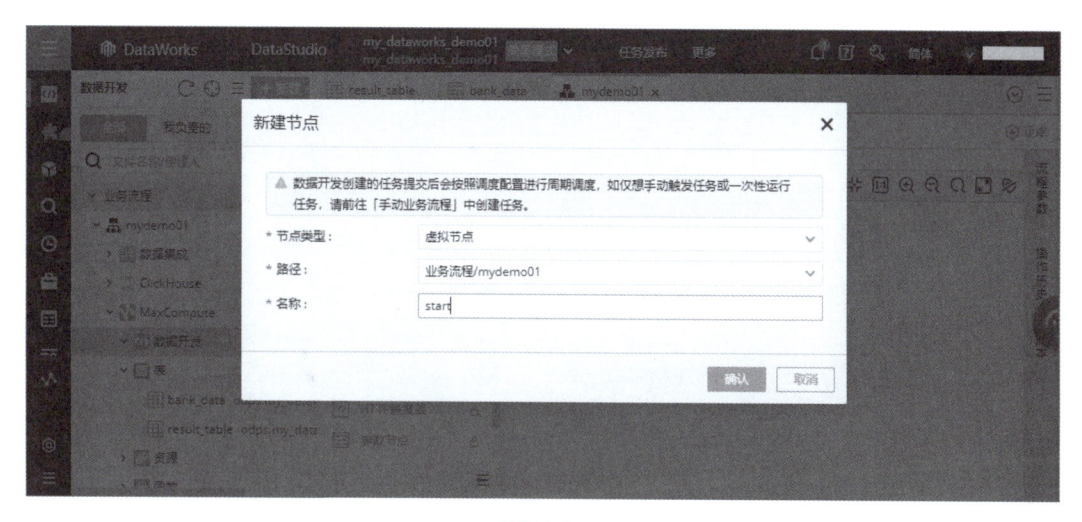

图 11-35

（3）双击虚拟节点的名称进入节点的编辑页面。选择节点编辑页面右侧的"调度配置"选项。

（4）将"时间属性"选区中的"重跑属性"设置为"运行成功或失败后皆可重跑"，如图 11-36 所示。

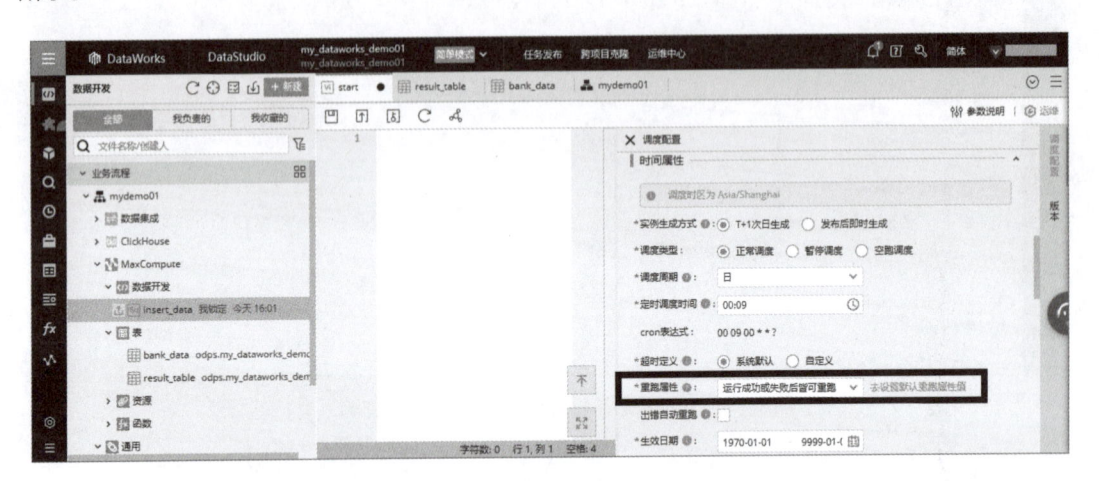

图 11-36

（5）在"调度依赖"选区，单击"使用工作空间根节点"文字链接将虚拟节点的上游节点设置为工作空间根节点，如图 11-37 所示。

图 11-37

（6）单机工具栏中的"保存"按钮保存虚拟节点的设置。

（7）按照同样的方法新建 ODPS SQL 节点，并命名为 insert_data，如图 11-38 所示。

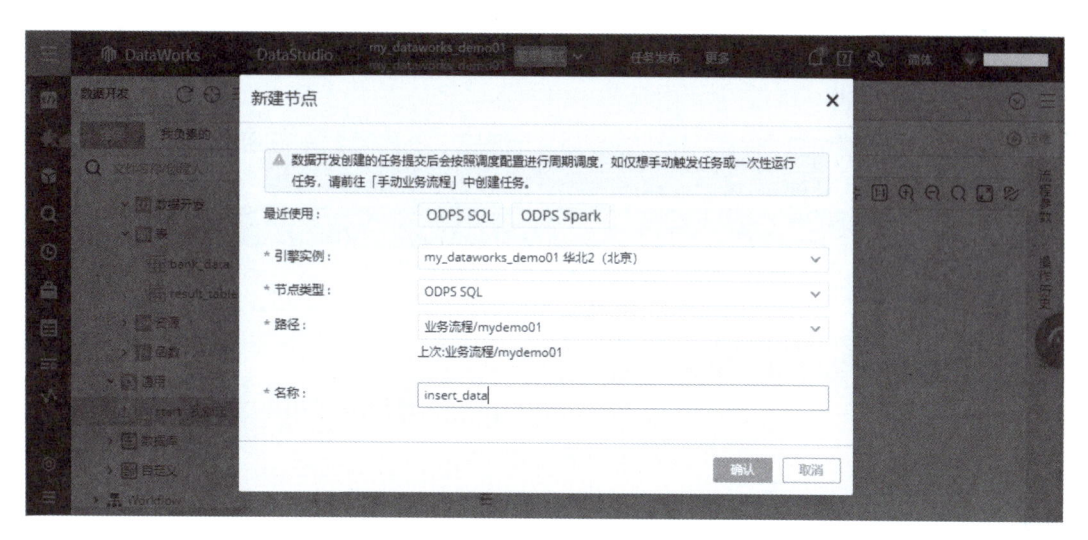

图 11-38

（8）拖曳连线，将 start 节点设置为 insert_data 节点的上游节点，如图 11-39 所示。

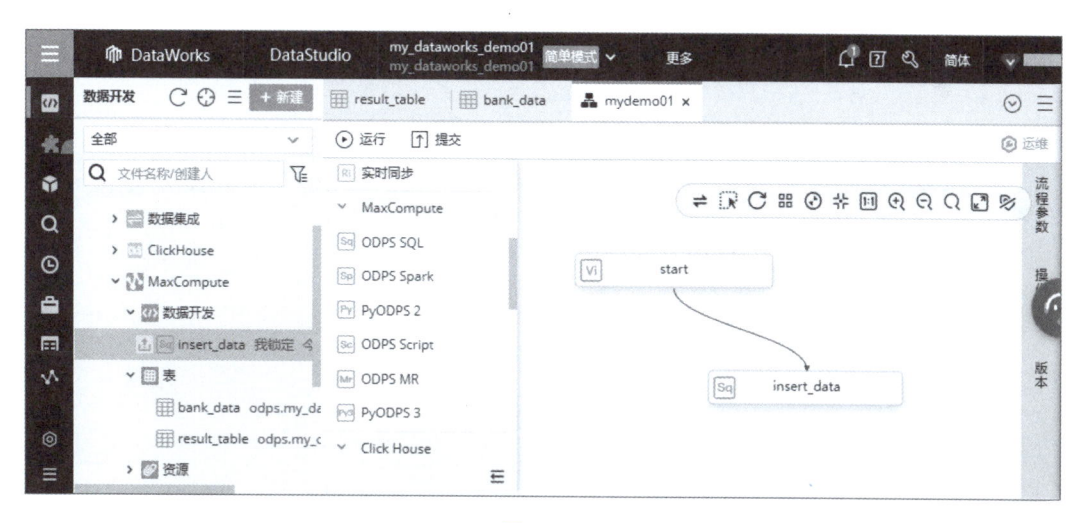

图 11-39

（9）在开发面板上双击 insert_data 节点，进入节点的编辑页面，输入下面的 SQL 代码。

```
--将数据插入到 result_table 中
insert overwrite table result_table
```

```
select education,count(marital) as num
from bank_data
where housing = 'yes' and marital = 'single'
group by education
```

（10）单击工具栏中的"保存"按钮防止 SQL 代码丢失，如图 11-40 所示。

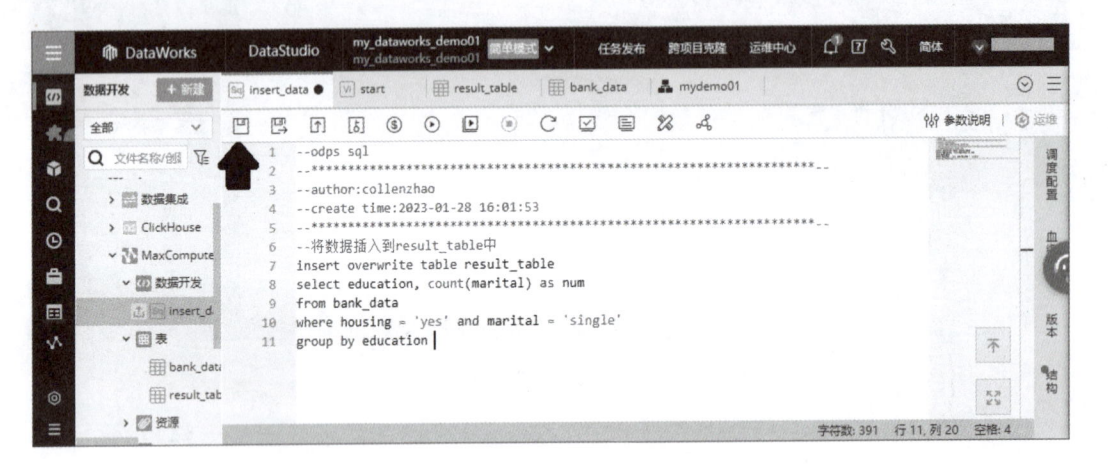

图 11-40

（11）单击"运行"按钮测试 ODPS_SQL 节点的任务，如图 11-41 所示。

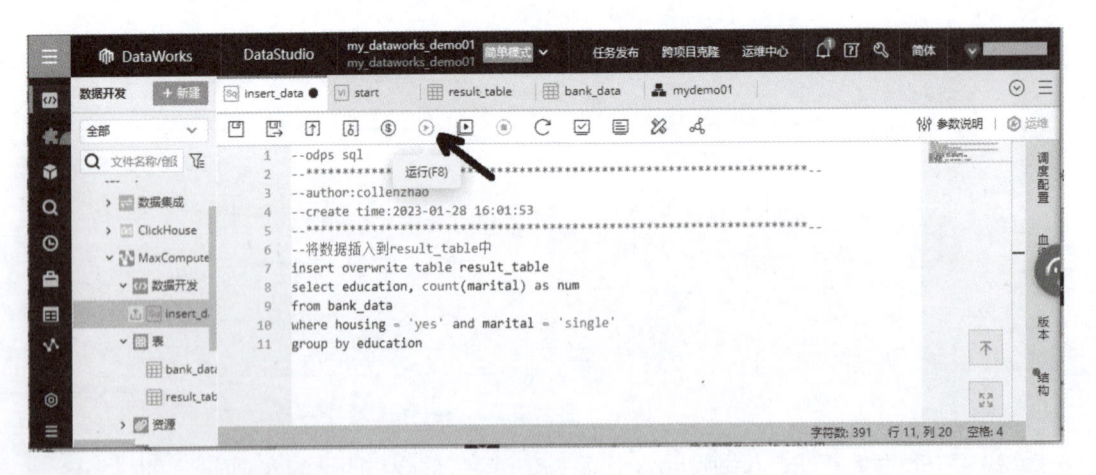

图 11-41

> 运行任务节点会产生相应的费用，如图 11-42 所示。

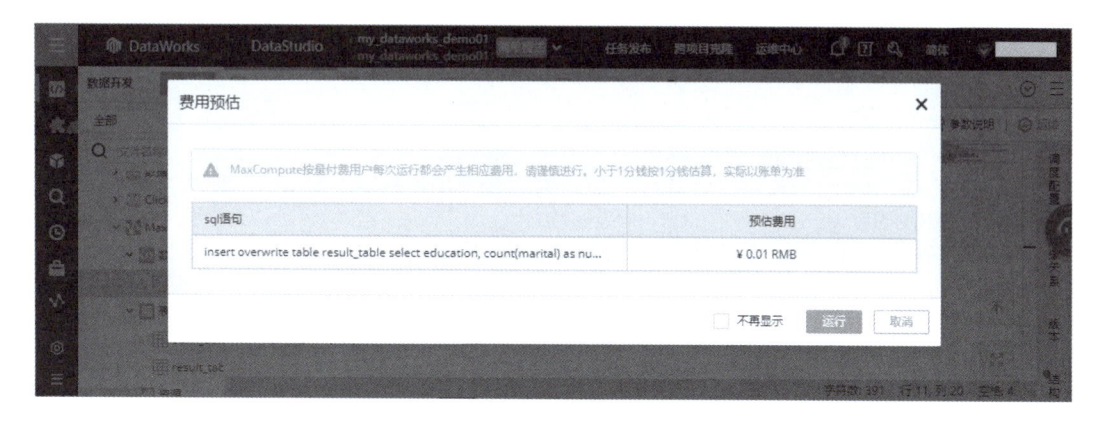

图 11-42

（12）运行结束后，即可在页面下方查看运行日志和结果，如图 11-43 所示。

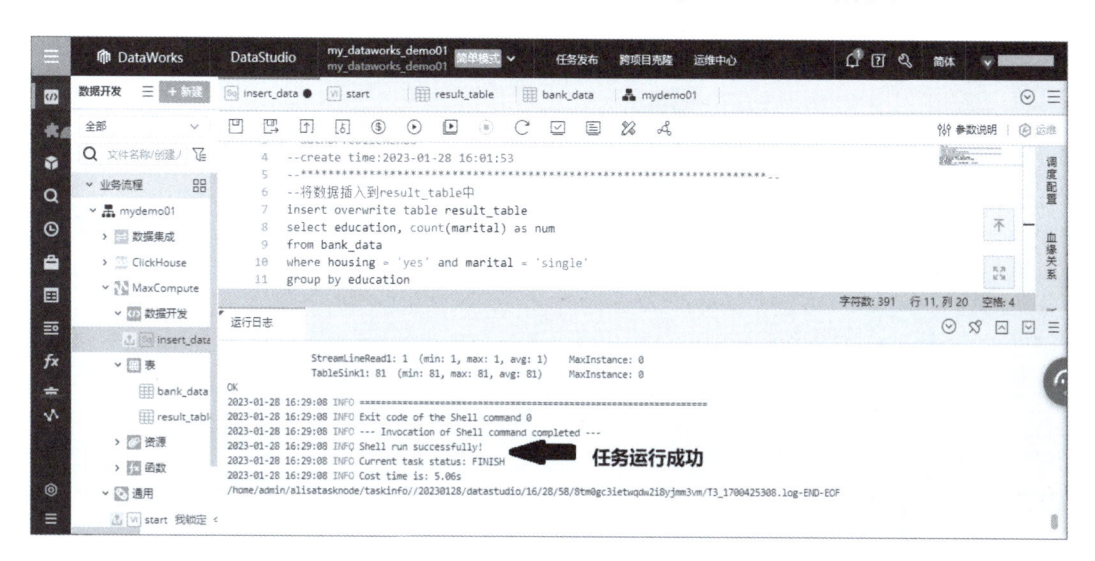

图 11-43

（13）通过 MaxCompute 命令行工具查看任务输出的结果。

```
my_dataworks_demo01>select * from result_table;
```

输出的结果如下。

```
+------------------------+----------+
| education              | num      |
+------------------------+----------+
| university.degree      | 2399     |
| basic.4y               | 227      |
| basic.9y               | 709      |
| unknown                | 257      |
| professional.course    | 785      |
| high.school            | 1641     |
| basic.6y               | 172      |
| illiterate             | 1        |
+------------------------+----------+
```

11.3.4 提交业务流程

在业务流程开发并测试完成后，就可以将业务流程进行提交。具体的操作步骤如下。

（1）在业务流程开发页面中，单击"提交"按钮，如图 11-44 所示。

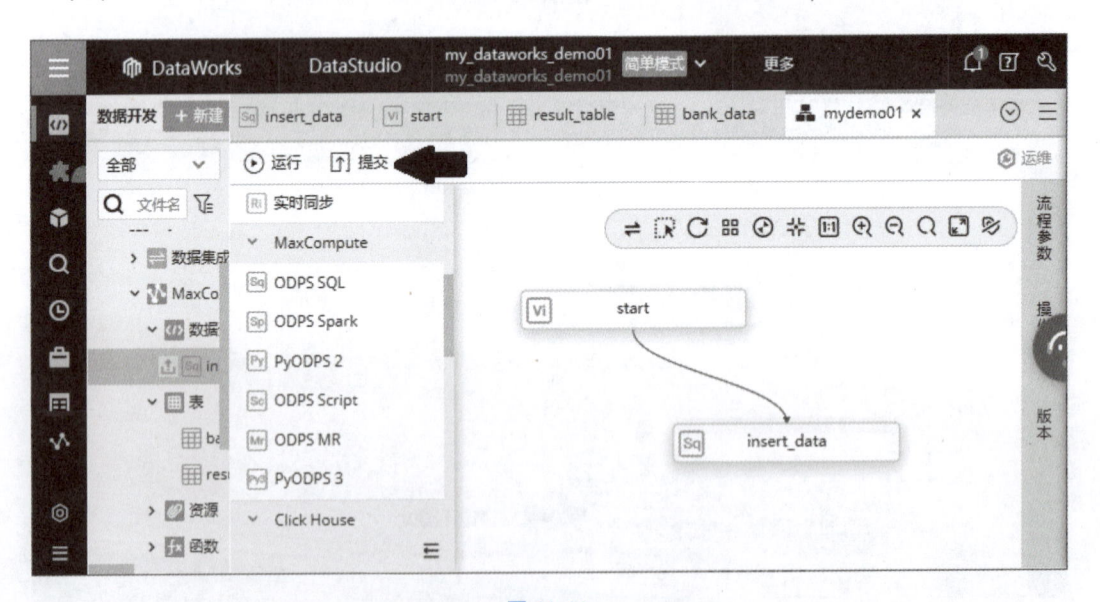

图 11-44

（2）在"提交"对话框中，选择需要提交的节点，输入备注，并勾选"忽略输入输出不一致的告警"复选框，如图 11-45 所示。

（3）在业务流程提交完成后，将会显示成功和失败的任务信息，如图 11-46 所示。

图 11-45

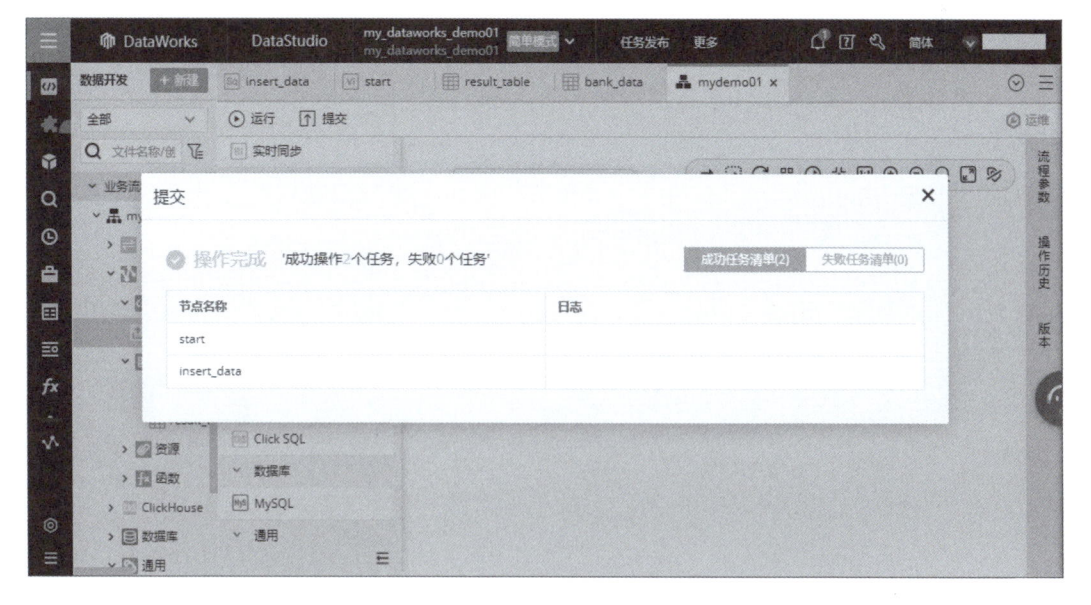

图 11-46

> 本节开发的业务流程相对比较简单，读者可以根据实际需要增加更多的任务节点来开发业务流程。例如，在图 11-47 中增加一个数据集成的离线同步节点，将 MaxCompute 中 result_table 表的数据同步到 MySQL 中。

图 11-47

第 12 章
数据可视化分析平台 Quick BI

Quick BI 是一个专为云上用户量身打造的新一代智能 BI 服务平台。Quick BI 可以提供海量数据实时在线分析服务，支持拖曳式操作，具有丰富的可视化效果，帮助用户轻松自如地完成数据分析、业务数据探查、报表制作等工作。

12.1 Quick BI 简介

用户通过 Quick BI 可以无缝对接各类云上数据库和自建数据库，大幅度提高数据分析和报表开发效率。零代码拖曳式的极简操作，让业务人员也能轻松实现大数据分析。

12.1.1 什么是 Quick BI

Quick BI 是一款全场景数据消费式的 BI 平台，秉承"全场景消费数据，让业务决策触手可及"的使命，通过智能的数据分析和可视化能力帮助企业构建数据分析系统，用户可以使用 Quick BI 制作漂亮的仪表板、格式复杂的电子表格、酷炫的大屏、有分析思路的数据门户，也可以将报表集成在用户的业务流程中，并且通过邮件、钉钉、企业微信等分享给同事和合作伙伴。

Quick BI 可以让企业的数据资产快速流动起来，通过 BI 和 AI 结合挖掘数据背后的价值，加深并加速在企业内部各种场景的数据消费。Quick BI 的管理控制台如图 12-1 所示。

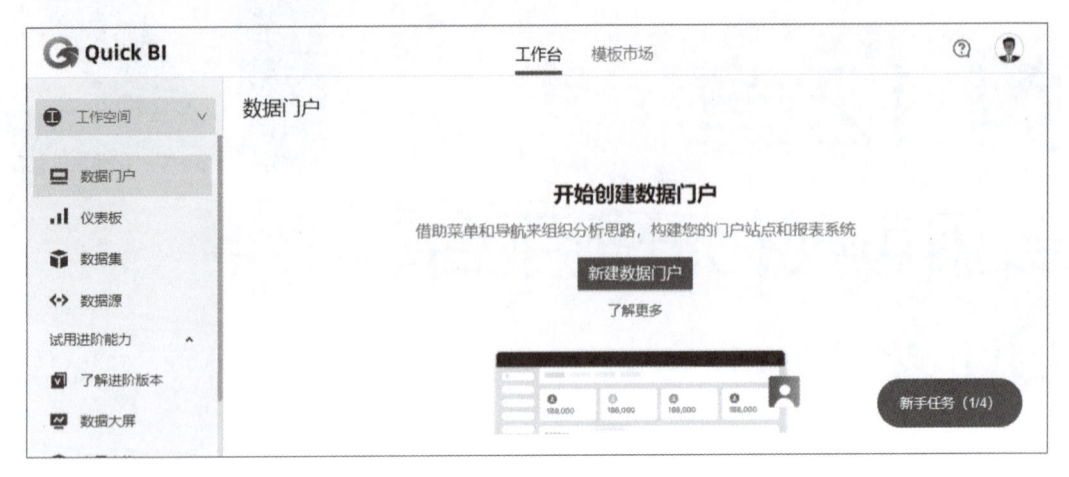

图 12-1

12.1.2 Quick BI 的基本对象

Quick BI 是一个基于云计算的灵活的轻量级的自助 BI 工具服务平台，它包含的基本对象有数据源、数据集、电子表格、仪表板、数据门户等。下面分别进行介绍。

1. 数据源

用户在使用 Quick BI 分析数据时，需要先指定原始数据所在的数据源。Quick BI 中提供了多种添加数据源的方式。

（1）从云数据库添加数据源。

（2）添加来自自建数据库的数据源。

（3）上传本地文件。

Quick BI 创建数据源的页面如图 12-2 所示。

> 从图 12-2 中可以看出，Quick BI 几乎支持市面上所有类型的数据库。

2. 数据集

用户可以将各种不同的数据源中的表创建为数据集。在数据集列表中，用户还可以对已添加的数据集进行编辑、移动和删除操作。使用 Quick BI 创建的数据集如图 12-3 所示。

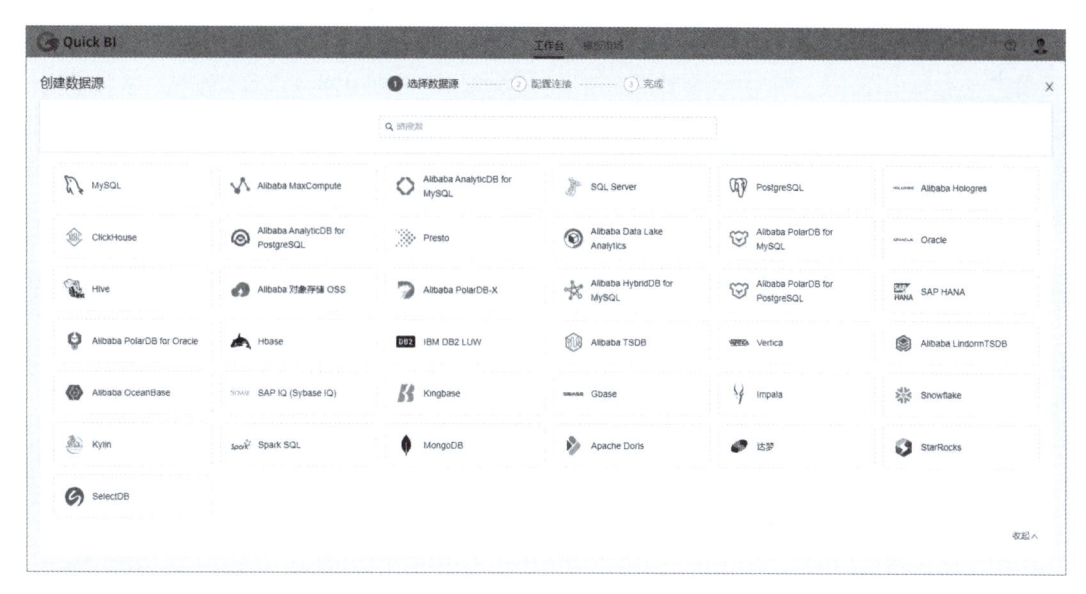

图 12-2

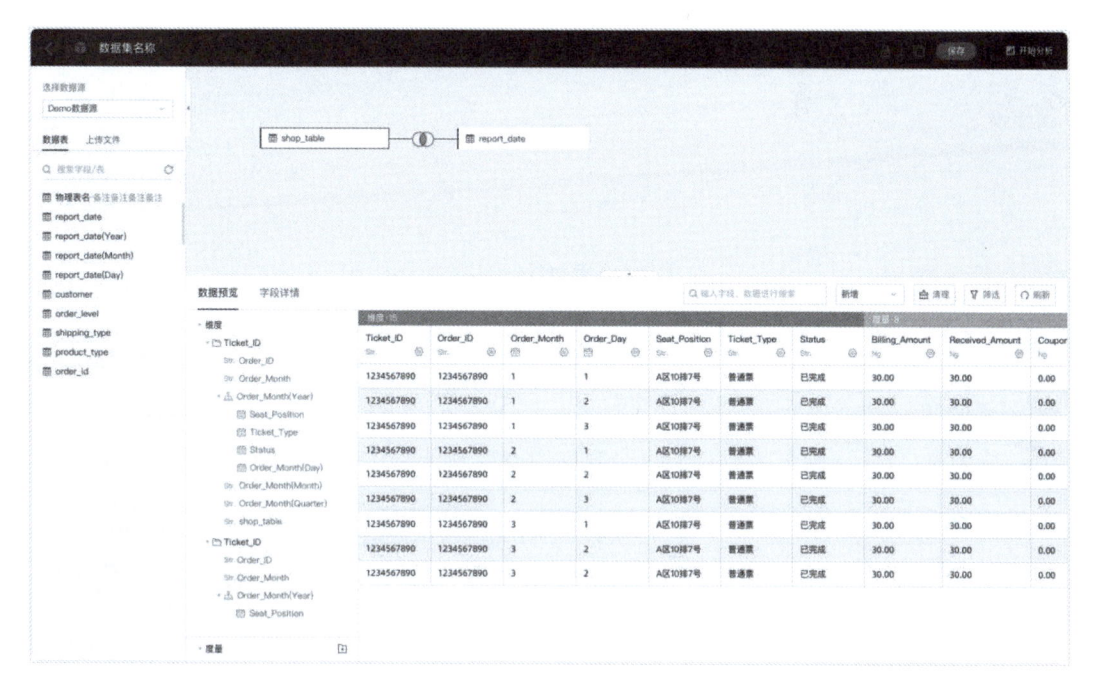

图 12-3

3. 电子表格

电子表格类似于 Excel 的在线报表设计器。它支持灵活、个性化的报表样式配置，支持在线和本地多元化的分析模式。业务人员可以自助完成"格式复杂，信息量大"的中国式报表，实现各类报表的制作。用户在选中一个数据集后即可使用电子表格对数据的内容进行分析。Quick BI 的电子表格如图 12-4 所示。

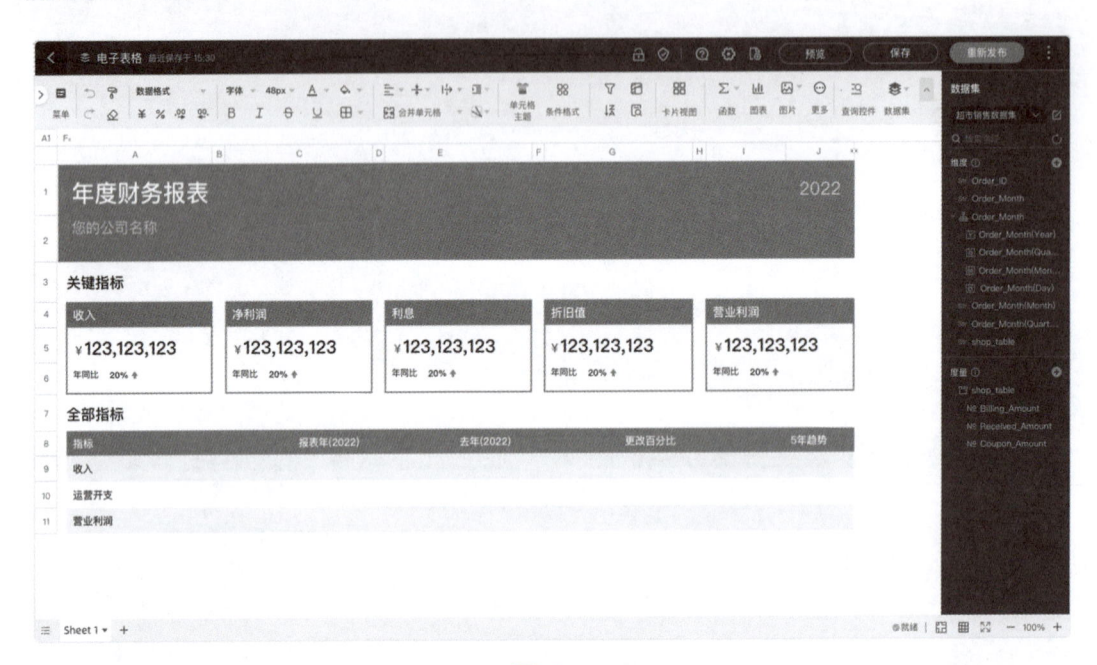

图 12-4

> 电子表格仅适用于 Quick BI 高级版和 Quick BI 专业版。

4. 仪表板

仪表板采用了更加灵活的磁贴式布局来显示报表数据的交互，它不仅可以将数据以可视化的方式呈现，还可以通过各种数据筛选和查询，使用各种数据展现方式，突出数据中的关键字段。Quick BI 的仪表板如图 12-5 所示。

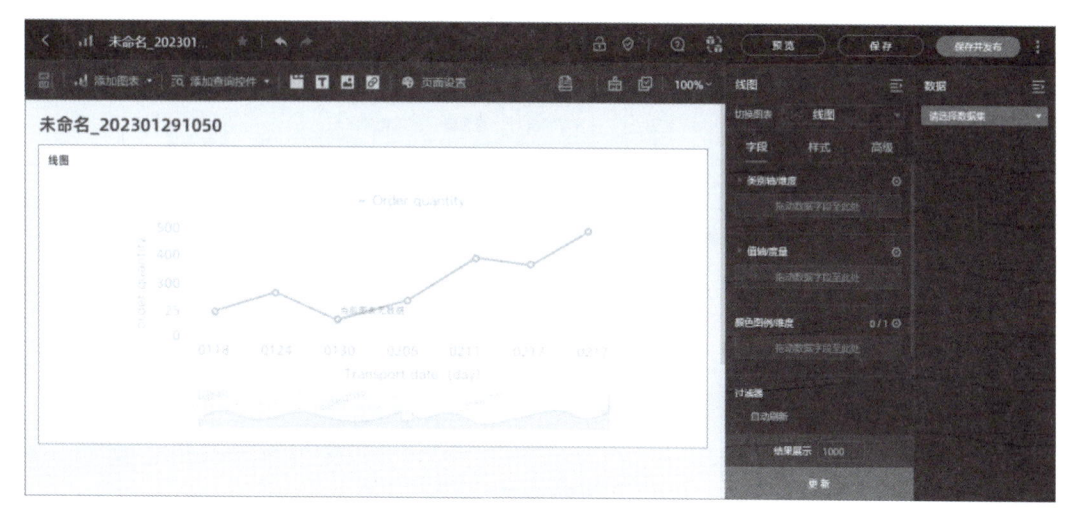

图 12-5

5. 数据门户

数据门户也叫数据产品。用户可以使用数据门户功能构建应用,例如经营分析系统。数据门户不仅可以引用 Quick BI 中的数据结果,也支持外挂链接。Quick BI 的数据门户配置页面如图 12-6 所示。

图 12-6

12.1.3　Quick BI 的体系架构

Quick BI 体系架构由 4 个不同的模块组成,分别是数据连接模块、数据处理模块、数据展示模块和权限管理模块。Quick BI 的体系架构如图 12-7 所示。

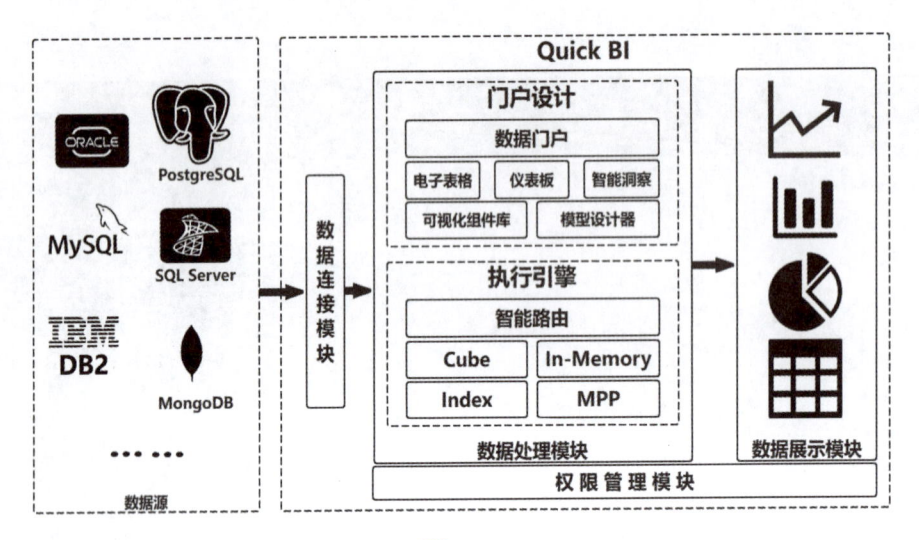

图 12-7

下面详细说明每一个模块的功能和特性。

1. 数据连接模块

数据连接模块负责适配各种云数据源，包括但不限于 MaxCompute、RDS（MySQL、PostgreSQL、SQL Server）、Analytic DB、AnalyticDB for PostgreSQL、HybridDB for MySQL 等，封装数据源的元数据/数据的标准查询接口。

2. 数据处理模块

数据处理模块是 Quick BI 最核心的一个模块，它由 3 个不同的引擎组成，如表 12-1 所示。

表 12-1

引擎名称	说　明
查询引擎	负责数据源的查询过程
数据预处理引擎	负责数据源的轻量级 ETL 处理，目前主要支持 MaxCompute 的自定义 SQL，未来会扩展到其他数据源
数据建模引擎	负责数据源的 OLAP 建模过程，将数据源转换为多维分析模型，支持维度（包括日期型维度、地理位置型维度）、度量、星形拓扑模型等标准语义，并提供计算字段功能,允许用户使用当前数据源的 SQL 语法对维度和度量进行二次加工

3. 数据展示模块

数据展示模块支持将电子表格、仪表板、数据门户分享给其他登录用户访问，支持将仪表板公开到互联网供非登录用户访问。数据展示模块支持的数据分享方式如表 12-2 所示。

表 12-2

分享方式	说　明
电子表格	提供在线电子表格的相关操作功能，包括行/列筛选、普通/高级过滤、分类汇总、自动求和、条件格式等数据分析功能，并支持数据导出，以及文本处理、表格处理等丰富功能
仪表板	将可视化图表控件使用拖曳的方式组装为仪表板，支持线图、饼图、柱形图、漏斗图、气泡地图、色彩地图、指标看板等 40 多种图表。支持查询条件、TAB、IFRAME、PIC 和文本框五种基本控件，支持图表间数据联动
数据门户	可以将仪表板使用拖曳的方式组装为数据门户，支持内嵌链接（仪表板），支持模板和菜单栏的基本设置

4. 权限管理模块

权限管理模块分为组织权限管理和行级权限管理。其中，组织权限管理负责组织和工作空间的两级权限架构体系管控，以及工作空间中的用户角色体系管控，实现基本的权限管理，实现不同的人看不同的报表内容。行级权限管理负责数据的行级粒度权限管控，实现同一张报表，不同的人看不同的数据。

12.1.4　Quick BI 的应用场景

Quick BI 拥有众多用户，丰富的功能特性满足了用户在不同场景的需求。Quick BI 主要可以被应用于以下 3 个场景。

1. 数据即时分析与决策

企业在业务数据化运营中，经常需对用户留存率、活跃率等进行数据报表分析，而 Quick BI 的数据展现方式丰富，操作便捷，很好地满足了用户全程数据的自助分析与即时决策的需求。它有效地解决了企业业务人员取数难；报表产出效率低，维护难；图表效果设计不佳，人力成本高的问题。

2. 报表与自有系统集成

企业在运营过程中，期望用最低成本、最快速度搭建一个可展示、可分析的简易 BI 系统，迅速将公司重要业务数据集成展现在公司的管理系统中，为各业务线和各区域的人员提供数据支持。Quick BI 具有上手简单、快捷，可以满足不同岗位的数据需求，学习门槛低的特点。利用 Quick BI 与内部系统集成结合进行数据分析，极大地提高了看数据的效率。同时，利用统一的系统入口，可以解决员工使用多系统的麻烦，利于使用与控制。

3. 交易数据权限管控

数据对支付平台来说至关重要。运营团队需要通过数据去掌握业务的发展情况，以及时发现异常并解决问题。作为数据团队，除了分析数据，还需要对数据权限进行管控。基于此需求，Quick BI 能够轻松实现数据权限行级管控；适应多变的业务需求；保障跨源数据集成及计算性能。

12.2 【实战】使用数据可视化分析平台 Quick BI

Quick BI 是一款专为云上用户和企业量身打造的新一代自助式智能 BI 服务平台，其简单易用的可视化操作和灵活高效的多维分析能力，让精细化数据洞察为商业决策保驾护航。下面将使用一个真实的数据分析案例来演示如何使用 Quick BI。

12.2.1 项目背景与需求

这里将使用阿里云提供的零售企业样本数据进行演示。通过分析 2019 年 8 月企业的订单信息和流量渠道信息等数据，找到企业运营状况不佳的原因，最终指导相关业务部门制定决策和采取行动，以提高企业整体的利润。

12.2.2 连接数据源

在使用 Quick BI 进行数据分析和报表搭建前，需要先连接数据源。

> 阿里云提供一个默认的云数据源 MySQL。如果不想使用默认数据源，则可以在目标地域创建一个数据源。

具体的操作步骤如下。

（1）选择 Quick BI 管理控制台左侧的"数据源"选项，进入"数据源"页面，单击"新建数据源"按钮，弹出"创建数据源"对话框，选择"MySQL"选项，如图 12-8 所示。

图 12-8

(2)数据源类型选择阿里云。

(3)按照表 12-3 配置 MySQL 数据库的连接参数。

表 12-3

参 数 名	描 述	示 例
显示名称	数据源配置列表的显示名称。名称由汉字、数字、字母、下画线（_）或短横线（-）组合组成	Demo 数据源
数据库地址	部署 MySQL 数据库的外网地址	rm-uf609996l63c3d2q52o.mysql.rds.aliyuncs.com
数据库	部署 MySQL 数据库时自定义的数据库名称	quickbi_online_demo
用户名	登录 MySQL 数据库的用户名	quickbi_train
密码	登录 MySQL 数据库的密码	quickbi_train
数据库版本	选择数据库版本： 选择 5.7，表示兼容 MySQL 5.7 及以下版本。 选择 8.0，表示兼容 MySQL 8.0 版本	5.7

(4)配置完成后，单击"连接测试"按钮，显示"数据源连通性正常"，如图 12-9 所示，单击"确定"按钮。

图 12-9

（5）在"数据表"列表中可以看到"Demo 数据源"中的数据表，如图 12-10 所示。

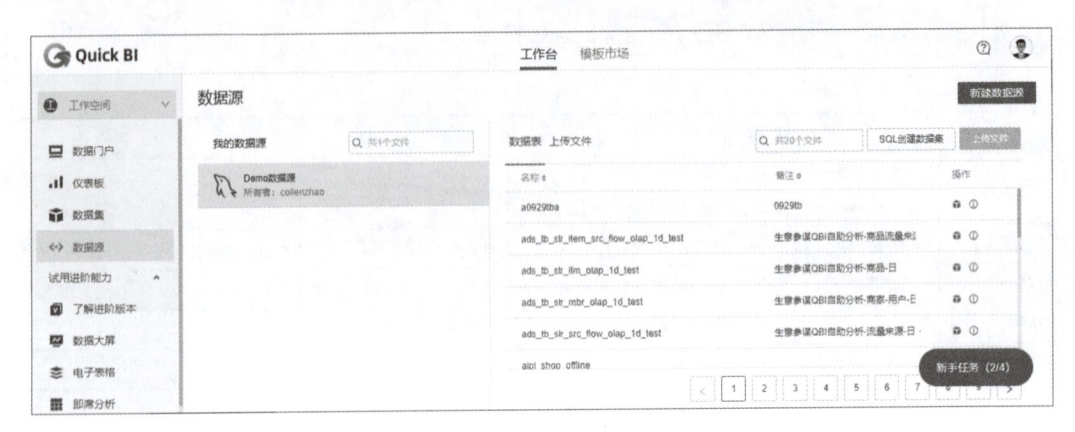

图 12-10

12.2.3 数据建模

连通数据源后，当需要分析的数据存储在不同的数据表时，可以通过数据关联，把多个数据表连接起来，形成模型，进行数据分析。具体的操作步骤如下。

（1）在"数据源"页面中，选择"demo_订单信息明细表"作为目标数据表，单击其后的"创建数据集"按钮，如图 12-11 所示。

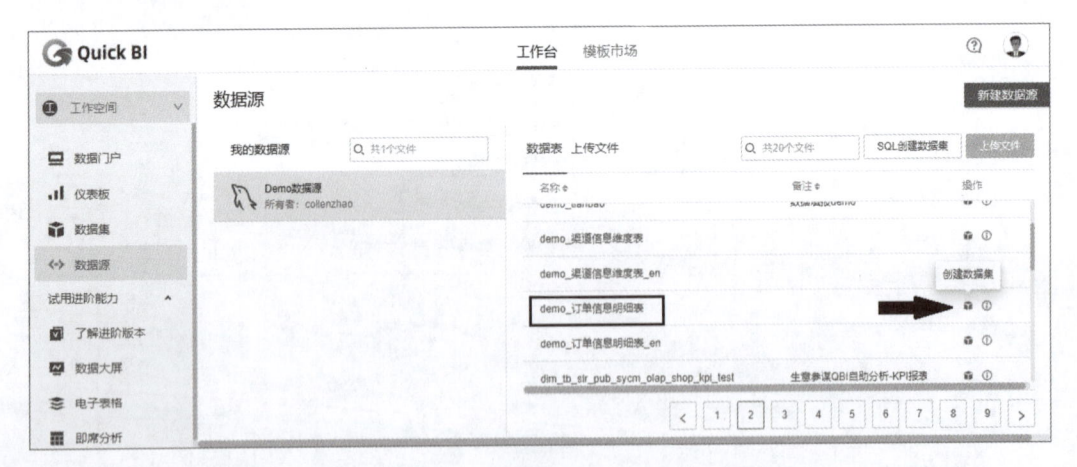

图 12-11

（2）进入数据集编辑页面，将"demo_渠道信息维度表"拖曳到表关联的面板中，如图 12-12 所示。

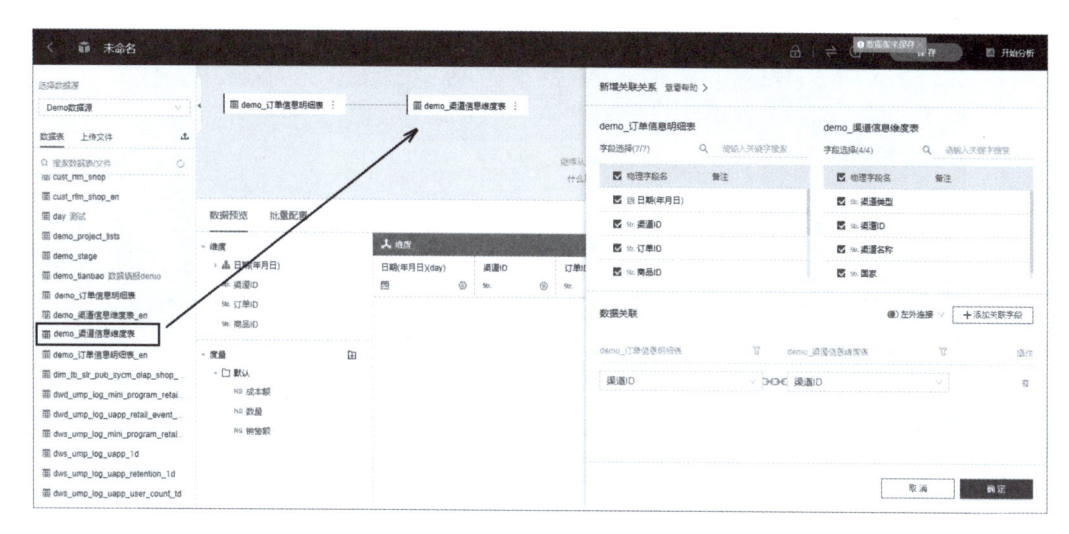

图 12-12

（3）在右侧的"数据关联"选区中选择"左外连接"选项，并设置关联的字段，如图 12-13 所示，单击"确定"按钮。

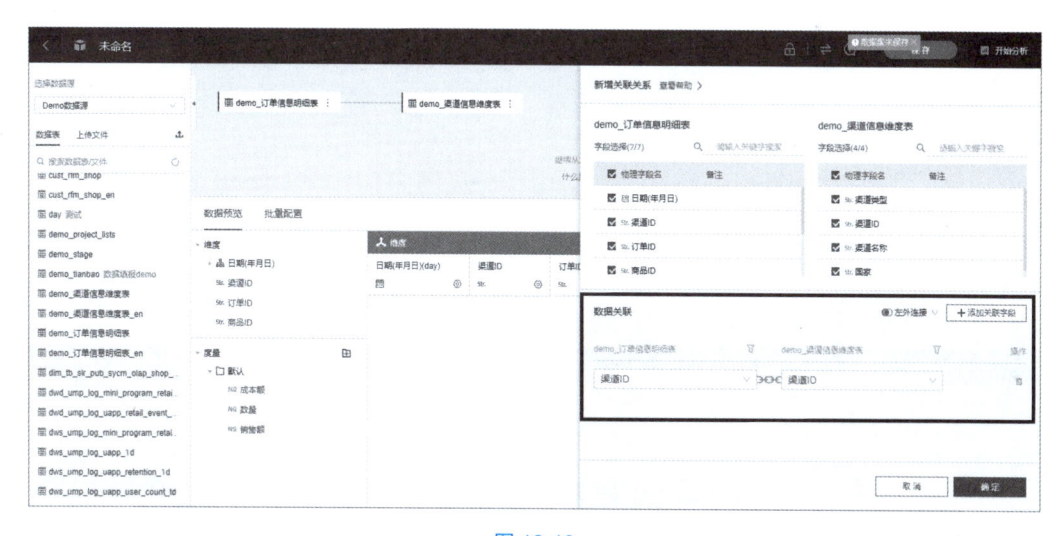

图 12-13

（4）单击页面右上角的"保存"按钮，弹出"保存数据集"对话框，在对话框中输入数据集的名称，如"demo_毛利率分析"，如图 12-14 所示。

（5）单击页面右侧的"刷新预览"按钮，就可以预览数据集的数据，如图 12-15 所示。

（6）单击"新建计算字段"按钮，就可以在数据集中增加新的字段，如图 12-16 所示。

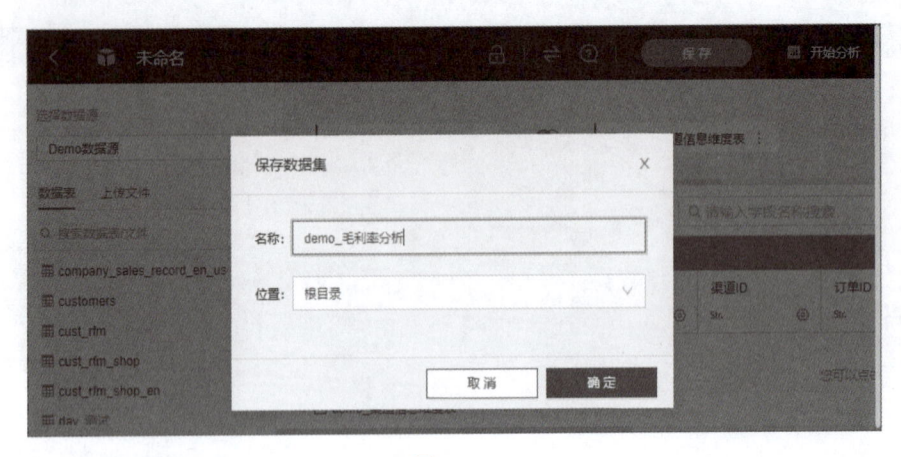

图 12-14

图 12-15

图 12-16

（7）在"新建计算字段"对话框中，新增毛利额字段，如图12-17所示。

图 12-17

> 毛利额的字段表达式为 SUM([销售额])-SUM([成本额])

（8）按照同样的方式新增毛利率字段。

> 毛利率的字段表达式为(SUM([销售额]-[成本额]))/SUM([销售额])

（9）字段添加成功后，单击页面右上角的"保存"按钮。

12.2.4 数据可视化分析

数据集创建成功后，就可以通过创建仪表板，添加不同的图表来展示数据，并通过联动进行数据可视化分析。具体的操作步骤如下。

（1）在数据集编辑页面中，选择右上角的"开始分析"选项，在弹出的下拉列表中选择"创建仪表板"选项，如图 12-18 所示。

图 12-18

（2）为了更好地展示各月的销售额、毛利额、毛利率 3 个关键指标的走势数据，这里使用指标趋势图进行呈现。在仪表板编辑页面中，选择"添加图表"选项，在弹出的下拉列表中选择"指标趋势图"选项，如图 12-19 所示。

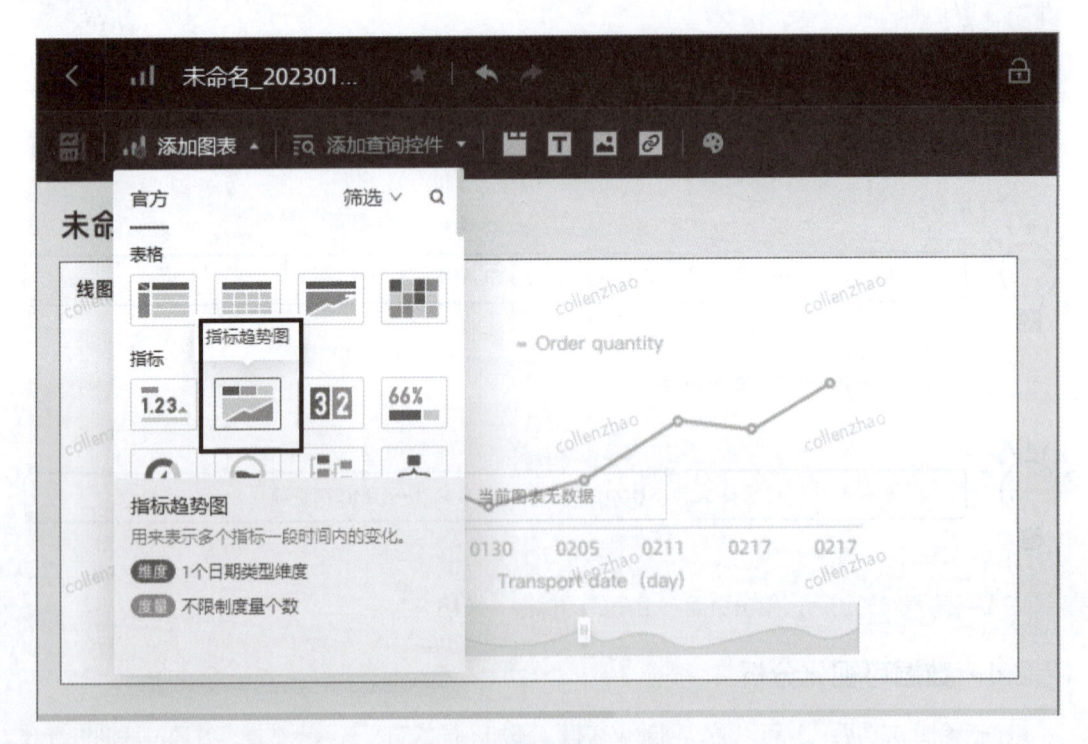

图 12-19

（3）在"字段"选项卡中，配置"日期/维度"和"指标/度量"，单击"更新"按钮。此时就可以展现出指标趋势图，如图 12-20 所示。

图 12-20

（4）单击"保存"按钮，在"保存仪表板"对话框中设置名称，如"毛利额异常下滑诊断分析"。

（5）选中指标趋势图，在"高级"选项卡中勾选"开启副指标展示"复选框，如图 12-21 所示。

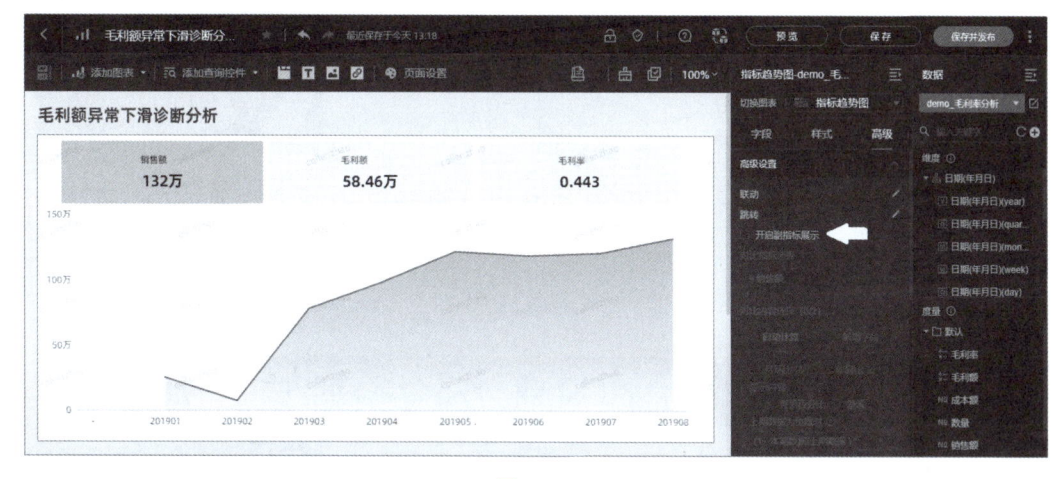

图 12-21

（6）在"对比指标选择"下拉列表中，选择"销售额"选项，并勾选"月环比"和"选择涨跌标记"复选框，如图 12-22 所示。

（7）重复第 6 步，按照同样方式设置"毛利额"和"毛利率"字段。设置完成后如图 12-23 所示。

（8）创建气泡图展示不同渠道类别的销售额、毛利率、毛利额的数据。选择"添加图表"选项，在弹出的下拉列表中选择"气泡图"选项，如图 12-24 所示。

图 12-22

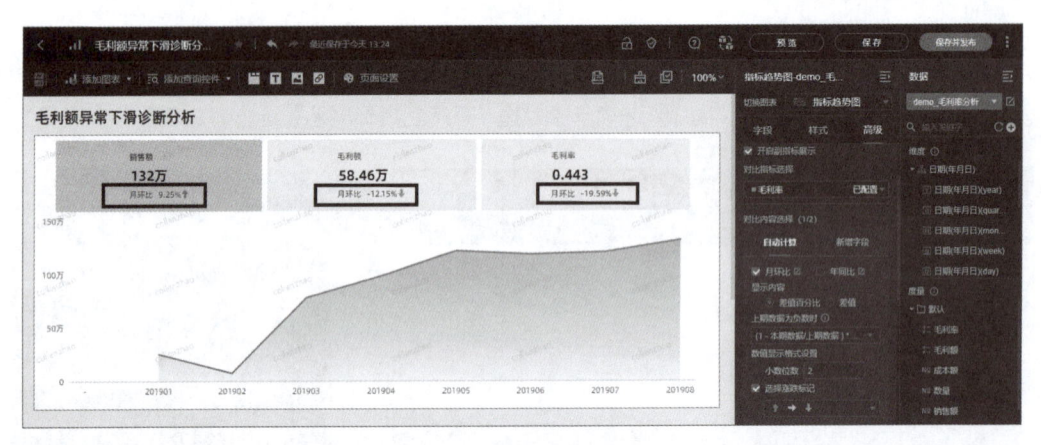

图 12-23

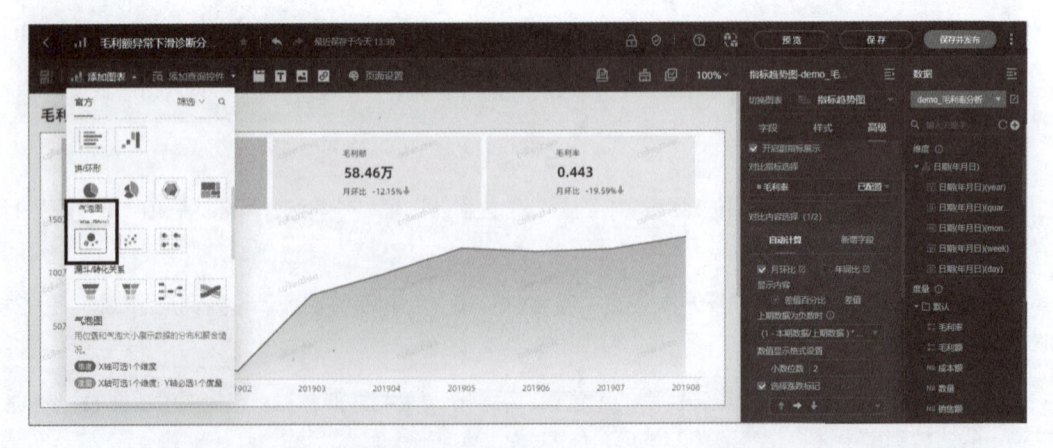

图 12-24

（9）将气泡图的名称设置为"渠道类别销售&毛利四象限图"，并根据表 12-4 设置气泡图的字段。

表 12-4

字　段	值
X 轴/维度或度量	毛利率（聚合计算）
Y 轴/度量	销售额（求和）
类别/维度	渠道类型
颜色/维度或度量	渠道类型
尺寸/度量	毛利额（聚合计算）
过滤器	日期（年月日）(month)

（10）单击"字段"选项卡中"过滤器"选区的 ▼ 按钮，设置过滤器，以查看 2019 年 8 月的数据，如图 12-25 所示。

图 12-25

（11）先单击"更新"按钮，然后单击"保存"按钮。此时的气泡图如图 12-26 所示。

（12）选择"样式"选项卡，将图例设置为居右显示，并勾选"开启四象限"复选框，如图 12-27 所示。

图 12-26

图 12-27

（13）为了更好地展示各个渠道下销售额、毛利率和毛利额的详细数据，创建一张新的气泡图，用于分析渠道明细销售额和毛利额数据，如图 12-28 所示。

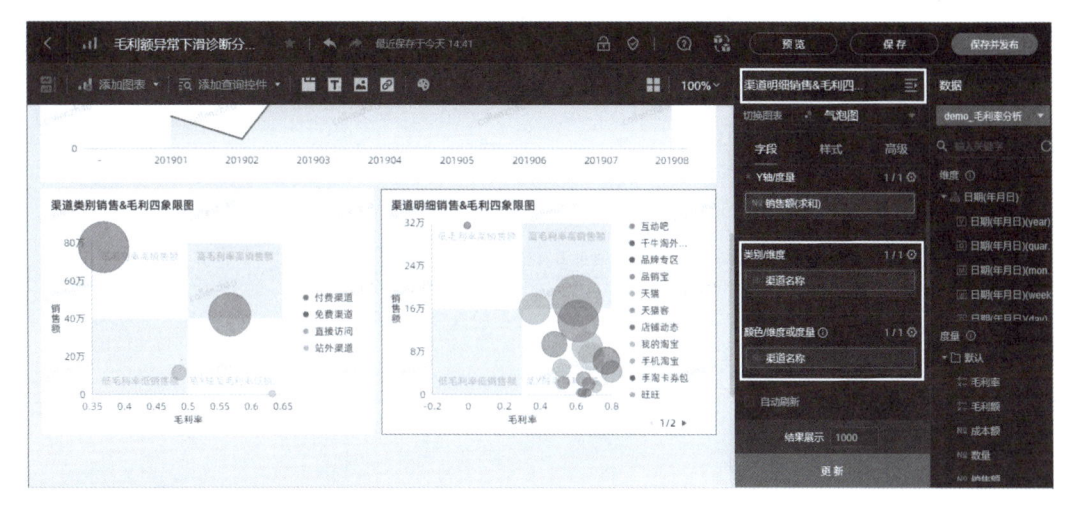

图 12-28

> 为避免重复操作,可以复制上述气泡图并将"渠道类别"字段替换为"渠道名称"字段。

(14)配置"渠道类别销售&毛利四象限图"和"渠道明细销售&毛利四象限图"的联动,以便更好地分析各个渠道在 2019 年 8 月的销售额和毛利率。在"高级"选项卡的"高级设置"选区中,单击"联动"右侧的"编辑"按钮,如图 12-29 所示。

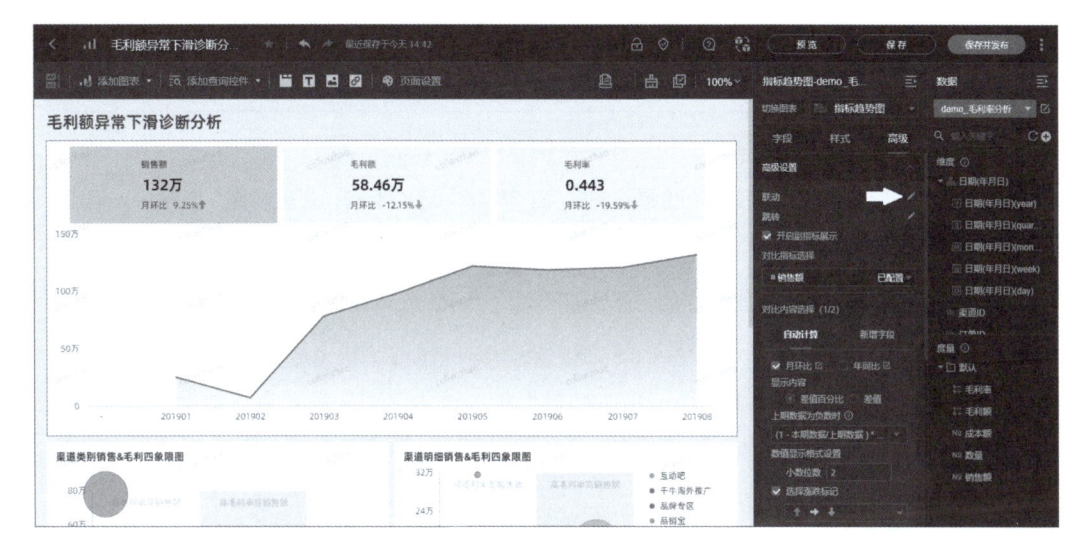

图 12-29

（15）在"图表联动设置"对话框中设置联动的方式，单击"确定"按钮，如图 12-30 所示。

图 12-30

（16）联动配置完成后，单击指标趋势图中 2019 年 8 月的数据点，可以看到"渠道类别销售&毛利四象限图"和"渠道明细销售&毛利四象限图"中的数据已被过滤为 2019 年 8 月。

> 分析"渠道类别销售&毛利四象限图"的各个渠道类别在 2019 年 8 月的销售额和毛利率数据后，发现免费渠道在高销售额低毛利率象限，属于异常区间。因此，配置"渠道类别销售&毛利四象限图"和"渠道明细销售&毛利四象限图"的联动，查看 2019 年 8 月免费渠道下各个渠道的销售额和毛利率数据，分析异常受哪些渠道影响。

（17）选择"渠道类别销售&毛利四象限图"，在"高级"选项卡的"高级设置"选区中，单击"联动"右侧的"编辑"按钮，如图 12-31 所示。

（18）按照图 12-32 设置图表联动，单击"确定"按钮。

（19）联动配置完成后，单击"渠道类别销售&毛利四象限图"中免费渠道的数据点，可以看到"渠道明细销售&毛利四象限图"中的数据已被过滤为 2019 年 8 月免费渠道的数据，如图 12-33 所示。

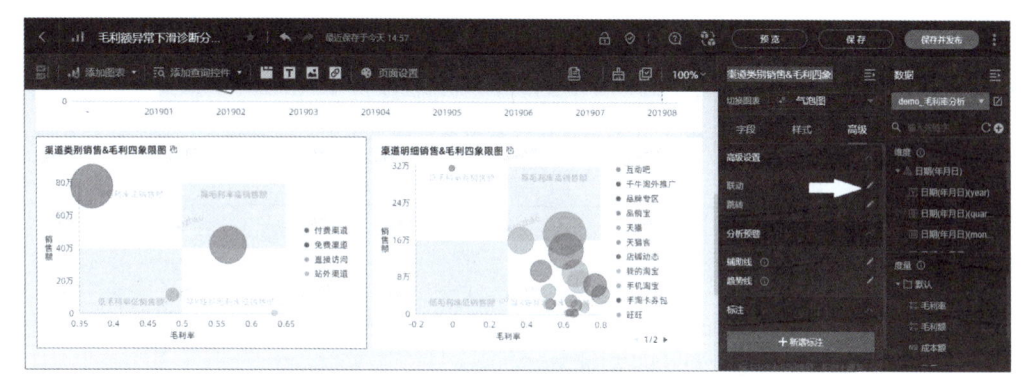

图 12-31

图 12-32

图 12-33

> 分析"渠道明细销售&毛利四象限图"各个渠道在 2019 年 8 月的销售额和毛利率数据后,发现手淘卡券包在高销售额低毛利率象限,属于异常区间,最终导致毛利额异常下降。

12.2.5 发布共享仪表板

分析完成后,可以将仪表板搭建成数据门户,并导出用于存档。如果随着时间发展,数据出现了其他异常,用户可以将仪表板分享给他人协同编辑。

具体的操作步骤如下。

(1)单击右上角的"保存并发布"按钮。

(2)选择 Quick BI 管理控制台左侧的"数据门户"选项,进入"数据门户"页面,单击"新建数据门户"按钮。

(3)按照图 12-34 的指引添加并设置门户菜单。

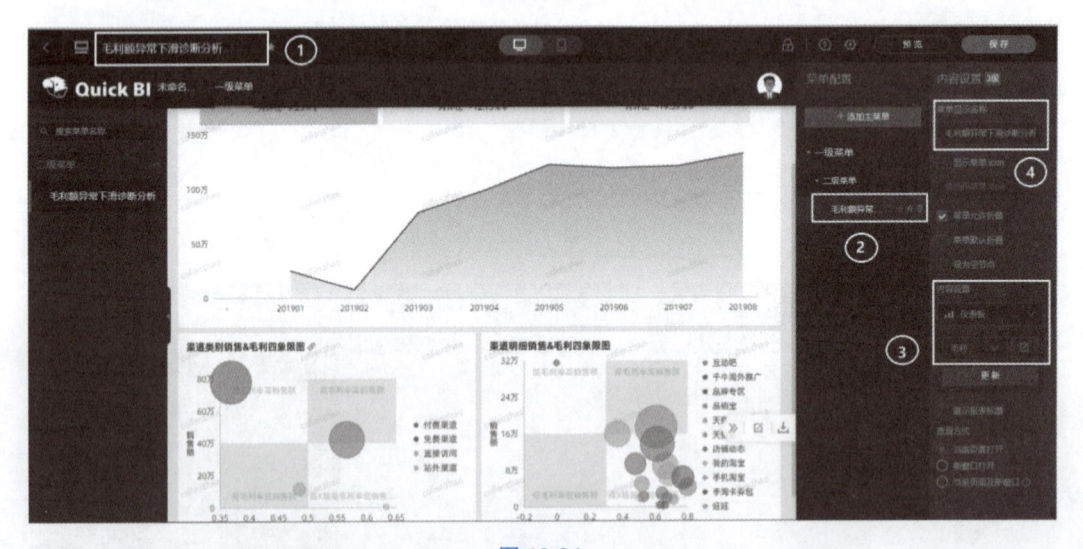

图 12-34

(4)单击"导出"按钮 导出数据门户,如图 12-35 所示。

(5)弹出"导出"对话框,设置"导出名称""文件格式"和"导出渠道",单击"确定"按钮,如图 12-36 所示。

第 12 章　数据可视化分析平台 Quick BI | 415

图 12-35

图 12-36

（6）创建好的仪表板可以分享给团队中的其他成员使用，如图 12-37 所示。

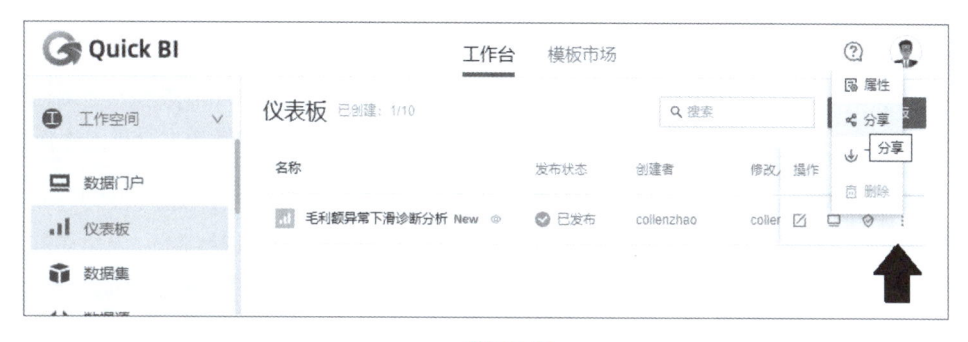

图 12-37

第 13 章
机器学习平台 PAI

机器学习平台 PAI（Platform of Artificial Intelligence）是面向开发者和企业的机器学习/深度学习工程平台，提供包含数据标注、模型构建、模型训练、模型部署、推理优化在内的 AI 开发全链路服务，内置 140 多种优化算法，具备丰富的行业场景插件，为用户提供低门槛、高性能的云原生 AI 工程化能力。

13.1 机器学习基础知识

机器学习（Machine Learning） 是让计算机能够自动地从某些数据中总结出一定的规律，并得出某种预测模型，进而利用该模型对未知数据进行预测的方法。它是一种实现人工智能的方式。

13.1.1 什么是机器学习

百度百科对机器学习做了如下解释。

> 机器学习是一门多领域交叉学科，涉及概率论、统计学、逼近论、凸分析、算法复杂度理论等多门学科，专门研究计算机怎样模拟或实现人类的学习行为，以获取新的知识或技能，重新组织已有的知识结构使之不断改善自身的性能。它是人工智能核心，是使计算机具有智能的根本途径。

机器学习是人工智能的一个子集。这项技术的主要任务是指导计算机从数据中学习，利用经验来改善自身的性能，不需要进行明确的编程。在机器学习中，算法会不断进行训练，从大型数据集中发现模式和相关性，根据数据分析结果做出最佳决策和预测。机器学习应用具有自我演进能力，它们获得的数据越多，准确性会越高。机器学习技术的应用无处不在，例如家居生活、购物车、娱乐媒体及医疗保健等。

13.1.2 机器学习的常见算法

目前，机器学习大致可以分为以下 4 类，如表 13-1 所示。

表 13-1

类　别	说　明
有监督学习 （Supervised Learning）	当已经拥有一些数据及数据对应的类标时，就可以通过这些数据得到模型，再利用这个模型去预测新数据的类标，这种情况被称为有监督学习。有监督学习可以分为回归问题和分类问题两大类。在回归问题中，预测的结果是连续值；在分类问题中，预测的结果是离散值。常见的有监督学习算法包括线性回归、逻辑回归、K-近邻、朴素贝叶斯、决策树、随机森林、支持向量机等
无监督学习 （Unsupervised Learning）	在无监督学习中是没有给定类标训练样本的，这就需要对给定的数据直接建模。常见的无监督学习算法包括 k 均值聚类算法、EM 算法等
半监督学习 （Semi-supervised Learn-ing）	半监督学习介于有监督学习和无监督学习之间，给定的数据集既包括有类标的数据，也包括没有类标的数据，需要在工作量（如数据的打标）和模型的准确率之间取一个平衡点
强化学习 （Reinforcement Learning）	从不懂到通过不断学习、总结规律，最终学会的过程就是强化学习。强化学习很依赖于学习的"周围环境"，强调如何基于"周围环境"做出相应的动作

13.2　机器学习平台 PAI 基础知识

机器学习平台 PAI 是阿里云人工智能平台，提供一站式的机器学习解决方案。

13.2.1　初识机器学习平台 PAI

PAI 起初是阿里巴巴集团内部（如淘宝、支付宝和高德）的机器学习平台，致力于让公司内部的开发者更高效、简洁、标准地使用 AI（Artificial Intelligence）技术。随着 PAI 的不断发展，2018 年 PAI 正式商业化，目前已经积累了数万的企业客户和个人开发者，是中国云端机器学习平台之一。

PAI 底层支持多种计算框架。

（1）流式计算框架 Flink。

（2）基于开源版本深度优化的深度学习框架 TensorFlow。

（3）千亿特征样本的大规模并行计算框架 Parameter Server。

（4）Spark、PySpark、MapReduce 等业内主流开源框架。

用户只要准备好训练数据（存放到 OSS 或 MaxCompute 中），所有建模工作（包括数据上传、数据预处理、特征工程、模型训练、模型评估和模型发布至离线或在线环境）都可以通过 PAI 实现。

13.2.2　PAI 的架构

PAI 的体系架构如图 13-1 所示。

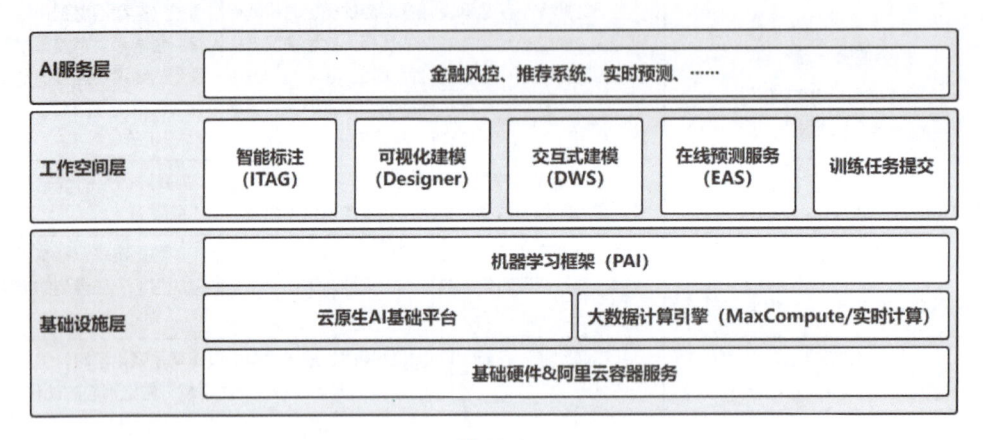

AI服务层	金融风控、推荐系统、实时预测、……
工作空间层	智能标注（ITAG）｜可视化建模（Designer）｜交互式建模（DWS）｜在线预测服务（EAS）｜训练任务提交
基础设施层	机器学习框架（PAI） 云原生AI基础平台｜大数据计算引擎（MaxCompute/实时计算） 基础硬件&阿里云容器服务

图 13-1

PAI 的体系架构从下至上可以分为以下 3 层。

1. 基础设施层

基础设施层涵盖硬件设施、基础平台、计算资源及计算框架。PAI 支持的硬件设施包括 CPU、GPU、FPGA、NPU、容器服务 ACK 及 ECS。在 PAI 上可以使用的计算框架包括 PAI-TensorFlow、PAI-PyTorch、Alink、ODL、AliGraph、EasyRL、EasyRec、EasyTransfer、EasyVision 等，用于执行分布式计算任务。

2. 工作空间层

工作空间是 PAI 的顶层概念，为企业和团队提供统一的计算资源管理及人员权限管理服务，为 AI 开发者提供支持团队协作的全流程开发工具及 AI 资产管理服务。PAI 工作空间和 DataWorks 工作空间在概念和实现上互通。

3. AI 服务层

PAI 广泛应用于金融、医疗、教育、交通、安全等各个领域。阿里巴巴集团内部的搜索系统、推荐系统及金融服务系统等，均依赖于 PAI 进行数据挖掘。

13.2.3 PAI 的功能特性

PAI 的算法经过阿里巴巴集团大规模业务的沉淀，不仅支持基础的聚类和回归类算法，也支持文本分析和特征处理等复杂算法。PAI 支持的机器学习算法如图 13-2 所示。

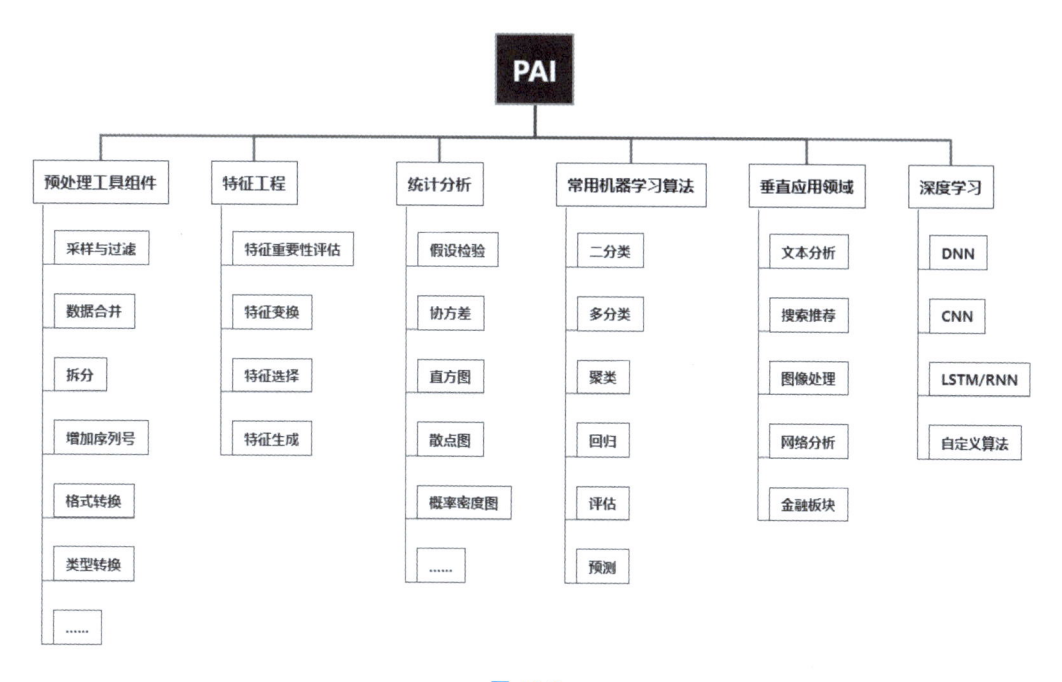

图 13-2

PAI 支持丰富的机器学习算法、一站式的机器学习体验、主流的机器学习框架及可视化的建模方式。根据机器学习全流程，PAI 分别提供了数据准备、模型开发和训练及模型部署阶段的产品。

（1）数据准备。PAI 提供了智能标注（iTAG），支持在多种场景下进行数据标注和数据集管理。

（2）模型开发和训练。PAI 提供了可视化建模 PAI-Designer、交互式编程建模 PAI-DSW、训练任务提交，满足不同的建模需求。

（3）模型部署。PAI 提供了云原生在线推理服务平台 PAI-EAS，帮助用户快速地将模型部署为服务。

13.2.4 PAI 的基本概念

PAI 中涉及的基本概念有很多，这些概念主要分为了两个大类：管理类和开发类。开发类中所包含的概念如表 13-2 所示。

表 13-2

概　念	描　述
数据集 （DataSet）	用于标注、训练、分析等的数据集合，支持将存储在 OSS、NAS、MaxCompute 等存储介质中的结构化、非结构化数据或目录注册为数据集。同时，PAI 支持统一管理数据集的存储、版本、数据结构等信息
工作流 （Pipeline）	构建 DAG 来实现组件之间上下游逻辑调度的对象，是一个静态概念。构建完成后，PAI 支持对它进行重复提交运行
工作流草稿 （PipelineDraft）	在设计器画布上操作的编辑状态的工作流对象，支持重复编辑生成不同的工作流
组件 （Component）	在 PAI 工作流和工作流草稿中编辑，是工作流任务执行的最小单元。组件分为以下两种不同的类型。 （1）预置组件（Build-in Component）：PAI 预置了基于阿里巴巴最佳实践的多类组件，涵盖从数据预处理到模型训练及预测的全流程。 （2）自定义组件（Custom Component）：PAI 支持用户基于代码和镜像，自己定义可以被工作流组合编排的组件
节点（Node）	被拖曳到设计器画布上的一个组件，形成工作流中的一个节点
工作流快照 （SnapShot）	工作流草稿每次运行时会记录工作流草稿完整的配置信息，从而形成工作流快照。这些信息包括节点配置、运行参数、执行方式等，可以用于工作流草稿的版本记录及配置回滚
工作流任务 （PipelineRun）	一次工作流的任务执行。可以通过设计器提交工作流草稿并运行，或者通过 SDK 直接提交工作流并运行，生成一个工作流任务
作业（Job）	运行在各种计算资源中的任务
实验对照组 （Experiment）	兼容 MLFlow 中的概念。针对模型准确率等评估指标，用户可以将两个及以上的训练任务投递至实验对照组中进行对比分析
任务（Run）	一个任务指一次任务执行，兼容 MLFlow 中的概念，必须归属于某一个实验对照组。用户可以使用任务跟踪 PAI 上提交的训练任务，也可以在本地使用 MLflow Client 直接创建任务
模型（Model）	模型是基于数据集和算法代码通过训练产出的结果，可以预测新数据
Processor	在线预测算法结果的程序包，通常与模型文件一起部署，从而获得模型服务。PAI 支持以下两类 Processor。 （1）预置 Processor：针对常用的 PMML、TensorFlow 等模型，EAS 提供了预置的 Processor。 （2）自定义 Processor：如果 EAS 提供的预置 Processor 无法满足模型部署需求，用户可以根据 Processor 的开发标准自定义 Processor
模型服务 （Service）	模型服务包含模型文件和 Processor 代码，用户可以对模型服务进行创建、更新、停止、启动、扩容及缩容操作
镜像（Image）	PAI 支持将 Docker 镜像作为 AI 资产进行管理
实例（Instance）	计算资源被启动的最小单元

13.3 使用机器学习平台 PAI 实现智能推荐

在了解到了机器学习和 PAI 的基本知识后，本节将结合一个具体的使用场景来演示 PAI 的强大功能。这里将使用 PAI 提供的协同过滤算法和 ALS 算法来实现商品的智能推荐。

13.3.1 使用协同过滤算法实现商品推荐

协同过滤算法是一种基于关联规则的算法。以购物行为为例，如果用户甲和用户乙都购买了商品 A 和商品 B，则可以假定用户甲和用户乙的购物品味具有一定的相似性，利用这种相似性就可以构建一个相似度矩阵，从而完成商品的推荐。

1. 基于用户和基于物品的协同过滤算法

在利用协调过滤算法构建相似度矩阵实现商品推荐时，有两种不同的方式，即基于用户方式的协同过滤和基于物品方式的协同过滤。下面分别进行介绍。

1）基于用户的协同过滤

基于用户的协同过滤的基本思想相当简单。基于用户对物品的偏好找到邻居用户，然后将邻居用户喜欢的物品推荐给当前用户。从计算的角度看，就是将一个用户对所有物品的偏好作为一个向量来计算用户之间的相似度，找到邻居用户后，根据邻居用户的相似度权重及他们对物品的偏好，预测当前用户没有涉及的物品，计算得到一个排序的物品列表作为推荐列表。表 13-3 给出了一个例子。

表 13-3

用 户	物 品			
	物品 A	物品 B	物品 C	物品 D
用户 A	√		√	推荐
用户 B		√		
用户 C	√		√	√

根据表 13-3 可以画出图 13-3。对于用户 A，根据用户的历史偏好，这里先根据计算得到一个邻居用户——用户 C，然后将用户 C 喜欢的物品 D 推荐给用户 A。

2）基于物品的协同过滤

基于物品的协同过滤的原理和基于用户的协同过滤的原理类似。只是在计算邻居用户时从物品的角度，而不是从用户的角度，即先基于用户对物品的偏好找到相似的物品，然后根据用户的历史偏好，推荐相似的物品。从计算的角度看，就是将所有用户对某个物品的偏好作为一个向量来计算物品之间的相似度，得到物品的相似物品后，根据用户历史的偏好预测当前用户还没有表示偏好的物品，计算得到一个排序的物品列表作为推荐列表。表 13-4 给出了一个例子。

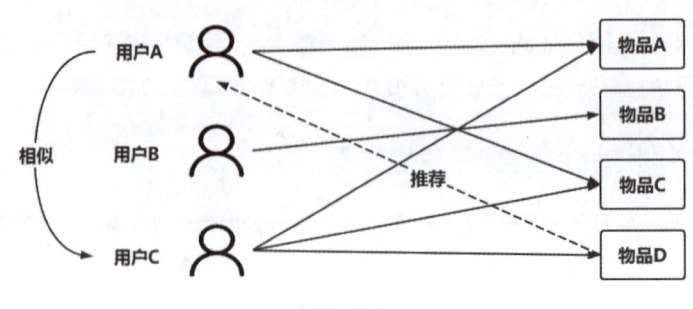

图 13-3

表 13-4

用　户	物　品		
	物品 A	物品 B	物品 C
用户 A	√		√
用户 B	√	√	√
用户 C	√		推荐

根据表 13-4 可以画出图 13-4。对于物品 A，根据所有用户的历史偏好，喜欢物品 A 的用户都喜欢物品 C，得出物品 A 和物品 C 比较相似，而用户 C 喜欢物品 A，就可以推断出用户 C 可能也喜欢物品 C。

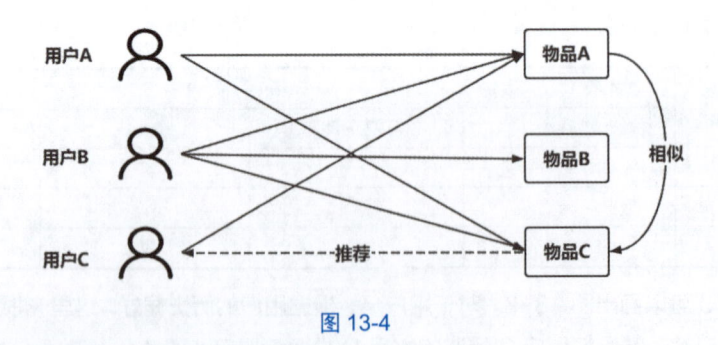

图 13-4

2. 使用 PAI 基于协同过滤实现商品推荐

下面将通过具体的操作来演示如何使用 PAI 基于协同过滤实现商品推荐。

（1）登录 PAI 的管理控制台，并创建一个工作空间，如图 13-5 所示。

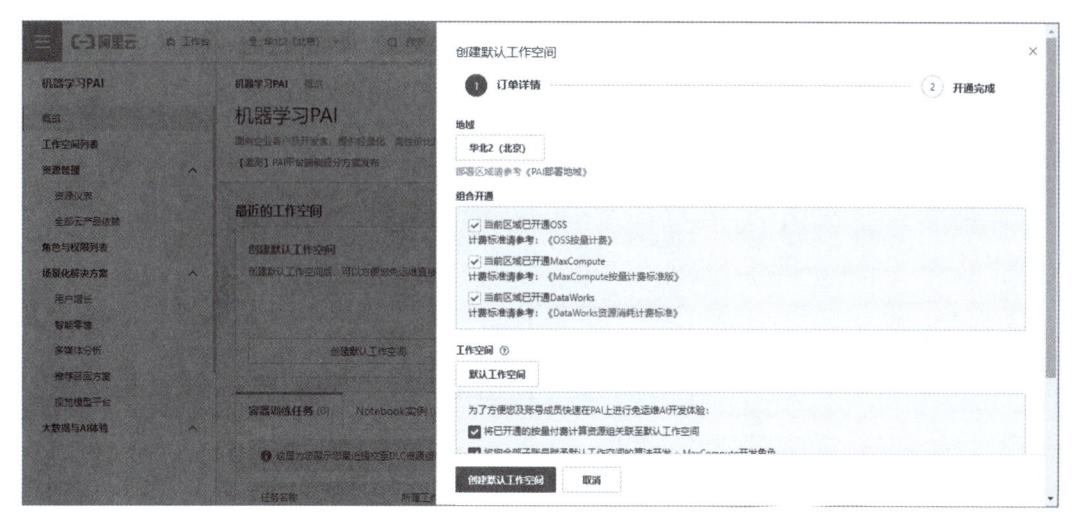

图 13-5

> 这里为了方便进行演示，直接创建一个默认的工作空间。

（2）进入工作空间，在左侧的导航栏中选择"模型开发和训练"→"可视化建模（Designer）"选项，进入"可视化建模（Designer）"页面，如图 13-6 所示。

图 13-6

（3）在"可视化建模（Designer）"页面的"预置模板"选项卡中，单击模板列表中"推荐算法-商品推荐"选项下方的"创建"按钮，如图 13-7 所示。

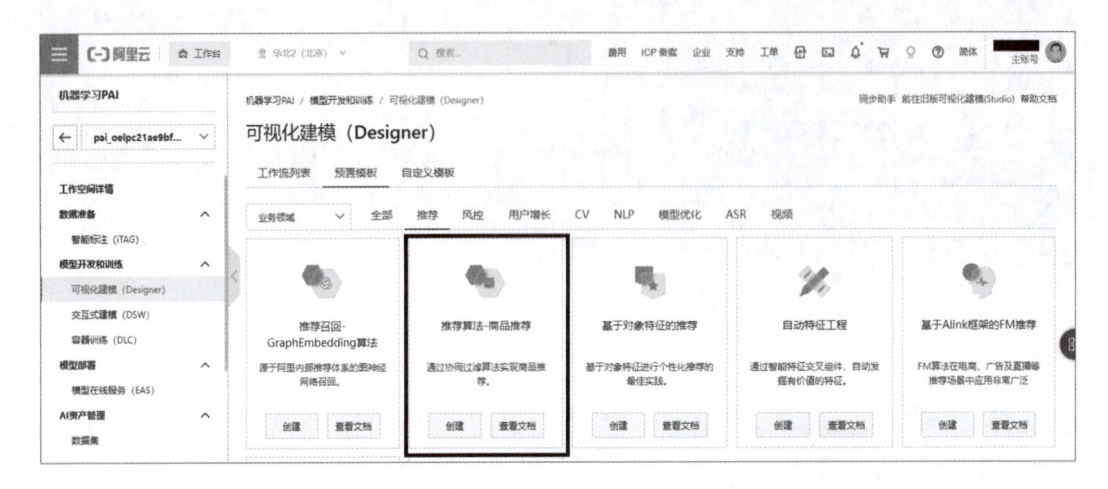

图 13-7

（4）弹出"新建工作流"对话框，保持默认参数设置，单击"确定"按钮，如图 13-8 所示。

图 13-8

（5）单击"进入工作流"按钮，如图 13-9 所示。

（6）系统将根据预置的模板自动构建工作流，如图 13-10 所示。

图 13-9

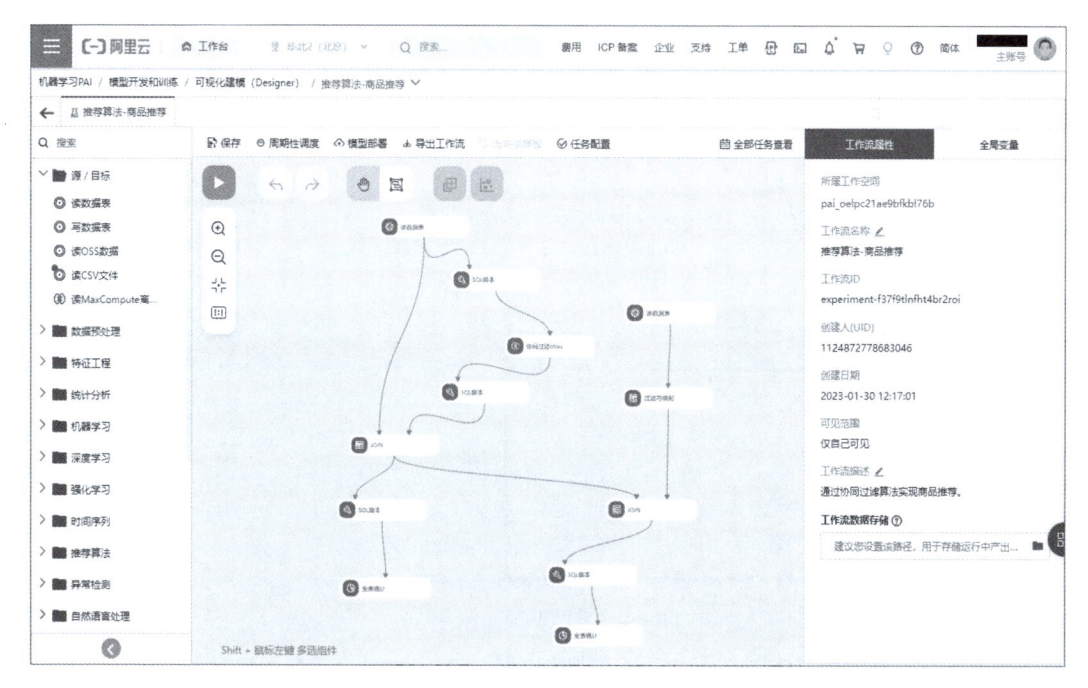

图 13-10

（7）单击画布上方的"运行"按钮 ，运行工作流，并等待工作流运行完成。

（8）右击"读数据表"节点，在弹出的快捷菜单中选择"查看数据"→"ODPS 源的输出"命令，如图 13-11 所示。

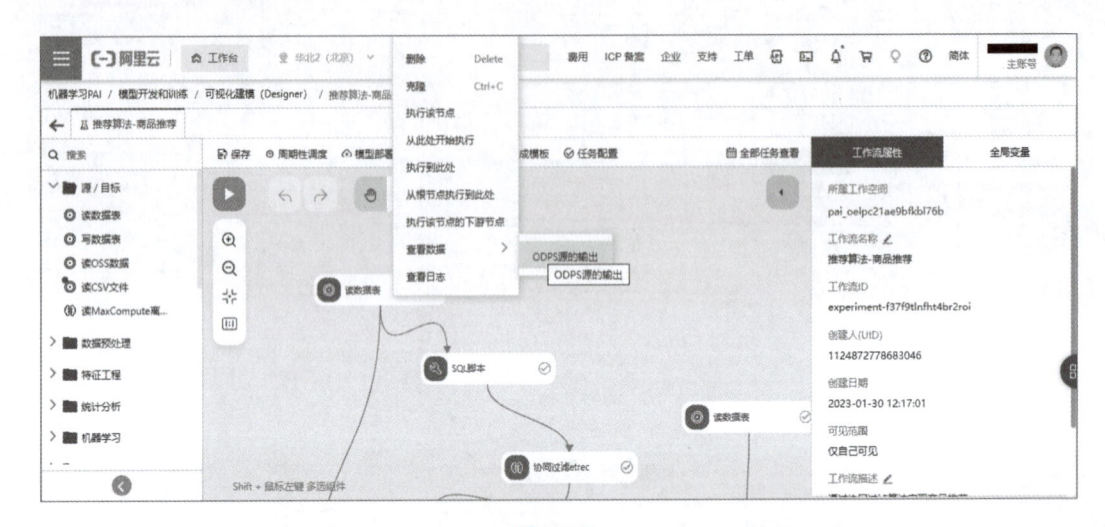

图 13-11

（9）此时处理的数据源的数据将显示在页面下方，如图 13-12 所示。

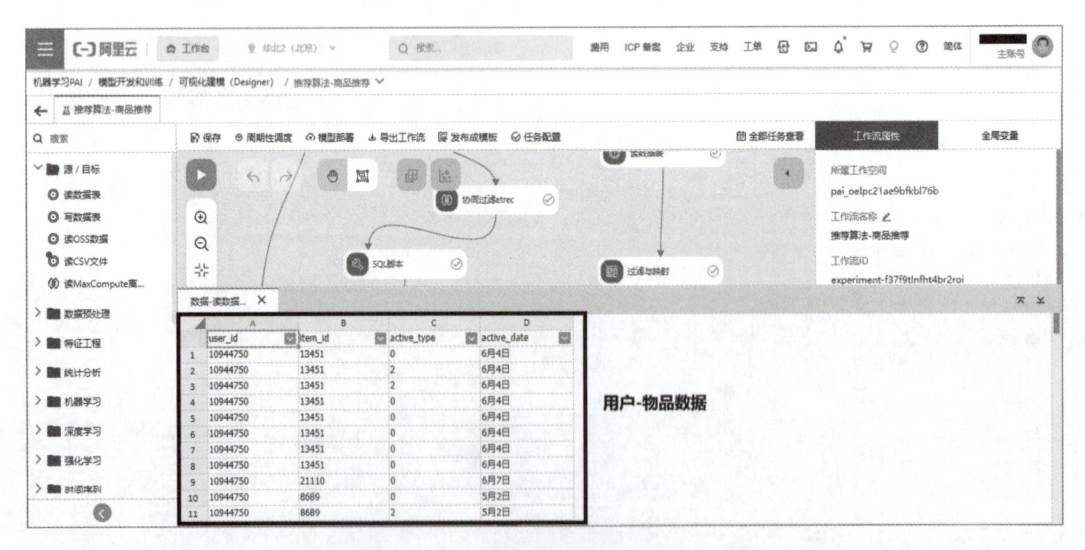

图 13-12

（10）右击画布中的"全表统计"节点，在弹出的快捷菜单中选择"查看数据"→"全表统计输出"命令，即可查看生成的推荐列表，如图 13-13 所示。

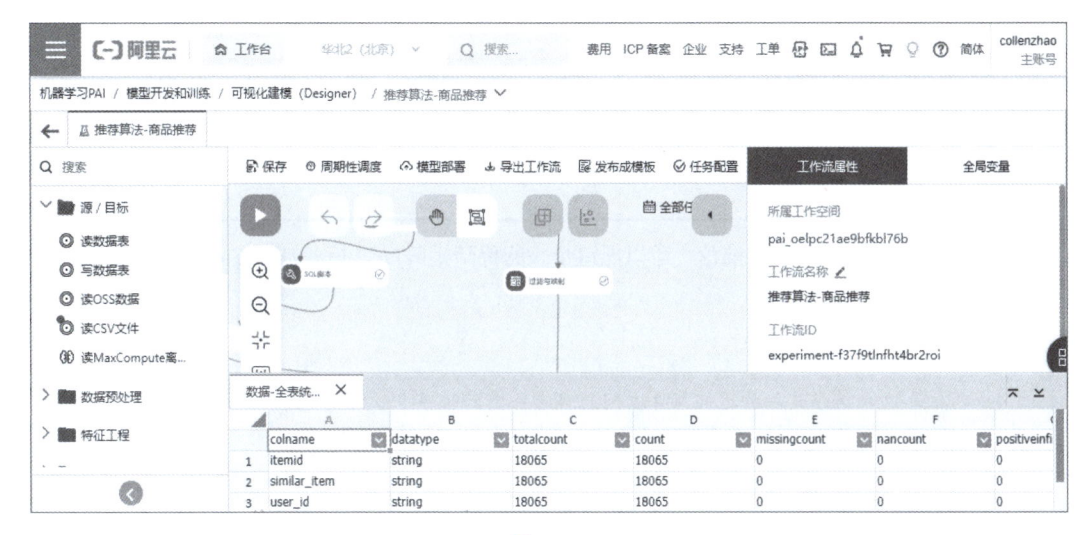

图 13-13

13.3.2 使用 ALS 算法实现商品推荐

利用协同过滤算法实现商品推荐就是要预测用户喜欢但是没有发现的物品,使用该算法的前提是构建一个相似度矩阵,而该相似度矩阵的构建需要获取用户以往的购买信息。但在实际情况下,尤其是在系统冷启动时,往往是缺少这样的购买信息的。因此构建的相似度矩阵不能很好地反映用户与用户、物品与物品之间的相关性,从而造成推荐结果不准确。解决这一问题的办法是采用 ALS 算法实现商品推荐。

1. ALS 算法的基本原理

ALS(Alternating Least Squares)算法的原理是对稀疏矩阵进行模型分解,评估缺失项的值,从而得到基本的训练模型。该算法兼顾了用户和物品两个方面,因此也可以叫作混合的协同过滤算法。

以电影打分为例,原始数据是每个观众对每部电影的评分矩阵 R。因为每个观众不一定看过这部电影,且每个观众不一定对该部电影进行评分,所以该评分矩阵可能是稀疏矩阵,如表 13-5 所示。

表 13-5

观众	电影				
	阿凡达	阿甘正传	乱世佳人	美丽心灵	万圣节 8
观众 1	7	7	5		4
观众 2		1			
观众 3	4		6		4

续表

观众	电影				
	阿凡达	阿甘正传	乱世佳人	美丽心灵	万圣节 8
观众 4		7		4	
观众 5		5			6

为了使用稀疏矩阵 R 进行推荐，可以把这个大的稀疏矩阵 R，拆分成两个小一点的矩阵 U 和 V，如图 13-14 所示。

> 这种拆分是一种近似拆分，因此存在一定的误差。

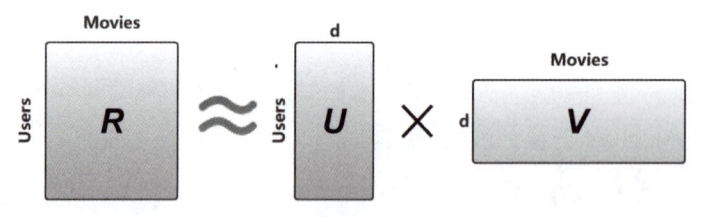

图 13-14

其中，U 矩阵代表用户的特征，包括 3 个维度：性格、文化程度和兴趣爱好，如表 13-6 所示。

表 13-6

观众	维度		
	性格	文化程度	兴趣爱好
观众 1	U11	U12	U3
观众 2	U21	U22	U23
观众 3	U31	U32	U33
观众 4	U41	U42	U43
观众 5	U51	U52	U53

V 矩阵代表电影的特征，也包括 3 个维度：性格、文化程度和兴趣爱好，如表 13-7 所示。

表 13-7

维度	电影				
	阿凡达	阿甘正传	乱世佳人	美丽心灵	万圣节 8
性格	V11	V12	V13	V14	V15
文化程度	V21	V22	V23	V24	V25
兴趣爱好	V31	V32	V33	V34	V35

> U 矩阵和 V 矩阵的维度是一样的。

这样，U 矩阵和 V 矩阵的乘积就可以近似表示 R 矩阵。这样的表示是存在误差的，因为对于一个 U 矩阵来说，并不可能仅仅使用 3 个维度就代表着一个人对一部电影评价全部的维度，比如还有地域等因素。这个误差可以使用均方根误差（RMSE）表示。

> 拆分的维度越多，RMSE 就会越小，推荐的效果就越好，但计算量也越大。因此，在实际应用中并不是拆分的维度越多越好，只要 RMSE 满足要求即可。

在使用 ALS 算法的时候，寻找最合适的拆分方式的过程叫作训练模型。得到模型后，就可以使用该模型来完成商品的推荐。

2. 使用 PAI 基于 ALS 算法实现矩阵拆分

下面将通过具体的操作步骤来演示如何使用 PAI 基于 ALS 算法实现矩阵拆分。这里将会用到测试数据文件 ratingdata.txt。该文件包含 3 个字段：userID（用户 ID）、itemID（物品 ID）和 rating（评分数据）。文件内容如下。

```
1,101,5.0
1,102,3.0
1,103,2.5
2,101,2.0
2,102,2.5
2,103,5.0
2,104,2.0
3,101,2.5
3,104,4.0
3,105,4.5
3,107,5.0
4,101,5.0
4,103,3.0
4,104,4.5
4,106,4.0
5,101,4.0
5,102,3.0
5,103,2.0
5,104,4.0
5,105,3.5
5,106,4.0
```

（1）在"可视化建模（Designer）"页面上，单击"新建工作流"按钮，在弹出的下拉列表中选择"新建"选项，如图 13-15 所示。

图 13-15

（2）弹出"新建工作流"对话框，在对话框中输入工作流名称，单击"确定"按钮，如图 13-16 所示。

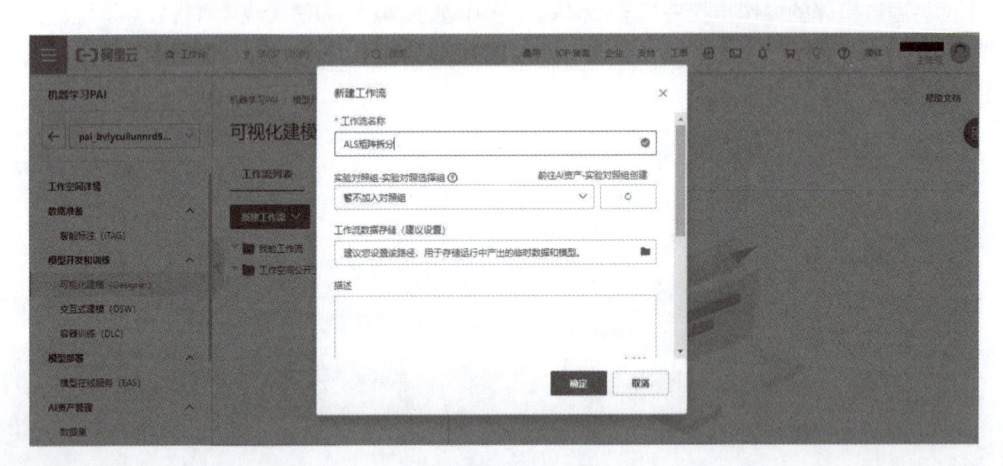

图 13-16

（3）进入工作流。

（4）将"源/目标"列表中的"读 CSV 文件"组件拖曳到画布上，如图 13-17 所示。

（5）选中"读 CSV 文件-1"节点，在右侧的"参数设置"选项卡中，单击"文件路径"文本框右侧的 ■ 按钮，如图 13-18 所示。

（6）弹出"选择 OSS 目录或文件"对话框，在对话框中选择"上传文件"选项，将 ratingdata.txt 文件上传，单击"确定"按钮，如图 13-19 所示。

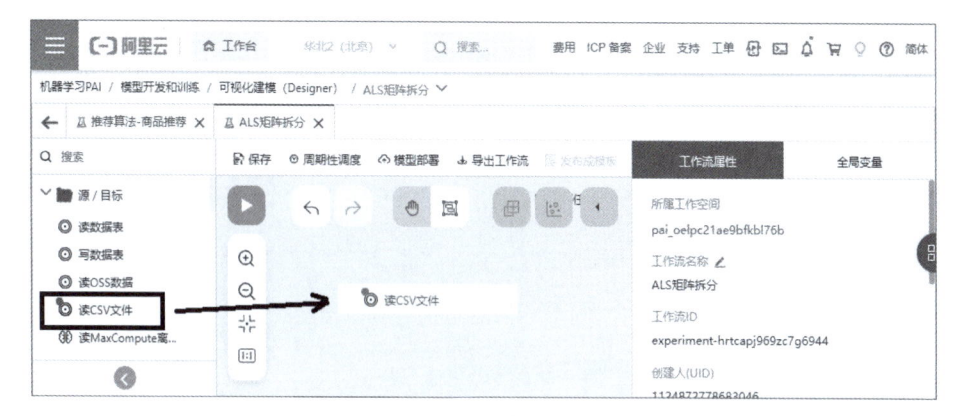

图 13-17

图 13-18

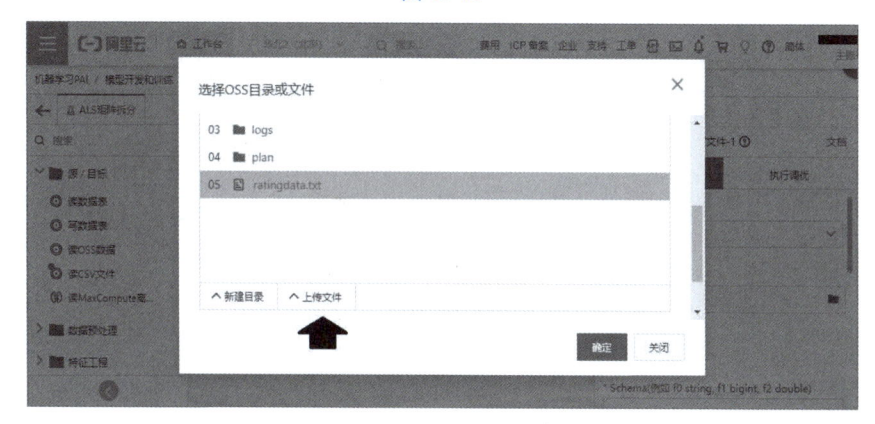

图 13-19

（7）在"参数设置"选项卡的"Schema(例如 f0 string, f1 bigint, f2 double)"文本框中设置数据格式定义，如图 13-20 所示。

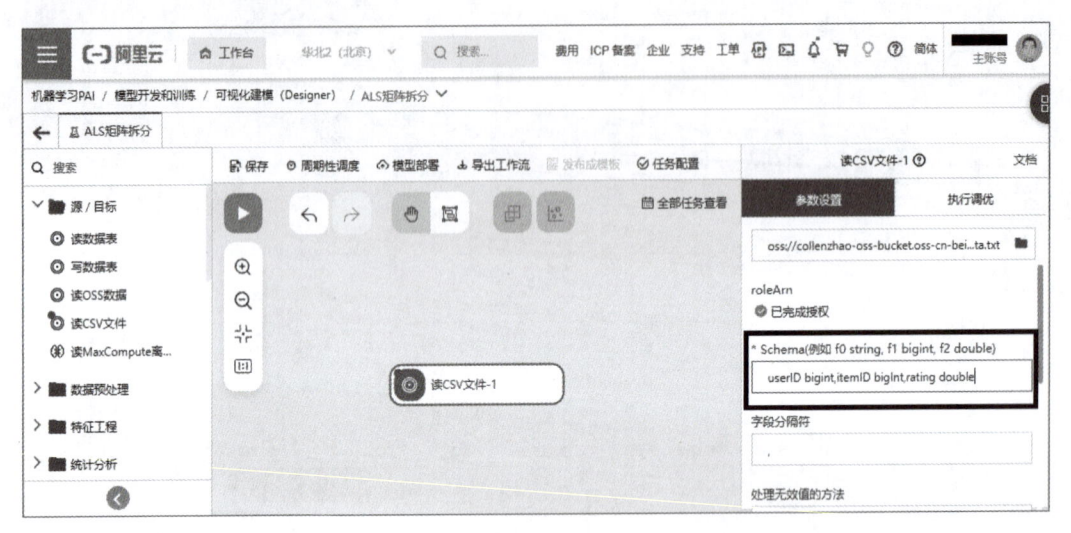

图 13-20

（8）右击"读 CSV 文件-1"节点，在弹出的快捷菜单中选择"执行到此处"命令，如图 13-21 所示。

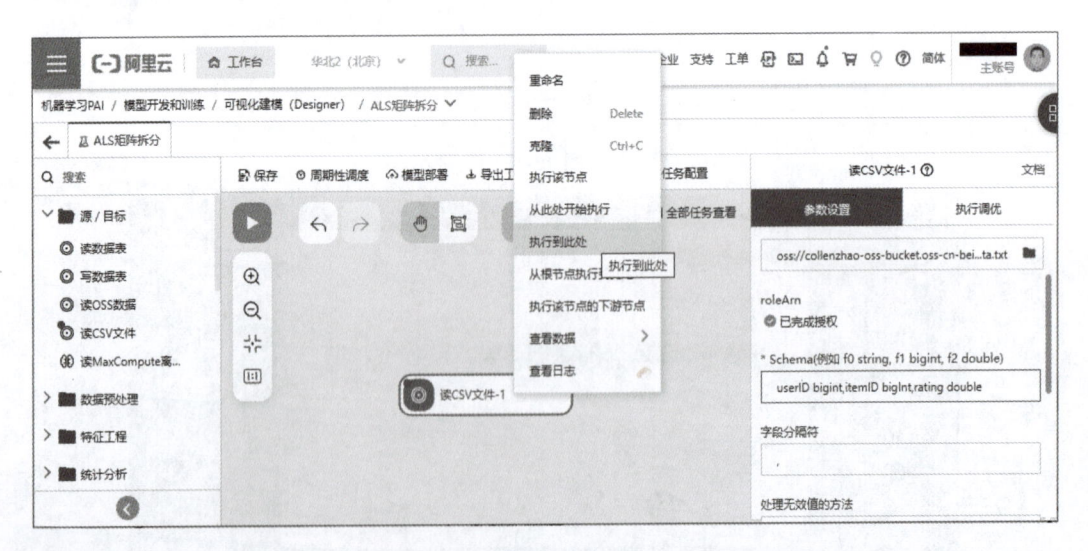

图 13-21

（9）执行完成后，读取的 CSV 文件数据如图 13-22 所示。

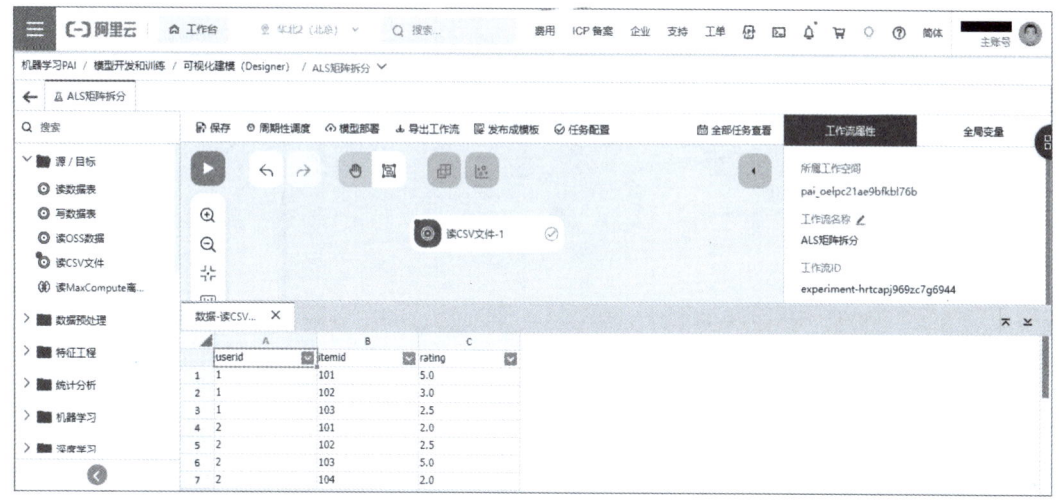

图 13-22

（10）在画布中增加一个"ALS 矩阵分解（旧版）"节点，如图 13-23 所示。

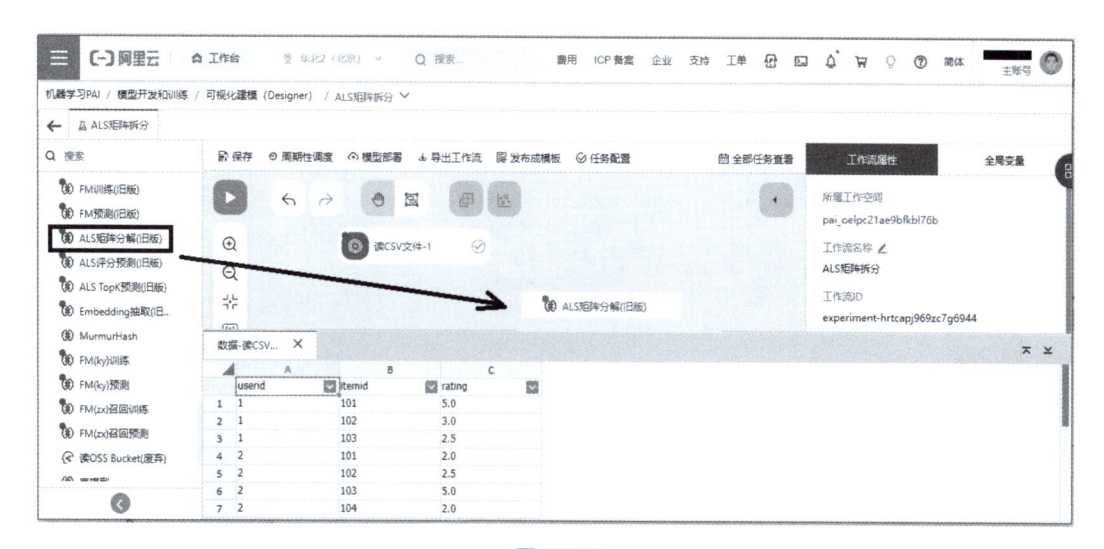

图 13-23

（11）连接"读 CSV 文件-1"节点和"ALS 矩阵分解（旧版）"节点，并在右侧设置"ALS 矩阵分解（旧版）"节点的相关字段，如图 13-24 所示。

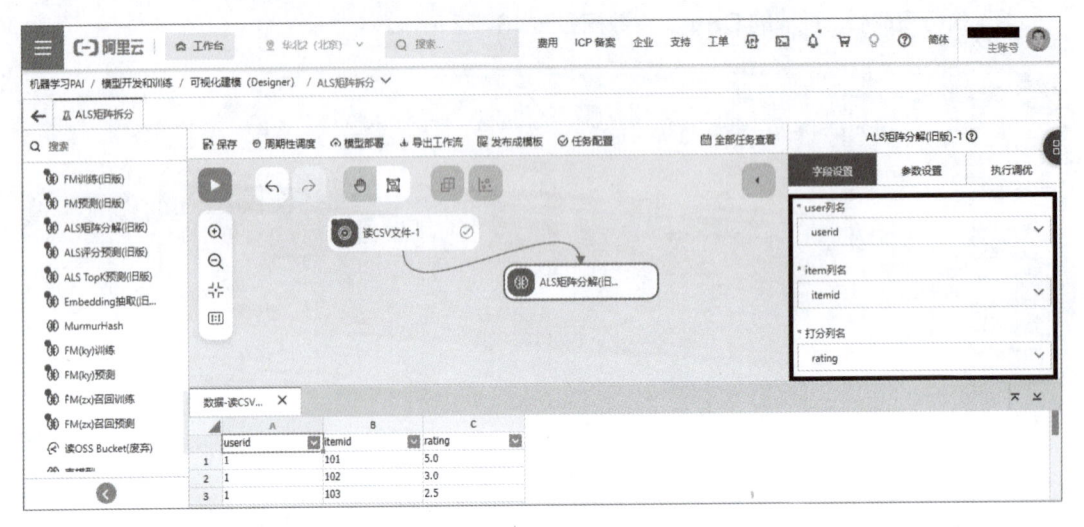

图 13-24

（12）单击"保存"按钮。

（13）右击"ALS 矩阵分解（旧版）"节点，在弹出的快捷菜单中选择"执行到此处"命令，如图 13-25 所示。

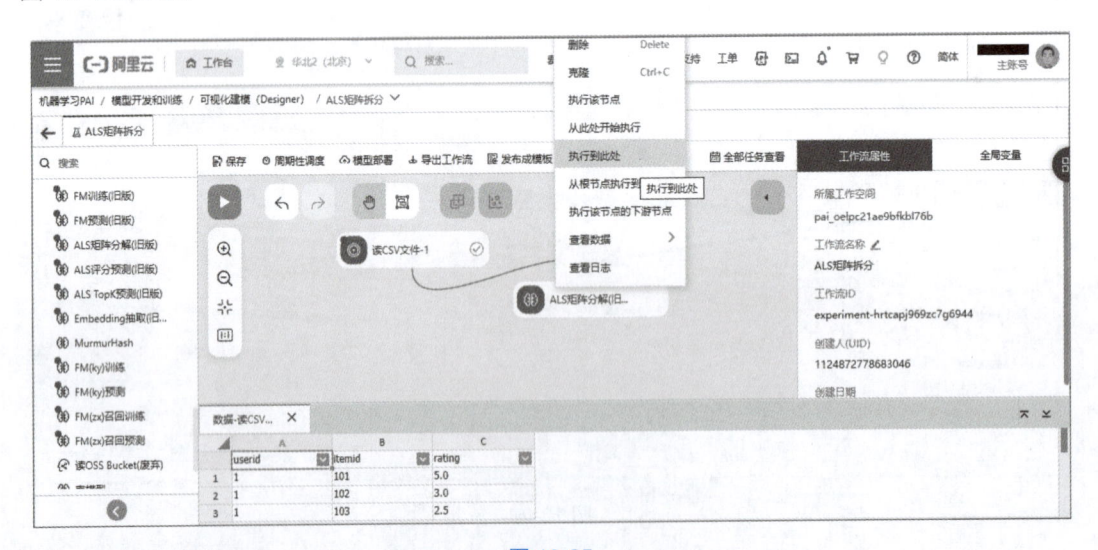

图 13-25

（14）执行完成后，就可以观察到拆分后的矩阵，如图 13-26 所示。

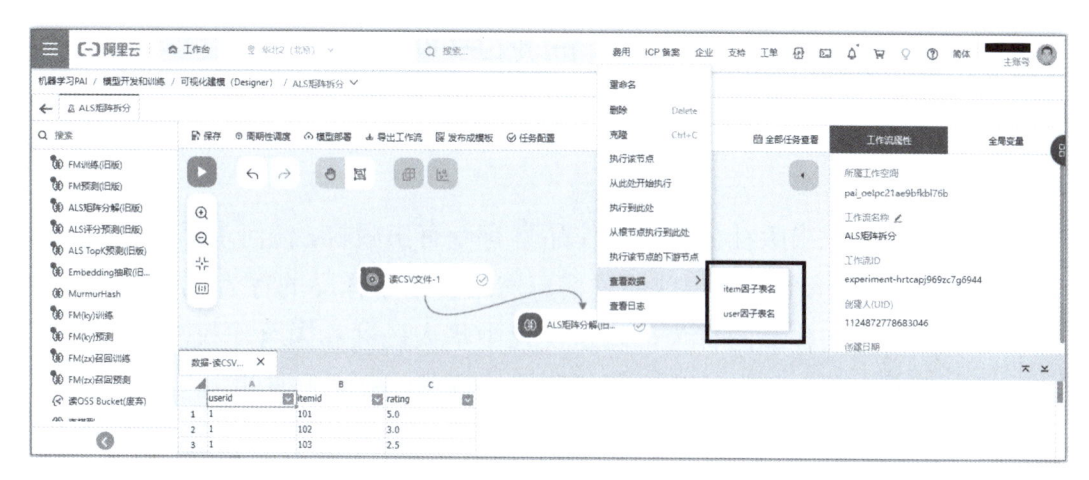

图 13-26

拆分后的矩阵数据如图 13-27 所示。

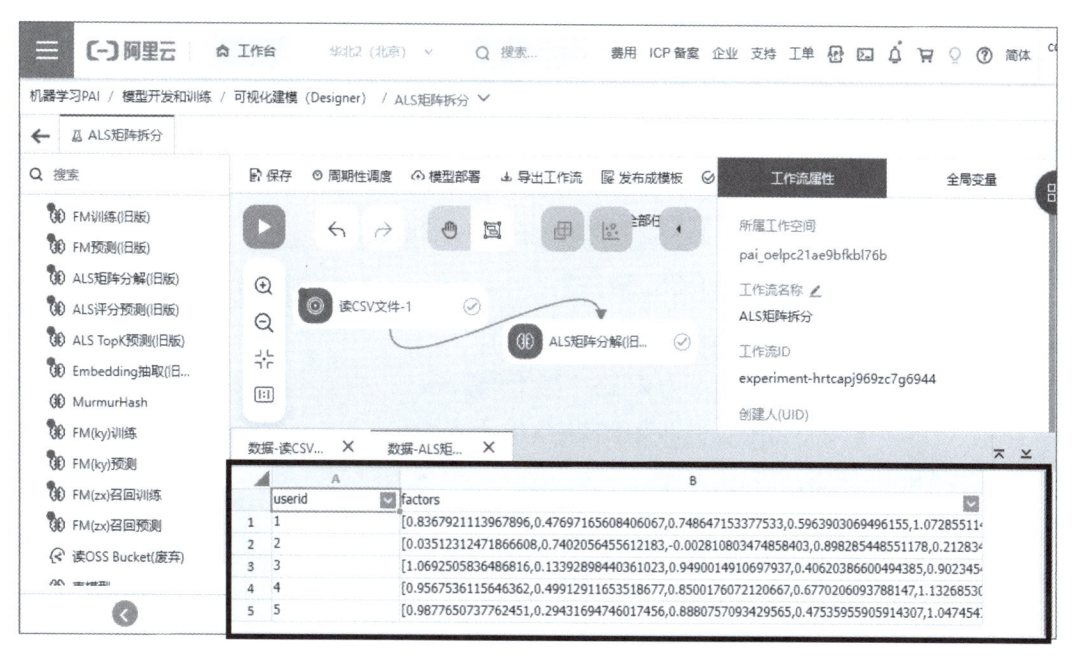

图 13-27

反侵权盗版声明

电子工业出版社依法对本作品享有专有出版权。任何未经权利人书面许可，复制、销售或通过信息网络传播本作品的行为；歪曲、篡改、剽窃本作品的行为，均违反《中华人民共和国著作权法》，其行为人应承担相应的民事责任和行政责任，构成犯罪的，将被依法追究刑事责任。

为了维护市场秩序，保护权利人的合法权益，我社将依法查处和打击侵权盗版的单位和个人。欢迎社会各界人士积极举报侵权盗版行为，本社将奖励举报有功人员，并保证举报人的信息不被泄露。

举报电话：（010）88254396；（010）88258888
传　　真：（010）88254397
E-mail：dbqq@phei.com.cn
通信地址：北京市万寿路173信箱
　　　　　电子工业出版社总编办公室
邮　　编：100036